The Social Politics of
Anglo-Jewry
1880–1920

For Frances

The Social Politics of Anglo-Jewry 1880–1920

Eugene C. Black

Basil Blackwell

Copyright © Eugene C. Black 1988

First published 1988

Basil Blackwell Ltd
108 Cowley Road, Oxford, OX4 1JF, UK

Basil Blackwell Inc.
432 Park Avenue South, Suite 1503
New York, NY 10016, USA

British Library Cataloguing in Publication Data

Black, Eugene C. (Eugene Charleton), *1927–*
 The social politics of Anglo-Jewry 1880–
 1920.
 1. Great Britain. Jews. Social conditions,
 1880–1920
 I. Title
 305.8'924'041

 ISBN 0–631–16491–X

Library of Congress Cataloging in Publication Data

Black, Eugene Charleton.
 The social politics of Anglo-Jewry 1880–1920/Eugene C. Black.
  p.   cm.
 Bibliography: p.
 Includes index.
 ISBN 0–631–16491–X
 1. Jews—Great Britain—Politics and government. 2. Jews—Great
Britain—Societies, etc.   3. Great Britain—Ethnic relations.
I. Title
DS135.E5B56   1989
305.8'924'041—dc19

Typeset in 9½ on 11 pt Ehrhardt
by Opus, Oxford
Printed in Great Britain by T.J. Press Ltd, Padstow, Cornwall

Contents

List of Tables

Preface

The Social Politics of Anglo-Jewry, 1880–1920 grew out of a much more extensive study on which I have been engaged for some years, an enquiry I plan to title, *From Voluntarism to Collectivism: British Social Politics, 1885–1922.* As I pursued my research into Britain's transition from a society working principally through social discipline and voluntaristic institutions to a modern collectivized one functioning principally through legal disciplines, one extraordinary exception stood out. British Jews as a community cared to an astounding and unique degree for the needs of their own community. Not only did they do this far longer than most groups within British culture, but they managed the task while being inundated by East European co-religionists. Understanding the cooperative international network that processed immigrants took me to the splendid archives of the Alliance Israélite Universelle in Paris. The issues Zionism posed for communal leaders took me beyond the London and Paris communal archives and into those of the British and French governments.

This book examines the ways in which a small, highly acculturated, London-based Jewish elite developed a variety of institutions to socialize the Jewish community. Anglo-Jewry's objectives were simple: to create patriotic Britons and to preserve Jewish culture. I use the term 'acculturate' advisedly. Some Jews assimilated, resolving the difficulties and tensions of being a people apart by compromises at the expense of Jewish observance and Jewish identity. Intermarriage and apostasy always threatened or appeared to threaten British Jewish identity. What Anglo-Jewry sought to create and, in many ways, succeeded in doing, was to establish a subculture within British society. British Jews could, so Anglo-Jewry contended, fulfil themselves as Jews of the diaspora, an accepted and respected part of British society and the Western world while preserving the bonds of Jewish history, tradition, and belief.

Those assumptions, not to mention the institutions that proclaimed them, came under increasing challenge as the Jewish community changed. It multiplied in size and changed in cultural background. Jewish newcomers were no longer principally of Dutch and German origin, wholly or substantially adapted to Western ways and values. By the 1880s they came in overwhelming numbers from the *stetls*, the ghettos, of the Pale of Settlement in the Russian Empire or other parts of Eastern Europe. Their traditions, their culture, their way of life were different, a challenge, even an affront, to westernized Anglo-Jewry. These aliens also seemed to rouse, or threaten to arouse, anti-Semitism in British social and political life. That appeared to place at risk a century of Anglo-Jewish achievement in successful acculturation.

For a generation Anglo-Jewry laboured to resocialize these East European co-religionists. Jewish newcomers, however, displayed an extraordinary capacity to adapt themselves. Through what proved to be a creative tension of growth and development, both were changed. For Anglo-Jewry this meant, among other things, a slow, often grudging, democratization. It also offered, even demanded, new roles and greater importance for Jewish women in what had been overwhelmingly the domain of men. The task at hand, educating and assisting tens of thousands of newcomers, also changed the old order almost as profoundly as it conditioned the new. Women and children, while still closely bound in family and kinship networks, achieved greater and greater independence. Provincial Jewish communities, particularly in the larger cities, demanded a greater voice in communal affairs.

Anglo-Jewry, however, displayed a capacity to adapt. As Zionism came to present an alternative to diaspora acculturation and assimilation, Anglo-Jewry found itself under direct political challenge. Strained to its utmost to meet its continuing communal obligations while answering the needs of a nation at war, the Jewish leadership confronted the aspirations of the great powers that favoured the opportunistic exploitation of Zionism. International affairs thus came to play a crucial role in the internal history of British Jews.

Many able scholars have examined aspects of the problems I have pursued. Cecil Roth, V. D. Lipman, Chimen Abramsky, William Fishman, Aubrey Newman, and Martin Gilbert merely begin a list. Lloyd Gartner, Bernard Gainer, Jerzy Zubrzycki, and John A. Garrard, to mention but four, have dealt with Jewish immigration and the anti-alien movement. Stuart Cohen, Ben Halpern, Jehuda Reinharz, Bernard Wasserstein, and David Vital, among others, have dealt with Zionism and its impact on Anglo-Jewish politics. Bill Williams for Manchester and Ernest Krausz for Leeds have brought the latest historical scholarly methods to bear as they have retrieved the vibrant life of provincial British Jewry from the shadow of London domination. I am intellectually indebted to all of them and personally beholden to many for their advice and kindness.

I must pay specific tribute to three pioneers in particular whose work has guided us all and will continue to lead students through the complexities of British Jewish history. Vivian David Lipman has helped to bring order out of social and institutional chaos. My study of Jewish immigration proceeds from ground well broken by Lloyd P. Gartner, and any student of the politics of immigration restriction must begin, as did I, with Bernard Gainer. The influence of all three will be strongly felt in these pages.

So many individuals have helped so much that I cannot thank them all. To them, however, are due many of the strengths of this book, and none shares in its flaws. My colleagues at Brandeis University have been particularly supportive. Dean of Faculty Ann Carter twice furnished Mazur Grant support. The Tauber Institute provided a summer grant that enabled me to begin my archival work. Stephen

Schuker offered encouragement and useful criticism on matters relating to foreign policy. Bernard Wasserstein, whose advice has been invaluable, patiently reviewed parts of the manuscript in draft. Ben Halpern, a treasured colleague for many years, has been a thoughtful, sometimes dissenting critic, always helpful and attentive. Jehuda Reinharz has been most encouraging. Susan Tananbaum, whose own research on the socialization of Jewish girls and women in London should prove to be an important contribution, has pointed me more than once in a useful direction.

Many colleagues from other institutions have offered assistance and suggestions. Chimen Abramsky, Israel Bartal, Wladek Bartoszewski, Malcolm Brown, Michael Burns, Brian Cheyette, Harvey Chiswick, David Doughan, Todd Endelmann, David Engel, Martin Gilbert, Nancy Green, Sylvia G. Hiam, Elie Kedourie, Lionel Kochen, Mark Levene, Heinz Lubasz, Michael Marrus, Aubrey Newman, Anthony Polonsky, David Sorkin, Michael Stanislawski, David Vital, Geoffrey Wigeder, Robert Wistrich and Steve Zipperstein might be singled out in particular. Neither my rabbinical father-in-law nor brother-in-law, Jerome and Jonathan Malino, bears any responsibility for my discussion of British Jewry, although each has been more than helpful on important points of detail. James Glickman cast his novelist's eye over my manuscript.

Some archivists have been particularly considerate and helpful. No single person has done more for me, or for the many other scholars who have worked in the Mocatta Library, than Trude Levi, whose command of the materials is exceeded only by the warmth and grace of her personality. David Massell, Executive Secretary of the Board of Deputies of British Jews, gave me access to Board archives, assisted me with my labours, and patiently suffered my disruptions of his facilities. Georges Weill, Conservateur en Chef et Directeur des Services d'Archives de la Ville de Paris et du Département de la Seine and Archivist for the Alliance Israélite Universelle, has proven himself an exemplary colleague and adviser as well as a friend. Mme Levyne, who does so much to make the Alliance a scholar's delight, displayed rare sensitivity and tolerance for my needs. Michael Heyman and his staff at the Central Zionist Archive in Jerusalem were even more accommodating than their sparkling new facilities.

Basil Blackwell has proven an author's delight. Seán Magee, the editor, Ann Bone, the copy editor, Ruth Bowden, the desk editor, and Sophie Hartley, whose labours have proven so important for artwork and illustrations, have done everything possible to expedite the processing of the book.

Above all, my particular good fortune is to have in Frances Malino both a partner and a professional colleague. Her advice and comments as well as her support and forbearance have proven invaluable. This book is infinitely the better for her suggestions, although she shares not at all in whatever defects may remain.

Waban, Massachusetts, USA

Acknowledgements

Some of the material in chapters 12 and 13 was presented in public lectures at Worcester College, Oxford and the International Conference on the History and Culture of Polish Jews in Jerusalem and has appeared in different form in my article, 'Lucien Wolf and the making of Poland: Paris 1919', *Polin: A Journal of Polish-Jewish Studies*, II (1987), 3–36. Portions of the Samuel Montagu biographical section have been presented as public lectures to the Jewish Historical Society of England and the Center for European Studies at Harvard University and will appear in slightly different form in the *Transactions of the Jewish Historical Society of England*.

The author is particularly grateful to the custodians of the following archives for permission to publish copyright material that they hold: the Board of Deputies of British Jews; the Library and Archive of the Alliance Israélite Universelle; the British Library Board (for permission in particular to print extracts from the Burns papers); the Public Record Office at Kew; the House of Lords Record Office and the Beaverbrook Trust (Lloyd George Papers and Beaverbrook Papers); the Anglo-Jewish Archives (the Stettauer papers, among others); the Mocatta Library at University College, London (the Gaster Papers and the Lucien Wolf Papers, and others); and the *Jewish Chronicle*.

The author and publishers would like to thank the following for their kind permission to reproduce photographs: BBC Hulton Picture Library 1, 8, 10, 11; The Illustrated London News Picture Library 13; London Borough of Tower Hamlets Local History Library and Archives 2, 3, 9; Museum of London 12; University College London, Mocatta Library 4, 5, 6, 7.

JEWISH EAST LONDON

SCALE

This Map shows by Colour the proportion
of the Jewish population to other residents of East
London, street by street, in 1899.

EXPLANATION OF COLOURING.

Proportion of Jews indicated.

95% to 100%.

75% and less than 95%.

50% and less than 75%.

25% and less than 50%.

5% and less than 25%.

Less than 5% of Jews.

NOTE.—In all streets coloured blue the Jews form a majority of the
inhabitants; in those coloured red the Gentiles predominate.

Introduction

Few in numbers and rigorously managed, British Jewry had nevertheless become, by the nineteenth century, a subtly diverse and mobile community. The oldest group, generally Sephardi Jews of Spanish and Portuguese ancestry, migrated to England principally from Holland during the Cromwellian and later Stuart years of the seventeenth and eighteenth centuries. This Sephardi oligarchy, intimate, highly structured and mutually reinforcing, dominated Anglo-Jewry from the resettlement into the nineteenth century. Dutch and German Ashkenazim drifted towards London in increasing numbers through the eighteenth century, enriching and complicating communal life. Bit by bit they added their own institutions to those the Sephardim had already established.

As they prospered, wealthier German Jews, principally bankers and stockbrokers, came to share power with the Sephardi 'Grand Dukes'. Then they began to reshape communal institutions to their own preferences. While great Sephardic names – Montefiore, Magnus, Mocatta, Henriques – continued to play leading roles in Anglo-Jewish institutions throughout the later nineteenth and early twentieth centuries, Sephardi Jews more generally gave place to the increasing numbers, wealth, prestige and ideas of Central Europeans. Disraeli, Lopes, Ricardo and Samuda merged into the English elite. Other Sephardim held aloof from their Ashkenazi co-religionists, withdrawing further into their world of synagogue and cousinhood. The lion of nineteenth-century Anglo-Jewry, Sir Moses Montefiore, himself a Sephardi who denounced Sephardi exclusiveness, deliberately married an Ashkenazi, and bequeathed much of his fortune to enhance the 'assimilation' of Portuguese and German Jews. Central European Ashkenazi Jews – Rothschild, Samuel, Cohen – became, meanwhile, increasingly the ascendant Anglo-Jewish families.

The world of Anglo-Jewry, whatever its tensions of background and leadership, remained socially assimilationist and religiously conservative throughout the nineteenth century. Formal religious traditionalism held almost unchallenged sway, although that Orthodoxy was shaped into a very English mode. Only two exceptions escaped the weight of neo-Orthodoxy. One synagogue, that in Upper Berkeley

Street in the West End, encompassed London's Reform movement from 1842. While attracting some restive Sephardi and Ashkenazi families, the secession never flourished as some hoped it might. Unlike Reform Judaism in Germany or the United States, English Reform, while retaining its proud independence, drifted through the late nineteenth and early twentieth centuries towards a communally acceptable conservatism. Another movement, the Jewish counterpart to late nineteenth-century Christian Modernism, evolved from a former student of Benjamin Jowett, who had done so much to advance 'the new criticism' in Anglicanism, at Balliol College, Oxford. This student, Claude Goldsmid Monte-fiore, one of the most cultivated figures of turn-of-the-century Anglo-Jewry, combined both Orthodox and Reform, Ashkenazi and Sephardi backgrounds. He brought his enthusiastic patriotism and strong religious commitment to the cause when he founded the Liberal Jewish Synagogue in 1910 as a bastion for Jewish religious progressivism.

As was likely to be the case for any successful, adapting small minority, a modest but constant attrition nibbled at Jewish numbers.[1] Anglo-Jewry's doctrinal and cultural conservatism, however, undoubtedly minimized such inroads. Jews married Jews and raised their children in traditional observance. While the Jewish elite anglicized itself and its community, Anglo-Jewry demanded a place for Jews as Jews within British society. Anglicization as a policy, moreover, developed by degrees, moving more rapidly and into more aspects of British Jewish life with the Ashkenazi ascendancy. As late as 1803, Sephardi schools taught students in Ladino. The first English sermon in synagogue was not preached until 1819, and Bevis Marks, the great Sephardi monument, held out against sermons in the vernacular until 1831. The programme of anglicization, once in place, still moved within well-defined limits. The British Jewish elite was proud to be a clearly defined subculture within British society, part of it yet separate from it. Anglo-Jewish pride was stirred, not because Benjamin Disraeli became Prime Minister, but because Lionel Nathan Rothschild was elected and re-elected to Parliament as a Jew and would not take his seat until any qualified Jew could sit. His son 'Natty', as an intimate of the Prince of Wales from Cambridge University days in 1861, unlocked the closed doors of the highest society for the Jewish elite. Three Rothschild daughters married English aristocrats, pointedly retaining their Jewish faith.

How this community defined itself, how it developed and reinforced its character, and the ways in which it responded to external and internal challenges are the subjects of this study. The first chapter deals briefly with some of the principal figures of Anglo-Jewry, and the second with the secular and religious institutions through which that elite formally governed the Jewish community. The third chapter introduces the Jewish Board of Guardians, the most expensive and most ambitious communal philanthropy. British Jews made much of the fact that they cared for their own. No other group within British society addressed so many social needs so effectively from its own resources. Established in 1859 to deal with Ashkenazi poor or newcomers who had no synagogue connection, the Board of

---

1 Todd Endelmann is currently completing a work on apostasy among British Jews. For this period, see his study, 'Communal solidarity and family loyalty among the Jewish elite of Victorian London', *Victorian Studies*, 28/3 (1985), 491–526.

Guardians soon came to define the principles of communal social welfare and to administer many of them.

The Jewish Board of Guardians addressed the immediate needs of those who had fallen behind in life and did so in ways intended to impress upon its beneficiaries the virtues of self-help. Adopting the prevalent social philosophy of the Charity Organisation Society, the Board distinguished between 'deserving' and 'undeserving' cases, treating even those found worthy of assistance in ways that encouraged them to become independent as quickly as possible. Moral socialization accompanied communal aid. Through schools, the subject of chapter 4, and clubs, considered in chapter 5, the process of socialization was extended to the youth and, as time went on, to adults. Education anglicized the community, while affirming its Judaism. Not only did children learn the English language, but they were taught British ways. The solid Victorian virtues of cleanliness, industry, discipline and good order made not merely a better person but also enabled the individual to get on in the world. In ways like this the community could stand proudly as Britons and Jews, respected and respectable members of British society.

That which was done in the name of order and decorum was also imposed to maintain communal deference and elite control. To say this suggests a social tension, a conflict between classes of the community, for which the evidence is, at best, murky. Social welfare everywhere partook of social manipulation, and public assistance programmes in late Victorian and Edwardian Britain were scarcely model humanitarian enterprises. School systems invariably impart some social values as a conscious or unconscious part of their curricula.

A panoply of other, often overlapping voluntary institutions addressed specific problems. Communal philanthropies, the focus of chapter 6, cared for orphans and the aged, the sick and disabled, the hungry and the homeless. Charities served sabbath meals, built model housing, furnished lying-in benefits, provided medically competent *mohelim* to perform ritual circumcision, comforted the mourning. Anglo-Jewry continued to expand its communal resources throughout the 1890s, reaching out to minister to the physical and spiritual needs of its co-religionists and, particularly, to newcomers. Through synagogues and secular organizations, like the Board of Guardians, the schools, and the clubs, the Jewish elite sought to manage and control, to socialize and anglicize the newcomers. As numbers of Jews in Britain multiplied after 1881, organizational evolution and a seemingly inexhaustible philanthropic purse grew in proportion. Whether in social welfare or education, medical care or poor relief, economic opportunity or religious ministration, the community strove to answer all wants while imposing its order and values.

The first part of this book examines these evolving institutions and evaluates their purposes and effectiveness. While Jewish institutions never provided all social services for the Jewish population, they answered an impressive proportion of needs. Anglo-Jewry was not merely dedicated; it was lucky. State assistance was already available in such crucial areas as schools and health even before the great surge of Jewish migration began in the 1880s. In the decades that followed, numbers, costs, and the growing range of provided services, for Jews just as for the population as a whole, ultimately outran the resources and ingenuity of voluntarism. The communal leadership and communal purse could sustain fewer and fewer social services without state assistance. Anglo-Jewry came increasingly to cooperate with and ultimately to depend upon central and local authorities to serve and socialize its community.

Much of that socialization emphasized self-help, a lesson that British Jews took to heart and practised, sometimes to elite applause, sometimes to Anglo-Jewish annoyance or distress. Chapter 7 discusses some of the more striking ways in which the broader community came to care for and express itself. Institutions such as Friendly Societies were encouraged and popular. Anglo-Jewry had mixed views about trade unions. So, as things turned out, did Jewish workers themselves. Political radicalism much annoyed the elite, but it, too, struck no deep root in the community before the First World War. Working against secularism and radicalism was deeply-ingrained religiosity, which could also prove a focus for resistance to anglicization. Communal socialization, by the early twentieth century, had come to be a mixture of elite-imposed and self-generated ideas and institutions.

That generation, both within the elite and broader community, that had enriched, modified and extended the ideas, values and institutions of British Jews shared the great changes going on within British society. Chapter 8 discusses a dramatic if ill-comprehended development, the increased role and scope for Jewish women and related developments in the socialization of children. On the one hand, the expanding role and greater scope Jewish women came to enjoy was of a piece with developments in British society. But, on the other hand, strong traditions acted in particular ways to hobble their independence and circumscribe any drive towards equality. Not surprisingly, growing independence developed hand in hand with new institutions for moral and social control.

The second part of this book considers Anglo-Jewry and its working institutions confronting the specific internal and external problems of immigration. The problem, in the first instance, was simply one of numbers. At the heart of Anglo-Jewry's growing if self-imposed burden lay the alien question, the substance of chapters 9 through 11. Newcomers drained communal resources. For the first half of the nineteenth century, the alien poor were more often than not Dutch and German Ashkenazim. That fact inspired the initial formation of the Jewish Board of Guardians. By the second half of the nineteenth century, immigrants coming into or passing through the United Kingdom were overwhelmingly East European. After the assassination of Tsar Alexander II, vicious state and popular persecution and pogroms accelerated what had begun as and continued to be a quest for economic opportunity and a better life. From the events of the 1880s, however, grew a myth that political and religious abuse alone triggered and sustained Jewish migration. But the movement from Russia, like the movement within Russia, was a rational economic choice accelerated by irrational politics. By the 1880s this wave from the Pale swept across Central and Western Europe to the shores of the United States. As the numbers grew, each country of reception, from neighbouring Germany and Austro-Hungary to the further European, American, even African and Asian states of debarkation, grew restive.

For Great Britain, this meant an increase from a relatively stable Jewish population of 65,000 in 1880 to at least 260,000 on the eve of the First World War. Anglo-Jewry sought to discourage Jewish immigration or to assist it to move, as expeditiously as possible, to other shores. Jewish numbers, if not considerable, were highly concentrated and increasingly visible. More than half of the Jews lived in London, principally in two parishes of the borough of Stepney. This concentration revived a stereotype of the Jew which Anglo-Jewry had spent two centuries attempting to erase. The image of the Jew, not merely as strange and different, but as menacing, unfairly competitive, even criminal, threatened the successful acculturation and assimilation of the community. Could the labours that produced the end of religious tests in British political and cultural life be partially undone? So it appeared as the nineteenth century drew to its close. By the 1890s, the matter of restricting alien immigration into England became a serious British political issue for the first time in modern history.

Unionist and Conservative party leaders formulated an approach that they believed spoke to British needs. They offered fleeing Jewry part of Kenya, an East African refuge, while approving Jewish efforts to develop settlements in the British Empire, the United States and Latin America. At the same time, they adopted immigration restriction as a party issue. To a greater degree than most authorities admit, this transparent singling out of immigrant Jews was less a manifestation of anti-Semitism, overt or veiled, than a reversal of high Victorian assumptions and practices. Immigration restriction was the easiest and most politically palatable way to initiate a broader attack on the mid-Victorian gospel of free trade. Protection, whatever camouflage it might wear, was intended to preserve things British from foreign competition. Both Conservative party leaders and the Anglo-Jewish elite preferred to pick and choose the 'better sorts of immigrants' for their own country and community. Immigration restriction had, in fact, long been communal practice. Anglo-Jewry preferred to continue making such choices itself as it had done through policies of encouraging emigration and repatriating those who could not adjust to life in Britain.

Anglo-Jewry acquiesced, even cooperated, in the government's early twentieth century efforts to limit immigration. Doing so, however, rendered an ageing leadership politically vulnerable. The growth of viable, aspiring provincial Jewish communities had already generated political tension. Immigration restriction, however, polarized the Jewish community in ways that nothing had done before. Neither political radicalism nor trade unionism had yet made substantial headway among London Jews, native or foreign-born. Trade unionism proved durable only in provincial communities like Leeds. There the small Jewish middle class resented London-oriented Anglo-Jewish condescension, and a substantial, cohesive tailoring trade union spoke a significantly different political language at least into the early twentieth century. Manchester was to become the headquarters for the political campaign for Jewish institutional decentralization or democratization, and Liverpool's foreign Jews in 1904 even challenged the authority of the Chief Rabbi in court.

More than anything else, the veiled and uneasy alliance between the Jewish leadership and the politics of immigration restriction helped to energize and politicize Jews in Britain. That is the substance of chapters 10 and 11. Immigration restriction willy-nilly defined two British Jewish worlds: that of native Jews, generally English by birth or long residence, and that of the alien Jews of East European origin, more recently arrived in Britain, generally concentrated in the

London ghetto. Newcomers found themselves defined as different. Like it or not, they discovered or had imposed upon them a political sense of self. Their new community, even as it developed in a world of Anglo-Jewish institutions, had no difficulty finding would-be spokesmen within itself and among discontented British Jews to challenge the Anglo-Jewish elite.

Substantially alien East End London increasingly answered its own needs. Like the newcomers of generations before, East Europeans got on in the world. They were less dependent on Anglo-Jewish philanthropy and more generally able to cope for themselves. What had been small assertions of independence or nostalgia assumed new importance. Some had clung to traditional observances and Yiddish culture in defiance of Anglo-Jewry's anglicizing thrust. Others asserted themselves through radical ideology and challenged Anglo-Jewry's political conformity. An increasing sense of the masses as a body apart from, if not hostile to, communal leadership encouraged establishment jacobins. The old elite were practical men of affairs, suspicious of intellectuals and given to regarding professionals as their servants. The new community appeared to offer political scope for the ambitious and disaffected. The issue of convenience for some, of commitment for others, became Zionism. One aspect of this problem is the subject of a study by Stuart Cohen,[2] which describes the conflict between middle-class professionals, who staked their claim to usurp the leadership of Britain's Jews on a commitment to Zionism, and the traditional leadership of high politics, banking and finance who, with some noteworthy exceptions, regarded Zionism as alienating and dangerous.

The third part of the book, chapters 12 and 13, deals with the broader scene upon which this drama was played out. The complicated struggle for communal control was a matter of international as well as domestic politics from the beginning of the twentieth century. British, French, German, Austrian and American Jewish organizations had worked together, with considerable success, to organize and manage East European Jewish migration. Diplomacy and great-power politics played a substantial role in Anglo-Jewry's struggle to control its community. Disputes about what position the community should take before the Royal Commission on Alien Immigration in 1903 and activist outrage at Anglo-Jewish responses to the Kishinev pogrom the same year defined the domestic and foreign policy lines on which communal politics would be fought in Britain.

In 1914 war heightened the crisis and disrupted the traditional cooperative network of Central and West European Jewish leaderships and simultaneously raised Zionism to the sphere of practical politics. Anglo-Jewry, understanding what was at stake, attempted to coordinate its policies with those of allied belligerent and neutral Jewish elites. In domestic matters, they succeeded. Anglo-Jewry maintained control of all communal organizations. The broadening umbrella of welfare state protection, articulated during and immediately after the war, helped to pay the bills, even as it contributed to the continuing erosion of actual communal control.

Foreign policy was another matter. Anglo-Jewry had long lobbied the British government on matters concerning co-religionists abroad. Anglo-Jewry, working with its European and American counterparts, had addressed the issue of Jewish

2 S. A. Cohen, *English Zionists and British Jews: The Communal Politics of Anglo-Jewry, 1895–1920* (Princeton, 1982).

migration and created an impressive network for processing refugees. Anglo-Jewry, however, could influence British foreign policy only to the degree that its agenda could be represented as in Britain's best interests. Wartime diplomatic needs made Zionism appear to be an attractive option for western governments. Anglo-Jewry, fearing the domestic as well as international implications of Jewish nationalism, struggled in cooperation with its French counterparts to limit the diplomatic commitments of their governments to Zionism. The Balfour Declaration in November 1917, pledging the British Government to support the establishment of a Jewish homeland in Palestine, appeared to be a disastrous defeat for the anti-Zionist elite, but Anglo-Jewry quickly recovered and regrouped. Cutting its losses on Palestine, Anglo-Jewry held firm against the broader programme of Jewish nations and enjoyed at least momentary success at the Paris Peace Conference of 1919.

Anglo-Jewry's power, however, could never be fully retrieved. A façade of stability and control remained, but by the early 1920s, the world of Victorian and Edwardian Anglo-Jewry was drifting away. The generation of Jewish magnates who forged the Anglo-Jewish institutions was dead or dying. Rigid elite control was incompatible with the social mobility and increasing affluence of British Jews. London centrism could not be sustained given the growing richness and vitality of provincial Jewish life. Democratization, with all its implications, was as inescapable for Jewry as for Britain itself. Forms and institutions remained, persisting into and beyond the Second World War. But the substance was eroding well before the dramatic surge of Zionism offered a focus for class tension and political discontent. The growth of collectivism blunted traditional voluntaristic instruments of social control. In spite of those changes, cutting so deeply into institutional life, the community continued to plod forward, little altered in outward form or appearance. Ingrained habit and momentum may be partial explanations, but something else explains the residual strength of voluntarism. Anglo-Jewry's religious and cultural institutions stood the test of time into and beyond the First World War because they were effective.

But this study is more than the saga of an elite and the institutions through which it functioned. Those acted upon became leaders themselves. Immigration restriction arrived in the United Kingdom in 1905, and the flow of East European newcomers, which had already begun to diminish at the turn of the century, further declined from 1907 to the First World War. The aliens of the 1880s and 1890s adapted on their own terms to British life, influenced, perhaps even dominated, by Anglo-Jewish conceptions. Their children drew on both the old world of their parents and the new world of contemporary Britain, sometimes becoming more English than the English, sometimes remaining restless people uneasily suspended between different cultures. Some would find salvation in Zionism, others in Marxism. The quest, whatever form it took, was yet another of the tensions in the process of subsequent Anglo-Jewish history.

The study of that adaptation is another story.

1

A Dramatis Personae

The world of Anglo-Jewry was human and small. That size and character were simultaneously a strength and a weakness. The tightly-knit, interconnected cousinhood that dominated the community did not make all of the decisions, but it made many of them, and its will gave effect to most of the institutions that shaped the lives of all British Jews. Accustomed to lead, conscious of their obligations, demanding deference, this handful of families and individuals played a disproportionate role in the lives of all of its people. But neither capacity nor taste for commitment and leadership was heritable. The generations who articulated and managed the elaborate infrastructure were dead or dying by the war years. Their successors, if ambitious, often elected to act on a broader stage than British Jewry provided. Those who succeeded to the leadership ultimately proved unable to resist the aspirations of provincial Jews for a greater role in communal governance and the demand for a place in decision-making from the very groups Anglo-Jewry had been at such pains to socialize. Like other elites, however, Anglo-Jewry continued to rule by habit and momentum through and beyond the First World War.

The 'Grand Dukes'

At Queen Victoria's Diamond Jubilee in 1897, no one had the slightest doubt who should present the Loyal Address of Her Majesty's Jewish Subjects. Nathaniel Meyer (Natty) Rothschild (1840–1915), first Jewish peer to sit in the House of Lords (1885), was the presiding partner of the Rothschild Bank at New Court. The Rothschilds had already undergone their apotheosis from banker to institution. Natty's father, Lionel Nathan Rothschild (1808–1879), had been the first Jew elected to parliament and a protagonist in the enactment of the Jewish Disabilities Act of 1858. That pioneer of Jewish emancipation also continued the aggressive and expansionist banking policies of his father, the founder of the London House. By the 1880s, the Rothschilds remained monumental figures in London and international finance, but New Court turned away from dynamic banking. The three sons of Lionel Nathan made their highly conservative, personal decisions in the partners' room. From their great Piccadilly mansions and their estates in the Vale of Aylesbury, the Rothschilds became Victorian monuments, generous, eccentric, and always slightly larger than life. They moved in the highest circles in the land. Natty and the Prince of Wales had been friends since their days together at Cambridge University. Albert Edward, the future Edward VII, struggled through a blizzard in 1881 to reach the wedding of Leopold (1845–1917), Nathaniel's youngest brother, at the Central Synagogue. For the first time a member of the English royal family had attended a Jewish service. All three brothers – Nathaniel, Alfred, and Leopold, the 'Edwardian Rothschilds' – died during the First World War. Their passing marked a generational change, not only in that eminent family, but in Anglo-Jewry itself.

Alfred de Rothschild (1842–1918), Nathaniel's younger brother, although one of the three managing partners, concentrated on expenditure rather than investment. A handsome bachelor, he devoted himself to dilettantism. His appointment as a Governor of the Bank of England was abruptly terminated in 1889 when he used that position to ascertain what an art dealer had paid for a painting he later sold to Alfred. His entertainments were lavish and appropriate to an age of plutocracy. Although an expert on French eighteenth-century art and furniture, he lacked that sense of restraint that would translate his aesthetic ambitions into lasting monuments. His country house, Halton, which Alfred constructed to rival his cousin Ferdinand's Waddesdon Manor, managed to be excessive and ultimately vulgar, rather than grand. Alfred de Rothschild figured much less than his brothers – save on charitable lists – in the world of Anglo-Jewry. Alfred did, however, take an active and intelligent interest in British foreign affairs. He championed a policy of cooperation with Germany and intimidation of Russia. He seems not to have been involved, as was his brother Nathaniel, in the diplomatic arm of Anglo-Jewry, the Conjoint Foreign Committee, preferring to act as a private individual, particularly with his friend, Joseph Chamberlain. Active in spurring City resistance against loans to Russia, Alfred regarded that benighted country not merely as a vicious oppressor of Jews but as the most serious threat to world peace.

Leopold de Rothschild, the most popular of the three brothers, paid attention to politics and to the Jewish community but concerned himself principally with sport. A notable owner and breeder of racehorses, 'Mr Leo' considered his election to the Jockey Club in 1891 one of the greatest moments of his life. An automobile pioneer in England, he almost single-handedly drove the speed limit from fourteen to twenty miles per hour in 1902. His passion for motoring led him to form an automobile association in 1904 which, in 1907, became the Royal Automobile Club. From 1879 to his death in 1917, however, he shouldered a major communal burden as one of the honorary treasurers of the Jewish Board of Guardians. At the turn of the century, his generous patronage of Jewish youth clubs meant the difference between their success and failure. In 1917, Leopold found himself thrust into the centre of communal politics. Anti-Zionist leaders recruited him as a counterweight to his nephew, Walter (the second Lord Rothschild). The move did not deter the Zionists, but Leopold's illness and death deprived the anti-Zionists of one of their more influential voices just as conflict erupted into civil war at the Board of Deputies, the nearest organization British Jews had to an elective governing body.

Nathaniel Lord Rothschild, banker of highly conservative stamp and collector of all things magnificent, was England's leading Jew. Given England's international position, this gave him the dubious privilege of being regarded as the lay leader of world Jewry. An immigrant Polish Jew attending services in a small London synagogue, so runs an oft-repeated story, heard those about him whispering, 'The Lord is come.' Believing the messiah had arrived, he prostrated himself upon the floor, then peeped up to see the substantial girth and black beard of Lord Rothschild bemusedly staring down at him. Nathaniel not only conducted most of the bank's business affairs; he also played to the hilt his dominant role in Anglo-Jewry. He succeeded his uncle, Anthony, as president of the United Synagogue. Lacking a sense of humour, autocratic, and didactic, Nathaniel Baron Rothschild conserved family resources, avoided imaginative banking, and devoted himself to his charities. A strong champion of the Chief Rabbi – Hermann Adler was his selection – Rothschild took an active hand in the broad world of Jewish social institutions. Whether it was the Jews' Free School, the largest single elementary and secondary school in England, or the Russo-Jewish Committee which did so much to fund and organize the processing of refugees, whether the Jewish Board of Guardians or the Jewish Religious Education Board, the name of Rothschild would lead the list. Not only did Rothschild write the largest cheques; he made management his personal concern.

Some Rothschild schemes – a vast synagogue in Whitechapel Road for immigrant Jews to be associated with a 'Jewish Toynbee Hall' settlement house, for instance – miscarried, caught up in a combination of West End indifference and a communal political challenge from Sir Samuel Montagu. These banking titans, however, always set aside their struggle for pride of place within Anglo-Jewry when great issues arose. Even during a decade of struggle over Rothschild's East End scheme, the two worked harmoniously on the thorny political and organizational issues of alien immigration. Rothschild produced £30,000 for the proper launching of the Landau-Montagu Poor Jews' Temporary Shelter. That invaluable institution nurtured transmigrants who lacked access to regular Jewish relief institutions and who were only waiting for opportunities to move onwards from their Eastern European past to their overseas future. Rothschild effectively represented Anglo-Jewry on the Royal Commission on Alien Immigration. Montagu was one of Anglo-Jewry's most effective witnesses before it. Thanks to Rothschild's efforts and dedication, the Commission report, in 1903, conceded essential points that Anglo-Jewry wished to make about its people.

Whatever the personal limitations of Rothschild brothers, the family could fill in for deficiencies by summoning European reserves. Cousin Ferdinand de Rothschild (1839–1898) from the Vienna branch came to England to marry Evelina, Lionel's oldest child. Unlike Alfred, Ferdinand had 'unerring taste in art'.[1] Waddesdon Manor impressed both Queen Victoria, who was reduced to begging for an invitation to visit, and generations of critics. Ferdinand, who became naturalized as an Englishman on his marriage, gained Nathaniel's seat as member of parliament

1 Frances, Countess of Warwick, *Afterthoughts* (London, 1931), 87ff, compares the two. The most thorough current study of the nineteenth-century family is R. Davis, *The English Rothschilds* (Chapel Hill, 1983). For Rothschild family involvement in Eretz Israel, see S. Schama, *Two Rothschilds and the Land of Israel* (London, 1978).

for Aylesbury when his cousin became Baron Rothschild. Although he is principally remembered for the figure he cut in English high society, Ferdinand also devoted considerable time and effort to Anglo-Jewish business. Evelina herself and Ferdinand after her death took an active role in educational and medical Jewish charities.

Nathaniel disapproved of Zionism, although Theodor Herzl, the movement's founder, impressed him as a person. Herzl's *Address to the Rothschilds* (1896), however, was to find a warmer reception with Nathaniel's son, Lionel Walter (1868–1937), who succeeded as the second Baron Rothschild. Walter, the hopelessly indulged older son, was dragged most unwillingly through what his father regarded as training for his future obligations. His lack of interest in banking ultimately led his father to make an appropriate settlement on him, while disinheriting him in favour of Walter's younger brother, Nathaniel Charles (1877–1923). The title, of course, still descended to Walter, but the Bank went elsewhere. The title, in fact, followed in its wake. Charles succeeded as senior partner in the Rothschild Bank, and Charles's son was to succeed as the third Lord Rothschild in 1937.

'Mr Walter' was impossibly shy. Although a tall, handsome man, he conversed with great difficulty, almost invariably staring at the floor. His words sputtered out, either in a self-conscious whisper or, more rarely, in an overcompensating, window-shaking roar. From his earliest youth he seems to have related more easily to insects and animals than people. Well tutored by Professor Albert Newton, the great naturalist at Cambridge, Walter later began systematically to assemble what would become the Tring Zoological Museum. He had an engaging sense of his own eccentricity. He enjoyed being photographed driving a coach and four zebras through Tring Park. Walter served as member of parliament, his most memorable speech being on the subject of small fish. Walter, however, could be cultivated and used in politics. Weizmann and Balfour enchanted him, Balfour's 'Dear Walter' letters not only talking politics but touching on the miscellaneous concerns of kindred intellectuals. This extremely shy, almost totally apolitical Rothschild, during the few years that he stood forward on the public stage, was to be the focus of the great British Zionist controversy. The legend that, having received the Balfour Declaration on 2 November 1917 for which he had campaigned so long, he retreated from public attention to Tring Park and his zoological collection is inaccurate. Having helped to foment the revolt of the Jewish Board of Deputies in May 1917, he continued to play an active role on that body through the Paris peace settlement of 1919. He supported his presidential choice at the Board of Deputies, Sir Stuart M. Samuel, in domestic as well as foreign affairs. Rothschild held steadfastly to the Declaration, although he strenuously resisted the more advanced claims of Jewish nationalists. Irony and coincidence have often played a great role in history. One of the odder historical accidents is that the only important pro-Zionist English Rothschild happened to be titular head of the family at just that moment when Zionism became a matter of practical politics.[2]

---

2 The death of Leopold de Rothschild just as the 1917 dispute reached its peak removed the most outspoken Rothschild anti-Zionist. Leopold's widow, Maria, continued to fight the Zionist Organization. One unidentified Rothschild 'defined a Zionist as "an American Jew who has given an English Jew money to get a Polish Jew to Palestine." ' V. Cowles, *The Rothschilds* (New York, 1973), 207.

THE ARISTOCRACY

Sir Julian Goldsmid, Bt

'A Prince in Israel', as the *Jewish Chronicle* called Sir Julian Goldsmid, was unique in a world of individualists. A righteous man, his interests were broader and considerably more cultivated than many of his equally religious fellow philanthropists and community leaders. The Goldsmid family had been much involved in the creation of the University of London, that pioneering enterprise in British secular education. Sir Julian was no less committed to Jewish education to which he gave generously of his time and money. Goldsmid was a strong man, determined, even stubborn, without being autocratic. Without florid oratory or wilfulness, he usually got his way by judiciously asserting his strong personality. One of the ablest chairman of public meetings, his unostentatious firmness won the confidence of those with whom he was dealing, whether it was in the House of Commons, the Berkeley Street Synagogue, the Anglo-Jewish Association, or the board of directors of the Brighton Railway Company.

Goldsmid was the fifth generation of his family settled in England. Although originally from Polish Jewish background, Goldsmid's family joined the Marrano fugitives who founded the Amsterdam Jewish community. Settling in England in the mid-eighteenth century, the family moved from success to success in London banking. Sir Isaac Lyon Goldsmid, the first baronet, was one of the founders of London University and the principal pioneer of Jewish emancipation. The title descended to Sir Francis Goldsmid, Julian's uncle, who died childless. Isaac's younger son, Frederic, the father of Julian, served briefly as member of parliament for Honiton, played an active role in educational and Jewish affairs, but died when Julian was only twenty-seven. Uncle and nephew were very close, Sir Francis coming to play, to a considerable degree, the role of a surrogate father. Julian's sisters married appropriately through the cousinhood, one of his favourites becoming the wife of Frederic D. Mocatta.

The Goldsmids, while ever proud of their Jewish identification and role, moved in the highest circles of British society. Sir Julian was a friend of the Duke of Cambridge. The Prince of Wales visited him at his country seat. Sir Julian enjoyed country pursuits, and proved himself a mountaineer of some accomplishment. Goldsmid was also drawn, from early young manhood, into the world of Whig–Liberal politics. Following closely the lead of his uncle, Sir Francis (from whom he inherited the baronetcy), Julian was active on the floor of the House of Commons on behalf of persecuted Jews. Sometimes cooperating and sometimes competing with Baron Henry de Worms and other Jewish members of parliament, Julian took a strong line in favour of unrestricted alien immigration, dwelling at length and in well-informed detail on the economic benefit Britain derived from East European newcomers. Sir Julian had broad interests in matters of diplomacy and imperial policy, spoke on them with some expertise. Ultimately he broke with Gladstone on the issue of Irish Home Rule, joining the Liberal Unionists. Sir Julian became a great favourite in parliament, achieving renown as chairman of committees. Had not ill health overtaken him, he would almost certainly have become Speaker of the House of Commons.

In his philanthropic connection with the University of London, Sir Julian was, among other things, one of the great benefactors of the medical school. Goldsmid succeeded Sir James Paget as vice chancellor of the university, a post he held until his death. A fixture of the great institution on Gower Street, Goldsmid was also uncompromisingly dedicated to Jewish education. He joined his father and uncle on the board of the Jews' Free School in 1861, but the Jews' Infant Schools commanded his greatest interest. After thirty-five years of service as committee member and officer, he was elected president of the Schools in 1883. Sir Julian also presided over the West Metropolitan Jewish School in Red Lion Square, passing the reins and financial responsibility for that institution over to his sister, Isabel Goldsmid, when it was reconstituted as the Jewish High School for Girls in Chenies Street.

Sir Francis pointed Julian to yet another of his most important activities by taking a leading role in founding the Anglo-Jewish Association in 1871. Ostensibly created to revive the waning prestige of the Alliance Israélite Universelle in Britain after the defeat of France in the Franco–Prussian War, the Anglo-Jewish Association also served the important function of providing Reform Jews, excluded at the time from the Board of Deputies, with an institutional forum in which to take positions on major issues involving British Jews. Julian was its first vice president. Succeeding Baron Henry de Worms as president in 1886, Goldsmid drew on his experience in the Anglo-Jewish Association and parliament to broaden and enrich each on matters pertaining to the Jews of Eastern Europe. Julian also inherited his uncle's devotion to the cause of Roumanian Jewry. He used every contact and any opportunity to the day of his death to mitigate the lot of those unfortunates. The determination that Lucien Wolf, Anglo-Jewry's foreign policy spokesman, displayed in the Paris peace negotiations of 1919 to secure full civil rights for Roumanian Jews and minority rights in each of the succession states of Eastern Europe was, to a great extent, a Goldsmid legacy.

As president of the Anglo-Jewish Association, Goldsmid not only revived and extended the range of cooperative educational projects with the Alliance Israélite, he also brought the Anglo-Jewish Association into a prominent role in administering the funding and settling of Jewish refugees overseas. Goldsmid persuaded Baron de Hirsch to accept a vice presidency of the Anglo-Jewish Association and to transfer a considerable bloc of the shares in the Jewish Colonisation Association to that body. Active in the organization of the Mansion House Committee to aid Russian refugees and president of the successor Russo-Jewish Committee founded in 1882, Goldsmid directed the funding and flow of emigrants for a dozen years. Only Lord Rothschild and Sir Samuel Montagu were to be involved so completely both in the *haute politique* of Russo-Jewish affairs and the day-to-day management of the flow of human beings.

Goldsmid's patient and persistent diplomacy helped to construct the international cooperative network of Jewish organizations to manage the flow of emigrants and refugees. He applied the same skills to Anglo-Jewish controversies. The Russo-Jewish Committee, for instance, ran a parallel relief and social service operation to the Jewish Board of Guardians but conducted it on somewhat more enlightened and generous lines. Board executives felt not merely their philosophy but their honour impugned, a contretemps that threatened to divide Anglo-Jewry into warring camps. Sir Julian's political tact not only patched over the differences but, by 1893, also changed the way the Board of Guardians administered its affairs.

This deeply believing man, who drew close to Claude Montefiore towards the end of his life, imparted dynamism to the Reform congregation even as a young man. Once again, he followed in the footsteps of his uncle who had served as chairman of the synagogue committee. That body needed Goldsmid. The more liberal spirits of the Orthodox United Synagogue were often philosophically far in advance of Berkeley Street Reform Judaism. Sir Julian spoke to the reformers in the language of reform, but he simultaneously sought to bring Orthodox and Reform closer together. Goldsmid 'combined intellectuality and humanity, the predominance in it of great ideals without the sacrifice of magnificent tolerance.' Sir Julian negotiated the constitutional amendment that brought the Reform Jews on to the Jewish Board of Deputies. At the same time, he upheld that congregation's autonomy by declining to take part in the selection of a new Chief Rabbi. Through Goldsmid's tireless negotiations, however, the Reform Jews took part in the Jewish Religious Education Board, the first time that all Jews were represented on a body formed for religious purposes.

Sir Julian Goldsmid achieved 'a perfect equilibrium between his intellect and his emotions'. Wise, kind, and just, he had the strength of his convictions but never bullied others when he put them forward. No one bullied him. Lord Rothschild might have browbeaten others into supporting his grand design for the East End, a costly and injudicious project. Goldsmid and Sir Samuel Montagu argued against it, presented alternatives, and ultimately carried the day.

A champion of intelligent philanthropy, no Anglo-Jewish leader believed more strongly than Sir Julian that education held the key to a better future, not merely for Jews but for all mankind. Goldsmid brought his determination and commitment to the national as well as the communal scene. As acting Speaker of the House of Commons, he called Joseph Chamberlain to order, the only time that freewheeling statesman was so restrained. That same Sir Julian, who at one moment attended to the vast demands of national, even world politics, simultaneously tended the minutest details of the Jews' Infant Schools or the Alliance Israélite educational institutions in the Ottoman Empire.[3]

Sir Samuel Montagu, Bt, First Lord Swaythling

Sir Samuel Montagu, Bt, first Baron Swaythling (1832–1911) was the most important of the Samuels, a Liverpool family which drifted into London and specie banking. His nephew, Sir Stuart M. Samuel, Bt, also a banker who assumed Montagu's seat in parliament as member for Whitechapel, would preside over the Jewish Board of Deputies after the struggles of 1917. Another Montagu nephew, the statesman Herbert Samuel, the first professing Jew to hold cabinet rank, was also the first minister to suggest that the British government adopt Zionism as its policy. From active Liberal party service, Herbert Samuel would move on to become first high commissioner under the Palestine mandate.

Samuel Montagu demonstrates how history mistreats those who become unfashionable. Although active all his adult life in the United Synagogue, he also

---

3 The quotes are from the obituary editorial. *Jewish Chronicle* (*JC*), 10 Jan. 1896. Goldsmid's will had a net estate value (taxed at eight per cent) of £1,093,493 11s 6d. *JC*, 6 Mar. 1896.

created his alternative world of the Federation of Synagogues. He had strong views about rabbis, looking upon those he respected as moral authorities who should understand that real authority belonged in the hands of communal lay leaders. Montagu understood how to use rabbis as instruments of social policy as he repeatedly demonstrated in his management of the Federation of Synagogues. Montagu believed in an unamended Jewish tradition. He studied Talmud, the commentary on the *Mishna* which represents those teachings second in importance only to Torah (the Bible) for observant Jews. His first teacher went to Clifton, and that fact alone made Clifton the public school for Montagu's sons. Montagu continued regular study with the much-respected Reverend B. Spiers until very late in life.

That study reinforced his theological rigidity and moral inflexibility, qualities that grew more pronounced towards the end of his life. Montagu was not in the least bothered by accusations of fanaticism and bigotry, arguing that he did not court popularity. People must take him as he was.[4] Montagu's last will and testament underscored these less attractive qualities and helped neither his public image nor historical reputation. Montagu was a deeply believing man. But in our secular age, belief is unfashionable, so Montagu becomes for twentieth-century historians an oppressive capitalist, concealing authoritarianism behind a façade of religiosity. His monumental work among the East End poor is written down or off and ascribed to cynical manipulation. Montagu was an anti-Zionist, although he hedged his bets by buying choice Jerusalem property. Opposing Zionism cost him, as it would his brilliant son Edwin, a modish place in subsequent hagiography. Authoritarian Sir Samuel was, rigid, simplistic in his beliefs, and capitalist to the teeth, but he deserves better than historians have allowed him.

People of letters have often done badly by Samuel Montagu. Even his name, so his daughter records, was a schoolmaster's error. Montagu Samuel was mistakenly enrolled as Samuel Montagu. The family, for some reason or another, did not object and Montagu enjoyed being singled out in this way. When created a baronet in 1894, Sir Samuel had his name recognized by Letter Patent. As time went on, Montagu nourished myths about his life and even seems to have come to believe them. He represented himself as a self-made man in his constant evocation of the virtues of self-help. He came in fact from the prosperous middle classes. His father was a Liverpool watchmaker and silversmith who provided the start-up capital for the Montagu bank. Samuel's wife came from the powerful and prosperous Cohen family. He does qualify as a self-made multimillionaire. He came to London as a very young man and established a foreign exchange business, Samuel and Montagu, with his brother, Edwin Samuel. His brother-in-law, Ellis A. Franklin, another of the Anglo-Jewish gentry and a pillar of communal Orthodoxy joined the partnership in 1862, lending the bank character and respectability. The firm, reflecting young Montagu's personal domination, became Samuel Montagu and Co. He created one of the great foreign exchange houses and the undisputed leader in the world silver market. Montagu the banker was a man of total probity and considerable wisdom. He built carefully in a field much given to boom and bust. He displayed, *Banker's Magazine* observed in 1888, an

4 L. H. Montagu, *Samuel Montagu, First Baron Swaythling. A Character Sketch* (London, 1912), 31.

unerring understanding of and intuition about indirect exchanges, the capacity to make greater profits by capitalizing on disparities in conversion and reconversion rates of foreign currencies.[5]

Montagu grew rich in the City, and the City was the richer for having him. In spite of the vagaries of English weather, Royal Exchange transactions were made in an open court, the great bankers and brokers sheltering from the elements in the protective embrace of its columns. Montagu had the Royal Exchange roofed in at his own expense. Then, as a further monument to his public career as a banker and member of parliament, not to mention as a reminder of Jewish contributions to British life, Montagu commissioned Solomon J. Solomon, a leading Jewish academic artist of his day, to decorate the improved facility with a mural. His theme, aptly chosen, was Charles I demanding the surrender of the four citizens: London's refusal to do so not only restated City freedom but became a landmark in the history of English liberty. In these gestures, as so much else, Montagu displayed both shrewd political instinct and his impressive capacity to use publicity. He made himself readily available to journalists and was invariably sought out for statements on currency matters. He wrote regularly on financial subjects for periodicals, even contributing several articles to *Palgrave's Dictionary of Political Economy* and the *Encyclopaedia Britannica*. One of England's ablest and most outspoken bimetallists and champions of the metric system, he served on the Royal Commission on Gold and Silver (1887–90), spoke before any chamber of commerce that would listen, and even carried his cause to the Trades Union Congress assembled at Swansea. He was instrumental in improving the condition of London costermongers, a cause his nephew Stuart M. Samuel would adopt preparatory to succeeding Montagu as member for Whitechapel in 1900. Montagu believed in trade unions, and advocated a system of free employment registry offices well before the creation of labour exchanges. Like many who believe they themselves have risen on their own, 'he had little sympathy with the man who failed to get on.' A classic liberal, he believed that anyone, given the opportunity to do so, could succeed by application and industry.

Like the rest of the Anglo-Jewish elite, he was connected and reconnected through the cousinhood of marriage. His brother-in-law was Lionel Louis Cohen (1821–1887), a pillar of the United Synagogue, strong man in developing the Jewish Board of Guardians (which evolved into a Cohen family enterprise), and future member of parliament. Cohen connections and business success brought him to the centre of Jewish philanthropy in 1859 at the age of twenty-seven. Involved with the original Jewish Board of Guardians, Montagu established the loan system that became so central in board work. Together with the Reverend A. L. Green and Nathan S. Joseph, he introduced and refined the board's policy of

5 Indirect exchanges might mean, for instance, exchanging marks for pounds but doing so by converting the marks to francs, francs to dollars, and dollars to pounds to take advantage of favourable exchange rates on each. S. E. Franklin prepared a brief summary of the early history of the firm in 1967. Adam Spielmann, Montagu's brother-in-law, trained Samuel as a bullion broker before he left to become manager of the London branch of the Paris firm of Monteaux. When Monteaux decided to manage the London branch with a member of the family, Montagu asked his father for funds to start on his own. But Montagu was not yet twenty-one, and his father was hesitant to risk £5,000 without greater security. In 1853, Louis Samuel lent Edwin, Montagu's elder brother, the funds to start Samuel and Montagu on condition that E. A. Franklin be a partner. Franklin added the appropriate gravity and standing of a communal lay leader of undisputed probity. See, Samuel Montagu & Co. Ltd. Papers, 114 Old Broad Street, London EC2P 2HY.

systematic visitation. Long a member of the inner circle of the United Synagogue, by the age of thirty (1862) he was elected to the Board of Deputies, originally representing Manchester and ultimately the Spital Square Synagogue in London.

Montagu philanthropy invariably touched the core of communal needs. He founded the Jewish Working Men's Club in 1870, over which he presided until his death. He knew that he understood East End Jews better than most of his fellow Anglo-Jewish aristocrats. He had few illusions about but great sympathy for underprivileged co-religionists. His public position made him one of the community's leading spokesmen on great issues, and no single person did more to articulate, design, and implement communal social policy. He sat as member of parliament for Whitechapel from 1885 to 1900. A member of the House of Commons Select Committee on Alien Immigration in 1888, he was also a key communal witness before the 1902–3 Royal Commission.

When Montagu spoke, even critics listened. Montagu went to Russia in 1882 and 1886 at the behest of the Mansion House Committee, the City of London organization concerned with assisting refugees. He visited Jewish settlements from Palestine to North America. He did much to organize the stream of westward migration. His second trip to Russia, which covered thousands of miles and visited every major city and town of Jewish settlement, became a triumphal procession unsettling for Russian authorities. Government officials first harrassed him, then finding that official and unofficial efforts to intimidate Montagu only made him firmer of purpose gave 'Jew Montagu' forty-eight hours to leave the country. Never before had a member of parliament been so treated. Montagu raised the issue on the floor of the House of Commons, and only pleas from friends in Moscow dissuaded him from creating a serious international incident.

The Mansion House Fund for the relief of Jewish victims of Russian pogroms became the Russo-Jewish Committee. Montagu succeeded Sir Julian Goldsmid as president, serving until ill health forced his retirement in July 1909. In the committee, Montagu had no greater supporter than his successor, Lord Rothschild. Aiding Russian Jews – and most of the funds to do so came through the Russo-Jewish Committee – was too important a matter to be yet another area of rivalry between the banker princes. The peripatetic Montagu travelled to the wilds of Sioux country in 1884 to study existing and potential colonies for Russo-Jewish settlers. He negotiated with Jewish leaders and government officials in Montreal, Chicago and New York to develop effective machinery for processing and placing immigrants and refugees.

With Hermann Landau (1844–1924), a fellow banker and the first Pole to become part of the Anglo-Jewish elite, Montagu revived and reorganized the Poor Jews' Temporary Shelter, the way station for many migrant and transmigrant Jews as they reached London on their way from Eastern Europe. Montagu, as member of parliament, served his constituency and the nation well. He secured a reduction in naturalization fees from the Gladstone government in 1886, eased stamp charges on bills of exchange in ways that helped London remain the financial centre of the world, and helped to bring the acquisitions of the wealthy to the public by introducing legislation dealing with bequests to the nation. He also made certain that national monuments were accessible. Montagu arranged to have Tower Gardens opened to the public, to the delight of East Enders, and he sponsored the development of the riverside promenade. He knew his people, for he walked among them and dealt with them throughout his adult life. He understood them better than other princes of the community who stood, however benevolently, at a distance, embarrassed if not outraged by their vulgarity.

Montagu communicated with those East End denizens, not simply as the member for Whitechapel, but as a man who shared their deep religiosity. Although he himself shared in the anglicization of establishment Orthodoxy, he understood how foreign and threatening it must appear to the immigrant. And so he pursued his own way to bring East End Jews, as he often put it, 'under wise influences'. Once again with Hermann Landau and assisted by the clothier and East End politician, Mark Moses, Montagu had a formula. The Federation of Synagogues, which he created, nurtured and sustained until his death in 1911, was his effective way of bringing order from theological institutional chaos, anglicizing suspicious aliens, and fostering the spiritual and social values he felt best.

Judaism was at the core of Montagu's being. A life member of the council of the United Synagogue, he was active in founding the Brighton, St John's Wood, and particularly the New West End Synagogue. For many years he served as vice president of the Jewish Association for the Diffusion of Religious Knowledge, the predecessor of the Jewish Religious Education Board. Montagu headed the Initiation Society, which sought to bring medical competence as well as theological propriety to ritual circumcisions, for nearly thirty years. He also presided for more than a generation over the Shechita Board which regulated *kashrut* observance. Careful attention to kosher dietary rules, like sabbath observance, lies at the core of Orthodox Judaism. The Shechita Board oversaw the licensing and inspection of kosher butchers and their premises.

As with everything else, Montagu took the details personally and seriously. He could be seen, almost any week, hectoring a wayward butcher on the minutiae of the rules. Montagu always travelled with Dr Asher Asher, the great 'civil servant' of the United Synagogue. Both took great pride in their careful observance. Montagu proudly recalled that they often ate only bread and onions in 'deference to religious scruples'. On his voyages to North America and the Middle East, he made special arrangements for his meals, just as he ascertained that his sons, Louis, then Edwin, when travelling around the world would have kosher food for each meal prepared by a Jewish butcher.[6]

Highly opinionated, tough-minded, uncompromising on principles, Montagu often boasted that he had never left a promise unfulfilled and had never failed in an engagement. He could not be cowed, as various community worthies and the Russian government discovered. Rothschild–Montagu confrontations sometimes shook the Anglo-Jewish world, but the two invariably acted together when the situation demanded it. They agreed on the things that mattered: havens for religious refugees, immigration restriction, and the principles upon which poor and immigrant Jews should be socialized. They differed, in so far as they did at all, on how these things were to be accomplished and, to a lesser extent, in whose debt the

6 S. D. Waley, *Edwin Montagu: A Memoir and an Account of his Visits to India* (London, 1964), chapter 1. See also, 'Sir Samuel Montagu: a sketch and an appreciation', *JC*, 19 Dec. 1902 and the obituaries, *JC*, 13 Jan. 1911 from which the quotes are drawn.

community should stand. Montagu served on the board of Rothschild's 4% Industrial Dwellings Company, founded to provide model housing for poor East Enders. Rothschild acted as honorary president of Montagu's Federation of Synagogues. Their communal alliances and cooperation almost never crossed into the social sphere. Rothschild and Montagu chose not to move in the same private circles.

Montagu's sense of duty often made him stay a course he disliked but never where he felt that a moral wrong had been done. He quit the Jewish Board of Guardians over a dispute about the care of deserted children. He dragged his Federation of Synagogues out of the Jewish Religious Education Board because two members of its executive committee held what Montagu considered to be heretical theological opinions.

He took pride in his family and its achievements, although he feared, correctly, that his most brilliant son, Edwin, was at best religiously indifferent and that his remarkable daughter Lillian, with her promotion of Liberal Judaism, was theologically dangerous. A devoted Liberal in politics, Montagu contributed generously to party coffers, at a time when Liberalism was shifting from the laissez-faire he admired to a collectivism he considered socially enervating and debilitating. He was a devout Orthodox Jew who believed in the literal interpretation of scripture in the age of 'the new criticism'. He expected loyalty and deference in an age of increasing social mobility and democratization. He had an intelligent businessman's suspicion of intellectuals, although he was more of one himself than he would have been willing to acknowledge. He detested Zionism almost as much as socialism at a time when both were counting more and more among 'his people'.

Yet he was in all these things, like the Rothschilds, part of the greater English elite. While he ruled no domain as vast as the Rothschild's Vale of Aylesbury, he took an active role in country life. Montagu was an excellent horseman. His patience and love of detail made him a keen angler and expert fly-fisherman. Few could compete with him on even terms at the billiard table. His country seat, from which he took the Swaythling title, lay in Hampshire. In the country he followed the regimen of a good English lord of the manor. He sat upon the County Bench for Southampton and presided over the Southampton Horticultural Society. In the great tradition of the English elite, he straddled City and country. He was Justice of the Peace and Deputy Lord Lieutenant for the County of London, a member of the house committee of the London Hospital, and one of the first trustees of the People's Palace, Mile End. Like the Rothschilds, Montagu was a collector. In Montagu's case, his collection of silver, one of the finest in the world, was bequeathed to the nation through the Victoria and Albert Museum.

Montagu's uncle, Moses Samuel (1796–1860) had translated Moses Mendelssohn's *Jerusalem* and other works into English and edited a Hebrew literary magazine, *Cup of Salvation*. Sir Samuel Montagu, Bt, first Baron Swaythling, filled and offered that cup of salvation to tens of thousands. British Jewry owed much of its shaping and character to that sensitive master of detail, gifted with imagination and fixed in moral purpose.

Frederic David Mocatta

Frederic David Mocatta (1828–1905), the 'prince of Jewish philanthropy' was, so Claude Montefiore commented, 'the most eminent English Jew in nobility of character; he stood head and shoulders above all the rest of his community.' He commanded respect throughout Jewry and London by the range and thoughtfulness of his benevolence. 'Far from mere giving,' continued Montefiore, 'he was almost restless in doing good.'[7] Mocatta was a philanthropist, not simply a Jewish philanthropist. He gave his money and his deep moral sense of commitment without hesitation, often borrowing against his future income to meet current charitable needs. The son of one of the oldest and most eminent Sephardi families in England, his grandfather founded Mocatta and Goldsmid, the bullion brokers to the Bank of England, a firm that prospered dramatically as the British economy grew. Like his father, he entered the family firm in his mid-teens. In spite of his early apprenticeship in the world of business, his father and private tutors educated him well. Learned, cosmopolitan and well-travelled, he wrote about Jewish history and culture and collected materials concerning it. He amassed an extraordinary collection during his lifetime, principally Hebrew books, that became the nucleus of the Mocatta Library at University College, London. Like his father, he regularly attended London's Reform Synagogue. Religiously conservative himself in spite of his Reform affiliation, Mocatta attempted to achieve a unification of synagogues comparable to the consolidation of philanthropic enterprises to which he dedicated his life. In 1876 he tried, unsuccessfully, to amalgamate the Board of Deputies of British Jews and the Anglo-Jewish Association, which would constitutionally and politically have reunited the community. Although he failed in his broader ambition, Anglo-Jewry thereafter spoke with a united institutional voice on matters relating to international Jewish interests and foreign affairs. The Conjoint Foreign Committee, with equal representation from the two parent bodies, would, for the next half century, be Anglo-Jewry's foreign ministry and, in some respects, its cabinet.

Mocatta's philanthropy was his family. He and his invalid wife, a daughter of Frederick David Goldsmid, MP, had no children. Charity and social service became Mocatta's life. After thirty years at Mocatta and Goldsmid, he retired at forty-six to devote himself entirely to his great passions, philanthropy and Jewish culture. No leading English Jew had a broader vision of charity, although Mocatta's philanthropic conceptions never moved substantially beyond conventional Victorian philosophy. As one of the leading members of the Charity Organisation Society, the national committee advising all British philanthropies, he resisted notions that the state should assume wider social responsibilities and commitments. While never sharing the Victorian conception that moral deficiency explained most poverty, he understood that charities were falling far short of the needs of the 'deserving' poor.

---

7 Quoted in Ada Mocatta (ed.), *A Memoir of F. D. Mocatta* (1928–1905) (London, 1911), 17, quoted in V. D. Lipman, *A Century of Social Service 1859–1959: The Jewish Board of Guardians* (London, 1959), 139n. Mocatta exemplified the 'philanthropic' assimilationists to Theodor Herzl, the founder of Zionism. 'Mocatta impressed me,' Herzl recorded in his diary, 'somewhat like an officious second at a duel.' R. Patai (ed.), *The Complete Diaries of Theodor Herzl*, translated by Harry Zohn, volume I (New York and London, 1960), 408–9.

Accepting the starker implications of classical economy, he sought salvation in migration. The problem, as he saw it, was that British Jewry was growing at just that time it should be sending greater numbers onwards to lands of opportunity. Mocatta, who had been introduced to Herzl, saw Zionism as an impractical chimera. He understood that Jews must be allowed to escape from Russia and offered to contribute £10,000 should the community raise the £1 million that contemporary opinion estimated it would cost to do the job.[8]

His greatest work was in the organization of philanthropy rather than any novel sense of social service. He spent his life struggling against duplication and overlap, and he was personally responsible for unifying Jewish organizations in much the same line of social work.[9] One of his favourite charities, the Home for Aged Jews, was the product, in the first instance, of a merger of the Jewish Workhouse with the Hand-in-Hand Asylum. Unlike many if not most Anglo-Jewish philanthropists, Mocatta preferred to be inconspicuous. He would assist organizations in trouble, resolve conflicts, or even develop new bodies, and then, once matters were in hand, step modestly into the background. His colleagues in the Charity Organisation Society had never seen anyone so willing to spend day in and day out in the dull tedium of committee meetings or doing the grubby administrative chores of philanthropies.[10] Mocatta worked for years on the visiting committee of the Jewish Board of Guardians, believing that only by firsthand, case-by-case examination could he understand what must be done and how to do it.

No organization lay closer to Mocatta's heart than the Charity Voting Reform Association, a non-sectarian enterprise of which he was the moving spirit. The Voting Reform Association ultimately even recruited the Archbishop of Canterbury in its campaign to eliminate the invidious practice of subscribers voting to decide who should benefit from a charity. Even in death, Mocatta continued his campaign, offering the Jews' Hospital and Orphan Asylum £1,000 if it would, within ten years, end that practice. He bequeathed almost £35,000 to seventy-five charities, commenting on each and singling out others that he would have remembered had they not clung to subscriber voting.[11]

Mocatta, like Montagu, spent much time among the poor and immigrants of the East End. Like Montagu he clung to voluntaristic individualism and rejected state collectivism. Mocatta, however, unlike Montagu, had a keen sense of poverty. While he never rejected the distinction between the 'deserving' and 'undeserving' poor and believed each case must be determined on its individual merits, he realized that philanthropy was falling further and further behind what must be done in cases about which there could be no question. Mocatta believed that the wealthy should tax themselves to relieve poverty, although he had no illusions that others would do so to the extent he did. Mocatta saw trouble brewing in the social *malaise* of the 1880s and feared the socialist doctrines that immigrants brought from Eastern Europe and publicized throughout the East End. Corresponding with his close

8 He gave a more than generous proportion of the £108,000 actually collected.

9 The Mocatta Library has a Table of Metropolitan Jewish Charitable Institutions compiled by the Statistical Committee of the Jewish Board of Guardians (JBG) for the early 1870s showing more than thirty-five relief organizations dispensing an income in excess of £17,000.

10 Obituary notice, *Charity Organisation Review*, February 1905, 107.

11 *JC*, 17 Feb. 1905.

friend, Charles Stewart Loch, the moving spirit and president of the Charity Organisation Society, Mocatta toyed with various solutions, even a graduated income tax that would ascertain that 'the care of suffering' be shifted to 'society as a whole, and not left to chance as it is now.' But, in fact, Mocatta was staunchly opposed to labour legislation, thought the eight-hours movement an 'absurdity', and was astounded that the London County Council should even think of constructing working-class housing. He told Loch that state-funded old age pensions were 'a damned heresy which all thoughtful people should be bound to oppose with all their might'.[12] Mocatta, ironically, seems never to have appreciated the degree to which state funding and state money even in his time sustained the broad panoply of voluntaristic organization.

But no single Victorian philanthropist, as David Owen reminds us in his exemplary study, 'gave more lavishly of his time and money, and none more effectively combined personal service and monetary benevolence with concentrated, almost excruciating efforts to gain an understanding of the larger issues.'[13] Mocatta was generous of heart and kindly of soul. He feared the demoralizing effect of indiscriminate giving and believed that only as benevolence became a science could it also become effective. And to that end he dedicated his life.

Claude Goldsmid Montefiore

No name reverberated through Victorian Jewish history more resoundingly than Montefiore. Sir Moses Montefiore (1785–1885) overshadowed every figure in Anglo-Jewry. His residuary legatee, Joseph Sebag-Montefiore, played a major role in London banking and political matters. Justice of the Peace for London, Kent, and the Cinque Ports, Sebag-Montefiore was Sheriff of Kent in 1888 and one of the Commissioners of the Court of City Lieutenancy. President of the Board of Deputies until his death, Sebag-Montefiore's contacts were so many and so effective that the Italians named him, in 1896, honorary consul-general to London for the Kingdom of Italy.

The great Montefiore heir was also Sir Julian Goldsmid's legatee. Claude Goldsmid Montefiore (1859–1939) left his greatest mark as spokesman for advanced liberal Jewish theology, as a leader in movements for communal education, as a moral crusader and as an outspoken British patriot. Combining in himself the Sephardic and Ashkenazic traditions, this pioneer of Jewish theological reform and modernization strove without hesitation to realize, in all of its dimensions, the concept of English Jew. Montefiore announced a religious revolution from the pulpit when he preached 'One God: One Worship' at the West London Synagogue on 1 February 1896. Reverberations echo to the present day.

---

12 Mocatta–Loch correspondence in Mocatta, *Mocatta*, 31–45.

13 David Owen, *English Philanthropy, 1660–1960* (Cambridge, Mass., 1964), 428. Owen's brilliant sketch of Mocatta links his work with that of the Jewish Board of Guardians and places both in the mainstream of the history of nineteenth-century philanthropy (410–28). Ada Mocatta's obituary collection (see note 7) and the obituary notices in the press, particularly *JC*, 17 Feb. 1905, and *Charity Organisation Review*, February 1905, are the most convenient biographical summaries.

The bond of religion is not merely wider than the bond of race, it is of totally different kind. Their union in any monotheistic religion is arbitrary and galling. The bond which unites Englishman to Englishman – be they of whatever creed or race – Saxon or Norman and Dane are we – is one thing: the bond which united Catholic to Catholic and Jew to Jew is, or should be, another.

But though ideals transform facts and guide them, they are not facts themselves. In Judaism the needed and logical separation of religion and race, the triumph of the one and the disappearance of the other, still awaits accomplishment. It is obvious that the very idea of it was absurd until the days of emancipation. The Jews had first to become citizens of the lands in which they dwelt, feeling and responding to the bond and duties and the thrill of nationality at least as fully and acutely as their fellow citizens of a different creed.

Small wonder that Montefiore, more strongly than any Anglo-Jewish leader, would resist, denounce and fight the emergence of Jewish nationalism. For those who sought refuge from anti-Semitism and the tremors of his age in a Jewish state and Jewish nationalism, Montefiore argued the case for Jewish universalism.

> Remember first of all that it is religious idealism alone which will cure us Jews of those rather prevalent failings of ostentation and display, sins ven[i]al in themselves, but sometimes leading to loose living and materialistic ideas, and thereby providing an additional stimulus to the venomed activity of the foe. Religion has been, is, and will continue to be, the greatest ethical power over the mind of man. The lover of God will not be the servant of Mammon. The lover of God will not be the slave of lust. The honour of woman is safest with the lover of God.
>
> And in the second place remember that national religions are incongruous with modern civilization – nay more that a national religion is incongruous with our own creed. The more Eastern and oriental our religion is in forms and customs, the more it plays into the hands of the anti-Semites. The more our forms and customs tally and correspond with the forms and customs of Eastern races, the more handle you give to the attacks of our enemies, the less chance you afford for the propagation of the true Jewish religion.[14]

Montefiore's historic theism was not an attenuated mixture of Judaism and Unitarianism with a high sense of moral purpose, as some critics suggested, but an attempt to discover a dynamic basis upon which to harmonize Jewish theology and ethics with modern philosophic criticism and scholarship. Montefiore demanded a religion that would bring outsiders in, not drive insiders out. Patriotic, even jingoistic, ethical, with more than a touch of heavy-handed puritanism, humane in the best liberal tradition of the nineteenth century, Claude Goldsmid Montefiore sought to make English Jews the paragons of British society.

Unlike most of the privileged Anglo-Jewish elite, Montefiore did not adopt the social habits of the English upper classes. The Rothschilds were country gentlemen.

---

14 C. G. Montefiore, 'One God: One Worship. A Sermon Preached at the West London Synagogue on Saturday, February 1, 1896'. Printed with comment in *JC*, 14 Feb. 1896.

Montagu rode well and delighted in hunting. Montefiore, quite possibly because he was so intensely engaged in the study of moral issues, despised hunting. He held 'purposeless' country weekends in contempt. Abstemious himself, he felt that drink, the lubricant of privileged social gatherings, corroded moral character. Gambling, one of polite society's vices, destroyed winner and loser alike. Like many other latitudinarian religious thinkers, he preached and practised a strong and somewhat narrow moral code. From this grew his obsession with the moral instruction of the young, his lifelong commitment to children's education, his concern with sexual discipline, and even his contribution of his suburban Stamford Hill estate to be a reformatory for girls.

Cultivated and sophisticated, Claude Montefiore carefully formulated views he considered to be right. Once refined, he clung to them with a rigour a seventeenth-century Covenanter would have envied. Jews must be the moral pathfinders for all humanity. That was their higher purpose. Zionism and Jewish nationalism, Montefiore was convinced, threatened not merely the social and political achievements of Western Jewry; they placed Judaism itself at risk. So, as president of the Anglo-Jewish Association from 1895 to 1922, he fought such ideologies before, during and after the Balfour Declaration. However fixed his own views, Montefiore personally supported scholarship and learning, even when it ran counter to his opinions. Although his own scholarly interests were Judaism in the early Christian era, Montefiore felt that he needed to understand rabbinic theology better. So he brought Solomon Schechter, the founder of Conservative Judaism, to England in 1882, launching him on his long, successful career in Britain and the United States. Montefiore never lost sight of his own purpose, whatever the distractions might be. He pioneered Liberal Judaism. One of his most active lieutenants proved to be Lily Montagu, Sir Samuel's dynamic social-worker daughter. Lily had a more than spiritual interest in Montefiore, who was then a widower. Their public attitudes and philanthropic views coincided, but the match, in spite of Lily's best efforts, did not take. Montefiore chose Florence Fyfe Brereton Ward, sometime vice mistress of Girton College, Cambridge. Miss Ward received instruction from the Reverend Morris Joseph and was received into the Upper Berkeley Street Synagogue. Lily Montagu remained single and expressed her love for Montefiore through their joint enterprises – Liberal Judaism and the moral instruction of youth.

DYNASTIES AND INSTITUTIONS

The Cohens and the Jewish Board of Guardians

The Jewish Board of Guardians was, in its own way, a cousinhood. The president actually managed the institution, and through most of its years a member of the Cohen family presided. Since Anglo-Jewry's cousinhood was so inextricably linked by marriage, the Cohen familial connection was broad indeed. In addition, other 'inevitable' leaders, like Frederic D. Mocatta, brought their own networks of committed kin. Mocatta, vice president of the board, was brother-in-law of Mrs Lionel Lucas (1835–1918), who not only patronized but supervised much of the women's work at the board with a firm hand. Mocatta's nephew, David Frederick Schloss (1850–1912) brought civil and communal expertise to the board. He was a barrister, a civil servant at the Board of Trade, and an acknowledged authority on labour and industrial problems. Schloss had also been one of the investigators on Booth's famous survey of London. Involved in the government enquiries about immigration and British Commissioner to the 1910 International Congress on Unemployment held in Paris, he sponsored and directed much of the public health work of the board from 1884. Alexanders, Raphaels, Keysers, Lucases and Schlosses, not to mention Franklins (related to Waleys and Montagus) and Samuels, served on the board from generation to generation and brought in-laws and relations to aid the cause.

Whether because of this or in spite of it, a limited number of families provided the bulk of board support and leadership. But such has almost always been the case with successful eleemosynary institutions. The extensive list of donors, published with individual contributions specified, was an important community statement. 'Aid societies' for the board, as for other charitable causes, mobilized small donors with their halfpennies or half-crowns. Thus could the common people of the community assist in what all regarded as a great cause and make their individual statements of respectability. Slightly more substantial contributors arrayed themselves behind one communal leader or another, through whose good offices and encouragement money was raised. In this way, with its overtones of familial politics, communal gentry jostled one another in amicable competition.

Ephraim Alex, the founding president, provided much of the patient diplomacy and political leadership that was to bring the Board of Deputies into being, but that institution bore from its beginning the determined stamp of Lionel Louis Cohen. First as secretary developing and articulating board policies, and then for eighteen years as its second president (1869–87),

> the ethics of the Board as to the treatment of the poor might, in a great measure, be assigned to him for their origin; the policy of the Institution has been determined and shaped by the aid of his marvellous administrative ability, his guiding principle having been to centralize and to co-operate with kindred societies for the purpose of checking and suppressing mendicity and indiscriminate charity, and to found such a centralization as to prevent the idle partaking of the charity intended for the unfortunate.[15]

At the United Synagogue, in London Conservative Party politics, in stock exchange matters and as designer of Anglo-Jewry's social welfare dreadnought, Lionel staked a wide claim for the Cohen clan. Whether Sir Benjamin L. Cohen, Bt, Lionel's younger brother, Conservative member of parliament, and leading figure on the London Stock Exchange, would have succeeded as third president had Cohen leadership not by then have come to be assumed, one cannot tell. When Lionel died in 1887, there seemed no question about the matter. Sir Benjamin's personal mark on the Jewish Board of Guardians was not some new approach to social work and relief. He constructed an impressive monument. He personally

---

15 JBG, *Annual Report for 1887*, quoted from L. Magnus, *The Jewish Board of Guardians and the Men Who Made It* (London, 1908), 82.

gathered the resources to construct the modern facilities for the board opened in 1896 without intruding upon organizational capital funds or deflecting operational contributions and subscriptions. In matters of policy, he opted for those things that had worked. Sir Benjamin Cohen stepped down at the time when the board found itself increasingly pressed beyond available resources. By 1897, the facts could no longer be avoided. However broad a basis of small contributions might be constructed, the Board of Guardians depended on substantial contributions from major benefactors for its ongoing work and the continued capitalization of endowment. Larger contributors were cutting back on their subscriptions, and financing board work required increasingly dangerous raids into endowment. Anglo-Jewry did not regard this as a failing vote of confidence in the Cohens. It turned to Sir Leonard Lionel Cohen, son of Lionel and the president from 1900 to 1920. Sir Leonard proved an able, if hard-pressed, leader who forced the board to reconsider the range of its activities, while trying to give it a renewed sense of purpose. He pioneered timely new ventures, particularly in health care. He guided the organization through much of the initial conscious contruction of the welfare state, preserving, as far as possible, the values the board had proclaimed since its implementation while sliding costly social welfare activities partly or almost completely into the hands of the state. Sir Leonard did much to define the broad outlines of the twentieth-century partnership of the increasingly collectivist state and the residually voluntaristic Board of Guardians.

The dynasty continued through the twentieth century. Vice president Sir Arthur Stiebel succeeded Sir Leonard in 1920, but in 1926 Miss Hannah F. Cohen, daughter of Sir Benjamin, became one of the two vice presidents. She succeeded Stiebel as president in 1930, the first woman not only to hold high office in but to run the Board. She stepped down in 1940, surrendering the presidency to Sir Lionel Cohen (later Lord Cohen of Walmer, president 1940–7), the son of Sir Leonard, and grandson of Lionel Louis Cohen, the man who, more than any other, had made the Jewish Board of Guardians.

RELIGIOUS LEADERS

The Chief Rabbi

The Adler family dominated the nineteenth-century Chief Rabbinate. The rabbi of the Great Synagogue had already come to be recognized in the London and provincial Ashkenazic comunity as the chief religious authority in the country when Nathan Marcus Adler took office in 1845. The constitutional structure of what would become the chief rabbinate of the British Empire, Bet Din (chief rabbinical court) and all, was in place. Dr Nathan Adler, as Chief Rabbi (1845–80), promulgated a set of regulations in 1847 defining his supremacy in all matters of ritual and practice. Nathan Adler blended Orthodox Judaism into English life, calling rabbis ministers and clerics, dressing them in the mufti of Anglican clergymen, introducing the vocabulary of the Established Church into British Orthodox Judaism, and even endorsing an ecclesiastical architecture that suggested Anglican substance with Jewish symbols. Adler believed that sustaining traditional

Orthodoxy in religious practice was best accomplished through judicious adaptations to British culture and a high degree of centralization of religious authority. This demanded, among other things, an Anglo-Jewish rabbinate, but, as a way of enhancing his own authority, he carefully appropriated the title to his own gift. Ministers with the title of Reverend presided over synagogues. Adler took the lead in promoting the Jews' College to train them.[16] Those seeking rabbinical certification, however, could only secure it on the continent or by Adlerian fiat. Not until the beginning of the twentieth century were statutory arrangements agreed upon that defined the English training prerequisites for the rabbinate.

The Adlers also pursued institutional centralization. Nathan Adler pressed for the systematization of Jewish charity through what would ultimately become the Jewish Board of Guardians. The United Synagogue was also much of his making. The United Synagogue Act of 1870 statutorily defined the function and relationships of the principal London Orthodox synagogues. In doing so, the parliament did more than ratify what had been past practice. As Jews established communities in outer London and the provinces of Britain, the United Synagogue aided them to construct new component synagogues.[17] As far as the Adlers could achieve it, Orthodox Jewry was shaped institutionally to resemble Anglicanism, with the Chief Rabbi a Jewish Archbishop of Canterbury.

The Adlers, father and son, shaped the pre-1914 institutions in their authoritarian image. Nathan M. Adler, a distinguished scholar and rabbi of Hanover, possessed the international standing and social elitism Anglo-Jewry sought and needed as it aspired to be an accepted and established subculture within British society. The common treasure of the community, Nathan observed when speaking to the Sephardi congregation, was the Torah. What bound them together as Jews was the same religion, the same holy language, and the same history.[18] But Nathan never publicly aspired to achieve Sephardi–Ashkenazi union. He sought only close cooperation. Within the rapidly growing Ashkenazi community, however, he had a well-defined agenda. The minister, as he insisted upon calling the spiritual head of each congregation, must set a public example through his own life. He was the guardian of the holy law and must preserve the sacred inheritance 'undimmed and uninjured'. Education, in the broadest sense, must come under rabbinical purview. The Jewish home was 'the first and most important school', 'our little

16 C. Roth, 'The Chief Rabbinate of England', in I. Epstein and E. Levine (eds) *Essays presented to J. H. Hertz, Chief Rabbi* (London, 1942); V. D. Lipman, *A Social History of the Jews in England, 1850–1950* (London, 1954), 34–40. Nathan Adler, however, sought to recruit middle-class Jewish boys to an appropriate Jewish preparatory school and move them on to the rabbinate. As Jews became middle class, they preferred to share English elite education, and Jews' College perpetually teetered on the brink of disaster on just such issues of social recruitment. For one interesting exception, see I. Finestein, 'Joseph Frederick Stern 1865–1934: Aspects of a Gifted Anomaly', in A. Newman (ed.), *The Jewish East End 1840–1939* (London, 1981), 75–96.

17 The standard history is A. Newman, *The United Synagogue* (London, 1980), although C. Roth, *The Great Synagogue, 1690–1940* (London, 1950), is still useful. For the Adler family, see also M. N. Adler, *The Adler Family* (London, 1909).

18 N. M. Adler, *The Bonds of Brotherhood: A Sermon Delivered in the Synagogue . . . of the Spanish and Portugese Congregation . . .* (London, 1849), 5ff, 14.

Temple the school for adults'.[19] Nathan preached order and decorum in religious and secular affairs. When Nathan retired in 1880, the chief rabbinate passed, although not without considerable debate and controversy, to his younger son Hermann. The choice was well made, for the next generation of British Jewish history demanded a gifted Chief Rabbi who would not question the values and assumptions on which Anglo-Jewry rested. Hermann's older brother, Marcus, no less able intellectually but perhaps of less severe mettle, turned his attention to Stepney Jewish Schools and actuarial statistics, with both of which he achieved singular success.

Dr Hermann Adler presided over the massive growth of the Jewish community and moved generally in harmonious tandem with the Rothschild communal leadership. Autocratic in style and conservative in politics, Chief Rabbi Hermann Adler presided over the greatest expansion of the British Jewish community. As much as any man, he was to mould the spiritual response of Anglo-Jewry to the dramatic problems of modernization. Adler was a missionary. He toiled and preached with but one end in view, to make West Enders and East Enders alike 'loyal subjects and steadfast Jews'.[20] He fought all forms of 'irreligion', pressed for traditional content and ritual in Judaism, and believed, above all, that the highest form of Jewish culture was to be found in the enlightened diaspora.

Adler disliked the immigrant Jews who disrupted the tidy fabric of the community and displayed an unpleasant propensity to trigger doctrinal controversy. He detested Zionism which he considered 'absolutely mischievous'.[21] He could talk to the immigrants in their own tongue, and he was not above appealing to universally acknowledged East European rabbis for theological support when it suited his purposes. Adler was suspicious of secular reformers and had as little as possible to do with Reform Judaism, even to the extent in 1902 of ostracizing the West London Synagogue of Reform Jews. His father had fought the Reform movement. The son now battled both Reform and twentieth-century Liberal Judaism. Adler rejected latitudinarianism and 'the new criticism'. He accused Claude Montefiore of omitting the 'essentials of faith and practice', of rendering Judaism indistinguishable from Ethical Culture or Unitarianism.[22] Just as he stood four-square for an Orthodoxy he and his father had anglicized against the winds of intellectual change, London preoccupied him at a time when provincial Jewry was growing in size and pride. In an increasingly democratic age, he remained an uncompromising believer in elite governance. 'I would not,' Adler argued,'unduly exalt the functions of the Jewish pulpit. But the danger of our times is not that the pulpit be unduly exalted, but lest, by the apathy of its incumbents, it be unworthily lowered.' 'Whenever the preacher's voice is heard in the sanctuary,' he continued, 'it must be to teach the doctrines of Judaism in all their purity and integrity.'[23]

19 N. M. Adler, *Predigt beim Antritte seiner Amtes also Ober-Rabbiner in Grossbritannien gehalten in der Great Synagogue of London am 4ten Tamus 5605 (8ten Juli 1845)*. (London, 1845), 5–15. Adler preached his inaugural sermon in German. All his sermons published thereafter were in English.
20 [Charles] Booth Papers, B 197/11 in the Library of the London School of Economics and Political Science.
21 Anglo-Jewish Association (AJA) council meeting, 11 July 1897. AJA Council minute books, III, 56–7 in the Mocatta Library, University College, London; *JC*, 16 July 1897.
22 Letter to the editor, *Daily Telegraph*, 28 Oct. 1909.
23 H. N. Adler, 'The Functions of the Jewish Pulpit', *The North London Pulpit. A Special Series of Sermons Delivered at the North London Synagogue*, No. 3 (7 May 1892) (London, 1892), 8–9.

One acute observer found him a man 'of great energy and fervour. He treats nothing lightly and becomes impressive in his intensity.'[24] Learned, but literal minded, he had an ambiguous relationship to and view of foreign Jews. Adler feared them. They endangered the work of generations. They were given to ecclesiastical indiscipline. They threatened Anglo-Jewry's harmonious world view. Adler's answer was authority rigorously imposed. His strong centralization quite possibly deprived the synagogues of much flexibility which might have enabled them to be more responsive to rapidly evolving communal needs. Adler's iron hand provided British rabbis less imaginative scope than they might otherwise have had. Ever jealous of challenges to his authority, real or imagined, Adler unwittingly created gratuitous opportunities for those whose visions and values were different. When he died, in 1911, after pontificating for more than thirty years, not only the Adler dynasty and style but the constitutional powers of the Chief Rabbi became a matter of heated debate. Chief Rabbi Herz, imported from the United States via South Africa, preferred cooperation and negotiation, even Zionism.

The age of the Adlers, however, had not passed. Another Adler had come to play a major role in both Jewish and London life. Nettie Adler, daughter of the Chief Rabbi, embodied in her life and activities an important shift in focus in Anglo-Jewish life. A progressive in the spirit of the turn of the century, she sat on the Education Committee of the London County Council. Much involved in the more constructive aspects of contemporary feminism – the National Union of Women Workers and the National Union of Women's Suffrage Societies – Nettie Adler brought her skill as a professional social worker and teacher to London local government and the influential and exemplary public educational policies that London would pioneer. She symbolized, in a profound sense, the changes taking place in the social politics of Anglo-Jewry. Women were emerging to take their place, even in the conservative Jewish world, with men. She was strategically placed to continue traditional Adler leadership, to administer part of the transition from voluntaristic philanthropy to the welfare state.

Moses Gaster

Rabbi Dr Moses Gaster (1856–1939) never wielded the power of the Adlers. Spiritual leader of the Sephardim, Gaster was never fully master even in his own house. Nor did he ever play the role he was certain that he deserved in the world of Anglo-Jewry. Gaster was extraordinarily learned, financially improvident, notoriously temperamental, infinitely proud, and has not been treated well by historians. Born in Roumania, he taught at the University of Bucharest and was an acknowledged authority on Roumanian literature. He was dismissed and expelled from the country in 1885 for protesting against the mistreatment of Roumanian Jews. Gaster's erudition and status brought him, first, an appointment in Slavonic Literature at Oxford, then, in 1887, appointment as Haham (Communal Rabbi) of the quarrelsome and problematical English Sephardi community, although he was himself Ashkenazi. The Sephardi leadership preferred worthy decorations as rabbis. The knotted brow on Gaster's portrait in the Spanish and Portugese Jews'

24 Booth Papers, B 197/29.

Congregation bears artistic witness to his tortured relationship with it. Gaster delighted the lower orders in his flock, but the genteel and arrogant leadership quarrelled with him on one issue after another.[25] The remarkable fact of Gaster's career was not his ultimate retirement as Haham in 1918 but the fact that he had lasted so long.[26]

London's Sephardic Synagogue was certainly not his preference. A man of extraordinary intellectual gifts and capacity, he had great hopes for the Judith Montefiore College in Ramsgate. His effort to turn it into a Jewish institution of higher learning for the training of rabbis (1891–6) failed, dissolving in a confusing welter of accusations and stories of Gaster's unwillingness to discipline his students. Disputes about diplomas and qualifications, painful recriminations, and controversy that cast credit on no one sullied the columns of the *Jewish Chronicle* through the winter of 1895–6.

Matters were no better when it came to Zionism, of which Gaster is one of the less remembered and certainly less celebrated pioneers. Gaster fought almost everybody in the movement at one time or another. His running battles with Lucien Wolf come as no surprise, but Gaster was, if anything, harder on friends than foes. Gaster believed, with some justice, that he held the 'true' Zionist dream aloft when Ugandan and Mesopotamian compromises were under serious discussion. Herzl might compromise, but Gaster would not. His savage struggle with Leopold Greenberg of the *Jewish Chronicle* added little to either's reputation. Gaster never forgave, was never wrong, was always the victim of rogues and knaves.

Fact followed prediction in Gaster's case. He was, in fact, regularly betrayed. Weizmann, who had stood with him in the early divisions within the English Zionist Federation and for whom Gaster had helped to secure British citizenship, cut him down on the eve of the Balfour Declaration. Gaster's special relationship with Herbert Samuel, which grew out of the friendship of their wives, not to mention close associations cultivated for years with such strategically placed civil servants as Lawrence Oliphant at the Foreign Office, played a crucial role in converting the British government to the Zionist cause. Gaster carried the day with Sir Mark Sykes, and Sykes became the foremost champion of Zionism within the closely knit Cabinet staff–Foreign Office taskforce that managed Middle Eastern policy.[27]

During the war, while Herbert Samuel and Lucien Wolf were attempting to impress alien Jews from London's East End into either the British or Russian army, Gaster led the resistance. He argued the injustice of conscripting aliens alone for

25 See, for instance, the considerable resentment of the annual meeting of the Elders in January 1905 over allowing the Haham renewal of his lease for the house at 193 Maida Vale for £40 plus rates and taxes. The house and repairs cost the congregation £1,813 8s 7d. *JC*, 3 Feb. 1905.

26 Gaster's easily wounded vanity was doubly affronted when Rabbi Dr Adler, the Ashkenazic Chief Rabbi, was invited to dine with Campbell-Bannerman rather than Gaster himself. Gaster had laboured diligently, even against a Jewish candidate, to secure the return of Liberal MPs. Gaster even believed that he had been instrumental in preventing the return of Gerald Balfour in the election of 1906, a modest hyperbole. Perhaps, he suggested plaintively to Winston Churchill, this could be attributed to the Liberal Prime Minister's bad staff work. They confused the Chief Rabbis. Gaster to Churchill, 26 Feb. 19, Gaster Letter Book, March 1905 to June 1906, 654–5. Gaster Papers, in the Mocatta Library, University College, London.

27 Gaster to Sykes, 3 July 1915; 3 Nov. 1916; 3, 9, 31 Jan., 1 Feb. 1917. Gaster Letter Book, Aug. 1915 to Nov. 1916, 720–1; Nov. 1916 to May 1918, 8–9. 184–5, 207, 268, 272–3, 279.

the British army and the immorality of forcing them to fight for a Russia that had oppressed and persecuted them.[28] Even after conscription came to Britain, Gaster helped to orchestrate a campaign against military service through the Foreign Jews Protection Committee against Deportation and Compulsion, which continued to gain widespread popular support from alien East European Jews.[29] That support became, in the course of the war, a vital factor in Jewish internal politics. Gaster also brought Sokolow from Russia, and arranged meetings with British officials, only to find that Weizmann, James de Rothschild, and Sokolow had blocked him from what Gaster considered to be his deserved presidency of the English Zionists and even removed him from the primary executive council.[30] His anger was unappeasable, if understandable. That he made many of his own difficulties and that he lost so many battles should not, however, in any way diminish his importance in the life of Anglo-Jewry during these great years of transition.

THE COMMUNAL CIVIL SERVANTS

Nathan Joseph and Lucien Wolf

While but two among many dedicated and effective servants of Anglo-Jewry, Nathan Joseph (1834–1909) and Lucien Wolf (1857–1930) left their indelible marks, Joseph in domestic and Wolf in foreign policy. Both were born in England. Both were totally acculturated and proudly Jewish. The Joseph family was a cadet branch of the cousinhood, Nathan Solomon Joseph being a brother-in-law of Chief Rabbi Hermann Adler. Nathan's father, a substantial merchant, married into the Raphael banking family. The nine children were privately tutored, a common way of educating the progeny of prosperous Anglo-Jewry. Nathan continued to University College, London achieving a distinguished record in civil engineering. Graduating at twenty, Nathan trained as an architect. In a career spanning fifty years, he achieved deserved renown as Anglo-Jewry's leading architect and its most wide-ranging social engineer. Joseph never flagged in his commitment to improving the social and spiritual life of the community of which he was a part. He sought to improve the quality of Jewish spiritual life and served as honorary secretary to Jews' College from 1861 to 1869. Joseph worked closely with Montagu in the early years of the Jewish Association for the Diffusion of Religious Knowledge and was himself the author of many of that institution's tracts. At first highly Orthodox, he moved increasingly towards liberal and reform positions and was, with Claude G. Montefiore, a founder of the Jewish Religious Union. His book, *Religion, Natural and Revealed*, suggests the extent of that theological and philosophical migration. Early concerned with issues of socializing poor and immigrant Jews, his quarrel with Lionel Cohen in 1870, when Joseph defended the small East End Orthodox

---

28 Among other things, Gaster thereby displaced Lucien Wolf as head of the National Union for Jewish Rights. Dywien to Gaster, 15, 31 Aug., 21 Sept. 1916. Gaster Papers 36/328/1, 105/328/1, 86/329/1.

29 Bezalel to Gaster, 10 May 1917, Gaster Papers 45/327/2; Slvko to Secretary of State, War Office [7, 10 Sept. 1917], Gaster Papers 215.

30 Gaster to Sokolow, Dec. 1917, Gaster Papers.

synagogues against 'establishment Synagogue imperialism', anticipated the Rothschild–Montagu dispute over the United Synagogue or Federation of Synagogues approach to socializing Jews of the East End.

Joseph was an accomplished architect. His monuments still stand, impressive reflections of Victorian and Edwardian styles and values. He designed the buildings for the Guinness and Iveagh Trusts. The Central, Bayswater, and New West End Synagogues were his creations. Experienced in designing model working-class housing, he created the blocks of flats for the 4% Industrial Dwellings Company, Anglo-Jewry's venture into model subsidized buildings to house and socialize East End workers. While one historian who knew them well referred to them as ugly monuments to paternalism, they represented the state of the art in their own time and a decided improvement over the dangerous rookeries they replaced.[31]

Joseph learned his social engineering in the field and brought to it the ongoing literature of social amelioration. When Sir Samuel Montagu initiated the visiting committee of the Jewish Board of Guardians in 1861, Nathan Joseph was one of the original members. While he served both the Jewish Board of Guardians and United Synagogue on a variety of investigatory committees, his particular interests were health, sanitation, and the relationship of environment and behaviour. Whatever the issue of the moment, Joseph could be found at the heart of it. As secretary then chairman of the sanitary committee of the Jewish Board of Guardians, he persuaded Anglo-Jewry to use its influence to attack the worst housing conditions and landlord abuses. Joseph lobbied for enabling legislation that would permit local authorities to take legal action. When it came, Joseph led the agitation to induce borough and council authorities to take action. As if his work on the sanitary and visiting committees, his efforts to design and develop public and private working people's housing, and his own successful architectural firm were not demanding enough, he was also deeply involved in several important philanthropies. The Jews' Hospital and Orphan Asylum, of which he was vice president, depended upon him for almost half a century. Directing education and apprenticeship policy for that institution, he was responsible for shifting the burden for its support onto the Board of Education. He himself patronized promising Jewish scholars and younger Jews who taught at board schools.

Joseph played a central role in designing Anglo-Jewry's policies and institutions for managing immigrants and refugees. Among the founders of the Mansion House Committee in 1882, he served as chairman of the executive of its successor body, the Russo-Jewish Committee and of the Conjoint Committee of that body and the Jewish Board of Guardians. His leadership and activity in the several institutions involved guaranteed that Anglo-Jewry's major institutions pursued essentially uniform, coordinated domestic policies from the 1880s to his death in 1909 and beyond. To the extent that any single person could be said to have

---

31 J. White, *Rothschild Buildings: Life in an East End Tenement Block, 1887–1920* (London, 1980), 24.

developed, defined and articulated Anglo-Jewry's social policy, that individual was Nathan Solomon Joseph.[32]

Joseph's counterpart in Anglo-Jewish international policy was Lucien Wolf, Anglo-Jewry's foreign secretary. Born in London on 20 January 1857, he was the eldest son of Edward Wolf of Canonbury, then a solidly middle-class Jewish enclave. Edward Wolf, who married the daughter of a Viennese banker, left the Habsburg domains for England after 1848. He furnished his children English bourgeois comfort of continental sophistication. First educated in English private schools at Gloucester House, Kew, and Highbury College, Lucien then attended the Athenée Royale in Brussels and the Institut Rosenfeld in Paris. Cultivated, cosmopolitan, fluent in several languages, Wolf was an excellent scholar, a distinguished if somewhat antiquarian historian, and a well-connected journalist. One of the founders of the Jewish Historical Society of England, he brought to his tasks an enthusiasm for scholarship and facility of expression that still command respect today. He revelled in mixing with communal notables, strongly identifying with them. His began his journalistic career at the age of seventeen, serving as sub-editor and leader writer for the *Jewish World* from 1874 to 1893. When he became the editor (1906–8), he enjoyed no more success than his predecessors in competing with the *Jewish Chronicle*, a journal for which he also frequently wrote. He was active in London and continental journalism, being simultaneously the foreign editor of the *Daily Graphic* during its heyday from 1890 to 1909 and London correspondent for *Le Journal* of Paris from 1894 to 1898, successfully juggling these assignments with his work for the *Jewish World*. He wrote regularly on colonial and foreign affairs for *The Times* and contributed many articles to the *Fortnightly Review* under the pseudonym 'Diplomaticus'. His close connections with the Reuters news agency provided him with both information and contacts which he turned to good account both in diplomacy and journalism. He made the cause of persecuted Jews his own. A classical liberal in politics – he referred to himself often as a disciple of the Manchester School – Wolf believed that human history was a record of improvement, that the diaspora was a permanent fact, that Jews were an essential and important part of the cultures in which they lived. Emancipation and acculturation would, he felt certain, ultimately come to the Jews of the benighted states of Eastern Europe, and Jews would prosper there as they had done in Western nations. From early in his adult life, Wolf committed himself to celebrating Jewish achievements in Western society and politics and hastening the process of true emancipation, equality and acculturation in the East.

His weapons were his agile pen and a bent for diplomacy, both quickly recognized by friend and foe. No one used either talent more effectively. Documentation was his forte; eloquence rendered it compelling. No task was too difficult. He knew his languages, and he created a network of informants. He created *Darkest Russia*, the best informed and most articulate organ denouncing the Russian political and religious persecution of Jews. So complete were his files that

32 See, particularly, Joseph's obituary in *JC*, 18 June 1909. Herzl had ambiguous views about Joseph whom he felt exemplified 'stupid charity' and those 'Jewish relief committees [which] must subordinate themselves to us, or they will be dissolved.' He called Joseph 'a likeable, completely anglicized, slow-thinking and prolix old man'. Theodor Herzl, *The Complete Diaries of Theodor Herzl*, ed. R. Patai, trans. H. Zohn, 5 vols (New York, 1960), vol. I, 278.

he could, in response to almost any international issue, prepare a well-documented position paper articulating and defending Jewish interests. Cosmopolitan and gracious, Wolf was equally at home in the drawing rooms of Anglo-Jewry and the exclusive corridors of the Foreign Office. Not surprisingly, the Ripon family selected Wolf to write the life of the first Marquess with whom he had often worked so harmoniously.[33] Wolf's abilities, his style, and his command of the facts in issues immediately relevant to Jews brought him to the council of the Anglo-Jewish Association in 1886, where he remained until his death. He seemed the logical choice to be secretary for the Conjoint Foreign Committee of the Board of Deputies of British Jews and the Anglo-Jewish Association in 1888 and its successor, the Joint Foreign Committee, when that body replaced the Conjoint in 1917. He was frequently called the Ambassador of the Jewish People, a deserved soubriquet. As much as any single person, Wolf came to play a dominant role in the diplomacy not merely of Anglo-Jewry but, to a considerable degree, of French Jewry as well. These matches were easily made. Most of the Anglo-Jewish elite and the more active members of the Alliance Israélite Universelle shared Wolf's values, philosophy and opinions. Wolf also never forgot who held formal authority. He talked with and wrote almost daily to those who mattered, cleverly insinuating that his policies and initiatives were really their own. Claude G. Montefiore of the Anglo-Jewish Association and David L. Alexander, president of the Board of Deputies, never wavered in their support of Wolf, and when Alexander was driven from the presidency in 1917, Wolf carefully rebuilt that same relationship with Alexander's successor, Sir Stuart Samuel. In the same way, Wolf's intimate relationship with Jacques Bigart, the secretary of the Alliance Israélite, essentially fused the policies of Anglo–French Jewry during and after the First World War. The Quai d'Orsay considered Wolf to be a man of utmost importance. John Headlam-Morley, treaty draftsman for the British peace delegation, called Wolf the effective author of the Minority Treaties imposed on the Succession States in 1919. Lord Robert Cecil thought of Wolf as one of his key League of Nations experts on refugee questions. Rabbi Stephen Wise, who had crossed swords with Wolf on Zionist issues in 1919, appreciated Wolf's qualities. Awarding him the honorary degree of Doctor of Hebrew Letters in July 1930, Wise announced,

> Lucien Wolf, English Journalist, Jewish Historian, international diplomatist, veteran soldier in the cause of righting injustice to the Jew, for half a century wise and skilled and untiring pleader by word and pen for Jewish rights, Jewish statesman labouring in many lands and for many peoples that Justice be done to Israel.[34]

Wolf richly deserves his important place in diplomatic history. He sometimes fought out hard issues face to face, but his great skill was negotiation, finding the points of shared common interest and building an agreement from them. His

---

33 L. Wolf, *The Marquess of Ripon*, 2 vols (London, 1921). Wolf was also a mason, not in one of the specifically Jewish lodges, but in the Author's Lodge of Freemasons, of which he served as master in 1911–12. Wolf listed his 'recreations' for *Who's Who* as 'Anglo-Jewish history, genealogy, and heraldry', an appropriate reflection of the way in which he chose to see himself – an upper middle-class Englishman, proud to be a Jew.

34 Quoted from *JC*, 29 Aug. 1930.

suppleness, his deftness of manoeuvre, his capacity almost to toe dance through seemingly intractable issues with impossible people made him an effective 'foreign minister'.[35] Those same qualities provided Wolf with a sense of self that could, at times, be almost overbearing, a confidence that left him not only playing but revelling in the role of 'Mr Oversecretary'. Wolf cultivated those images, relishing even their tart side. He never hesitated to pontificate, however tactfully, on the basis of his substantial and rarely understated expertise. He fought Zionism and Jewish nationalism throughout his career, compromising only, at the beginning of the twentieth century, with Israel Zangwill's Jewish Colonisation Society. That body, Wolf conceded, served the necessary temporary role of creating havens, preferably far from the British isles, for victims of religious and political persecution. In all these things he proceeded from a simple axiom. Jews should act prudently, should seek the attainable, must constantly strive to bring to Jews throughout the world the 'benefits' of disaspora acculturation.[36]

35 Mallet to Wolf, 6 Nov. 1909, Board of Deputies of British Jews (BDBJ) Papers C 11/5/1, in the Archives of the BDBJ, London; Report of the Conjoint Foreign Committee (CFC), 1901–10; Alliance Israélite Universelle (AIU) à BDBJ, 3, 6, 9 Jan. 1906, BDBJ C 11/2/2; L. Wolf, Address to Lord Grey, 11 Jan. 1913; Mallet to Wolf, 17 Jan., 6 Feb., 9 June, 24 July, 29 Oct. 1913; Wolf to Alexander, 26 Nov. 1913, BDBJ C 11/2/4. Records of the Joint Foreign Committee, Dec. 1913 to 23 Feb. 1916; *The Times*, 24 May 1917.
36 Wolf to Meyerson, 19 Feb. 1913, BDBJ C 11/5/2.

2

Anglo-Jewish Governance

British Jewry was many things. Class, residence, and form of worship divided Jew from Jew. East End and West End are a shorthand used to describe state of mind and degree of acculturation even more than place of residence. Differences, all observers agreed, could be heard, seen, and smelled. Just beyond the overcrowded immigrant and working-class core in Whitechapel and St George's-in-the-East served by Yiddish-speaking peddlers, hawkers and small shopkeepers lay a more anglicized ring of artisans, small shopkeepers and merchants. Although a Jewish working-class community could be found just to the north in Tottenham, further north still, in Highbury, Canonbury and Dalston, lived impeccably respectable middle-class employers, substantial shopkeepers, and some professionals. A community of perhaps 5,000 in 1880, it had increased to about 30,000 by 1921. This was the heartland of Jewish respectability. Once transplanted this far, many remained, having successfully escaped ghetto sounds and odours. Others were in social transit, pausing only to recommence their familial migration towards such affluent north-west suburbs as Hampstead.

Just west of the City in areas like Bloomsbury, professionals and entrenched middle-class merchants and manufacturers had established themselves by the mid-1890s. The most successful and wealthiest Jews mingled with the English elite in Piccadilly, Hyde Park, Kensington Gardens, and even Belgravia. Modish Maida Vale and developing St John's Wood housed middle- and upper-middle-class businessmen and professionals. The affluent Jewish colonization of Hampstead and Golders Green grew apace in the early twentieth century, as Jewish fashion followed that of other prosperous, upwardly mobile Londoners. Further to the west in Hammersmith, artisans and petty tradesmen rubbed elbows with modestly prosperous merchants. To the south-east of the ghetto and in the borough of Southwark, a comparable if slightly less affluent mixture of artisans, small employers and shopkeepers developed another stable community, served by its own schools and synagogues, part of, but slightly detached from, their social peers to the east and north.

Anglo-Jewry encouraged dispersion to attack the overcrowding and exploitation in the congested East End. That concentration seemed to many the principal social fact impeding the anglicization of immigrant Jews. In what Anglo-Jewry felt to be the best interests of all concerned, Anglo-Jewry preferred to move East Enders on to the provinces. Failing that, it sought to disperse them to other parts of greater London. 'In the country,' Chief Rabbi Hermann Adler told Charles Booth's investigator, 'foreign Jews become anglicized much more rapidly than in London, and it is desired to make London approximate to country condition as much as possible.' Dispersion, however, meant moving lower-class Jews further to the East, not blending them into the upwardly mobile migration from Whitechapel to Hyde Park. To that end, communal services were planted in such areas as West Ham, Poplar and Peckham.[1]

A tiny community – probably less than 20,000 – in 1850, two-thirds of London's Jews would, by best estimate, have lived in the 'ghetto', the East End or contiguous parts of the City of London. When the great migration began in the 1880s, the same proportion of the 45,000 London Jews could still be found there, but the northern and western migration was well under way. The Jewish population of the greater East End in 1900 had almost trebled to about 125,000, but it would rise no further. What self-motivation and Anglo-Jewry could not accomplish, a changing environment did. Housing stock steadily diminished, replaced by commercial and industrial property. Slum clearance accelerated the process in the twentieth century. Wartime bombing completed the job in the 1940s. The 280,000 inhabitants of the borough of Stepney in 1911 (already reduced to 250,000 by 1921) dropped to 200,000 by 1938 and fewer than 99,000 by 1951. These same facts, however, also help to explain the difficulty of moving working-class Jews out. Although employers moved to more salubrious settings, their factories, workshops, warehouses and offices remained in and around the East End.[2] The 4% Industrial Housing Company, Anglo-Jewry's effort to upgrade housing stock by building new estates, discovered that it had no difficulty finding tenants for the properties it developed within the old East End, but when the Company attempted to plant settlements to the east and north, it was far less successful. East End Jews, even when offered good housing, playgrounds, synagogues, and kosher butchers, showed little desire to move, despite accessible and inexpensive underground, tramway or bus transportation.

Although London Jewry probably represented no more than sixty per cent of the Jews of Britain, a proportion that remained more or less constant through the century from 1840 to 1940, provincial Jewry was still diffuse, the largest communities being the few thousands in Liverpool, Manchester, Birmingham and Leeds by 1880. Provincial Jewry, moreover, lacked the entrenched elite leadership of London. Those who succeeded in the provinces often moved to London. Provincial Jewry may have deferred to London for much of the nineteenth century, but London arrogance rankled aspiring leaders. By the turn of the century, London–provincial controversy had generated substantial pressure for constitutional modification and ideological orientation in Jewish institutions. That

1 Interview with the Chief Rabbi (Dr Adler) at Finsbury Square, [1896]. Booth Papers C 196/7.
2 Lipman, *Social History*, 168–71 summarizes this information.

provincial rebellion, compounded by a Zionist–Assimilationist division within Anglo-Jewry itself, won a brief, if pyrrhic, victory in 1917 at the Board of Deputies. Little had actually changed. London continued constitutionally to dominate British Jewry until well after the First World War.

SECULAR INSTITUTIONS

The Board of Deputies of British Jews

The elected representatives of British Jews, the Board of Deputies, evolved from the Committee of Diligence appointed in 1746 to watch over the interests of British Jews. Organized cooperatively by Sephardic and Ashkenazic Jews at the accession of George III in 1760 as the London Committee of the Deputies of the British Jews, this oligarchic 'parliament' was the principal institution through which Jews as an organized body interacted with the British government and wider British public. At first only Orthodox synagogues were represented. Reform Jews could not sit on the board until 1886. The Board of Deputies, to which the Registrar General granted authority to license for Jewish marriage, refused, after the Reform schism in 1842, to grant the secretary of that congregation authority to certify marriages according to the Jewish rite. This issue remained contentious even after the Berkeley Street Synagogue received representation on the board. Chief Rabbi Hermann Adler reopened the religious disputes in 1902. Only in the 1940s would the matter finally be set aside. 'Second-class' status for Reform Jews helps to explain the importance of the Anglo-Jewish Association. Through that body, formed in 1871, Reform Jews could claim their place in the constitutional management of the community. Liberal Jews, the disciples of Claude G. Montefiore and the redoubtable Lily Montagu, achieved board recognition in 1911. By that time, however, the board had begun to make places in its assembly for such lay institutions as Jewish friendly societies, and a new Chief Rabbi, more given to accommodation, assumed office.

Whatever its vagaries and however oligarchic and London-oriented the Board of Deputies might be, its claim to represent the community was never disputed. Board management, its methods, its elections and the breadth of its constituencies became, by the twentieth century, an increasingly heated subject of communal debate, but all parties acknowledged the Board of Deputies to be the 'parliament' of British Jews and sought to achieve their goals through, not against it. At the United Synagogue, a Rothschild ruled; at the Board of Deputies, a Montefiore. With the death of Sir Joseph Sebag-Montefiore in 1903, however, the line was broken, and David Lindo Alexander, a distinguished barrister who had long effectively run the board, was elected president. Alexander, staunchly Conservative in politics, rigorously Orthodox in religion, and uncompromisingly assimilationist and anti-Zionist, simultaneously broadened the range of board activities while attempting in all that mattered to preserve tradition, deference and control.

The Board of Deputies, although a lay body, enjoyed a measure of religious authority. The board was the agency through which the Registrar General dealt with the Jewish community. Although the rabbinical court, the Bet Din, ruled on religious matters and acted as a court of arbitration for civil matters between Jews, the Board of

Deputies handled legal issues concerning marriage and had formal responsibilities in the certification of new synagogues and burying grounds. In such matters, the board worked cooperatively with the Chief Rabbi and, on issues concerning the Sephardim, with the Haham. The board, although jealous of its jurisdictional responsibilities, scrupulously avoided intruding on matters that it acknowledged to be under the jurisdiction of the Bet Din. To the degree that religious issues translated into important secular and political ones – the most obvious but by no means the only examples being sabbath observance and Sunday trading – the Board of Deputies dealt with them.[3] While most such concerns involved business, when factories could be open or the right of Jews observing their sabbath to conduct their enterprises on Sunday, Jews also confronted ignorance or insensitivity in other areas. University calenders and examinations rarely took account of the Jewish calender, so the board negotiated with university authorities in an effort to minimize conflicts for Jewish students. The 1896 metropolitan survey for the equalization of rates, for instance, was scheduled for the second day of Passover. The board secured a postponement. Statistics about Jews were an increasingly important matter of public debate, so the board took the lead in providing volunteer assistants to census enumerators in East London in 1901 to ascertain that returns would be as accurate as possible. From 1884, the board arranged holy-day furloughs with the War Office for Jewish troops.[4]

The Board of Deputies was Anglo-Jewry's domestic political lobby. It negotiated matters touching upon Jewish interests with government departments and local authorities. The board lobbied parliament on matters of communal moment, although it preferred to work behind the scenes through friendly members of parliament or sympathetic peers. Sometimes the board preferred to appeal to Jewish members; at others, it sought out friendly Gentiles. Anglo-Jewry, proud of its substantial political and social gains, had no inclination to place them gratuitously at risk. The board wished to have as few issues as possible identified as 'Jewish interests'. Little good was accomplished, so the board believed, by excessive Jewish political visibility. This understandable strategy of deflecting potential anti-Semitism could also become a rationalization for avoiding difficult issues. More importantly, the board sought, in political publicity or negotiations, to identify its constituents as British first, Jews second. The board cooperated with public authorities whenever possible.

At one level, Anglo-Jewry did well at making a virtue of necessity. The much publicized evils of the sweated trades, for instance, embarrassed the Jewish elite. They disliked the public attention that private and official enquiries focused on Jewish sweating in the clothing trades. Anglo-Jewry understood that the labour-intensive, subcontracting systems of production in clothing and the boot trade provided constantly expanding demand for workers and created opportunities for newcomers in a setting where Jewish observances could be respected. Although the leadership believed sweating to be the cause of social, even moral, problems, it also wondered what other system could have provided such scope for self-help and

---

3 See, e.g., BDBJ B 2/18/1 for files concerning Sunday observance, 1879–1911, and BDBJ B 2/18/2 for general issues concerning street trading, principally, but not exclusively, touching on sabbath issues.

4 On this last point, the board strenuously objected to the United Synagogue's efforts to intrude on its business. BDBJ minute book, 17 Feb. 1896.

created so many opportunities for upward mobility. The elite had no economic stake in the sweating system save the indirect gains achieved by having so many poor employed rather than being a burden on communal resources.

Even had Anglo-Jewry been willing to live with the social and economic conditions sweating engendered, it could not accept the public image of the Jewish community that the system produced. Something had to be done. On the one hand, Anglo-Jewry did what it felt it could to change the practice. That turned out to be very little. On the other hand, Anglo-Jewry went out of its way to ensure that sweating was understood to be a national, not merely a Jewish, practice and problem. The leadership pointed to sweating in areas other than tailoring and among people other than Jews. That was all very true. Government and private investigators censured Jew and Gentile alike. The Board of Deputies and the Jewish Board of Guardians cooperated in giving the widest possible publicity, in English and Yiddish, to factory and workshop regulations. Anglo-Jewish authorities worked as closely as possible with government factory, sanitary and school inspectors.

In this as many other problems, however, the Board of Deputies responded to an issue thrust upon it. Not before the early twentieth century, and hesitantly and sparingly even then, did the Board of Deputies actually take the initiative acting in anticipation of needs. Nor was the board alone in this policy. Other Anglo-Jewish agencies did the same, responding after unfavourable publicity or some public authority brought communal problems to light. The Jewish Board of Guardians sanitary committee attacked squalid living conditions in the East End only after the Royal Commission on the Housing of the Poor had already been appointed and communal inaction would have been a matter of public reproach.

The Board of Deputies conducted its regular monthly and special meetings under the rules of parliament. Save in extremely rare instances, meetings were fully reported in the Jewish press, ostensibly bringing public scrutiny to bear on its proceedings. The board actually functioned through a committee system that accentuated executive control. Executive officers of the board made up half the members of each committee, the others being individuals with particular competence or interest in that area. While this facilitated cooperation and avoided potential jurisdictional conflicts, it gave the executive control over what matters would come before the board, when, and in what form. Committee meetings, moreover, were closed to outsiders, and committee minutes were unavailable to other deputies.

The law and parliamentary committee was the board command post on important domestic matters. When other committees, such as the education committee or the immigration committee, dealt with matters at law or of potential legislation, then those committees sat jointly with the law and parliamentary. Although committee recommendations had to be voted up or down at a meeting of the deputies, much board business never came before the body. Board executives often dealt discreetly with the public official or body concerned. Ultimate control rested firmly with the executive. Although the temperature of debate rose from the early twentieth century, particularly after Zionism became a divisive political issue, heat alone failed to unseat the old guard before the great explosion of 1917. Even that revolt of the deputies ultimately meant no more than a change of some personnel. The oligarchy continued to rule. Gradual accommodation to more democratic representation slowly rendered the board more responsive to the rich variety of interests and attitudes within the Jewish community, but the process proved slow in coming. Slow change is ultimately as or more decisive than sudden revolution. By the 1940s the old system of management sustained by deference was gone beyond retrieval.

The Board of Deputies acted to protect Jewish civil liberties and, increasingly as time went on, came to be drawn into anti-defamation work.[5] Self-confidence helped; continental anti-Semitism probably helped more. English anti-Semitism traditionally had a sneering, condescending edge, almost a 'genteel' character. Ostensibly scholarly literature could feed or appear to validate it. Thus the board, for instance, fought a long, at least partially successful campaign against the publication of Richard Burton's *Human Sacrifice amongst Sephardim or Eastern Jews* (London, 1897).[6] In such matters the board tried to pick its targets with care, passing by instances it considered to be of no moment. The board in 1896, for instance, investigated a swindler describing himself as secretary of the Anti-Jewish League and was delighted that the government decided to prosecute for felony. Board representatives tactfully suggested that West End theatres might wish to modify 'unfortunate' characterizations of Jews. On occasion, board officials made embarrassing errors, as when they misidentified and denounced Reverend Canon Malcolm MacColl as the author of a 'disgusting' article, 'The Modern Jew', in the *Quarterly Review*.[7]

The board was ever sensitive to public opinion, and in this quarter it attempted to anticipate problems. Board officials were less clear about how best to deal with verbal and occasional physical violence in the East End. All, naturally, were deplored, but improvement demanded action beyond the capacity of the board or the Jewish community or of Britain itself at the turn of the century. Immigrant and working-class competition for insufficient housing and work in such marginal but highly competitive trades as tailoring, cabinet-making and bootmaking produced occasional ugly outbreaks on the perimeter of Jewish East End settlement. The world of the East End was one in which a trifling advantage could mean success, an accident or small misfortune, failure. Costermongers, petty traders and small shop-keepers existed in a highly competitive environment in which trouble could all too easily arise. Late nineteenth-century Stepney was, in many ways, an explosion waiting to happen. Public authorities, fortunately, also understood this. Exemplary police work at the time of the infamous Whitechapel murders restrained what otherwise might have been serious 'Ripper Riots' in 1888. Agitation fomented in support of legislation restricting alien immigration at the turn of the century helped to trigger nasty incidents. A group of newly-arrived immigrants being conveyed to

5 Colin Holmes went to great, perhaps slightly overdrawn, lengths to show the range and depth of British anti-Semitism in *Anti-Semitism in British Society, 1876–1939* (London, 1979), and Dr Brian Cheyette at Leeds is currently doing some very instructive work on Jewish stereotypes and images in British literature. Steven Gilbert Bayne's interesting doctoral dissertation, 'Jewish Leadership and Anti-Semitism in Britain, 1898–1918' (Columbia University, 1977) develops an elaborate argument about the shift from defensive thinking and responsive politics.

6 See, e.g., BDBJ Minute Book, 11 Apr. 1897; Law and Parliamentary Committee, 3 June, 4 July, 27 Oct. 1897, BDBJ C13/1/4. The Burton problem continued, surfacing again in 1909. Law and Parliamentary Committee, 8 July, 4 Oct. 1909, BDBJ B 2/10/8.

7 *JC*, 24, 31 Jan., 7 Feb. 1896.

the Jews' Temporary Shelter were showered with brickbats. Jewish pioneers venturing forth to previously all-Gentile parts of Stepney occasionally found their houses damaged and furniture destroyed. While Jewish leaders always ascertained that such cases came to the attention of the police, they felt they could do little more.

On occasion, political considerations forced Anglo-Jewry to take an aggressive stand on an issue where its natural inclinations were to be quiet and carefully defensive. Much of the Jewish community grew restive in the face of the growing challenge of modernity to sabbath observance. Sabbath observance, like *kashrut*, lay at the heart of being Jewish. But Jewish sabbath observance and the Christian sabbatarian agitation of the late nineteenth century worked against one another. Closing for the Jewish sabbath, were it not to penalize observant Jews economically, ran at cross-purposes with Christian campaigns for Sunday closing legislation. Anglo-Jewry was, generally, pleased to see East End agitation for more rigorous sabbath observance. The Chief Rabbi found his concerns and those of the East End were one on the matter. He organized and found considerable West End support for his Jewish Sabbath Observance Society. The president of the Board of Deputies, although interested, felt that aggressive agitation might reopen the still-festering sores of anti-Jewish agitation remaining from the struggle over the Aliens Act. Holding the line against Christian sabbatarian proposals that threatened Jewish Sunday trading rights, Alexander believed, was the limit to which political influence could be employed. Demanding more – a full-fledged dual system of sabbath observance – would never be accepted and would inspire anti-Semitism. The position of the Board of Deputies, although judicious, undercut Adler's leadership in the sabbath observance movement and underscored the cultural division between an 'assimilated' Jewish establishment and East European observant newcomers.

The Board of Deputies concentrated on what it regarded as the defence of community interests. Constant bickering over amendments to protect Jewish traders from the various Sunday closing bills with which Lord Avebury and other Christian zealots cluttered the parliamentary calendar forced the board's executives into action they would have beeen glad to avoid. Key Jewish members of parliament carefully watched such private bills. The Chief Rabbi, on the other hand, no longer had control of the East End sabbath observance movement. As an independent movement developed among the East End workers, the leadership had to act, for its communal authority was at stake.

First, the Board of Deputies informed the Jewish Trades Union Sabbath Observance Society that their proposed mass meeting on 'the proposed Sunday Legislation and to urge a better observance of the Sabbath' would 'be inopportune and unnecessary at the present time in view of Earl Crewe's Speech and that the question of Sabbath Observance was a religious question which did not come within the view of the Board.' Then the board told Adler that he need no longer delay his society's proceedings and offered whatever further assistance it could. After that, the trade unionists were informed that the board was supporting Adler's Sabbath Observance Society, and the workers would be well advised to do the same.[8]

8 Law and Parliamentary Committee, 20, 25 Mar. 1907, BDBJ C 13/1/6.

To reduce sabbath observance, in effect, to a political matter of negotiations, to deal with Sunday trading as a matter of expediency, underscored not merely a contemporary dilemma, but a constant problem for diaspora Jewry. How best can Jewish practices be integrated in a Christian society? Sabbath and secular issues could easily become tangled in ways that touched Jewish sensitivities and needs. Various shops bills, often introduced by such defenders of Jews as Sir Charles Dilke or Winston Churchill, sought to limit excessive hours for shop assistants and ease the often harsh conditions under which they worked. But those proposals also raised sabbath observance questions that vexed the Jewish leadership. Some Jews proposed adopting Sunday as the Jewish sabbath and evading a host of difficulties through calender legerdemain. Few considered the idea seriously. The late nineteenth and early twentieth centuries saw regular efforts to impose stricter rules about Sunday closing, each of which demanded modification and amendment if Jewish rights and sensitivities were to be respected. Not only did Judaism as ritual emphasize sabbath observance; Jews regularly had to confront the problem of squaring their business lives with a Christian calendar. A highly observant Jew who closed his business on *shabbat*, Sunday, the Christian and Jewish holy-days, and the various legal bank holidays, would shut down one third of each year.

Sabbath observance had conflicting and contradictory implications for the community and its leadership. Increasing pride and Jewish self-assertiveness help to explain its popularity within the community. But therein lay yet another problem. Anglo-Jewry strove to make Judaism unobtrusive and inoffensive to the British while simultaneously nourishing its vitality. Highly acculturated Jews generally came or attempted to come to terms with the apparent contradictions involved. But to the degree that Jews were forced to consider themselves as Jews, they tended to become restive with the one-sided compromises being forced on them.

The Jewish national revival, which so many leaders believed to threaten the very basis of British Jewish culture, also stimulated Jewish self-consciousness, in spite of its secular roots and philosophy. Anglo-Jewry needed to find acceptable ways of accommodating three elements: communal needs, increasing self-consciousness in a growing and less homogenous Jewish population, and the pressures of contemporary politics. By 1911, Board of Deputies leaders hit upon what it considered a perfect compromise of Jewish and Christian sabbatarian needs. A division of labour could serve both while giving greater scope for Jewish opportunity. Board executives urged their friends in high places to bring substantial numbers of Jewish men and women into public employment. Christians would work on Saturdays and Jews on Sundays to keep the Post Office, public transportation, and other public services humming.[9]

9 Herbert Samuel, then Postmaster General, encouraged Alexander to bring a deputation on those matters, and Robert Sebag-Montefiore, who took an active role at the London County Council, planned to take up London transport issues there. Law and Parliamentary Committee, 20 June 1911, BDBJ C 13/1/7. Claude G. Montefiore, considering sabbath observance crucial to his Liberal Judaism, toyed with the notion of shifting the Jewish sabbath to Sunday to harmonize with British society but failed to convince even himself. C. G. Montefiore, *Liberal Judaism. An Essay* (London, 1903).

The Anglo-Jewish Association

Established West European Jewry had everywhere, by the mid-nineteenth century, come to terms with its place as people of the diaspora. With varying degrees of comfort, the elites prospered in their host cultures, accepted acculturation, if not assimilation, and defined with considerable precision those rituals, that learning and those customs that identified them as Jews. West European Jews had gained, were gaining, or were having pressed upon them, the political rights and social expectations of their class. The founding of the French Alliance Israélite Universelle ('All Israel are comrades') in 1860, the first modern international Jewish organization, derived from a heightened sense of Jewish consciousness, the confidence of achieved position and security, and something approximating a sense of clear and present danger.[10] The Alliance came into being to work everywhere 'for the emancipation and moral progress' of Jews. Education, publications and diplomacy would be their weapons. Adolphe Crémieux, founder and president from 1863 to 1880, brought his parliamentary and ministerial experience and connections. France responded. Never would the Alliance play a more impressive role in foreign affairs than it did during the Congress of Berlin in 1878.

The Anglo-Jewish Association, which was to play such a dominant role in the international politics and philanthropy of Anglo-Jewry diplomacy, originated in 1870 as a branch of the Alliance Israélite Universelle. Both organizations represented affluent and acculturated Jewish elites within their host cultures. Both prided themselves on their Jewish commitments as well as their integration into French and British national life. Both engaged in wide-ranging charitable activities, particularly the development and support of educational institutions abroad. From their earlier days, they struggled directly and through diplomatic channels to secure full civic and religious freedom for Jews everywhere in the evolving Balkan and East European states.[11] The Anglo-Jewish Association, unlike the Board of Deputies, provided English Reform Jews with an institution from which to lead the British Jewish community in which they were equal partners with their Orthodox colleagues. The resolutely Reform Sir Julian Goldsmid assumed the presidency in

10 The Damascus affair of 1840 reminded the more fortunate Western Jews just how precarious Jewish life could be. While blood libels – the recurring anti-Semitic myth that Jews murder Christian children to use their blood in rituals – in the far-away Lebanon might seem remote, urged only by less civilized people or bigoted, hysterical and vicious Capuchins, the French consul in Beirut, Ratti-Menton, had joined in the campaign. Closer to home and clearly within the ambit of Western civilization, the Mortara case in 1858, in which papal police kidnapped a Jewish child and refused redress to the family, reinforced the need for international Jewish organization to safeguard Jewish rights. Since both the Damascus affair and the Mortara case involved French as well as Jewish interests and since France was, however transiently, the major continental power, the idea of a French-based organization in which the more fortunate emancipated and enlightened Jews would work for the benefit of their suffering co-religionists seemed reasonable and proper. Sir Moses Montefiore, who had played so active a role in the diplomacy of those matters, had his personal differences with Adolphe Crémieux but still considered French leadership appropriate.

11 The Goldsmid-Crémieux correspondence from 1863 in [Archives de l']A[lliance] I[sraélite] U[niverselle] Angl[eterre] I/J/3 demonstrates the range of concerns and French initiatives. The Serbian files from Goldsmid à Crémieux, 15 mars 1863 into and through the 1870s are particularly interesting. The petition from the Anglo-Jewish Association to the King of Serbia, 29 Oct. 1872 can be found in AIU Angl I/D/5/3892. For preparations for the Congress of Berlin, see, *inter alia*, AJA to AIU, 22 Jan. 1878, II/D/23/5964.

1886; Ellis Franklin, the very soul of Orthodox philanthropy, served as treasurer; and a member of the Sassoon family was usually on the executive. Albert Löwy (1816–1908), who served as secretary until 1886, brought the dignity of continental scholarship, Central European connections, and cultivation to the association. He helped to create and reinforce the elite network through which information, money and policy could flow as Western Jewish establishments attempted to control an unprecedented flow of immigrants and refugees.

While Palestine settlements, schools and relief figured regularly on the Anglo-Jewish Association agenda, such matters, always coordinated with the Alliance as well as German, Austrian and American organizations, were never treated as issues touching on Jewish nationalism. Such a concept would contradict the strongly assimilationist assumptions on which the several cooperating institutions stood. The Anglo-Jewish Association proved unabashedly elitist and almost implacably anti-Zionist. Like the French Alliance, the German Hilfsverein and the Austrian Allianz, the Anglo-Jewish Association sprang to the colours in 1914 demonstrating that they were patriots first and an international community of Jews only second. For almost forty years, such organizations did what they could to aid Jewish refugees and ease Jewish resettlement so long as the wanderers moved onwards to other countries than their own. So intimate was international coordination and cooperation, reaffirmed in daily correspondence and annual or semi-annual meetings, that the ties of Western and Central European Jewish leaders seemed indissoluble. But the day war came, the relationships instantly collapsed as each Jewish organization flocked to its national belligerent cause.

The Anglo-Jewish Association acted, as it regularly announced in annual reports and general meetings, on matters concerning the status of Jews in the world overseas and philanthropy, particularly Jewish education, overseas. The association centrepieces in philanthropy abroad were the Evelina de Rothschild schools in Jerusalem and in Baghdad. But education in Asia and Africa, important as it was, remained the formal, not the motivating, association purpose. The organization's more important role was to furnish an institution through which all Anglo-Jewish leaders could share in the formal and visible management of British Jewish affairs. Politics brought the Anglo-Jewish Association into being and sustained it once there, particularly foreign affairs in matters concerning Jews. The elite of this highly structured community created an institution to bridge the Anglo-Jewish Association and the Board of Deputies of British Jews. The Conjoint Foreign Committee, which the presidents of the Board of Deputies and the Anglo-Jewish Association chaired at alternate meetings, consisted of seven representatives of each organization. Safely removed from the public forums of parent body meetings, the Conjoint Foreign Committee, arguing the need for confidentiality in diplomatic negotiations, also remained free from ongoing community scrutiny. When the political contest with Zionism reached its peak during the First World War, the presidents and Lucien Wolf, the secretary, also kept secret minutes with matters and conclusions not reported to the constituent bodies.[12] The Conjoint Foreign Committee, moreover, became a discreet forum, a quasi-cabinet in which

---

12 See the minutes and secret minutes in AJ/204. The BDBJ 'C' files have many copies of the constitutional arrangements in their several stages of negotiation and resolution.

Anglo-Jewish leaders could consult and formulate broad policies safely removed from publicity and communal oversight.

Foreign affairs, however, remained the principal concern. No sooner was the Anglo-Jewish Association organized than it found itself brought into the politics of the Middle East in the aftermath of the Crimean War. Since the Turks had been unwilling to concede Russian Jews citizenship, the conclusion of the Peace of Paris (1856) raised the issue of who was to act for the abused Jews of the Holy Land. The Alliance and the Association prodded the victorious allies to assume responsibility for the protection of Jews as well as beleaguered Christians. Anglo-Jewish Association pressure worked. The British consul in Jerusalem responded by giving his protection, but the situation both in Europe and the Ottoman domain became far too complicated for such casual arrangements.

The new Bismarckian world demanded continued Jewish activity in foreign affairs. French defeat in 1871 and the diplomacy of the Congress of Berlin (1878) reshaped the structure and balance of international politics. To the obvious complications of an unpredictable world, Eastern Europe became a setting for the systematic persecution of Jews. Official and unofficial pogroms spawned panic waves of Russian Jewish refugees.[13] Most organized Jewish international activity came to involve problems relating to assisting unprecedented numbers of human beings on the move. While most Jews emigrating from Russia or Roumania moved to central and western Europe or to countries across the ocean, others drifted into the domains of the Ottoman Empire.

They were not well received there, less because they were Jewish than because they were perceived to be Russian. The British, given their influential position in Constantinople, spoke, albeit in muted tones, for these immigrants, but the British government had no interest in defending Russian refugee Jews in Palestine or anywhere else at the expense of what they considered to be the needs of British policy. The Ottoman government, never happy with Russians and particularly annoyed by the substantial incursion of Russian Jews, sought to limit the number of resident Jews in Palestine. The British consulate warned in 1885 that British protection would be withdrawn after five years for those Jews under forty-five years of age. The Anglo-Jewish Association and Board of Deputies bargained unsuccessfully with the Foreign Ministry over the next two years to ease the plight of refugee Jews.[14] Pressure continued with no success. By 1888, Ottoman authorities demanded that passports for Jews in Jaffa and Jerusalem must indicate that the holders were Jewish. For the next six years, the Conjoint Foreign Committee, a foreign policy advisory body of the Anglo-Jewish Association and the

---

13 Both British and French Jewish leaders worked vigorously, although with little success, to persuade the Foreign Office and le Ministère des Affaires Etrangères to intervene on behalf of persecuted Russian Jews. The leading Jews even attempted personal diplomacy. See, e.g., Mocatta à Loeb, 10 jan. 1882, AIU Angl II/D/34/631. When an Anglo-American Protestant delegation visited the Kaiser to persuade him to petition on behalf of Protestants in the Russian Baltic provinces, the AJA attached an address on behalf of Jews. July 1871, AIU Angl II/D/21/1984.

14 Jews had to register and were prohibited from residing in Palestine for more than thirty days. See, particularly, the discussion with the Foreign Office on 13 December 1887, BDBJ B 2/9/8; see also C 11/12/54 and C/14 *passim*.

Board of Deputies of British Jews, processed memorials and petitions from Jews as far afield as Morocco and Persia, as well as a flood of grievances from Palestine.[15]

The Turks responded to incoming Jews like every western country by turning to immigration restriction. By 1886, the Conjoint Foreign Committee was urging the Foreign Office to use its influence to ease restrictions the Turks had placed on 'working Jews'.[16] That seemed a reasonable compromise, and the committee prided itself on its political realism. Given stiffening Ottoman resistance to any immigration of 'poor Jews' and those with limited or no skills, the committee concentrated on attempting to secure relief for the distressed already in the Ottoman Empire, organizing acceptable migration schemes for refugees, and attempting to persuade the British government (as they would continue to do until 1917) to remonstrate with Russia about its anti-Semitic policies.[17]

But the cancer of persecution was spreading, not receding. As Roumania also escalated its violence against Jews, the Conjoint Committee lobbied feverishly with the Foreign Office. If Russia was too important, too unresponsive to justice, or too powerful, surely Britain could influence if not coerce little Roumania, whose systematic violation of civil liberties guaranteed by the Congress of Berlin were a matter of public record and shame.[18] The Roumanian case would be the school in which the Conjoint Committee studied the problem of minority rights clauses in international settlements. Roumanian persecution would remain a central concern for the Committee and its French colleagues into, through, and beyond the First World War. This obsession reflected their abiding commitment to doing that which was right even more ardently if it also appeared to be possible.

The Conjoint Foreign Committee spurred the Anglo-Jewish Association and the Alliance to develop Jewish communal networks to regulate the movement of refugees with the clear purpose of moving them onwards and out of Europe. The

15 For a file of such memorials and petitions, see BDBJ C 11/2/1 and particularly Pauncefot to the AJA, 19 June 1889. For the case of Isaac Amar in Morocco and the AJA deputations to Salisbury and Earl Granville, see *Ninth Annual Report of the Anglo-Jewish Association... 1879–80* (London, 1880), 7–8, 16–29.

16 BDBJ C 11/1/8. The death of Adolphe Crémieux (1796–1880), president of the AIU and twice French Minister of Justice, saw the Alliance retreat from its forward role in politics and diplomacy to concentrate on educational, relief, civil rights and anti-defamation work. The Alliance had performed yeoman service in diplomacy, particularly in the Balkans. To some extent, I believe, the British Conjoint Foreign Committee moved into the vacuum the shift in Alliance effort created. Small matters of procedure, so revealing in diplomatic history, suggest this move in the centre of gravity. See, e.g., Montefiore's view of shortcomings in AIU protocol, Duparc to Bigart, 11 Apr. 1902, AIU Angl I/D/18.

17 The British moved more slowly than the French on the matter of relief. By the 1860s, however, British institutional relief for Jewish victims of natural disaster had become almost a matter of course. Some £5,225 went to Palestinian Jews ravaged by cholera and beset by locusts in 1865. More than £2,000 was subscribed and distributed in the famine of 1874. The Association of British Jews also engaged a Safed and Hebron physician to tend the poor of those communities. BDBJ C 11/1/8. Anglo-Jewry, however, still worked principally through the AIU. See, e.g., Adler to Bigart, 28 Jan, Loeb à Adler, 31 jan 1892, AIU Angl I/B/54bis/7769. Even as late as the turn of the century, the Alliance was seen by outsiders to be the principal agency involved in Palestinian relief. See, Francis Denman of the Society for Promoting Christianity among Jews to the président of the Alliance imploring him to take action in Safed, 19 Dec. 1902, AIU Angl II/D/38/9810.

18 For the minutes of the Conjoint Foreign Committee, see AJ/204, in the Mocatta Library, University College, London. BDBJ C 11/2/2 has the records of the Joint Foreign Committee, 1901–10, particularly the Foreign Office responses and negotiations in 1902 and 1907 and the Private and Confidential Memorandum on the Treaty Rights of the Jews of Rumania, November 1908.

English side of this task would ultimately be committed to the Russo-Jewish Committee, itself an amalgam of leaders whose institutions socialized and processed immigrants. European governments permitted, even abetted this process. Governments responded less well when organized Jewry sought to enrol their support in checking anti-Semitism in other countries, particularly when national interests demanded cultivation of the criticized power.

The Jewish elites of Britain and France confronted a paradox. They understood perfectly well that their own countries would resist substantial Jewish immigration, the only viable option. The elites had come to understand, even to share, the sensitivities of their host cultures. Neither the British nor the French Jewish establishment wished to be embarrassed by unmanageable masses of 'the great unwashed', so some alternative had to be found. Israel Zangwill's Jewish Territorial Organization, a body intended to find and develop settlements for Jewish refugees anywhere they could establish communities and prosper, cut across the Jewish nationalist sentiment and deflected some of what otherwise might have swelled the Zionist stream.[19] Narcisse Leven, president of the Alliance, chaired the international board of the French-sponsored Jewish Colonisation Association (ICA). The British, like other West Europeans, shared both its costs and benefits. The ICA also enabled the Alliance and French Jewish leadership to avoid the Jewish nationalist implications of Palestinian questions against a rising Zionist tide by resettling refugee Jews in Latin American or African alternatives, even in Kurdistan and Iraq. Fertile as that Mosul district might be, however, and underpopulated as it was, the problem of brigandage and despoliation remained almost unsolvable. The Alliance, nevertheless, invoked not merely French authorities, but even the British Board of Trade.[20]

Under the presidency of Baron Henry de Worms, who resigned in 1885, the Anglo-Jewish Association grew and prospered, soliciting and securing support from Jew and Gentile alike.[21] Blood accusations, the libel that Jews practised ritual murder, were denounced as soon as they were publicly known. The association protested at the alleged forced conversion of Falashas, the Black Jews of Ethiopia, in 1881. Alliance schools received financial support, and Anglo-Jewish Association schools came into being from Morocco to Bombay. By 1885, the association argued that its principal concerns were the prevention of persecution and the improved education of young persons in foreign countries. The Anglo-Jewish Association, like its parent Alliance Israélite Universelle, saw itself as furthering and hastening

19 See, e.g., the *Twenty-Eighth Annual Report of the Anglo-Jewish Association, 1898–1899* (London, 1899) which even annexed various settlement society reports.

20 Ultimately this same Mosul region would become a focal point in Anglo–French diplomatic disputes, first during the famous Sykes–Picot negotiations during the First World War and then, subsequently, in the tortuous efforts to revise that ill-considered agreement. By that time, however, the prospect of oil, not Jews, soured international relations. J. Niège to Board of Trade, 4 Aug .; A. W. Fox (BT) to Foreign Office, 12 Oct. 1906. [United Kingdom. Public Record Office.] F[oreign] O[ffice] 406/30/52–56 in the UK Public Record Office. The British and French shared an enthusiasm for Baron Maurice de Hirsch's various settlements.

21 Baroness Burdett Coutts, for instance, one of wealthiest women in England, was also a committed philanthropist. She established a 'compassionate fund' to help Jewish victims of East European and Middle Eastern wars in 1878. *Thirteenth Annual Report of the Anglo-Jewish Association, 1883–1884* (London, 1884), 6–8.

the liberalization of the East. Once those benighted empires and countries reached the cultural and institutional level of nineteenth-century West European liberal civilization, anti-Semitism would wane, all races and religions would share the benefits of growth economics, social mobility and political emancipation. That assumption continued to move the overwhelming majority of Anglo-Jewry.

The Conjoint Foreign Committee came to be acknowledged at the Foreign Office as the official body speaking for British Jews on matters of foreign policy. Sir Julian Goldsmid assumed the Anglo-Jewish Association presidency in 1886, with Lord Rothschild, Sir Samuel Montagu, Frederic D. Mocatta, and two Sassoons on the board. Lucien Wolf now sat on the council. Russia and Roumania came to figure more and more prominently on the agenda, with the association finally conceding in 1892 that it could accomplish little save in facilitating emigration and resettlement through the Russo-Jewish Committee. Diplomacy proved more effective in Morocco, Egypt, Greece, Persia and the Ottoman Empire.

Gains on the perimeter, however, threatened to be offset by losses in Europe itself. Anti-Semitism wore various disguises in liberal Europe. The French Chamber openly discussed revoking the civil rights of Jews. The mayor of Vienna campaigned and won on an anti-Semitic platform in 1895, although the Anglo-Jewish Association believed that anti-Semitism was becoming less a religious or even a racial attack than it was an evolving part of a general crusade against capitalism.[22] Claude Goldsmid Montefiore assumed the presidency of the Anglo-Jewish Association in 1895 on the death of Sir Julian Goldsmid. He found that all was far from well in this institution of the rich and powerful. The Anglo-Jewish Association confronted an annual deficit of £700 and, given the period of mourning for its late president, it could use no festive occasions as an opportunity to recapitalize itself. He appealed, therefore, through the columns of the Jewish press, for community aid in furthering the 'sacred cause of education' both secular and religious for both sexes 'in Eastern countries'.[23]

Organizational difficulties were not purely financial. Mancunian restiveness prevented the Anglo-Jewish Association from lapsing into political torpor. Dr Joseph Duhlberg led a movement in 1900 demanding more information on council proceedings. Just as subsequent Zionist challenges would come, in part, from a Manchester base, so the Anglo-Jewish Association found itself challenged by restive Mancunians. While the Manchester branch approved Anglo-Jewish Association educational labours, it attacked Association restraint in foreign policy. Like the Glasgow branch in 1903, Manchester feelings ran so high that its local branch criticized the council in early 1905 for having failed to organize a protest rally after the attacks on Kishinev Jews.[24] Such complaints, the luxury of those excluded from responsibility, rankled, but they also were the warning tremors of the earthquake to come in 1917, when provincials, quite as much as Zionists, assaulted the bastions of Anglo-Jewish power to demand more than a token share in the power to make decisions.

---

22 See, particularly, the *Twenty-fourth Annual Report of the Anglo-Jewish Association, 1894–1895* (London, 1895).

23 *JC*, 28 Feb. 1896.

24 The parent body responded, rather tartly, that the Kishinev Jews themselves asked that public protest not be made, fearing that that would aggravate an already appalling situation. *JC*, 24 Mar. 1905. See also Cohen, *English Zionists*, 139–40.

The Anglo-Jewish Association and Conjoint Foreign Committee had, in fact, sought the behind-the-scenes cooperation of the American and Western European governments when they attempted to negotiate with Serge Witte during the meetings at Portsmouth, New Hampshire, to end the Russo-Japanese War. Discreet diplomacy, however, could not be conducted in the glare of publicity, and Englishmen, as private citizens, had a limited capacity to influence the domestic policies of a foreign state. For public consumption, the Anglo-Jewish Association could only protest that what influence could do they had accomplished. They had procured 'redress for outrage and prevented threatened excesses', but where the association wished to achieve most, its powers and influence were most limited. The association took heart, however, from the more than 9,000 students in its schools. Even at the cost of a £1,000 annual deficit, they were the hope for a better future.[25]

THE EXERCISE OF SPIRITUAL AUTHORITY

The Ancient and Honourable: The Spanish and Portuguese Synagogue

The Spanish and Portuguese Synagogue, the monument to former Sephardi domination, played a diminished role in communal matters. Aloof and proud, the Sephardim stood apart, always a group within Jewish social and cultural life, contributing leaders, money and institutions, but caring principally for their own in their own way. Although some Sephardim, following the Montefiore example, married Ashkenazim, most did not, preferring to wed amongst themselves. Migration did not reinforce Sephardi numbers. Social success and acculturation drew many of the livelier and more ambitious away from their aloof, independent community and into the secular world.

The Reform movement, precipitated to a great extent by malcontent Sephardim, drew almost equal numbers of Sephardi and Ashkenazi in the 1840s, but the Sephardim could ill afford such attrition. Some Reform Synagogue leaders appreciated the implications and gravity of the problem. Frederic D. Mocatta, for one, expediently bridged that gap by simultaneously belonging to and worshipping in the Reform congregation of his father and the Spanish and Portuguese Synagogue. Secular success and the relative openness of upper-class society made apostasy an increasingly tempting option. The Disraelis, the Ricardos, the Lopes and the Samudas drifted away. The entry of the 'grand dukes' into elite English culture enormously enriched British social life but worked to the relative impoverishment of many traditional Jewish institutions.

Every year produced another financial crisis in the current accounts of the Spanish and Portuguese congregation. Reorganization and the quest for financial solvency dominated the mid-1890s. Lack of interest and lax administration led to the closing of Montefiore College in Ramsgate in 1896, an institution which, in spite of Haham Gaster's lofty ambitions, never became a great college for rabbinical

25 *Thirty-Fourth Annual Report of the Anglo-Jewish Association, 1904–1905* (London, 1905); AJA annual meeting, 29 Oct. 1905. *JC*, 3 Nov. 1905. See also, *JC*, 7 Apr., 30 June, 25 Aug., 15 Oct., 17 Nov. 1905.

training.[26] Matters did not improve over the next decade. The annual meeting of Elders in January 1905 revealed the continuing decline of interest and concomitant financial difficulties. The notables continued to drift away. Sir Edward Sassoon found his parliamentary duties too demanding to continue as president. The treasurers recited a dismal story of raids on capital funds to meet current operating costs and little prospect of better days ahead. The historically quarrelsome congregation fussed about petty details and renewed its grant of £900 to the congregational board of guardians. The synagogue's board of guardians remained solvent thanks to substantial discretionary donations from Sebag-Montefiore and the estate of Judah Varieas.[27] The Spanish and Portuguese Synagogue, however, could capitalize on its own history. Its original properties were now immensely valuable. Land adjoining its historic cemetery, for instance, could be sold to the Great Eastern Railway for £7,000. That sale furnished more than enough capital for a new cemetery in the more salubrious surroundings of Golders Green and provided much of the money for new school and synagogue construction.[28]

The Spanish and Portuguese, although losing families and individuals to the Reform congregation, even to apostasy, made little effort to adapt itself either in ritual or policy to the evolving world of British Jewry. Since the newcomers were overwhelmingly Central or Eastern Europe Ashkenazim, the Sephardim felt no need to engage themselves in broad philanthropic schemes. Through the years they considered merging their charitable institutions with those of the Ashkenazim, but usually did not. The Spanish and Portuguese sustained their own schools, their own board of guardians, and their own small philanthropies. Sephardi representatives sat on the Board of Deputies, and, at the turn of the century, the Jewish Religious Education Board. Individual Sephardim played significant roles in the life of the British Jewish community. None figured more importantly than its Haham, Rabbi Dr Moses Gaster (1856–1939), although he was himself an Ashkenazi. His outspoken championship of Zionism and Jewish nationalism, moreover, was unlikely to win him friends among Spanish and Portuguese lay leaders or the magnates of the Anglo-Jewish Association on whose board he also sat. But it did secure him at least transitory popularity among the restive British Jews in the years before and during the First World War. But that was the end. He retired in 1918, and the Spanish and Portuguese leadership heaved a collective sigh of relief.[29]

---

26 Converting its freehold property in Bevis Marks to income-producing warehouses, the congregation absorbed a short-term capital drain and six per cent income loss in anticipation of future enhanced revenues. The congregation sold property in Mile End to raise capital for congregational schools in Spitalfields. Here the need was considerable, for although government inspectors gave the girls' school high marks, the infants' school grant was cut for its 'unsuitable buildings'. Total revenue for 1894 (£5,273) was compared with 1895 (£4,959), over half of which in both years came from rents and endowment. The Bevis Marks properties represented a £12,207 investment. Expenditure included almost £1,500 for salaries and £575 for pensions. The total *Finta* (contributions from members) were £1,446. Additional offerings produced £675. *JC*, 6 Mar. 1896.

27 Minutes, annual meeting of the Elders. Spanish and Portuguese Synagogue, 29 Jan. 1905. *JC*, 3 Feb. 1905. The Spanish and Portuguese Board overrun was more than £450 in 1904 and had required the sale of £600 of stock in 1903, none of which was replaced.

28 Annual meeting, 8 Mar. *JC*, 13 Mar. 1896.

29 Gaster Letter Book, Mar. 1905 to June 1906, 654–5.

The United Synagogue

Pride of place belonged to the Spanish and Portuguese congregation, but Ashkenazim dominated British Jewry first and foremost through the United Synagogue. The first step towards combination was the agreement of 1834 by which the three principal Ashkenazic synagogues apportioned the costs of religious and charitable obligations. The Great Synagogue bore half the total, the Hambro and New Synagogues one quarter each. The three, while continuing to recruit new members, ended poaching practices by agreeing not to rent seats to members of either of the other congregations. The agreement was soon outdated, for it did not accommodate the steady outward migration of more affluent Jews.

Chief Rabbi Nathan Adler had a far wider vision than this. He aimed at nothing short of establishing a unified Orthodoxy for the entire British Empire under his leadership. Orthodox Jewry would be socially and culturally an equivalent of Anglicanism. While assuming an uncompromising resistance to Reform Judaism, Nathan Adler designed and executed an elaborate reconstruction of Orthodoxy to adapt it to British culture. His clergy wore neatly trimmed beards when they were not clean-shaven. They were 'ministers', and addressed as 'reverend'. They wore Anglican clerical mufti when out of the synagogue. Smiling rabbis in reversed collar stare out from religious class photographs utterly indistinguishable from Church of England parsons with their confirmation flock. The vocabulary of Anglican usage was applied to Ashkenazic Orthodoxy. Discipline, order and decorum in the manner of the Church of England were brought to synagogue services. Even synagogue architecture began, in some instances, to assume suspiciously Anglican forms. Adler believed that such changes were symbolic ways of adapting to British culture without compromising *halachah*, the rules governing Jewish observance. Jews would not be strangers. They would be as one with the people among whom they dwelt. But they would be Jewish, living Jewish lives, fully adapted people of the diaspora. They would indeed be English people of the Jewish persuasion and faith, appropriately integrated in and yet defined apart from the culture in which they lived.

The Adlers, father and son, also had a more subtle agenda. By reserving the title of rabbi, in so far as they could, to themselves, they established and confirmed their own authority over Ashkenazic Orthodoxy and concentrated spiritual and doctrinal power in their own hands. The Chief Rabbi became, in this way, the Anglo-Jewish equivalent of the Archbishop of Canterbury in the Church of England. English Jewish 'ministers' demeaned by this state of affairs could secure rabbinical credentials by attending continental Jewish institutions. East European immigrants looked askance at anglicized Orthodoxy and were ill disposed to defer to a native clergy apparently lacking rabbinic credentials. By so clearly subordinating their English rabbis, the Adlers, although enhancing their own position and authority, had in effect so undercut rabbinic authority that East End Jews often sought advice or adjudication from well-known East European rabbis. Hermann Adler, on more than one occasion, found it expedient to seek support of his rulings from eminent East European rabbis when attempting to impose his authority upon alien Jews.[30]

---

30 Adler had done so, for instance, when issuing his *issur* (a condemnation of butchers violating the rules of Shechita) which led to a famous and very significant legal case, Fineberg v. Adler et al. tried at the

Communal hopes that Jews' College might recruit the best and the brightest were doomed. Anglo-Jewry came to understand the cost of Adlerian ecclesiology, yet only in the late 1890s did a coherent demand grow for the regular certification of English rabbis through Jews' College. The Jewish press stirred and rumbled. Professor Israel Gollancz, Goldsmid Professor at University College, London, actively campaigned for change, and by 1903 agreement was finally reached. The Chief Rabbi granted rabbinical certificates, not simply when he needed to qualify English 'ministers' for his Bet Din, but on completion of appropriate training and examinations.

The Anglicanization of Orthodoxy also meant the rationalization and unification of synagogues. By 1866, Chief Rabbi Nathan Adler proposed that the wardens of all Ashkenazi synagogues unite their congregations under one management to bring order and regularity into both ecclesiastic and philanthropic affairs. Lionel Cohen, who had already fought to establish the Jewish Board of Guardians, helped forward Adler's campaign among communal lay leaders. On the ecclesiastical front, negotiations between the constituent bodies produced a formula acceptable to the Charity Commissioners. The agreement of 1870 provided:

> the objects of the Institution to be called the United Synagogue shall be the maintaining, erecting, founding and carrying on in London and its neighbourhood, places of worship for persons of the Jewish religion who conform to the Polish or German ritual, the providing of means of burial of persons of the Jewish religion, the relief of poor persons of the Jewish religion, the contribution with other Jewish bodies to the maintenance of a Chief Rabbi and other ecclesiastical persons, and to the communal duties devolving upon metropolitan congregations, and other charitable purposes in connection with the Jewish religion.[31]

United Synagogue prestige was doubly confirmed since the Rothschilds immediately assumed its presidency. Save for a brief interregnum from 1876 to 1879, when Sampson Lucas headed the council, the Rothschild ascendancy remained unbroken until after the First World War.

Communal titans – Rothschild and Montagu – disagreed on what role the United Synagogue should play in the East End. The political testing ground was Rothschild's East End scheme, a plan centring on a massive new synagogue, to be planted by the United, that would minister to the spiritual and social needs of poor and immigrant Jews. Montagu was initially rebuffed in the United Synagogue, although his resistance to Rothschild's East End plans for the United ultimately prevailed in that body's governing council. Sir Samuel offered a new creation, his Federation of Synagogues, as an alternative East End programme. Montagu's

---

Liverpool Assizes on 25 February 1904 before Mr Justice Bigham. See, particularly, the account and commentary in *JC*, 4 Mar. 1904.

31 On this general issue, see my essay: E. C. Black, 'The Anglicization of Orthodoxy: the Adlers, Father and Son', in the forthcoming volume by F. Malino and D. Sorkin (eds), *From East and West* (Oxford, 1989). The statute establishing the United Synagogue is 33–34 Vict c 116, 'an Act for Confirming a Scheme of the Charity Commissioners for the Jewish United Synagogues', 14 July 1870.

Federation accepted the authority of the Chief Rabbi but offered an alternative path for alien integration into British Jewish religious life to that of the United Synagogue. In one form or another the debate about the East End scheme rattled through Anglo-Jewry's halls from 1886 to 1896, sometimes in grandiose, sometimes in more restricted forms. In one proposal there was to be a great synagogue and an elaborate Jewish Toynbee Hall. Alternatively the synagogue shrank in size, and the general settlement house gave way to organizations or individuals addressing specific social needs. In some versions the emphasis lay on committed people, in others on elaborate facilities. All parties agreed that 'something' must be done for the poor and migrants of the East End. Everybody also acknowledged that the West Enders must shoulder most of the burden, but each specific proposal generated a negative majority once the actual costs were spelled out. Rothschild–Adler blandishments proved to no avail. West End Jewry ultimately would not pay their price.

The United Synagogue council decision was sound, although not necessarily for the right reasons. The Anglo-Jewish gentry had no desire to spend their money to satisfy the Rothschild–Montagu pride of place. Montagu's Federation of Synagogues alternative offered an effective compromise in the acculturation of East European immigrant Jews. Montagu had a solution for the problems of exisiting East End *shtiblech* or conventicles (*hebrot*), the religious facilities that served most of the poor and newcomers. He would provide the capital to fund their conversion into small, regular synagogues that would simultaneously answer the demands of faith and the sanitary and building inspectors. Under those circumstance, why should the seatholders of West End synagogues bear the costs? Nor would Anglo-Jewry underwrite a great 'missionary enterprise' in the East End. The elite paid the bills for a host of philanthropic institutions. Toynbee Hall, that model non-denominational settlement house, was already in place, and Anglo-Jewry's capacity to establish and staff a university settlement was unclear. Recent Jewish university graduates by the turn of the century tended to display, with several striking exceptions, a growing disinclination for a life of communal service. The debate dragged on unresolved, while East End Jewry was, to a greater and greater degree, working out its own destiny in its own way. That being so obviously the case, a substantial, costly effort seemed less and less justifiable.

United Synagogue imperialism was forestalled, principally because the council was unwilling to finance lavish projects of dubious value. United synagogues were available if desired by East Enders, but the grand design was dropped. The United remained undisputably ascendant in the world of middle- and upper-class Jews. Not all Ashkenazic synagogues formally associated with either the United or the Federation. As late as 1920, twenty-one London congregations remained independent of either. Almost all, however, participated in the conferences of Anglo-Jewish ministers which Chief Rabbi Hermann Adler and his successors summoned annually from 1910 onwards 'to review the orthodox position and strengthen its defences'.[32] The United Synagogue not only enjoyed religious authority; its administrative methods and organization influenced all communal activity. The United had, from its beginning, a well-articulated, adequately paid

---

32 E. N. Adler, *London* (Philadelphia, 1930), 206.

'civil service', which even enjoyed an elaborate superannuation plan. Committed professionals helped to make the United Synagogue an inspiration and model for many of the best contemporary and subsequent philanthropic organizations.[33]

Growth was orderly, judicious and fiscally sound. The council laid so much emphasis on budgetary discipline that finance often appeared to be the principle, not merely a principal Anglo-Jewish policy. The United Synagogue expanded from five congregations holding funded property of £39,000 in 1870 to an organization of sixteen synagogues thirty-five years later. The United Synagogue council considered each proposal for a new synagogue, then advanced the cash needed to augment the capital the proponents could raise. Each new congregation then amortized its debt. 'Recoupment' worked so effectively to build a growing, viable organization that only £5,000 had to be written off by the early twentieth century. Expansion, in spite of some capital attrition, saw United Synagogue income grow by almost two and a half times, from £15,000 to £34,000. Richer synagogues could carry poorer ones through bad times.[34] By the mid-1890s, the United Synagogue was financially comfortable enough to take stock of its commitments without feeling harried.

Any annual budget night put Anglo-Jewry's priorities on display. When the United reviewed its obligations in February 1896, for instance, feelings ran high. The treasurer could point to a year which began with a surplus of just over £4,000 and ended with a balance slightly in excess of £5,000, the highest in the history of the United Synagogue. Like a good Chancellor of the Exchequer, he proposed assessment reductions to 17.5 per cent instead of the 18 per cent of 1895 by taking £500 from that surplus for the current budget. His own numbers, however, warned against that policy. Seven of the constituent synagogues provided all of the surplus, while six others had deficits. Those were modest enough, the old Hambro', that historic monument to Jewry's London past, accounting for almost half the red ink. Sentiment was expensive. The treasurer's cure: more fiscal discipline and hopefully more revenue. The United Synagogue, the treasurer reminded a council delighted to hear such things, carried far too much of the national and imperial Jewish religious burden itself. Unattached congregations did not, for instance, contribute their share to the Chief Rabbi's fund. Perhaps British and Empire synagogues should be charged fees for services the Chief Rabbi provided.

Matters were worse in regard to support for Jewish communal services. The treasurer insisted that the United should not continue to meet everybody's burdens. It must tend to its own business. United Synagogue capital was not appreciating. Debt needed to be restructured as a first fixed charge. Were the United Synagogue not to bring these matters into hand, it would shortly lose the capacity to advance the money for new synagogues as they were needed. The building fund remained solvent only because new, prosperous synagogues amortized their obligations more rapidly than scheduled.

33 See, e.g., Great Synagogue, *Report of the Committee in Reference to the 'Duties and Emoluments Annexed to the Office of Secretary . . . to be Considered by the Vestry 5th February 5626–1866* (London, 1866). One of the more influential early statements of the need for 'rational' communal organization and administration was Henry Faudel's *Suggestions to the Jews for Improvement in Reference to Their Charities, Education, and Central Government. By a Jew* (London, 1844).
34 Budget night meeting, 7 Mar. *JC*, 10 Mar. 1905.

Treasurers, on such occasions, make it their business to threaten fiscal catastrophe. The debates through each budget line revealed how synagogue officials viewed philanthropic priorities. First on the United's list was the Jewish Board of Guardians. Synagogues created it, and synagogues sustained it through its earliest years. The board remained a substantial charge, but £1,250, impressive as it might seem, was now only seven per cent of the charitable expenditure of the United, a significant proportionate reduction from the ten per cent of the previous decade. The council froze its contribution, moreover, just when demands for and costs of board services were rising and board deficits cumulating at an unnerving rate. No one, however, attacked the Board of Guardians on the floor of the meeting. The same could not be said for the infant Jewish Religious Education Board whose £650 occasioned unwarranted criticism of its work. Nor did the Board of Deputies escape criticism, questions being asked whether the certification of secretaries – the only explicit service the Deputies rendered the United Synagogue – was worth the £160 annual subscription. Jews' College, which was still unable to recruit students from the Jewish elite, continued to receive only its halved allotment of £100. Ellis Franklin pleaded that Jews' College was the only hope for training an English rabbinate. The United, as it happened, was voting its preference. The more affluent congregations, in particular, preferred to import distinguished foreign rabbis rather than spend money to train English ministers they had little intention of hiring. Since Anglo-Jewry did not send its sons to Jews' College, why should it squander money there? Capitalizing on the momentum of the meeting, the treasurer, Franklin Davis, singled out the United's niggardly grant of £15 to the poor of the Holy Land. The poor of London, he argued, had a greater claim on United Synagogue resources than the poor of Jerusalem. If, he continued, the United wished to support Jerusalem Jews, moreover, the amount proposed was so trivial as to be an insult.

The council of the United Synagogue, made its preferences clear. Its first obligation was to preserve and strengthen its constituent congregations. Religiously and symbolically this translated into preserving but anglicizing Orthodoxy, making the United Synagogue the Jewish equivalent to the Church of England. Decorum and form dominated ritual. Questions and answers in the Christian mode crept into the marriage ceremony. Simeon Singer's authorized edition of the Prayer Book, with its English translation, was among other things an effort to standardize form, emphasize ecclesiastical discipline and replicate, for Jewish ritual forms, the Church of England Book of Common Prayer. Singer's Prayer Book also answered the needs of those whose Hebrew had faltered or been forgotten along the way and made, without ever actually saying so, yet another concession in the anglicization of Orthodoxy.

Chief Rabbi Nathan Adler's policies roused significant communal resistance. Annoyance with his programme of anglicization turned Hermann Adler's succession to his father as Chief Rabbi into a political crisis. Rothschild exerted all his influence for Adler and ultimately prevailed. Lay leaders and Chief Rabbi worked in harmony for the rest of the century. Anglicization remained in place, making English Orthodoxy as unique in its way as Anglicanism was among Christian Churches. Institutionally this translated into answering communal needs with the minimum of risk. While allowing some place, temporarily, for sentiment in the case of the Hambro' Synagogue, the council declined to entertain any expensive, expansive programme likely to incur recurrent, possibly growing, deficits.

On a smaller scale, new initiatives were already being taken. Adler conducted regular meetings of United Synagogue ministers engaged in any form of communal or visitation work to compare notes and plan strategies. Even more striking was an area in which British Jewry lagged slightly but not too far behind the host culture. Jewish women were playing a greater role in existing organizations and developing new philanthropies specifically responsive to needs of women and children. Anglo-Jewry finally recognized, in the course of the 1890s, that women had come to play a major, and perhaps even the most effective, role in teaching and socializing the newcomers. One by one the governing boards of Jewish schools and philanthropies added women to their numbers.[35] But conceding women greater scope and authority raised, by implication, troublesome questions about the role of women in Orthodox Judaism. While women seat-owners had always participated in the governance of the Reform congregation, should they also be allowed to vote in United Synagogue elections?

At the same time, Anglo-Jewry's religious arm sensed that some vital part of its mission lay on the boundary between spiritual and secular life. While communal educational and charitable institutions delivered religious messages with their social services, that was not the whole story. The Federation of Synagogues hoped to counteract secularization by organizing itself in some relationship to the image of the newcomer, while working to integrate him into English life. The Federation existed among and ostensibly as a part of East End culture. The United Synagogue, whose leadership contributed extensively to the secular social institutions, also attempted to address itself to a growing spiritual gap. One response, patterned after contemporary Christian social activist institutions, was rabbinical. The United Synagogue, as part of its East End Scheme proposals, repeatedly debated the question of an East End Jewish settlement, modelled on Toynbee Hall. The debate, both at United Synagogue council meetings and in the broader Anglo-Jewish community, often pivoted on the need for personal involvement, not simply more philanthropic institutions. The argument dragged on. All agencies, by the end of the 1890s, pleaded as ardently for more committed workers as for money.

The Adlers had made their clergy preach and given the sermon a place of prominence in United Synagogue services. Now Hermann Adler began to demand that they be social workers as well. While all East End schemes had included some enhanced, substantial role for Jewish ministers, a renewed flurry of conversionist activity, while as ineffectual as previous ones, spurred the institution of Adler's Committee of Workers among the Jewish Poor. The Thrawl Street Centre in Spitalfields, the principal legacy of the many East End Schemes, opened in 1902. As transient projects had before, the centre provided a facility for Jewish ministers, in their rare free moments, to counsel the poor. Early statistics were scarcely encouraging. Only 667 new cases sought the services of 'the committee of workers' the 325 days the centre was open in 1904. Since the centre offered 'no pecuniary assistance . . . which relieves it entirely of the charge of tending to pauperise', but

---

35 Lead article, *JC*, 13 Mar. 1896. East End controversy or no, when the individual balloting came for the fifteen members of the Board of Shechita, Sir Samuel Montagu, Bt, led the list, closely followed by Board of Guardians president B. L. Cohen, Ellis Franklin, and Henry Lucas. Council meeting, 11 Feb. *JC*, 14 Feb 1896.

freely inculcated 'a spirit of self-help and self-reliance amongst the poor', even its limited impact was impressive. Given the response, the organizers

> deemed it wiser to forbear, at the present juncture, from launching into anything more ambitious, but to remain content, for the time being, . . . with the knowledge that there is a steady growth of appreciation of the Centre among the poor, and of capacity for just this special kind of work among the members of the Committee. Many of the cases are kept in view continually, direct touch being maintained with the poor in their home-life and their general affairs.[36]

The committee, to give it credit, understood that education worked both ways at the Centre. Not only were the poor being taught that these middle-class Jewish ministers could provide counselling and friendship, but the clergymen learned that their enterprise was 'too great, too sacred, and too exacting to be seriously attempted in anyone's leisure'.[37]

But what, in fact, was Thrawl Street actually intended to do? Certainly the clergy were not there to provide social services, grants in money or kind, or to duplicate any of the myriad of already overlapping agencies in the East End. Thrawl Street did give the West End ministers a sense of 'doing good', and that improved rabbinical morale. But, as one veteran rabbi who knew the East End well observed, the things West End clergy knew how to do were not what the East End needed. The Jewish poor had trouble with discontinuity, the occasional and capricious aid or guide. The poor required no teaching about Judaism; that, as those who knew them best constantly reminded philanthropists, was ingrained in their bones. The West End needed that kind of ministry. The East End was short of workers who could guide the poor through the labyrinth of daily life and living, who would be understanding confidants of their problems on their terms. The End End needed workers who did not lecture, but that, unfortunately, was what West End ministers did best.[38]

So Thrawl Street did what it could. Sincere rabbis gave the best advice they could, tried to listen, to understand and to help. They suggested where to go to find jobs, to seek help, to get care. They listened to people's troubles. And all the time they worked to anglicize the East Enders, to inculcate the values that animated Anglo-Jewry, stressing the importance of knowing English, doing things the English way, of becoming English. From modest enough beginnings – about 700 cases a year in 1904 – the Committee of Workers among the Jewish Poor almost quadrupled its caseload by 1910. It also moved into the Jewish Institute on Mulberry Street, where Dayan Feldman presided purposefully and effectively. The steady articulation of the welfare state changed the nature of committee cases, as it did for all settlement social workers. The number of applicants for employment, previously one of the largest categories, shrank markedly as Board of Trade labour exchanges began their work. Organized sabbatarianism also contributed as a newly-established Sabbath Observance Employment Bureau endeavoured, as the committee had formerly done, to match workers only with observant employers.

36 *Thirty-Fifth Report of the United Synagogue* [for 1904] (London, 1905); *JC*, 3 Mar. 1905.
37 *JC*, 3 Mar. 1905.
38 Reverend A. A. Green, Debate at the Old Boys' Club, Oxford St, Whitechapel, 9 Dec. 1905. *JC*, 15 Dec. 1905.

Increasingly the Committee of Workers stepped into the remaining gaps in the social welfare programmes. In the first decades of the twentieth century, medical care generally and the campaign against tuberculosis in particular drew increasing communal attention and resources. The rabbis sought as best they could to ascertain that the Jewish ill received Jewish care. They forwarded applicants for health care, when possible, to the health visitor of the Jewish Board of Guardians and, otherwise, sought to recommend deserving cases to hospitals, conscious always of the medical programmes of conversionist agencies working among the poor.[39] Conversionist activity, which expended enormous resources for a highly limited return, remained a matter of great communal anxiety. Sir Isidore Spielman, for example, wished to form a committee to counteract the work of missionaries among the Jews. Anglo-Jewry, while sympathetic and prepared to take legal action wherever that was appropriate, felt that conversionists fed on Jewish poverty, the insufficiency of many social programmes and a continued lack of adequate religious training. Curing such underlying problems all involved the expenditure of much money. That, the Board of Deputies of British Jews observed, 'was beyond the scope of the Board's work'.[40]

The Federation of Synagogues: 'The Cause of the Small Man of Great Faith'

Sir Samuel Montagu, although he remained involved with and a major participant in the United Synagogue, believed it failed to serve the people it had left behind and the newcomers who were descending in ever multiplying numbers upon the old East End. London synagogues were inconveniently located and priced beyond the means of most immigrants. But even those who could have paid, Montagu realized, preferred more familiar places and forms of worship. The increasingly anglicized usages of the United Synagogue were not merely strange, they were offensive. Newcomers clung to old ways. After the family, the religious *hebra*, a loose association that served as both synagogue and friendly society was their great bond. Beatrice Webb, that pioneering social investigator, had a keen eye for matters religious. She has left a much-cited description of a *hebrot* into which she had ventured one Saturday morning, 'stifled by the heat and dazed by the strange contrast of the old-world memories of a majestic religion and the squalid vulgarity of an East End slum'.[41] Her account combines the diffidence of her class and arrogance of her racial prejudices with her intellectual and emotional grasp of the place and meaning of religious experience. She graphically conveys the clamour, confusion, and even smells of those vital back street religious institutions that provided such an important centre in the life of the poor and the alien.

39 Annual meeting, Committee of Workers among the Jewish Poor. *JC*, 20 Jan. 1911.
40 Law and parliamentary committee, 20 May 1912, BDBJ C 13/1/6.
41 See, C. Booth (ed.), *Life and Labour of the People of London*, I (London, 1893), 567–9. The section is quoted extensively in L. P. Gartner, *The Jewish Immigrant in England, 1870–1914* (London, 1960), 188–9, and Gartner's chapter 5 ('The Religion of the Immigrant') remains the richest and most rewarding general discussion of the subject. My debt to Gartner for lay and religious institutional understanding on these points is more than obvious. The Federation of Synagogues Archives – Joseph E. Blank's minutes from 1887 to 1912, two volumes of minute books from 1887–1923, and three letter books from August 1892 through July 1916 – are at 64 Leman Street, London, classified in the Mocatta Library as AJ/93.

Thrown together with scant resources, these conventicles remained small, noisy, offensive ties to the old world of the Pale rather than the new world of Anglo-Jewry. In Eastern and Central Europe, the conventicles usually had ties of some sort to the communal synagogue and accepted its religious leadership. The Hasidim from Lithuania preserved their rules, organization and costume wherever they settled, but such firm independence was rare. English conventicles that became gatherings of the East Enders looked backwards to the lands from which migrants had come. They challenged British ecclesiastical authority. English Orthodoxy seemed strange to them, and the Adlerian policies of anglicization rendered them stranger still. The conventicles could not afford to hire and pay rabbis of their own, and they suspected the hidden or not-so-hidden agenda of the English Jewish clergy. When they needed rabbinic rulings, they turned back to the familiar, to the rabbi of their old home town or one of the more eminent East European rabbis.[42] But the poor Jews and new Jews hungered for preaching, and they delighted to crowd into the vast, usually almost deserted shell of the Great Synagogue in Duke's Place for the opportunity to hear any passing well-known *maggid*, those enormously popular travelling preachers. Anglo-Jewry, for some undefined reason, never seriously considered using that synagogue as its own effective missionary bastion. Instead, annual meetings of the United Synagogue regarded that historic monument which was steadily losing paying members as an embarrassing liability rather than a great communal asset and complained about the costs involved in keeping the doors open. Immigrant Jews had little interest in joining such an 'establishment' synagogue. The £3 10s cost of a seat made the question purely academic.[43] The new synagogues that London and provincial Jews created as they moved out, even the conventicles that sprang up in provincial centres, by contrast, increasingly revolved within the orbit of the United Synagogue and under the authority of the Chief Rabbi.

The London conventicles were originally visible signs of success and upward mobility among the German and Dutch Jews of the late eighteenth century and first two-thirds of the nineteenth century. As members prospered, they abandoned their conventicles for the prestigious and more costly world of the synagogue. The conventicles became the legacy of one generation of newcomers to the next, to be abandoned as they migrated upwards and outwards from alien to English Jew and from lower to middle class. Although many an acculturated English Jew might have begun his life in this new land in conventicles, Anglo-Jewry anxiously pressed new Jews to move beyond them.[44]

While communal debate, particularly in the columns of the *Jewish Chronicle*, sputtered on and off, a British Medical Association investigation made some community action imperative. *The Lancet* for March 1884 published a serious indictment of public health in the East End, pointing directly at Jewish overcrowded

42 As was the case, for instance, in the dispute leading to Fineberg v. Adler et al. in 1904. See footnote 30 above. See also, Gartner, *Jewish Immigrant*, 187.

43 Gartner, *Jewish Immigrant*, 201; *JC*, 18 May 1883.

44 'The sooner the immigrants to our shore learn to reconcile themselves to their new conditions of living, the better for themselves. Whatever tends to perpetuate the isolation of this element of the community must be dangerous to its welfare.' *JC*, 23 Jan. 1880. See also *JC*, 6 Feb. 1880, 25 Feb. 1881, quoted to much the same effect in Gartner, *Jewish Immigrant*, 200–1.

housing and poverty. Something had to be done. The Jewish Board of Guardians and other philanthropies addressed the nuts and bolts issues of social and economic conditions. Nathan Joseph's sanitary committee initiated its campaigns for better health and improved housing, while Rothschild mobilized the sluggish United Synagogue to lead a charge against 'spiritual destitution' in the East End.

Thus began more than a decade of East End plans or projects. Rothschild understood how politically vulnerable Anglo-Jewry might be. Poor Jews and 'strange Jews' could endanger the public image and achievements of Anglo-Jewry. Self-help and the cushion of charitable institutions which had served the small Jewish community of England no longer appeared to answer public needs. Break the *Landsmannschaft*, the bond of the old homeland, that lies at the heart of the conventicles, argued Chief Rabbi Hermann Adler, and the way lay open to proper socialization.[45] But while secular institutions and increasingly elaborate mechanisms of social control were to be constructed over the next generation, the United Synagogue proved unwilling to develop an extensive missionary programme among the poor and immigrant Jews. East End plans, debated back and forth for years, ultimately crumbled on the somewhat specious issue of constructing a 'vast' and costly new synagogue to serve the spiritual needs of the East End. Various peacemakers – Nathan S. Joseph from the Board of Guardians and Russo-Jewish Committee, the Reverend Simeon Singer with his impeccable East End connections, and Hermann Landau of the Poor Jews' Temporary Shelter (who attempted to reach an accommodation from the Federation side) – repeatedly sought to harmonize Anglo-Jewry's purposes to no avail.

Sir Samuel Montagu understood that West End Anglicanized Orthodoxy and culture did not answer East End wants and needs. The East End was his constituency, and he strove to make it so in the spiritual as well as political sense. Montagu's devout and narrow religiosity gave him an insight most other Anglo-Jewish millionaires lacked. He assumed, with engaging if uncharacteristic credulity, that the system of belief which led him to holiness worked the same way for every Jew. An educated, even a sophisticated man, he believed in the literal interpretation of the Bible. In this he stood as one with pious East Enders.[46] Montagu sought to mould the conventicles into an independent group of small synagogues, financially self-sufficient, and institutionally responsible. Responsible, in Montagu's mind, meant doctrinally Orthodox, culturally quasi-anglicized, and ultimately satellites of the greater world of Anglo-Jewry. Montagu's co-workers in this enterprise, like Montagu himself, lived in closer daily contact with the new people of the East End. Montagu and his allies were already well established within the Anglo-Jewish establishment, but they also had both a strong commitment to and sensitivity about the immigrant community.

Hermann Landau (1844–1924) was the moving spirit with Montagu in establishing the Poor Jews' Temporary Shelter in Leman Street that was to play so vital a role in the lives of immigrant and transmigrant Jews. Mark Moses, who, like Landau, was born in Poland, had strong political connections with Montagu in East End politics. Moses, as one of the most prosperous clothing contractors of the area,

45 Gartner, *Jewish Immigrant*, 202.
46 Montagu, *Samuel Montagu*, chapter 2.

also understood the subtle workings of Whitechapel politics and the East End economy. All three preferred to cajole and entice rather than bully and threaten, although none was above using coercion when necessary. Montagu personally funded cooperating conventicles. He was himself a member of forty synagogues. Through purse and personality, he deftly combined cooperation and control.

The Federation of Minor Synagogues, as it was known for its first two years, encouraged the study of Hebrew, Talmud Torah schools, and the familiar Orthodoxy, but simultaneously demanded English as the language of Federation business, the abandonment of Yiddish, and subtly introduced its own form of Anglo-Jewish socialization. Much was useful. Factiousness was to be settled by arbitration. Sanitation and education became moral obligations. Rothschild understood and approved, even accepting the honorary presidency of the Federation. When Montagu sought to answer a crucial need arising from the unwillingness of insurance companies to underwrite fire insurance for East End shops and dwellings, he turned to Rothschild's Alliance Assurance Company for the necessary guarantees and offered subsidized policies to Federation members.[47]

The Federation of Synagogues was a cleverly designed compromise. It brought immigrant conventicles under the general spiritual authority of the Chief Rabbi and his Bet Din. Montagu knew that rabbinical authority could make his Federation work, but he realized that he must import rabbis who would function effectively with the members of the Federation. He first brought the Rabbi M. Lerner from Alcase from 1890 to 1894 shrewdly placing him under the authority of Chief Rabbi Adler. In one stroke he blunted Adler's potential resentment at the circumvention of the Chief Rabbi's control of the rabbinical title and reinforced the Adlerian ideal of an English rabbinical hierarchy. Seeking experienced ministers immediately accepta-ble to the East End community, Montagu then brought Rabbi Avigdor Chaikin from the Jewish immigrant community in France in 1901. Adler, who was then compromising with Jewish lay leaders by defining clear standards for rabbinical appointment, placed Chaikin on his Bet Din, simultaneously giving status to the Federation and greater authority to his ecclesiastic court. Rabbi Meir Jung from Hungary, paid from a Montagu bequest, followed him in 1911. When Montagu expanded his Federation into provincial Britain through what was called the affiliation scheme, one of the powerful inducements he had to offer those scattered congregations was the occasional service of the Federation rabbi.

Montagu and Adler cooperated easily. The Federation had directly and indirectly extended the Chief Rabbi's authority and prestige. The Federation, moreover, had done what the United Synagogue had been unable to do, define an acceptable compromise between the religious culture of Eastern Europe and the Anglicanized Orthodoxy of the United Synagogue. Since Chaikin, then Jung, sat as a judge on the Chief Rabbi's Bet Din, East Enders were more likely to bring their disputes before that ecclesiastic court and to abide by its decisions.

---

47 Alliance Assurance promised support to the extent of £7,000 for a Society (chaired by Montagu's nephew, Stuart M. Samuel) to operate in connection with the Federation. Premiums were to be at 7s 6d per cent with minimum policies of £100, maximum of £2,000 and no claims to be honoured of £10 or less. *Biannual Report of the Federation of Synagogues* (London, 1898). For the discussions, see particularly, *JC*, June–July 1898. Cecil Roth, *The Federation of Synagogues* (London, 1937) remains the standard authority on the subject.

Overriding considerable resistance, Montagu also secured Federation representation on the Shechita Board, although only after an ultra-Orthodox separatist movement challenged the constituted religious authorities. From thence Montagu's Federation secured its place on the Flour Committee, the equivalent for sharing in the supervision of and profits from matzos (unleavened bread). Small and impecunious synagogues throughout Britain were invited to shelter under the umbrella of his Jewish Congregational Union, but only the Reading congregation struck deep and prosperous root. The Union did, however, enable Montagu to organize a dispersion committee which worked, on as cost effective a basis as possible, to remove Jewish families from the overcrowded East End of London to new homes, new jobs and receptive synagogues in provincial cities.

By the early twentieth century, Montagu had integrated his institution into the religious structure of Anglo-Jewry. Sir Samuel's conception had triumphed, a victory made clear as the ultra-Orthodox separatist Machziké Hadass was finally brought into affiliation with the Federation and under the authority of the Chief Rabbi. Montagu believed the way the newcomers believed. He had no patience for his daughter Lily's flirtations with religious modernism. The old ways were right. That appealed to newcomers who were almost as bewildered by Anglican Orthodoxy as by English secular life. Montagu was also a consummate salesman in such matters. He resonated with the immigrant Jewish hunger for great preaching. He recruited Chaim Maccoby, an East European living legend, and then persuaded Maccoby, once the *maggid* was well established in London, to begin preaching in English, not Yiddish.[48]

The Federation proved an immediate, if expensive, success. Within one year, it claimed thirty synagogues with 2,120 members and several more loosely affiliated conventicles. Doubling its membership over the next ten years, the Federation could claim almost 6,000 members in fifty-one constituent bodies when Montagu died in 1911. Even more important, Montagu slowly amalgamated existing conventicles and dissuaded East Enders from forming new ones. He knew how to use carrots and sticks. Montagu money provided architects for facilities or assistance to bring buildings up to the standards demanded by health authorities. By no means all applicants were accepted and the terms imposed demanded significant contributions from the congregation. Should conventicles fail to avail themselves of Montagu's generosity, the sanitary department of the Jewish Board of Guardians or or the local health authority was likely to come to call.[49]

The work suited Montagu, answering both his personal needs, particularly his competition with the Rothschilds, and his genuine desire to address the spiritual wants of the Russo-Jewish aliens.[50] Through the Federation, Montagu accomplished what Rothschild and the United Synagogue had been unable to do and what the uncompromising Chief Rabbi, Hermann Adler, had previously been unwilling

---

48 Montagu, anxious that his achievements not be lost, bequeathed £2,000 to the Federation to pay Chaikin, Maccoby and their successors. 'Swaythling's Will', *JC*, 10 May 1911.

49 Royal Commission on Alien Immigration, *Parliamentary Papers* (1903), IX Cd. 1743, [herafter cited as RCAI], q 16674; *JC*, 15 Nov. 1889; Gartner, *Jewish Immigrant*, 204–5. Gartner notes that Montagu's gifts of £2,000 during the first two years of the Federation probably equalled almost half of their total expenditure, page 205.

50 Federation of Synagogues, *Laws and Bye-Laws* (London, 1895).

to do. He had created a 'half-way house' that worked, a staging area in the cultural anglicization of East European Jews, combining the familiar with the British. Montagu's Fabian approach and sensitively designed, although carefully controlled, institutions brought substantial numbers of poor Jews and migrant Jews effectively under Anglo-Jewish theological control.

All Jewish leaders did not applaud. Benjamin Cohen, president of the Board of Guardians, argued that Montagu and the Federation brought 'cleavage and disunion'. By pandering to East End preferences, Montagu actually prevented poor Jews 'from becoming members of the body politic', thus retarding their necessary anglicization.[51] Cohen may have resented Montagu leaving the Board of Guardians or possibly he extended their parliamentary differences as members for opposing parties. Whatever the explanation, Cohen was wrong. Montagu played a brilliantly constructive role, from the Anglo-Jewish perspective, in unifying or attempting to bring together splintering groups of British Jews. His rigorous Orthodoxy and his willingness personally to go out among the people of the East End counted just as much as his long purse and readiness to use firm measures to secure his goals. They really were 'his people'. 'Mentor', the *Jewish Chronicle* columnist, recalled an incident during the House of Commons debate on the Aliens Bill. Most members of parliament were sleeping, as was their wont during speeches. Montagu was on the floor being characteristically didactic. Suddenly his manner changed. 'I know these people intimately,' he said firmly. 'I have been in and out among them all of my life. I am proud not just to be their friend, but prouder still that there are many amongst them whom I reckon as my best friends.' His words brought the House up sharply. This City millionaire whose slightest whisper could shake the money markets of the world, standing among jaded politicians, proudly declared his personal friendship with these marginal people.[52] Therein lay Montagu's secret. He was perfectly sincere, utterly honest, and those with whom he dealt knew it.

In 1890, Montagu the peacemaker sought to achieve a reunion of the Orthodox synagogues, pleading for the excommunicated Upper Berkeley Street congregation. In 1904–5, he played the principal role in concluding the agreement between the Shechita Board, of which he was president, and the Machziké Hadass, an ultra-Orthodox splinter group that broke with British Jewish authorities in 1891. By the end of the 1870s, the needs and size of the Jewish population were straining the world of kosher butchers. The Shechita Board, which regulated such matters, after much debate, abolished all fees and perquisites paid to wholesale butchers and revised the system of taxation and payment. Jewish butchers, with supplies now better organized, paid the board a tax of one penny per pound on meat bought. Three quarters of the income went to the United Synagogue, one quarter to the Spanish and Portuguese Synagogue.[53] Benefits were reciprocal. The kosher market was regularized. Useful communal revenue was generated, the well-regulated

---

51 Federation board meeting, 26 Jan. *JC*, 31 Jan. 1896. For some sense of Montagu's command and policies, see [Federation of Synagogues], *Biennial Report* [1894–6] (London, 1896) in Booth Papers B 196.
52 *JC*, 20 Jan. 1911.
53 *JC*, 24 Jan. 1879. Shechita issues were points upon which Ashkenazim and Sephardim closely coordinated their policy, both for London and Manchester Such matters play a substantial role in Gaster–Adler correspondence. See, e.g., Gaster Papers 89/93, 83/101, 67, 74, 87/182, 69/200, 11/237, 22, 30/265.

system of *kashrut* indispensable, and the board's authority enhanced. But as the community grew and as it became more 'Russo-Polish' through the 1880s and 1890s, controversy arose. Montagu protested at the exclusion of the Federation of Synagogues from representation on the board, warning that trouble would lie ahead were East European voices not to be clearly heard. As if to prove his point, a group of Ultra-Orthodox within the alien community charged the board with lax practices and, by refusing to deal through the board, challenged the structure of rabbinic authority in London. The Machziké Hadass, the True Upholders of the Religion, as they called themselves, forced the matter before the highest authorities and threatened to accept no answer but their own. Once again Montagu brought his sincerity, his patience, his belief, and his purse to the struggle. When he was done, Machziké Hadass was contractually back in the fold.[54]

Montagu's religious views gave him a keen sense of precisely those points of Anglo-Jewish Orthodoxy most likely to offend traditionalists. Mixed choirs, for instance, endorsed by Adler, unsettled the observant. Montagu would have none of it in Federation synagogues but accepted the United Synagogue arrangement that mixed choirs would be appropriate so long as a partition separated the male from the female singers. Montagu also smote doctrinal laxity, as he saw it, as harshly as he could. When that shining knight of the Jewish community, Claude G. Montefiore, with Montagu's own daughter, Lily, sponsored a broad-based religious revival through their Jewish Religious Union, Sir Samuel angrily demanded that the Federation of Synagogues cancel its subscription to the Jewish Religious Education Board. That body, he shouted, had elected two board members 'who had openly denied the fundamental principles of Judaism'. Only three votes were cast against him.[55]

Montagu had, as on other occasions, both a personal and an ideological agenda. The opportunity to score leadership points against Montefiore must have pleased Montagu almost as much as this opportunity to demonstrate how much better he was at running organizations than others. Montagu, after all, had passed his Association for the Diffusion of Religious Knowledge over to Chief Rabbi Adler to become the Religious Education Board. Just as the Jewish Board of Guardians led those institutions ministering to the physical needs of the Jewish community, the Jewish Religious Education Board assumed responsibility for the spiritual education of their co-religionists, particularly those needs which went beyond synagogue programmes. So many Jewish children received no formal religious instruction that some much enhanced communal programme was clearly demanded. Evolving from the Association for the Diffusion of Religious Knowledge, which established its first

54 Gartner, who had access to substantial Machziké Hadass materials, argues that only financial collapse brought the 'Upholders of the Religion' back into line. Gartner, *Jewish Immigrant*, 209–14. Bernard Homa, who contributed to Machziké Hadass records to the Anglo-Jewish Archives in the Mocatta Library, argues for the degree of independence preserved. B. Homa, *A Fortress in Anglo-Jewry: The Story of the Machzike Hadath* (London, 1953). While Montagu used financial leverage among other things, he managed to bring Machziké Hadass under the umbrella of the Federation, to reestablish the authority of the Chief Rabbi over the congregation, and even to settle the bitter *shechita* issues which had done to much to trigger the dispute in the first instance. Historians who see Montagu as an authoritarian capitalist bullying the poor underestimate the power of his personality, the values he shared with East Enders and his very deft political skills.

55 *JC*, 3 Mar. 1905.

school in 1876 in the premises of the Old Castle Street board school, the Jewish Religious Education Board coordinated its activities with both the state and independent schools. By 1878, a committee had purchased the site for the Stepney Jewish School, bringing forth substantial contributions from most of the leading figures in Anglo-Jewry.[56]

Jewish women played a major role in the educational campaign. Not only did they write much of the literature that the Religious Education Board was to use, they instituted the Jewish Study Society. Lady de Rothschild not only worked with voluntary schools. She developed the sabbath school programme. She started the first such programme with Mrs Horatio Montefiore and Mrs Isidore Harris in 1857. To meet metropolitan needs, the Association for the Diffusion of Religious Knowledge later extended the programme, but almost all children attending their schools came from such institutions as the Jews' Free School. Other improvised schools were not particularly successful, although the path of original Jewish migration out of the East End can be tracked by institutions established and managed by committed women from Southwark, to the West End, to North London, and Hackney.[57]

Montagu, whom the *Jewish Chronicle* once denominated 'The Caesar of the Community', sought and achieved results. He pressed Federation representation upon Anglo-Jewry's various social institutions, often against considerable resistance but invariably to good effect. Both as minority voices in management and as the recipients of many of the services, Montagu drew the foreign and the poor more closely within the ambit of Anglo-Jewry. This involvement made a difference. While East End contributions to welfare organizations paled beside the beneficence of West End philanthropists, the numbers who gave were substantial, growing, and produced much financial support. Through their giving, East Enders, as Montagu insisted they would, gained a sense of importance and belonging, matters of no small importance in making English Jews. The Federation, moreover, reminded the community as a whole of the significance of elementary things Jewish and just how important they were. When the Sabbath Observance Committee, for example, slid into disrepair and disuse in 1897, Montagu and the Federation took the lead in demanding communal sabbath discipline.[58]

56　The Old Castle Street school was near the present site of the City of London Polytechnic. The school managers gave facilities for the teaching of Hebrew and religion. Roughly 500 of the 700 boys and girls attending the board school were Jewish, but even after compulsory attendance was in place, only 450 of the 700 children were on class registers, and only 300 attended classes regularly. The Chief Rabbi complained ruefully that only ten per cent of the Jewish students availed themselves of this religious instruction. N. M. Rothschild and Sons led the list for Stepney Jewish School with £250, a sum matched by a daughter of Baroness Mayer de Rothschild. The £50 standard brought in the Moses brothers, Sir Julian Goldsmid, David Cohen, Charles Samuel, Nathaniel Montefiore, Frederic D. Mocatta and A. D. Sassoon. £950 was in hand before the Chief Rabbi launched his public appeal. *JC*, 3, 17 Jan. 1879.

57　*JC*, 21, 18 Feb. 1879.

58　*JC*, 30 July 1897. This point is developed in more detail in connection with the social institutions themselves in chapters 3–6. The *Jewish Chronicle* editorially applauded the Federation. 'But with the weeding out of undesirable synagogues, with the educative principles at work, and with the lessons of restraint, self-government and organisation constantly impressed upon its embers it is probably enough that it will gradually and steadily evolve into a strong, trustworthy, and self-dependent institution.' *JC*, 18 Oct. 1898.

Reform and Liberal Judaism

The great German-inspired Reform movement of the early nineteenth century took root in its synagogue in Upper Berkeley Street in 1842 and the creation of a provincial one in Bradford a few years later, but Reform never flourished and prospered in the way Reform Judaism did in Germany or was to do in the United States. It eliminated the distinction between Sephardim and Ashkenazim, and the Reform Synagogue could boast some of Anglo-Jewry's greatest names – Goldsmid and Mocatta, for instance – but it proved doctrinally too conservative to attract the disaffected. Its prayer book was essentially an abridged Sephardi one challenging little in doctrine beyond length of service. Dropping observance of the second day of holy-days precipitated the greatest controversy and Chief Rabbinic criticism. The Reform Syngagogue enfranchised lady seatholders from its institution, a move that not surprisingly made Upper Berkeley Street, if anything, even more conservative. Mrs Lionel Lucas stood prepared to denounce any hint of concession or change.

The Spanish and Portuguese community lifted its ban against the Reform congregation in 1849, and Reform Jews initially supported Jewish charities through the Bevis Marks Synagogue. Communal needs being what they were, Reform Jews were soon reconnected with the several principal philanthropies. Any attempt to deny priority of place to such leading Anglo-Jewish families as Mocatta, Goldsmid, Montefiore, Magnus or Henriques would be preposterous. The Anglo-Jewish Association provided Reform leaders a place in the institutional management of Anglo-Jewry after 1871. By 1885, Reform Jews sat on the Board of Deputies. Although Chief Rabbi Adler displayed, at best, uneasy tolerance for the Reform congregation, every principal Orthodox synagogue attended the 1892 service celebrating fifty years in Upper Berkeley Street. The Sephardim, moved by sentiment, Mocatta, and economy, buried their antagonism. The Spanish and Portuguese congregation jointly purchased a new cemetery in 1895 with their Reform co-religionists.

English Reform Judaism, through the First World War, posed no doctrinal challenge to the Orthodox order and added nothing, as an institution, to the content of Anglo-Jewish social philosophy. Mrs Lionel Lucas even managed to draw the line against additional English being added to Reform services. The slightest whisper of any doctrinal modification brought the old guard out in force. Attendance might decline, interest fall off, but the retention of the old service was, Mrs Lucas reminded the 1903 annual meeting, 'a matter of life and death'. No real concessions were forthcoming, and the Reform Synagogue, while glorying in pedigree and endowment, bade fair to join the Spanish and Portugese congregation in splendid, gradual atrophy and decline. Reform Jews, as individuals, played dynamic roles in the Jewish leadership but did so through the political and social institutions with which they were engaged.[59]

59 D. Marmur (ed.), *Reform Judaism: Essays on Reform Judaism in Britain* (Oxford, 1973); A. M. Hyamson, *The Sephardim of England* (London, 1951), 280–1; Roth, *Great Synagogue*, 255; C. Bermant, *The Cousinhood: The Anglo-Jewish Gentry* (London, 1971), 76. The thought that the Jewish Religious Union, the opening door to Liberal Judaism, might be allowed to use the Berkeley Street premises provoked Mrs Lucas to protest, 'If you lend the synagogue to them you may as well lend it to the Church.' She then observed, 'The spirit of unrest would never have existed if you had not allowed innovations.' Berkeley Street Synagogue, annual meeting of seatholders, 29 Mar. 1903. *JC*, 3 Apr. 1903.

Anglo-Jewry, Orthodox and Reform, laboured mightily on each social front. As the struggle over immigration restriction heated up at the end of the nineteenth century, the leadership demanded even greater philanthropic effort to make the community immune to public criticism. So intense and far-reaching was the campaign that several community leaders began to wonder if the Nation were not struggling to win a world while losing its own soul. They could not even have asked such questions had Anglo-Jewry not had so secure a sense of place within British society. For Sir Samuel Montagu and those who thought like him, the only answer was to stay with the strength of tradition. Jewish nationalists averred that Judaism could be nothing without a land of its own, not that they, as individuals, necessarily wished to move there. If not, they argued, Jews elsewhere in the diaspora would always be victimized, whatever appearances might exist to the contrary.

Still others felt that Jews must stand proudly as Jews nourished by and reinforced in their tradition but also as British Jews who were British in every sense of the term. Oswald J. Simon, founder in 1899 of the Sunday movement, displayed his confidence in the cordial integration of the British and Jews when he proposed a frontal assault on the host culture. Jews should reduce Judaism to its simplest monotheistic formulations and should actively proselytize among disaffected Christians. Judaism, so defined, could be the universal religion of the future. Save for a handful of suburban enthusiasts, Simon found no followers. Anglo-Jewry admired the subculture it had made within British society. Far from attacking anyone except brutal Russians, barbaric Roumanians, or other persecutors far from British shores, Anglo-Jewry preferred to construct a defensive perimeter. Such a strategy was not without cost. Intermarriage and apostasy nibbled around the edges of the community where attractions of assimilation, reinforced by secularist modernism, overcame the constraints of acculturation.

Claude G. Montefiore, who as much as any single individual, spoke for the lay community on matters concerning the young, sought to find a latitudinarian answer through the Jewish Religious Union. He feared the steady erosion of the Jewish spirit among successful Jews and hoped to bring them back both to belief and more than *pro forma* participation in Judaism. Montefiore devoted much effort to preaching in the East End, but the problem he sought to address lay in the West End. Like others, Christian or Jewish, who felt their spiritual roots crumbling away beneath their feet in a dramatically changing world, Montefiore hoped to come to terms with the new world and fit Anglo-Jewry to its dimensions. Perhaps modernized showmanship would open the way to serious spiritual ministration. Montefiore sought hymns, anthems, and rituals that might rouse the flagging Jewish spirit and bring both numbers and enthusiasm to synagogue worship.

Miss Lily Montagu agreed and brought her contagious enthusiasm and considerable community prestige to Montefiore's Religious Union platform. Miss Montagu had not succeeded in snaring the widower Montefiore. He preferred a past vice head of Girton College, Cambridge, who converted to Reform Judaism. Lily Montagu settled for second best, a shared commitment to the cause of Liberal Judaism. Sir Samuel Montagu, her father, refused to have anything to do with such an organization. Orthodoxy stood on its own merits as far as he was concerned. Sir Samuel knew his own mind and felt that others should be of the same opinion. The religious problem, if there were such a thing, was to tailor the individual to fit

Judaism, not to desiccate Judaism or turn it into a secular spectacle to render it palatable to effete West Enders.[60] Sir Samuel's faith was the old religion, and he cast himself in the role of the Biblical patriarch. For those he conceived to be latitudinarians, he was a Jeremiah. Yet this uncompromising combatant conceived of himself as a great peacemaker within the Jewish community, a man who stood between the great world of grand dukes and millionaire bankers (of whom he was one) and the small world of the frightened immigrant, clinging to familiar rituals, language and culture.

Montefiore, on the other hand, was a man of utmost cultivation, aware of the latest currents in theology and philosophy. No less committed to strengthening Judaism than Montagu, Montefiore called religious indifference the greatest problem. For that he had a modern solution. 'Combination' was the answer of the day. Look around you, Montefiore urged, and what do you see? On all issues, political, economic, social and labour, union was essential for survival. His Jewish Religious Union would seek out a consensus for Judaism, a body of dogma upon which all could concur, and thus retrieve those who had become estranged. With Montefiore raising the banner, many Anglo-Jews rallied to his cause as volunteers and contributors. The Religious Union began its campaign in 1902 giving public addresses to any group which might listen. The first result, not surprisingly, was a flurry of outraged letters and editorials in the Jewish press. Chief Rabbi Hermann Adler blasted the Liberals for desiccating Judaism, not deepening it. Claude Montefiore and Lily Montagu were not to be dissuaded. 'They desired to prove that Judaism was a living force,' announced Lily at a meeting that rejected a compromise with the Reform Synagogue, 'capable of affecting modern life and not dependent on the survival of Oriental customs.' The Liberals wanted nothing to do with the religious smugness and self-complacency that had smothered Anglo-Jewry. Liberal Judaism would serve God and a modern community. Theirs was a living faith.[61] For those who preferred not to listen or to think for themselves, the Religious Union prepared tracts and pamphlets carrying the word to a culturally varied audience.

Since music buoyed the spirit, volunteers mobilized a Religious Union choir. A generous budget transported Montefiore's inspirational group to various gatherings. Given such great effort, first year results seemed disappointing. Perhaps, thought Montefiore, the matter was simply one of inadequate money. With engageing naivety (and in spite of Lily Montagu's warning), he doubled the minimum subscription to five shillings, effectively cutting out any Jews not impeccably middle class from participation. The Union priced itself out of its intended market and became little more than a self-congratulatory group of *engagés* patting one another on the back and preaching to the converted.

By 1905, Montefiore admitted that he had underestimated the strengths of obstacles to their work, that the evils they attacked were more deep-rooted and

---

60 Montagu, who had a proprietorial interest in the New West End Synagogue, snatched the Reverend S. Singer away from the Union in April 1903. See Montagu to Singer, 15 Apr.; Singer to Montagu, 15 Apr. 1903. printed in *JC*, 24 Apr. 1903.

61 For the rejection of a compromise with the Berkeley Street Synagogue, see Jewish Religious Union meeting, 5 Apr. 1903. *JC*, 10 Apr. 1903. For the Chief Rabbi's view, see H. Adler, 'The Old Paths', 6 Dec. 5663 [1902]. printed in *JC*, 12 Dec. 1902.

complex than they had assumed. 'We must go forth and try and create a desire for public worship,' he told the annual meeting. 'We must reason, argue, urge, and induce, and it comes to meaning a good deal more work than we had originally supposed.' Their mission to the East End had reclaimed but thirty or forty souls in 1904. Considering the effort and money expended, Montefiore was doing no better than the conversionists. The *Jewish Chronicle* observed the tone of 'chastened optimism' in its 1905 meetings, and added

> the Union has not yet become, if it ever will become, an effective remedy for our religious ills. We must not forget that this body has had the most influential backing, and has been allowed to go its own way without interference or attack by the rest of the community.

If Jews are falling away from their faith, the *Chronicle* continued, it was not for the lack of what the Union wanted to provide.

> They are not waiting to be lured by Hebrew sirens to the religious shores; and for that reason we do not think it logical or reasonable to tamper with established religious practice in order to bring them back to Judaism.

One thing Montefiore had right. Every leading voice in Judaism felt a pressing need for a revival, not simply of Jewish faith but of Jewish culture. The Religious Union, however, was, so its critics believed, merely a drain upon the resources better devoted to the Jewish Religious Education Board, a body upon which Montefiore also sat.[62]

The constitutional structure of Jewish governing bodies, lay and religious, while incomplete and certainly not in any sense controlling the life of every British Jew, provided the first framework of communal governance. Some institutions overlapped. Others, the Anglo-Jewish Association, for instance, were in theory responsible only to their membership. Many Jews who thought of themselves as such lived outside the formal structure of synagogue or conventicle. Yet however incomplete or incongruous the institutional arrangements might be, they worked.

62　*JC*, 3 Mar, 1905; General Meeting, Jewish Religious Union, 21 Feb. 1905. JC, 24 Feb. 1905. See also Ellen M. Umansky, *Lily H. Montagu and the Development of Liberal Judaism in England* (Ann Arbor, 1981).

3

Philanthropy and Social Control

Anglo-Jewish philanthropy was renowned for the scope of its beneficence. In a variety of overlapping forms, it touched the needy, the hungry, the mad, the orphans, the blind, the sick, not to mention the great rituals of life from birth to burial. Anglo-Jewry believed that it had no choice. After the Poor Law Amendment Act of 1834, secular authorities could and usually did apply a workhouse test to the needy whom private charity could not or would not assist. Those to be relieved at public expense could be required to enter the workhouse. Lest the poor be tempted to abuse public funds, conditions and diet in the workhouse were designed, by carefully calculated administrative rules, to be more unpleasant than those of the poorest people who remained independent and self-supporting. Jews thrust upon the poor law workhouse for relief might be unable to follow their special observances or their dietary laws.[1] The leadership could not deny its poor the facilities for observance and remain true to its own principles. The Jewish poor, moreover, floundering in their world of deprivation were perpetually fair game for conversionists, who pressed an aggressive East End programme. Intensive proselytizing, whether by the Anglican missions or the several Nonconformist operations, while a source of anxiety for the Anglo-Jewish leadership, produced

---

1 C. H. L. Emanuel, long-time secretary and solicitor to the Board of Deputies, observed that the Board of Deputies negotiated an understanding with the Chancellor of the Exchequer in 1834 to allow Jews freedom from sabbath work and to provide kosher food in the workhouse, an agreement reconfirmed when a Board of Deputies deputation went to the Poor Law Commission in 1842. L. Emanuel, *A Century and a Half of Jewish History*, 22, 44–5, quoted in Lipman, *A Century of Social Service*, 12n. Lipman's study remains the standard work on this topic.

trivial results for much effort.[2] Christian missionary enterprise in the East End produced few real conversions but regularly prodded Jewish institutions into responsive action.

British Jews had historically cared, to a great degree, for their own. The Jewish community, appealing against the reimposition of the aliens tax in 1690, pleaded that the hundred souls who constituted the poor Jews were 'indigent poor people who are maintained by the rest and are in no way chargeable [to the parish poor rates]'. Sephardi authorities, by 1770, however, distinguished between the indigenous poor and newcomers. In an effort to thrust responsibility for maintenance on family or friends, they refused to provide poor relief to migrant Jews coming to England from Holland 'who left that country without good cause'. The Ashkenazim, rapidly increasing in numbers during the eighteenth century, took no concerted measures to control the influx of their co-religionists. As on almost all matters, the two communities stood apart. Each attempted to shift as much of the burden for relief as possible on to the other. Joshua Van Oven, one of many distinguished philanthropists who were to argue in the nineteenth century for rationality and unity, appealed to the community in 1802 to establish a Poor Board 'to conduct which it would be expedient to incorporate several gentlemen for each synagogue, which should constitute a Board for the management of all the Jewish poor in the metropolis.'

The Sephardim declined to subsidize what they regarded as Ashkenazi social irresponsibility. The only Ashkenazi charities at the time were the Bread, Meat, and Coals Charity, founded in 1780 (which continued to function through the Victorian era), the Talmud Torah School (limited to orphans) which would later evolve into the Jews' Free School, and the Jewish Soup Kitchen. Asher Goldsmid founded the Jews' Hospital 'as a home for the aged poor and as an industrial school for the young' in 1795. In each instance, however, these charities barred the foreign poor. The three great synagogues busily shunted the problem from one to another. Synagogue overseers of the poor were expected to develop new and interesting ways of 'circumventing importunity'. Henry Faudel, who was to render invaluable services to the Jews' Hospital, repeated Van Oven's plea in 1844: he proposed a general council of British Jews to manage all Jewish charities 'to secure an efficient centralisation with wholesome and necessary control'. The existing system of laissez-faire, he argued, produced more problems than benefits. It encouraged mendicants and idlers instead of training productive artisans and assisting the industrious.[3]

Fifteen years later the community finally decided to deal with the issue of 'the strange poor'. The Great Synagogue voted to establish a conjoint committee to manage such matters in January 1858 and to create the Jewish Board of Guardians in

2 The London Society for the Propagation of Christianity among the Jews, for instance, celebrated its centennial in 1901. Its East End garrison, at that point, numbered nine ministers, seven medical men, fifteen lady workers, nine lay missionaries, six agents, five schoolteachers and three 'dispensers'. See Dep CML 35/6 in the Bodleian Library. East End Jews appear to have thought little of availing themselves of missionary relief and medical care, taking the leaflets, listening to the prayers, and departing none the worse for wear. C. T. Lipshutz (sometimes spelled Lypshutz) at the Barbican Mission to the Jews, Prebendary Webb Peploe's most effective proselytizer, alienated almost every other missionary by his dubious advertising and tactics. See, e.g., the 1899 material in Dep CMJ d 21/13.

3 [H. Faudel], *Suggestions to the Jews for Improvement in Reference to Their Charities, Education and Central Government: By a Jew* (London, 1844). For the quotes above and a general account, see 'A sketch of the early history of the Jewish Board of Guardians', *JC*, 20 Mar. 1896.

February 1859. Its first chairman, Ephraim Alex, was overseer of the poor for the Great Synagogue. Alex argued that the immediate problem was to understand 'the statistics of poverty'. To that end, he secured a one year experimental grant from the three principal Ashkenazi synagogues. Alex, whose political skills had proved crucial in securing the vote creating the board, became president, and Lionel L. Cohen, the strategist and tactician of improved relief systems, was named honorary secretary. The board met on 16 March 1859 and began operations on 1 July, holding its first relief 'rota' a week later. The experiment, however, was hesitantly launched. The supporting synagogues demanded that the board report and have its powers reconfirmed every six months.

Whatever misgivings Anglo-Jewry may have felt and however tentative its support for the institution, recipients of the board's charity learned, from its opening session, to feel the opprobrium of poverty. The board's unsalubrious setting must have been as discouraging to applicants as to its patrons. The institution was initially housed, almost as an afterthought, in a draughty wood and glass extension, partitioned off from the Jewish Soup Kitchen in Black Horse Yard, Whitechapel. Supplicants were not permitted to forget who they were and their dependence on the more fortunate members of the community. Standing before the seated 'rota', the poor were made to feel the full indignity of their position. With the passage of time, the board refined this initial psychological conditioning. Those seeking loans to make themselves self-sufficient were spared the humiliation of attending the general relief hearings. A stern sense of duty made the founding members a hardy and determined lot. One generation educated the next. Algernon E. Sydney, a delegate of the New Synagogue, provided personal continuity from the original hesitant voluntaristic experiment to the welfare state, serving as honorary solicitor and a board member from its founding in 1859 until his death in 1916.

The board fulfilled a desperate social need. The early Victorian community sought to meet the problem by expanding its synagogue-based and related charities, but these tended to be specialized, duplicatory, and (particularly as the Jewish population exploded in the last decades of the nineteenth century) increasingly inadequate to cope with communal poverty. Several social observers in the middle of the nineteenth century pointedly commented on Jewish industriousness, and on how loth Jews were to turn to charity, often contrasting them to English 'layabouts' or 'feckless' Irish. They also recognized that Jews cared for themselves. Both conclusions about Jews were correct, although misleading. Private benevolence was widespread, and small charities sprang up to meet this or that need, but the poor confronted a bizarre and highly political world of relief. Samuel Montagu, who had learnt from experience, 'used to get impatient with the multiplication of societies, which he firmly believed existed for the sake of their secretaries.'[4]

Through the first half of the nineteenth century, charity had been literally on a 'catch-as-catch-can' basis. Synagogue beadles distributed small amounts of cash relief each week by handing, often merely tossing, coins to a seething, clamorous crowd at the synagogue gate, a random system of relief ill-calculated to aid the weakest. Other charities turned relief into high or low politics. Many had elaborate balloting for their benefits, precipitating campaigns of competitive distress.

4 Montagu, *Samuel Montagu*, 51.

Advertisements in the *Jewish Chronicle*, for instance, would solicit votes for a forthcoming balloting, pressing the claims for support of one candidate or another and, incidentally, displaying the various leading figures in the community who had endorsed that deserving soul. But what happened to the orphan, the blind girl, the consumptive boy, the old woman or disabled costermonger unable to find influential sponsors or run advertisements in the Jewish press? Perhaps a private patron would appear but perhaps not.

Almost all charities began with the assumption that Jews were members of or attached to one or another of the synagogues. Many of the poor, therefore, had no communal source of aid.[5] This was particularly the case for 'strange Jews'. These migrant foreigners, originally Dutch or German, became, as the century wore on, Jews from the vast centres of Eastern Europe. Not only did they arrive in unprecedented and growing numbers, they were more foreign, more strange, less tractable than their predecessors. Throughout the nineteenth century, Anglo-Jewry created institutions – schools, hospitals, retirement homes, a panoply of specialized charities – that proliferated, sometimes in duplication of one another, without any overall plan.

Almost all imitated the conventional, although much criticized, policy of Victorian charities by awarding each subscriber a vote in selecting beneficiaries. Philanthropy thus conveyed a sense of power as well as performing a *mitzva*, the obligation of the observant Jew. The Sephardim, who had relatively little new migration and an upwardly mobile community, had fewer needy and felt less pressure for change. Most nineteenth-century institutional growth occurred among the 'German' Jews. Given the fact that more than two dozen Ashkenazi charities, exclusive of schools or friendly societies, doled out approximately £30,000 by the middle of the nineteenth century in a somewhat haphazard manner and probably another £20,000 in private charity, organized philanthropy cried out for rationalization and reform.[6]

Thus it was that after several false starts in the late 1840s and 1850s, Lionel L. Cohen, 'the High Priest of the secular government of our community', animated the Jewish Board of Guardians to give order to the proliferating and overlapping Jewish charities.[7] He was the first of a family dynasty that presided over the board. Anglo-Jewry came to entrust this task to the Cohens. Five of the seven presidents between 1859 and 1947 were descendants of Louis Cohen, and no one of them served less than eight years as president. The organization of philanthropy also grew out of a general demand for rationalization in Anglo-Jewry. The same sentiment that sought more orderly philanthropy also led to the formation of the United Synagogue in 1870. The United Synagogue, in turn, inspired the first amalgamation of older charities, that of the Jews' Hospital and Orphan Asylum, a curious if surprisingly effective pairing.

5 Patrick Colquhoun describes at length the condition of poor Jews, barred by prejudice or by their own religious observance from entering the general labour market, driven to live by their wits and all too often turning to crime at the end of the eighteenth century. *The Police of the Metropolis*, 5th edn (London, 1797), 158–60.

6 *JC*, 25 Sept. 1859. Abraham Benisch, the editor, ran a series of editorials during the previous two years pleading at almost interminable length for a central charitable coordinating body.

7 *JC*, 10 Jan. 1879.

The problem of consolidation, however, was never fully resolved. The vested interests of dozens of organizations and hundreds of subscribers were at stake. Every donor, in meeting his or her moral obligation as a Jew, also earned social prestige. Each enjoyed that small access to power that the right to vote for beneficiaries entailed. Each had a self-importance not easily or readily surrendered. Institutions, once created, not only recruited volunteers but generated paid positions for secretaries, fund raisers, pledge collectors and various administrators. Administrative expenses were perpetually discussed, but few institutions showed a capacity, between 1880 and 1914, to cut costs by eliminating staff. The general thrust was understandably in the opposite direction. All institutions recruited and deployed volunteers, but most came to feel the need for better-trained professional workers. Even the Board of Guardians further professionalized itself between 1890 and 1912. Although volunteer visitors continued to play their traditional investigative role and although the managing committee continued to sit on the relief rotas, the investigations and recommendations came increasingly from trained social workers. Professionals, moreover, had a sense of self-importance that translated into demands for higher salaries. What the Board of Guardians discovered was no less true of other philanthropies. The Jewish Religious Education Board, for instance, found, much to its annoyance, that its ill-paid teachers unionized in 1910.

Rigour in oversight was order of the day for the Board of Guardians from 1859. Jacob Loewenthal, the first clerk and investigating officer, set a standard to which future officers and professionals would repair with pride. Fluent in several languages, assiduous in investigation, dedicated to making the institution work, Loewenthal guaranteed, as much as any communal servant could, that the board's work would meet with approval from the most sceptical donor. The board liked to train its own. Board employees early acquired and long sustained those habits and that cast of mind which Anglo-Jewry sought to inculcate in the community. Morris Stephany, whose rigorous standards as secretary to the board from 1877 to 1918 were a legend in the community, began his apprenticeship as an office boy in February 1867. Like the United Synagogue that spawned it, the board had its own professional civil service, complete with superannuation scheme, to develop and sustain consistency and institutional morale.

The board had been founded ostensibly to deal with the problem of the foreign poor. The moving spirit of the institution, Lionel Cohen, had accepted this limitation only long enough to gain community approval. Once the board was in place, Cohen argued that confining aid to 'the strange poor' would establish a dual system of relief, create unnecessary friction and duplication, and undoubtedly wreak severe hardship upon the poor themselves.[8] On this point, however, Anglo-Jewry remained divided. Existing philanthropies represented strong vested interests. Board of Guardians 'imperialism' was then and thereafter regarded with much suspicion. Cohen pleaded, lobbied, even bullied. Anglo-Jewry accepted Cohen's broader plan only with some misgivings and an implied agreement not to encroach on existing philanthropies without their consent.

8 L. Cohen, *Scheme for the Better Management of All the Jewish Poor, Report Presented to a Sub-Committee of the Great Synagogue, appointed 14th of July, 5619* [1859] (5th January 1860) printed for private circulation.

The board made clear its commitment to responsible management and community control in the appointment of its first committee. Samuel Montagu, on his own initiative, had begun a practice of personally investigating each applicant for aid. The visiting committee, established in February 1861, translated this into institutional policy. Frederic D. Mocatta, who more than any other single figure embodied the spirit of Jewish philanthropy, accepted the chairmanship. With such members as Samuel Montagu, Lionel Van Oven and Julian Goldsmid, Anglo-Jewry's leading social activists personally committed themselves to ensuring that resources would be frugally and effectively employed. Communal leaders pledged their time, effort, and money. Anglo-Jewry often contrasted their personal involvement in actual operations to the way in which American Jewish philanthropists committed their money but not themselves to active charitable work.[9] 'Visitation' was Anglo-Jewry's key. Community confidence was assured by the guarantee that community leaders like these would personally investigate cases before and after support was given.[10]

The Jewish Board of Guardians moved circumspectly. For its first few years, those congregations that would become the United Synagogue in 1870 contributed most of its funds. From its inception, however, the board sought to build an independent financial base through bequests, subscriptions, and donations. The board drew, in addition, substantial amounts from various public authorities, delighted to subsidize part of the cost when the balance would be borne by a private charity. Much of the development of the British welfare state grew through such partnerships in which ratepayers and taxpayers subsidized existing voluntaristic enterprises. But public authorities, however benevolent, intruded on the freedom of voluntaristic organizations. They insisted on knowing what was done with public money. State inspection ultimately meant increasing state definition of standards and sound management.[11]

The board's relationship with and use of state aid proved ultimately to be its salvation. In formal and public terms, however, the Jewish Board of Guardians existed to care for its unfortunate co-religionists and to prevent them from having to turn to state aid. From its inception, the board had delicate problems of public relations. On the one hand, it had to advertise its importance and need for growth by pointing to tasks yet undone. On the other hand, however real those pressures

9 Joseph to Loeb, 22 Oct. 1884, AIU Angl I/H/7/10,000.

10 Lewis Emanuel served as honorary secretary. The original committee also included two Josephs, another Cohen, David Hyam and H. H. Collins. See, generally 'A sketch of the early history of the Jewish Board of Guardians', *JC*, 20 Mar. 1896. Charity Commission, *Return of the Endowed Charities in the County of London of 19 September 1901* (London, 1901) has a long chapter on the Jewish Board of Guardians.

11 The JBG, for obvious reasons, never admitted the degree to which local authorities subsidized or supplemented its relief, but Jacob Franklin, an economist and statistician who founded and chaired the board's committee on legislative and parochial affairs, ascertained, from the late 1870s, that the JBG drew all possible assistance from local Poor Law authorities. *JC*, 10 Aug. 1877; Lipman, *A Century of Social Service*, 71. The Whitechapel Poor Law Union return to the Home Office for 1895 suggests much use of medical facilities (which the JBG felt to be appropriate) and little of the workhouse. Statistics were maintained by country, not ethnicity, but recipients from Russia, Poland, Austria and Holland were reported to be almost all Jews. Of 798 individual cases, 679 (85 per cent) received out-patient medical assistance, seventy-two (9 per cent) were admitted to the infirmary, and a mere twenty-seven (3 per cent) admitted to the workhouse. Alien Jewish cases represented 92 per cent of all alien cases handled in the Whitechapel Union. *JC*, 27 Mar. 1896.

might have been, the Jewish Board of Guardians was at considerable pains, especially in its early years, to suggest that matters were reasonably well in hand, that the board could, in fact, do its job. Were the board clearly to acknowledge that it could secure state support, private contributions might dry up. If it implied that it had accomplished its task, the board's annual appeals for money would fall short of its needs. It must never suggest that Jewish philanthropy could not care for the Jewish poor, for communal self-sufficiency was indispensable to the public image of British Jews.

Annual reports and annual meetings trod this delicate tightrope surprisingly well, conveying simultaneously the sense of great needs and of a task well done. The board represented itself as meeting community obligations only by straining every nerve and squeezing every farthing but nevertheless meeting its commitments. The board observed, in 1864, that there was nothing 'exceptional' in the condition of the Jewish poor, and that the poor in 1867 'were less in want of the absolute necessities of life than before'. The board in those early years also minimized the impact of immigration, although the problem of 'strange Jews' had brought it into being. And the board could not be blamed for failing to anticipate that East European immigration would shortly all but overwhelm it.[12]

Charity, even after the creation of the Jewish Board of Guardians, was far from under control. The difficulties were institutional and philosophical as well as economic. Those who considered social issues, while acknowledging the many problems, still advocated extending the philosophy and control of the Jewish Board of Guardians to the remaining multitudinous small enterprises.

> Disunited and eccentric action in charitable institutionalism tends to pauperise the community. We must [argued 'Nemo' in 1879] raise the poor and suffering from the misery of dependence. We can alone elevate – not by lavish giving and facile acquirement, but – by that wise forethought, careful supervision, and intelligent administration consequent upon intelligent organisation. From the chaos of poverty to create order, to strip pauperism of its wretchedness, to encourage the growth of industry, to inculcate and foster thrift, to inspire the rising progeny of beggars with notions of independence, all this is avowedly to be the work of the Board.[13]

Lionel Cohen found board expenses rising to £3,000 by 1879. To draw more support from Anglo-Jewry, he emphasized the need to 'raise' the poor, not 'degrade' them. The problem of poverty went to the very soul of the community.

> The charity which merely salves over the evil of distress instead of radically curing it is not considered by many co-religionists the very perfection of benevolence, is yet recognised, by too few of them, as being a positive evil instead of a positive benefit.[14]

Curative social policy must be based upon sound principles, or Gresham's Law would go to work. We must shut

12 Board of Guardians for the Relief of the Jewish Poor (hereafter cited as JBG), *Seventh Annual Report* (London, 1864), 9, 24; *Tenth Annual Report* (London, 1868), 9–10.
13 'Nemo' to the editor, *JC*, 3 Jan. 1879.
14 'The Jewish Board of Guardians', *JC*, 10 Jan. 1879.

the little sly doors through which the trading beggar may creep and pass undetected among the crowd, elbow the worthy and necessitous poor – necessitous through no fault of their own – and then succeed by clamour and cunning, by the exposure of self-made sores to excite the unreasoning pity of beholders who will not give themselves the trouble to enquire into the causes below the surface, or who have not the capacity to deal with one of the largest questions of our modern civilization – how to ameliorate the condition of the poorer classes.[15]

The board, however, did not enjoy the luxury of other Victorian charities, the capacity to throw its 'undeserving' poor on the workhouse. Ultimately it would acknowledge using municipal Poor Law Union workhouses only in rare and exceptional cases as a disciplinary sanction when all other measures had failed. The board found itself, therefore, forced to create a system which would minister to all the poor and yet not create a class of permanent paupers. Few private philanthropies displayed such imagination in developing novel and useful policies and practices. None showed more intelligent management and single-minded, if flexible, pursuit of a coherent social philosophy. The Jewish community might be relatively small, but no single Victorian philanthropy, outside of the field of education, operated on so vast a scale for so many people.[16]

The Jewish Board of Guardians became the classic philanthropic Victorian pioneer. Its philosophy was universally applauded and often imitated.[17] Investigation and visitation were its hallmarks. Such casework in the field brought generations of volunteers to impressive levels of competence. The agency maintained detailed records on every case (and on every unsuccessful applicant). Relief should be 'adequate', itself a highly relative term, but serve, wherever possible, to enable the recipient to regain 'independence'. Cash contributions, save in the form of loans, were only a last resort. Money itself was almost never used even for relief allowances. Anglo-Jewry had long before adopted the common philanthropic practice of acquiring blocks of 'tickets' for food or fuel redeemable at shops within the community. By such devices was 'misuse of relief' supposed to be avoided. Such efforts failed. An underground market discounted food and coal tickets for cash. The bath tickets which each applicant had to use before receiving relief seem to have had no market value.[18] Seeking relief, moreover, brought the applicant under Anglo-Jewish scrutiny and 'discipline'. Regular home 'visiting' went hand in hand with the application for relief. Once the committeeman or social worker was inside the door, applicant and family became fair game for regulation

---

15 *JC*, 3 Jan. 1879.

16 Hannah Hyam, one of the first women to serve on the JBG executive committee, reminded all Jewish women social workers how quickly and easily the wrong lessons could be learned. 'Children are very quick to comprehend a situation of this kind, and will not be slow to perceive that laziness, carelessness, dirt are rewarded and that the shifting of their most sacred responsibilities on other shoulders is not considered blameworthy by the lady or gentleman who allow – almost encourage – their parents to act this way.' 'Organisation in charitable work', *JC*, 30 May 1902. To understand this general problem, see David Owen, *English Philanthropy, 1660–1960*, to which I am much indebted.

17 J. H. Stollard, *London Pauperism amongst Jews and Christians* (London, 1867) is an excellent, if hyperbolic, example.

18 Lipman, *A Century of Social Service*, 56n.

and 'improvement'. The longer one needed relief, the more extensive and detailed this external oversight and management. Any case being relieved for more than six months was reinvestigated and revisited.

British social observers and philanthropists approved. The Jewish Board of Guardians created the standard to which all such institutions aspired. Investigation, complete records, adequate relief and home visiting became the publicized watchwords of the national Charity Organisation Society.[19] Founding president Ephraim Alex suggested two other principles to deal with the issue of immigrants 'flooding' to England to live on charitable bounty. No case should be relieved unless the recipient had been resident for six months, a curious exclusion by a body ostensibly established to deal with the newly-arrived poor. That provision in the board's constitution meant no relief even for the 'deserving' poor immigrants. As newcomers arrived in significant numbers, other agencies had to be created to answer their needs. Alex's second recommendation, while never formally adopted, was held in reserve and acted on when the occasion seemed to warrant. Recalcitrant cases – president Alex called them 'confirmed paupers' – should be passed over to the Poor Law authorities. Here the board stood on sensitive ground. It avoided publishing such statistics, and local Poor Law Union returns, while indicating some Jews in their institutions, do not provide usable numbers. The board unquestionably used and could always consider employing the 'workhouse threat'.[20]

Few social agencies showed more capacity to experiment and improve their approaches and policies than the Jewish Board of Guardians. Unlike other English charitable institutions, the board had to create imaginative options to deal with the 'undeserving poor' if it were to avoid dependence on the workhouse sanction. Almost all Jewish philanthropic institutions functioned on the assumption that their constituents wished to be 'moral', to improve themselves. They were correct. Most did. All Jewish institutions sought to underline the virtues of self-help. The Board of Guardians, no less than Anglo-Jewry's schools and synagogues, considered education to be one of its major functions, constantly to proclaim and demonstrate communal approval of those who were self-reliant and self-sufficient. The relief of distress, the board believed, 'should be thoughtful as well as emotional'. Benefactors, no less than the poor and ignorant, required education were relief to be effective.[21]

Twenty years after the establishment of the Jewish Board of Guardians, the Sephardi congregation conceded that the benefits of efficiency outran the glories of tradition. The Spanish and Portugese Synagogue established its own board of guardians amalgamating as many as possible of the Board of Elders charities under one roof. Daniel Castello, the moving spirit, was delighted and paid tribute to both the inspiration and cooperation of the 'Board of Guardians for the Relief

---

19 Four years after the implementation of the JBG, the Liverpool Central Relief Society attempted to develop a comparable city-wide programme. Owen, *English Philanthropy*, 424.

20 Lipman gives no information on the extent of this practice. Lipman, *A Century of Social Service*, 27ff. The board would scarcely have publicized such data, preferring to emphasize the number repatriated or 'dropped from the rolls'. Once the Aliens Bill debate began, however, proponents of immigration restriction could always find Jews in workhouses. See chapters 9 to 11 below.

21 'The Jewish Board of Guardians', *JC*, 10 Jan. 1879.

TABLE 3.1   Jewish Board of Guardians income, outlay and capitalization

	1865	*1870*	*1875*	*1880*	*1885*	*1890*
Income (£)	3,578	6,372	8,920	11,184	14,095	17,526
Expenditure (£)	3,020	5,184	7,330	11,186	13,104	17,391
Administrative Costs (£)	757	1,063	1,230	1,840	1,494	1,838
as % of Expenditure	25%	21%	17%	16%	11%	11%
Increase in capital (£)	313	1,104	4,695	10,095	24,138	32,217

Sources: Lipman, *Century of Social Service,* 107; JBG, *Annual Reports.*

of the German Poor'.[22] The board example was contagious. It arrived at its time of testing, the 1890s, with a record of sound management and administration, disciplined costs and a steadily enhanced capital position.[23]

The board understood that direct benefit aid and cash grants did not address the issue of poverty but merely made it tolerable. Like other sensitive contemporary charitable enterprises, it feared that relief would engender pauperism. Testing the borderland between the 'deserving' and 'undeserving' poor consumed much time and administrative effort. Both the board and community leadership felt that their most important work were those activities 'which aim at making every Jewish citizen, as far as possible, a self-supporting and self-respecting unit of the population'. The board would point with greatest pride to the psychological as well as the economic impact its loan, industrial and sanitary departments had on the community as a whole.[24]

The Industrial Department

The industrial department grew from an experiment in 1861, which more than any other clearly embodied board philosophy and intentions. A donor provided ten sewing machines. The board then saw that they were fruitful and multiplied. The work committee, as it was then called, carefully screened applicants and lent them machines for two shillings a week until the original cost was repaid. The machine then became the borrower's property, and the board bought another. In less than three years, twenty-six machines were in circulation, instilling 'a spirit of resourcefulness and independence'.

> The self-respect of the lessees is maintained by keeping them aloof from the general recipients of relief, and a large class of poor, probably now amounting to one thousand persons has been enabled gradually to become self-supporting.[25]

22 Some of the charities consolidated, such as the *Mehil Sedeca* and the *Honen Dalem,* reached back more than 150 years. Castello also secured the cooperation of two of the trustees of the LARA fund established for various benevolent purposes. *JC,* 21 Feb. 1879.
23 Lipman, *A Century of Social Service,* 107.
24 As it did in JBG, *Annual Report for 1904* (1905) with much applause from *JC,* 17 Mar. 1905.
25 Magnus, *Jewish Board of Guardians,* 27–8.

The board discontinued this practice when the Singer sewing machine company itself adopted a comparable buying-by-instalment hire-purchase policy, and turned to teaching applicants for aid to capitalize on that opportunity.

The work committee began in 1868 to supervise the training of Jewish girls as seamstresses. Once again, the board paid careful attention to subtle distinctions as part of its never-ending education of the less fortunate. Those being instructed were spared the 'humiliation of attending the Relief Committees with the indiscriminate crowd of general applicants'.[26] By 1872, the work committee had moved beyond sewing machines and seamstresses to become the industrial committee, one of the showpieces of Jewish philanthropy. In one area after another, the industrial committee employed its funds to repeat its sewing machine success. The committee purchased and lent tools and equipment to carpenters and cabinet-makers, to shoemakers, printers, umbrella-makers, and bookbinders.

One problem confronting fledgling Jewish entrepreneurs was their inability to give security to workshops and warehouses to purchase the goods necessary to start in business in the first instance. The industrial committee began underwriting small security deposits. As trades became crowded, the committee used a donation from Baroness de Rothschild to apprentice boys and girls 'to trades other than tailoring and cigar-making and to their subsequent advancement in these trades'.[27] Poor parents often moved their children into such occupations because they could apprentice them without having to pay a premium. This subtle intrusion of the board into the family simultaneously promoted communal economic and social development and added yet another small measure of Anglo-Jewish control. By 1882, the committee had developed an elaborate apprenticeship programme for girls as well as boys. Parents were constantly urged to choose well-paying professions for their children. The ambitious programme was intended to be self-supporting. Premiums for new and increasingly varied apprenticeships were recouped by apprentices' earnings. Gifts and private subscriptions could create new activities on an opportune basis. A shorthand class was established to begin feeding Jewish youngsters into the rapidly expanding service sector. Workrooms, subsidized by their own products, came into being.

The industrial department depended on the cooperation of the established although still active businessmen in the community for effective channeling of boys and young men into apprenticeships in the skilled trades. Friends of the board, thus, contributed not merely money but influence. Tradespeople in handicraft industries would be asked to accept industrial department boys as 'outdoor apprentices'. Under such conditions the department could maximize its resources, providing premiums appropriate to the trade to be learned but not defraying costs of board and lodging. Those not themselves engaged in such trades were asked to use their influence to solicit apprenticeships from tradespeople with whom they dealt. The board welcomed non-Jewish employment so long as the Jewish apprentices were not expected to work on sabbath or holy-days.[28] Apprenticeship grew, as a board activity, from its inception in 1863 to the last years before the First World War.

26 JBG, *Eleventh Report* (London, 1869) sets forth its views at length.
27 Magnus, *Jewish Board of Guardians*, 31.
28 When pressed to find places, as they were in early 1905, the department would appeal through the Jewish press for assistance from all readers. See, e.g., Hermann H. Meyer to the editor, *JC*, 3 Feb. 1905.

TABLE 3.2   Jewish Board of Guardians apprenticeship

Year	No. of apprentices	Programme cost (£)
1863	1	10
1873	85	1,319
1888	103	1,461
1893	131	2,107
1898	230	3,001
1903	236	2,945
1908	371	3,239

Source: Jewish Board of Guardians, *Annual Reports.*

Within twenty years of the board's institution, it publicly admitted a serious issue. Jewish tradesmen and merchants would not hire enough Jews, a problem that persisted until East European immigration brought in an ample supply of novice and cheap labour. When questioned, Jewish employers responded about Jewish workers:

> They are not so faithful, so obedient, or so capable as the professors of other creeds. But the supreme fault found with them is that they are not satisfied like other men, to drudge all their lives for a moderate salary. They betray too great an anxiety to set up in business for themselves, to the detriment of their masters' commercial interests as soon as they have accumulated sufficient experience and capital.[29]

The industrial department also attempted to move labour towards more promising enterprises. Apprentices had usually sought places in tailoring or shoemaking. The department did everything possible to discourage newcomers from entering overcrowded trades. By the early twentieth century the department had been able to place more apprentices in areas with better prospects for growth.

Nathan Joseph believed that the industrial department moved too little and too late. He proposed altering the entire strategy for apprenticeship in 1901, but neither his strident criticism of policy nor devaluation of department achievements led to the changes he sought. Joseph happened to be correct. The department wasted board funds each time it placed an apprentice in tailoring or bootmaking. Poor parents had no need of the board's assistance if they chose to place their sons in those trades. Joseph was also right, if impolitic, to publicize the other side of apprenticeship statistics. While more and more young people were placed, a steadily increasing proportion failed to complete their indentures, and over 40 per cent of apprenticeships outstanding were cancelled in any year.

Joseph suggested that the industrial committee remember that Jews, as history showed, did not delight in servitude and that apprenticeship should function within realistic market terms. Were premiums raised to £25, boys and girls would gain access to more and better trades, shorter terms of indenture, and something

29 'Sabbaticus' to the editor, *JC*, 21 Feb. 1879.

resembling market wages and hours. When a boy who would earn 7s a week as a board apprentice could walk out and earn 18s for performing the same task, Joseph argued, the board was unlikely to recruit suitable candidates. Over-long hours, Joseph continued, deprived apprentices of opportunities to improve their vocational skills and advance themselves. Even the industrial committee conceded that apprentices working a twelve-hour day rather than ten and a half hours could not attend the technical classes that the board itself tried to arrange. Joseph's public criticism achieved at least part of its desired effect. The 1904 annual report proudly announced apprentices placed in seventy-seven different lines of work, the only tailor's apprentice, symbolically enough, 'a crippled lad'.[30]

The industrial committee, however, also managed the workrooms in which, from the 1870s, girls learned fine embroidery as a way of improving their capacity to earn premium wages. As in apprenticeship, earnings were modest and below market rates. That deterred working-class girls but, ironically, attracted better-to-do young ladies, pleased with the prospect of pocketing three or four shillings a week for themselves while learning skills they wished to develop before marriage. On the other hand, the board workrooms offered a haven for handicapped persons, providing a workplace free of market pressures. But that was not the committee's principal objective. Without careful oversight, its workroom facilities might become a charitable enterprise rather than a school for enhanced productivity.[31]

The workrooms of the industrial department produced a substantial stock of men's, women's and children's clothing but also created two awkward problems, one of distribution and the other of social philosophy. The workrooms were essential for training, but what should be done with their output? In an age increasingly sensitive to prison labour and other forms of subsidized competition, this created a problem in public relations. For the industrial department, the difficulty was doubly complicated. Marketing workroom products competed directly with the very tailors and clothiers whom they were asking to employ their workroom trainees and apprentices. Workroom output, to avoid this conflict of interest, went only to relief and charitable agencies, particularly the women's guilds of the several synagogues.[32]

Social philosophy proved a trickier issue. Mrs Lionel Lucas, social activist in philanthropy and highly conservative in social policy, came to rule the workrooms. Not only did her contributions fund several board operations; she had been a major benefactor in building the board's new facilities. Mrs Lucas used the workrooms to enforce her particular social views. Mothers should never, in her opinion, work outside the home. Girls should never be encouraged to avoid family responsibilities. Thus Mrs Lucas fought against the Jewish Crêche, which, by providing infant day care, allowed mothers to take jobs outside the home, and campaigned tirelessly against Jewish girls' clubs. Both institutions were important in assisting Jewish girls and women to adapt to British society, and both proved

---

30 JBG, *Annual Report for 1904* (1905); discussed and praised in *JC*, 17 Mar. 1905. For Joseph's criticisms, see JBG, 13 May, 11 Nov. 1901 reported in *JC*, 17 May, 15 Nov. 1901 and Samuel Oppenheim's responses. Oppenheim to the editor, 9 June 1901, *JC*, 14 June 1901.

31 Magnus, *Jewish Board of Guardians*, 35–7, 102–3; Lipman, *A Century of Social Service*, 119–23.

32 See, e.g., the notice soliciting Guild patronage in *JC*, 17 Mar. 1905.

instrumental in a slow evolution of Jewish women's independence and women's rights. That was not Mrs Lucas's intention. She, like the philanthropic males of Anglo-Jewry, enjoyed both authority and rights but disliked extending them too far.

Mrs Lucas's social philosophy, moreover, seemed to answer board needs. Widows, particularly young women lacking skills, cost the board money. The trifling cash benefits the Board of Guardians allowed, moreover, trapped these women in a cycle of unproductive poverty. Mrs Lucas's workrooms provided the easiest, least domestically disruptive, and, in the short term, the most economical answer to a vexing problem. The workrooms enabled the board to evade an unpleasant reality. Only by applying the same social philosophy to men and women, aiding all to become truly self-sufficient, could the board effectively attack those 'inducements to pauperism' that it so criticized. Only by assisting women to find opportunities in what was still a highly discriminatory workplace, as various Jewish philanthropies attempted to do in the decade before the First World War, could the industrial department actually perform its job. It only began to do so. Supervised apprenticeship for girls, for instance, was almost an afterthought. A 'ladies' subcommittee' to oversee girl apprentices and follow up on individual cases was established only in 1903.

Apprenticeship posed increasing problems for the board. Whether for boys or girls, as Nathan Joseph warned, the industrial committee had to adapt itself to contemporary market reality and should plan, not for the present, but for the prospective economic future. Youths resisted the length of training and rigours of contracts when jobs with opportunities for immediate pay and personal independence beckoned. That hobbled industrial committee efforts to upgrade employment skills and move Jewish boys away from the overcrowded tailoring, boot and furniture trades. The industrial committee had great hopes. It sought to function free of the stigma of charity, ultimately to act as the apprenticing agency for the whole Jewish community, an ambition it never realized.

The committee became more skilled in exploiting other communal and state resources, although its mode of operation changed little. Apprenticeship premiums were usually loans, to be repaid by the apprentice once he achieved independent earnings. Some training costs were shifted on to the Jewish and board schools. Vocational programmes were encouraged, and Nathan Joseph urged a conference of the industrial committee and board officers in 1901 to cultivate systematic and routine cooperative contacts with individual schoolteachers as well as schools. Joseph understood the advantages that could, indeed must, accrue both from better coordination of communal resources and from using wholly or partially state-funded programmes to further communal policies.

The Sanitary Department

The sanitary department was another frontline of the campaign to bring the poor and the foreigner up to acceptable standards for English Jews. Anglo-Jewry understood that few areas posed a greater threat to the communal image as well as to community health. In the first instance, they recognized simple medical facts. Substandard housing and living conditions jeopardized lives – and not merely those of the poor. Such conditions also sustained a stereotype of the Jew that the community had struggled hard to erase. Popular concern with the national well-being came to be increasingly translated into crude, social Darwinist terms. The 'dirty' Jew, particularly the 'dirty foreign' Jew, threatened himself, his neighbours – Jew or Gentile, even the nation. 'Keeping them out' would somehow or other improve the economy, prevent decay of housing stock, improve employment for native English in the clothing trade and make Britain stronger and more secure in an increasingly dangerous world. Anglo-Jewry understood the danger of such simplistic rhetoric. It was bad enough that such sentiments came from the bigots and ignorant. When the British Medical Association's journal published its special sanitary commission report on the Polish colony in the East End in 1884, the community immediately leapt into action.[33]

The board had, in fact, already made its own tentative starts on housing problems well before the *Lancet* article appeared. It all started with elementary medical care. Three years after its founding, the board agreed to assume reponsibility for the medical relief of the poor previously given by the City synagogues. Even by 1862, however, the board wondered if its resources should be used for this purpose. What, after all, was 'Jewish' about medical assistance? Only the inability of poor Jews to speak English justified this board expenditure. As private and state social agencies have invariably discovered, providing any service creates its own demand. Just over 5,000 people were attended during the first full year of medical service. Between 1865 and 1870, applications for all other forms of aid rose from 12,030 to 13,594 or 13 per cent; patient visits and patient attendances over the same five years increased from 17,320 to 30,564 or 76 per cent.[34] No other area had expanded so explosively, and no other area seemed so intractably abused. Conventional visiting controls could not be brought into play. Desperate cases could not be seen on premises cluttered with minor ailments, real or fancied.

Following its own instincts and the recommendations of the Charity Organisation Society, the board drew up new guidelines. Applicants for medical relief who could afford to pay for it – the guideline being family income in excess of thirty shillings per week – must do so. They were encouraged to work through friendly societies or provident dispensaries which would, for a small weekly fee, provide medical care for all members of the family. The poor would have to apply for relief, submitting to case investigation and a means test. The immediate effect seems to have been faster treatment for the ill who had to be attended at home. Since the board found 'nothing of a specifically Jewish character in mere dispensing of drugs and the giving of medical advice', in 1879 it turned the medical care of the Jewish poor over to the district medical officers appointed under the Poor Law.[35] Gathorne-Hardy's Act of 1869 removed public medical aid from the workhouse stigma of poor relief by enabling local authorities to provide parochial dispensaries for the poor. As with education, state intervention saved the day in this high cost sector of social welfare.

The Board of Guardians, so accustomed to keeping Jews away from poor law assistance, still hesitated, pondering the implications of that statute. After seeing medical attendances rise another 34% in 1871 while applications for all other forms

33 *The Lancet*, 3 May 1884; *JC*, 16 May 1884.
34 See the extended discussion in JBG, *Twelfth Annual Report, 1870* (London, 1871). Magnus offers some curious percentages. Magnus, *Jewish Board of Guardians*, 115
35 Lipman, *A Century of Social Service*, 60–3.

of relief declined, the board put prudence and principle together. Medication and treatment, it decided, were not specially Jewish or non-Jewish. A smallpox outbreak and a cholera scare delayed its decision, but the board, with United Synagogue approval, abandoned outdoor medical relief in 1873. By 1879, shortly before the great East European migration, the board officially turned to state relief. Medicine was no longer directly a board benefit. Sir Henry A. Isaacs, elected to chair the medical committee in 1880, presided over a body that never met, the functions of which reverted to the board's executive committee in 1882.

The board had, thus, shortly in advance of the great immigration, committed itself to a policy that it would only act in cases where 'religious issues' were involved. Services meeting the religious test, such as the provision of kosher food to Jewish patients in various London hospitals, continued and expanded. The board itself subscribed to the Royal Maternity Society to obtain tickets for midwife attendance for the poor.[36] Its early experience with runaway medical costs taught the board a timely lesson. Only the most rigorous controls and narrow definitions would enable it to survive. The spirit of self-help and discipline Anglo-Jewry sought to inculcate in its community was bred in the bones of its principal social-work agency.

Cholera epidemics, a trigger for public health activism throughout England, also forced Anglo-Jewry to confront sanitary issues within its own community. Nathan Joseph contended, as early as 1865, that illness was the fundamental cause of poverty, this a generation before Beatrice Webb would advance professional social work by making the same point with statistical demonstration. He also showed how the geography of epidemic coincided with the area of worst public health. Joseph's suggestions reinforced what the board learned every day from its own visiting committee. A sense of the issue, however, did not imply a solution readily at hand. Statutory provisions to deal with 'nuisances' were inadequate. Three principal measures – Torrens's Artisans Dwellings Act of 1868, Cross's Artisans' Dwellings Act of 1875, and the Housing Act of 1890 – were in the future. Only when they were in place could the power and resources of government be deployed on a broad scale and an effective campaign to spur state activism begin. That was to prove costly beyond any estimates, and the housing problem remains uneasily suspended between public and private effort with the state defining minimal standards and the market dictating amenities.

Nathan Joseph, then an aspiring architect and board civil servant, warned as early as 1865 that board visitors should make thorough reports on the homes of the poor and take steps to have obvious defects remedied. But Joseph was asking that since the corrupt vestry and district panels charged with such matters under the Metropolis Management Act of 1855 were unlikely to act, the board should appoint its own sanitary inspector. For two years, George Parsons, recommended to the board by the City of London Medical Officer of Health, struggled to bring order out of sanitary chaos. The cholera outbreak of 1866 inspired the board to move. The costs were high, although the achievements were significant. Parsons inspected approximately half of the dwellings in which Jewish recipients of board relief lived.

---

36 Magnus, *Jewish Board of Guardians*, 119. The food services came from several charities. Among others, one founded by Baroness Lionel de Rothschild provided food for invalids. Pupils of the Jews' Free School learned their cooking in the kitchens. Most patients apparently survived. *JC*, 17 Sept. 1858; Stollard, *London Pauperism*, 65 quoted in Lipman, *A Century of Social Service*, 63n.

Of the 471 buildings – approximately 14,000 tenements – Parsons discovered sanitary violations in 343 (72.8 per cent). Board action, given the Joseph–Parsons initiatives, dramatically limited the spread of the 1865 fever and 1866 cholera epidemics among the Jewish population. Once the danger had passed, however, the board, as an economy measure, released Parsons and consigned his work to its already overtaxed medical committee.[37]

The board, of course, could bring significant coercive influence to bear. Board visitors investigated the dwelling of any individual applying for relief. They made clear what should be done, undoubtedly with more than a little hint that it must be done. Convincing individuals to clean their dwellings, to whitewash their walls and to repair the defects of their quarters did not necessarily go to the heart of the matter. While the visitors could educate tenants about landlord responsibilities, moving landlords to act was another matter. Until elaborate statutory provisions were enacted and adequate administration evolved, the state's coercive mechanisms were, at best, random and capricious, sometimes also corrupt.[38] A substantial reduction in available housing stock, moreover, aggravated the East End problem. Model dwellings and developments, for Anglo-Jewry as for other committed philanthropists, barely scratched the surface of the problem.

Immigration ended evasion. By 1884, the board could no longer resist the need to professionalize its sanitary inspection services.[39] Once appointed, moreover, sanitary committee inspectors entered dwellings and workshops alike, demanding and securing considerable improvement. For some years no greater evidence could be provided confirming the power of voluntarism and communal deference in British Jewry. No one, as Gartner observes, ever seems to have considered challenging the authority of these board agents, a tribute to the power of deference as a form of social control. They had no legal coercive powers, but they did have the authority and prestige of the Board of Guardians. Looming not far behind that were such imposing figures of Anglo-Jewry as Sir Samuel Montagu and Frederic D. Mocatta whose will was not lightly to be thwarted and who themselves stood between the worlds of the East End and the West End and interpreted the one to the other.[40] Sustained by banker princes and the board, sanitary inspectors moved with as much authority as any voluntary organization could muster.

Questions of housing and sanitation, while always central to board thought, were matters to which that body addressed itself only episodically until it reestablished its sanitary committee in 1884. Even then the more pressing question appears to have been public relations, the unflattering image of the 'Jew' contemporary social investigators were painting for the British public. Sweating,

---

37 Lipman, *A Century of Social Service*, 64–5.

38 Royal Commission on the Housing of the Working Classes, First Report, *Parliamentary Papers* (1884–5), XXX (C. 4402), 34. Complaints that members of the various local governing bodies themselves owned property in violation of public health standards were chronic throughout London; see pages 22–3. On the general issue, see Owen's discussion in *English Philanthropy*, chapter 14.

39 Several key members of the board, like A. E. Franklin, the honorary treasurer, were involved with the Mansion House Council on the Dwellings of the Poor and other organizations established at the behest of the Charity Organization Society in 1882.

40 Gartner, *Jewish Immigrant*, 152–3. On this point see the testimony of JBG president Leonard Cohen before the Commission on Alien Immigration. RCAI (Cd. 1742), II(1903) qq 15,400–14,404.

overcrowding and understandable public anxiety about deteriorating standards of public health in the Jewish East End demanded that Anglo-Jewry take some positive action.

Fearing renewed anti-alien agitation, the sanitary committee attempted in 1892 to repeat the earlier board success in the 1866 cholera epidemic. The committee inspected thirty-two workshops and 2,317 houses, and invoked the much improved statutory provisions and authorities to remedy that which was wrong. The steady extension of public authority intervention meant that a modest board effort could produce significant results. The Local Government Act of 1888 replaced the old Metropolitan Board of Works with the new, vigorous London County Council, and the London Government Act of 1899 substituted borough councils for the plethora of vestries and boards of works.[41]

Public health issues, however, unlike medical care itself, were not something for which public-funded remedies were conveniently available. The Royal Commission appointed in 1884 to consider the housing of the poor began looking into and publicly deploring the sweatshops and tenements of the Jewish East End. Communal embarrassment led the board to reconstitute its sanitary committee. Even the stubbornly independent Spanish and Portugese Board of Guardians acted in concert. A new joint sanitary committee survived until 1901. Then, when the Board of Guardians began contemplating costly programmes of medical aftercare and to combat tuberculosis, the Sephardim withdrew. The board pressed on undaunted, discussing both problems and solutions with the Whitechapel District Board of Works. Their correspondence revealed serious problems, a range of concerns, and much sanitary committee and district board concern to shift responsibility away from themselves. The two most positive results were that the Whitechapel inspector attacked some of the worst abuses, particularly in the water supply, and Lord Rothschild undertook to develop the 4% Industrial Dwellings Company Ltd, Anglo-Jewry's response to the provision of increased and better housing for the deserving poor.

As numbers grew and particularly as many requiring medical attendance either could not or would not deal with non-Yiddish-speaking doctors or apothecaries, the issue of medical assistance arose yet again. The executive committee reviewed the problem at length in 1891, took testimony from those organizations principally involved, and reaffirmed its position that there was nothing Jewish in the provision of medical assistance. Parochial medical relief was more than adequate, and Jewish poor suffered no discrimination in its distribution. Local authorities, however, invoked their own means test before admitting patients to Poor Law Union infirmaries.[42] The Jewish poor, to learn the meaning of responsibility, should join provident dispensaries. The executive committee rejected the argument that missionary dispensaries endangered the religious commitment of Jews, although Samuel Montagu, thinking of his Federation of Synagogues, and Hermann Landau

---

41 Lipman, *A Century of Social Service*, 64–6, 88; S. E. Finer, *The Life and Times of Sir Edwin Chadwick* (London, 1950), 502.

42 London poor law guardians objected heatedly to the admission of non-destitute patients, and repeatedly brought the issue to the attention of the police. See, e.g., the correspondence from 1887–1900, ME[tropolitan]PO[lice] 2/244 in the Public Record Office.

of the Poor Jews' Temporary Shelter were to put that argument with increasing firmness over the next several years.

Landau, in particular, refused to let the issue drop, reintroducing it in public meetings and the Jewish press in 1896. While almost all Anglo-Jewry preferred the self-insuring system provident dispensaries provided, a few, like Landau, contended that the Yiddish–English barrier was real. Yiddish speakers were second-class citizens who received third-class medical attention. Montagu, usually a defender of the provident principle, took issue with the Cohens and Mocatta on the grounds that medical care might be a chink in communal armour against clever conversionists. Yiddish-speaking missionaries, he feared, could make inroads among the poor aliens of the East End. The board resisted.

> The Board believes that the proposed movement will tend to pauperise the poor, will strike a blow at the Provident Societies which so powerfully foster a spirit of thrift among the East End population, and will be in opposition to that principle of unsectarianism in medical charity, which has happily made such rapid progress in recent years.[43]

The board remained true to its principles of 1859. It cooperated in founding the Jewish Provident Dispensary in 1897 which was incorporated into the Metropolitan Medical Provident Association. Medicine demanded self-help and patient responsibility. Social work was first and foremost moral education.

The executive committee did acknowledge one defect in medical care for the Jewish poor in 1891. Nursing was inadequate, and something should be done. Into that breach stepped that formidable lady of Jewish philanthropy, Mrs Lionel Lucas. She furnished at her own expense three full-time nurses from 1891 until 1906. When finally granted supplementary funding, Mrs Lucas doubled her nursing staff.[44] Concern, particularly for maternity cases and aftercare, helped to inspire the Sickroom Helps Society, which worked with Mrs Lucas's staff from 1896 to provide home care for recently discharged hospital patients and for mothers in the first days after giving birth.

The board's new cause – one to which it paid greater and greater attention and to which it contributed a substantial portion of its budget – was the early diagnosis, treatment and containment of tuberculosis. Leonard Cohen made it his personal crusade, firmly seconded by the omnipresent Nathan Joseph. A subcommittee examined the reported increase of tuberculosis among the Jewish poor in 1897. Although its findings were ambiguous on tuberculosis itself, the report did emphasize the considerable spread of a variety of pulmonary ailments, including tuberculosis, among the Jewish poor and working classes. Such considerable advances were made in local authority sanitary inspection that the board was able, by 1905, to congratulate itself on leading London in the right direction. The board also eliminated one salaried male sanitary inspector and substituted two volunteer female health visitors. The future course was charted towards improved sanitoria, preventive medicine, and medical aftercare.[45]

43 JBG, *Thirty-eighth Annual Report, 1897* (London, 1898), 19.
44 The president paid fulsome tribute to Mrs Lucas at the 1905 JBG annual meeting. *JC*, 31 Mar. 1905.
45 JBG annual meeting, 26 Mar. 1905. *JC*, 31 Mar. 1905.

From the limited beginnings of the sanitary department, where the board attempted to act in advance of the local authorities or national investigations, the department gained respect and functioned in close cooperation with national and local institutions.[46] The sanitary inspector initially prodded the landlord, dispatching a standard letter that itemized defects in a property. In many instances this sufficed. Should the owner prove recalcitrant, the inspector prepared a formal report. David Schloss, secretary of the sanitary committee (1884–1904) examined it, approved it, and forwarded it to the local Medical Officer of Health. Carrying the weight of a board document, it invariably sufficed to move the local authorities, although often less effectively than the sanitary committee desired. The Whitechapel Board of Works, for instance, took a more relaxed view of industrial nuisances than the Jewish Board of Guardians. Increasingly in the 1890s, the sanitary inspectors encountered workshop resistance, and government inspectors found themselves legally circumscribed in available grounds for action.[47] London County Council, however, once it displaced the old metropolitan borough councils in 1889, proved a highly amenable partner. So effective was the London County Council, indeed, that the board found its investigative function redundant. Now able to leave sanitary supervision to local authorities, the sanitary committee moved in fact as well as in name to being the health committee, principally devoted to preventative medicine and problems of individual health care. Tuberculosis, the modish medical problem of the day, came to command the board's attention. There the board would pioneer treatment and aftercare. Even after the decisive entrance of the state into medical care with the passage of the National Insurance Act of 1911, tuberculosis remained a Board of Guardians obsession.

Few if any welfare agencies were as imaginative and as responsive to the findings of contemporary social observers. When Beatrice Webb, for instance, contended that half the existing destitution in the nation was produced by illness and that tuberculosis alone accounted for one-seventh of all poor law expenditure, the board could proudly show that it had shifted the focus of its activities to public health. Even the allowances committee which dealt with cash outlay tried 'to build up the family physically to prevent a fall to pauperism, especially when consumption has removed the head or when he is permanently incapacitated by illness'.[48]

The Visiting Committee: Social Control as Policy

Once an individual applied for aid for himself or his family, he quickly discovered, if he had not known before, that the board had no compunction about regulating minute details of family life and organization. Samuel Montagu and the Reverend A. L. Green experimented with visiting on a private basis themselves, bringing such valuable information back to board rotas that the executive committee created the visiting committee. That body immediately became central to board administration as well as the agency through which new, enthusiastic volunteers, accompanied by a

---

46 Miss Hilda Joseph (notice once again the continuity in family social work activity), a health visitor of the Jewish Board of Guardians, for instance, was elected a member of the Royal Sanitary Institute in 1904. *JC*, 13 Jan. 1905.

47 Lipman, *A Century of Social Service*, 124–9.

48 JBG, Annual Meeting, 26 Mar. 1911. *JC*, 31 Mar. 1911.

veteran visitor, were taught the realities of board work. Committee members not only reviewed worthiness to receive benefits but visited the premises of those receiving aid, repeatedly, if they deemed it appropriate or necessary. Not until 1896 was initial investigation placed in the hands of a professional.[49]

The visiting committee itself, however, had been reorganized in 1893, moving beyond routine semi-annual reinvestigations. New general principles were laid down, not as hard and fast rules but as guidelines. The amateur veterans of decades of investigation were withdrawing. Newcomers needed pamphlets to explain what their predecessors had learned by action. Board resources being limited, visitor's handbooks included a list of current Jewish charities and other philanthropies available to Jewish applicants. Frederic D. Mocatta, devoted as ever and determined to have the best possible information available for committee members, personally sponsored instructive lectures and paid for their publication.[50] Through the mid-1890s these touched, among other things, on the best methods of dealing with those out of work, the causes of infant mortality among Jews, how to provide better infant care when mothers must earn a living, overcrowding, the increase of tuberculosis among Jews and (to reaffirm board traditions and policies) the value of apprenticeship.

The visiting committee investigated both board relief cases and, after the reorganization of 1893, those that the Conjoint Russo-Jewish Committee–Board of Guardians proposed to consider. Visitors investigated misuse of loan funds and did not hesitate to bring legal action against anyone who violated the strict terms of their agreement.[51] Given the board's dedication to the principle of self-help, loan fund investigations in some years represented almost half the cases considered. Visiting took Anglo-Jewry, not merely its salaried servants, into the homes of their poor. Once there, they attempted to determine how family life should be organized. They would, in many instances, essentially take control of children's lives, bringing boys who they feared might have 'to shift for themselves' to the attention of the industrial committee that they might be apprenticed for suitable trades.

Board benefactors who were also experienced visitors grew increasingly restive with their traditional preponderance of chronic cases. They desired more scope, and they also sought more recruits. They wished to feel themselves involved with improving, not merely sustaining, the community. Such internal demands coincided with reforming demands from community experts. The crisis of Russian refugee immigration in 1892–3 forced the board to reassess its priorities and purposes. Initially, the issues involved focused on emigration and repatriation, the board fearing that its resources would be drained by Russian and Polish Jews flooding into the East End. The Russo-Jewish Committee, which had caught the imagination of so many Anglo-Jewish leaders, demanded a humane communal policy for newcomers. Its secretary and principal spokesman, Nathan Joseph, also demanded

---

49 'at a salary not over 35 shillings per week.' JBG monthly meeting, 13 Apr. 1896. *JC*, 17 Apr. 1896.

50 Frederick S. Franklin to the editor, *JC*, 20 Nov. 1896. A complete file no longer appears to exist at the Jewish Welfare Board, but the individual presentations, as made, were published in full in the *Jewish Chronicle*.

51 See, e.g., the JBG prosecution of Harris Rauchwerk and Abraham Davis 'for attempting to procure charitable relief under false pretences'. Judgement was rendered for the JBG, which demanded restitution of its £5. Rauchwerk got off, but Davis was fined £5 or one month in prison. *JC*, 3 Jan. 1896.

that the board modernize its casework techniques. Since Joseph had also done so much to frame Board of Guardians policy, one might have expected him to achieve this with ease. This was decidedly not the case. After more than a year of stormy controversy, ultimately calmed by the resignation of the board's intractable and uncompromising secretary, Lionel Alexander, and the exertions of the two presidents Sir Julian Goldsmid and Benjamin L. Cohen, the Board of Guardians and Russo-Jewish Committee composed their differences. Nathan Joseph brought to the visiting committee modern casebook and casework techniques in 1893. In doing so, he expanded the investigatory and administrative functions of the visiting committee. That simultaneously met old guard ambitions and answered needs for institutional efficiency.

Newcomers willing to make the substantial commitment of time and effort were increasingly hard to find. Those with the leisure and resources had many options and too many claims upon their services.[52] To some extent, the feminization of social work helped to fill this volunteer gap. Women, in a much-needed innovation, were finally brought from coordinate to regular membership. The board had, somewhat hesitantly, created a ladies conjoint visiting committee in 1882 that acted with the lady visitors of the United Synagogue. Like the gentleman, the ladies, with salaried assistants to manage the details, visited poor Jews in institutions to which they were confined and in their homes. As with other social and education institutions, the Lady Visitors sought to give

> such advice as might promote thrift and personal cleanliness, and may add generally to their comfort, to encourage habits of self-supporting industry and to offer to the poor in institutions, instruction, consolation and advice.[53]

Joseph's reforms brought women to the board's visiting committee, while the older body continued alongside with its traditional institutional visiting functions. The move proved timely. A growing concern about Jewish infant mortality made instruction for mothers in health care and childrearing a visitor priority. Board-sponsored East End mothers' meetings date from 1895, and by 1897, the visiting committee, previously hesitant on the point, established a Jewish day nursery.[54] By 1900, the first two women, Mrs Alice Model and Miss Hannah Hyam, both experienced social workers, had been added to the board executive itself. The board had finally begun fully to comprehend the useful role women could play in its activities and developed new areas in which their talents proved particularly useful.

In other areas, however, necessity rather than sensitivity led to accommodation and improved cooperation. Jewish Board of Guardians 'imperialism' remained

52 The issue dominated the 13 November 1905 JBG meeting. One of the more interesting contributions to the debate was Hannah Hyam's insistence on the value of visitors who lacked formal training in social work. *JC*, 17 Nov. 1905.

53 Quoted from Lipman, *A Century of Social Service*, 115. On the general issue of the feminization of philanthropy and social work, see Frank Prochaska, *Women and Philanthropy in Victorian England* (London, 1980).

54 Part of the difficulty in establishing a Jewish crêche lay in the formidable obstruction of Mrs Lionel Lucas, about whom see more in chapter 8. JBG, *Annual Report for 1897*, 68; Lipman, *A Century of Social Service*, 113–16.

suspect among the almost one hundred Jewish philanthropies, but board investigative resources were invaluable. No philanthropy had the board's experience, its records, or its staff of trained visitors. Other Jewish philanthropies, with Board of Guardians approval, turned to board experts to investigate their applications. Cooperation worked to the benefit of all institutions, if not recipients. Uniform standards and conditions for relief could be defined, and duplicatory aid eliminated. Individual files grew as information about the least fortunate members of the community was consolidated in the board's archives. Even the Soup Kitchen for the the Jewish Poor acknowledged in 1895 that indiscriminate charity promoted pauperism and gratefully thanked the board for its investigative cooperation. The soup kitchen ten years later changed its mind. Feeling that the board was overly severe on the temporarily destitute, it declined to send the board or allow its investigators to inspect the soup kitchen's weekly list of cases. Few others resisted. The Boot Fund, the Aged Needy Society, and the 'Penny Dinners' remained aloof, but other organizations had entered into cooperative agreements by the first years of the twentieth century.[55]

The Loan Committee: Teaching Self-reliance

The Jewish Board of Guardians sought not to relieve but to cure poverty. The board strove to avoid any form of aid that might 'pauperize' the recipient or create passive dependency. To the degree that poverty was a state of mind, the circumstances of relief were rendered deliberately demeaning to reinforce the incentives for independence. To prevent abuse, cash aid was given only in exceptional cases. Direct aid grants were issued as food or fuel tickets. Since self-sufficiency remained the object, the Jewish Board of Guardians preferred loans to other forms of relief. David Benjamin's £100 benefaction in 1859 became the nucleus of the board's special loan fund.

Initially the board feared that its charity might be misused and preferred to advance goods rather than cash, another version of the works committee sewing machine enterprise. During its first seven years, the board granted 1,767 loans totalling £2,263, some with and some without security. The Eleazar loan fund, capitalized with £1,000 in 1866, demanded the appointment of a special subcommittee, ultimately the loan committee, to manage matters. Its first chairman, I. A. Boss, defined loans as a category of aid apart from conventional relief. Borrowers, perhaps to avoid 'moral' contamination, were not permitted to mix with the ordinary applicants for relief. The second chairman brought his vigorous business methods and considerably more money to the loan fund. Sir Samuel Montagu presided over a steady reduction of bad debts to a point at which they and costs of administration amounted to a mere 3.75 per cent of total outlay.[56]

Simon Simons succeeded Montagu in 1885 and accelerated the cycling of loan funds. Both the number of individuals served and the money available steadily expanded. From January 1885 to the end of December 1890, 2,924 beneficiaries

55 *Annual Report of the Soup Kitchen for the Jewish Poor, 1895–1896* (London, 1896) and *JC*, 9 Oct. 1896; JBG, annual meeting, 25 Mar. 1905. *JC*, 31 Mar. 1905.

56 Montagu, Wolf Harris, Francis L. Cohen, the family of Moses Joseph, and Baron Hirsch's bequest contributed substantially to loan fund capital and made possible the greatly expanded operations.

received £12,133. During the next five years, the number of loans granted increased by 26 per cent to 3,670, and the amount lent grew 23 per cent to £14,874. Funds loaned increased tenfold between 1860 and 1895. The maximum for a single loan, under Simons's administration, rose to £25, which better approximated to actual small business needs, and the form of repayment was altered. The old Eleazar loan fund, now the capital of 'the special loan department', was used for those who could not offer security for their loan, while the other, more substantial resources were lent against pledged property. 'Special loans' were made in amounts from ten shillings to five pounds 'for trade purposes', the recipients either shopkeepers 'in a small way of Business' or hawkers. Losses on these special funds ran much higher than for secured loans, about 15 per cent per year, an amount the board believed tolerable 'given the class this benefits'. The board took understandable pride in its loan policies, stressing the overall percentage of bad debts – a trifling 2.5 per cent – as a measure of its success.[57]

The loan committee, as it worked with its new, principally alien, clientele emphasized that effective loan policies demanded a more imaginative and creative approach to sanitary inspection and health care:

> the class of borrowers we have been granting loans of later years are of a very much poorer class than hitherto, and in many instances I do not think I over estimate if I say fully one third of our applicants are in a sickly state of health, unfortunately suffering from consumption brought on by working in unsanitary workshops and the following of such trades as tailors, pressers, cap makers, boot finishers, etc.[58]

The newcomers, whatever their disabilities, proved worthy beneficiaries of board trust. Thrift, enterprise, and upward social mobility were theirs with or without board exhortations. Board success, through its loan committee, in accelerating alien enterprise and self-help was one area in which Anglo-Jewish aspiration and immigrant ambition reached a happy meeting of the minds.

Money and Morale

Hidden behind apparent board success lay several problems. Although annual appeals for emergency support, warmly endorsed by the Jewish press and communal leadership, met reasonable response in the routine financial crises after the mid-1890s, the board could never have continued to function without the rapid evolution of the welfare state. The board had initially depended on the United Synagogue, but that subsidy – about £1,400 – although it fluctuated slightly, never increased. A sagacious investment policy and a commitment to capitalize bequests, not to mention its austere administrative policies, enabled the board to operate within its means until the 1890s. Continued financial success, however, came to rely

57 JBG, *Annual Report for 1905* (London, 1906); *Report on the Endowed Charities in the City of London, 1905*; *JC*, 29 Dec. 1905; Report of J. M. Ansell to the visiting committee, 11 Nov. 1896. Ansell conluded with an appeal to the visiting committee to be more rigorous in the cases sent to it by the loan committee. *JC*, 13 Nov. 1896.

58 Report of J. M. Ansell, chairman of the loan committee. JBG monthly meeting, 12 Oct. 1896. *JC*, 16 Oct. 1896.

TABLE 3.3   Impact of aliens on Jewish Board of Guardians relief funds

Year	Cases	No. of individuals	% of Russo-Polish aliens		Total
			Resident in UK 7 Years +	Resident in UK 7 Years −	
1894	5,157	32,510	40.8	35.7	76.5
1895	4,794	34,418	41.2	36.5	77.7
1896	4,366	35,063	27.9	47.4	75.3
1897	4,286	33,380	30.0	49.3	79.3

Source: Jewish Board of Guardians, *Annual Report for 1897*, 41ff.

on spot benefactions for current expenditure. The board, for instance, managed a surplus of £625 in 1895, but only through expedients unlikely to be repeated. Anonymous 'friends of the board' enabled it to clear a £1,000 bank overdraft advanced to keep the industrial and loan departments in business. Daniel Marks gave £1,050, and a further £500 from 'friends of the board' brought revenue over £21,600, covering almost a seven per cent deficit.

Benjamin N. Cohen, to whom fell the unenviable task of presiding over the board as it fell further and further into debt, conceded that the board executive had historically turned to individual members to tide it over budget deficiencies, a reminder that even the carefully audited board books do not reveal the entire scope, nature or cost of board operations. Sir Julian Goldsmid and Maurice Beddington, both deceased, Cohen reminded the board, had been among a 'rapidly diminishing group who allowed the Secretary of the Board to come to them for sums amounting to £200 to £300 per year as relief to private deserving cases that came before the Board'.[59] Traditional sources of income, while still indispensable, no longer paid the bills. As late as 1871–2, the United Synagogue grant, originally more than half the funds available to the board, represented just over 40 per cent of total revenue. That £1,273 had fallen to less than seven per cent of board relief disbursements by 1895.

Where could economies be achieved? The board's 11 per cent overhead and administrative costs compared very favourably with any such institution, public or private, then or since. Board members recognized, by the mid-1890s, that they were as extended as they could be without some substantial change in income. Greater and greater efforts were made to repatriate applicants to Russia or encourage emigration for those who could not seem to make their way in London.[60]

59 Private quarterly accounts were given to such befactors. Discretionary funds like these, Cohen mused, enabled the secretary to make those £25 grants which might take a recipient from penury to independence and prevented the individual from becoming a dependent of the board. The discretionary funds also allowed the executive to distinguish between those who should and should not be processed through the deliberately 'demeaning' relief rotas. JBG, monthly meeting, 10 Oct. *JC*, 14 Oct. 1898.

60 Almost no 'native' applicants were refused aid. Only six cases (five old, one new) in 1896 (1.9 per cent of those investigated, then refused) and nine (five old, four new) in 1897 (2.2 per cent) were natives as opposed to 349 (227 old, 22 new) 'foreign' in 1896 (77.8 per cent) and 322 (306 old, 16 new) in 1897 (78.9 per cent). 'Native' cases relieved actually rose from 578 (11.2 per cent of the total) in 1894 to 636 (14.8 per cent) in 1897. JBG, *Annual Report for 1897* (London, 1898), 41ff.

TABLE 3.4   Jewish Board of Guardians repatriation and emigration, 1894–1897

	1894	1895	1896	1897
Repatriation				
Men	490	335	460	533
Dependent wives	103	80	61	74
Children	261	111	131	158
Emigration				
Men	79	88	87	109
Dependent wives	13	35	29	36
Children	36	72	34	64
Widows	3	6	1	6
Children of widows	5	4	2	13
Single women	10	8	7	9
'Deserted' women	61	79	93	98
Children of deserted women	113	172	207	194
Orphans or deserted children	0	0	6	6
Destination of emigrants:				
United States	127	145	149	176
South Africa	16	27	38	21
Australia	12	9	3	17

Source: Jewish Board of Guardians, *Annual Report for 1897*, 44ff.

Grants for fixed or temporary allowances, in spite of all efforts, continued to creep upwards. Widows became a steadily growing burden on resources. The 266 on the rolls in 1875 reached 400 by 1885, but by 1895 the number had reached 639. The board had, fortunately, not yet been forced to draw down capital. Funded property and real estate acquired for £4,200 had reached almost £43,000 in market value by the mid-1890s.[61]

The board liked repatriation, which was always 'voluntary'. Those who could not adapt and were poor prospects for emigration, board leaders argued, should not remain burdens on the community. British Jewry, under ideal conditions, offered each newcomer a chance. That was the extent of social obligation. Almost 92 per cent of cases the relief committees considered for repatriation were dispatched, fares and maintenance paid, to the Russian Empire, at a cost the board considered a bargain when compared to ongoing and prospective maintenance. A few, slightly more than 2.5 per cent, were relocated elsewhere within the United Kingdom, much the same way that Sir Samuel Montagu's dispersion committee sought, through the Federation of Synagogues, to offer new opportunities in the provinces for those eking out a marginal existence in the East End. Independently of the Russo-Jewish Committee, which cared for 'refugees' as opposed to 'immigrants', and other bodies processing transmigrants, like the Poor Jews' Temporary Shelter, the emigration committee of the Jewish Board of Guardians also attempted to move

61 JBG, *Annual Report for 1895* (London, 1896).

part of its own actual or potential caseload onwards. The board was particularly anxious to break the common practice whereby the husband or father emigrated, usually to the United States, but left his family behind. Once self-sufficient, he would then usually, but not always (as the board dolefully observed), send for those left behind. American Jewish social agencies applauded this practice, as it imposed less strain on *their* overtaxed resources, but Anglo-Jewry would not cooperate. Women and families left behind, even temporarily, were registered on board books, until the twentieth century, as 'deserted'. Lest breadwinners forget their responsibilities, the board dispatched such families on as quickly as possible.[62]

Government transfer payments in partial support of various services the board rendered became an increasing although still small portion of board income before 1906. From 1906 onwards, the board came increasingly to depend on larger grants or the government itself absorbing expensive services. Some income, although never substantial, came from aid societies for the board in the East End and other parts of London which collected small contributions from hundreds of individuals. The aid societies, although good for morale, were more important as symbols of community engagement and commitment than as sources of income.

The Jewish Board of Guardians, in fact, shared a problem common to many distinguished eleemosynary institutions. From its foundation until the First World War and even beyond, most of the money – and it was considerable – to capitalize and operate the board came from about forty families. The same might be said of almost every major charity, but none was as ambitious in design and achievement as the Board of Guardians. The board made much of its independence, of the fact that it was Anglo-Jewry's social welfare institution resting on the support of the whole community. But the board began as a financial dependant of the United Synagogue, and its survival ultimately depended on more and more of its functions being absorbed or substantially funded by the growing welfare state.

By 1905, the Jewish Board of Guardians was reeling. Overextended, committed to activities it could not prosecute effectively, the board still sought to command and control Jewish charity. The efficiency of centralization would eliminate waste. The community, even many of the board's most important friends, would have none of it. Leonard Cohen, who would preside over board destinies until 1920, despaired of the future. His frugal management had reduced the £2,000 current accounts deficit of 1903 to £1,500 in 1904. The board's bankers, however, had grown increasingly restive in the face of continued overdrafts and threatened to increase the interest to 5 per cent. Only Cohen's personal appeal to Lord Rothschild for £1,000 and Edgar Speyer for £500 tided the board over this crisis.[63] When the various overdrafts and internal indebtedness to capital accounts were sorted out, Cohen reported as early as November 1904, £10,000 was needed, £5,000 to wipe out 'a harassing debt' and the balance just to meet board expenses for the winter.

Part of Cohen's problem was generational. As the old Anglo-Jewish magnates retired or died, the extent to which individual board officers had personally underwritten small as well as substantial expenses became more evident. The Cohens themselves and selected friends, for instance, underwrote the construction

---

62 JBG, *Annual Report for 1897* (London, 1898), 44ff.
63 The Van Oven estate also contributed £7,000, but that augmented severely taxed capital funds.

and furnishing of the new board facilities in 1895 and 1896 without appealing to regular subscribers and contributors. Every wealthy member of the board also dipped into his or her purse to meet needs that never appeared on the books as board expenses. Frederic D. Mocatta, while he lived, underwrote visiting committee professional instruction and the printing of its pamphlets and handbooks. Mrs Lionel Lucas, president of the ladies visiting committee from 1880 to 1913, not only directed but paid for the domestic help and visiting nurses the board and the Sick Room Helps Society furnished. Sir Samuel Montagu, in addition to his several donations to the board loan funds, financed many of the minor costs and needs of the loan department. None of these contributions appeared as official expenditures, but they represented, as the board discovered in the twentieth century, substantial demands against current income once the benefactors were no longer there.

Financial strain generated unprecedented displays of public ill-will in the early twentieth century. Many problems ran together. Anti-alien agitation raised the communal temperature. Political rifts developed in the communal leadership itself, polarized by divided counsels on what responses British Jews should make to the Kishinev pogrom of 1903. Anglo-Jewish solidarity, the essential precondition for smoothly functioning voluntaristic institutions, was beginning to crumble. A quarrelsome board meeting in January 1905 heard with little enthusiasm an appeal from the Jews' Temporary Shelter for assistance in processing the large influx of Russian reservists and conscripts fleeing service in the Russo-Japanese War.[64] Money matters frayed nerves. To make matters worse, relief agency policies seemed to be working at cross-purposes. All problems appeared overwhelming. Substantial numbers somehow must be helped to emigrate at just that time when anti-alien agitation was gaining a second lease on life. The Mile End by-election was being fought, to general appearances, solely on the alien immigration issue. Resources were taxed to the limit, and the downturn in trade reduced East End contributions and increased East End welfare needs and demands.[65]

The board rejected the notion of deflecting immigration by eliminating or reducing aid for the aliens. Its own statistics showed that record demands for its services came principally from economic conditions which drove marginal England-resident Jews to the wall.[66] Although the number of applications for board relief declined through the first years of the twentieth century, fixed allowances and charges – the costs of relieving individual cases – tended to rise. Only as the state came to assume more and more of the burden of social welfare, particularly of the high-cost sectors, could the board remain viable and solvent.

Simultaneously the board became aware of the extent to which it had already moved from relief to welfare. As it became more conscious of that shift, the board

64 The Temporary Shelter appealed to the board, the Anglo-Jewish Association, and the Russo-Jewish Committee on 10 January 1905 for assistance in processing individuals through its overtaxed facilities.
65 Minutes, meeting of the JBG, 22 Jan. 1905. *JC*, 27 Jan. 1905; see also the editorial of 13 Jan. 1905.
66 The 1904 caseload ran 20 per cent above that of 1903, with particularly heavy demands on cash grants. At first glance the numbers suggested that aliens were the problem. Of 6,018 cases assisted, 4,383 were Russians or Poles. But in fact, although the caseload increased by 905, only 163 were actually new cases. Russian and Polish recipients, moreover, rose by only ten (barely 0.2 per cent), native Jewish claims rose 21 per cent and resident foreigner cases by twenty-five.

recognized that the amateur and philanthropist were less appropriate managers for the enterprise. Volunteer assistance steadily gave way to professional social work. The administrative staff of 1913 approached thirty in contrast to the nine of 1891. Investigation and visiting passed into the hands of an ever-growing trained group of workers rather than the enthusiastic philanthropic interventionists and 'visitors' of mid- and late-Victorian England. Much was gained, but something – spontaneity, perhaps – was lost.[67]

For its first thirty years the board had been in the forefront of innovation in social work; for the next thirty, it fell further and further behind. In some ways, the board became a victim of its own success. To some extent institutional arrangements it had itself created came to constrain the board. The Jewish Board of Guardians very slowly adapted its administrative attitudes, arrangements and commitments to move into the new world of the welfare state. Old habits and well-established practices would have been hard enough to break. Since, however, its traditional obligations did not go away – applicants for relief still stood in supplication at the brass rail before a seated rota (even into the twentieth century)[68] – and since the number of Jews resident in London for more than six months had swollen beyond the imagination of the board's founders, just 'doing its job' monopolized energy and resources and limited the board's capacity thoughtfully to reconsider what it was doing and why. Where the Charity Organisation Society formerly held the Board of Guardians up as an example to all, by the mid-1890s it was urging the board, like other philanthropic enterprises, to improve visitation techniques and make casework files rigorous studies. The board, continued the Charity Organisation Society, should ascertain that the investigator was present when the decision to assist or not was made. Board records were both inadequate and in disarray. The board should maintain complete case files both for reference by any involved in decisions and as a basis for systematic case conferences and comparisons.[69] Subjective, *ad personam* judgements had no place in modern social work.

Professionalization on such a scale came very slowly to the board. For one thing, it cost far too much for a board that took such pride in its low administrative overheads. Pressure from within the community, however, proved irresistible. The Russo-Jewish Committee, as it designed constructive policies to address the issue of Russian refugees, forced the board to re-examine both its policies and assumptions. The committee and the board had to work together, and committee leaders knew all too well how the board functioned. Tempestuous meetings and challenges in 1892 and 1893 ultimately produced an interesting compromise. Nathan Joseph, who as architect and social worker had done so much for the board before turning to serve the Russo-Jewish Committee, forced the board to reorganize while acting

67 See JBG, *Annual Reports, 1890–1914*, particularly the increasingly statistical reports from 1913, and Lipman, *A Century of Social Service*, 142–3.

68 This practice of symbolic humiliation to receive relief came under increasing editorial attack from the *Jewish Chronicle*, not to mention from professional social workers, in the 1890s. Asher Myers, then editor of the *Jewish Chronicle*, always championed JBG fund-raising, but he stung JBG veterans with his pointed, small editorial criticisms. Frederic D. Mocatta, generous as a philanthropist could be, felt the relief rota practice to be absolutely correct. It expedited the conduct of business. The aged or ill women (nothing was said about sick men) were allowed a chair. F. D. Mocatta to the editor, *JC*, 14 Apr. 1893.

69 Report of the Charity Organisation Society for 1895–6 discussed in Lipman, *A Century of Social Service*, 110.

TABLE 3.5   Emigration, repatriation and loans as Jewish Board of Guardians strategy

Year	Cases	No. of Individuals	Emigrated	Repatriated	No. of loans	Amount lent (£)
1863	1,659	—	230	—	225	301
1873	2,072	6,631	741	—	88	667
1883	2,822	10,529	1,239	1,158	319	1,406
1888	3,513	12,921	1,254	1,567	633	2,452
1893	4,881	18,852	1,532	2,391	837	3,128
1898	4,462	16,241	1,701	2,461	1,676	7,348
1903	5,113	18,250	2,630	4,334	3,033	19,500
1908	4,248	19,408	1,065	2,960	2,531	16,912
1913	3,348	13,931	172	123	3,079	21,617

Source: Jewish Board of Guardians, Annual Reports.

for the committee, then himself returned to direct the board's visiting committee from 1893 until his death in 1909. By that time he had successfully moved the Board of Guardians towards professionalization, redefined specialization and systematic case work.

As the Liberal government undertook an increasingly broad legislative and administrative social agenda after 1905, and particularly after the December 1910 election, the agenda of the Jewish Board of Guardians both extended and eased. The more dramatic new social legislation, however, proved more significant for the future than the present. The most substantial immediate gains, in terms of transferring costs and responsibilities, came at the level of local government, where the reconstituted London local authorities, by the beginning of the twentieth century, absorbed costly public health and sanitation costs. But a new government ultimately willing to make a greater commitment to social welfare meant that the board could, in the future, limit some commitments to 'topping off' inadequate public benefits. So, too, the Aliens Act of 1905, which Anglo-Jewry recognized as being, if properly administered, in its own best interests, worked dramatically to retard immigration and transmigration, the source, whatever public denials it might choose to make, of much of the board's difficulty. Numbers alone were thereafter unlikely to overwhelm the board. The individual caseload, if not the total outlay, actually showed a modest decline in the decade before 1914.

Both national insurance and old age pensions, bellwethers of the welfare state, had limited immediate impact. Too many Jews were not British subjects, nor had they been resident long enough to qualify for benefits. Unemployment insurance originally covered a handful of industries and those ones with few Jewish employees. Only when Lloyd George's coalition considerably broadened the scope of unemployment coverage in 1920 did a substantial portion of poor British Jews benefit. Even then the self-employed and small traders lay beyond the scope of welfare legislation. Board expenditure continued to rise until many of such high-cost welfare benefits had been substantially shifted to the state. For one thing, although individual cases declined, Jewish demography being what it was, the total

TABLE 3.6   Jewish Board of Guardians, expenditure on relief and total contributions

Year	Expended on relief (£)	Contributed (£)
1893	16,700	14,743
1898	16,358	12,338
1903	22,203	16,749
1908	27,350	18,809
1913	26,415	16,888

Source: Jewish Board of Guardians, *Annual Reports.*

numbers of dependants continued to expand until the 1920s. Fewer and fewer of those relieved, moreover, could either be moved on or sent back.

The board, not surprisingly, concentrated its efforts in two areas: attacking what it perceived to be underlying causes of poverty, particularly health-related issues, and bolstering, through small loans, Anglo-Jewry's continuing commitment to the principle of self-help. The Baron de Hirsch estate bequest of £90,000 in fresh capital for the loan department set that part of board policy on a sound fiscal footing. The board could meet its ongoing commitments in the twentieth century only by dipping into capital.

In 1906 it conceded its difficulty and openly abandoned its traditional policy of funding legacies. Thereafter the board employed bequests, as necessary, to meet current charges.[70] The board attempted to apply its resources more imaginatively and effectively. Tentative experiments and new directions that the board had undertaken, such as its attack upon tuberculosis, could be further advanced with funds released from other commitments. The sanitary committee reconstituted itself as the health committee, avowing in name a substantial change in function and emphasis. Board pioneering often produced new state support. The board joined forces with local authorities in developing tuberculosis dispensaries in Whitechapel and Stepney, opened a cottage home at Walton in 1911 for tubercular children, and by 1914 had an active after-care committee for consumptives. Lady health visitors were added in 1904, the nursing staff strengthened, and cooperative programmes refined with local government health authorities.

These new departures enabled the board to launch a fresh campaign for financial support with the prospect of 'curing' poverty and reducing welfare costs. After watching its expenditure for artificial teeth quadruple between 1907 and 1910, the board subsidized milk distribution and bought a major dairy firm to serve the East End. State old age pensions began to ease board cash outlays after 1908, and the National Health Insurance Act of 1911, while discriminating against aliens, cut some actual and potential board obligations. Labour exchanges reduced the place of

70 The board consumed over £100,000 of legacies to meet current expenditure between 1919 and 1929. The fiftieth anniversary (1909) and the seventieth (1929–30) saw bold campaigns to recoup which succeeded principally in reducing the deficits for those years. See Lipman, *A Century of Social Service*, 155–6.

and need for board workrooms. State institutions, more efficient than the board could possibly be in matters of job placement, however, undercut one important board commitment. Labour exchanges had no interest in ascertaining that Jewish applicants found employers who respected sabbath or holy-day observance.

Traditional areas of strength became problems. The industrial department, once the pride of the board, had held up apprenticeship as embodying the principles of self-help. But by 1910, the department was marking time, bemoaning a steady 50 per cent cancellation rate, usually ascribable to the 'misconduct of boys', and waiting until the system of trade schools would be more generally established and attendance at them made compulsory.[71] The market, not the welfare state, made the short-term difference in this instance. By creating an unprecedented demand for juvenile labour, not to mention the needs of military enlistment, the war of 1914 removed the immediate problem from board control, although it would compound board difficulties during the testing years of demobilization in the early 1920s.

On the other hand, the expanding range of state concerns also created new 'Jewish needs'. Increasingly, legislative concern about children raised new and old issues in troubling form. Should Jews care for their own wayward young, or should they attempt to make arrangements with existing secular or other denominational facilities? The same questions could be posed about hospital and other health care. Spiritual ministration, dietary provisions, observance of Jewish holy-days and the sabbath each disrupted, to some degree, the routine workings of established non-Jewish institutions. But the capital costs and ongoing expenses of creating and operating specifically Jewish institutions, often to serve a very limited number of individuals, could be overwhelming. Not surprisingly, Anglo-Jewry preferred, in such matters, to provide for Jewish needs within existing institutions, rather than undertake the responsibility for building and maintaining Jewish borstals for juvenile offenders or specifically Jewish hospitals for the Jewish ill and infirm. The Board of Guardians, admittedly battered by wartime disruption and needs, declined a London County Council invitation in 1915 to start a home for mentally deficient Jewish children.

The Jewish Board of Guardians entered the 1920s confronting the tasks of demobilization, redefinition of function and purpose, and refining cooperative programmes with government authorities. The heroic years of the nineteenth century had passed when a phalanx of philanthropic volunteers, animated by a sense of who and what British Jews should be, worked through the board to aid those in need while socializing them in Anglo-Jewry's image. The Jewish Board of Guardians had pioneered programmes and policies widely imitated by Victorian and Edwardian social agencies. Like those who set it in operation, the board had aged, become less resilient and less imaginative, although more professional. The board survived, at great strain, the testing years of massive immigration. The Board of Guardians had witnessed and had been the vehicle for providing Jewish women with greater freedom, scope and authority. The board could justly claim that it had

71 See *Fifty-second Report of the Jewish Board of Guardians* (London, 1911), *Forty-seventh Report* (London, 1906), and Leonard Cohen's presidential address at the annual meeting of 26 March 1911. As 'medical and cognate relief' soared to £2,050, Cohen explained that Beatrice Webb argued that half of existing destitution could be ascribed to sickness, and that tuberculosis accounted for one-seventh of all Poor Law expenditure. *JC*, 31 Mar. 1911.

helped to create a general public impression of Jews as purposeful, responsible, industrious, even moral. However demeaning conditions of assistance might have been, the Jewish Board of Guardians proved an effective institution in the tasks it had undertaken. Those in need found assistance, small traders and businessmen and apprentices were provided with opportunities. The board, by any broad scale of evaluation, succeeded.

The Board of Guardians, however, was but one of several Anglo-Jewish institutions developed to socialize the community. Schools, clubs and a host of specialized philanthropies worked in a great common purpose, the articulation and refinement of an acculturated Jewry, conditioned to succeed in British life while preserving the heritage of diaspora Jewish culture.

4

Education: The Mind and the Soul

We desire to train as well as to teach; to form character as well as to impart knowledge.
L. B. Abrahams at the Maccabæans education night dinner, 29 January 1898

While much temporizing and considerable laissez-faire obtained in the socialization of adult Jews, their children were taken firmly in hand. Anglo-Jewry had three demands, one qualitative and two substantive. Schools should instruct the Jewish young well; they must also teach them how to be British and how to be Jews. Schools were the front lines in the campaign to shape the Jewish subculture. Anglo-Jewry depended on them to impart the skills necessary to make Jewish children effective and productive members of British society. But the schools and ancillary socializing institutions were also designed to shape and cultivate youth in a mode and image that both Jews and Britons would applaud.

Through much of the nineteenth century, Anglo-Jewry had to create its own strong system of independent schools. The Jews' Free School, a favoured Rothschild philanthropy, stood proudly as its central ornament. Other schools were developed to meet the needs of the growing Jewish population, both in the East End itself and for the upwardly mobile, scattering into other parts of the metropolis. Jewish institutions, like other independent schools, received government grants so long as they met defined academic standards and satisfied government inspectors. A British system of state education did not come until the last third of the century. Anglo-Jewry could not have been more fortunate. State schools rather than more Jewish voluntary schools enabled the community leadership to meet what would have been the otherwise impossible task of schooling immigrant children.

Only in 1870 did Britain create a state elementary education system. Attendance became compulsory between 1876 and 1880. The new mandatory system granted subsidies to approved independent schools while also empowering local authorities to construct secular schools. Since independent schools were, with few exceptions, Christian and usually Church of England, attendance also generally meant participating in the religious education and training that the school offered. The Victorians fancied themselves a believing people, so state schools, called 'provided schools', also gave very general non-denominational Christian religious training. Given British denominational heterogeneity and concern for freedom of conscience, a variety of safeguards permitted parents to exclude their children from religious instruction. Jews, as a matter of custom and ultimately of administrative regulation, attended instruction only in the Old Testament. The same rules obtained wherever local authorities employed independent ('non-provided') denominational schools to meet local educational needs. Students of other religions were not to be obliged to attend that school's denominational activities.

After 1880, the Jewish population doubled, then doubled again. Anglo-Jewry, wealthy as it was, could never have furnished the resources to expand its parochial school system to meet Jewish educational needs of the 1890s and beyond. Fortunately for the community, the state shouldered most of the burden. Compulsory education, through provided schools wherever necessary, was in place long before Jewish immigration poured into the East End. Schools would be there to serve their children, even if they were not quite the institutions Anglo-Jewry would have preferred. Mandated, non-sectarian religious education presented Anglo-Jewry with no great difficulty. It had only to bear the costs of providing for the more adequate religious education of Jewish boys and girls. Even that proved a formidable task. Jewish religious education was expensive. Christians needed only the vernacular. Jews needed Hebrew language instruction as well as religious training. In a rapidly growing community, available resources trailed behind perceived community needs. Into that gap between adequate religious instruction and available community resources, in the mind of anxious leaders, crept the conversionist missionaries.

Balfour's Education Act of 1902 extended mandatory education to secondary schools. That much-needed and long-delayed measure arose in part because Anglican independent schools, to which the Cecil family specifically and the Conservative party rather more generally were committed, faced increasing financial difficulties. The survival of many seemed at stake. But denominational schools meant all denominational schools, so the Act of 1902 drew support from Roman Catholics with their parochial schools. The measure also propped up overextended Jewish independent schools. Under the legislation, non-provided schools now drew their operating financial support principally from taxes expended through local educational authorities.

While those bodies paid most of the bills, certain capital costs and maintenance still fell on the school managers and their boards. Local authorities, moreover, defined what physical as well as curricular standards were for all supported schools. Without exception, Jewish schools found themselves confronting sharply increased costs to bring their physical facilities to approved levels, a reflection of Anglo-Jewry's past educational budget priorities.[1] Jewish schools, however, retained full control of their religious curriculum. Local educational authorities had to allow 'reasonable facilities' for teaching religion during school hours, and school

---

1 Jewish schools were somewhat, although not seriously, undermaintained. As the Act came into force, each Jewish independent school found itself forced to make unanticipated expenditures. In addition, the Jews' Free School student body grew, for example, by 33 per cent between 1883 (when it had last added to its buildings) and 1896. The Education Department demanded that facilities be brought up to standard, imposing 'sanitary' costs alone of £2,200 (18 per cent of the previous year's total budget). *JC*, 2 Oct. 1896.

managers retained control of that instruction. In Jewish schools, this was understood to include Hebrew language training and permitted several school hours each week for religious instruction.[2]

Even in secular institutions, politics and social geography being what they were, Jewish headmasters and headmistresses came, over the years, to direct an increasing number of the East London county council schools. By the early twentieth century, many of the East End elementary board schools were 'Jewish'. Jewish management and predominantly Jewish student bodies at state schools in Whitechapel and St George's-in-the-East comforted parents and the community, but Anglo-Jewry still needed to develop and fund a religious education programme for Jews in London County Council schools.

The task of providing 'Jewish education' in state schools fell, first, on the underfunded Jewish Association for the Diffusion of Religious Knowledge, which was re-established as the Jewish Religious Education Board. Changing the name did not, however, balance the budget. The board selected and paid elementary schoolteachers to provide the religious instruction mandated by the Education Acts. That demanded recruitment and training. Neither proved easy or inexpensive. The Religious Education Board, in spite of repeated pulpit appeals and the enthusiastic support of the *Jewish Chronicle*, confronted a growing gap between needs and current resources. The board could never catch up with Jewish numbers. The demographic explosion in the East End alone would have imposed almost impossible demands, but the dispersion of Jewish settlement to new areas, each of which required its own facilities, meant the facts of Jewish life outdistanced contemporary ingenuity and outran available resources.

Anglo-Jewish social policies, seen as desirable, even necessary, in themselves, thus aggravated Religious Education Board difficulties. Welfare agencies, for instance, worked assiduously to disperse the population of the overcrowded East End and urged Jews to move to new districts. Samuel Montagu even organized a dispersion society to assist members of his Federation of Synagogues to migrate to other parts of London or Britain. But easing the burdens of Stepney, when Jews moved elsewhere in London, placed more burdens on the overloaded Religious Education Board. Teachers, materials, and facilities had to be provided everywhere. It all cost money. Asking Jews to prosper and move outwards, the Chief Rabbi reminded a captious board meeting in January 1905, 'entailed the terrible responsibility on the community of seeing that the children should not be allowed to go without religious instruction'.[3]

While the Education Act of 1902 rescued the Jewish independent schools, it also left the nine self-important governing bodies of those institutions rattling about London with little to do. Once upon a time, each had recruited the resources and managed its school. Now an Act of 1903, expanding on the general principles of the Act of 1902, placed administrative oversight for all schools in the hands of the Education Committee of the London County Council. School managers still had to

---

2 For a sense of the Board of Deputies' painstaking lobbying see, *inter alia*, the proceedings of the law and parliamentary committee, 1 July 1901, BDBJ B 2/10/4; 17 June, 24 July, 27 Oct. 1902, 7 Oct. 1906, BDBJ C 13/1/5.

3 *JC*, 27 Jan. 1905. Gartner, *Jewish Immigrant*, 220–31 discusses these issues.

satisfy inspectors by bringing the various Jewish independent institutions up to standards, but beyond such tedious details, each governing board found itself with little beyond ceremonial responsibility. Drains, roofs and sanitation were far from the most effective rallying cry for subscriptions and donations, nor did they enhance the governors' sense of their own importance.

Anglo-Jewry understood that Conservative government policies, in propping up underfunded Anglican schools, happened, incidentally, to preserve Jewish parochial schools. Balfour and fellow proponents of the 1902 Act sought to salvage Anglican institutions driven to the wall by rising educational costs. To accomplish this, they cleverly designed a measure to attract political support from non-Anglicans. Nor had they miscalculated; any religious denominations which had heavily invested in elementary and secondary education breathed a sigh of relief. For Anglo-Jewry, national educational policy after 1870 taught a lesson repeated many times over. Jews could transfer costly social welfare to the state while still appearing to care for their own community. Exchequer and local authority grants preserved a voluntary system strained to or beyond the breaking point. Education, one of the most expensive areas of capitalizing social overhead, was a dramatic case in point.

Sir Henry Campbell-Bannerman's Liberal government, which took office at the end of 1905, was committed to the 'secularization' of all schools receiving government assistance. While the partisan political temperature rose, Anglo-Jewry looked more closely at what this might actually mean. The rhetoric, as was so often the case in passionate Liberal–Conservative debates, suggested a substantive difference that was not there. The Board of Deputies realized that the government's attempt to modify the system in 1906 was actually a potential boon, not a liability. By eliminating the distinction between provided and non-provided schools in a coordinated system of undenominational education, Anglo-Jewry could benefit yet again. Capital and maintenance costs, under the Liberal proposal, would be transferred to the state. Jews had no quarrel with secular management of education so long as Jewish religious and Hebrew education were safeguarded, and they were.[4] From time to time, a Jewish leader would suggest eliminating Jewish voluntary schools altogether. Anglo-Jewry never seriously considered that option, but the fact that it could be seriously made was significant. Liberal 'secularizing' education bills, Anglo-Jewry realized, served community interests quite as well as Conservative 'religious' ones. Sir Charles Elliot, a Conservative party champion of denominational education and treasurer of the London School Board, pleaded for Anglo-Jewish support in fighting the Liberal 'secularist' proposal in 1906.

> You are standing shoulder to shoulder with other religious denominations to perpetuate the principle of religious instruction. I see a danger, if another

---

4 The Cowper–Temple clause troubled committed religious dogmatists. The protection of religious freedom also granted a parent the legal right to prevent his child from having any religious education. The executives of the Board of Deputies saw the opportunity, by slightly amending the bill, to force Jewish parents to provide religious education for their children, whether they desired it or not. Report of the law and parliamentary committee on the Education Bill, 1906, 16 May 1906. BDBJ C 13/1/6. As Sydney Webb informed the *Jewish Chronicle*, none of the Jewish voluntary schools was in serious trouble when the time came to absorb them into the London County Council system. The capital expenditure demanded to bring the schools up to LCC standards were modest enough, although Lord Rothschild complained that the drains at Jews' Free School had never been so rigorously inspected. *JC*, 21 Apr. 1905.

[Liberal] Government were restored to power, of its trying to confine education to its secular side only. . . . There can be no greater evil than the imparting of only secular knowledge in the schools.[5]

Anglo-Jewry, however, had looked beyond the rhetoric to the reality. Under the Liberal bill, non-provided denominational institutions could continue to offer religious instruction. Only now, the entire costs could be shifted from the shoulders of Jewish philanthropy to the state.[6]

Jewish philanthropy prospered in fruitful partnership with the state. Local authorities, after all, shared Anglo-Jewry's social goals. They, too, wished to see workers improve their prospects and move from marginal trades to better ones. Local government initiatives continually transferred costs from Jewish organizations to the ratepayer. By 1897, for instance, the London School Board, spurred by its Progressive majority, specifically addressed the issue of upgrading skills in overcrowded trades. Going to the heart of the matter, the board engaged an experienced, skilled cutter to teach evening classes that would broaden the capacities of those trapped by the excessive subdivision of labour in East End tailoring. Women's dressmaking evening classes offered young ladies training that would enable them to work either at home or in West End firms. For a mere twopence per week, young men were taught wood-carving, carpentry and furniture design. The school board even offered a Remington typewriter to any school able to form an adult education commercial class in shorthand, typing and bookkeeping, provided only that each student already be able to take shorthand at eighty words per minute.

Jewish philanthropy adapted itself to such opportunities, augmenting incentives and filling gaps. Evening classes in East End board schools, for instance, had extensive programmes to teach foreign Jews English by 1895. The London School Board and the Russo-Jewish Committee both saw these as part of a programme to anglicize the immigrants and to help them move onwards from their slum housing and overcrowded trades. Since the London School Board did not recognize classes in elementary English or fund anything below the level of the fifth form, a substantial portion of the cost fell on the Russo-Jewish Committee. The school board provided facilities. The committee paid the fees for those students who could not pay their own. The committee, to recruit effective staff, also supplemented the salary of any teacher who could speak Yiddish. One way or another, the Russo-Jewish Committee subsidized some 600 students in twenty-five classes at approximately 2d per attendance by 1897. The classes were a striking sight.

> One scarcely knows which to admire most – whether the men or the women, the grizzly beards and the married matrons trying to squeeze their bulky forms into the children's desks at which they sit, or the bright boys and girls, only just turned fourteen, who, having been at school till half-past four, and finished their lessons for the next day, are back again at half-past seven, such is their eagerness to acquire knowledge.[7]

5 Jewish Religious Education Board (JREB) festival dinner, 15 Feb. 1905. *JC*, 17 Feb. 1905.
6 See the Runciman Papers, University of Newcastle-upon-Tyne Library, for the negotiations on the Liberal proposals. H. F. Wright reminded Runciman that only Roman Catholics and Jews actually wanted 'Church teaching'. Wright to Runciman, 26 May 1906, WR 14.
7 *JC*, 1 Jan. 1897.

They acquired more than skills. Beginners were first taught English using a Russo-Jewish Committee *Yiddish–English Manual*. More advanced classes were taught how to adapt to British life. Students, usually younger ones, could be found studying such manuals as *The Laws of Every-Day Life*. Those who already had four or five years of training in the English language were given *The Life and Duties of a Citizen*. The Russo-Jewish Committee believed that, once literate in English, the newcomer 'picks up a knowledge of civic duty from the newspapers and the experience of daily life, which is of more practical use than the information imparted at school. But for the foreign immigrant such theoretical instruction is undoubtedly useful.' The distinction was sensible enough. While the 'greener', the newcomer, needed to understand habeas corpus and trial by jury, the Russo-Jewish Committee concentrated on thirteen- to sixteen-year-old boys and girls when teaching Stuart history enlivened by magic lantern show.[8]

The schools not only socialized and anglicized the children, they 'elevated' the family. Nettie Adler, daughter of the Chief Rabbi and community stalwart on the London School Board, suggested the obvious and subtle ways in which the change was wrought. On any given morning, a school manager might appear to find two or three strangely dressed 'little people' in the hall of the boys' or girls' department, the boys perhaps wearing Russian blouses, the girls bedecked with coral earrings and necklaces. They were among the fortunate children, immediately admitted to school. Six months later, when seeing what progress had been made,

> you will find that they have become to all intents and purposes little English men and women, passing in a few weeks through the lowest standards, and soon taking as much pleasure in football or cricket at the Tower-Moat, or in 'tip-cat' in the streets, as the most veritable British-born citizen of them all.[9]

But this was only the beginning. Through the children, 'higher concepts of morality, cleanliness, and industry' could be conveyed back to the home. East End parents had great respect for education, and Anglo-Jewry should exploit that in every possible way. Parents should be brought to school to see their children at work. School savings banks promoted self-help and were, in effect, savings of parents, not children. The Education Department had precisely that in mind when establishing them. The school visitor was a 'friend', unlike the investigator for the Board of Guardians. The student and her mother would listen to the 'ladies' of the school.

ARTICULATING A SCHOOL SYSTEM

The British Jewish establishment had its long-established anglicizing educational institution, the Jews' Free School in Spitalfields. An impressive institution, the largest elementary school in England at the beginning of the twentieth century, its curriculum embodied the perfect balance, in establishment eyes, of things English

8 One correspondent recommended that the Jewish Board of Guardians make more use of all courses, even to the extent of making attendance a precondition for relief. *JC*, 1, 8 Jan 1897.

9 Nettie Adler, 'The schools as a means of elevating the family,' paper to the JBG visiting committee. *JC*, 3 June 1898.

and Jewish. Moses Angel (1819–1898), headmaster for fifty-one years, regarded education as mechanically as the school clocks which he personally wound every day. Students were 'very regular or very irregular'. They were often also very impressive. Israel Zangwill studied there and has bequeathed us, in his autobiographical reflections, a picture of the living, pulsating, exciting world of the Jews' Free School. Annual prize-giving ceremonies invariably brought an address from some old graduate, reflecting on how Angel's school had dispatched him, regular or irregular as he might have been, a better person committed to success. Moses Angel dedicated himself, not merely to socializing the respectable, but to developing a vocational curriculum that would enable his charges to succeed. He transformed the Talmud Torah he took over in January 1840 from a 'sink of ignorance' to what was by government reports the largest and best-managed elementary school in the United Kingdom. Jews' Free, in addition, served as a vital community centre. Jewish Religious Education Board sabbath classes met there. Children's Happy Evenings provided an escape from overcrowded homes and an alternative to juvenile street hooliganism. The Jewish Lads' Brigade needed the Free School large hall for its weekly drills. Another charity used Free School facilities to provide regular concerts for the poor.[10]

Angel's successor as captain of the flagship of the Jewish educational fleet, Louis B. Abrahams, was outspoken in advocating the Anglo-Jewish orthodoxy he was determined to have taught. He told assembled parents, benefactors and schoolchildren at the annual prize-giving ceremonies of 1905 of the Free School's place in their lives. Then, scarcely pausing to take a breath, he gave his view as to what they should be doing. The responsibility for bringing up thousands of children, he reminded his audience, was shared between teachers and parents. The school had done its part: it had gained eight additional London County Council scholarships. Physical education was producing sounder bodies to accompany agile minds. Now parents must do theirs. Home training must supplement and support the school's training. Parents must reinforce habits of personal cleanliness and tidiness. They should say nothing children should not hear. They must take responsibility for their children during leisure hours. Keep them out of the streets. Now that transportation had become so inexpensive, parents should move to the suburbs and live in more salubrious settings. The headmaster urged his audience to discard Yiddish, 'that miserable jargon which is not a language at all' and which created 'a dividing line' between them and their fellow English subjects. As they turned away from Yiddish, they should also throw off their 'foreign habits' and 'foreign prejudices and become English – truly English'. To those who had told Abrahams they were 'too old to change', he urged them to make the effort to give their children 'a fair chance to grow one with the people among whom they dwell'.

> Strengthen the efforts of the teachers to wipe away all evidences of foreign birth and foreign proclivities, so that [your] children shall be so identified with everything that is English in thought and deed, that no shadow of anti-Semitism might exist, that [your] boys and girls may grow up devoted to

10 See, particularly, the discussion of the Jews' Free School (JFS) annual report for 1895–6 in *JC*, 2 Oct. 1896, Angel's obituary in *JC*, 9 Sept. 1898; Gartner, *Jewish Immigrant*, 221–4. The early minute books (1831–60) of the JFS are AJ/138/1–2 in the Mocatta Library.

the flag which they are learning within these walls to love and honour, that they may take a worthy part in the growth of this great Empire, whose shelter and protection [I hope] will never be denied them.[11]

Anglo-Jewry early in the nineteenth century considered creating a school which would serve Jewish 'infants'. Anglicization would move more rapidly if children were not left too long exclusively with their parents. Frances Barnett, later first headmistress of Jews' Free School and a pioneer in children's education, took a room at Bell Lane 'and personally collected out of gutter and garret thirty young ragamuffins under school age and taught them as best she could their letters and their manners.' Institutionalizing such a programme demanded money, so there matters stood until the opening of a conversionist school. That threat, always so effective in opening Anglo-Jewish philanthropic purses, worked once again. Frances Barnett had already interested Anna Maria Goldsmid, also a devotee of educational reform. She, in turn, bestirred her brother, Sir Francis Goldsmid and Walter Josephs. They arranged for some rooms, roughly fitted out in a warehouse off Houndsditch. And thus, in 1841, the Jews' Infant Schools (actually two schools under one administration) came to be launched. Miriam Harris, the first teacher, had up to two hundred students. When it shifted to Commercial Street the school accommodated a thousand. Adding a branch in Whitechapel Road in 1867 and constructing a new facility in Buckle Street brought enrolment to over 1,600 children aged from three to eight being prepared to enter the Jewish school system. Matthew Arnold, the famous poet and the first government inspector of Jews' Infant Schools, strongly approved. By 1896, more than two thousand children were receiving secular and religious instruction at Jews' Infant Schools.

Jews' Infant also served as a training college for Jewish teachers and a pedagogical pioneering enterprise. Over seventy would be engaged at any time in observing and practice teaching. Not surprisingly, Jews' Infant quickly adopted the latest techniques. The school introduced Froebelian methods to kindergarten instruction, long before they were more generally imitated in English education. Anglo-Jewry took infinite pride in how well the little ones looked at work, hemming, knitting and sewing. Children aged three to eight learned discipline and their place in society. Fees at this voluntary institution remained modest thanks to growing government grants and endowment income that covered 75 per cent of costs. Claude G. Montefiore succeeded Sir Julian Goldsmid as president of Jews' Infant Schools in 1896, bringing his determination to impart effective moral as well as secular education to Jewish children. Montefiore regarded the institution as a success on both counts. Three-quarters of those who attended Jews' Infant Schools continued into the Jews' Free School.[12]

---

11 *JC*, 7 July 1905. The JFS entered the age of state underwriting some £3,000 in debt and needing a £15,000 capital drive to meet future needs. One Rothschild-sponsored banquet turned the trick. *JC*, 12, 31 May 1905.

12 In 1895, Jews' Infant Schools (JIS) received £2,100 from the government, donations and subscriptions of £1,030, and earned endowment income of £1,420, a state–community 60–40 ratio. Claude G. Montefiore reviewed the history of the JIS at length at the festival dinner of 20 January 1897 which rebuilt sagging endowment funds. *JC*, 22 Jan. 1897. See also, *JC*, 12, 15 Jan. 1897, 10 July, 23 Oct. 1896; Lipman, *Social History*, 48–9.

Five other elementary schools, constructed either to meet increasing East End demands or to accommodate the spread of Jewish settlements through the metropolis, were far smaller than either Jews' Free or Jews' Infant Schools. Perhaps the most famous was the Westminster Jews' Free School, a venerable foundation created when an older boys' institution merged with a newer one for girls in 1846. Under the kindly management of Jacob Woolf for thirty-five years until his retirement in 1905, it grew from four hundred to six hundred students. London County Council officials believed the facilities to be overtaxed and insisted that Westminster Free reduce its rolls to just over five hundred in 1910. Government grants covered half the school's budget. Forced to devour capital to meet annual needs, the school needed all the marginal assistance it could find.

Collateral philanthropies eased ongoing expenses. Schoolchildren, for example, ate at the nearby Emily Harris Home. Even the poorer children were expected to pay one penny per week for five dinners, the balance of costs coming from the Penny Dinners organization. The few who could not afford this received their meals free. The Jewish Schools boot fund and special school charities provided shoes and clothing for poor children. Demands for assistance were so numerous that the care committee, which selected the children to receive various benefits, had to employ a professional visitor to assess the merits of claims. Subscriptions consistently proved inadequate, and Westminster Free, although enjoying substantial Davidson, Montefiore and Waley backing, never could build a substantial endowment. Headmaster Woolf preached and practised Matthew Arnold's dictum that 'conduct is three parts of life.' The Westminster Jews' Free School drew consistently high marks from government inspectors, but Woolf valued still more the kind of people his students became. Nor did he rest content with what had been accomplished while his students were enrolled. Westminster Jews' Free must, he believed, continue to exert a moral influence over its boys throughout their lives. To do this, he urged the creation of a boys' club for the West Central area, which would continue to provide a salubrious setting and some measure of continuing education for young men and women. Through Claude G. Montefiore, who increasingly appointed himself Anglo-Jewry's spokesman on matters educational, Woolf's wish was granted, and the Westminster Jews' Free continued to play a role in its graduates' lives through their adolescent years.[13]

Stepney Jewish Schools, on the other hand, emphasized vocational instruction well before such a curriculum was generally offered in London primary schools. With a keen sense of employment prospects and the market, school authorities sought to move their charges away from overcrowded traditional trades into woodworking and metalworking. Stepney Jewish Schools, with its curriculum designed for working-class children, also furnished a pool of potential teachers for the London County Council system. London County Council recruited the most promising between the ages of twelve and thirteen and subsidized their secondary education. Founded in 1867, Stepney came by the beginning of the twentieth century to serve almost nine hundred East Enders usefully and well each year.

Not only did Stepney pioneer vocational education, it integrated 'muscular Judaism' into its curriculum. H. H. Burdett, director of the nearby People's Palace

13 *JC*, 3 Mar., 29 Sept. 1905, 3 Mar. 1911.

gymnasium, worked closely with the headmaster to develop a programme which would produce Jews 'who, while devoted to English sports would be none the less devoted to their ancestral faith'. Immigrant children, 'weakly and pale-faced' as they were, might seem poor material with which to work with, but they took to Indian club, fencing-stick and polo ball. Athletics, so Burdett and Headmaster W. Ashe Payne contended, rounded out the integration of immigrant youth into English society.[14] Anglo-Jewry believed it.

They also believed in W. Ashe Payne, the headmaster. Non-Jewish and a son of one of England's more distinguished families, Payne drew community applause when Stepney Jewish was still a middle-class school with an academic curriculum and even more for his highly successful conversion of it into one of the East End's most effective institutions. Conventionally suspicious East European immigrant parents warmed to him. His pedigree and talent made him doubly attractive to those seeking to mould the children of newcomers to Anglo-Jewish ideals. Payne sought to develop the highest standards of character in his students, while simultaneously furthering an elaborate vocational and commercial curriculum. As Payne's twenty-fifth anniversary as headmaster approached, letters to the Jewish press suggested how widespread and deep his impact had been. His advocacy of broad programmes in athletics and physical education reverberated throughout Jewish voluntary schools, and the growing emphasis on the social value of sports was a factor in the selection of Joseph Bernberg, with his strong athletic credentials, as principal and headmaster of the South London Jewish Schools. Sir Edward Stern, president and a major benefactor of Stepney Jewish, saw the results in 'the happy, cleanly look of all the children and . . . the intense interest they seemed have have in their work'. Stern understood the role of the Schools. He was glad to see, as he presented the 1905 graduation prizes 'that manual and technical instruction were as much cultivated as mental instruction'. His condescension appears to have had no demonstrable impact upon the noisy friends and parents, delighted to have the opportunity to socialize with one another.[15]

14 Prize-giving, Stepney Jewish Schools (SJS), 1 June 1896. *JC*, 5 June 1896; General meeting, SJS, 1 June 1905. *JC*, 9 June 1905. Marcus Adler (1837–1911), elder brother of the Chief Rabbi, founded the school. An actuary and fellow of the Royal Statistical Society, Adler founded the London Mathematical Society. He designed the LCC system of train and tram fares that proved of such benefit to the working classes and that helped to make possible their dispersion, thus easing slum congestion. Adler's success derived in part from the relative ease with which he could recruit substantial support from the leading Anglo-Jewish families. See, e.g., the building fund drive list, *JC*, 17 Jan. 1879.

15 Prize ceremony, SJS, 10 July 1905. Payne displayed an extraordinary capacity to recruit extra help and the resources of others. Metalworking classes, for instance, were held at the People's Palace. By 1896, the Schools received £1,506 from government grants towards its total £2,436 expended (62 per cent), all testimony to Payne's success in managing the enterprise. SJS that year proposed to take over and build on the site of dilapidated cottages adjoining the school. By doing so, the school would improve the neighbourhood, add places for 300 more children, and earn £600 more from the government. Annual meeting, SJS, 8 Apr. 1897. *JC*, 16 Apr. 1897. When approving Stepney progress at a fund-raising ball in 1898, much was made of Stepney's pioneering development of physical drill, swimming, cookery and laundry work among Jewish schools. *JC*, 28 Jan 1898. The industrial committee of the Jewish Board of Guardians issued a pamphlet stressing the importance of every boy and girl learning a good trade and the importance of apprenticeship. The tract offered JBG support for those who could not afford to pay a premium, 'To parents of children leaving school' (London, January 1901) in Yiddish and English for distribution through each Jewish school. Mocatta BA 28 JEW in the Mocatta Library. Payne, after being headmaster for thirteen years, claimed that he had become Barmitzvah. *JC*, 17 Oct. 1902, 14 July 1905. On Bernberg's appointment at South London with its more than 250 students, see *JC*, 7 Nov. 1902.

Bayswater Jewish Schools, founded in 1867, addressed itself to the needs of more successful families that had wended their way into the West End. Serving three to four hundred children, it found the double impact of demography and mobility made planning difficult. New immigrants, many young and with large families, pressed hard on East End facilities. That was understandable. West End prosperity brought different problems. As Jews moved into the middle classes, they also limited family size. Once mobile, moreover, Jewish families were prepared to move on, less attached to their immediate communities, and less willing to extend themselves financially to support local institutions. Bayswater Jewish Schools responded by specializing in the slightly older students. The Sephardi congregation paid £25 to educate all children from the Spanish and Portuguese Orphans Society. Bayswater took its declining infant population by bus to special schools at Notting Hill, while itself recruiting students from scattered West End Jewish families.

Prosperity did not emancipate the middle classes from Anglo-Jewish tutelage. The apparatus of oversight, stewardship, and benevolence, so clear in the East End institutions, also operated on the more fortunate. The school's care committee visited the home of each new student. Having made clear to the parents, however subtly, what community expectations and standards were, the school addressed itself to the attitudes of the children. The girls' department organized a benevolent fund to which students contributed from one farthing upwards. The money was used to purchase clothing or spectacles for those who could not afford them, underlining the distinction between privilege and its obligations as against dependence, deference, and gratitude. This not-very-subtle sociology lesson was made easier because the poor represented so small a minority of the student population. Only fifteen of 370 attending were fed without charge in 1910–11, and only forty-five came under the somewhat more capacious umbrella of the Children's Country Holiday Fund. That benevolent enterprise dispatched children who could not otherwise get a summer holiday to Eastbourne for 5s 8d apiece. Bayswater's strong academic programme regularly received 'excellency grants' from government school inspectors. On the other hand, it had been somewhat behind the times in introducing an elaborate sports programme, but a new headmaster, in keeping with the times, brought Bayswater his enthusiasm for athletics and physical education in 1910.[16]

Buck's Row school, on the other hand, was one of the municipal schools which picked up students as Jews moved eastwards from Whitechapel in the early 1880s. The Jews' Free School may have been the recognized centre for Jewish children, but Buck's Row school, given the facts of Jewish migration, came to be a Jews' Free in miniature. Buck's Row had the advantage over Stepney Jewish of students from marginally more prosperous and substantially better-motivated families. The headmaster delighted in the 'material improvement in the tone of the children. They are more amenable to good, wholesome discipline, and are better behaved, whilst their parents take a greater interest in the work of the school.' By 1910, over seven thousand Jewish students had passed through the institution, many of them

---

16 *JC*, 28 Aug. 1896; *JC*, 7 Apr. 1911. Almost a third of the students were fed at school in 1910–11, suggesting that many came from too far away to return home at noon.

maintaining close ties with it even after migrating to different parts of the world.[17] Whitechapel Foundation School, a non-denominational independent school, also served East End Jews from the 1870s, but such institutions were not favourably regarded. They were expensive and seen as potential centres for conversionist activity, whatever safeguards might be promised for the religious preferences of parents.[18]

Anglo-Jewry had a hard lesson to learn. Educational institutions, as other groups and societies have also discovered, demand substantial fixed investment. But the societies that use schools are mobile. The Jewish High School for Girls, for instance, closed at the end of the 1896–7 school year. Founded in 1845 by leading members of the West London Synagogue, the school, originally called the Metropolitan Jewish School, served middle-class Jewish families. Some seventy boys and ninety girls attended on average, but enrolment began to sag. The boys' side closed in 1881, but Miss Isabel Goldsmid, daughter of Sir Francis, donated new premises in Chenies Street in Bloomsbury to serve 180 to 200 girls. The school, open to all denominations, received high marks from inspectors but never recruited full classes. Elementary education could elicit communal philanthropic support, but high-school education was another matter. As directors, Goldsmid and Mocatta might create confidence in the Jewish High School for Girls, but they could not recruit the children of the upwardly mobile. Jews were moving on from the Gower Street region. Non-Jews – and they were always a quarter to a third of the students – could not make up the difference. Although enrolment rose slightly in the 1890s, fees could not begin to meet charges, and Jewish middle-class parents, who had by then moved west, south-west and north-west to more affluent parts of London, preferred to send their daughters to schools nearer to home. With attendance rarely reaching eighty and facilities always less than half full, the Jewish High School for Girls and Day Training College for Teachers joined the Jews' College School of the City of London, abandoned long before, as institutions discontinued when Jews moved on.[19]

Only schools in what continued to be the concentrated centres of Jewish population saw student demand steadily outrun the supply of places. Every Jewish school outside the East End suffered financial problems. Some contended that their problem was a lack of facilities, not of potential students. Westminster Free claimed a waiting list of a hundred or more potential students. Given Westminster Free's central location, that may have been true, but the Bayswater example was more commonly the case. Jewish upward social mobility and outward migration meant several things. The population became less fixed in place, less predictable in family size, and increasingly drawn into other cultural worlds. Planning Jewish parochial

17 *JC*, 20 Jan. 1911.
18 The school fee was £2 1s for parishioners, £2 8s for non-parishioners, both well beyond the reach of most East End Jews. In addition to the school fee, the parent or guardian was required to deposit £1 as 'a guarantee against loss or wilful damage of books or other property'. The curriculum would appeal only to parents who saw their children continuing beyond elementary education. Whitechapel Foundation offered a wide range of modern languages, mathematics, physical science, history, geography, English language and literature, drawing and Latin. Although scripture was taught, no boy was required to attend religious instruction against the wishes of his parents. *JC*, 10 Jan. 1879.
19 *JC*, 30 Apr. 1897.

education became increasingly difficult. Potential consumers, having once cut their original East End roots, displayed increasing independence of choice. As Jews moved into more affluent areas, they also came increasingly to share the institutions and aspirations of their neighbours.[20]

Anglo-Jewry's leading families more often than not retained tutors for their children. They also turned to the same selective schools the British elite attended. Rothschild sons went to Harrow, Montagu's to Clifton, where 'Polah House' accommodated Jewish students. Those marginally lower in Jewish society also aspired to elite education. The steady growth of advertisements for preparatory schools in the early twentieth-century issues of the Jewish press testified to their successful upward social mobility and determination to plant their sons at the ancient universities. As more and more within the community aspired to premium education, institutions arose – always with appropriate religious blessings and endorsements from acknowledged community and educational leaders – to answer the need. Reverend John Chapan, former headmaster of the Jews' Hospital and Orphan Asylum, established Hillsboro' College in West Dulwich, while Samuel Barczinsky, in the salubrious seaside environs of Brighton, offered the Wellesley House school which would provide Jews with public school teaching, proper preparation for both Cambridge and Oxford examinations, while giving due attention to Jewish needs and education. Ascott House school in Brighton, emphasizing its university and public school staff, secured testimonials from many leading English Jews.[21] Schools and press served each other's interests. Jewish newspapers rewarded the education trade, which produced so much advertising revenue, with regular coverage of prizes won, scholarships achieved, or other newsworthy notes.

Originally such secondary institutions were principally for males, but by 1904 Miss Berkowitz's Tivoli House school in Gravesend offered Jewish young ladies what she described as education 'of the highest quality'. For the elite, however, women's education continued to be what it had been for Lily Montagu, private

---

20 One mother complained in 1879 that Jewish schools were too far removed from areas in which increasing numbers of Jews lived. Like mothers then and since, she believed that children should not have to commute so far through cold and inclement weather and that travel by underground rail was unwholesome, 'even for adults'. *JC*, 17 Jan. 1879. In 1904–5, the Jews' Free School had 3,452, and the Jews' Infant Schools 1,763. The Bayswater Jewish Schools (32), South London Free Schools (64), the Spanish and Portuguese Schools (311), the Stepney Jewish Schools (889) and the Westminster Jews' Free School (621) completed the list. In addition the Old Ford and North Bow Jewish classes met three times a week with 350 students, and the various Chedarim and Talmud Torahs together with classes attached to various synagogues for religious instruction rounded out the list of institutions providing Jewish education. Some of the smaller schools found their expenses outran their resources even with the government grants. See, e.g., the annual meeting of the governors of the Westminster Jews' Free School, 23 Jan. 1905. *JC*, 3 Mar. 1905.

21 Hillsboro' emphasized its 'staff of great scholastic ability', 'careful attention to domestic and sanitary arrangements', athletics, and 'judicious regard to physical development'. Jewish youth were obviously to emulate their 'muscular Christian' peers. The Whitechapel Foundation School in Leman Street, on the other hand, offered solid secondary education with no pretensions to elite socialization. Open to 'all religious tenets', it did not compel any boy to attend religious instruction against the wishes of his parents. See the advertisements, e.g., in *JC*, 3 Jan. 1879. Maurice Jacobs, the principal of Ascott House School, recruited the Chief Rabbi, the Haham, and Rabbi Morris Joseph and backed them with D. L. Alexander (Board of Deputies), Arthur Cohen (the Soup Kitchen), Montefiore, Montagu, de Rothschild and Arthur Sassoon, among others. *JC*, 24 Feb. 1905.

schools to the age of fifteen, followed by four years of tutors at home.[22] Fashionable Anglo-Jewish wives, for their part, combined self-interest with educational philanthropy. They created a Domestic Training Home that would furnish education and moral guidance for poor Jewish girls and, incidentally, provide privileged Jewry with a supply of trained servant girls. Jewish girls, however, displayed little interest in the home. More and more girls sought to enter the rapidly growing world of clerical work. Pitman's Metropolitan School in Southampton Row, among others, offered its complete commercial curriculum for the swelling number of Jewish would-be white-collar workers. Pitman's, moreover, displayed a keener sense of who was employing whom. Popular evening classes at reduced rates trained students who had already taken their regular courses for the civil service.[23]

The two great universities had abolished their last formal discriminatory tests against Jews by 1880. Barriers had fallen or soon tumbled at prestigious schools. Certainly Anglo-Jewry had little cause for complaint. The great public schools, always socializing grounds in merging the plutocracy and the aristocracy, increasingly drew the children of exotic elites both at home and abroad to their nourishing bosoms. Sir Samuel Montagu, acting for the community, negotiated arrangements for Jewish boys to be exempted from compulsory chapel at St Paul's School in 1882. Cheltenham had a Jewish house, Clifton special provisions for Jewish students. Professor Israel Gollancz developed an elaborate programme of Jewish secular and religious instruction at Harrow. Anthony de Rothschild was head boy at Harrow in 1905, a mark of the degree to which Anglo-Jewry's leaders had come to mutually comfortable terms with British elite culture.

Both Oxford and Cambridge had synagogues to serve their students before the end of the century. That may have comforted parents more than students. Herbert Samuel escaped his rigid Orthodox upbringing at Balliol College, Oxford, and Edwin Montagu fled as far from the Jewish community as he could when attending Trinity College, Cambridge. Westminster School absorbed substantial numbers of the more recently arrived West Enders. St Paul's School, which had responded earlier to complaints about compulsory chapel attendance, quickly accommodated Jewish unease about proposed Saturday sports programmes in 1901. Headmaster Randall of Charterhouse, however, told the Board of Deputies that parents of boys attending his school were forewarned about compulsory chapel and that he was strongly opposed to 'segregating' Jewish boys. Sir Philip Magnus undertook the private negotiation of a compromise.[24] By the late nineteenth century, Jews slid easily and comfortably into Britain's class-tracked educational system.

22 E. M. Umansky, 'Lily H. Montagu and the Development of Liberal Judaism in England', doctoral dissertation, Columbia University, 1968, pp 61–2. Tivoli House, among others, advertised regularly in the *Jewish Chronicle* from the mid-1880s.

23 *JC*, 6, 20 Jan., 15 Sept. 1905.

24 H. S. Q. Henriques, 'Jews and Education in England', confidential report for the law and parliamentary committee [1901], BDBJ C 11/2/14. The Governors of St Paul's School actually wanted to give the boys more opportunity to play organized games and, in an effort to accommodate, offered Scripture as the subject for Saturday morning work. Law and parliamentary committee, 3 Dec. 1903, BDBJ C 13/1/5. A *Jewish Chronicle* leading article drew attention to Roman Catholic distress over quest for education that guaranteed social status at the price of compromising their religious integrity. It warned that Jews must be equally aware of the problem. *JC*, 6 Oct. 1905. For Charterhouse, see the copies of the July-August 1902 correspondence between Dr G. H. Randall and Alexander incorporated into the minutes and BDBJ minute book, 18 June 1902, 15 Feb. 1903. Harrow dealt with the issue of segregation by closing Jewish House in 1903 but preserving and defining the special rights, liberties and obligations of Jewish boys.

In centres of Jewish population, the growing Jewish community was far outrunning the capacity of Jewish-sponsored schools. Jewish children, particularly immigrants' children, depended upon other schools. Some were denominational Christian schools, but most attended the more than a hundred local elementary schools run, first, by the London School Board, then by the London County Council Education Committee. The early cultural heroes of the East End – Selig Brodetsky or Israel Zangwill, for instance – emerged from the nurturing womb of the Jews' Free School. Between the 1890s and the First World War, an elaborate system of scholarships grew up, enabling poor but clever children to secure free places in secondary, technical and higher education. Of some 2,399 children, for instance, who received Technical Education Board and London County Council grants at eleven plus in schools of the borough of Tower Hamlets, Irving Osborne estimates, using the rather dangerous test of 'Jewish-sounding names', that 1,063 (44 per cent) could have been Jewish.[25] Many, moreover, would have been competing at schools in which overt or veiled anti-Semitism, usually disguised as hostility to aliens, made even attempting to secure a grant almost as difficult as succeeding.

Education stood high among Anglo-Jewry's commitments at least in part because it served as one of the best weapons in the arsenal of socialization and community management.[26] More than three-quarters of the more than 25,000 Jewish pupils in East End elementary schools attended London Board schools or Christian 'National' schools by the beginning of the twentieth century. The overwhelming majority (almost 85 per cent) attended 'Jewish' board schools or Jewish voluntary schools. Anglo-Jewry had ultimately managed, in fact, to shift the burden for educating seven out of every ten East End Jewish children in a 'Jewish' environment on to the payer of rates or taxes. Board schools found themselves forced to adapt to the social reality of their location. The first board school erected in the Jewish quarter, for instance, was at Old Castle Street. 'The Christian system' it employed for some years proved a failure. The school could not be filled. After appointing a Jewish headmaster and adapting itself to the community, school places were not only oversubscribed but Old Castle Street invariably drew high commendations from school inspectors. Adaptation was far more rapid after that. By the first years of the twentieth century, board schools in Whitechapel were overwhelmingly Jewish, those of St George's-in-the-East were rapidly becoming Jewish, and the process was repeating itself in Mile End, and even reaching as far as Bow. Jewish parents generally preferred Jewish voluntary schools when space was available, but in 1902, the five purely Jewish voluntary schools in East London were full with their 6,180 pupils. Sixteen board schools were also 'practically Jewish'. That meant the Jewish holidays were observed and details of curriculum and conduct were adapted

---

25 I. Osborne, 'Achievers of the Ghetto', in Newman (ed.), *Jewish East End*, 163–72.

26 Critics, as critics will, contended that the board moved with too fine a sense of money spent and too little a sense of need. John Simon, for instance, felt that far too little attention was paid to South London, where the board simply increased the number of students to more than 14,000 while cutting the number of teachers to less than 240. The majority of the board, he continued, posing as champions of a religion that puts cleanliness next to Godliness, will not allocate a trivial amount for soap and water. Jewish schools were filthy and overcrowded. Proclaiming themselves a religion that feeds the hungry, they refuse to provide school breakfasts. 'The Jews', MS Simon 107, f 3, in the Bodleian Library, Oxford.

'to suit the wishes of Jews'. Those sixteen board schools had over 15,000 pupils. In six other East London board schools, another 2,600 Jewish students attended in numbers ranging from nearly 60 per cent of the school to less than ten per cent. Anglo-Jewry's principal concern for these children was to ascertain that they received adequate religious instruction. More than 1,600 Jewish children even attended Christian 'National schools' in the area, being almost two-thirds of the pupils attending St Stephen's, Spitalfields.[27]

While Jewish children had excellent records in those county council schools in which they represented a majority of the students, they felt or were made to feel uncomfortable in those in which they were a minority. Children responded with truancy. Anglo-Jewry sought to encourage school managers to display understanding and, where necessary, to relax their code.[28] Problem children in overwhelmingly Jewish schools, on the other hand, were taken firmly in hand. When the headmistress of the Deal Street school in the East End reported a student 'to have contracted dirty and thieving habits and to be untruthful', a committee of the Board of Deputies resolved to interview her to see if he could be charged for committal to the Hayes Industrial School, the Jewish community's reform school for boys.[29]

Anglo-Jewry's stratified educational system lacked internal flexibility. The child, when 'tracked', was also, to some degree, 'trapped'. To deal with rare anomalies, the Education Aid Committee, founded in 1898, functioned as a somewhat capricious deus ex machina 'to assist embryo genius to mount to the top of the ladder, not to drag mediocrity laboriously up a few rungs'. With each award came elite supervision. A member of the committee or a member of the Maccabæans, the club which had sponsored the organization, was appointed 'guardian' of the recipient, for 'in this way a controlling and guiding influence is exercised which is of even greater value than the money grant.' The committee had no difficulty in finding deserving cases. Communal hearts glowed about the boy violinist who, barred from conservatory training in Russia, had paid his way across Europe to London by performing. There he supported himself by giving violin lessons at one shilling an hour. The committee, satisfied that the lad had serious talent, undertook his musical education. Who could fail to admire the daughter of a shoemaker 'whose gift for modelling struggled for expression'. She made slippers by day and created designs by night. She also won first prize in an art competition of the London Board Schools in 1903. A mere £15 answered her professional training needs. Thirteen would-be geniuses applied in 1904, of whom four were considered favourably. A son of poor parents who had won £70 in open competition to attend

27 Jewish children represented more than a quarter of the more than 98,000 pupils in East London. Of those Jewish children, a trifle more than one-third were born abroad. Evidence of S. Mather, division superintendent of Tower Hamlets division of the London School Board, to the Royal Commission on Alien Immigration (RCAI), 11 Dec. 1902.

28 Law and parliamentary committee, 12 Jan. 1909, BDBJ C 13/1/6. 'A good schoolmaster,' commented Sir Joshua Fitch to the Maccabæans at their self-congratulatory education night dinner in 1898, 'is one who possesses ample knowledge, good teaching, power, sympathy with every form of childish weakness, except sin, and faith in the possibilities even of the humblest scholars.' *JC*, 4 Feb. 1898.

29 The Glass Case. Law and parliamentary committee, 24 July 1907. The committee was quick to defend Jewish students whose cases were mishandled and quite prepared to carry matters to the national Board of Education. See, the case of the Jewish student transferred from East Ham Technical College to a LCC school. Law and parliamentary committee, 5 Dec. 1907, BDBJ C 13/1/6.

Balliol was awarded a supplementary grant to maintain himself. The daughter of a capmaker displayed great promise as a violinist. Educated at a foreign conservatory at the expense of a Christian friend, she returned to London only to be so caught up in her family's poverty that she could not arrange a concert début. Once she was accepted as a student for a year by one of the most distinguished violinists of the day, the committee raised the funds to maintain her 'in a suitable home' for eighteen months.[30]

CARING FOR UNDERPRIVILEGED STUDENTS

Support for genius was all very fine, but the community confronted a far more demanding and less tractable problem. Anglo-Jewry had to provide, in the most literal sense, for the poorest members of its community and do so without the gratification of immediate return. What child could attend school in rags? As late as 1910, a hundred pairs of shoes had to be distributed to the poorest of the slightly more than five hundred students at the Westminster Jews' Free School.[31] Committed ladies, mobilized through synagogue auxiliaries and individual school committees, distributed hand-me-down clothing to children who would otherwise be unable to attend. Beyond this elementary problem of appearance lay the simple issue that the East End had hungry children who were unlikely to be able to consume knowledge if they lacked food.

The London School Board, although slow to act, was among the first in England to address the problem of feeding school children. A school board inquiry of 1889 produced the London Schools' Dinners Association. That organization, tight-fisted as charitable providers tended to be in Victorian Britain, proved to be a frugal yet an effective enterprise. Subsequently, the school board created a committee, with representatives from itself, the various schools, and the several municipal and private relief agencies involved, to approve and process requests, ascertaining that each case of need had been validated. Even when the London County Council assumed the powers of the old London School Board, the committee continued to function, supervising the work of committees at individual schools. Those committees investigated the needy cases, prepared lists of underfed children, and arranged for their dinners at school.

Independent schools, of course, had to make their own arrangements before the Education Act of 1903 (which empowered the London County Council to administer the schools within its jurisdiction). The Chief Rabbi's wife organized the Jewish Penny Dinners Society which provided Jewish schools a kosher noonday meal for impecunious Jewish schoolchildren. Women managed Penny Dinners, just as they staffed the various school and synagogue organizations, which furnished

---

30 The Maccabæans began work on the project in February 1895, launching the organization the following year. Education Aid Society, *Seventh Annual Report* (London, 1905); *JC*, 24 Dec. 1897, 28 Apr. 1905. The Education Aid Society Papers are in AJ/35, in the Mocatta Library.

31 The school, finding the work of selecting children for various benefits too overwhelming for its volunteer care committee, employed a paid visiting social worker to conduct investigations. Westminster Jews' Free School, annual meeting, 23 Jan. 1911. *JC*, 3 Mar. 1911.

poor children with clothing and shoes.[32] Demand immediately pressed hard on needs, and women adopted the traditional philosophy of assistance. Each individual was to be as self-sufficient as possible. Wherever possible, children paid for themselves and, through penny contributions, for some less fortunate fellow student. While training in philanthropic responsibility began at home, the Penny Dinners saw that children continued to learn it at school. The sense of status and place was reinforced over and over again for giver and recipient. Underfed children received most of their meals free but the rules of the Jewish Board of Guardians animated all charities. Free meals were dispensed, Mrs Adler assured anxious donors concerned about profligacy, only after personal investigation of the condition of the families or 'on recommendations of ladies who work in the East End'.[33]

Whatever the niggling economies and however severe the investigations, Penny Dinners could not feed all the hungry Jewish schoolchildren from its own resources. Only after January 1905 did a London County Council subvention make it possible for what shortly became the Jewish Children's Dinners Association to feed the necessitous.[34] Ironically, just when London County Council rescued Penny Dinners, the *Jewish Chronicle* was proclaiming,

> as far as the Jewish underfed children are concerned there is absolutely no call for State Intervention – a course which many enquirers into the general question of the feeding of school children have been urging of late.[35]

The editorial could not have been more incorrect. State intervention alone made it work. School meals were provided by statute in 1906. Where Jewish charities served some 87,750 meals in 1905, London taxpayers made it possible for Jewish philanthropy to provide over 377,275 in 1910. Tagging along behind school meals came clothing, bundles for the deserving being generated by synagogue ladies' auxiliaries and the workrooms of the Jewish Board of Guardians. The Jewish Schools' boot fund carefully examined the shoeless, preferring to distribute its 2,000 pairs annually to orphans or children of the permanently disabled.[36]

32 Women of the Adler, Meyer and Jacob families always figured among the officers, but the trustees included Birnbaum, Waley, Harris, Mocatta, Löwy, Clifford and Hass, a representative Who's Who among the names in Jewish philanthropy. As was true of Victorian women's charities in general, the donation and subscription lists show substantially smaller individual gifts, usually ranging from two guineas downwards. See, F. Prochaska, *Women and Philanthropy*.

33 *JC*, 31 Mar. 1905. Of slightly more than £650 received in 1901, over £100 was paid in by the children themselves. Approximately 42 per cent of the more than 47,000 meals served that year were free dinners to underfed children. Jewish Children's Penny Dinners, *Annual Report for 1901* (London, 1902).

34 The LCC committee distributed funds from what by then had come to be called the Referee Children's Free Breakfast and Dinner Fund.

35 'The feeding of school children', *JC*, 28 Jan. 1905 found 5.25 per cent of Jewish as compared to 5.32 per cent of non-Jewish children 'underfed'. The number of free meals represented 50 per cent of the total. Most of the balance went into partial subsidies to sliding scales of contributions. Jewish Children's Dinners Association, *Annual Report for 1910* (London, 1911). The work of the Children's Dinners Association was replicated for outlying Jewish schools by ladies' committees attached to their governing bodies. Bayswater, for instance, provided over a hundred meals five days a week, but all the children contributed something on a scale from one penny to eightpence.

36 The distribution figures for 1897 and 1900 were almost identical. Jews' Free School had its own boot and clothing committee and was not included in the totals. Infants' Schools, not surprisingly, consumed the most (360), followed by the Gravel Lane and Settle Street board schools (180 each). Jewish Schools' Boot Fund, *Ninth Annual Report (1897)* (London, 1898), *12th Annual Report (1900)* (London, 1901).

A Jewish branch of the Children's Happy Evenings Association, Jews' Free School happy evenings, allowed individual patrons an opportunity either themselves or through hired performers to provide special entertainments for the schoolchildren and opened school facilities for occasional supervised recreation. After some half a dozen years' experience, Nettie Adler could report in 1897:

> There has been a great improvement in the orderly demeanour of the children when assembling for marching purposes in the Hall, and the arrangement of boys into small squads, each headed by a helper, has been found to work satisfactorily. The 'quiet rooms' continue to give much pleasure: painting, bead work, and games of draughts and dominoes always attract a large number of children. Several ladies are present at every gathering, and by undertaking the same branch of play at each evening, are thus able to gain the sympathy and friendship of the children in their respective rooms. During the summer months the playground is a source of unending pleasure, and, as usual, football reigns supreme favourite among the boys.

Special monthly entertainments that year included a conjuror in April, three magic lantern shows, and 'an excellent nigger representation' after which buns, chocolate and oranges were distributed to the children.[37] The concept of wholesomeness, the reinforcing qualities of nature, and a vision of a world beyond the overcrowding and grime of East London came through the Jewish branch of the Children's Country Holiday Fund. When the programme started in 1889, 105 children were sent to the seaside. Volunteers furnished suitable resort facilities, provided kosher food, and oversaw the fortnight's holiday. Almost 1,400 a year – invariably more than the budgeted 1,000 – were dispatched by the turn of the century. Children saved their own farthings and halfpennies. Families scrimped to round out needed contributions, whether sixpence or three shillings. Once again a useful social lesson, the virtues of kindliness and unselfishness within the family, had been taught.[38]

For children below school age, still other provisions had to be made. East End working mothers and their infants were encouraged to use the Day Nursery for Jewish Infants in Whitechapel. One of Lady Rothschild's benefactions, the facilities were, conveniently enough, owned by the London Hospital. A doctor and nurse oversaw the medical conditions of mothers and their infants. Use of the crèche brought the mother and her family under a measure of community oversight and supervision. Volunteer visitors periodically inspected the homes from which infants came. The staff of the London Hospital suggested a fumigation chamber for the children's clothes. Nursing mothers were always provided with facilities in which to

---

37 1896 had been a peak year. Seventeen happy evenings served 4,770 children for the trivial cost to the organization of £28 15s. That allowed the Jews' Free School Happy Evenings to provide contributions to four nearby board schools for festivities of their own. Subsequent years delivered fewer entertainments but continued, as the frugal executive reported, to serve the children at a cost between 1.3 and 1.8d per child per occasion, 'fourteen happy evenings for 3,920 children and ten entertainments in 1897, fifteen for 4,335 in 1898, and thirteen in 1900 for 3,710'. Jews' Free School Happy Evenings, *Sixth Annual Report, 1896*; *Seventh Annual Report, 1897, Eighth Annual Report, 1898*; *Tenth Annual Report, 1900*. (London, 1898–1901); *JC*, 15 Jan. 1897, 21 Jan. 1898, 13 Jan. 1899, 18 Jan. 1901.

38 *JC*, 29 May 1896, 5 Nov. 1897, 3, 10 June 1898.

feed their children. The nursery, however, found that so many mothers arrived in the evening 'not in fit condition', that by 1910 they were finally provided with meals and an opportunity to rest before nursing their young. Even here, the rule of self-help still obtained. Mothers had to bear part of the cost themselves. The balance came from private donations. The Jewish Crêche proved to be a subtle index of the state of the economy. Full employment meant strained facilities. In the economic recovery of 1904, for instance, when work was plentiful, over 900 mothers used the facilities in July. As more young women moved into the workforce, demand accelerated. The 2,200 mothers who used the facilities in 1904 swelled to 6,550 in 1910. The crêche added a kindergarten to handle the slightly older children.

Community oversight and supervision began early and, through infants, reached into an ever-widening circle of working-class families. The results were, from the point of view of the community and inspecting medical officers of health, truly remarkable. The health of the children and their physical well-being testified to the nursery's success. Infant mortality declined. The health of mothers improved. In an age increasingly conscious of the problem of physical deterioration, Anglo-Jewry had addressed the problem and, incidentally, begun to shape the lives of its community.[39]

JEWS' COLLEGE

Religious ministration, so important to Jewish socialization, depended on a supply of trained clergy and a well-articulated system of Jewish education to serve both Jewish voluntary and board schools. Anglo-Jewry had an ambiguous relationship with its principal rabbinical training institution. Created in 1856, Jews' College had a history of ups and downs, with far too many of the latter. Professor Israel Gollancz was determined to understand why English Jews, with their commitment to learning and veneration for their religious institutions, could not create a major and respected centre. Jews' College was brought to Tavistock Square and associated with University College, London. Neither a central location nor attachment to a major centre of learning produced an institution such as American Jews had created with the New York seminary half a century before. The explanation was immediately at hand. Abler English Jews avoided the ministry. The children of the wealthy and more powerful rarely even considered it. Most English-trained ministers lacked status. Ministers, even when granted the title of rabbi, were often regarded as cultural decorations, a kind of synagogue status symbol. When seeking a minister for a major synagogue, Anglo-Jewry was likely to recruit a distinguished veteran or an exciting European.[40] Lay leaders, not ministers or rabbis, dominated congregations and their business. Intellectuals puzzling about the English ministry understood one reality. Forces of demand conditioned supply. The life of the

---

39 Annual meeting, Jewish Day Nursery, April 1905; Annual meeting, Jewish Day Nursery, May 1911. *JC*, 7 Apr. 1905, 19 May 1911.

40 A practice Anglo-Jewry continued well through the twentieth century. One case in point would be that distinguished scholar, Dr Alexander Altmann, who fled from Berlin to become Communal Rabbi of Manchester before moving on to the United States and a professorship at Brandeis University.

minister at a provincial synagogue for a paltry £100 annual salary with little prospect of promotion to the great world of the United Synagogue was hardly an incentive. The minister of a small provincial congregation, Nathan L. Cohen, reminded Jews' College students

> must needs be almost an expurgated edition of human nature. He must cultivate patience, tact, invariably a fair judgement, and, above all, that very difficult attribute, a true sense of proportion, and always imperturbable courtesy in the face even of unwelcome opposition. . . . He must abstain, as a rule, from acute, at least, secular controversies, under the danger of losing his influence for good with those from whom he may differ. His part . . . was to conduct the service, and to attend to religious requirements, to teach and train the young, to visit and comfort the suffering and those in trouble, to evoke high conduct and to do religious observance, and he is to do all this mainly by periodical sermons warranted not to exceed twenty minutes![41]

Such a rabbinate would never attract the ambitious or privileged.

The sociology of the English ministry being what it was, Anglo-Jewry compounded the difficulty by maintaining three rabbinical training institutions: Jews' College, Arias College in Hampshire, and the Sephardi Montefiore College in Ramsgate. Arias College could not recruit students, and Montefiore College, weak enough under the best of circumstances, was wracked by scandal and controversy. Even closing Arias College and Montefiore College failed to go to the heart of the matter. Jews' College still recruited 'misfits', 'incurables' and 'tradesmen' – scarcely the building blocks for a powerful clerical order. Not until 1902 did Chief Rabbi Adler finally define the requirements of the rabbinate in such a way that courses at Jews' College and University College could make a prospective 'minister' eligible for the title of 'rabbi'.

That did little to resolve the problem. What was Jews' College to do? Its options seemed limited. Its future held the prospect of being little more than a ghetto within the University of London system. Sir Adolph Tuck, who single-handedly kept Jews' College afloat in the early twentieth century, had to exert all his influence to prevent the United Synagogue, as an austerity measure, from slashing the trivial subsidy it did provide. Hobbled financially, unable to recruit strong candidates, Jews' College could not move beyond its limitations. An accumulated deficit and cheeseparing economies in teaching and bursaries made conditions at Jews' College almost unbearable by 1910.

Every interested party had ambitions for Jews' College, but those dreams ran in very different directions. Where one suggested making it a more serious intellectual enterprise through the addition of Arabic and Assyriology, another contended that only the addition of serious social studies to the curriculum could equip a twentieth-century rabbi with the tools needed to carry out his ministry. Intellectuals debated with righteous, single-minded passion. Not one of them understood that neither tinkering with the curriculum nor demanding respect for 'the ecclesiastical

---

41　Prize-giving, Jews' College, 3 May 1903. *JC*, 8 May 1903.

order' (itself an interesting use of Christian rhetoric) addressed the issue. The fewer than twenty students enrolled were symbols of the crisis at Jews' College.[42]

THE JEWISH RELIGIOUS EDUCATION BOARD

The formal task for bringing Jewish education to Jewish children ultimately fell to the Jewish Religious Education Board, established in 1894. Given the commitment of Anglo-Jewry to anglicization and the preservation of Jewishness, nothing should have commanded more support from the community leaders. Designed to encompass the broadest possible consensus of leading Jews, the board became, as a result, a battleground between the dogmatic and increasingly testy Sir Samuel Montagu and almost everybody else. Montagu considered that Claude Montefiore and Israel Abrahams, members of the board of governors, 'had openly denied the fundamental principles of Judaism'.[43] Montagu had both a personal and an ideological agenda in his dispute. The opportunity to score leadership points against Montefiore may have pleased Montagu. Montagu also despised the Liberal Judaism of Montefiore and that of his own daughter. Montagu also could not have failed to be aware of the emotional interest his daughter Lily had in Montefiore and the fact that when Montefiore remarried, he preferred someone else.

Montagu also felt betrayed in the institutional shuffle. He had passed the Association for the Diffusion of Religious Knowledge over to Chief Rabbi Adler to be reorganized as the Religious Education Board. Having surrendered control, he now saw the organization 'in the hands' of individuals whose doctrinal views he regarded as dangerous and detestable – of those scarcely fit to choose what should be taught to the young. Montagu's quarrel, at bottom, was spiritual. He refused, for the rest of his life, to allow his Federation of Synagogues to support any more latitudinarian conception of the true faith. Nor was Montagu alone. Other critics touched upon utility rather than religion and warned that the Jewish Religious Education Board was a decade ahead of its most important constituency.

> There is the large section which clings with all of the passion of orientals to the narrowed Judaism of the worst of Ghettos; there is another which has been overwhelmed by the spirit of freedom of this country; there is a large intermediate body composed of those who were liberal even in the Ghetto, and of those whose inherited affections have not been wholly neutralised by the influences of their surroundings.[44]

---

42 Israel Gollancz held a well-publicized symposium in November 1905 which produced a welter of complaints and an intellectuals' tower of babel. The simple fact was that the community would not support the cost of a major institution, and the rabbinate never, during this period, attracted the new aspirant applicants who might have reversed this. See, *inter alia, JC*, 12 May, 1 Dec. 1905 and then compare *JC*, 3 Mar, 2 June 1911. Necessary centralization had at least begun. Montefiore College in Ramsgate had not, in spite of Gaster's ambitions, become a great centre for rabbinical training, and simply transferred £1,000 of its income to Jews' College each year. Arias College, in the bucolic bliss of Hampshire, closed in 1905 for lack of funds. *JC*, 22 Sept. 1905.

43 *JC*, 3 Mar. 1905.

44 Herschkowitz to the editor, *JC*, 14 Aug. 1896.

Above all the board needed information. East End Jewish children were accustomed to long study and Talmudic discussion and highly suspicious of the ways of anglicized Jews. On the one hand, this opened entrepreneurial opportunities. Any *melamed*, observed one East End social worker, newly arrived from Poland can set up his religious school in a tiny room and draw fees from as many pupils as he can cram in. Alien parents place confidence in them, for they have a reputation for piety and knowledge and that 'certain odour of sanctity that goes with that reputation, but neither in their appearance, nor in their manners, nor in their methods of teaching do they seem to possess those attributes we deem needful in the schoolmaster.' Some of these Chedarim were of considerable quality, the Brick Lane Talmud Torah, for instance, handling a thousand boys between five and thirteen for which the local community had raised £6,000. Chief Rabbi Adler had nothing but scorn for a system of religious education which had not changed in two hundred years. On the other hand, as more than one critic pointed out, Jewish voluntary school Hebrew religious instruction was so deficient that 70 per cent of students at the Jews' Free School also attended a Talmud Torah or Chedar after school. United Synagogue religion classes were often a 'disgraceful subterfuge', offering a premium to parents to have their children inadequately instructed.[45]

While the Jewish Board of Guardians led those institutions ministering to the physical needs of those of the Jewish community in want, the Jewish Religious Education Board assumed responsibility for the spiritual education of their co-religionists, particularly those with needs beyond the working of the synagogues. If Montagu took himself out, Sir Joseph Sebag-Montefiore brought the Spanish and Portuguese in. Sir Philip Magnus undertook the supervision of teacher training, although Claude G. Montefiore personally contributed most of the fees.[46] The Religious Education Board confronted communal ignorance, which led parents to leave their children in board school Christian religious classes. Montagu was outraged that Jewish children occasionally won the hymn-singing awards. The Federation of Synagogues distributed ten thousand handbills in Yiddish and English among its members in 1897 calling attention to the Cowper–Temple 'conscience clause' in the Education Acts that allowed parents to withdraw their children from denominational instruction to which they objected and explaining how Jewish parents should use it. Belatedly, the Chief Rabbi followed suit.[47]

The Association for the Diffusion of Religious Knowledge had earlier addressed this problem in a somewhat scattergun way. The omnipresent Nathan Joseph helped to launch its first school in 1876 in the premises of the Old Castle Street board school, but results were, to say the least, uneven. Only ten per cent of the five hundred Jewish students attending joined Hebrew and religion classes. By 1878, a committee had purchased the site for the Stepney Jewish Schools, bringing forth substantial contributions from most of the leading figures in Anglo-Jewry, but

45 See, particularly, Mrs N. S. Joseph's paper, 'The Chedarim', and the discussions in the conference on Jewish elementary education, 26 June 1898. Special supplement, *JC*, 1 July 1898.

46 Jewish Religious Education Board, *Eighth Annual Report. 1902* (London, [1903]), 35. The JREB initially established a 6,000 student target. Where 4,555 students received subsidized instruction under the old Association for the Diffusion of Religious Knowledge in 1893, 5,100 attended JREB classes in 1895. JREB, *First Annual Report, 1895* (London, 1896).

47 *JC*, 5 Nov., 3 Dec. 1897.

enhanced effort produced no more than three hundred students attending regularly. Sabbath schools, yet another area touched by Lady de Rothschild's charity, supplemented the association's efforts. Lady de Rothschild inaugurated the first with Mrs Horatio Montefiore and Mrs Isidore Harris in 1857. To meet metropolitan needs, the Association for the Diffusion of Religious Knowledge later extended the programme, but it was merely teaching more to those already receiving instruction. Almost all children attending their schools came from such institutions as the Jews' Free School. Other improvised religious schools were not particularly successful, although the path of original Jewish migration out of the East End can be tracked by institutions established and managed by committed women from Southwark, to the West End, to North London, and Hackney.[48]

The Association for the Diffusion of Religious Knowledge could not adapt itself to the dramatically expanding needs of Jewish children. The association may also have suffered from the public stands of its own leadership. Sir Samuel Montagu's dogmatic positions on a variety of issues may or may not have precipitated the move from David L. Alexander of the Board of Deputies and the executive committee of the United Synagogue to redefine and reorganize the institution, but they certainly helped. Most Jewish children attended board schools by the early 1890s in spite of all efforts to expand Jewish voluntary schools. The Jewish Religious Education Board attempted to step into this widening gap, coordinating its activities with both the state and independent schools. It institutionalized the religious classes of Jewish children attending secular schools and, at the time same, developed a programme to train teachers for its religious classes.[49]

In spite of substantial initial funding from the organized synagogues, other contributions proved difficult to secure. The Education Act of 1902 finally brought home to the community the extent of its needs and responsibilities. That statute also made possible the diversion of resources that, prior to state funding, would have gone to the various Jewish independent schools. Administering the distribution of funds under the Act of 1902, moreover, gave the Jewish Voluntary Schools Association increased importance. In cooperation with each other, the association

48 *JC*, 21, 18 Feb. 1879. The Old Castle Street school was located near the present City of London Polytechnic. *JC*, 3 Jan. 1879. For the Stepney site, N. M. Rothschild and Sons led the list with £250, a sum matched by a daughter of Baroness Mayer de Rothschild. £950 was in hand before the Chief Rabbi launched his public appeal. *JC*, 17 Jan 1879. See also H. M. Adler, *The Cry of Our Board School Children: A Sermon Preached at the St. John's Wood Synagogue* (Dec 1, 1894) (London, 1894).

49 Board school children were presumed to need Hebrew religious instruction, but, as Mrs Nathan Joseph reminded the community in 1898, 70 per cent of Jews' Free School students received such inadequate instruction that their parents sent them to a Talmud Torah or Chedarim after school. *JC*, 1, 8 July 1898. The board began with the 300 oldest of the almost 450 Jewish children attending the Baker Street school in Stepney. The very young would presumably be brought into tuition as they advanced in the school. Sir Philip Magnus organized the committee to train Jewish teachers. Most of his recruits were men from King's College, London, but one came from Yorkshire College (shortly to become Leeds University), and two women were from Cambridge. Jewish Religious Education Board, *First Annual Report* (London, 1895) in the Mocatta Library. The teacher training committee student books are in AJ/89/2 (Men, 1894–1908) and AJ/89/3 (Ladies, 1898–1920) in the Mocatta Library. The Hebrew Teachers' Association was restive with Anglo-Jewish constraints, arguing in 1898, for example, that Talmud could not be taught without the help of Yiddish and that the language of instruction should be left to the individual teachers. That was not acceptable and helps to explain why Sir Philip Magnus and others went to such care in the selection and training of teachers under JREB auspices. *JC*, 19 Aug. 1898.

and the Religious Education Board were able to develop uniform communal standards about what 'adequate' religious education should be. It still all cost the community money. A festival dinner in 1902 raised £12,000, but that was gone within three years. By 1905, the Religious Education Board undertook a three-year capital campaign to raise £16,000.[50]

The *Jewish Year Book* reported over 30,000 Jewish pupils in London in 1905, of whom 8,000 attended the Jewish schools. More than 22,000 attended London County Council schools. Fifteen of these lay in the borough of Stepney. Three schools in the East End had 1,100 Jewish students but lacked any provision for their religious instruction.

> The managers speak in terms of high praise of their intelligence, of the regularity of their attendance, and of the rapidity with which the foreign children acquire a knowledge of the vernacular and adopt English manners. A portion of these scholars acquire some knowledge of Hebrew in the various Talmud Torah Classes and Chedarim in the East End. But the religious training there given is inadequate.[51]

By 1910, the number of Jewish children receiving elementary education in the metropolis had, the *Jewish Year Book* reported, risen to almost 37,500, although the number attending all forms of religious education declined from almost 24,000 to 22,000. An estimated 5,000 received private tuition, but this left 10,500 Jewish children for whom no religious educational provision had been made. That estimated gap was never closed.[52]

Chief Rabbi Adler reminded the community that they had appreciated what was at stake when the conversionists battened on the Jewish poor and the recent immigrants in the East End. Although the conversionists still nibbled around the edges, they were no longer the great problem of the past. The community had repulsed them. The spiritual needs of the poor remained. Their religious hunger must be fed as surely as the victims of poverty demanded help from the Jewish Board of Guardians. Winter was a season of physical and spiritual privation. The community must answer both calls.[53] Once £10,000 had actually been pledged through private solicitations, the special appeal could, wheeling out the big guns of the community, count on a fund-raising banquet to raise the other £6,000. For those indifferent to the religious appeal, the leadership spoke with unconscious candour.

> Quite apart, too, from the religious aspect of the matter, we must have some regard for the terrible moral dangers that abound in this 'modern Babylon,' and against which the Board, by withdrawing children from the streets, and imparting to them religious instruction, wages a useful war.

50 The JREB expended more than £5,000 per year by 1904. With the dispersion of the London Jewish community, new classes were needed in new schools, but the demands of the East End already overtaxed resources.

51 From time to time the JREB appointed a subcommittee 'to look into the system of religious and moral teaching pursued' that, after much soul-searching, would report itself satisfied. See, e.g., JREB, *Eleventh Annual Report, 1905* (London, [1906]), 16.

52 I. Harris (ed.), *Jewish Year Book for 5666* (London, 1905); *Jewish Chronicle Year Book for 5672* (London, 1911).

53 Sermon, New West End Synagogue, 28 Jan. 1905. *JC*, 3 Feb. 1905.

Claude G. Montefiore, Adler reminded his audience, had already underscored the importance of that moral instruction for Jews as a minority within British society.

> Every Jewish scamp, every Jewish money-lender, every Jewish cheat, does more harm to Judaism than a Christian scamp, a Christian money-lender, a Christian cheat does harm to Christianity. Contrawise every Jewish hero does us more good. This is the necessary condition of minorities. So may you recognise and understand your importance and your responsibilities.[54]

Estimates varied. No one knew, first of all, exactly how many Jewish children there were or how many were receiving religious instruction. The same child, for instance, would be counted separately for each place in which he or she attended religious class or Hebrew instruction. Whatever the number, Anglo-Jewry realized that substantial, possibly increasing, numbers were slipping away without any religious instruction whatsoever. Such anxieties, regular fare in the letters column of the *Jewish Chronicle*, helped to inspire triennial crash funding programmes.

Successful drives usually depended on Anglo-Jewish unity. In 1905, Samuel Montagu was more than usually distressed. He felt betrayed, which he translated, as he often did, into a betrayal of Judaism. Just what did 'religious education' for children actually mean? While Montagu took no exception to Mrs N. L. Cohen's *Infants' Bible Reader* or any of the other spiritual pabulum the board served, he was unhappy. Montagu had at one time presided over the Association for the Diffusion of Religious Knowledge, so he was quite certain that he knew what should be taught. When the association was converted into the Religious Education Board, Montagu thought he had communal commitment for strict Orthodox religious education and for generous support of Talmud Torahs. Montagu continued to demand Orthodoxy in religion and berate the board for failing to meet the spiritual needs of three-fifths of London's Jewish children. He refused to enrol his Federation of Synagogues in the great common cause, although the lost £35 subscription mattered little.[55]

While the board refused to be rattled on the issue of dogma – a specious argument since the Chief Rabbi passed on all matters of curriculum and instruction and Haham Gaster had been added to the executive committee in 1898 – it fretted about the 60 per cent of Jewish children who as late as three years after the Act of 1902 still apparently received no formal religious instruction. The formidable Nettie Adler, daughter of the Chief Rabbi and vice president of the board, now sat on the Education Committee of the London County Council, so Jewish views would be effectively heard in the management of London's education. But the board could not serve a wider constituency without expanded resources and consolidating the resources of the several formerly independent Jewish schools. Within five years the Religious Education Board had its own teacher training college and, to its great annoyance, a teachers' association, which demanded that teachers not be demeaned 'in their professional callings as public servants' and that they be properly paid. The board supervision committee rejected the request. Economies were demanded and

---

54 JREB prize-giving, 8 June 1901; *JC* editorial, 13 Jan. 1905. See also, *JC*, 3 Feb., 10 Feb. 1905.

55 Elkan Adler immediately made up the loss, acidly observing, 'Sir Samuel Montagu had grown very scrupulous in his old age. He seems to think "who drives fat oxen should himself be fat." ' The Chief Rabbi, who certainly knew, denied that Montagu had been given any such understanding. *JC*, 10, 17 Mar. 1905.

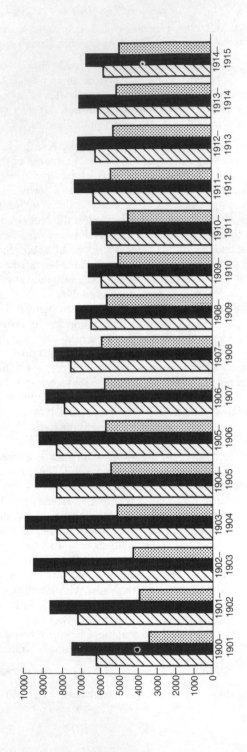

FIGURE 4.1 Jewish Religious Education Board statistics

provided. The number of children taught declined, although the Jewish student population declined very little if at all. Teachers' salaries were cut by 11 per cent in 1909.[56]

By the turn of the century, with its programmes in place, the Religious Education Board never managed to enrol much more than one third of its potential student population. Students actually attending crept briefly over 8,300 in 1904–5, but then began to decline. Of the founders, Ellis Franklin died in 1908. Claude Montefiore and Claude Lousada, instrumental in so much policy and major contributors, resigned the same year. Triennial dinners that usually fell short of their fund-raising goals meant cumulating financial deficits. The board, whose regular income was under £1,700, resisted efforts to establish a system of student fees. Bequests were devoured to meet current expenditure.

Then matters seemed to turn around. The death of Samuel Montagu (then Lord Swaythling) in 1911 saw the Federation rejoin the board. His son, Louis, the second Baron Swaythling, assumed the vice presidency of the Religious Education Board. He hoped to restore peace and harmony within the Jewish establishment. He re-established the Federation subscription and office on the board. His talents were immediately enlisted in the special appeal for £15,000 that spring, but even the Rothschild–Swaythling reunion fell short by almost £2,000. Anglo-Jewry had to wait for demography, the steady decline in the population of Jewish schoolchildren, to catch up with philanthropy. In the course of time it did. St Mary's School closed its doors in 1907, and the London County Council shut down the first 'Jewish' board school, Old Castle Street, at the end of the 1912–13 academic year. The economies achieved by school closings in the old East End heartland, however, were offset by new demands on the frontiers of London Jewish settlement.[57] Meanwhile the Federation recommenced its small subscription, and student enrolments climbed back over 6,000 for three years. Reunion, however, merely camouflaged the inexorable decline. The fact of the matter was that the board had fewer and fewer potential pupils. Statistics of student attendance, moreover, tended to be misleading. An undetermined number of those attending Religious Education Board classes were also enrolled in Jewish parochial schools such as Stepney or Jews' Free, received synagogue language and religious instruction, or were students at East End Chevras or Talmud Torahs.

The Jewish Religious Education Board, however, could take pride in many achievements. To answer its needs, it had subsidized the education of upwards of forty young men and women studying to teach Jewish children at English universities each year. From this trained cadre would come both teachers and community professionals to serve the next generation. The board was also never too poor to be patriotic. When London County Council established a school for Belgian

---

56 JREB, *Sixteenth Annual Report, 1910* (London, [1911]); JREB Teachers' Association, annual meeting, Toynbee Hall, 29 Jan. 1905. *JC*, 3 Feb., 24 Mar. 1911. By 1904, the board had actually outrun its resources. With 9,893 children in class and forty-six men and women being trained by the teachers' training committee, the board found itself forced to turn down all requests for more classes and additional rooms where institutions were already in place, let alone to extend its work in other districts. JREB, *Tenth Annual Report, 1904* (London, [1905]); *JC*, 17 Mar. 1905.

57 JREB, *Thirteenth Annual Report, 1907* (London, [1908]); *Eighteenth Annual Report, 1912* (London, [1913]); *JC*, 24 Feb., 24 Mar., 7 Apr., 12, 26 May, 2, 16 June 1911.

Jewish refugee children in 1914, the Religious Education Board, pleased to find that the boys and girls understood English, undertook their religious instruction.[58] The board, moreover, with the cooperation of the Jewish Study Society, mobilized the scholarly resources of the community to develop syllabi, particularly in Jewish history, that helped to furnish a keener sense, for children and adults, of who and what they were.

58 JREB, *Twenty-first Annual Report. 1915* (London, [1916]), 17–18.

5

Club Life: Moulding Youth
and Shaping Character

YOUTH GROUPS

Anglicization of immigrant and native-born Jewish children proceeded, in the first instance, through their compulsory elementary education. As numbers of Jewish children expanded, that education was increasingly conducted in the state-managed, non-denominational schools. Results were instantaneous, dramatic, and cumulative, feeding back into the Jewish families themselves. Not merely the children but through the children the parents were being instructed. Headmasters testifying before the Royal Commission on Immigration, for instance, spoke without exception about the extraordinary dedication, discipline and achievements of their Jewish pupils. Self-congratulatory testimony might be expected under such circumstances, but the headmasters clearly considered themselves unusually successful.

But what happened when school stopped? How did the community continue to reinforce the process of anglicization while sustaining the Jewishness of its youth? Anglo-Jewry developed a remarkable sensitivity to adolescents. Just down Leman Street from the Jews' Temporary Shelter stood the Jewish Girls' Club, which came to be known as Lady Magnus's Club after its redoubtable founder and president. From 1888 it sought to cultivate the three Rs: religion, refinement, and recreation. East End working girls had evening meetings to be told scripture stories while they did needlework. 'It was,' mused an enthusiastic commentator almost twenty years later, 'a delightful combination of the practical and the ideal.'[1] It was originally called the Jewish Girls' Friendly Society, and every girl joining paid one penny each week, although benevolence provided the bulk of club funds. Volunteer 'ladies' actively assisted the superintendent, reading, singing, and chatting with the girls. From the beginning, an annual country excursion was laid on to expand the horizons of members. 'Everything was done to improve and refine them.' In January 1885, Lady Magnus and the Chief Rabbi's wife instituted tea meetings in Bayswater

1 'The religious side of club life', *JC*, 31 Mar. 1905.

for selected East End girls. For those who could not cope with West End culture shock or could not spare the time from work, volunteer ladies combined the decorum of tea with Bible lessons at Jews' Free School. Finally, in 1888, the tea meetings, sewing classes and Bible study amalgamated in the Jewish Girls' Club. Lady Magnus's Club, like its many imitators, enrolled girls from fourteen to eighteen. The aim of all youth clubs, as Lady Magnus later described it, was

> in the first place to check and not accumulate the sharpening influences of early independence; they are meant to calm all that makes for competition and excitement, and to awaken a sense of pleasure in what is restful and beautiful; to help to worthy thinking rather than to the amassing of information; to direct lagging feet to really profitable paths; they are designed, in short to civilize and to spiritualize rather than to stimulate these keen-witted boys and girls, as, fresh from school discipline, they enter on their university of the streets.[2]

How were those Arnoldian virtues of sweetness and light to be brought to the ill-lit streets of the East End? From the simple beginnings of scripture and sewing, a steadily expanding range of useful and purposeful services came through club auspices. Sunday teas, sewing, cooking and 'musical drill' were offered every evening.

While carefully avoiding patronage or preaching, religious instruction continued to be the preoccupation of the carefully managed executive committee, but classes expanded from plain and fancy needlework into other 'practical' domestic arts. Cooking was particularly favoured. Quite as important, however, was instruction in English and lectures on contemporary topics. A night class in French started in November 1890. The library grew to the delight of the managers and the pleasure of intellectually curious working girls. A savings bank, instituted to inculcate habits of thrift, was preaching to the converted. By the early twentieth century, the active members among these East End working girls – tailoresses, typists, cigarette makers, shop assistants, buttonhole-makers and bookkeepers – were accumulating an average of more than one pound each per year. Exercises, gymnastics and drill came to be increasingly in favour. On Sunday afternoons the club offered mixed (and well chaperoned) social gatherings, it being thought, as Lady Magnus reported, that the 'opportunities they afford help to create the nice tone of the girls.'[3]

Lily Montagu offered the next generation her West Central Jewish Girls' Club. Emily Harris, a devoted social worker in the East End, was an apostle of instruction through example. She sought out Anglo-Jewish *grandes dames* who would provide Sunday 'occasions' for East End working girls. Lily, at nineteen, was one of her disciples. From such occasions, she recruited family support to create the West Central Jewish Girls' Club. Her somewhat embarrassing, quasi-autobiographical novels, particularly *Broken Stalks*, published in 1902, suggest that first the club, then Liberal Judaism as commitments were ways in which she compensated for her frustrated passion for Claude Montefiore. Although she could not share his life, the widower Montefiore having married Florence Ward, Lily Montagu would share Montefiore's commitments in philanthropy and communal work.[4] Carved out of the heart of Soho, the club formally existed, Lily Montagu explained, 'to help the girls to realise a complete life, to realise their physical powers and powers of brain and hand and heart, their desire for service and their capacity for enjoyment'.

Lily repeated Lady Magnus's three Rs, if in the somewhat more cumbersome rhetoric of her social activism and liberal Judaism. Our work, Lily Montagu argued, is development. Jewish philanthropy and the government were willing to help meet the requisite costs. At the dedication of the new facilities in Dean Street, Soho, in January 1896, the 130 members present attested to the sentiment of the inaugural prayer.

> Be Thou the guardian of our daughters and sisters, who shall often gather within this building for rest and innocent pleasures, and loving companionship, and mutual helpfulness and improvement. Here may they take sweet counsel together; here may they come under the influence of sympathetic and unselfish friends; and here may they find some compensation for whatever hardship or dullness there may be in their daily lives, while they joyfully confess that within these walls, at least, their lines have fallen unto them in pleasant places. O protect our sisters all from the temptations and pitfalls of a great city. Give to this place a refining and hallowing influence upon their characters, so that not only they may learn to respect themselves, but may so bear themselves in the world that by their example the respect and reverence of others may be secured for all womanhood.[5]

The Reverend Simeon Singer warmed to his improving theme of the value of an evening club 'as a means of drawing city girls from the temptations of music-halls and dancing-saloons, and on its value as an educational and social force.' President Harris and honorary secretary Lily Montagu proudly offered the uplifting alternatives of gymnastic apparatus, a large classroom 'furnished with cooking stove, dresser, etc.', another library, and a sitting room for the older girls. Lily Montagu and her sister offered fortnightly Bible classes, not, Lily ruefully conceded in 1901, very well attended, 'but we are not discouraged.' Every evening those attending met in the club room for prayer 'in order that real meaning be brought home to our members'. Faith moved hand-in-hand with sound management, a Montagu trade mark. A concert appeal cleared the 'terrible debt' incurred to rebuild the premises in 1900. Ongoing maintenance could be defrayed by sub-letting club facilities during the day.

Lily translated that successful concert into an annual fund-raising event at the Royalty Theatre. There, to the rousing applause of subscribers and friends, one programme opened with twenty members singing an enthusiastic, if heavily Yiddish-accented rendition of 'Ye Mariners of England'; another featured an

4 In general, see L. Montagu, *My Club and I: the Story of the West Central Girls' Club*, 2nd edn (London, 1954).
5 *JC*, 24 Jan. 1896.

'unconvincing scene' from *A Midsummer Night's Dream* and a rather more impressive athletic demonstration from forty 'muscular Jewesses'. Although Yiddish was discouraged and English emphasized, Hebrew was encouraged. A short drama written for the occasion 'in pure Hebrew' brought one of the more decorous moments of the reign of King Solomon to the delighted, if uncomprehending, 1902 audience.[6]

Once again, the state came to the assistance of voluntarism. The Education Act of 1902 provided a new source of funding for such clubs. By giving 'continuing education' classes, the West Central and other clubs qualified for state aid. Lily drove her club from fifteen members crowded into a room in Devonshire Street in 1892 to 220 in 1900, but government funding helped to push the numbers up to more than 480 in 1910.

Obviously the club 'afforded innocent and wholesome recreation in a district with dangerous attractions and grave temptations.'[7] But the West Central did much more than that. It taught English to foreigners. Lily Montagu first went to the Russo-Jewish Association where, given the importance of her request and the fact that her father was president, she was unlikely to be turned down. She secured a modest £24 grant, but this marked only the beginning. The Education Act of 1902 enabled Jewish clubs, like Jewish schools, to pass educational costs on from students, members or the Jewish community to the taxpayer. The West Central expanded its curriculum to include a wide variety of practical arts through LCC Board of Education grants. These began at £49 in 1903 and grew to nearly £200 by the eve of the First World War. No longer dependent exclusively upon volunteer enthusiasts, Lily Montagu was able to use her grants to employ three LCC teachers on a part-time basis.

A ramblers' club visited picture galleries and attended concerts in winter and arranged outings and holidays in the summer. The industrial department sought out situations and apprenticeships and found more than two hundred positions for club members in 1910 alone. Needlework classes, a staple of such organizations, paid their costs through the sale of the girls' work. In spite of state aid and the pennies of its members, like all such agencies, the West Central depended on the contributions of generous Jews for most of its endowment and income, and the giving community was quick to express its approval or disapproval. Some would-be patrons withheld support when they discovered that the West Central had a drama class. Lily defended her policy, arguing that 'the class was valuable in inculcating self-control and other useful qualities' and 'produced nothing but good'.

These were working girls, and Lily insisted that they take the responsibility for their own governance. Since a few were 'occasionally noisy, even rough, perhaps even rude', some of the ladies and gentlemen who came to observe before opening their cheque books looked askance. Her club was not recruiting saints, Montagu

6 *JC*, 28 Jan. 1898, 22 Feb. 1901, 28 Feb. 1902, 27 Feb. 1903; West Central Jewish Girls' Club, *Seventh Annual Report* (London, 1901).

7 The handbook for such organizations was Maude Stanley, *Clubs for Working Girls* (London, 1890), strongly endorsed by the *Charity Organisation Society* in *Charity Organisation Review*, VI (1890), 111. Lady Albina Hobart Hampden, 'The working girl of today', *Nineteenth Century* (1898), also beat the drum for more girls' clubs.

exclaimed at the annual display in 1905, 'if it were so, she would be obliged to resign the secretaryship forthwith.'[8] The Montagus, as a tribe, had a delightful capacity to be stunningly direct.

Lily Montagu, in fact, successfully taught girls 'self development and service'. In contrast to adolescent boys in their clubs, girls were not in the least self-conscious about the importance of religious education and religion itself in their lives and enthusiastically welcomed and participated in religious classes and services. The feeling of comradeship, so carefully nurtured in the club, was sustained through continued involvement even after active membership ended. An Old Girls' group regularly returned to help with the club and demonstrate in themselves and their lives how much the organization, the values it imparted, and the fellowship it provided had meant to them. In so far as camaraderie could be measured in terms of success in team sports, the West Central tended to monopolize prizes in sport and handiwork at annual girls' club competitions.[9]

For girls and boys, clubs continued the behavioural instruction begun in school, emphasizing order, self-discipline, thrift and independence constrained by deference. Drink was never a widespread problem among Jewish youth as it was for so many in the British working classes; on the other hand, gambling was an endemic Jewish problem. Sexual discipline, for both sexes, was a matter of great concern. Given increasing independence as more adolescents moved into the workforce and spent substantial portions of the day away from parental control, contemporary social workers saw clubs for working girls, in particular, as 'a good antidote to the perils of injudicious and premature lovemaking'.[10] Not surprisingly, Anglo-Jewry turned first to girls' clubs. From the outset, Jewish girls' clubs acted to bring the power of example to bear on working-class girls at an impressionable and restless age. The presumption that middle- and upper-class Jewish women had something more important to offer their poorer co-religionists than they could receive at home led Helen Lucas, the defender of tradition at the Reform Synagogue, patron of the Jewish Board of Guardians, and social worker for forty years, to protest. Such clubs, she argued, only served

> to destroy home and family life, and influence, which used to be such a splendid feature among our children. If, instead of teaching our working girls to despise their homes, the promoters of these clubs would visit the girls they desire to benefit in these homes and encourage them to help their mothers, as they can do in various ways when their day's work is over, we should not want rescue homes and societies as alas! we do now. These clubs teach the girls to seek their pleasures away from their homes and engender the habit of going out at night where dangers await them in every street.[11]

Her criticism precipitated a debate in the editorials and correspondence columns of the Jewish press in the spring of 1898, the weight of argument running strongly

8 *JC*, 14 Apr. 1905.
9 West Central Jewish Girls' Club, *Annual Report for 1910* (London 1911); *JC*, 24 Mar., 14 Apr., 9, 16 June 1911.
10 *Charity Organisation Society Review*, VI (Jan-Dec 1890), 111.
11 Helen Lucas to the editor, *JC*, 29 Mar. started a heated discussion which reverberated until mid-May. *JC*, 1, 15 Apr. 1898.

against her. Whether one or two girls had actually wound up 'on the streets', the statistical risk of the girls' clubs being a stepping stone to prostitution were remote. One gentleman, active in the Jewish Association for the Protection of Girls and Women, let slip the actual unspoken fear. Girls who should become wives and mothers might become neither but instead turn into 'new women'. The evidence, whether that carefully assembled by the National Union of Women Workers, or that produced by clubleaders presumed that possibility might be true and built from that assumption. Every settlement house demonstrated how clubs were effective instruments for social instruction and moral persuasion. The community was the richer for them.

> To a tired, impatient, impressionable young woman, after a long day spent in factory or workshop, airy rooms, comfortable chairs, a sense of space and leisure, must be in themselves influences which make for righteousness. A sensibly managed club supplies a real want just at its most pressing time and need. It offers books and rest and change, and just that amount of discipline, to newly released school-girls which is the alphabet of courtesy and a continuation class, so to speak, to self-control. It gives girls the companionship – whether by means of actual classes or by the mere intimate moving about among them matters little, so long as it is companionship – of women more happily circumstanced, better dressed, better educated, better mannered perhaps, yet with a hundred sympathies in common and with some things it may well be, in which the teachers are the learners.[12]

Lily Montagu conveyed a clearer sense of what managers of girls' clubs hoped to accomplish in her short novel *Naomi's Exodus* (1901) than in any of her more formal, official pronouncements. Naomi's family keeps a small chandler's shop in a Jewish quarter of West London (appropriate for Soho as opposed to Whitechapel). She is discontented, unhappy with the restrictions of ritual, the dreariness of obligation and the narrow, dissatisfying state of affairs in which she finds herself. Her metamorphosis will be to discover that her soul can find fulfilment and development, even in her little ghetto shop. The great moral Samuel Smiles preached so untiringly and effectively to the Victorians was repeated once again. Building moral character, not material accomplishment, translated into success in life. What matters is what you are, not what you have.

This powerful lesson was reinforced in yet other ways. As part of its programme of encouraging greater use of loan funds, the Jewish Board of Guardians briefly experimented with two branch loan departments. This, the board felt, would stimulate self-help without any implied taint incurred through visiting the board's own headquarters. The West Central Jewish Girl's Club was selected as one of the offices in 1900. Lily Montagu's young ladies were also taught a sense of social responsibility and the philanthropic obligations of even marginal economic success through the West Central's special relationship to the Emily Harris Home. The

---

12 'K.M.'[Lady Magnus], 'A word about girls' clubs', *JC*, 15 Apr. 1898. Mrs Lucas, who rarely let anything that annoyed her pass, continued to criticize girls' clubs, employment of women away from their homes, or any facilities, such as the Jewish Crèche, which facilitated mothers 'shirking' their family responsibilities by providing day care for infants and pre-school children.

Harris Home, named after Lily's late mentor in club work, provided a temporary residence for a limited number and meals for a substantial number of otherwise homeless or unsupervised girls of working age. Such an institution

> is an absolute necessity in the Soho District, as it is the only mode in which we can attempt, with any hope of success, to combat the terrible conditions that exist for girls living and working in the neighbourhood. There is no other Jewish Home where respectable girls out of situations, or living too far from their own homes can lodge for a small charge. Many girls come from undesirable homes, and are much benefited by the moral and physical advantage they receive.[13]

An employment bureau sought out positions for Harris Home residents and applicants who sought its help. Constant efforts were made to promote some sense of home life and home feeling among the residents.

The home began its slightly peripatetic existence in 1902 before settling down just off the Tottenham Court Road. Rose Davis, its matron and guiding spirit until 1910, started as a member of the West Central in 1894 and kept up her membership in that organization as an 'old girl'. By 1910, in spite of unsettling management turmoil, the home still managed to shelter some sixty-six girls in the course of the year while providing almost 20,000 meals.[14] Some of the transients were girls from abroad seeking work in England, but most were simply adolescents without parents or guardians. The Harris Home, for obvious reasons, came to play an important role in the 'rescue and protection' activities of the Jewish Association for the Protection of Girls and Women. The same self-consciousness about Jewish involvement in prostitution and the publicity that entailed which would lead the Montefiores to establish Stamford Hill (the first Jewish industrial school for girls), gave the Harris Home an increasingly important place among Jewish philanthropies. The overtones of this rescue and rehabilitative function, particularly in the Soho area, underscored an important moral lesson for the West Central girls and gave them a not-very-subtle sense of superiority.

Youth clubs were, like so many Anglo-Jewish institutions, family fiefs. The Sassoons patronized the Butler Street Jewish Girls' Club, directly modelled on Lady Magnus's pioneering enterprise, which attempted to provide girls with 'that social atmosphere which was so much needed'. Unlike other clubs, Butler Street began on a large scale. A large new building for the Jewish Soup Kitchen provided, one might say required, this strategy. The soup kitchen's first-floor rooms were available. Ample facilities, however, demanded a substantial membership from the beginning. Anglo-Jewry's women saw that it happened. Lady Sassoon provided the patronage; Katie Solomon and Nettie Adler did the work; Lily Montagu offered experience and advice. Women social workers brought in a nucleus of almost a

13 Emily Harris Home for Jewish Working Girls, *Third Annual Report* (London, 1905). Emily Marion Harris died in November 1900 having worked so hard to help make the West Central the £1,000 per year, 250-member operation it had become. West Central Jewish Girls' Club, *Seventh Annual Report* (London, 1901); *JC*, 7 June 1901, 17 Feb. 1905.

14 Feeding was a major occupation of the Home which provided the meals for the Westminster Jews' Free School and Jews' College as well as girls who worked in the Soho area. Emily Harris Home, *Ninth Annual Report* (London, 1911); *JC*, 24 Mar. 1911.

hundred girls – clubs usually started with a select dozen or so – each of whom they had known for at least three years. The initial cadre was expected, in turn, to bring in more promising candidates. Girls living in tenements, explained Nettie Adler, leading member of the Education Committee of the London County Council, needed a place in which to read, to think, and to enjoy social recreation. The club provided some intellectual activities, which made it eligible for government education grants, but did not compete with London County Council evening schools. Miss Adler well understood how to keep separate her areas of responsibility. The Chief Rabbi demanded that members prove themselves 'really good and worthy English citizens'. How should they do so? Through the 'quietness in their demeanour and dress. If there were one thing that befitted the true lady it was abstaining from and shunning anything that was showy or gaudy in their dress, noisy or obtrusive in their behaviour.'[15]

Butler Street may have helped the noisy and rough East End girls learn genteel manners; it also taught them something about the feminism of the day. Dayan Feldman gave them the word on women's suffrage, and Margaret Macdonald of the National Union of Women Workers and wife of the future Labour Prime Minister held a lecture and discussion of the factory laws. Otherwise the story was much the same: instruction ranging from cookery to Bible, activities from gymnastics to needlework, job placement service, a well-patronized library, a thrift club, and a bond of friendship that grew steadily larger, 'a real force for good'.[16]

Girls' clubs were too effective to be lost simply because Jews moved further from the East End or adolescents were much more likely to be at school or at home than at work. The activities changed in emphasis, not in kind, to reflect the different class background. Anglo-Jewry's agenda encouraged liberty and responsibility but rarely preached equality. The Kilburn Recreation Club for Girls had its thrift fund and active library. Pleasure rather than utility crowded its classes. Singing, drilling and elocution augmented the domestic arts. In the fashionable West End, the Beatrice Jewish Girls' Club assembled for its annual meeting and entertainment on Sunday, 26 March 1911. The club was here primarily a place for enjoyment with provision for sabbath afternoon services, first aid and hygiene classes, but – once again with the assistance of the LCC Education Committee – singing, English cookery, needlework and German were among subjects taught.[17]

All girls' clubs shared certain features. Each placed considerable emphasis on religious instruction and the importance of religion in life. In the great Victorian tradition, women were taught to uphold the deepest moral values of the community

---

15 Lady Sassoon hoped, in particular, that her club would 'give a sort of home to those girls who happen to be unfortunately friendless, to enable them to complete the instruction, which, owing to stern necessity, they left too early to finish; and above all to attain that paramount object that all educational systems set before them, viz., the training and moulding of character.' *JC*, 19 Dec. 1902. Butler Street had the usual subscription of 1d per week and an entrance fee of 2d. The club was open every evening but Friday with specialized activities systematically laid on: Monday features dressmaking, letter-writing and Shakespeare; Tuesday – cookery, Hebrew, and embroidery; Wednesday – drill and first aid (Miss Adler did not suggest whether the two were causally related); Thursday – basket-making and singing. Saturday night was devoted to literary and social gatherings, and Sundays were set aside for planned social occasions. A fortnightly scripture class was regularly planned. *JC*, 12 Dec. 1902, 22 Dec. 1905.

16 *JC*, 13 Jan,15 Dec 1905; 17 Mar 1911.

17 *JC*, 3, 31 Mar 1911.

and to pass them on, in turn, to their own children. Their education in the more formal and utilitarian senses was extended, even deepened, through club life. Girls found their domestic skills broadened and their intellectual horizons expanded. Anglo-Jewry, through the instrument of the girls' clubs, brought its conception of refinement and behaviour to both the middle and lower classes. Adolescents learned an important social lesson. Respectability was the goal. Rowdiness, vulgarity and noise suggested a lingering affinity for a life of which the community disapproved. Refinement, taste and discretion brought approval and made one's life easier and social advancement obtainable. Recreational outings carefully inculcated, among other things, notions of what should be aesthetically preferable. Club girls learned the virtues of the outdoors, even how holidays should be most profitably spent. Under the watchful eye of volunteer ladies on Sundays or occasional evenings, adolescent girls learned 'appropriate' modes of social intercourse with adolescent boys. All clubs taught the importance of the healthy body as well as the alert mind and moral character. Drill, gymnastics and exercise were offered each evening. And while all clubs shared certain features, subtle distinctions separated one club from the next, distinctions that reflected gradations of class. Through the clubs the community reminded adolescents not merely of universally shared values and culture, but who belonged where doing what.

Boys' clubs addressed themselves to similar problems, although since adolescent males were presumed to be continuing education or going to work, the need for them initially seemed less pressing. Claude Montefiore, devoted to the moral welfare and education of the young, joined Felix A. Davis to develop several of these organizations. The institutionalized mobilization of boys in clubs, however, began with the Jewish Lads' Brigade in 1895. Boys' brigades were increasingly popular in Britain in the 1890s, one of several manifestations of a growing obsession about Empire and national efficiency.[18] The Jewish contribution to the widespread military organization of youth, the Lads' Brigade served, at least in part, to demonstrate that Jews were as patriotic as their fellow Englishmen. Founded by Colonel A. E. W. Goldsmid and forwarded by Lt Col. Cecil Sebag-Montefiore, these smartly uniformed Jewish adolescents marched past prejudice and resentment. The nineteen pioneers who attended the first encampment at Deal in 1895 had swollen to well over 1,500 by 1910 and could no longer even hold their summer encampment in one place. As Montefiore reminded a festival dinner in 1902, the primary object of the Jewish Lads' Brigade

> is to instil habits of honour, cleanliness, and orderliness in the rising generation of the community. Our second object is to improve the physique and consequently the health of our boys.... The Jewish mind ... is like a valuable jewel which, if enclosed in a rotten case, is liable to be lost. Our third object is to keep in touch with our boys after they leave school. The children

18 See, J. Sprighall, *Youth, Empire and Society: British Youth Movements, 1883–1940* (London, 1977); O Anderson, 'The growth of Christian militarism in mid-Victorian Britain', *English Historical Review*, 76 (1971), 46–72. General Lord Methuen stressed the value of such organizations in correcting shortcomings in family discipline in 'Training the youth of England', *Nineteenth Century and After*, 57 (1905), 238–43. The Home Office was bombarded with such suggestions. See, e.g., the files in HO 45/10790/301145 in the Public Record Office. The Women's Industrial Council strongly endorsed drill for girls. See its *Eighth Annual Report* (1902), 8.

of the poor leave school at an earlier age than those of the well-to-do, and during the years that intervene between boyhood and young manhood many of them, for want of another place to go to, pass their leisure hours in the streets. It is for these that the Jewish Lads' Brigade was established, to inspire them with an *esprit de corps*, to provide them with a place of meeting where they cannot drift into evil courses. Our fourth object – and a particularly good one – is to foster a wholesome sympathy between the different classes of the Jewish community.[19]

Each of the points struck a resonant chord: self discipline, moral behaviour, social responsibility, physical and mental fitness, and a strong sense of fellowship. The organization aspired to be 'the highest expression of the patriotism of the Jew'. The brigade was one of the most timely and important statements of the Jewish community at the turn of the century. From it a disproportionate number of young men would march off to fight in and become casualties of the Boer War. Anglo-Jewry approved. When the brigade appealed for £5,000 to put its affairs in order in October 1905, the money was in hand within a month. The brigade was not simply a Jewish but a national statement. 'Its stiffening of the Jewish muscle,' trumpeted the *Jewish Chronicle* enthusiastically, 'comes opportunely at a time when the prophets are lamenting the physical deterioration of the nation.' What the brigade did for Jewish physique and health figured large among its proclaimed virtues. It rid East End lads of their 'ghetto bend'.[20]

Over the next half a dozen years, the numbers grew, and financial demands expanded even more. A committee of ladies, which by the early twentieth century had become a necessary adjunct of any important organization, undertook to collect 40 per cent of the capital in the new fund-raising drive of 1911. The Jewish Lads' Brigade did not, however, avail itself of army support. As it did to other organized youth brigades, the War Office offered the Lads' Brigade recognition, certification and support. After some debate, Anglo-Jewry elected not to avail itself of state support. The reasoning helps to explain why the community leaders would assume the somewhat awkward stance they did in regard to immigration restriction. The stake was Anglo-Jewish control of its own community. Anglo-Jewry preferred, in this instance, to pay rather than compromise communal authority over Jewish

19 *JC*, 24 Jan. 1902.

20 *JC*, 6 Oct. 1905. The brigade grew out of Colonel Goldsmid's presentation to the physical education subcommittee of the Maccabæans, and held its first meeting on 16 February 1895. Frederick D. Mocatta financed it. Sergeant Major Brock drilled it. Even its first annual report proclaimed, 'The lads learnt habits of cleanliness, obledience, and good behaviour. The influences brought to bear on them were wholesome, and cannot fail to work for good in after years.' Quoted in *JC*, 17 Mar 1896. The minute books and papers, including scrap books and photographs, of the Jewish Lads' Brigade from 1897 to 1936 are in AJ/34 in the Mocatta Library. The JLB also provided a convenient way of shelving Rabbi Benjamin Schewzik, whose chequered career had taken him from quarrelling with Gaster about Montefiore College to quarrelling not only with the Anglo-Jewish philanthropic leaders but with his employers at the Arbitration Bureau of the Self-Help Association in the East End. Schewzik's undeniable skills among the East End poor were pressed into service when he was appointed recruiting staff officer of the JLB with the honorary rank of lieutenant. *JC*, 6 Aug. 1897. National attention focused increasingly on the issue of physical condition and health after the confronting the excessive rejections of would-be recruits for the army during the Boer War. See, particularly, Interdepartmental Committee on Physical Deterioration, PP (1904), XXII (Report and Appendix, Cd. 2175; Minutes of Evidence, Cd. 2210; Appendix, Cd. 2186).

institutions. The brigade formally declined War Office recognition and aid on the grounds that doing so would mean a constitutional change 'converting what was a purely social organisation into a more or less military one'.[21]

The price seemed small for preserving this public demonstration of Jewish patriotism under complete and total community authority. The Lads' Brigade, moreover, had itself absorbed many of the functions of youth clubs. When the Liverpool company was on parade in 1896, its chaplain reminded the assembled lads, 'the boy who was neat and smart in apearance, obedient to those over him, punctual and regular at his work, was the boy who would attract the favourable notice of employers.'[22] The brigade ran employment registers and did much to advance the job careers of its members. The brigade, moreover, like other national youth groups, ostensibly did much to mitigate class conflict by lowering barriers between the poor and better-to-do. So Jews marched in smart uniforms under fluttering Union Jacks, expended an impressive amount of ammunition on the newly-constructed rifle range at the Jews' Free School, drilled and manoeuvred at summer encampments – patriotic Britons but uncompromisingly Jews.

The brigade also served yet another purpose, marking a reassertion of virtues considered to be uniquely masculine in an age in which the increasing importance of women was being uncomfortably acknowledged.

> The Brigade is a practical body, making solely for manliness, and appealing in no way to the tawdry sentimentality of our drawing-room philanthropists; it is based on no dreamy theory as to the ameliorative effects of herding together the unclubable. Its originators and executive prefer to employ the iron rule of discipline rather than the softening influence of female patronage.[23]

The dramatic contrast was everywhere repeated. The 'wild boys of the East' could best be transformed into clean, presentable, orderly young men through the rigour of military order. 'No one could have believed,' remarked the Reverend Simeon Singer to the New West End Synagogue on the occasion of the July 1898 synagogue parade, 'that many of these bright and erect lads belonged to the class from which are also recruited the slouching guttersnipes who loaf about the lanes and alleys of the East End.'[24]

Regular youth clubs followed hard on the heels of the Lads' Brigade. The Brady Street Lads' Club in the heart of Whitechapel started with seventy members in 1896. Throughout Brady Street's early years, approximately one third of the members also belonged to the Jewish Lads' Brigade. Oxford House, the settlement house at Bethnal Green, lent Brady Street its gymnasium once a week and its

---

21 *JC*, 12 May 1911.
22 *JC*, 14 Oct. 1898.
23 *JC*, 28 July 1898.
24 The 1897–8 annual report argued that the Jewish Lad's Brigade worked so effectively 'by accustoming young boys to discipline, by bringing them together in organised bands, by drilling their bodies out of physical sloth, a feeling for manliness and honour is created, which influences their whole bearing and conduct and substitutes high-toned sentiments of responsibility and respect for authority, for mean and sordid thoughts.' Colonel Goldsmid, when organizing the North London Branch of the JLB informed the Dalston Synagogue, 'Their aim was to keep the lads away from the pernicious influence of the public-house, and to instil into their minds habits of cleanliness, discipline, and obedience to orders from their superiors.' *JC*, 14 Feb, 17 June, 8 July 1898.

grounds at Walthamstow for cricket and football. Athletics dominated club activities.[25] That made Brady Street attractive. Lady Rothschild's patronage helped, for it gave Brady Street access to facilities. The 4% Industrial Dwellings Company, that intelligently conceived Rothschild corporation which had done so much to capitalize low-rent housing estates for East Enders, provided expanded premises in Durward Lane, Whitechapel, which included a gymnasium and roof garden. Lady Rothschild provided £250 each year by 1905, almost 60 per cent of the club's ordinary revenue, and the more than three hundred members put in over £60 in their weekly pennies. Sir George Faudel-Phillips, who had done extensive work for the deprived, opened the new facilities. After discussing the virtues of sparring and punctuality – he found them related virtues – Sir George proclaimed that a club taught its members to depend on one another. The club also inculcated the virtue of winning in competition, but always winning squarely, an unconsciously ambiguous but also characteristic contemporary observation.[26]

Toynbee Hall, the original and greatest of the East End settlement houses, helped to inspire the Victoria Working Boys' Club in 1901. The Chief Rabbi solicited Leopold de Rothschild, Stuart M. Samuel and Daniel Marks to assist in planting the club squarely in the heart of the East End on Commercial Road. Intended to provide recreation for the working lads of the neighbourhood, the Victoria grew steadily to a maximum of 350 members by 1911. A waiting-list of about a hundred hoped to share the athletic facilities and recreational opportunities of the club, particularly the annual summer camp at the Isle of Wight. With Charles Sebag-Montefiore as honorary secretary, the club emphasized the *esprit de corps* it inspired among its members, 'imbuing them with that spirit which made ideal English characters'. The Victoria Club moved quickly to expand beyond the usual fourteen to eighteen age constraints. It opened a children's 'kiddie's' club to 150 which developed a pool of anxious recruits, and it cultivated its 'old boys' network not only in London but throughout the world. Those contacts helped in the important work of directing young men towards trades with greater opportunities and the best markets for their skills.[27]

By 1901 Chief Rabbi Adler was urging those interested in 'the rising generation' forward in a campaign to target undersocialized areas and 'to prevent the descent into hooliganism and crime at this impressionable age'. Brady Street was the model, and Brady Street also defined the costs, estimated to be £300 per year, that should

---

25 Brady Street claimed 90 to 150 members by its Second Annual Report (1898). Ernest Lesser, the honorary secretary boasted to Lady Rothschild, 'In addition to the great influence which they exercised upon the character and physique of the members, such institutions did more to anglicise the alien than all the time and labour which philanthropists devoted to other methods.' *JC*, 20 May 1898.

26 *JC*, 24 Nov. 1905.

27 Seasonal trades such as tailoring and bootmaking were strongly discouraged. By 1911, the club tried to direct its members towards learning a good trade, learning it entirely rather than just some aspect of it. The club pushed its members towards becoming mechanics, machinists or plumbers. It also encouraged emigration for the greatest opportunities. West Canada happened to be particularly in favour. *JC*, 29 Nov. 1901, 24 Feb. 1911. Early in the club's history, Reverend Canon Barnett, the activist Anglican social reformer of the East End, hoped that the club would be distinguished 'by the good conduct and gentlemanly behaviour of its members.' It would, thereby, 'make London a cleaner, healthier, and ultimately a more beautiful place.' Fourth annual prize-giving and display, 17 Jan. 1905. *JC*, 20 Jan. 1905.

be raised to maintain each facility.[28] Lionel de Rothschild opened Hutchison House Club for Working Lads on 28 June 1905, with a flourish and display by its members who were also in the Jewish Lads' Brigade. Rothschild addressed those in the community concerned that Jewish philanthropic resources might better be spent to aid the sick and the poor. Clubs were social prophylaxis.

> We hope to catch the youth of the immediate neighbourhood, and to help them to rise in the world, to help them out of the temptations which they find in the street, the music-halls and the public-houses. We want to instil into the boys ambition, the pride of being Jews and the pride in being Englishmen. [Cheers] We want to teach them the qualities of endurance and sportsmanship.[29]

Rothschild called for the privileged Jews to subscribe and for volunteers, particularly from those young gentlemen who had attended Harrow and Cheltenham, each of which had both a strong Jewish component and taught the virtues of social activism and responsibility. Within five years Hutchison House had overstrained its facilities with three hundred active members and realized it could double its size were bigger facilities available. From recreation and 'muscular Judaism', Hutchison House expanded its educational, religious and cultural programmes. The library proved popular. A thrift club inculcated 'good habits'. The club had its own summer camp. Hutchison House served its little community well and also provided many young gentlemen with a sense of social purpose and commitment as volunteer workers.[30]

Each club had its particular features. Sponsored by and using the facilities of the Stepney Jewish Schools, the Stepney Jewish Lads' Club had a stronger religious education programme and more commitment to religious services and prayer than most. That was testimony to the formidable role the Reverend J. F. Stern played in Stepney's promotion and development. But the Stepney club shared in the gymnastics, sports and recreational programmes of the less overtly observant clubs. Stepney even had its own minstrel troupe with some twenty talented performers. 'Black face' humour seems to have had a strong transatlantic appeal among the ethnic working classes and particularly among Jews. Stepney's bank had 'many £5 depositors'. The club sponsored its own special country holiday. Stepney's strong moral commitment may help to explain its anti-gambling league. While the community saw drink as a peculiarly Christian vice, its leaders acknowledged gambling to be a serious Jewish problem.[31]

The West Central Jewish Lads' Club had a slightly more up-and-down existence than Lily Montagu's Girls' Club which served the same area. The simplest explanation is probably the opening of the West Central Jewish Men's Club in 1905

28 *JC*, 1 Feb. 1901.
29 *JC*, 30 June 1905.
30 Hutchison House Lads' Club, *Annual Report for 1910* (London, 1911); *JC*, 19 May 1911.
31 The Stepney Jewish Lads' Club Papers are in AJ/250 in the Mocatta Library. See also, *JC*, 10 Jan. 1902, 31 Mar. 1905. The anti-gambling crusade among Jewish clubs assumed many of the characteristics of teetotalist campaigns among Gentile youth groups. Brady Street, which had from its beginning a by-law providing for the dismissal of any boy found betting on club premises, also instituted an Anti-Betting League. *JC*, 19 June 1903.

that consistently siphoned off older Lads' Club members. Men's clubs offered more scope and less supervision. Once again, Leopold de Rothschild played an active role in planting a boys' club on a firm footing. For the West Central Boys' Club, the emphasis was on discipline, recreation and physical exercise. The West Central, the only Jewish club entered, was placed third in the Federation of London Working Boys' Clubs football league in 1901. Mrs Nathaniel Montefiore loaned the West Central a house in Fitzroy Square rent-free, which enabled the two hundred members to pursue their vocational and general classes as well as indulge their passion for manly sports indoors as well as out. The club had its own Jewish Lads' Brigade company which helped to explain the constant use of a rifle range and, perhaps, the club's considerable success in boxing.[32]

As with girls' clubs, lads' clubs showed a different emphasis when established in the more affluent West End. The Hammersmith and West Kensington Jewish Young Men's Club was organized in February 1911 to meet a need for 'greater cooperation' between the young men of the neighbourhood, to gather them together and 'foster the spirit of comradeship', to help them to

> realize their corporate responsibilities as men and Jews, develop their moral character, and show them how best to defend the interests of the faith to which they belonged.
> Among the objects of the club will be to foster a spirit of comradeship among Jewish lads of the district, the holding of lectures and debates on Jewish subjects, and the promotion of athletics.[33]

Clubs succeeded both in what they did within the Jewish community and the effective way in which they presented Jewish youth to England. The various Jewish clubs competed with striking success in the various activities of the Federation of London Working Boys' Clubs in such diverse sports as cricket, football and swimming. In a culture which has always placed a premium on athletic achievement, youth clubs were an important way to demonstrate the Jewish contribution to a better English life.

Anglo-Jewry understood just how important this sportsmanship statement was. The generally serious *Jewish Chronicle* began to run a regular sports column in the early twentieth century. The Jewish Athletic Association, founded in 1899, attempted to pick up the communal gap left after the organization of the Jewish Lads' Brigade. While the lads' brigade represented 'physical training on military lines' the Jewish Athletic Association 'was more in the nature of physical training on an athletic basis'. Founded to encourage athletics among constituted clubs (and not merely youth clubs), the athletic association was Anglo-Jewry's statement for 'muscular Judaism'. Taken on by the Maccabæans, that assembling place for Jewish professionals and intellectuals, in 1900, the response was so overwhelming that the Maccabæans' committee had to draw up a constitution with a view to establishing leagues and more organized competition. With predictable fervour, they organized

32 West Central Jewish Lads' Club, *Third Annual Report* [1900] (London, 1901); *Fourth Annual Report* [1901] (London, 1902); *Annual Report for 1904* (London, 1905); *Annual Report for 1910* (London, 1911). The West Central Jewish Working Lads' Club scrapbook, 1900–8, has rich accounts and memorabilia of club doings. AJ/136, in the Mocatta Library.

33 *JC*, 3 Mar. 1911.

school and club sections, hoping to recruit provincial branches, and to draw upon community support to provide healthy bodies for Jewish men and women. The Waley-Cohen family, which figured so prominently in the Jewish Board of Guardians, adopted the Jewish Athletic Association. Like the Board of Guardians, the athletic association had ambitions beyond its resources. By 1910, the association managed the athletic affairs of nineteen affiliated clubs, twenty-six boys' schools, and twenty-two girls' schools.[34] The association influenced, as Felix Waley its president proudly observed, thousands of young men and women for the better. It assisted schools by providing money for team fares, gave swimming tickets to schools and clubs for the various municipal pools, and provided equipment for soccer, cricket and basketball teams. Although it was unable to raise the funds or find the space for its own playing grounds, the London Playing Fields Association allowed it a virtual monopoly of the Elms, Walthamstow, recognized at the time as one of the best playing grounds in London.[35]

Youth clubs and organizations, like schools, taught that which was not available at home. The Jewish Lads' Brigade, a direct copy of the Church Lads' Brigade, brought boys out of the East End to camps with military discipline and camaraderie. Given the number of those from Russia and Poland who had fled from Eastern Europe to avoid military service, parents must have viewed the brigade with some suspicion, in some instances even prohibited sons from joining. For boys, however, the brigade was an escape from the crowded dwellings and streets of the East End. The brigade offered the drama of uniforms, martial music and fellowship wrapped in the mystique of patriotism. Patriotism was, after all, an ultimate expression of anglicization. Not only the brigade but other boys' clubs had managers, themselves often public school products, pushing Jewish boys into the Territorial Army.[36]

The organization of youth was, to a considerable degree, the work of the liberal spirits of the Jewish elite. They had grown up in the age of the settlement house, been inspired by Toynbee Hall, and felt that 'sense of social sin among persons of property' to which Beatrice Webb referred. Youth clubs were, in this sense, one of the more important ways in which the active philanthropic families merged their interests and ambitions with many among the younger Jewish elite. Fresh from the inspiration of their Jewish mentors at Harrow and Cheltenham, reminded at Oxford or even at Cambridge that young educated gentlemen must take seriously the needs of their world and society, they moved into politics and social activism. Basil Henriques, son of the great Sephardi family, was inspired by the example of Claude Montefiore to work among Jewish youth. Schooled at Harrow and Oxford, he turned to social work. Like so many others, Jewish and non-Jewish, he served his apprenticeship at Toynbee Hall. He was then to create the Oxford and St George's Club in 1914, built upon all those examples stretching back to the Jewish Lads' Brigade and the Brady Street club. His generation of Anglo-Jewry had few abler missionaries to the young.[37]

34 Jewish Athletic Association (JAA) annual meeting, 20 Mar. 1911. *JC*, 24 Mar. 1911.

35 JAA annual distribution of medals, 24 Jan. 1911. *JC*, 27 Jan. 1911. See also JAA annual distribution, *JC*, 17 Dec., 22 Dec. 1905, 13 Jan. 1911.

36 See the 'discussion groups' section in Newman (ed.), *East End*, 135–40.

37 Henriques Papers, Anglo-Jewish Archives in the Mocatta Library; L. L. Loewe, *Basil Henriques* (London, 1976); R. Loewe, 'The Bernhard Baron Settlement and Oxford & St. George's Clubs', in Newman (ed.), *Jewish East End*, 143–6.

SOCIETIES FOR ADULTS

Beyond clubs to mould and continue to socialize adolescents lay yet another world of adult institutions carefully articulated to combine education and conviviality. In the great tradition of artisanal self-help, the Free Lectures Association, which customarily met at the Jews' Infant School on Commercial Street in the heart of the East End, brought, until 1879, intensive discussion of current issues and serious music or dramatic readings to a considerable and highly receptive audience.[38] Institutions such as the Jewish Working Men's Club and Institute resembled both in their organization and proceedings those many voluntary organizations zealous mid-Victorian clergymen developed to educate and improve their parishioners while raising trifling sums for worthy causes. Mr H. L. Hyam, for instance, organized a Saturday evening in January 1879 which offered the assembled individuals and families piano solos, Mark Antony's oration, vocal duets and an inspiring recitation while raising funds for local charities. All activities were conducted in English, touched English themes, and served to reinforce the constant anglicization of the community while reminding those assembled that they were also Jews.

New working men's clubs developed and old ones expanded to provide approved forms of socialization and recreation. The club provided, among other things, healthy recreation, social improvement, and an appropriate alternative to idleness or worse. Samuel Montagu took the lead. In February 1872, he began the Jewish Association Reading Rooms in Hutchison Street, Aldgate. Montagu, with perhaps a conscious sense of irony, donated a former public house free of rent and rates that would provide reading rooms open to men and women, 'for wholesome Sabbath recreation'. A fluctuating membership averaging two hundred, however, could not sustain the operational costs, and Montagu believed firmly that those who used such facilities should themselves underwrite its ongoing expenses. Members openly objected to the presence of teenagers which they found offensive. Whether men also objected to sharing the facilities with women is unclear. Whatever the case, the venture did not flourish.

In 1874, Montagu created the Jewish Working Men's Club in place of the reading rooms. He drew on the example established by London philanthropists in 1862 with their Working Men's Club and Institute Union, an umbrella organization to coordinate the establishment of adult institutions carefully articulated to combine education and conviviality. The Jewish Working Men's Club was, from its organization, closely associated with that umbrella organization. Montagu's club continued in the union, sharing in its success and difficulties until 1902. Then, quite suddenly, the club withdrew from the union, never to rejoin it. Whether the Jewish Working Men's Club took offence at the role some other London working men's clubs played in developing anti-alien agitation is not clear. The growing democratization of the club may have made it less amenable to the deference union leaders expected to be paid to their ideas. Democratization, however, made the club

---

38 See, e.g., *JC*, 3, 10, 17 Jan. 1879.

no less deferential to its benefactor. Montagu and the West Enders were invariably elected as the honorary officers.[39]

Lionel L. Alexander directed the day-to-day operations until his death at the end of the nineteenth century, adapting it to what appeared to be the needs of the times. A ladies' social room was added in 1897. An associated cycling club swept the more adventurous into the country for recreation. Originally established in the reading rooms' premises, the club's 1,000 to 1,500 members needed more space and better facilities. A public subscription to which Montagu was the principal donor built a new centre in Great Alie Street, Aldgate. There it stood until it closed in 1912, serving 'for the purpose of social intercourse and recreation, and in no sense to take the place of instructions whose aims were educational'. Neither alcohol nor gambling was permitted on the premises, but regulation went no further. Montagu felt healthy recreation a better instrument for temperance than the formal pledges of abstinence, then so much in vogue. Montagu even stood neutral when the proposal to sell drink was raised in 1897 for financial reasons. The membership, preferring the strong anti-drink line of Stuart M. Samuel, would have none of it. Billiard-playing, moreover, accounted for more than £300 of annual club revenue. By the end of three years, over 1,150 members had joined, although membership peaked in 1887 at 1,500. When, as Montagu hoped they often would, members wanted 'something more and higher', the organization would and did respond. Lectures, debates and musical events dotted the club calendar, always to the applause of the Jewish press. The club gave an enthusiastic if qualitatively marginal performance of *HMS Pinafore* in 1905 to raise money for the clothing department of the Jewish Board of Guardians. The club also functioned as a friendly society, although in this case insufficient numbers joined the self-insurance medical society, so that sub-section was wound up. Three-quarters of club income was annually spent either on the various self-insuring subscriptions or on games and recreation. Athletics waxed and waned from year to year depending on members' whims. A swimming club appeared, disappeared, and reappeared, although drill and exercise clubs were more consistently well attended.[40]

Increasingly, as members exerted more influence over club activities in the years before the war, the programmes moved in the political directions that concerned them rather than towards Anglo-Jewry's conventionally approved topics. Theodor Herzl held his first great Zionist meeting there. The Poale Zion Association used the Jewish Working Men's Club for a protest meeting against the administration of the Jewish Colonization Association in Argentine Jewish colonies, to which so many East Enders had been encouraged to migrate. What the members wanted, however, was more sport and less uplift, so the club moved increasingly into recreation and athletics. It continued to serve the important function of providing a socially acceptable meeting ground upon which marital matches could be considered and made. Its Sunday evening concerts at which West End performers entertained for charity attracted hundreds. Dances heightened conviviality. Any reader of *Israel*

---

39 Harold Pollins suggests that club members saw no benefit to association with the union. They had no desire to patronize drinking clubs, and members of other union clubs probably had no desire to share Jewish Working Men's Club sobriety. 'East End Jewish Working Men's Clubs, Affiliated to the Working Men's Club and Institute Union: 1870–1914', in Newman (ed.), *Jewish East End*, 189.

40 *JC*, 1 May 1896, 22 Jan., 19 Nov 1897, 22 Apr. 1898, 7 Apr. 1905; Montagu, *Samuel Montagu*, 50.

Zangwill's *The Children of the Ghetto* (London, 1892) will recall his charming description of a Purim Ball and carry away a sense of how much the club meant in East End life.[41] One of the most popular entertainments ever held, ironically, was S. B. Bancroft's public reading of Dickens's *A Christmas Carol* during the holidays of 1896–7.

Yet neither democratization nor education nor recreation ultimately saved the club. It remained Montagu's institution, a throwback to the deference expected of and demanded from upwardly mobile, anglicizing Jews of the East End. Montagu's death sapped institutional vitality, flexibility and financial reserve. Public libraries had more books. Toynbee Hall had university extension courses. Upper-working-class and middle-class anglicizing Jews were following their betters out of the old East End, the successful moving west or north, others migrating further east or south.

Montagu also played a critical role in the history of the most durable of East End Jewish clubs, the Netherlands Choral and Dramatic Society. He brought the two societies together and gave them their new facilities in 1887. The Netherlands Choral Society, formed in 1869 to train choristers and provide entertainment for charitable institutions, and the Netherlands Dramatic Society, founded in 1881, had originally used Dutch as their language. Montagu's price for his aid included an opening of the membership to English people, Germans, Poles and others. He insisted the Netherlands, thereafter, 'conduct their proceedings in the English language'. The Netherlands managed itself, although always with the benevolent oversight of Montagu or his nephew, Stuart M. Samuel. Only men could be members. Principally a recreational institution trading in fellowship and entertainment, the Netherlands sold alchohol (one of the more reliable ways of balancing institutional books), permitted card-playing (in spite of communal anxiety about gambling), and appears to have furnished an unofficial political base for Stepney Liberals. Samuel furnished a library. Someone, undoubtedly either Montagu or Sir Stuart, paid for ambulance classes that inspired two Netherlands members to go off to the Boer War in 1902 in the Medical Corps. Club membership fluctuated from approximately 700 in 1890 to a brief peak of 1,095 in 1901, then lagged to 600 and less by the end of the decade.

The Netherlands operated 'strictly on Trade Union lines,' seeking 'to inculcate those principles into all our members'. That translated, not into class solidarity and socialism, but self-help and personal responsibility. Membership dues were higher than those of the Jewish Working Men's Club, and members themselves seem to have come from that East End Jewish borderland of lower middle class and artisan. The Netherlands club had its 'tontine' sick and benefit funds. As a more prosperous organization should do, the club, in its most affluent days, subscribed £50 a year to its own favourite charity, the Jewish Soup Kitchen. Affiliated with the Working Men's Club and Institute Union, members of the Netherlands regularly subscribed to the union's convalescent home. Samuel Strelitski, a Dutch tailor, known to one

---

41 They had much to complain about. The contracts between the colonization organization and the colonists were in Spanish, which the Jewish colonists rarely understood. The homesteads, moreover, had an aura of indentured servitude about them, and the immigrant received no compensation for improvement, regardless of how much time and money he put into it. *JC*,13 Jan. 1911. For an interesting discussion, see Pollins, 'East End Clubs', in Newman (ed.), *Jewish East End*, 173–92.

and all as 'Uncle' presided over Netherlands operations through most of its years to the First World War. Closely associated with Montagu – an Elder of the Federation of Synagogues – Strelitski was generally viewed 'as the unofficial head of the Dutch Jews in the East End of London'.[42] He was also son-in-law of the superintendent of the Jewish Soup Kitchen, which may explain Netherlands' partiality for that charity.

Serving an area of expanding Jewish needs, in 1905 Leopold de Rothschild joined Felix A. Davis, the youth and club enthusiast, to sponsor a new working men's club for the West Central area. The boys' and girls' clubs were already in place. To provide for the recreational and social needs of working male adults, the premises at 113a Tottenham Court Road were equipped to answer the 'legitimate needs' of working males, serving as an alternative to the gambling 'clubs' or drinking establishments that tended to corrupt or to reflect unfavourably on the Jewish community.[43] The new premises answered the good purposes of social engineering and architecture. Members, the nucleus drawn from 'old boys' of the Brady Street club, could bask in the glow of premises fitted throughout with electric light, having ample facilities for billiards, such games as chess or draughts, even an all-purpose hall which served for concerts, lectures or as a gymnasium. Well-furnished reading rooms invited contemplation, although the fitted refreshment room pointedly banned intoxicants.[44]

The club management, while delighted to encourage culture, had its own agenda of what must be presented. Dr C. W. Saleeby, an eminent authority on the then-fashionable notions of eugenics, spoke pointedly to a large meeting about alcoholism, infant mortality, and immunity from disease. The Jews, he reminded his audience were 'the best selected race in existence'. Their progress was remarkable, and they owed it to being oppressed. Now the oppresser had disappeared: 'The future of humanity rested with the upbringing of the young, and the high standard of Jewish motherhood, backed up, no doubt, by exceptional fatherhood, had resulted in the fundamental survival of the Jewish race.'[45] The time Jewish mothers spent breast-feeding their children produced notably low infant mortality. Non-drinking parents produced the best type of child. Mixed marriages undid the qualities the race had developed.

Felix A. Davis, the president of the West Central, devoted much effort to forwarding youth movements. Mens' clubs, to him, were extensions of boys' clubs. They brought 'muscular Judaism' to late adolescents and young adults and

42 The Dutch government created Strelitski a Knight of the Order of Orange Nassau in 1904 in public recognition of that role. *JC*, 9 Sept 1904. For the Netherlands, see Pollins, 'East End Clubs', in Newman (ed.), *Jewish East End*, 182–6; *JC*, 24 Feb. 1882, 22 July 1887.

43 Justice Denman, not always the most tolerant magistrate in London, took particular note at Marlborough Street police court on 17 January 1905 of what he held to be a Jewish alien proclivity for fighting and gambling, suggesting that parliament badly needed to bring in legislation enabling magistrates to deport such undesirables. *JC*, 20 Jan. 1905.

44 Felix A. Davis presided over the new club with Leopold de Rothschild and Claude Montefiore looking over his shoulder as vice presidents. Their remarks on the club opening suggested how self-consciously Anglo-Jewry was looking over its collective shoulder during the debates on the Aliens Act of 1905. The facilities themselves were impressive, covering three floors at an annual rental of £230. *JC*, 10 Feb. 1905.

45 Saleeby continued from this dubious point to announce, even more incorrectly, that Jews owed their relative freedom from tuberculosis to the fact that the dietary laws required that their meat be examined before it was eaten. *JC*, 17 Feb. 1911.

continued the purposeful socialization of young men. Davis thought evening classes unnecessary. The members wanted recreation after working all day. Half a dozen years after organizing the West Central, Davis contended that the club succeeded in what it set out to do, to provide 'real service for the West Central district', which meant providing purpose and social discipline for young adults. The club was evolving its own traditions and ideals, Davis contended, which would inevitably influence the later life of its members. To promote that sense of group solidarity, they even initiated the *West Central Magazine*, run in conjunction with the Fitzroy Square Jewish Men's Club. The journal combined didactic morality, sports news, and yet another way for 'old boys' to remain part of the club community. The West Central expanded to fill leisure wants and needs with 'appropriate' and supervised activities. Healthy inter-club athletic competition, a holiday fund, even a series of club rambles helped to mould 'good English Jews'.[46]

Both male and female clubs patterned themselves on non-Jewish models and adapted them to Anglo-Jewish needs. Clubs continued a process of socialization begun in schools. For the better established adults, freemasonry rather than friendly societies or community clubs answered social needs. Masonry represented an assimilated entry into liberal, even cultivated, society while preserving the immediate company of familiars. At the same time, fraternal orders provided burial and sickness benefits.[47] Many lodges were exclusively or principally Jewish; others were integrated. Both provided Jewish masons with status and sociability within the framework of British culture. The Jewish press applauded, publishing in each issue the doings of each lodge and the passage of individuals up the ladders of degrees and office.

The social organization of the community placed contributors to synagogue, school and charitable institution in the position of providers and managers with their own internal hierarchy of prestige, power and wealth. The more privileged English Jews created and were, in a variety of ways, themselves shaped by this network of voluntary institutions. Other organizations evolved with Jewish westward and northern migration from the old East End. 'Several Jewish gentlemen of North London think a musical and literary society would be desirable.' With this advertisement, the North London Jewish Literary Society sprang into being with its two-guinea subscriptions for gentlemen, one guinea for ladies. Jewish bourgeois culture announced its arrival in Islington. At the same time the well-established West Enders delighted in a performance of the comic opera *Les Cloches de Courneville* at the Sir Moses Montefiore Literary and Art Society.[48]

Such organizations spread and developed with the resettlement of Anglo-Jewry's more affluent members. From individual entries, the world of Jewish literary societies came to be recorded in a regular column of the *Jewish Chronicle*. Literary societies were cultural footprints in the path of Anglo-Jewry's upward social mobility, eloquent testimony to progress and achievement. From the older City Jewish Social and Literary, one's eye could run outwards to the West End Jewish Literary, the South Essex Jewish Social and Literary, the Finsbury Social and

---

46 West Central Jewish Men's Club, sixth annual meeting, 19 Mar. 1911. *JC*, 24 Mar. 1911.

47 Joppa Lodge, held at the Albion Tavern, Aldersgate Street, had a benevolent fund in excess of £1,300 by 1878. *JC*, 10 Jan. 1879. The *Jewish Chronicle* reported the monthly meetings of each lodge.

48 *JC*, 24, 31 Jan. 1879.

Literary, the Hammersmith Jewish Literary. The South Hackney Jewish Social and Literary Institute marked yet another frontier post for north-east London. Consecrated and opened in the summer of 1905, the Institute, with marvellously unconscious irony, appropriated the building that was formerly the Hackney Conservative Club. The institute bought the building, furniture, 400-volume library, and all with the hope that the facility would 'become the centre of Jewish communal activity in Hackney'.[49]

The Reverend J. F. Stern sought to transplant the culture of the privileged more directly into the East End. Understanding the subtle distinctions of class and value within what West Enders too often saw as an undifferentiated ghetto, he organized the East London Jewish Communal League in 1894. Initially intended to provide a forum for local cultural events, Stern also used the league to develop commitment to charitable and social work among the better-off residents of the East End. The league unquestionably helped to spur the growth of aid societies for the major Jewish charities, but its history was uneven at best. By 1901 Stern had convinced the league to lower the minimum age for members from eighteen to sixteen in an effort to recruit young alumni of the boys' and girls' clubs.[50] Recapturing enthusiasm, however, extended the necessary range of activities beyond available resources, and greater expectations could not of themselves produce more substantial results.

By the end of the nineteenth century, a Union of Jewish Literary Societies was clearly in order. Intellectuals, too, could have their portion of organized Anglo-Jewry. Through the union and various related organizations, successful Jewish intellectuals and cultural patrons hoped to define the Anglo-Jewish mind and consciousness. The Jewish Historical Society of England began its discussion and researches. The Society for Jewish Statistics sought to bring modern social science to the service of the community. The Jewish Study Society and the Union of Jewish Literary Societies dreamt of purposeful programmes in the service of the community.

Leadership and membership were, not surprisingly, highly duplicatory from one of these organizations to another. Israel Abrahams and Lucien Wolf, for instance, dominated the Jewish Historical Society. They also, together with Israel Gollancz, hoped to unify the diverse constituencies of Jewish intellectual life in the Union of Literary Societies. From 1902 to 1905, they struggled to bring together Zionists and anti-Zionists, Orthodox and Reform, amateurs and professionals. Overwhelmingly focused on London, the union also sought to integrate the increasingly vibrant Jewish intellectual life of the provinces to forge a complete Jewish community and to bring 'a purer and refreshing atmosphere sweeping over the arid tracts of Anglo-Jewish life'.

The Jewish Historical Society of England evolved from cultural pride. It spoke to the impressive achievements of nineteenth-century Anglo-Jewry and the twin heritage of being English and Jewish that it was determined to uphold. To build Jewish pride and British Jewish consciousness, the Jewish Historical Society worked up an affiliation scheme to transmit a knowledge of Jewish history throughout the

---

49 *JC*, 9 June 1905.
50 East London Jewish Communal League, eighth annual meeting, 16 Mar. 1902. *JC*, 21 Mar. 1902.

country. The society appealed to every community to form its local society. For a mere three guineas, the local organization would receive three copies of the *Transactions*, three copies of other publications at member's rates, admission to the London society, the right to submit papers for presentation, loans of copyright lectures and notes, lantern slide shows for the cost of carriage only and an invitation to join in the exciting enterprise of historical research.[51]

Lucien Wolf, having shaped the Jewish Historical Society, wished to step down as president in 1896. He felt that the position should rotate annually, He had succeeded in making the study of medieval Anglo-Jewish records a serious part of Jewish history, and Wolf had made the *Transactions of the Jewish Historical Society* an important journal for English historians.

> To my mind the chief duty of the rising generation of Jews is to cultivate the Jewish historic spirit. There will be no future for Judaism or re-habilitation of the race without it. I earnestly appeal to you for the study of our inspiring traditions, for the loving care of our great heritage.[52]

The Historical Society wanted records preserved, an admirable undertaking. A Jewish museum stood high on the cultural agenda, testifying simultaneously to the importance of tradition, monument, memory and pride. In anticipation, a Jewish exhibition was proposed for the Whitechapel art gallery in the autumn of 1906. The union sought 'to broaden the outlook on life of our young men and women, and to strengthen their attachment to their race and its ideals.' Of course it was also 'a dignified means of counteracting the conversionist propaganda . . . by establishing reading-rooms, holding lectures and by other means that come within the orbit of their work.' Intellectuals, too, enrolled themselves in the task of shaping English Jews. Members volunteered to teach English to naturalization clubs. They provided lectures for the youth clubs, tried to provide stability for the weak East End literary societies, and generally gave organized scope to Jewish cultural expression for their approximately forty constituent organizations.[53]

The union had also initially been formed to understand why the Jewish literary movement appeared to be in decline. Its conclusions seemed intelligent enough. So many small literary societies proliferated that resources were stretched far too thin. Consolidation of existing rather than the formation of new organizations should be the order of the day. What the union failed to understand was that these literary and social societies, unlike the union itself, were not created with an intellectual agenda. They were social organizations which, however pretentious in prospectus, were statements of cultural status. When the aspiring North London Jewish Literary and Social Association – a more candid title than most – was being launched, one sage organizer 'hoped that the usual fate of such societies – that of rising in a sky of intellectuality and setting in a sea of matrimony – would not befall the sun of the proposed Association.'[54]

The union's views on the literary societies gave a technically correct diagnosis without ever appreciating the real problem. The union was far more comfortable

51 *JC*, 30 Apr. 1897.
52 See the report on the 4 Jan. 1896 meeting in *JC*, 10 Jan. 1896.
53 *JC*, 23, 30 June 1905.
54 *JC*, 23 July 1897.

when sifting out an agenda of scholarly purpose. Perhaps they should write a textbook of elementary Jewish history. Children's lectures should be prepared for synagogue classes or special children's services. The union and Jewish Historical Society should arrange for lectures in Jewish history to be given to all schools.[55] These were tasks intellectuals understood and could, perhaps, accomplish.

The Maccabæans, founded in 1891, represented the acknowledged secular professional and intellectual elite of Anglo-Jewry. They were not the writers and teachers and intellectuals of the Union of Literary Societies, save on a highly selective basis.

> It is a body of Jewish professional men who have formed themselves into a society for their own up-lifting and for such advancement of their ideals. Jewish businessmen [mused president M. D. Spielmann in 1905] have no such society of their own, as they are popularly supposed to do pretty well without one (laughter); but we are glad to have included a few of them – kindred spirits – in our ranks.[56]

Professor Meldola, the distinguished scientist who replaced Professor Israel Gollancz as president in 1910, believed that the Maccabæans had more than justified their existence by serving as a meeting ground for intellectuals. Not only did social discourse among those in widely varied fields of endeavour sharpen and deepen each participant's capacity, but the Maccabæans as an organization enabled Anglo-Jewry 'to publicize to the world how much we appreciate the professional achievements of our community.' While the organization from time to time debated controversial issues of communal interest – the power of the media, for instance, and whether Jews should or should not formally respond to 'wilful cruel and slanderous mis-statements which have become more and more common in the yellow press'[57] – its most important work lay in two related areas. The Maccabæans, led by its president, Colonel A. E. W. Goldsmid, founded the Jewish Lads' Brigade. With the great stalwart of Jewish philanthropy, F. D. Mocatta, as one of the founding members, the Maccabæans, not surprisingly, also assisted in the formation of institutions that brought cultural contributions to social service. The Maccabæans helped to organize the Jewish Historical Society and the Education Aid Society. The organization also considered the merits of establishing Jewish Toynbee Halls in the East End, opting ultimately to applaud and support rather than to take action and initiate.

The Maccabæans took great care in their other principal task of shaping the Jewish public image.

> The Macccabeans, I have always understood, are a voluntary association, in the main, of professional men, for the purpose of putting forward our best

---

55 Council meeting, Union of Jewish Literary Societies, 25 Sept. 1905. *JC*, 29 Sept. 1905. Against this surge of Anglo-Jewish intellectual purpose, little pockets of resistance began to form. The Hebrew Speaking Society, for instance, gained a sufficient following over the next years to hold an impressive mass meeting in January 1911. *JC*, 6 Jan. 1911.

56 Maccabæans art dinner, 19 Feb. 1905. *JC*, 17 Mar. 1905.

57 A point on which there was considerable difference of opinion. Maccabæans, 'The Jews and the Press', 2 July 1905. On balance, the community leaders preferred to leave anti-defamation work to the Board of Deputies. *JC*, 7, 14 July 1905.

side, from the intellectual point of view, to the world; and showing that Jews are not entirely a commercial community but have another aspect to their existence.[58]

Impressive assemblies celebrated the arts, *belles lettres* and individual Jewish achievement at dinners that brought Anglo-Jewry's elite together with their peers in British life and culture. One of the more triumphant moments was the large dinner in January 1911 to celebrate the appointment of Rufus Isaacs as the Attorney General. The first Jew to hold this office, Isaacs was warmly applauded by the leading legal figures of Anglo-Jewry and the foremost lawyers in the land. Lord Alverstone, Lord Chief Justice (whom Isaacs would shortly replace), and Sir Edward Carson waxed eloquent on the merits of Isaacs.[59] Anglo-Jewry had never before been so well or substantially represented in the British government as it had come to be in Asquith's government.

58 *JC*, 24 Feb. 1911.
59 Simon diary, 15 Jan. 1911. MS Simon 2, f 1; *JC*, 20 Jan., 24 Feb. 1911.

6

Communal Philanthropies

Communal philanthropies coexisted and overlapped with synagogue charities and such overarching institutions as the Jewish Board of Guardians. While performing different tasks, they shared certain characteristics. The more affluent provided for the less fortunate. Each charity distinguished between the deserving and undeserving poor. Every philanthropy sought to render its recipients self-supporting as quickly as possible. All organizations considered themselves, in a profound sense, educational institutions teaching the less fortunate what they must do while ministering, as economically and efficiently as possible, to their immediate needs. Each institution contributed to Anglo-Jewish social discipline. But for all the common purpose and social philosophy, they remained what that stern critic of East London philanthropy, Mrs Bernard Bosanquet, called 'sprinkling charities'.

> Soup kitchens, philanthropic societies, country holiday funds, ragged school funds, funds from all the enterprising newspapers, and funds from all the political clubs in the district; church funds and chapel funds, missionary and mothers' meetings, all are engaged in pouring money into a slough of poverty which swallows it up and leaves no trace of improvement. No one is the richer for all the thousands of pounds squandered in the parish, for it is given away in miserable little doles which are incapable of keeping any man to solid ground, and only help to 'keep him down.' Almost as bad are the spasmodic incursions from the West End to relieve the misery of the East.[1]

Mrs Bosanquet indicted religious and secular philanthropy alike as unsystematic, pauperizing and harmful. The Jewish Board of Guardians shared her fears, but the Jewish community never surrendered to Board of Guardians imperialism. Closer examination of community charities suggests that some of Mrs Bosanquet's criticisms were well merited, some unfair, and others simply incorrect.

1 Mrs B. Bosanquet, *Rich and Poor* (London, 1896).

HEALTH

Anglo-Jewry, as we have seen, adopted ambiguous policies towards health care. Contemporary standards of medicine being what they were, community preferences may have made little difference. Medicine, argued the Jewish Board of Guardians, knew neither race nor religion. Medical care, moreover, should be a matter of personal responsibility and self-help. The prudent individual received medical assistance through his trade organization, friendly society or provident association. Those institutions, however, varied widely in benefits offered and the quality of care provided. Money and tight budgets were the principal problem. Physicians contracted to the Friendly Societies Federation before that body collapsed, for instance, were underpaid and, as a result, offered generally indifferent treatment. Inferior drugs accompanied substandard medical care. Beyond the patent limitations of professional competence, even such medical care as was provided left much to be desired. Both the doctors the Board of Guardians employed during its brief foray into providing medical care and the physicians whom the Jewish benefit societies engaged displayed a partiality for the dram of whisky, gin or brandy as universal cures.[2]

For those who had not provided or could not care for themselves, Anglo-Jewry believed that the Poor Law Union workhouse infirmaries and the metropolitan hospitals, generously supported either by Anglo-Jewish taxpayers or philanthropy, should serve. The board learned from its brief experience in providing medical care how difficult costs were to control. It felt no qualms and displayed no hesitation in shifting that burden back to the local authorities. The times, moreover, were right. British society mobilized, on the heels of cholera outbreaks and a spirited public health campaign, to provide medical care, such as it was, for the poor. Although administered through the poor law authorities, medical assistance, unlike poor relief itself, brought neither social stigma nor political disabilities. Edwin Chadwick, the reforming civil servant and secretary to the Poor Law Board, ceaselessly urged public health improvement from within the government. Poor Law Unions were in place, and cost-conscious governments were unlikely to create duplicatory institutions. Poor Law Union medical care, however, remained free from the statutory disabilities of poor relief. Such extra-parliamentary bodies as the Association for the Improvement of London Workhouse Infirmaries pressed the case for public medical care upon the politically conscious public. Between them they created an 'improved' system of which Anglo-Jewry was delighted to avail itself. By doing so, the leadership transferred one of its potentially most costly forms of social welfare from the community to the state.[3]

2 See, e.g., the correspondence on friendly societies medicine *JC*, 12 May 1911.
3 Chadwick to Twining, 1 Sept. 1866. Louisa Twining Papers in the Fawcett Library, City of London Polytechnic. Ernest Hart was one of the leading agitators in the campaign for an association to forward the cause. See his article, 'Metropolitan infirmaries for the pauper sick', *Fortnightly Review*, IV (1866), 459–63. The extra-parliamentary campaign drew widespread support from community leaders. Charles Dickens,

The timing proved doubly fortunate. Just as state-provided education was in place immediately before the rising tide of immigration swept into the East End, medical care for the needy was also shifted to the ratepayer. Poor law guardians immediately felt the impact and objected to the admission of non-destitute patients to their facilities. Anglo-Jewry, always sensitive to public perceptions of the Jew, made every effort to minimize the extent to which Jews appeared to be taking advantage of state medical care.[4] Once having started, moreover, the state steadily extended the range of medical services it offered. The Administrative Provisions Act of 1907, for instance, initiated the school medical service. Over 850 school doctors and 1,250 school nurses tended children attending board schools by 1914. School medical service funding brought better provision to the special schools for the blind, the deaf and the physically impaired, simultaneously augmenting the educational grants to those special Jewish institutions. With provision already in hand for subsidized pre-natal and maternity care, the Asquith government brought pre-school children under the public medical umbrella for the first time in February 1914 when the Treasury allocated £5,000 'to be distributed in aid of schools for mothers'. Actions which sprang from motives of humanity and social efficiency continued for the sake of national survival. The war concentrated public attention on the health of the nation. School medical care expanded downwards. Some 180 health centres administered through 120 schools by 1916 provided care for pre-school children.[5] Efforts like these not only meant new state initiatives but strengthened the fruitful partnership of local authorities and Jewish philanthropies. Maternity and child care had become popular issues in each political party since 1907 with a steadily expanding agenda. Over and above the services provided through national insurance after 1911, local authorities provided health visitors and subsidized professionally qualified ones serving the Jewish Board of Guardians. Local government authorities established or made grants to existing maternity and infant welfare centres and provided or helped to provide for the attendance of licensed midwives, while carefully avoiding duplication of assistance under national insurance.[6]

John Stuart Mill, Thomas Hughes, and the Archbishop of Canterbury contributed their efforts. James Kay Shuttleworth, like Chadwick one of the great pioneering civil servants, helped to guide the campaign. See, e.g., Association for the Improvement of London Workhouse Infirmaries, *Report of a Public Meeting . . ., March 3rd, 1866* (London, 1867); *The Management of the Infirmaries of the Strand Union, the Rotherhithe and the Paddington Workhouses; being an Outline of the Proceedings of Official Inquiries . . . into Allegations of Ill-Treatment and Neglect and Mismanagement of the Sick Poor . . .* (London, 1867).

4 See, particularly, the Infirmaries file, 1887–1900. ME[tropolitan]PO[lice Papers] 2/244 in the public Record Office. Christopher Addison, who would become the first Minister of Health in 1919, summarized the complicated state health provisions just before the outbreak of the war in *The Health of the People and How It May Be Improved . . .* (London, 1914).

5 Arthur Henderson's confidential memorandum, Maternity and Infant Welfare Work, of 22 July 1916. CAB[inet Papers] 37/152/16, in the Public Record Office, and Walter Long's memorandum of 21 June 1916, CAB 37/150/9, summarize the work of the education authorities and Local Government Board.

6 See, for an overview, Lord Rhondda's secret memoranda GT-1056 (14 June), GT-1268 ([4 July]), and Hayes Fisher's response, GT-1662 (9 Aug. 1917), CAB 24/16/1–5; CAB 24/18/289–98; CAB 24/22/256–8.

Through the 1880s and 1890s, Anglo-Jewry worked vigorously to extend medical self-insurance for East Enders. How better to urge the virtues of self-help? Health care was yet another form of education and socialization. Workers were urged to enrol in friendly societies with medical plans. Other social organizations stepped in as well. Samuel Montagu's Jewish Working Men's Club promoted its own plan. Like many Montagu philanthropies, it flourished so long as Sir Samuel helped to foot the bills. Frederic Mocatta and others, including Montagu, enjoyed greater success when they capitalized and sponsored a provident medical association requiring but a twopenny weekly contribution from each beneficiary.

Nagging doubts remained. Some champions of the East End poor argued about *de facto* segregation, the creation of two classes of dispensary care. Exisiting facilities benefited principally English-speaking Jews. Yiddish-speakers, they argued, were unable to communicate or humiliated when they sought medical care or medicine. Embarrassment, false dignity, or both, prevented them from availing themselves of help. The failure to provide a free Yiddish-speaking dispensary for the East Enders opened the way for the conversionists. Christian conversionists, a recurrent Jewish phobia, fluttered about the unfortunate like so many vultures, ever ready to seize on some unanswered need. Now they offered a free dispensary. Hermann Landau, Montagu's ally and president of the Poor Jews' Temporary Shelter, considered that to pose a real threat. During 1896 and 1897, public meetings and the columns of the Jewish press reverberated with heated debate. Mocatta offered help to underwrite another branch of the Metropolitan Provident Dispensary in the East End with Yiddish-speaking doctors, but Landau resisted, holding out for his free dispensary. Montagu, flush with Federation of Synagogue success, supported Landau. Finally Sir Benjamin Cohen's firm veto from the Jewish Board of Guardians decisively tipped the balance, and the plan was dropped. Anglo-Jewry once again reaffirmed its belief in the principle of participatory self-help.[7] This stand committed the Jewish leadership to subsidizing self-help enterprises but spared communal resources for new medical departures. It was a great thing for people to be kept independent, said Frederic Mocatta, speaking for the communal leadership in 1902, and there was no reason because a family was poor that they should be treated as if they were receiving alms.[8] Ultimately those experiments,

---

7 'The Board believes that the proposed movement will tend to pauperize the poor, will strike a blow at the Provident Societies which so powerfully foster a spirit of thrift among the East End population, and will be in opposition to that principle of nonsectarianism in medical charity, which has happily made such rapid progress in recent years.' JBG, *38th Annual Report, 1897* (London, 1898), 18–9. For the report on the negotiations, see, *JC*, 12 Feb. 1897. For the opening of the new Jewish Provident Dispensary in October 1897, see *JC*, 3, Sept., 8 Oct. 1897, 18 Jan. 1898. The conversionist threat was probably not serious. Christian conversionist enterprise, real or exaggerated, however, proved a useful threat to mobilize philanthropy. One other issue in the debate, the argument that the non-English-speaking poor underused medical facilities, was possibly correct, although the various contributory and provident arrangements as well as the local hospitals had some Yiddish-speaking doctors and pharmacists. The Jewish institutional model remained that defined by the medical committee of the Charity Organisation Society, *Model Rules for Provident Dispensaries, June 1878*. (London, [1878]). Montagu derived some Cassandra-like satisfaction from the failure of the Jewish Provident Dispensary in 1903. Federation of Synagogues meeting, 17 Nov. 1903. *JC*, 20 Mar. 1903.

8 Jewish Provident Dispensary, annual meeting, 22 Feb. 1902. *JC*, 28 Feb. 1902.

particularly with the treatment of tuberculosis and medical aftercare, benefited not only the Jewish community but served as a model for subsequent public policy.

Anglo-Jewry, having argued that medicine knew no religion, also supported non-sectarian institutions to further its point. The St James's Philanthropic Society, founded in 1885, for instance, provided its own hospital care support plan, first at the London Hospital, and by 1905, in support of twenty hospitals serving the poorer central metropolitan area. When a deserving case came to its attention, the society issued a letter to the relevant hospital guaranteeing at least a portion of the costs of care. Working men were encouraged to subscribe even as little as one penny per week to 'help support institutions which were for their benefit'.[9] Non-denominational hospitals had long served Jewish needs. The London Hospital provided Jewish wards from 1842, steadily expanding space and facilities through the subsequent decades. Rothschild and Goldsmid wards served Jewish patients, male and female respectively. A Hebrew Trust Fund and annual contributions sustained annual costs. Leopold de Rothschild as vice president of the hospital and such luminaries as Sir Samuel Montagu and Sir Benjamin L. Cohen on the house committee provided Anglo-Jewry's imprimatur to an institution that, by 1904, served more than 1,700 inpatients and 51,000 outpatients, principally Jewish. One Sunday each June was 'Hospital Sunday', when every synagogue competed to raise funds for London hospitals.

Smaller hospitals also responded to Jewish needs. The Metropolitan Hospital opened Jewish wards serving some 100 patients each year, and a Yiddish-speaking staff physician held outpatient clinics twice a week, accounting for 11,000 visits in 1904. Charing Cross Hospital, which served Soho, established a new Jewish ward in 1903. The Brompton Consumption Hospital established its Jewish ward in March 1905. Hermann Landau contributed £1,000 in 1900 to construct a kosher kitchen for the German Hospital, and 'Hospital Sunday' provided the £100 per year maintenance charge. The East London Hospital for Children in Shadwell served substantial Jewish needs. Founded in 1868 with ten beds it served upwards of 35,000 outpatient attendances by the turn of the century. Although no special accommodations were made at the North-eastern Hospital for Children, ten per cent of the inmates were Jewish children. Jewish insane for whom private arrangements were not or could not be made were consigned to the Colney Hatch asylum. London County Council's asylum subcommittee even assisted it to construct an entirely new kosher kitchen in 1896, and the medical superintendant arranged that as many Jewish patients as possible would have their meals together.[10]

Despite the substantial community commitment to and services received from the various hospitals, a number of efforts were made to organize a specifically Jewish hospital. These campaigns were also, to some degree, another manifestation of the political challenge to the Anglo-Jewish establishment. While organized in the first years of the twentieth century, they began to acquire momentum only as the great late Victorian leaders passed away. The Association for a Jewish Hospital organized

9 Twelfth annual festival of the society, 14 June 1905. *JC*, 16 June 1905.
10 For the Colney Hatch arrangements, see *JC*, 27 Mar. 1896. On other hospitals, see, particularly, 'London Hospital and the Jewish Sick', feature supplement, *JC*, 20 May 1898, *JC*, 23 Mar., 10 June 1898, 'Jews and the London hospitals', *JC* , 23 June 1905.

in 1907 had raised £3,400 towards a £5,400 property within four years. Yiddish addresses highlighted each meeting, leaving no question about the challenge its middle-class leaders addressed to the traditional elite in form, values or substance. A West London branch, founded in Soho in 1908, faltered and collapsed but was reconstructed in 1911.[11]

Home care and nursing attendance loomed high on Anglo-Jewry's agenda in the 1890s, reflecting the growing feminine presence in philanthropy and social work. Two organizations, in particular, addressed nursing and home care needs. The East London Nursing Society, so Leonard Cohen reported to the Jewish Board of Guardians, nursed 700 cases in 1910 compared to 623 the previous year. Even those 623 required 15,800 visits. Alice Model, one of the great figures in turn-of-the-century social work, reminded him that the Sick Room Helps Society, a provident institution, did still more and, through its work, steadily reduced the number of maternity cases requiring Board of Guardians relief. The Sick Room Helps Society, modelled on the *Hauspflege Verein* of Frankfurt-am-Main, was a remarkable tribute both to the thrift of poor East End mothers and to the imagination and determination of a handful of stalwart Jewish women. Women social workers visiting East End homes commented on the loss of income and domestic disruption in families when illness, incapacity or recuperation required home care, forcing the wage earner to stop work. Maternity cases, in particular, pulled the father from work just as family expenses rose. For medical attention itself, the Royal Maternity Charity provided much East End assistance. The Royal Maternity dispatched medical officers and midwives to necessitous mothers, and Jewish women were disproportionately beneficiaries of this care. Of 4,120 cases in 1896, for instance, 903 (almost 22 per cent) were Jewish. The Royal Maternity Charity engaged four Jewish midwives, each of whom spoke Yiddish, to serve the community.[12]

The Royal Maternity Charity, however, provided care only through the time of delivery. Much post-natal home assistance could come from girls and women trained to provide home care and the most elementary practical nursing. A staff of trained practical aides meant that professionally qualified nurses could oversee a number of cases at minimal cost. The Sick Room Helps Society, funded by its founders and their friends, opened its provident branch in 1897. Poor mothers, understanding the benefits involved, contributed £31 in pennies, a considerable commitment from them but less than six per cent of society costs. By 1904, provident income had risen to almost £630 of the society's £2,200, a substantial 29 per cent. The Sick Room Helps originally aspired to answer general nursing and home attendance needs, but resources were soon badly overextended. The society staggered in 1899, unable to manage its financial obligations, although the provident branch sustained its operations without difficulty. Retrenchment and

11 *JC*, 19 May, 16 June 1911.
12 *JC*, 29 Jan. 1897. Cf. K. W. Jones, 'Sentiment and science; the late nineteenth century pediatrician as mother's advisor', *Journal of Social History*, 17/1 (1983), 79–96.

minor reorganization led the Sick Room Helps to concentrate on maternity nursing and home care.[13]

The Sick Room Helps attended all maternity cases coming under the notice of the Board of Guardians and all instances of ritual circumcision dealt with by the Initiation Society. By 1911 and the coming of national insurance, the greater proportion of Sick Room Helps assistance came through its provident branch rather than through the Board of Guardians. Nearly 5,000 members contributed £1,300, 36 per cent of total expenditure. Ten nurses and eighty 'helps' attended almost 3,300 cases. Volunteers performed all administrative services and paid overhead expenses out of their own pockets. The Sick Room Helps Society, thanks to a bequest, could embark, in 1910, on its own building and educational programme. A maternity ward and home for nurses in Spitalfields placed the society in the area of greatest need.

Like other Jewish philanthropies, Sick Room Helps assistance also introduced 'order into the homes of the poor in time of sickness', training the family in home management and child care while 'relieving the recuperating parent of considerable anxiety'. It worked. Infant mortality fell, and the society claimed a share of the credit. Trachoma, that 'immigrant blight', was better managed. Proper aftercare speeded recuperation and expedited self-help. Fathers remained at work, producing income and easing the potential Jewish Board of Guardians caseload. The board, therefore, happily provided a 10s grant for 'nourishment' on recommendation of the society. Administrative costs remained impossibly low because Jewish ladies contributed their time as well as their money. Necessitous cases received food through the Invalid Kitchen, a charity Baroness Lionel de Rothschild had established.

Sick Room Helps, however, was more than just another philanthropy. Although most of its organizers and supporters might have shuddered at the thought, Sick Room Helps struck a significant blow for Jewish feminism. Through that society, Jewish women, acting on their own initiative, significantly eased the life of the poor. Following their feelings and sensitivity, women comprehended a communal need and acted to meet it in ways in which men had not (perhaps could not have) done. The Helps, however, accepted the general axioms of communal philanthropy. The society moved into action only when the network of self-help had broken down, when friends, relatives, or neighbours were neither ready, willing, nor able to assume such responsibilities. Sick Room Helps served Anglo-Jewish needs. Alice Model and Bella Löwy had discovered yet another way in which the poor could be 'elevated'.[14]

13 For the overextension and redirection, see Sick Rooms Helps' Society (SRHS), *Sixth Annual Report, 1899* (London, 1900); *Seventh Annual Report, 1900* (London, 1901); *Eighth Annual Report, 1901* (London, 1902).

14 Helpers had instructions 'to clean and air the room or rooms, wash, dress, feed, and generally see after children too young to attend to themselves, see that the elder children are washed and sent to school: to wash dirty linen, cook the food for the family, and, if necessary, assist the doctor or nurse, though no professional work is attempted.' SRHS, *Eleventh Annual Report, 1904* (London, 1905); *Sixteenth Annual Report, 1910* (London, 1911); annual meeting, 28 Mar. 1911, *JC*, 31 Mar. 1911; JBG meeting, 8 May 1911, *JC*, 5 Nov. 1897, 12 May 1911.

The Home and Hospital for Jewish Incurables, organized in 1890, had a chequered early history. Lacking the usual community titans on its board, the Home and Hospital depended on the pennies of the poor more than most philanthropies, so financial constraints impeded its development. The first patients were admitted to two old houses in Victoria Park Road in 1891. Facilities were inadequate. Needs exceeded resources, and management disputes soon became public. By the summer of 1895, financial and administrative disorder demanded reoganization, and Anglo-Jewry stepped in. A committee of communal leaders – Frederic D. Mocatta, Barrow Emanuel and Lt Col. Charles Sebag-Montefiore – investigated and reported. Herbert H. Raphael, the first president, resigned, and the Home and Hospital was assigned to Montagu management.

Stuart M. Samuel, nephew of Sir Samuel Montagu, assumed the presidency. Lionel L. Alexander and Isaac Davis, much involved in the Jewish Working Men's Club and other Montagu enterprises, assisted in remodelling. Samuel recruited some major donors without ever forgetting the popular base on which the institution had been built in the first instance. The Costermongers' and Street Sellers' Union, with which Stuart Samuel was also much involved, made the Home and Hospital for Jewish Incurables its particular charity. From 1897 onwards, barrow people with their pushcarts paraded the streets on the first Sunday of each September in a massive demonstration and collection for the Home and Hospital. Small contributors, however, could not begin to carry the burden. The Home and Hospital could boast 500 subscribers, but people of modest means could only pay weekly, producing a total income of £200. Morally heartening that might be, but an expensive medical philanthropy could not operate on enthusiasm alone. A band of 'community ladies' volunteered to collect subscription arrears and to expand the contributing base.

Until substantially more money could be raised and better facilities procured, the Home and Hospital could manage only nineteen patients at a time. The medical officer and staff still achieved impressive results. Some inmates could be discharged as cured. All were tended with much care and considerable affection for 18s 6d per patient per week. The Passover *seder* (the ceremonial first-night dinner) of 1895, described in pathetic detail in the institution's annual report, touched the sensitivities and conscience of a broad public. Once the Montagu–Samuel connection had taken over, Anglo-Jewry tagged along. By 1900, £20,000 had been raised for a new building in South Tottenham, a mere twopenny ride from the heart of the East End. Designed with the latest innovations in mind – a mix of the latest in lifts, well-planned ramps for invalid chairs, spacious facilities set into an overpowering red-brick Elizabethan shell with over 200 feet of frontage – for a substantial £7,000 cost overrun, the Jewish community found itself with the model establishment in the kingdom. The Home and Hospital, while constructed and maintained by Anglo-Jewry, drew increasingly for its ongoing expenses from cooperative government agencies. Friends on the Whitechapel Board of Guardians undertook as early as 1897 to make a regular financial contribution to 'relieve ratepayers of the expense of attendance of patients at the Infirmary and to give poor people the benefit of attendance by people of their own creed.'[15]

The Jewish Home for Incurables served the dual purpose of caring for patients and providing a training school for Jewish nurses. Stuart M. Samuel called it a 'poor man's charity' when collecting fifty guineas from the East London fund-raising branch in 1898, and to listen to Samuel's speeches one would think costermonger parades carried the burden from one year to the next. Such rhetoric achieved two ends. East End efforts and contributions increased each year to the First World War. At the same time, wealthy donors, who had rarely given the home the time of day, much less any money, rallied to support this symbol of the people's philanthropy. By 1911, the Home for Incurables had eighty-two patients and some £20,000 in funded investments. Like so many other philanthropies, current expenses for the home devoured a third of annual legacies, hamstringing the campaign for fiscal viability.

All the twentieth-century blandishments were brought to bear to expand income. Alderman John Harris secured a subsidy each year from the Whitechapel Board of Guardians, on which he sat until his death in 1910. Just as the Home for Aged Jews learned much about improving its operations from the Home for Incurables, the Home for Incurables learned from the Home for Aged Jews the importance of bringing women on to its general committee. They brought a fresh infusion of ideas, energy, and cash. A theatre gala produced over £300. Once again, the less privileged were marshalled in an East London aid society. In this instance, the form and size of contributions suggests that the Home for Incurables appealed to the slightly better off. Quarterly, not merely weekly, subscriptions were a middle-class form of funding. Aid society leaders, mimicking the privileged, held parlour receptions. Businesses were persuaded to handle box collections. By 1910, the home's East End aid society raised more than £550 each year. Samuel understood his constituency and realized that the middle-class money was moving to Golders Green and Hampstead. A new north-west aid society was launched in 1911 to organize support. Occasionally a 'benevolent friend' organized a 'treat', such as the anonymous donor of a Purim poultry dinner, gramophone entertainments for the afternoon, and gifts for the institution staff.[16]

Care for the aged went hand-in-hand with ascertaining that working Jews survived to enjoy those benefits. By the mid-1890s, tuberculosis had become a major recognized health problem within the Jewish community, particularly in the slums of the East End. Frederic D. Mocatta, inspired by a paper on 'consumption', asked

---

15 Street collections came to be a general London annoyance, compounded by unemployment demonstrations, and police regulations were issued against them. Ironically this worked to reduce almost all East End philanthropic donations. *JC*, 29 Oct. 1897. See also, *Sixth Annual Report of the Home and Hospital for Jewish Incurables* (HHJI) (London, 1896), *Eighth Annual Report* (London, 1898), *Eleventh Annual Report* (London 1901), *Twenty-first Annual Report* (London, 1911). The Home and Hospital 'billed' local boards of guardians 19s 6d per patient per week, although some bodies, the City of London Guardians, for instance, balked at the figure. *JC*, 13 Aug. 1897. See also, *JC*, 3, 17 Apr. 1896, 17 Sept, 26 Nov, 24 Dec 1897, 21 Jan, 15, 22 Apr, 6 May, 8 July, 9, 16 Sept, 1898, 22 Feb, 1 Mar. 1901, 3 Feb., 5 May 1905, 17 Mar., 2 June 1911.

16 The expanding fortunes of the Home and Hospital are best followed in its annual reports, particularly from the *Sixth Annual Report, 1895* (London 1896) to the *Twenty-third Annual Report, 1912* (London, 1913). See also, *JC*, 3 Apr., 3 July 1896, 13 Aug., 26 Nov., 24 Dec. 1897, 21 Jan., 8 July, 9, 16 Sept. 1898, 1 Mar., 5 July, 29 Nov. 1901, 25 Apr., 19 Sept. 1902, 3 Feb. 1905, 17 Mar., 2 June 1911.

the Board of Guardians to print and circulate it among the board members and those serving on subordinate committees.[17] Nathan Joseph and Lionel Cohen mobilized the board, and the long campaign against tuberculosis was launched. The guardians publicly endorsed the policies recommended by the National Association for the Prevention of Consumption, and the hundred Board of Guardians visitors did their best as they went from case to case. The community created sanitoria, aftercare facilities, and a community nursing programme. Baroness de Hirsch funded Tudor House in Hampstead, which allowed the Jewish Convalescent Home to close the tuberculosis section of its Norwood home by the end of the nineteenth century. An umbrella philanthropy, the Jewish Convalescent Home, was formed to reorganize aftercare. The Jewish Seaside Convalescent Home at Hove, opened in May 1891 for adults and children, coalesced with the Samuel Lewis Seaside Home at Walton-on-the-Naze, with the joint operation called the Children's Convalescent Home. Sea breezes and recuperation came thus to be provided for some three hundred children each year. A special appeal for £8,000 temporarily funded the consolidated annual deficit of £1,150 per year.[18] The short-term expedients worked. By the time yet another shortfall developed, the government had committed itself to extensive programmes for consumptives and the medical care of children.

The Daneswood Sanitorium began the experimental treatment of consumptives 'by the best modern methods' in January 1905. In less than a year, experimentation had slowed, but the sanitorium became the foremost of such institutions in the country treating tuberculosis patients. Poor Jews, among whom the disease had grown at an alarming rate, benefited from this national showpiece, which admitted between seventy-five and a hundred new patients each year to 1914. Aftercare committee reports were very encouraging, but the budget committee confronted red ink. The Bischoffsheims gave the facility to the community, but its funds were exhausted within six years. The management owed the bankers almost £1,000, and further economies were impossible.[19]

Public health, as Anglo-Jewry realized, involved both reality and perceptions. Nathan Joseph, wearing his two hats as Jewish Board of Guardians sanitary expert and operating officer of the Russo-Jewish Committee, regularly called Anglo-Jewry's attention, not only to the real issues of public health, but to subtle and not-so-subtle ways in which the Jewish public image could be helped or hurt by its policies on such matters. First cholera and then, after 1894, misplaced fear of new outbreaks of bubonic plague, associated Jewish immigrants with contagion and implied that the medically 'unfit' immigrant menaced the British Isles. Much of the difficulty sprang from rumour and misunderstanding. A pneumonia outbreak in Southern Russia even frightened some government authorities who confused it with

17 *JC*, 13 Mar. 1896.

18 One philanthropist who modelled his efforts on the JBG example was W. P. Treloar. See his reflections in 'The cure of tuberculous children', *The Nineteenth Century and after*, LXXXIV (August, 1918), 288–95. One critic, however, argued that the board was guilty of 'spasmodic philosophy' and was merely dabbling with East End problems, not confronting them. *JC*, 11 Feb. 1898. See also Dr J. Snowman's lecture to the North London Jewish Literary and Social Union, 5 Jan. 1899. *JC*, 13 Jan. 1899. For convalescent home policies, see, in particular, *The Twenty-second Annual Report of the Jewish Convalescent Home* (London, 1904) which deals with the closing of the Norwood home, the shift to Hampstead, and the opening of Daneswood.

19 *JC*, 14 Apr. 1911.

the plague. Did not many Jews migrate from Odessa?[20] From such anxieties, warned Joseph, alien restriction could grow.

Disability, particularly when on the modest scale it tended to be within the nineteenth-century Jewish community, readily animated philanthropic sensitivity. The Indigent Blind Society, to take one instance, one of the more effective smaller charities, ministered to between fifty and sixty beneficiaries each year by the 1890s. H. H. Hyam and his brother David made the charity their particular commitment. Sir George Faudel-Phillips, Bt, Lord Mayor of London during the 1897 jubilee, presided. His presence enabled the society to increase its weekly pension from 8s to 10s and recruit the additional £300 that would cost each year. The commitment, however, thrust that conservatively managed organization into an annual deficit that forced it to compete in the yearly struggle for the philanthropic guinea and left it spending rather than funding subsequent bequests. But the £1,500 annual budget, like that of many other philanthropies, did not include all income or expenditure. Officers and board members celebrated their own lives by giving in cash or kind. David Hyam, treasurer of the society, for instance, awarded each pensioner five shillings on the occasion of his eighty-first birthday in 1905.[21]

HOUSING

With education and health, while maintaining a costly range of denominational institutions, Anglo-Jewry actually shifted by far the heaviest burden of social costs to the state. The increasing scale of state intervention, timed as it happened to be, allowed Anglo-Jewry the luxury of appearing to care for its own on a communal voluntaristic basis. Many critics agreed, arguing that Jewish charity was a magnet drawing East European paupers to London.[22] In the anti-alien testimony before the Royal Commission on Alien Immigration in 1902 and 1903, overcrowding and rack-renting, more than any other factors, fuelled the restrictionist fires. While philanthropists continued to underwrite voluntary institutions, more and more of those societies came to be partially, even substantially, dependent on public revenues. The more expensive sectors of public welfare, health, housing and education, were the first to be effectively transferred. Jews were not, the leadership continued to argue, a burden on the British public – a contentious point as agitation for immigration restriction grew. In the cheaper, often more visible areas of social welfare, Anglo-Jewry did indeed care for its own. Direct relief grants in cash and kind, aid for dependent children, old age pensions for those not beneficiaries of contributory schemes could be paraded before the community and the country. Jews, even their severest critics conceded, met their social responsibilities more completely than any other group in British society.

20 September 1899 outbreaks of 'virulent marsh fever', a diagnosis broadly applied to many ailments, some of which were found among occasional Jewish immigrants, routinely triggered restrictionist agitation when publicized. M[inistry of] H[ealth] 19/252 in the Public Record Office. For some of the more general official reports and discussions, see MH 19/247–8.

21 Annual general court, 20 July 1897. *JC*, 23 July 1897, 3 Feb. 1905.

22 See, e.g., Arnold White to the editor, *The Times*, 30 May 1887.

After education and health, housing remained the most expensive area of social need. Costs of improvement were potentially staggering. For Britain as a whole, particularly in metropolitan centres, rising housing costs outstripped wage gains. Britons were better fed and clothed for less as the nineteenth century drew towards its close, but housing cost more. Urban populations everywhere, especially in London, grew faster than available housing stock. Land use, moreover, was changing in all the areas adjacent to the City. Conversion of residential units into commercial or industrial space rendered the East End problem more acute at just the time that substantial numbers of immigrants were arriving, gravitating towards relatives and old acquaintances, and towards a culture safely Jewish and comfortably Yiddish.[23]

Anglo-Jewry had two housing strategies. It sought first, as in other matters, to move people on, if not overseas then to the provinces. Sir Samuel Montagu attacked the pressing problem of East End overcrowding by extending his network of synagogues into the provinces. He offered small synagogues the services of the Federation of Synagogues. Translated that meant access to the Montagu purse for the construction of approved and appropriate facilities and the services of the Federation rabbi. This new Jewish Congregational Union would unify disparate, often neglected small congregations and assist the poorer, and particularly foreign, Jews in the provinces. The Chief Rabbi approved since this brought those congregations officially under his authority. Anglo-Jewry applauded since Montagu could now establish a dispersion committee. While ostensibly nothing more than a subcommittee of the Federation and Union, Montagu's dispersion committee worked independently and with no publicity to move families out of the East End, onwards to new opportunities in provincial settings. The union guaranteed that the religious facilities immigrants clustered to the East End to find would be available where they settled. Through Montagu, Russo-Jewish Committee funds were available for resettlement, and through Hermann Landau, the Poor Jews' Temporary Shelter could select promising families wishing to stay in Britain and move them directly to provincial cities, not London. Costs were substantial. Landau estimated £30 per family, although Montagu believed that once the network was operating effectively, costs would be reduced.[24] At the same time, Anglo-Jewry continued to lobby local authorities, as enabling acts reached the statute book, to use their powers to improve the existing housing stock and to encourage urban redevelopment.[25]

---

23 Whitechapel's inhabited houses fell over 30 per cent from 8,264 (1871) to 5,735 (1901) while the population rose slightly over 4 per cent from 75,552 to 78,768. *Annual Report of the 4% Industrial Dwellings Company Ltd, 25 January 1889* quoted from K. D. Rubens, 'The 4% Industrial Dwellings Company Ltd: Its Formation and its East End Developments, 1885–1901', in Newman (ed.), *Jewish East End*, 193. These numbers, however, required considerable qualification. Edgar Harper, statistical officer of the LCC reminded the Royal Commission that 'house' had, at best, a hazy definition. A block of model buildings counted as one house in the returns. Although, by his calculations, the number of inhabited houses decreased in the boroughs of Stepney and Bethnal Green by 8.95 per cent, the actual housing stock was not reduced that substantially. RCAI, 15 Dec 1902.

24 *JC*, 25 Oct. 1901, 31 Jan., 21 Mar, 13, 20 June 1902.

25 The statutory advance only began with the 1875–6 Artisan and Labourers' Dwellings Improvement Acts, the Artisans' Dwellings Act of 1882 and the Housing of the Working Classes Acts of 1885 and 1890. Only the last actually provided for substantial urban clearance.

Individual philanthropists had already addressed the issue without any possibility of effectively correcting it. The free market, inspired by such demonstrative good intentions, could not work rapidly enough. The Crystal Palace Exhibition of 1851 displayed prize-winning designs for model artisan housing. Prince Albert took a personal interest in the problem. The Earl of Shaftesbury, Sir Sydney Waterlow, George Peabody and Octavia Hill developed model buildings and elaborate schemes of social management within them. But only Anglo-Jewry's most affluent philanthropists ventured into the field. Nathan Joseph, whose leadership of and activity in almost every department of the Jewish Board of Guardians made him that agency's greatest civil servant, was an accomplished architect as well as a social engineer. With Rothschild funding, he designed the Royal Albert Buildings on land acquired from the Metropolitan Board of Works in 1884. Frederic David Mocatta already served as a director in Sir Sydney Waterlow's Metropolitan Association for the Improving of the Dwellings of the Industrial Classes. Circumstances, however, demanded a more substantial approach, preferably one in which Anglo-Jewry attacked not merely a Jewish but a regional problem.

Anglo-Jewry's solution was the 4% Industrial Dwellings Company, founded in 1885. The leadership and the experts, spurred by Nathan Joseph who drew upon more than a decade of Jewish Board of Guardians sanitary committee reports, secured an East End commission of the United Synagogue to consider the condition of the Jewish poor. The community acted with unusual haste. The Prince of Wales was presiding over a Royal Commission on Housing, and, whatever the findings might be, any report about the East End could only cast the community in a bad light. Lionel Cohen, who assumed the family mantle as president of the Jewish Board of Guardians, delivered the United Synagogue report on 6 January 1885.[26] No effort was made to hide the unpleasant facts of overcrowding and filth in which too many East Enders lived. With the Royal Commission already sitting, the committee could scarcely do otherwise. Existing model dwellings, Cohen's committee reported, while answering the needs of the poor, could not provide an economic return and rent within their means. The fine hand of Nathan Joseph designed a way out. How could rents be reduced from the seven to eight shillings deemed too expensive in current model dwellings? Joseph's answer: reduce the net return on investment to four per cent, and excellent housing would be available at 5s per family unit.

Thus was born the idea that shortly became the 4% Industrial Dwellings Company Ltd. The Metropolitan Board of Works had a site at Flower and Dean Street. Rothschild assembled the philanthropic and professional leaders. Rothschild, Frederic David Mocatta, Samuel Montagu and Claude G. Montefiore blessed the plan. Algernon Sydney, solicitor for the Jewish Board of Guardians, agreed to act for the company. Nathan Joseph drew up the plans. The community would create the £40,000 capital by purchasing 1,600 shares at £25 apiece. The founders committed themselves for £25,000 and pledged the four per cent dividend. Nathan Joseph made drawings for 179 units and thirty workshops. Housing was constructed and available in just under two years, opening for occupation on 2 May 1887. The tenements succeeded from the start. Joseph's

---

26 The complete text is in *JC*, 27 Feb. 1885.

workshops proved a failure. They were converted into more tenements the following year, bringing the number of units to 198 at a total cost slightly in excess of the originally estimate.[27]

Since more than 1,000 applications were on hand for the 198 places by December 1887, Joseph felt confident than a second site would also succeed. The company acquired freehold land in 1888 which opened as the Brady Street Dwellings in March 1890. The £55,000 expended here created 285 units, principally three-room apartments. In the Brady Street facilities, moreover, a bath house furnished free hot baths, and a clubroom and library reinforced a sense of community and cultural improvement. Another 1,155 inhabitants, principally but not exclusively Jewish, could now enjoy salubrious dwellings for industrious artisans. Two slightly smaller complexes, Nathaniel Dwellings (1893) in Flower and Dean Street, which helped clear slums in the heart of Jack the Ripper's territory, and Stepney Green Dwellings (1896), which had more space, better amenities, and substantially higher rents, rounded out the original plan. The company deliberately included non-Jews among its tenants to avoid any charges of discrimination. By 1896, four blocks of flats housed more than 4,000, the overwhelming majority of whom were Jewish. Toynbee Hall, the great East End settlement house, offered its ultimate accolade when its representative to a Charity Organisation Society meeting in late 1901 testified not merely to the quality of housing, but to the quality of family life that the 4% Industrial Company had created – 'equal to or better than that of any place in England.' Preening itself, the *Jewish Chronicle* observed, 'the Jewish community can lay claim to be the only [religious body] that has taken up, in a practical manner, the housing of the poor question.'[28]

The planning, the social and the architectural engineering were overwhelmingly the work of Nathan Joseph. He and Algernon Sydney ascertained that company buildings and policies reinforced Anglo-Jewry's social philosophy. Under Rothschild's benevolent presidency, Joseph and Sydney attempted to extend company social development, moving into Stoke Newington and Camberwell. Stoke Newington, with its 326 tenements, should have been an ideal extension. Here were open spaces for play and recreation combined with the necessary facilities for 'Jewish' living. The United Synagogue built a new synagogue with schoolrooms. The active Dalston Synagogue and Federation synagogues served the area. A kosher butcher was on the estate. Local markets offered excellent food and goods at reasonable prices. Tram transport to East End work cost only a penny.

For the first time, however, the company had difficulty in filling flats. The January 1905 company meeting ascribed its difficulties to the depression of London trade and the transatlantic shipping fare wars which made emigration particularly

27 Only 1,280 shares (£32,000) were sold for the Charlotte de Rothschild Dwellings, the first site. The balance of funds was borrowed from the Jews' Free School capital on a ten-year, three per cent loan. On these and related matters see, Industrial Dwellings Society Papers (4% IDC), AJ/107 in the Mocatta Library, University College, London. See also, Rubens, 'The 4% Industrial Dwellings Company', in Newman (ed.), *Jewish East End*. Montagu, allegedly miffed by the state of negotiations on the East End scheme, resigned from the board in 1896, to be replaced by Claude Montefiore. *JC*, 7 Feb. 1896. The original debentures of £100,000 of which £95,000 were subscribed, was paid off on 1 Jan. 1900, and a new £135,000 issue was made. 4% IDC, *Sixteenth Annual Report*, 1900 (London, 1901).

28 *JC*, 8 Nov. 1901.

attractive. But the social engineers had, in fact, run slightly aground on the sands of East End working-class culture. East Enders did not commute, even by the penny tram or the plentiful omnibuses subsidized by the London Council Council. Proximity to employment, extended family and friends meant more than upgraded accommodation in unfamiliar settings. The *Jewish Chronicle*, anticipating policies British governments would attempt in the 1940s and 1950s, editorially urged Montagu's dispersion committee to shift some of its efforts from moving people to relocating factories. Like the mid-twentieth-century Labour government, Anglo-Jewry began to see strategically located workplaces as the key to the successful redistribution of people.[29] Company expansion continued, although the proportion of Jewish tenants in company dwellings fell sharply. A Camberwell estate attracted no Jewish families. It also had seventy families in arrears on rent, a rate twenty times higher than that of the company's heavily Jewish development at Stepney Green, although a modest enough figure for the region as a whole. Estates in Stoke Newington and Navarino, reportedly half Jewish and half Christian in 1910, although not fully let, had no bad debts or arrears. Lord Rothschild enthusiastically described 'his' tenants as 'a superior class of people'.[30]

Here the effort stopped. After 1910 no new construction was launched. Public housing played the role for which private model housing had previously been cast. The growth of the welfare state brought with it new taxes and duties that rendered such low-yield real estate investments less attractive. Perhaps most important, Nathan Solomon Joseph, Fellow of the Royal Institute of British Architects, died in 1909. In housing and in so many areas of social policy, his demise signalled the passing, not merely of a generation, but of its aggressive policy of social engineering and management. Anglo-Jewry was thereafter increasingly on the defensive, administering and attempting to sustain its extensive and expensive commitments. English Jewish social history would ultimately have been the same whether Nathan Joseph lived beyond his incredibly active seventy-three years or not. State institutions and revenue would increasingly underwrite and, to some degree, direct communal social policies. Joseph's death, however, removed the outspoken champion of a 'forward' voluntaristic social policy committed to shaping immigrant Jews in the image of Anglo-Jewry.

Just as the 4% Industrial Housing Company addressed the needs of its Jewish and non-Jewish tenants, concerned Jews carried communal as well as national concerns into groups attempting to influence public policy. Jewish leaders sat, for instance, on the most important London pressure group working to secure better housing for the underprivileged, the Mansion House Council on the Dwellings of the Poor. Sir Robert Fowler, Lord Mayor in 1883, with such stalwarts as Frederic Mocatta and Chief Rabbi Adler on his committee, launched what was widely regarded as his task force of self-selected busybodies. In its first year, the Mansion House Council formed district branches, and circulated handbills explaining housing law as it then stood, and giving prudential advice on how to avoid disease. The problem, needless to say, lay in the resistance of vested interests and encrusted

29 Twentieth meeting of the 4% Industrial Dwellings Company, 13 Feb 1905. 4% IDC Papers. AJ/107; *JC*, 17 Feb. 1905.

30 *Twenty-sixth Annual Report of the Four Per. Cent Industrial Dwellings Company* (London, 1911); annual meeting, 15 Feb. 1911. 4% IDC Papers. AJ/107; *JC*, 10, 17 Feb. 1911.

local authorities. With more than 2,500 frustrated cases in 1884, the council took a suggestion from the Royal Commission report on the housing of the poor. If sanitary authorities would not help, they should petition for a public enquiry. And so began the process by which, year after year, the Home Secretary found himself ordering an investigation of one community after another.

It all started in Clerkenwell in 1885, where 643 sanitary defects came to light. A petition from Mile End found 1,249, and the local vestry demanded that its medical officer of health resign. With this momentum, it was but a short step to the great Bethnal Green clearance scheme that grew out of the public enquiry of 1887. Non-Jewish slums were even worse. The 1888 investigation and that of 1889 for Woolwich helped to produce the Housing of the Working Classes Act of 1890. By then the self-selected busybodies were a convenient private tool of public policy. After Shoreditch and Ham in 1890 and Southwark in 1891, the Home Secretary, W. R. Ritchie, could secure both a Public Health Act and a new Housing of the Working Classes Act. By 1892, Mansion House Council complaints soared to 10,000 cases, twice earlier numbers. Three paid inspectors worked full-time supported by branch societies and correspondents throughout the metropolis. Regular advertisements called on the aggrieved to complain, and they did.[31] Through the Mansion House Council, Anglo-Jewry accomplished mutually reinforcing goals. On the one hand, the council concentrated public attention on slums and substandard housing as a general problem, bringing pressure effectively to bear on local authorities, government departments, even parliament, to address the issue.

Thanks to council efforts, taxpayers and ratepayers subsidized the improvement of poor people's housing, including that of the Jewish poor. An Anglo-Jewish social concern could thus be translated into a metropolitan crusade of which Jews were partial beneficiaries. At the same time, the Mansion House Council kept public attention and concern focused on an entire pattern of urban pathology, not concentrated as it otherwise threatened to be, on the Jewish East End.[32]

THE AGED

Respect and care for the aged had always been a cardinal principle within the Jewish community. This reponsibility devolved, in the first instance, on the family. Children and grandchildren cared for parents and grandparents who had not or could not provide for themselves. The aged spinster or bachelor, the man or woman

31 See, e.g., 'Mansion House Council on the Dwellings of the Poor', *JC*, 12 Feb. 1897. The attack from all sides appeared to produce results. The JBG, for instance, believed that Stepney conditions were much improved by the early years of the twentieth century. Only 46 per cent of the houses visited had sanitary defects in 1904–5 compared to 54 per cent in 1902–3. The question of overcrowding, on which the board worked in cooperation with the Mansion House Council on the Dwellings of the Poor, was much diminished after 1902. *JC*, 17 Mar. 1905.

32 The Mansion House Council on the Dwellings of the Poor, *Report, January 1901–June 1902* made it clear that St Pancras was the worst offender. Of the 10,327 inspections during the eighteen months under review in London, 1,728 (16.7 p^{er} cent) were improved in consequence. In Stepney, inspection was more rigorous and better results obtained. Of 1,019 houses inspected after complaints had been filed, 363 (35.6 per cent) were improved as a result.

who had the misfortune to outlive his or her family, or those whose children would not or could not care for them became communal obligations. Care for the Jewish aged, moreover, was not simply a matter of providing food, clothing and shelter. Ministration to the soul was an important as that for the body. Given the relatively small number of Jews in England early in the nineteenth century and the relatively high although declining death rate, old people not supported by their families were, whenever possible, aided or given supplementary support in their own homes, provided with places in almshouses, or cared for in institutions ultimately consolidated as the Jewish Home for the Aged.

One of Anglo-Jewry's more democratically sustained charities was the Aged Needy Society. Founded in 1829, although always needing that handful of generous subscriptions and bequests, it drew broad support from the community, principally through one penny a week contributions. Promoters showed schoolchildren and adults a frightening image of what the future might hold and offered them satisfaction and redemption – magnanimity for a copper. Although briefly hobbled by a competing body, the two amalgamated to make the Aged Needy, by 1880, one of the most popular as well as broad-based charities. With occasional large bequests and the benefits of a triennial ball, the society also had 1,800 subscribers paying from four shillings a quarter to three guineas a year. 'Decayed tradesmen, widows, and other deserving persons, who according to the laws of the institution, must have attained the age of sixty, are the recipients of the benefits of the charity.'[33] The five shilling a week allowance for each pensioner was unprecedented, indeed a figure to be much debated thirty years later when the British cabinet sought an economically manageable payment for those of seventy and older. Although the administrative costs were relatively high, annual subscriptions of £860 per year helped to maintain more than eighty pensioners by 1880.[34]

The organization, however, continued the system of subscriber election, and, with 1,800 voters, the matter of choices could be politicized around issues which had nothing to do with the merits of individual cases.[35] The long tradition, particularly within Jewish charitable institutions, of the donor being able to select the beneficiary persisted, reinforced by the relatively rare abuse of the voting system in general. The system of election, defenders argued, 'arouses warm interest in the charity' and 'confers a jealously guarded privilege' on the donor. At the beginning of the 1880s, only in the Jewish Home did a committee elect the new inmates, with results that the managers found highly beneficial. By the mid-1890s, the Aged Needy had succumbed to the need to have lady patronesses for its functions as well as the male community heavyweights for stewards. The access of ladies to society management, moreover, brought an important change in policy.

For the Jewish leadership and community, with a well-deserved reputation for genuine charity, to preserve a system of selecting beneficiaries that was neither

33 *JC*, 31 Jan. 1879.
34 The 1,800 subscribers (and voters) contributed £860, but eighty-four pensioners received £1,070 in 1878. The triennial ball in February 1879 brought out 400 guests and raised £800, essentially covering the gap. Working expenses were a trifle over £160. *JC*, 7, 14 Feb 1879.
35 As in the instance of the last election of 1878 in which a man of eighty-seven whom the investigating committee reported as 'helpless old man: strongly recommended' failed for the second time. He lacked powerful patrons willing to campaign for him. *JC*, 14 Feb. 1879.

useful nor humane puzzled leading philanthropists and their media supporters. The practice existed nowhere but in Britain. Florence Nightingale, who had much experience in such matters, had called it 'the best system of electing the least eligible, or, at any rate, the system for preventing the discovery of the most eligible.' The Charity Organisation Society fulminated against it. Gladstone denounced it as a nuisance. The Archbishop of Canterbury publicly attacked the practice in 1902 and announced that he never gave to a voting charity. Lord Shaftesbury, the great humanitarian, and F. D. Mocatta, the grand old man of Jewish philanthropy, denounced and made every possible effort to end the practice. The Aged Needy Society finally, and with considerable fears for its subscriptions and donations, succumbed to pressure and abolished the charity voting system.[36] Thereafter widows of pensioners continued to receive the benefit without having to go through the process of election. This burdened the budget just as many of the veteran subscribers were dying off. By then society pensions went to approximately a hundred pensioners, and resources were quickly exhausted. The usual triennial ball given to cover past deficits and build a small nest egg for the future had to be scheduled a year early in 1896.

For old people who could not house themselves or whose families could not or would not support them, almshouses, individual philanthropies, answered part of the need. Small and usually laying down prescriptions for entry, almshouses filled an important gap. As need and numbers grew, however, they, too, were caught up in the spirit of rationalization. The Joel Emanuel Alsmhouses, founded in October 1840, stood on the south side of Wellesley Square, one of the few patches of green in Whitechapel. By 1896, the surviving trustees no longer resided in London, and the philanthropy was passed over to the Charity Commissioners. Originally established for 'respectable Jewish people over the age of 60' the almshouses gave preference 'to persons of English birth or long residence in this country who have in times past maintained themselves in an independent position, and become reduced in circumstances through no fault of their own.' In addition to food, housing and medical care, the charity made an annual cash allowance of £13 17s for married couples, and £9 6d for single persons. To guarantee, however, that the almshouses were 'occupied by the class for whom they are intended', friends of the applicants for places were required to guarantee an additional minimum income. Inmates also signed a rigorous tenancy agreement, requiring all males, among other things, to attend daily morning and evening prayers as well as all sabbath and holiday services.

The Emanuel Almshouses had, by 1896, the almost unique advantage of income almost invariably far in excess of expenditure. With a capital surplus of £9,000 to £10,000, the reconstituted board of trustees hoped to sell the existing premises for warehouses and use the capital to build new facilities that would provide for greater numbers and also bring expenditure and income more evenly into balance. Thirty families were housed in new facilities, first in Wellclose Square, and then, when that area ran down, in 1904 in the then more bucolic setting of Stamford Hill. The

36 *JC*, 7 Feb., 13 Mar. 1896, 3 Mar. 1905.

Jewish Board of Guardians assumed responsibility for this facility only in 1922.[37] Another institution, the Jacob Henry Moses Almshouses in Mile End, established in 1862, was transferred to the Jewish Board of Guardians in 1895. Eight old people received housing and a five shilling per week allowance, on condition that they could raise another five shillings themselves. The principle and policy appealed to the board. Generally speaking, however, the board disliked such institutions. They were expensive, served limited numbers, and represented a disproportionate drain on limited resources. With great relief, the board finally closed and razed the Jacob Henry Moses Almshouses in the 1930s, rehoused the occupants in eight flats, and used a London Council Council mortgage to build subsidized housing. The Abraham Lyon Moses Almshouses built in 1838 on Devonshire Street in the heart of the original Jewish settlement handled yet a further twelve senior citizens. The Board of Guardians looked this gift horse squarely in the mouth. The facilities stood in need of extensive immediate repair, and would probably need to be replaced within twenty years. On the recommendation of its fiscally frugal almshouses committee, the board declined to assume responsibility until it was granted a special bequest of £2,500.[38]

By the mid-1870s, three other institutions, in addition to the endowed almshouses, provided for aged Jews. Frederic David Mocatta saw this division of effort between the Jewish Home, the Hand-in-Hand Asylum (for males) and the Widows' Home as costly and inefficient. He succeeded in bringing the Hand-in-Hand Asylum and Widows' Home together as one institution in 1876, but twenty years passed before the three amalgamated as the Home for Aged Jews. Part of the problem was location. The Hand-in-Hand Asylum and Widows' Home were in Hackney to the north of the East End, the Jewish Home on Stepney Green in the heart of it. While frustrated by the continued administrative division, Mocatta stood by the homes. His generosity enabled the Jewish Home in Stepney Green to survive. That institution tottered in its early days, barely able to meet annual expenses and burdened by an insecure tenancy. The managers laboured assiduously and, by the end of the 1870s, had recruited sufficient bequests and conducted enough benefit performances to raise its income to £1,400 per year, spending about £950 to handle thirty-five residents. Once the home showed itself capable of handling its annual costs, Mocatta gave £500 to acquire the copyhold interest in its property.[39] Amalgamation, when it came, produced unpleasant financial consequences. The economies achieved were far less than the income lost. Administrative expenses could be pared slightly, but overheads remained high until a new consolidated facility could be funded and constructed. Subscriptions and donations dropped sharply. The problem was immediate. Operating expenses demanded more than double the 1895 subscription–donation income, and no

37 Baron de Almeda (grandson of the founder), A. E. Franklin, Samuel Heilbut and Wolf Meyers were the new trustees. Mark Simmons, the trustees clerk, actually managed matters. The Emanuel Almshouses hoped to encourage further contributions by allowing testators to write a preference clause into bequests for any descendants of their own who might become 'reduced in circumstances'. *JC*, 16 Mar. 1896.

38 Lipman, *A Century of Social Service*, 135–6, 165. Sir Julian Goldsmid's £2,000 contribution in 1895, in my opinion, convinced the JBG to accept the Moses Almshouses.

39 The average age was seventy-four-and-a-quarter. Inmates cost 10s 6d per week to maintain. *JC*, 17 Jan. 1879.

further economies could be achieved until the Home for Aged Jews could be reconstituted in one building. Demography was already complicating a difficult situation. Relatively few immigrants were aged when they arrived. Demands for relief of the aged until the turn of the century, therefore, continued to reflect little more than the greater longevity of the native Jewish and long-time resident population. The lady of 102 who died in 1904 was exceptional, but the longevity was expanding and facilities were not. The Home was also the only Jewish institution providing for both the respectable aged and destitute poor. The balance between them, however, was shifting. What had formerly been a reasonable mix of paying and non-paying residents had by the mid-1890s become almost completely non-contributory.[40]

Legacies and endowment income, accumulated during the nineteenth century, gave the Home for Aged Jews more flexibility than many Jewish philanthropies. That income covered ordinary annual expenditure, so subscriptions, donations and paying inmates created a surplus in most years against future needs. The Home for Aged Jews budget does not convey a full sense of the extent to which it drew communal support. Local authorities as well as the community applauded the Stepney Home. The residents, as Frederic Mocatta disarmingly put it, 'appeared to be excessively happy'. They certainly proved very healthy, for even in severe winters the Home had little illness. The Whitechapel Guardians, for instance, annually voted it ten guineas for its exemplary service to the borough. That support, like the £250 the aid societies raised in small donations in 1910, appeared in the annual budgets. Home managers turned every fund-raising trick. Lotteries and entertainments were regular events. One concert in 1904 raised £330. But contributions, cumulatively substantial ones, also came in kind. Festive events – a wedding, an anniversary, the birth of a child – would be occasions on which Anglo-Jewish notables provided a dinner, an entertainment or an outing. Some such events were ways in which those already involved in the institution celebrated and magnified their role. Inmates, for instance, were treated to a poultry dinner with pastry to celebrate the marriage of Maurice Marks, nephew of the chairman of the house committee, to Rabbi Lipman's daughter.[41] But notables more generally drew the double benefit of publicity and charity, duly recorded in each issue of the Jewish press.

Growth, however, brought considerable new demands, ones that reached beyond normal annual giving. Lord Wandsworth gave the home his mansion in Nightingale Lane, 'Wandsworth', to be the future site of the consolidated institutions. That estate, which had originally cost more than £40,000, could only be adapted, as it stood, to accommodate forty to sixty aged people. That fell far short of the home's needs. Two dormitory wings had to be designed and constructed before the 150 to 200 old people could be accommodated. The home cleverly, if a trifle unfairly, attempted 'bargain' philanthropy, 'selling' its beds for £250 while reminding

---

40 One married couple, thirteen men and six women ranging in age from sixty to seventy-seven had been admitted during the course of 1895, and seventeen deaths occurred during the year, the deceased being an average age of eighty. At the beginning of 1896, 107 inmates including nine paying their own expenses and three married couples resided in the facilities. Home for Aged Jews, *First Annual Report (1895)*, (London, 1896).

41 *JC*, 20 Mar. 1896, 22 Dec. 1905.

contributors that the Home for Incurables had raised its bed price to £1,000. Demand for places, fortunately, rose slowly and in phase with the expansion of the Wandsworth facility. By 1910, that home housed 152 inmates, had completed the Hannah Davis wing for married couples, and brought modern technology to bear by adding an electric lift – making the Home for Aged Jews the model for its time.[42]

The selection of residents retained the traditional form of application and annual election, but, under Mocatta's determined pressure, the substance had changed. Each January the Home for Aged Jews announced the number of vacancies for men and women. Applications were filed, and the board selected the deserving cases. No longer, however, was balloting a form of patronage in which knowing the rich and prominent was the only safe way to secure a place. Mocatta, however, could violate the rules he championed in the interests of justice. Mental competence was a touchy point in cases of inmate admission. One 1896 case involved a ninety-one-year-old senile Jew confined in Homerton workhouse. The board finally agreed to admit him to the home but used the occasion to make a general rule to accept no paying applicants of questionable mental capacity. If families could pay the home, they could afford to make private arrangements rather than overstrain limited institutional resources. No sooner was the rule in place than a woman attempted to have her ninety-five-year-old father admitted as a paying inmate. The board declined, citing his mental condition, but the daughter, herself pressing seventy, could not keep him at home and had to have him admitted to the Highgate infirmary. Mocatta intervened. The man's age and disability should not, he argued, deny him the comfort of Jewish observances. Mocatta, as president, ordered his admission subject only to a physician certifying the man to be physically fit.[43]

CHARITABLE ASSISTANCE

Direct benefit societies ministered to the immediate needs of those in want. They provided food, clothing, and small amounts of cash. They were created through the years to supplement synagogue relief and serve those needy who did not, for one reason or another, qualify for or fall within the purview of the Jewish Board of Guardians. Some were of proud antiquity, reaching back to the early nineteenth century. Others appeared and disappeared in response to some perceived need or philanthropic inspiration. One of the 1896 newcomers to the list of social relief agencies, for instance, was the East End Bread, Meat and Coal Society, yet another organization which sought to bridge over temporary need.[44] Resident tradesmen and merchants simultaneously sought to display their own philanthropy, organized, sustained and funded from within the East End community, independent of West End grandees. Such organizations were not new. A small group of well-intentioned donors, not themselves in a position to make individual grand bequests, gathered in

---

42 Annual meeting, 26 Mar. 1905. *JC*, 31 Mar. 1905. Ordinary income was £3,682 in 1904, only a third of which came from subscriptions and donations. Ordinary expenditure the same year was £1,696. Home for Aged Jews, *Twenty-sixth Annual Report* [1904] (London,1905); *Thirty-second Annual Report* [1910] (London, 1911); *JC*, 17 Mar. 1905, 19 May 1911.

43 *JC*, 20, 27 Mar. 1896, 20 Jan. 1905.

44 The initiation 'smoker' was held at the Nag's Head, Houndsditch, on the 2 March. *JC*, 6 Mar. 1896.

1842 to create a 'consolidated' charity which could gain recognition comparable to the much publicized benefactions of the elite. For a generation these thirty-one donors pooled their contributions and divided nearly £400 each year in tickets for bread, coal and meals equally among themselves. These 'independents' resisted the blandishments of the Jewish Board of Guardians and those who pursued efficiency, defending the rights and importance of small charities.[45] Among the flourishing mid-century benevolent organizations was the Society for Providing Strangers with Meals on Sabbaths and Holydays, better known as the Sabbath Meals Society. It spent £333 to feed 2,316 in 1878.[46]

As acculturation and assimilation progressed, other institutions developed to meet particular problems of adjustment. The Jewish Volunteer Social Union provided help for Jews moving into the wider world of the host culture, serving the much-needed function of continuing to tie them to their Jewish world while reinforcing their life and work in highly diverse areas. Two men, for instance, who had enlisted in the Dorset Regiment were, through the intervention of the union, granted a rare permission to alter the enlistment papers on which they declared themselves Church of England and be officially recognized as Jews.[47] Some charities simply evaporated. The Motza Society, founded in 1840, closed its doors in 1896, a warning to anyone lightly assuming responsibility for institutional management. The society was founded to break a bakers' monopoly that had run up the price charged for Passover unleavened bread, forcing the poor to use potatoes. It succeeded, but once prices were reduced and stabilized the society was left in economic difficulties. Originally producing 600 sacks of Passover flour, its output fell to 100. Only half of that could be retailed, the other half being passed on to synagogues for their Passover charities at cost. Most board members resigned, declining to assume further debts. Two donors alone remained. They attempted unsuccessfully to keep the philanthropy afloat. Their appeals to the Rothschilds and Sir Samuel Montagu went unheeded. Less affluent community worthies nodded sympathetically but were also unwilling to salvage the wreck. Their redundant philanthropy collapsed, and they found themselves dragged into insolvency, personally responsible for the society's £1,800 arrears.[48]

Other institutions avoided entanglements with any specific benefaction. The Society of Promoters of Charity, founded in 1840, supplemented resources for many enterprises well into the twentieth century. A fashionable 'tertiary' philanthropy, it avoided risk while offering successful and upwardly mobile middle-class Jews public philanthropic recognition. Supporters in considerable numbers made contributions of one or two guineas at gala nights or through theatre ticket sales.[49] Slightly further down the social scale, the Tradesmen's Benevolent

---

45 *JC*, 24 Jan. 1879.

46 With income of £443 and expenditures of £405, the Society drew from a broad cross-section of the community. Its contributions consisted of small sums, rarely over £5. *JC*, 3 Jan. 1879.

47 H. J. Annenberg, a member of the committee, secured this rare concession. *JC*, 3 Feb. 1905.

48 P. J. Solomon, liquidated his half by selling a small income property producing £5 a week. His fellow trustee, A. Straus, may well have forfeited the property he pledged to the bankers. Solomon to the editor, *JC*, 6 Mar.; M. Davis to the editor, 13 Mar. 1896.

49 See, e.g., the advertisement in *JC*, 3 Feb. 1905. Association and setting meant much in such organizations. A January 1897 function, for instance, was pointedly held in what had been the Disraeli house in Portsdown Road. *JC*, 15 Jan. 1897.

Society, as the practical businessmen they were, adopted the ticket system recommended for all such organizations by the Charity Organisation Society. No handouts of shillings and sixpences to the indigent. As with most direct benefit organizations, winter was the season of need. Society giving and expectations accurately mirrored economic fluctuations and the severity of the weather. They had learned their philosophy in the pre-immigration school and applied it rigorously thereafter.[50]

Some Jewish philanthropists worried about the substantial number of poor who, for various reasons, good or bad, avoided applying to the conventional charities for relief. The wife of an outspoken champion of Jews' College and one of the United Synagogue's leading figures, Mrs Herman Tuck, determined to bring flexibility in relief policy. She singlehandedly struggled from 1891 against a degree of community indifference and even hostility from the leadership of established Jewish philanthropies. The community supported existing institutions, and Anglo-Jewry clung to its philosophy of means test and investigation. Mrs Tuck, a formidable lady, would not be denied. She regarded the communal leadership as insensitive, hiding humanity and equity behind the formalism of coldly Benthamite rules. Mrs Tuck did not disagree with the underlying question of investigation and benefits to the deserving. Nor did she question examining the use of the benefaction to ascertain that it had not been misapplied. Even her modest proposal to ease the 'humiliation' of relief was coldly received at first in 1890. She drew upon her own resources, then gathered some friends to help support her North London Grocery Relief Fund. The work prospered and more volunteers were soon needed. Within five years the fund was no longer regional and was working in harmony with the Jewish Board of Guardians, the visiting ladies committee, the Jewish clergy, and others 'who charge themselves with the duty of seeing that the relief administered is not misapplied'.

Fund distributions were made every Thursday from eleven to one during twenty weeks of the year at the Jewish Working Men's Club. There Mrs Tuck and earnest associates personally oversaw the business. Every man, woman or child with an appropriately certified ticket carried away a package of tea, coffee, sugar, rice, barley, beans and (pointedly) soap at a cost which ran to about £300 each year for the giving season. In its first five years, the fund issued 13,000 tickets at a cost of £1,200. On the eve of Purim (an occasion for gift-giving) 1896, Mrs Herman Tuck's sister-in-law Mrs Adolph Tuck handed a freshly minted shilling to each holder of a relief ticket and to many 'addressed a few encouraging words of advice'.[51]

Most Jewish philanthropies focused on the East End. One survived from the early nineteenth century that looked to other, more scattered pockets of London Jews. The Western Jewish Philanthropic and Pension Society, founded in October 1827, provided modest grants and pensions to the scattered poor of the West End and north-west of London. An unglamorous and underpublicized organization, the Western began as and remained a professional and middle-class activity rather than

---

50 In the winter of 1877–8, for instance, they used their £450 of net income to issue just over 7,200 tickets for bread, meat, groceries and coal, while the demand for 1878–9 ran closer to 9,000. *JC*, 7 Feb. 1879.
51 *JC*, 6 Mar. 1896.

one of the much-publicized fiefs of Anglo-Jewry. The Western survived, but proved less and less capable of answering its self-defined needs. The poor did not remain confined to the East End and were, by the late 1880s and early 1890s, dribbling out beyond the confines of that ghetto. Foreign poor with their Chevra Kadisha (relief) societies and Talmud Torahs, the Chedarim and their sweatshops had come to the West End. While the Jewish Board of Guardians ostensibly supported all poor Jews, its efforts were principally directed towards the highest concentration of poor in the East End. The Western Jewish Philanthropic, arguing that local communities better understood local needs, appealed for support from the broader community.[52]

None differed in conception, operation or philosophy from the prevailing norms of charity. The Soup Kitchen for the Jewish Poor created in 1893, however, often found itself at odds with prevailing institutional insensitivity and delay. Those who were hungry needed to be fed first, investigated later. It ministered to the immediate needs of the hungry from its quarters, first in Fashion Street and then, as needs grew, more commodious facilities on Butler Street, Spitalfields. The soup kitchen functioned seasonally, carrying the under-employed and unemployed through the pinched winter months. By the turn of the century, 1,100 to 1,200 families needed the soup kitchen for all or part of the winter. A special Passover relief distribution usually followed the season's closing. The one on 3 April 1898, for instance, assisted almost 2,500 families, some 1,000 of whom had been soup kitchen beneficiaries during the winter season and had but recently surrendered their 'kettles'. That 'large motley throng of deplorable looking men and hatless women with babies in their arms' stood five or six hours in line, waiting to be admitted in groups of half a dozen at a time. Superintendent Ellis of the soup kitchen picked out the impostors or double dippers, while cheery matrons distributed coffee, sugar, and potatoes, broken into 10lb to 40lb lots according to the size of the family.[53] The community, like Anglo-Jewry, took pride in the soup kitchen, and when its facilities were no longer serviceable gathered together to raise more than £10,000 in 1901 for the purchase of land and the construction of new facilities. The successful campaign meant that yet another girls' club could be launched and suitably provided for in the upstairs rooms of the building.

By 1904 the number of regular soup kitchen families had climbed to 1,450, surging to over 1,900 in 1905. Those numbers do not convey a full sense of what the philanthropy did. The Jewish Soup Kitchen fed regularly or on occasion more than 325,000 meals to 10,500 individuals. The charity, like its beneficiaries, lived a precarious hand-to-mouth existence. Princely benefactions meant two to five guineas, while the more conventional subscription or donation would range from half-a-crown to one guinea. Given annual expenditures reaching towards £3,500, the soup kitchen needed constantly to recruit new subscribers. Each winter the *Jewish Chronicle* faithfully reported the soup kitchen's financial inability to remain open through March. Each year the weekly list of contributors grew slightly longer, but the growing community and seasonal trades invariably strained even expanding resources. To some extent, the soup kitchen was the most sensitive barometer of

---

52 Its founder and first president was Samuel Ellis. J. W. Solomon, a well-known artist of his day, succeeded Ellis, to be followed, in his turn, by Professor Marks. In 1896, Marks, having served for twenty-two years, resigned the office to Reverend Isidore Harris. *JC*, 24 Jan. 1896.
53 *JC*, 8 Apr. 1898.

East End trade cycles, as in the downturn of 1904–5 when it received applications from persons 'who have resided in London many years, and have never before received relief from the Kitchen'.[54]

As Anglo-Jewry's philanthropic bill rose in spite of the substantial obligations absorbed by state and local authorities, demands grew for greater rationalization and discipline. The soup kitchen felt particularly pinched. On the one hand, as Hermann Landau, doyen of the Poor Jews' Temporary Shelter and vice president of the Jewish Soup Kitchen, argued, the soup kitchen did investigate whenever able-bodied males applied, and only provided food, never cash. The Jewish Board of Guardians complained that the soup kitchen declined to furnish lists of its beneficiaries, arguing that such information should be considered when the poor applied to the board for assistance. The soup kitchen management responded that it did not wish occasional users to be branded as paupers.

President Alfred L. Cohen consistently defended the soup kitchen's policy of investigation, reminding critics that the results were entered into the books of the institution which were open to the inspection of every subscriber. Cohen allowed that the occasional 'impostor' might slip through but felt convinced that the total could not exceed a dozen instances per year, scarcely a justification for a more elaborate system. While the soup kitchen argued for its own effective and inexpensive administration, that failed to speak to the issue of potential duplication. The hard hand of philanthropic discipline prevailed. The Board of Guardians insisted that proper relief 'consists in rendering applicants self-supporting as soon as possible, the test applied being not poverty, but distress.' By December 1905, the soup kitchen gave way and agreed to place its weekly list at the disposal of the Jewish Board of Guardians, conceding that, as a correspondent observed, 'Every penny given to an undeserving case is a penny taken from a deserving one – a double wrong is committed.'[55]

THE DISABLED

The milk of human kindness, so one argument runs, flows most easily for the disabled. To some extent this was true. The Indigent Blind Society, although economically managed, never demanded that those it served become self-sufficient.[56] Among the specialized institutions serving the needs of the Jewish community, the Jews' Deaf and Dumb Home on Walmer Road, Notting Hill, was close to many hearts.[57] Its original director, William Van Pragh, was the British

---

54 *JC*, 24 Feb., 6 Jan., 3 Feb. 1905. The Bayswater Synagogue, one of the few that regularly produced a surplus, adopted the soup kitchen as its own favoured charity. The rabbi's wife annually brought about two dozen young ladies and gentlemen to dispose of shilling tickets, producing, in 1896, £32. *JC*, 16 Mar. 1896.

55 'The Soup Kitchen and Communal Charity Organisation', *JC*, 29 Dec. 1905; A. L. Cohen to the editor, 1 Feb. 1897. *JC*, 5 Feb. 1897; Soup Kitchen for the Relief of the Jewish Poor, *Seventeenth Annual Report* [1904–5] (London, 1905); *JC*, 6 Oct. 1905.

56 *JC*, 3 Feb. 1905.

57 An organization for adults, as was so often the case, lagged far behind one for children. Dr Eicholtz presided over a social club for the Jewish deaf established in November 1903 'to provide amusement and recreation for adult Jewish males who suffer from deaf mutism'. When the Chief Rabbi inaugurated the premises on 29 November, he depended, ironically, on the Reverend F. W. G. Gilby of St. Saviour's Church for the Deaf and Dumb (Oxford Street) to interpret for the members. *JC*, 4 Dec. 1903.

pioneer of the oral instruction of the deaf and dumb. Baroness Meyer do Rothschild, who established the institution in the 1860s, sought to help the disabled to understand, to communicate, and, if possible, to function in society. How this should be done was no better resolved in the nineteenth than in the twentieth century. Jews began the lip method of instruction, a system widely imitated at the time, but debate continued about 'speaking' or 'signing'.

Frederic D. Mocatta, the greatest name in late nineteenth-century Jewish philanthropy, helped to lead the institution to new facilities and substantial obligations. Mocatta particularly favoured the home because it abandoned the charity voting system at his behest. A committee selected each child 'entirely on its merits', drawing its boys and girls from Britain and the Empire. Sir Edward Stern, one of the Anglo-Jewish gentry who had begun life humbly enough as a working man, made the cause his own. President of the home during the decades before the war, Stern observed that some thought intelligent deaf and dumb children should learn the oral system, while the less intelligent should sign. That, he argued cogently, was cruel in both cases. Children should be taught to understand what was said to them and to make themselves understood. The Jews' Deaf and Dumb Home existed to enable children to earn their livelihood in spite of their handicaps. They were, however, taught the very trades that Jewish Board of Guardians apprentices were being dissuaded from entering. On the eve of the First World War, girls learned to be embroideresses. Boys were trained as upholsterers, cabinet-makers, and bootmakers.

Although the home trained Jewish children from the provinces, even a few from South Africa, provincial Jewry never undertook its share of the costs. Deficits always haunted the home. Vigorous fund-raising, biennial balls and timely legacies kept arrears from accumulating, but £500 annual deficits haunted the nineteenth century, and £600 in annual red ink the twentieth. No such Jewish institution was more dependent on government grants for its survival before 1914. One third of home income by 1910 came from local authorities and the Board of Education. Government subsidies meant government oversight. The Board of Education, for instance, demanded in 1903 that the home expand facilities to ease overcrowding for the forty-six children in the institution and provide for eleven others awaiting admission. The £7,000 needed to expand facilities was raised only with the greatest difficulty. Numbers, moreover, continued to expand, finally stabilizing at approximately sixty-five. Children from more than half a dozen provincial Jewish communities were in residence, each bringing a subsidy from his or her local education authority, but the £30 all provincial communities contributed to the home was but a fraction of their share of the costs.[58] Spurred on by Home managers and committed philanthropists, however, East End Jews accepted the principle of self-help and mobilized an aid society that drew up to £150 each year in small weekly contributions. The pennies of the poor might not balance the books, but they made the moral statement that Anglo-Jewry wished to hear. Even the most

---

58 Jews' Deaf and Dumb Home, *Eighth Annual Report*, (London, 1879); *Thirty-third Annual Report* (London, 1904); *Thirty-fourth Annual Report* (London, 1905); *Fortieth Annual Report* (London, 1911). JDDH, annual meeting. Sir Philip Magnus, who had presided until 1897, stepped down, confronting a simple reality. The president must be, he remarked, a man of substantial means and more leisure than himself. *JC*, 7 May 1897.

humble were in yet another way tied into a network that reinforced elite values and community discipline.[59]

The Act for the Education of the Blind and Deaf (1893) made the institution eligible for government grants over and above the contributions from the local school boards that sent children to the home. Each child admitted, however, cost substantially more than government grants provided. While the average expenditure per child at the Jewish Hospital and Orphan Asylum was £28 in the mid-1890s, that of the Deaf and Dumb Home was £35. London School Board allocations were £11 per child for educational costs. As the Jewish community grew, moreover, the pressure to expand facilities was irresistible. One substantial addition cost £6,000 in the late 1890s. Sir Philip Magnus stepped down as president in 1898 to make room for Edward W. (later Sir Edward) Stern, hoping that Stern's own wealth and affluent business contacts would ease the financial strain. Stern, in turn, brought in other newly wealthy men who wished to promote their social status through philanthropic activity. He made Woolf Joel, a partner of the diamond speculator Barney Barnato, treasurer of the home to tap new South African Jewish wealth. Joel was no sooner on board than he was murdered. He had, however, put the home in his will, and that legacy became the nucleus for recapitalizing the institution.

Joel's bequest was, the home quickly learned, insufficient. The state dispatched unexpected bills. Jewish philanthropies, as they became eligible for public support, repeatedly discovered that government inspectors demanded substantial and costly improvements in facilities. Stern took matters firmly in hand. Since the Board of Education specified changes that would cost £7,000 to bring existing facilities up to standards, he opted to move the home to a new freehold property estimated to cost £11,000 including furniture. That would almost double the home's capacity by serving fifty-four, twenty-one more than the overcrowded older facility.

Sensible ambitions, however, aggravated fund-raising difficulties. The initial capital proved hard enough to raise, but more capacity meant substantially higher operating costs. Each child added extended the growing annual deficits. Slightly increased government grants, special fund-raising functions almost every year, and the conversion of legacies to current account tided the home over. By the end of 1904, the thirty children of 1895 had grown to twenty-eight boys and eighteen girls on the register, with eleven more children awaiting admission. Once again, the crowded Notting Hill facilities had to be expanded, and the management launched yet another £6–7,000 drive in 1904–5.

Building and improvement campaigns depended on the wealthy, but Sir Edward Stern succeeded in broadening the base of current support upon which the institution depended. 'Being a working man himself, he knew how hard it was for them to be able to spare a portion of their savings even for such an excellent work.' The Deaf and Dumb Home touched the hearts and purses of those of modest

59 The home emphasized its 'open admissions' policy, of which F. D. Mocatta so strongly approved, when soliciting contributions. The aid society, to attract the devout, observed that unlike other institutions, the home 'did not seek aid of apostate Jews and Jewesses'. *JC*, 24 Feb., 4 Aug. 1905, 14 Jan. 1916.

means. Proportionately the greatest help came through such East End organizations as the Jews' Deaf and Dumb Home Aid Society.[60]

CHILDREN

The popularity of the Deaf and Dumb Home lay in the fact that it served the disabled, but particularly disabled children. The communal heart also warmed to Jewish children thrown on their own resources. One of the few 'consolidated' charities, the Jews' Hospital and Orphan Asylum, served them. 'Orphan' was, to some degree, a misleading term, since 'single orphans' still had one parent alive, although that parent, usually disabled, a widow, or an 'abandoned mother', had to be incapable of supporting the child. The principal institution moved from Mile End to Lower Norwood, where it grew and prospered, providing allowances to a handful of aged and caring for an ever-increasing number of children. Although an intelligent consolidation of institutions, it long preserved the traditional system of balloting for beneficiaries before a special court of governors and subscribers.[61] Most of the great names could be found as sponsors and in attendance at annual courts. At the 1879 winter court, Lionel van Oven reported 195 children in the institution, twenty-eight of whom, even then, were placed there under the Pauper's Removal Act and sustained by public money.[62]

The merger of the Hospital and Orphan Asylum, long contemplated, had been repeatedly postponed, although the management of each institution was favourable. Since the most common consequence of merger was administrative streamlining and staff reduction, current employees and hangers-on in small and less efficient philanthropies usually had a vested interest in preserving their organization as it stood. In this instance, almost all involved put institutional welfare above personal convenience. Managerial fears focused, rather, on the potential loss of subscriptions

---

60 Jews' Deaf and Dumb Home, *Twenty-fifth Annual Report* (London, 1896) reviews the history of the home and discusses its prospects with considerable insight. JDDH, *Twenty-seventh Annual Report* (London, 1898) discusses the change in management and its implications, while JDDH, *Thirtieth Annual Report* (London, 1901) discusses the move to the freehold property, The Grange, near Wandsworth Common. East End aid societies and their growing importance in Jewish philanthropy testify to the 'embourgeoisement' of East End Jewry. From September 1903 through January 1905, the Home Aid Society raised £189, of which £131 came in the calender year 1904. The Home Aid Society, for instance, imitating the major organizations, held a dance in aid of the society at which it raised between £30 and £40. The gender ratio of any committee is usually the best indicator of the average size of subscriptions and donations. The Home Aid Society drew small individual gifts, and its committee was substantially middle-class and, unusually for such bodies, mostly female. *JC*, 24 Feb. 1905.

61 See, e.g., the summons for the special court on Sunday, 16 Feb. 1879 to elect sixteen boys and eight girls. A substantial (and presumably expensive) advertisement in the *Jewish Chronicle* of 10 January 1879 asked support for the election of one Sarah Hyman, whose mother was now dead and who, if not accepted on this ballot, would be too old for eligibility. In an impressive display of elite unity, she was recommended by Lady Rothschild, Samuel Montagu, the Haham, Sydney Samuel and Dr Asher who solicited proxies on her behalf. The Jews' Hospital and Orphan Asylum (JHOA) Papers (Norwood Archives) are in AJ/19 in the Mocatta Library, where the amalgamation scheme, sanctioned by the Charity Commissioners, 7 July 1876, is in file C/1.

62 After the merger had been completed (1878), the institution showed an income of £7,023 and expenditures of £6,259 in operating funds. Almost 20 per cent of the children in the Asylum were not actually orphans. Report of the general court, 16 Feb. 1879, Norwood Archives, AJ/19; *JC*, 21 Feb. 1879.

and donations. Donors were presumed to have strong attachments to 'their' institutions and to resent any loss of institutional identity and the relative importance of individual contributors. By the beginning of the 1880s, the merger was completed with none of the feared loss of income. With merger came amendment of the election procedure. The committee of management was enabled to act on its own initiative for 'double' orphans (children who had lost both parents) and any instances in which the poor law authorities paid the expenses. Other cases remained subject to ballot at semi-annual elections. Even here, the committee retained much discretion. It investigated each case to determine whether it was 'worthy'. Those not admitted the first time could accumulate votes for six elections. Many subscribers allowed the committee to vote their proxies, and the committee distributed them among those they deemed most eligible. The managers would have preferred to remove balloting altogether, but elections, like charity bazaars, were called a British institution and considered essential to stimulate subscriptions. Although subscriptions and donations represented only a quarter of Asylum income by the end of the nineteenth century, no one dared risk modifying institutional policy any further.

Since subscriptions and donations failed to keep pace with rising expenses, the Asylum was forced to spend rather than capitalize some of its legacies and to employ special occasions to meet ongoing needs. The Lord Mayor of London, Sir Faudel Phillips, for instance, used the occasion of his Mayoralty and a 'triumphant' first hundred years to make the annual general court on 9 February 1896 the occasion for raising almost £20,000, a badly needed remedy for tiresome deficits and arrears. Past obligations and debts nibbled the available new capital funds down to £16,000, and new facilties, much needed, were already on the drawing board. That left a potentially serious shortfall, for dividends and interest on bequests and endowment produced almost 45 per cent of annual income, while subscriptions, the children's orphan aid societies and life governorships accounted for only 34 per cent. Dipping into capital, the only available option, would merely make matters worse. Current accounts ran at almost a ten per cent deficit, discouraging when they were as persistent as they had been.

The philanthropy, however, had bold plans. Felix A. Davis would realize his dreams. The new centenary hall providing a school and services was his visible centrepiece. The steam laundry, for instance, would not merely serve the institution better, producing a great saving in outlay, it would also allow some of the girls to be trained as skilled laundry maids. Growing out of the centenary drive, the institution hoped to raise its subscription income by £1,000, allowing for the admission of thirty more children. Sir Benjamin Cohen of the Jewish Board of Guardians, a champion of balanced budgets and money first, buildings second, grumbled loudly at the 1897 general meeting about speculative development, reminded Norwood partisans that they lacked both the full sum necessary to construct Joseph's well-designed extension and any reserve for maintaining the new facilities. Depending on yet another special occasion, Lord Mayor Faudel Phillips's Mansion House dinner in May 1897, to raise a further £10,000, Cohen warned, was unsound philanthropic practice. 'Unsound' it may have been, but it served the purpose.

Norwood depended, more than most major Jewish philanthropies, on imaginative fund-raising. Supporters were more effectively mobilized because they had to be.

Norwood was one of the first of the older institutions to recognize the growing importance of women in philanthropy and social work. It appealed for their help in the field and in raising money. Female visitors were organized into a ladies' committee. Women were even finally brought on to the committee of management in 1901.[63] Children's orphan aid societies in every quarter of London contributed their pennies, halfpennies and farthings, urged on ultimately to become life members. Once again the East End worked the hardest, its local orphan's aid society being singled out on many occasions. Children were taught the meaning and demands of charity early. The North London Orphan Aid Society, founded in 1893 by the North London Synagogue, collected £976 10s 'chiefly in pence' for the upkeep of the Norwood Jewish orphanage during its first dozen years. Like nursing and clothing, orphans came to be considered as principally a female responsibility, and so, like clothing, the orphan aid societies enjoyed a broad base of support with very modest individual subscriptions. The children's aid societies existed, as their promoters publicly stated, not so much to raise substantial capital as to inculcate habits of charity among the young and, particularly, to inspire the parents to support Jews' Hospital and Orphan Asylum by their example. Boys and girls were much inspired by the report that nine children could be maintained on their donations. The Central Synagogue branch of the Children's Orphan Aid Society observed at the end of 1895 that Miss Edith Jacob, the indefatigable honorary secretary, had so organized matters that they had over two hundred members including six life members. By 1897, aid societies produced over £500 each year, covering over six per cent of Norwood's expenditure.[64]

The average number of inmates at the centenary mark was 267. About fifty, in any given year, attended under the Pauper's Removal Act, subsidized by one or another of the Poor Law Unions. More than five-sixths of the children came from London. The Asylum resisted admitting foreigners, having declared when the organizations were amalgamated that at least one of any child's parents must be or have been a British subject or resident for at least two years in the United Kingdom. The committee could waive the rule in any case of a 'double' orphan or if 'there are special circumstances to render such a course desirable'.

Eight aged out-pensioners also received £31 4s a year and a clothing allowance, the residuum of the Jewish Hospital. The physical facilities at Norwood were entirely devoted to children. Although 16 per cent of the girls and boys came from the provinces, provincial contributions lagged far behind that proportion of the budget. Of the twenty-five children who left Norwood in 1895, thirteen were apprenticed and one was taken on as a clerk by the Jewish Board of Guardians. Another was a printer's apprentice at the *Daily Telegraph*, while Alderman A. Leon

---

63　Anglo-Jewish resistance to bringing women into institutional management was striking. The debate, in almost every instance, used such rhetorical codewords as 'sentimental' and 'emotional' to explain why women were ill-suited for management. By 1900, however, they were on the council of the AJA and the JBG, and their role had expanded significantly in almost every philanthropy. The Jews' Hospital and Orphan Asylum was, if anything, excessively timid, altering its constitution to admit only three to the general committee and limit them to one on any subcommittee save for the ladies' committee. Norwood Archives, AJ/19; *JC*, 25 Jan. 1901.

64　Within two years, the Children's Orphan Aid Society income rose to £60. Each subscriber was, by 1905, asked to introduce at least one more in the course of the year. Report, Twelfth Annual Meeting, 8 Jan. 1905, Norwood Archives, AJ/19. See also, *JC*, 3 Jan. 1896, 13 Jan. 1905, 12 Feb. 1897.

Emanuel of Portsmouth found one other a position in the Royal Navy. Every effort was made to place boys in trades with good prospects, to break the demoralizing cycles of tailoring and bootmaking. The thriving bicycle industry seemed promising. An increasingly consuming society bought organs and pianos, so Norwood apprentices were placed in that trade.

The apprenticing committee felt that the Institution's work was undone when children returned to the 'unfavourable influences' of the East End. Norwood placed 'double' orphans as indoor apprentices from 1850 to 1891, returning the others to the surviving parent during apprenticeship. Neither policy satisfied the committee, for both threatened Norwood's careful socialization. The only supervision of the indoor apprentice was that of his master 'which cannot always be expected to be very efficient'. After five or six years in Norwood, returning the child to the supervision of its surviving parent 'does something to prevent the dissolution of family ties which often occurs when one member of a family is better cared for, and started in life more favourably than his brothers and sisters.' But returning to comparative disadvantage jeopardized everything Norwood had done. To circumvent this, the committee urged that a halfway house be established in which boys would remain under a measure of supervision while establishing themselves. The constantly overstrained budget never permitted it, but Simeon Lazarus opened a small house for apprentices in Coventry in 1891 with such good results that he opened a second at Stoke-on-Trent. That also brought Jewish boys into the pottery trades, an entirely new area for them with exellent job prospects. Norwood would have preferred to extend its supervised environment for girls by moving them into domestic service. Jewish girls, regardless of background, however, almost invariably resisted entering domestic service. Instead, the committee built into its Norwood curriculum a final six months for girls in which they would be housed separately, supervised by the matron, and taught household duties and cookery. Girls also worked in the new steam laundry, refining their skills in a service occupation in increasing demand.[65]

Norwood continued to live on the extreme margin of its resources. Transfer payments from the Jewish Board of Guardians and various Poor Law Unions for child care never met the cost per head. By late Victorian standards, Norwood was an exemplary enterprise providing facilities and services far superior to any others of its kind. Each year the Board of Education paid tribute to the quality of its education. Norwood trumpeted how much drill and exercise improved the carriage and bearing of its students. The institutional band, proudly sporting its new uniforms from Daniel Marks, helped to impart that martial spirit and patriotic pride that was to send 'old boys' off as enthusiastic volunteers to Britain's wars. Daniel Marks, donor of the gymnasium, was the organization's most distinguished 'alumnus'. He had prospered, and returned to act as honorary treasurer, and to help shape boys that they might succeed even as he had done himself. Each year the organization

---

65 JHOA, annual general court, 1896, Norwood Archives, AJ/19. *JC*, 14 Feb. 1896; annual general court, 1897. The apprenticeship book in the Norwood Archives is a fascinating case-by-case summary of placement and follow-up. One of the showcase examples was a boy who completed his apprenticeship in 1900 and was employed at Woolwich Arsenal at 42s per week. Norwood Archives, AJ/19. See also, *JC*, 12 Feb. 1897, 15 Feb. 1901. The *Jewish Chronicle* serialized a history of the Jewish Hospital and Orphan Asylum in March and April 1897. Norwood policies are discussed at length in chapter 4, *JC*, 16 Apr. 1897.

could parade still more successful apprenticeships, priding itself on the fact that so many boys whose indentures had expired continued to work for their masters 'at good wages'. Work training in place, Norwood developed holiday facilities in 1903. Isaac Davis contributed three houses in Margate to serve as a summer seaside home. Premium operations for larger numbers of children meant increasing demands on donors. By 1904, the East London Orphan Aid Society found itself strained beyond its resources. Never before had it been called on to serve 342 children. The society's houses for apprentices at Stoke and Coventry – all part of a programme of placing boys in trades with good prospects and dispersing the Jewish population – coupled with the costs of a vacation home at Margate, to which the orphans were processed during the summer in batches of thirty or forty at a time, escalated bills at an alarming pace. Society expenses outstripped its £9,000 income by almost £2,500.[66] By 1901, moreover, between four and five hundred Jewish children had been admitted to East End infirmaries or workhouses. The society had come to depend, to a greater degree than it cared to admit, upon receiving a subvention of approximately £900 that defrayed half the cost of poor law 'union' children placed in their institution. Through a legal formality, the society drew substantial local government assistance. Mothers had to take children to union workhouses or infirmaries in order to obtain redress against deserting husbands. That same formality, however, furnished ammunition to those seeking to restrict the immigration of Jews from Eastern Europe by showing that poor Jews represented an increasing cost to ratepayers. The society, to its credit, understood that attempting to hide or conceal this information would be the worst political course to take.[67]

In the early twentieth century, the state began to assume a larger and larger role in the supervision of children. Herbert Samuel's Children Act of 1908 consolidated and defined the by then impressive scope of legislation. Such reforms, necessary as they seem to any contemporary observer, did not sit well with the views of substantial numbers of the Jewish community. Some communal leaders actually seemed to be 'attacking' the integrity of the family, while so much Anglo-Jewish effort had been devoted to sustaining it. Nettie Adler, daughter of the Chief Rabbi and stalwart social reformer, was one of the moving spirits in the Committee on Wage-Earning Children, which sought to rouse public interest in and support for the Employment of Children Act. Limitation of child labour, however, was not the most popular of causes in the East End. Family income often depended on the small contributions children could make. The committee, moreover, sought to extend children's legal rights, a sentiment which, however modish in advanced British society, ran against the grain of the close-knit Jewish family. The committee

66 The society also supported twelve pensioners at £30 each per year as part of its shared expenses with the Jews' Hospital. Although preferring to 'disperse' its apprentices, the JHOA realized that most would remain concentrated in London, and as the institution moved into the twentieth century, it concerned itself with providing 'half-way housing' for boys and the oversight of a domestic trainer and paid visitor for girls as they went back into the East End. Norwood Archives, AJ/19; *JC*, 15 Feb. 1901.

67 'A few years ago,' contended Henry Isaacs of the JHOA, 'such a thing was never heard of in the community. The growing evil presented a difficult problem.' Minutes, annual meeting of the East London Orphan Aid Society, 29 Jan. 1905. *JC*, 3 Feb. 1905.

attempted, in 1905, to mobilize support for the campaign to secure separate courts of justice for children.[68]

Others also encountered familial cultural resistance. Some philanthropic women combined thinly disguised self-interest with socialization to appropriate deference. By the first decade of the twentieth century, domestic servants were becoming annoyingly expensive and in short supply. The Domestic Training Home at 1–3 Adelaide Road, Regent's Park, generously sponsored and supported by the wives of the fashionable, recruited Jewish girls to answer middle- and upper-class wants with the needs of the poor.[69] Attendance was poor; voluntary attendance poorer still.

Many philanthropies supplemented or reinforced ritual and religious needs. The Society for Relieving the Poor on the Initiation of their Children into the Holy Covenant of Abraham, for instance, known throughout the community as the Initiation Society, reached back to 1745. Although a Montagu bastion, the Rothschilds also provided generous support. As with the Federation of Synagogues, Sir Samuel's purse opened to cover deficits. The organization served two important functions. It trained and certified *mohelim* to perform ritual circumcision. Given some fatalities, extremely rare as they were, and occasional serious complications resulting from the ceremony, the organization, by bringing up-to-date medical standards to bear, answered a community need. In England, moreover, where circumcision was relatively rare among non-Jews before the First World War, malpractice invited invidious press comment, just the sort of publicity Anglo-Jewry wished to avoid. Initiation Sociey work divided almost evenly between training, underwriting the costs of ritual circumcision for the poor, and distributing lists of qualified *mohelim*.[70]

CONSOLIDATION

Jewish Board of Guardians critiques, the development of professional social work, and accumulated statistical and casework information might, of themselves, have reopened a vigorous debate about charity reform and consolidation. The day of the leisured amateur had or should have passed. Alice Model, who had already done so much to bring professionalization to health care, warned the Union of Jewish Women (itself an organization reflecting the changing times) about 'inexperienced enthusiasts' who wasted money and misdirected philanthropic energy. A swelling chorus of critics likened the evolution of Jewish philanthropy to the history of London metropolitan growth. Institutions evolved 'by haphazard accretion and without a definite plan'. Just as private builders added a development here or demolished another there, so social welfare grew up at the hands of private charity

68 *Report of the Committee on Wage-Earning Children* (1904); *JC*, 24 Feb. 1905.

69 Mathilda Moss acted as treasurer for the home, the subscription list for which reads like the directory of the rich and famous. *JC*, 6 Jan. 1905.

70 In 1895, for instance, the balance showed a slight surplus on expenditure of £288. Most (£161 10s) went for 'benefits', with £78 for salaries and commissions and £38 for printing and advertising. Initiation Society annual meeting, 2 Mar. The balance sheet reflected Anglo-Jewish generosity where important Jewish ritual was concerned. The society had an endowment of more than £1,600. *JC*, 6, 13 Mar. 1896.

builders 'who have founded societies here, there, and everywhere they pleased. The result is that the struggling, lumbering, planless metropolis is paralleled ... by a systemless and anarchical cluster of Jewish charities.'[71]

One general and another more specific factor gave substance to the movement for reform in communal philanthropy. Two decades of investigation, discussion and legislation broadened and deepened the social agenda of British politics. More and more aspects of day-to-day life came under investigative scrutiny and governmental management. The nation, not merely the Jewish community, was expanding its list of basic human standards and needs. The Liberal governments which came to office at the end of 1905 did not start with an elaborate collectivist agenda. Indeed, Campbell-Bannerman assumed office committed to little more than Irish Home Rule, free trade and being unlike Arthur Balfour. But specific demands and elaborate programmes were in the air. New social theories and specific human needs fused more and more with a new sense of what politics should be about in an increasingly democratic age. To that extent, communal debate about social welfare was merely a part of a larger national discussion propelled by professionalization and politics.

More important, perhaps, was a simple fact. The old leaders were dying off. They were not replaced. Their heirs, the wealthy and leisured, displayed far less interest in matters specifically Jewish, preferring to act on the national stage. Neither could the concentrated power of wealth and personality be duplicated by the next generation of community leaders. David L. Alexander, for instance, a barrister of great ability and a man deeply committed to the traditions of community leadership, was no Sir Joseph Sebag-Montefiore, his predecessor as president of the Board of Deputies. Sir Stuart Samuel, old Montagu's nephew, who succeeded Alexander as president in 1917, was not the overwhelming figure his uncle had been either in the world of specie banking or as a leader of Anglo-Jewry. Sir Stuart had worked effectively with several of the smaller East End Montagu fiefdoms, but while he certainly had more communal impact than Louis, second Lord Swaythling, he was never an overwhelming presence. Sir Edward Stern, who rose from relatively humble beginnings to business affluence and a major place in Anglo-Jewish philanthropy, had neither the wealth nor the hereditary communal prestige of the old oligarchy. Communal leadership and power, in short, was already attenuating or diffusing itself well before the provincial and Zionist rebellion at the Board of Deputies in 1917. The old elite, moreover, could probably not have handled matters much better. A broader group of successful businessmen and articulate professionals in London and the provinces was less and less willing to be told how the community was to work by a narrow, ageing London oligarchy. The restive did not speak with one voice, nor did communal deference vanish before, during, or even after the Great War. Anglo-Jewry, like the established English elite with which it turned out to share so much, continued to rule by habit, almost by momentum.

The extended early twentieth-century debate on Jewish philanthropy was, in this context, a much-needed discussion on the merits of the case and simultaneously a way of criticizing the old regime. The new generation felt entitled, by its talent and

---

71 'Training the philanthropic worker', *JC*, 24 Feb. 1905; 'Multiplying charities', *JC*, 13 Jan. 1905.

importance, to authority, respect, and status. Columns in the Jewish press, meetings of the Maccabæans, lectures, pamphlets and books provided legitimate forums for self-assertion. They had much to assert. The philanthropic network counted more than forty institutions by 1905, each of which had, in its way, become a vested interest. While well-intentioned volunteers performed many of the tasks and contributors ostensibly set policy, dozens of professionals found employment in these organizations. Contributors and volunteers had status and psychological commitments to their societies. For secretaries, caseworkers, fund-raising solicitors and collectors, philanthropic organizations were their livelihood. And so they grew, a tangled, rarely pruned thicket of benevolence.

Some areas of relief stacked one institution on top of another. No less than a dozen provided tickets for bread, meat, groceries and coal, some of them doing little more than turning them over, in bulk, to the Jewish Board of Guardians. The Sabbath Meals Society distributed almost 6,000 meals each year by the end of the nineteenth century. The Social Union Benevolent Society, a mid-1890s creation, passed out bread, meat and coal tickets 'to deserving poor irrespective of creed'. While four societies provided meals as relief in kind, they served, with the exception of the seasonal Jewish Soup Kitchen, highly specialized groups such as schoolchildren or refugees. Each major synagogue had its ladies' guild providing clothing for the needy, but so did the Jewish Board of Guardians and the Jewish Ladies Clothing Association. The Foreign Jewish Ladies' Benevolent Society spent some £250 each year, much of it devoted to the distribution of matzos but some in direct benefits. The seven different homes for the aged were slowly being consolidated, but a myriad of friendly societies, the Jewish Board of Guardians, the Spanish and Portuguese Jewish Board of Guardians, the United Synagogue, the Aged Needy Society and the Jews' Hospital and Orphan Asylum all provided pensions for the elderly in a patchwork, incomplete and uncoordinated manner. Well-intentioned amateurs stumbled over one another visiting, investigating, serving and ordering the unfortunate. No communal body directed the elaborate educational programmes.

Challenges to communal philanthropic anarchy were quickly repulsed. Anglo-Jewry tolerated no interlopers. As communal institutions competed for the philanthropic pound and while the United Synagogue and Federation of Synagogues quarrelled about East End schemes in the winter of 1896–7, two impatient Jews, S. Goldreich and E. Mendelssohn, who had gone out from Britain and prospered in South African gold, returned, aspiring to achieve communal status and respectability through Jewish philanthropy. They sponsored the Jewish Self-Help Association. Rabbi Benjamin Schewzik, undeterred by his battering in the scandals leading to the closure of Montefiore College in Ramsgate, took the operational lead in advancing the cause. With brash effrontery, the association challenged every standing Jewish philanthropy. Organized for the modest purpose of promoting

> the moral, social, intellectual, physical, sanitary and commercial improvement of the Jews of the East End and other districts of London, and in such other places in the United Kingdom as the Association may from time to time think fit and to relieve in any manner which the Association may from time to time deem practicable, the congestion and other social and economic evils arising

from the immigration or overcrowding of Jews who, either because they are unsuited to English life, or for any other reasons, are unable to support themselves or those dependent upon them.[72]

The Jewish Self-Help Association, with its modest £5,000 capital, announced an agenda that knew no limits. It proposed, among other things, to educate, provide meals, establish or subsidize public housing, organize apprenticeships and arrange a broad programme of cultural improvement. The *Jewish Chronicle*, weary of too much talk from the old guard and too few results, minimized the element of competition and argued that the association's activities could only enrich communal life.

Anglo-Jewry responded, belittling the South African scheme, criticizing such community luminaries as J. S. Ballin, Daniel Marks and H. G. Lousada who had, in one way or another, offered endorsement, support or advice. Sir Samuel Montagu ridiculed the association's pretensions to the United Synagogue and the Federation of Synagogues. Ellis A. Franklin, one of the lay community's leading moral spokesmen, animadverted on Rabbi Schewzik's character, imparting a devastating blow to Schewzik's authority. Neither Schewzik's complicated response nor journalistic editorial support could retrieve it. Montagu observed that this under-funded association sought working-class savings without offering any security and underscored various contradictions of aim and policy. To help the poor workman, the Self-Help Association purchased bread, motza flour, and coal in bulk, then sold it to him below market cost. Threatening every Whitechapel petty Jewish shopkeeper and tradesman with loss of business and possible bankruptcy was ill-considered policy. The association offered non-interest loans from non-existent capital and hoped-for future working-class deposits. Such talk unsettled the delicate East End credit system of small loans and pawnbroking. Mindless policies designed to court quick popularity generated resentment that outweighed whatever advantages Schewzik managed to accumulate through his labour and arbitration bureau. The labour bureau floundered from the start. When an applicant for relief 'of doubtful character' was rejected by the Jewish Board of Guardians, he walked around the corner to Schewzik's bureau where he was given short-term relief and a loan to establish himself in business.

But Schewzik's arbitration bureau gave the Self-Help Association some credibility. Ostensibly seeking to save foreign Jews, particularly those who knew little if any English, from routine humiliation in the local police and county courts, Schewzik offered arbitration in preference to litigation. Quite apart from offending the vested interests of some lawyers and interpreters, Schewzik simultaneously ran foul of Judge Bacon of the Whitechapel county court and the Chief Rabbi's Bet Din, the ecclesiastical court and arbitrating authority.[73] Schewzik's availability and willingness, even eagerness, to hound disputants into a settlement won him

---

72 Jewish Self-Help Association, Application for Limited Liability to the Board of Trade, 11 Feb. 1897. *JC*, 12 Feb. 1897.

73 Bacon's views can be found in his judgement quoted at length in *JC*, 5 Feb. 1897. Schewzik often rendered a decision at variance with Adler's Bet Din, leaving applicants a choice of rulings and undermining ecclesiastical discipline. See, e.g, the working man who sought and received a ruling that he did not need to sit *shiva* (to observe the conventional week of mourning) for his dead son. *JC*, 22 Jan. 1897.

considerable if fleeting local popularity among the more honest and better intentioned complainants and defendants.

Schewzik's authority and South African backers, however, could not withstand Anglo-Jewry's blistering criticism. Briefly unsettled and clearly angered at the insensitive interloper, local shopkeepers and tradespeople were not sorry to see the association go. Little trace remained by the spring of 1897. While many living close to the margin of subsistence regretted the transitory subsidized provisions and fuel, the Jewish Self-Help Association also revealed hidden fissures within the established Jewish community. When the *Jewish Chronicle* leader writer described the rise of the new association as 'a fairy tale', 'the dream come to realisation' that he saw was quite as much intended to cut the arrogant old oligarchy down to size as raise 'the moral and social elevation of persecuted Jews who have found a home in London'.[74] The fantasy faded as swiftly as it appeared. Schewzik himself turned his attention to recruiting for the Jewish Lads' Brigade, a modest enough ambition.

The rise and fall of elaborate East End schemes testified to communal uncertainty about what it should be doing and how best to do it. Overlapping agencies ministered, sometimes in contradictory ways, to the religious welfare of the community. In one of the more elaborate critiques of Anglo-Jewish effort, Ernest Lesser, who had worked in the field for several charities, suggested that Jewish philanthropy worked through the correlative ideas of *mitzva* (in this connection, the religious obligation to render service through good deeds) and *schnorrer* (one who makes a living by begging, often a confidence trickster). 'What system of philanthropy,' he asked, 'could be expected from people held in bondage by these two quaint but harmful influences?'

> With the spirit of the Schnorrer animating our poor, and wishy-washy sentimentalism clouding the minds of our rich, it is not to be wondered at that the era of preventative work in the communal field of philanthropy was so late in dawning. It is obvious that so long as a man firmly believes that he is doing *you* a service in coming to you for his charity, it is almost impossible to make him understand that you look at the matter from an exactly opposite point of view, that not only do you consider that you alone are performing the service, but that you actually want to put him into such a position that he may hereafter be independent of such services. From the point of view of the Schnorrer, the donor seeking to abolish him and his class is deliberately flying in the face of Providence.[75]

Lesser was doing no more than restating the rationale for creating the Jewish Board of Guardians, to make relief a matter of the brain, not the heart, to provide for the necessitous while avoiding pauperization. The will of the Cohens might dominate but had never and never would command all Jewish social welfare. Ultimately only through the higher rationalization of the welfare state could reformers seek to smooth out the hills and valleys of private benevolence.

74 *JC*, 19 Feb. 1897.
75 E. Lesser, 'A survey of our communal institutions', Maccabæans Paper. *JC*, 20 Jan. 1905.

7

Self-help and Self-assertion

East End Jewry was no passive community, moved hither and thither by economic needs or West End philanthropy and politics. Anglo-Jewry preached self-help and self-reliance, sometimes contributing to but often merely watching East End initiatives in economic, social, political, even religious life. John Dyche, who began as a penniless immigrant 'greener', celebrated his own career of self-help with two autobiographical articles paying tribute to those virtues Anglo-Jewry sought to cultivate in the community.[1] Anglo-Jewish leadership, however delighted it might be with what appeared to be East End acceptance of West End ethics, did not appreciate 'excessive' East End independence; still less did it care for any East End self-expression that threatened or appeared to blemish the public image Anglo-Jewry wished to present of itself and the Jewish community. Social deviance was never tolerated, the leadership putting itself to considerable trouble and expense to prevent crime and resocialize offenders. Jewish vigilantism in the late nineteenth and early twentieth centuries merged easily with mainstream movements for the regulation of moral behaviour. That much was to be expected. But Anglo-Jewry also denounced political radicalism, believing that it blemished the Jewish image as well as challenging the 'appropriate' order of things. Trade unions were generally seen as a mixed blessing, often tolerated because they were ineffective. Samuel Montagu, however, heartily approved of the 'new unionism' when he endorsed the London dockers' strike in 1889. Even religious zeal was brought to heel when it threatened the structure of Anglo-Jewish authority. In one area, however, East End and West End initiatives appeared happily to coincide – the friendly society with its ethic of cooperative self-help.

1 J. A. Dyche, 'The Jewish workman', *Contemporary Review*, 73 (1898), 35–50; 'The Jewish immigrant', *Contemporary Review*, 75 (1899), 379–99.

FRIENDLY SOCIETIES

As Lloyd George's national insurance plans neared fruition in 1911, Anglo-Jewry considered what the impact would be on that sprawling network of friendly societies so essential to East End workers. Well it might, for the legislation actually passed excluded aliens. Patient negotiations conducted principally by D. A. Ferscht on behalf of the Board of Deputies finally secured an amendment to the statute in 1918 so that it embraced all contributors. Beyond the supportive network of family and kin, the working man's friendly society remained his most important social institution after his synagogue. Not only did his friendly society insure him against illness or catastrophe; he met his friends there. The *Jewish Chronicle Year Book* for 1910 listed 320 Jewish friendly societies, a significantly higher figure than the 166 the Chief Registrar of Friendly Societies reported for the end of 1905. Most were still simple dividing societies, small individual accumulating accounts or mourning (*shiva*) and burial funds. A substantial proportion retained dividing or tontine principles rather than accumulating capital with a view to increasing future benefits. The sixty-eight Jewish lodges of different orders in 1905 had almost doubled to 136. Estimates suggested that there might be another 100 to 150 provincial societies. Neither set of statistics included the Jewish lodges of the Ancient Order of Foresters, which by 1911 had some 750 members with nearly £12,000.[2] Exactly what this meant in social terms is unclear. Just under 40,000 enrolments capitalized at £100,000 did not translate into 40,000 Jews enrolled in friendly societies with at least some modest benefits. Multiple membership was common, the employed worker dispersing his risks and benefits to secure adequate coverage in case of serious emergency.[3] Friendly societies, moreover, demanded regularly subscriptions. That meant friendly societies served those in steady employment with some

2 The Foresters trod upon Jewish sensitivities when they printed membership certificates with Christian iconography. After a long dispute that involved the Chief Rabbi and the Archbishop of Canterbury, the objectionable certificates were withdrawn. See *JC*, July–August 1898. Communal statisticians first attempted to assemble data in 1901. They more or less agreed that there were thirteen orders with seventy-one affiliated Lodges based in London and a further 117 independent societies covering 26,417 members. Multiple membership, however, reduced that figure to 22,783, a number that the correspondent felt 'practically covers the Jewish population of London'. *JC*, 11 Oct., 8 Nov. 1901. Dividing societies, although generally appealing to the less affluent, sometimes prospered. When the London Hebrew Tontine Society celebrated its tenth anniversary in 1898, for instance, it could boast over 870 members and an income of £3,000. Sick pay disbursements for £310, relief for members in distress £120, and £1,900 would be shared out at the next division leaving £1,450 in the reserve fund. Given this success, the committee proposed to establish a non-dividing branch of the society for those who could not afford the standard subscription where all but tontine benefits would be available for 4d per week. *JC*, 25 Mar. 1898. The Chief Registrar of Friendly Societies' statistics lagged well behind actual numbers. Many trade unions did not register their benefit societies. Synagogues had unregistered burial and *shiva* societies.

3 D. A. Fersht, 'National insurance', *JC*, 26 May 1911. Ten years before, the best statistical estimate was that 10 per cent of the more than 18,600 men in male societies were actually double enrolments, 5 per cent triple, 2.5 per cent belonged to four societies, and 1 per cent each to five and six societies, reducing total adult males enrolled in London in at least one society to just over 15,000, but that was considered close to full coverage. The Registrar General contended that the number was closer to 10,000, but conceded that the number of unregistered societies was substantial enough to make any estimate merely guesswork. *JC*, 11 Oct., 8 Nov. 1901.

surplus of income over expenditure. The newcomer, the irregularly employed, and the very poor still all too often lay outside this supportive network.

Jewish friendly societies, like so many other communal institutions, suffered from an incapacity to cooperate and consolidate. Individuality and competition reigned supreme in this prudential world of self-help. Jewish organizations, in this respect, were by no means unique. All friendly societies, whether Jewish or Gentile, competed for participants, the benefits they could offer, financial and otherwise, depending on the funds they could accumulate. Conservative financial policies might minimize risk and secure long-term benefits but they did not render an individual society more attractive. The friendly society, moreover, concentrated exclusively on benefits and could not provide the sociable ceremonials and organizational activities which played so important a role in the day-to-day life of workers and fed their sense of self-esteem. Lodge rituals, defining one's place in an elaborate hierarchy of status demarked by grandiose titles, were the medium through which humble people achieved prestige among their friends, co-workers and neighbours.

Friendly societies, however, were above all institutions through which poorer people dealt with financial risk. Burial funds of one sort or another were the first form of 'insurance' poorer people acquired in British or other western societies. Pennies paid warded off the horror of final anonymity, of 'dying in a ditch'. For those lacking even the pennies, almost all synagogues had burial funds for their poorest members, but by no means all Jews belonged to synagogues. Family burial insurance aided those without savings. The first additional benefits sought addressed catastrophe. As friendly societies evolved, they offered protection against other forms of temporary embarrassment or poverty. And so, both in financial and in social affairs, such organizations reinforced a sense of comradeship, of solidarity with one's peers, of mutual assistance in times of need and good fellowship. Some organizations were 'dividing societies', covering explicit needs, perhaps preserving a small emergency fund, but redistributing any surplus at the end of the year. Others were 'accumulating societies', bodies in which members built endowments for retirement as well as insurance against death, disability and illness.

Friendly societies, at all times, had far more members and a stabler membership than trade unions. Petty tradesmen, shopkeepers, skilled and unskilled workers enrolled and invested in them. Members tended to favour tontine or dividing societies, perhaps for the gambling touch involved, perhaps for the prospect of partial recovery of annual contributions. By the early twentieth century, women began to form their own, the 1907 report of the Chief Registrar of Friendly Societies listing three societies exclusively for them. Given Jewish habits of multiple enrolments, friendly societies represented a shrewd choice. They outperformed insurance annuities, a conventional middle-class investment, at the beginning of the twentieth century. Friendly societies did involve an element of risk, in that more marginal organizations had a distressing way of going bankrupt. Presuming that the institutions to which an individual belonged remained solvent through the member's life, the comparison is instructive. A man over thirty, an age by which an individual could be securely established in his line of work, who turned to an insurance company for an endowment policy would pay an average of 4s 5d per week for a policy of £150 maturing at the end of fifteen years. Presuming the worker survived to draw the benefit, he would receive £183 15s for £172 10s paid in premiums. He would, however, have no other coverage save for life insurance. A working man, on the other hand, who allocated 3s per week might invest one shilling in each of three benefit societies, a common practice at the time. His death benefit would be £50 from each of them as well as £10 payable to him in the event of his wife's death. He would receive a sick benefit of 15s per week for thirteen weeks. His coverage would include a mourning allowance of two guineas. Amounts varied widely, but he had access to something between £3 and £30 in the event of a severe financial emergency. His friendly societies offered medical aid at all times, provided disability insurance, paid for drugs and surgical appliances, and covered a physician's fee of one guinea in case of accident. Trebling the benefits, the worker who survived received £200 for £117 paid in during fifteen years.[4]

Authorities, communal or secular, understandably endorsed friendly societies. How better to encourage the industrious classes to care for themselves? Parliament had passed the Friendly Societies Act in 1801 to encourage and protect such organizations at a time when lower-class institutions were almost universally suspect. Prevailing political paranoia had simultaneously produced the Combination Acts outlawing trade organizations and proscribed suspect extra-parliamentary political associations. The first explicitly Jewish friendly society, the Pursuers of Peace, was organized in 1797, the Loyal United Lodge of the Sons of Israel registered in 1820, and the Lovers of Peace and Justice some three years later. A friendly society limited exclusively to Sephardim with the engagingly ambiguous title, Society 'Charity Escapes an Early Death', founded in 1830 still numbered over 300 members at the end of the century. Jews as individuals also joined secular societies. The next surge of organization began in the mid-1860s, reflecting in another way the larger, more complex Jewish community and the evolution of such communal institutions as the Jewish Board of Guardians and the United Synagogue to manage it. Provincial as well as London consolidation was the order of the day. The Birmingham Loyal Independent United Israelite Society, founded in 1853, managed to amalgamate the small and financially insecure local organizations into one body, ending the diffusion of resources through multiple memberships, and accumulating a paid-up capital of £1,500 by 1905.[5]

Cash benefits were essential, but friendly societies taught other equally important lessons and played a range of cultural roles. They inculcated, even enforced, sociability, cooperation, self-discipline and self-help.[6] They offered friendship,

4 A. Rosebury, 'The Jewish friendly societies: a critical survey', *JC*, 8 Sept. 1905, presents these statistics and an excellent general overview from which I borrow freely of the history of these organizations after the great migration of 1881.

5 John Hart, auditor of the Birmingham society, to the editor, *JC*, 15 Sept. 1905. See also, *JC*, 18 Mar. 1898. Registrar of Friendly Societies Brabrook mused about the old Jewish affinity for 'poetic names' citing, among others, the Righteous Paths Society (registered in 1836) and the Holy Calling Society (1858). *JC*, 11 Oct. 1901.

6 As in the early industrial workplace, a system of fines enforced appropriate behaviour both within and outside society premises. One characteristic society fined any member 3d for interrupting another. Anyone addressing the chairman as other than Mr Chairman could be fined 3d. Anyone 'making an improper remark outside of the Society's doors' might be fined half-a-crown. Parliament created friendly societies 'for the promotion of thrift among poor men', and provided that matters in dispute go to society arbitration rather than come before the courts where legal expenses would consume the organization's funds. Some, like Rind et al. versus Silverman et al. (The Dublin Hebrew Tontine and Benefit Society) in King's Bench Division before Mr Justice Kennedy, 23 Mar. 1903, did. The case and judgement dealing with 'improper arbitration' had significant implications. See *JC*, 27 Mar. 1903.

consolation in time of troubles or grief, and provided individuals with opportunities to express themselves, even to fulfil ambitions, in a supportive social setting. The widest range of opportunities were there for members of provident orders, friendly societies with branches, usually called lodges, under their control. Such organizations tended to appeal to the better established. Although the margin between contribution and benefits might be narrower, such orders were financially the most secure and in a position to offer the ambitious the greatest social scope within their panoplies of lodges, grand lodges and executive councils to carve out a place for themselves in public view and esteem. Secret rituals, bizarre costumes and private symbols gave members a sense of order and importance, and even satisfied ambitions within a private world of friends.

David Levy, sometime grand president of Order Achei Emeth, for instance, might well have been refused the right to land in England after the Aliens Act of 1905. But David Levy not only made his way in the working world of the East End, he became one of the great reformers of friendly societies. Levy landed penniless and illiterate. He educated himself, drawing where possible on philanthropic programmes, and worked through the world of the 'greener' to become a skilled tailor. Intelligent, ambitious, chock-a-block full of ideas, he drove to the top of Order Achei Emeth. As grand president, he abolished expensive and empty ceremonials in the order, reformed the 'old boy' oligarchy by introducing the elective principle, and actively engaged Order Achei Emeth in Jewish affairs. When Jewish reservists fled from Russia to avoid being called up in the Russo–Japanese war, for example, Levy organized a rescue operation, modest only in the sums it could raise but not in commitment and generosity of heart. An innovator prepared to ride over prejudice, Levy organized three ladies' lodges among the twenty in his order. He sought to reduce wasteful competition between the Jewish friendly societies and to improve cooperation among them. Having achieved closer cooperation, Levy sought to democratize the community just as he had worked to democratize provident societies. The friendly societies, he proposed, should demand representation at the Board of Deputies of British Jews and a voice in the management of the community.

The simplest Jewish benefit societies probably reached back to the resettlement itself. Simple mourning (*shiva*) and burial funds were administered through small *hebrot*, which acted as both religious and benefit societies. Given the traditional Jewish week of mourning, the bereaved family needed a small allowance. By the 1880s and the population explosion of the Jewish community, needs had greatly expanded. State aid came only through the ungenerous umbrella of the Poor Law. Prevailing political philosophy still believed that government best which cost least and subjected any social policy to a rigorous cost–benefit test. The prevailing ethic of voluntarism and self-help demanded self-taxation, and that demanded a framework of provident organizations through which to work.

The largest and most durable was Order Achei Brith, established in 1888 with thirty lodges, approximately 2,800 members, and a paid-up capital of £7,000. Trailing in members and far behind in capital was the Grand Order of Israel, whose twenty-six lodges included three in South Africa. Keenly competitive, the grand order offered substantial benefits for fairly small weekly contributions, giving it 2,640 members and funds of £3,850. David Levy's Order Achei Emeth and the

Hebrew Order of Druids each had over 1,100 members, but the druids, one of whose nineteen lodges was in Johannesburg, had half as much again paid-up capital. Lodges, moreover, became political as well as social statements. The Hans Herzl Lodge formed in 1905 was open only to Zionists. Each member had to subscribe to the Basle Programme, the compromise which did not require that the Jewish homeland actually be Eretz Israel. The London Labour Society pioneered sexual equality, opening a West End branch in September 1905 admitting men and women on the same terms, pledging itself politically to the trade union movement and to support labour politics. Each member paid ten shillings on entry which went immediately into the reserve fund. If the member emigrated, he or she was entitled to that ten shillings on three days' notice. To hold costs down, no benefits accrued for the first three months, and no fund accumulated. Reserves paid all benefits and management costs, and then each member was assessed for an equal share of what had actually been spent.

Most, although far from all, such organizations appealed more to settled and established individuals. Newcomers flocked to independent societies just as they preferred the comfortable cultural familiarity of the Federation synagogues. Such societies bore the names of Russian and Polish towns, a beacon to *Landsmanns-chaft*. The Cracow Jewish Friendly Society (founded in the 1860s) was, in 1905, by far the largest with some 380 members and an impressive capital of £1,550. Lagging behind came Warsaw, Denenburg, Vitebsk, Zhitomir, Siedletz, Plotsk, with other towns and villages trailing back into the communal immigrant past. These independent societies enjoyed a demographic advantage in that their members generally arrived in the prime of their productive life. Over time, this advantage waned. Youthful newcomers aged. Immigration, which had begun to decline at the turn of the century, dropped sharply after the Aliens Act of 1905. The thirty-year-old of 1880 was by then fifty-five, and there was no equivalent replacement stream of thirty-year-olds by 1910. Most independent societies remained solvent although hard-pressed as the First World War approached. Survival demanded that new members and contributions be recruited. To compete, they had to offer immediate benefits for slightly lower contributions, leaving themselves ill-provided to cope with future contingencies. Financial statements reflected growing deficits and raids on reserve funds. These weaker institutions became simultaneously more essential and increasingly at risk, for they served those denied benefits under the National Insurance Act of 1911.

Friendly societies were, of course, open to a broad group of subscribers. Trade societies restricted membership in their provident institutions to their trade unions. Their instability reflected the uneven progress of worker organization. Almost all functioned as 'dividing' societies, redistributing whatever modest surplus they might have just before Passover. Given the brief life of most Jewish trade unions, particularly in London, no other system would have been tolerated. The Cigarette-makers and Tobacco Cutters' Benefit Society, founded in 1887, like the trade union with which it was associated, although small, was financially the most sound, having some 100 members in 1905 and more than £600 capital. Although the trade was considered hazardous, tobacco dust then being viewed as a danger to workers' health, the benefit society had surprisingly infrequent calls upon its sick funds. Other organizations, the Cracow Society for one, refused to admit tobacco workers, although it did admit tailors. Actuarial experience showed that tailors more than any other group suffered from pulmonary tuberculosis. Organizations of masters, among friendly societies as with trade unions, were more stable, paid substantially better benefits, and prospered over time.[7]

TRADE UNIONS

The industries and crafts in which Jewish labour engaged, the inflow of immigrants with entry-level skills, and the strong Jewish working-class drive for upward social mobility and independence help to explain the rudimentary and generally unsuccessful history of Jewish trade organizations. Substantial numbers of working-class Jews never engaged in organizable occupations. Others, like costermongers, street salesmen or pedlars, organized principally to secure their rights to trade. Tailoring and bootmaking, the two most common East End occupations, were seasonal and volatile trades, difficult to organize under the best of conditions and almost impossible to unionize effectively with the constant flow of new immigrants. 'Greeners', as they were called, destabilized the labour force. They pushed established workers out or upwards into more skilled, supervisory, even entrepreneurial roles, while simultaneously preventing effective organization of the trade or improvement of basic wages and working conditions. While in economic terms this forced growth through displacement created a new domestic and export trade, in social terms this process translated into a harsh life for the least skilled. For most, the overall conditions of life, even in those circumstances, were an improvement over what they had endured in Poland and Russia. For some, as the trickle of individuals and families back to the world they had left behind demonstrates, it was not.

In this respect the Aliens Act of 1905 worked almost immediately to the benefit of labour. By discouraging or curtailing the inflow of unskilled labour, sweating could finally be constrained, wages and working conditions regulated and improved. Working-class Jews, however, proved singularly resistant to unionization. The most successful Jewish trade union, the Amalgamated Jewish Tailors', Pressers' and Machinists', which practically controlled the whole clothing trade, was in Leeds, not in London. Observant – its clubroom closed on the sabbath – the 2,000 members had a capital of £800 at the beginning of the twentieth century, enjoyed sick, unemployment and burial benefits, and stood well in the eyes of the community. A sustained economic downturn in the early years of the twentieth century began to strain both men and resources. A prolonged strike in 1903 aggravated the problem. Some of the most active and ablest members took advantage of the shipping rate war of 1904 to migrate to the United States, costing

---

7 The City of London Jewish Tailors' Society, instituted in 1867, had 180 members in the mid-1890s, all of whom were master tailors. They received a £1 per week sick benefit, four guineas as a *shiva* benefit and £20 as the death benefit for a member or his wife. Funeral expenses were paid, a tombstone erected (an interesting touch of status), and in case of serious illness, fees of 'an experienced physician' were allowed. This society, moreover, had a separate loan fund from which any member could borrow free of interest, the principal repayable in small weekly instalments. Society capital was in excess of £1,200. Annual meeting, 6 Dec. 1896. *JC*, 11 Dec. 1896.

the Amalgamated at least 150 members and reducing its treasury balance to £550. Master tailors, seeing an opportunity to re-establish control over at least the work rules in their shops, attempted to wind the clock back in a long 1911 lockout. The matter was ultimately resolved by invoking the Conciliation Act, establishing a conciliation board, and arbitrating the issues to a viable compromise.[8]

London working-class Jews, or a substantial minority of them, had ambitions that ran in other directions. London Jewish workers in general and newcomers in particular were unresponsive to trade union demands for solidarity. Their workplaces were small, lacking both the critical mass and stability of employment so essential in developing labour group consciousness. The network of London Jewish worker associations ran through family, kin, and landsman (those who came from the same town or village in East Europe), rather than a socialization of 'class' generated through workplace and functional fellowship. Upward mobility, even of limited sorts, inspired many males with ambitions to manage their own enterprises. Capital demands were modest, workplaces small, labour and opportunity available. While some communal leaders, as trade union organizers complained, worked to inhibit union growth and development, most did not. The Jewish press engaged principally in constructive criticism, although that did not necessarily sit well with marginally competent union organizers and leaders. Jewish ministers were accused of preaching against unionization, portraying trade organizations as anti-religious. Some did, but the evidence is murky as to what, if any, effect such sermons might have had. Anglo-Jewry, whatever its inclinations and prejudices, made little difference on this point. East End Jews, after all, lived in a world surrounded by examples of individual success that gave substance to the ideology of self-help. Their social betters preached the ethic; East End Jews practised it.

Immigrants, moreover, brought little experience of trade unionism. Their cultural baggage included a strong commitment to traditional Judaism and an abundance of political ideological division. Trade union leaders were often inclined to be Bundist, socialist, secular, and – as such things later came to matter within the alien community – anti-Zionist. Union activist secularism cut against the grain of strong community religious sentiment. As if this resistance did not present enough difficulties, the small minority of committed activists expended enormous effort in the easier task of quarrelling with one another rather than in the complicated problem of organizing a stubborn, difficult community. Wrangling moderates and radicals, socialists and anarchists excited contemporaries and have delighted historians but failed to overcome inertia and hostility, whether that of Anglo-Jewry or in the East End itself.[9] East End Jews, in many ways, replicated British artisanal and labour history of the earlier nineteenth century. Immediate needs were met

---

8 A joint board of employers and workpeople seems, in this instance, to have made matters worse, not better. See, e.g., *JC*, 31 Mar. 1905, 10, 17 Mar., 19 May 1911. The Amalgamated survived a short-lived challenge from the Leeds Tailoring Protective and Benefit Society, formed by members expelled from the Amalgamated in 1898. *JC*, 16, 30 Sept. 1898,1 Feb. 1901.

9 W. Fishman makes an eloquent, although I believe an excessive, case for the advanced political movements in the East End in *Jewish Radicals: from Czarist Stetl to London Ghetto* (New York, 1974). Lewis Lyons testified that trade unionists were on friendly terms with Zionists who had promised 'trade union conditions' when they got to Palestine. RCAI, 5 Mar. 1903. The weight of evidence points the other way. Zionism could most correctly be called a point on which trade unions, as trade unions, had no pronounced views.

through the established or new friendly societies. Trade unionism itself resembled so many Cheshire cats, appearing here, disappearing there, sometimes whole, sometimes fragmentary, and more often than not illusory. In politics East End Jews showed themselves surprisingly conservative, inclining to the 'left' only as advanced parties became impeccably mainstream.

Lewis Smith, a veteran of the Paris Commune, brought his zeal and experience to organize the tailors in 1874. His craft union survived a few weeks with some seventy-two small masters and workers. Two years later, again with ideological inspiration, the Hebrew Socialist Union tried once more, to be undone this time by peculation. After recruiting three hundred members in a few months, the union treasurer embezzled £80 of its funds and migrated to the United States, leaving ill-will, confusion, and a shattered union behind. Trade organizations appeared and disappeared more often and more rapidly once substantial numbers of immigrants arrived. Exploited and abused, workers concentrated in clothing, bootmaking, and cabinetmaking needed something, but the steady influx of 'greeners' and rising number of Jewish girls and women constantly entering the workforce undercut any union organization.

Unions appeared and disappeared with each trade cycle or in response to specific, often temporary, grievances. They were, more often than not, defensive, appearing with wage cuts or lay-offs and falling apart in times of prosperity. Cigar-makers, established well before the halcyon days of immigration, were able to sustain craft discipline, to bar the intensive subdivision of labour, and to preserve artisanal income and status. Their union-associated benefit society prospered. Cigarette-making machines and the increasing employment of women in that trade by the early twentieth century, on the other hand, made life for the Amalgamated Cigarette Makers' and Tobacco Cutters' Union far more difficult.[10]

The East London branch of the Boot and Shoe Operatives Union, established in 1888, had a fluctuating membership that at times approached three hundred. Being affiliated with the London Trades Council, however, it could better withstand the stresses of union adversity. Tailoring organizations continued to appear and disappear, competing with one another as well as powerful employer organizations. On occasion, masters and men acted together, as in an 1896 dispute when they combined to secure significant concessions from clothing manufacturers.[11] That

10 Jews had essentially introduced cigarette- and cigar-making to England. Jacob Kramich brought machine-made cigarettes to Players in Nottingham in 1882 and to Imperial Tobacco in Glasgow in 1888. RCAI (1903), qq 21,714–38. In 1890, Jewish men in the cigarette trade (few women were employed) received 6s per 1,000 and earned £3 to £4 per week. A Board of Deputies investigation in February 1911 to develop a response to a critical article in the *Standard* showed that the price per thousand had dropped to between 2s and 3s 6d, and workers were hard pressed to earn 30s per week. Filed as: Alien Criminal Cases, BDBJ B 2/1/9. By the end of the nineteenth century, the Cigarette Makers' were in an almost perpetual state of organization and reorganization and almost collapsed in July 1900. The Amalgamated Cigarette Makers' suddenly dissolved after a dozen years of modest activity in 1903. The women, who were usually paid about 75 per cent of the men's rate for comparable work, attempted to resurrect it in March 1903 with little success. *JC*, 8 Feb. 1901, 29 May 1903.

11 The problems remained much the same until the years immediately before the First World War. 'There really ought to be some sort of alliance between these middlemen employers and the workmen's organisation,' observed the *Yorkshire Evening News* about the tailoring trades, 'in order to prevent the prices being so cut down as to leave only a bare margin of profit for the employer.' 'The world of labour', *Yorkshire Evening News*, 2 Mar. 1911.

alliance, a tribute to the skilful diplomacy of Lewis Lyons, the union organizer and secretary, temporarily stopped the endemic and draining labour unrest that had nibbled the tailors' unions almost to death since 1891. The anger unionists felt towards their employers, however, ricocheted on to Lyons who was driven out. After another half a dozen years of disintegration, false starts on reorganization and repeated defeat in industrial disputes, some London politicians and trade union leaders pushed the fragmented tailors' organizations towards a new federation. Anger about anti-alien testimony before the Royal Commission on Alien Immigration far more than a rational choice of amalgamation produced an overflow meeting on 14 September 1902. Herbert Burrows came to preach socialism and worker brotherhood. Mrs W. Pemberton Reeves of the Women's Trade Union League, who presided, reminded a predominantly Yiddish-speaking audience in her flawless English that men and women must stand shoulder to shoulder. Alderman Heyday, an Independent Labour Party member of the West Ham town council called for the cosmopolitans and internationalists to combine against the capitalist, while a Midlands union organizer, who could at least speak Yiddish, denounced Lord Rothschild, meandered on about the need for a fair rents court, and urged aliens to become naturalized so they could throw the rascals out of parliament. The Military Uniform Tailors' Union, one of the few durable survivors of the 1890s, would have none of it. More anglicized workers turned against more recently arrived aliens. Union amalgamation in the largest single Jewish trade remained the fantasy of intellectuals.[12]

Internal divisions and faulty organization seldom inhibited irate workmen. London tailors might never develop an effective union, but they regularly disrupted business and occasionally tried police patience. The boot and shoe trade, wracked by savage competition and fed by a seemingly endless immigrant labour supply, saw locked-out workers combine for survival, temporarily win a union shop, and even attempt to form a cooperative productive society.[13] As was the case with tailors, particular sub-specialties which required some skills were best placed to survive trade and union organization boom–bust cycles. The Upper Machinists' Union, for instance, had a chequered history but never completely collapsed. When, in 1901, it reorganized to integrate women, the masters recognized the threat and organized themselves. The machinists, believing they were now united and could no longer be undercut by women workers moved increasingly aggressively. The masters, however, cultivated the less well organized Jewish Boot and Shoe Union to divide the workers. The Upper Machinists were outraged. Hobnobbing with the masters

12 For the Wonderland meeting, see *JC*, 19 Sept. 1902. The *Jewish Chronicle* had editorially preached against labour instability and pushed federation in the interests of all. *JC*, 29 Aug. 1902. See also, *JC*, 10 Jan., 25 July, 22 Aug., 16, 26 Sept., 17, 24 Oct. 1902. On the other hand, the trade union festival of 10 January 1902 at Goulston Street Baths, anticipated divisions between the more highly anglicized trade unionists and those 'mostly Oriental in character'. *JC*, 17 Jan. 1902. Lewis Lyons, who at crucial moments attempted to consolidate tailoring unions, lost much credibility when he testified before the Royal Commission in favour of limited immigration restriction. RCAI, 2, 5 Mar. 1903.

13 See, e.g., the tailors' strike in February 1899, MEPO 2/472. James Ramsay Macdonald and his wife Margaret had some interesting reflections on the threat of violence in trade disputes in their notes on the Trades Disputes Bill of 1903. Macdonald Papers, P[ublic]R[ecord]O[ffice] 30/69/1366. The Boot and Shoe Operatives' victory inspired a small boom in 1901 general trade union membership. *JC*, 25 Jan., 1 Feb. 1901.

'was derogatory to their interests', but by February 1902, the Upper Machinists themselves formed an alliance with small masters to stabilize the trade.[14] The Furriers' Union, on the other hand, was so vulnerable to dramatic seasonal variations and an entrenched piecework system that its height of ambition was simply to organize a board of arbitration. The United Cap Makers' Society, organized through the London Trades Committee when the Jewish society was about to collapse, sought to federate the fragments of the several small unions in the trade in 1901. Its principal achievement, however, was to produce a short-lived Yiddish weekly concerned entirely with Jewish trade union interests, and unity vanished as quickly as it had appeared.[15]

The cooperative movement, in its various manifestations, could boast considerable short-term enthusiasm but little staying power. The Factory and Workshops Act of 1901 created some legal difficulties for observant Jews in cooperative movements, but those issues were ultimately resolved between the Board of Deputies and the Home Office.[16] Most difficulties lay in the cooperatives themselves. The Jewish Co-operative and Industrial Alliance Society developed in 1903, gathering slightly over a hundred dedicated members during its first year. They were scarcely poor. Each took up two shares at £1 apiece, paying in subscriptions until they could establish 'a respectable shop'. Toynbee Hall social workers and women committed to the Co-operative movement urged the Alliance Society forward. But Toynbee Hall idealism and ambition – the cooperative planned to sponsor evening classes and lectures 'to educate and elevate the masses' – had limited appeal and costly consequences for the society's overstrained budget. The Alliance Society, moreover, enlisted in the East End dispersion movement, proposing to accelerate decentralization 'by delivering goods to members who live at a distance'.[17]

Five enthusiasts in a backroom launched Gray's Co-operative Society in 1905. Two years later it could show 146 members and £130 capital. The Jewish Co-Operative and Industrial Alliance Society opened new facilities in Whitechapel

---

14 The Boot and Shoe Workers are one of the better examples of the irrelevance of numbers to effectiveness in industrial organization. In November 1901 what was probably numerically the largest trade union in London – over 1,000 members – federated. By the end of the year only the Upper Machinists survived. *JC*, 21 Feb., 21 Nov. 1902.

15 *JC*, 14 Mar. 1902.

16 Policoff, secretary of the Manchester Jewish Tailors' Union brought the board's attention to the case of a Jewish workshop of the Co-operative Wholesale Society Ltd, opened in 1899 as a Jewish workshop under the control of a Jewish manager who was the nominal 'occupier' of the premises. Since the occupier must pay rent and be the actual employer of the workpeople and since the Jewish manager of a Christian-owned establishment could not be called an 'occupier' within the meaning of the Act (it being illegal for a Christian to register for sabbath exceptions), the workplace, the factory inspector ruled, must be closed on Sundays. Alexander negotiated matters with the Home Office, and a suitable resolution was found. BDBJ minute book, 16 July 1903.

17 Miss J. Halford (secretary of the International Co-operative Alliance), Miss M. Marsden (secretary of the National Co-operative Festival Association, and Miss J. P. McAdams (Brotherhood Trust) were among those who urged the Alliance Society forward. Miss Halford, to her credit, addressed the fifth quarterly meeting (at Toynbee Hall) in German. Anglo-Jewry had to admire such enterprise. Davis Abrahams, who addressed the same meeting in Yiddish, preached self-help and moral improvement, in spite of the fact that it made little business sense to use 2.5 per cent of profits for 'education'. See, particularly, *JC*, 15 Jan., 3 June 1904.

in late October 1905 attempting, as unsuccessfully as ever, to appeal to individualist and collectivist enthusiasm. The Alliance Society continued to seek worthy causes. Its profits were now to be dedicated to education and Zionism, which fortunately had other sources of income. Poor aliens both founded and comprised the membership of the Yiddish Co-operative and Industrial Society Ltd that started a fortnight later. Since its terms were strictly cash, it could never draw clientele needing at least occasional credit away from local shopkeepers. Limiting any member's investment to £200 may have seemed an appropriate statement of principle, but this food and provision society with a small benefit fund attached was not in a competitive position.[18]

Worker-organized institutions continually ran upon the shoals of individuality, division and over-ambition. By the turn of the century, however, masters' organizations were well established. They had to deal simultaneously with non-Jewish competitors and unfair practices among themselves, as well as the need to resist 'excessive' worker demands. Communal leaders had mixed feelings about labour organization, although they almost always endorsed masters' trade societies. Masters' organizations of and by themselves, however, did not answer all of what Anglo-Jewry perceived to be community needs. Combinations both of masters and men were needed to check sweating abuses, stabilize the East End economy, and protect Jewish interests in a secular society. Organized trades, for instance, were more susceptible to sabbath-keeping discipline.[19] Trade unionists, left to themselves, seemed all too often overly secular and drawn towards the will-o'-the wisp of socialism or other radical doctrines. Yet while Anglo-Jewry deprecated socialist ideology, it acknowledged problems in economic organization and benefits.

> The Jewish workmen are well known to be amongst the least inclined to organise for the purpose of aiding each other in obtaining better wages. In the tailoring, boot and cigar trades, the proportion of Jewish society is extremely small, and there are few trades where the wages range lower than in these.[20]

Even in the rare instances of labour success, advantages achieved were rarely consolidated. One of the most famous Jewish industrial disputes, the 1901 lock-out of boot and shoe workers, may have ended in union victory, but union membership collapsed before the end of the year.[21]

18 *JC*, 27 Oct., 3 Nov. 1905.

19 One effect of more rigorous sabbath observance was unrest among Gentile employees who lost Saturday wages, particularly in such trades as tailoring. Some systematic evasions of prohibited Sunday labour, for Christian women and youngsters, also appear to have been practised. The tailoring trade, in particular, tended to build its heaviest demand at the end of the week. See, particularly, the reports of Inspectors Clark, Livesey and Clarke Kennedy for East London in *Report of the Chief Inspector of Factories and Workshops* (London, 1911).

20 *JC*, 21 Mar. 1884.

21 P. Elman, 'The beginnings of the Jewish trade union movement in England', *Transactions of the Jewish Historical Society*, XVII, 53–62; Fishman, *Jewish Radicals*, 136 and part 2; Lipman, *Social History*, 116–9; and the contemporary G. Halpern, *Die Jüdischen Arbeiter in London* (Stuttgart and Berlin, 1903), Kapital 5. Differential regional wage rates were not so substantial as to accelerate the dispersion Anglo-Jewry would have preferred. The law and parliamentary committee on home work prepared elaborate statistics on this point for Sir Stuart Samuel to present as Jewish evidence in 1907, in BDBJ B 2/18/6.

To the despair of union activists, working-class Jews failed to understand what trade unions actually were. Most members

> join a union, pay a weekly subscription, but there the matter ends, and if anything goes wrong, they expect the Secretary to put it right. They are over and over again too anxious to start fresh unions without sufficient justification and give to the new body the name of an association or union. But it is neither. How can a union exist without unity, or an association unless the members are associated and combined together? The workman must realize that the first, the main, and the last essential to success is combination.[22]

Part of the difficulty lay simply in the fact that English trade unions were there to see, and the comparison frustrated Jewish trade unionists. They wanted to have instantly what had taken decades, even generations, to achieve and they sought it in volatile trades given to sharp competition and brutal economies. They would divide on issues of language, often refusing to tolerate discussion in English rather than Yiddish.

English trade union organizers who sought to assist Jews, particularly aliens, in their trades repeatedly found themselves victimized in just the same way as did Jewish organizers. T. O'Grady, secretary of the London branch of the Boot and Shoe Operatives, contended that the gains of a trade-wide strike in 1890 had been undone principally by defecting aliens. His union had, he estimated, spent £6,000 in assisting alien workers who left all too often to become small-scale sweatshop proprietors. Lewis Lyons contended that the problem was even more serious in the Jewish Tailors' Union. Aliens left the union to pay debts they had run up and went out to become independent sweaters. In both tailoring and bootmaking, however, the rapid development and extension of machine technology, quite as much as anything else, made possible the persistence and multiplication of small workshops. In both trades more and better (not inferior) products became available at lower prices. Consumers benefited at the cost of union organization. Jewish immigrants benefited much more as individuals from a market expanding more rapidly than either manufacturers or unions could control.[23]

The United Ladies' Tailors and Mantle-makers, which proved to be an unusually durable, if not very effective, organization started in 1889. Although membership peaked in 1891 at 550, the United still maintained an annual

---

22 *JC*, 23 July 1897. Jewish trade union organizers and secretaries were badly paid and roundly abused. Some of the more successful made ends meet by organizing and acting for several unions. S. Ellstein, for example, was simultaneously the organizer and secretary of the London Cigarette Makers', the East London Bakers', and the Military Tailors' Union at the beginning of 1904.

23 RCAI, 2 Mar., 5 Mar. 1903. See also the testimony of Solomon V. Anstell, RCAI, 19 Feb. 1903. Owners disliked sweating because it made the market so unpredictable. Unionists disliked sweating because it undercut all union goals. Jewish leaders, who often understood both the social and economic benefits and liabilities, disliked sweating because it reflected adversely on the Jewish image. Regulating sweating remained a serious Anglo-Jewish concern in the early twentieth century. See, e.g., the law and parliamentary committee discussions about the Commission on Sweating in 1907 and the Home Work Regulation Bill, 1908. 'The provisions of this Bill did not press more heavily on Jews than on non-Jews and that if it were possible to carry out its provisions in the manner intended by the Bill they would tend to improve the sanitary conditions under which work was done in the home.' Law and parliamentary committee, 12 June 1907, 19 Feb., 10 Mar. 1908, BDBJ C 13/1/6.

membership of three to four hundred through the pre-war period. The Ladies' Tailors and Mantle-makers, having carefully observed the world around them, carefully remained aloof from the siren song of political commitment or consolidated labour organization. Its relatively moderate policies enabled it to resist 'assaults on their rights', while avoiding the boom–bust history of such organizations as the Amalgamated Society of Tailors.[24] Boot and shoe workers repeatedly attempted to organize with steadily worsening results between 1886 and 1901. Other trades – tobacco, for instance, with its modest organizations of one to three hundred members – survived principally through the mutual forbearance of masters and men that minimized damaging trade disputes. Cabinet-making, on the other hand, was so broken into factions that the Master Cabinet Makers' Association, organized in June 1896, and the Jewish workers found their best interests served by acting in harmony to resist the efforts of non-Jewish cabinet-makers to drive Jewish masters out of business.

Jewish trade organization drew some benefit from government policies. Official efforts to standardize quality and create order among a multitude of government contractors, a movement which accelerated most dramatically in war, helped to nourish and sustain such moderate organizations as the Military and Uniform Tailors' Union. Late nineteenth-century efforts to form a union or society of women tailors, however, came to nought. Margaret Macdonald, investigating for the stores committee of the London County Council in 1902, even discovered that some contractors evaded regulated wages by having special Jewish staff and Jewish subcontracted labour working below the scale.[25]

Politics, particularly anarchist and socialist politics, sometimes generated misleading momentary enthusiasm for worker organization. Herbert Burrows would bounce out on any public platform to preach worker unity and the overthrow of capitalism, promising instant gratification through purposeful organization. Popular support, which more than once inspired union development, almost invariably proved chimerical. The great abortive strike of the International Tailors' Union in 1891, for instance, was not merely extremely expensive and violent. The quarrels to which it gave rise continued to divide Jewish tailors through subsequent

24 The Amalgamated brought in the West End coat tailors first, then their East End counterparts, but undoubtedly hurt themselves by then recruiting the Jewish Tailoresses Union. *JC*, 24 Feb. 1905. The Master Mantle Makers sought closer relations in 1903 with the London Mantle Makers' Union in hopes of stabilizing the trade. *JC*, 17 July 1903.

25 'I noticed that Messrs. Dolan had employed a special staff of about a dozen Jews and Jewesses upon the serge jumpers, which had been kept quite distinct from the rest of the contract. The total number on order, about 900, had all been made, at the time of my visit, and the prices paid had been according to the log, but upon looking through the work books, the amount earned by the finishers and button holers does not compare favourably with that earned upon other garments.' She encountered the same sort of problem in 1901 at Atkinson's, where she was unable to question the Yiddish-speaking Polish Jewish workers who ostensibly did not understand English. Margaret F. Macdonald to the stores committee, private and confidential, 28 Oct. 1901, Macdonald Papers. PRO 30/69/1366. See also *Report of the Select Committee on Government Contracts (Fair Wages Resolution)* (London, 1897); *JC*, 27 Nov., 4, 11, 18 Dec. 1896, 1 Jan., 26 Aug. 1897. The financial supplement of *The Times*, 31 July 1905, has a substantial discussion of the furniture-making industry and alien labour. While describing the displacement of English cabinet-makers earning £2 to £3 per week giving way to aliens earning 25s to 30s, the article also credited the shrinkage of foreign furniture imports and lowering of domestic prices to this change. See also Lipman, *Century of Social Service*, 116–17.

years. John Burns, the great union leader and later the first man from the working class to hold a cabinet seat, so burned his fingers by attempting to arbitrate in internal disputes that he developed an aversion to interference in Jewish trade union matters. To Burns's credit, however, he continued to be an outspoken defender of alien immigration even when some socialists and trade unionists ducked that sensitive issue.[26]

Jewish master bakers confronted not only the problem of dealing with their employees but the fending off of chronic harassment by the London Master Bakers' Protection Society. Trade unions appeared and disappeared with stunning regularity. The issue, in at least one principal instance, underscored problems of Jewish trade unions in highly competitive trades. Workers at M. M. Rosenberg's charged their employer with forcing them to work a seven-day week. Henry M. Cohen, secretary of the [Jewish] International Bakers' Union appealed to the Chief Rabbi in July 1901, informing him that the union proposed to boycott Jewish employers who violated the sabbath. Adler told Cohen in no uncertain terms that Jewish law prohibited boycotting any Jewish tradesman. Adler, who had previously worked with Montagu to secure sabbath observance agreements from East End Jewish employers, asked for the names and addresses of any master bakers who violated the sabbath. He summoned the master bakers to the Beth Hamedrash and laid down the conditions upon which they were entitled to have their bread labelled 'by permission of the Ecclesiastical Authorities'. Twelve master bakers signed a document agreeing not to bake on the sabbath or to permit workmen to enter their shops until the sabbath was over. Rosenberg went back on his word and ordered his men to work the next Saturday. The dispute dragged on through August and September with the union demanding that discharged workers be reinstated and that Rosenberg's new employees be required to join the union. Rosenberg refused, arguing that he could not pay that large a staff. The Chief Rabbi insisted, ultimately to no avail. The union collapsed.

Sabbath observance had also brought the London Master Bakers' Protection Society on to the field. They prosecuted Jewish master bakers who baked on Sunday under an antiquated seventeenth-century statute, the Bread Act. After a series of harassing prosecutions, the Board of Deputies aided the Jewish Master Bakers' Protection Society to defend itself, seeing all exceptions for observant Jews under the Factory and Workshop Acts in danger. Those statutes allowed Jews who did not work on Saturday limited Sunday working rights. Appealing from the magistrates to the divisional courts, the conviction of Simon Cohen was overturned in 1897. A four-year tacit agreement with the London Master Bakers under which no prosecutions were initiated against sabbath-observing Jewish bakers broke down in April 1902. Once again the Board of Deputies weighed in with the Jewish Master Bakers' Protection Society, defending against nine months of summonses. Once again they won on appeal. The London Bakers, having spent almost £640 on

---

26 The fight which started with a 'restoration committee' meeting at the Working Lads' Institute in 1891 adjourned to the Kay Street Radical Club. Husky club stewards maintained a measure of order, but the minority would brook no compromise in spite of Burns's assiduous negotiations. Four years later, the factions were still at it. Malcontents brought a libel action at the Old Bailey against one of the convenors of the meeting. Burns planned to testify for the defence, but the case was dropped. *JC*, 22 Dec. 1905.

prosecutions in 1902 alone, gave up the campaign in the courts and turned instead to support Lord Avebury's annual efforts to enact a stiffer Sunday observance law.[27]

The East London Jewish Bakers' Trade Union started in 1904 with general and widespread public sympathy. The men, not surprisingly, expected early concessions. The politically activist section took control and waived every opportunity for compromise. The activists, unable to believe that judgement would go against them, exhausted the union's public contributions and scanty resources by attempting to bring legal action against the masters with no understanding of the intricacies of the law and a stunning unawareness of the ways in which the courts were consistently ruling against labour. Presuming public support to be both permanent and generous, the activist leadership then squandered what remained of its resources and all of its credit in an effort to establish a cooperative bakery. The men drifted away in anger and frustration, and the union dissolved in February 1905.[28] Jewish labour leaders, on the other hand, sometimes showed the good sense to recognize their weakness. When the world of organized labour debated what action to take in the wake of the Taff Vale and Belfast cases in 1901 which appeared to remove legal immunity from striking trade unions, those unionists who attended came only with 'watching briefs'. Union leaders understood that they had neither the funds nor the organization to carry a battle into the world of courts and high politics.[29]

Masters, not hands, combined effectively. Mark Moses, one of Montagu's supporters in the formation of the Federation of Synagogues, organized the Mutual Tailor's Association, which evolved into the Master Tailors' League, sometimes called the Tailors' Improvement Association. Like other industrialist organizations, the Master Tailors sought simultaneously to regulate the trade in ways that would reduce the worst and most conspicuous abuses, to generate a more favourable public image of tailoring, and to control labour. The Trades Boards Act of 1910 enabled the Jewish Master Tailors' Association to extend its London operations and place its nominees on district trade commissions.[30] Masters and men in cabinet-making had problems with each other and with Christian firms with which they directly competed in 1896. The Hebrew Cabinet Employers' Association and the two principal Jewish worker associations agreed to a union shop, no subcontracting work out, and one apprentice or 'improver' for every five journeymen employed. The unions conceded that workers would neither leave jobs unfinished nor demand a higher rate once any project was started. Management controlled workplace rules and retained the right to discharge union men for cause.

---

27 See, particularly, R. versus Bros and Nosseck (*ex parte* Venters) (1901) and Cohen to Adler, 1 July, Adler to Cohen 4 July, Cohen to Adler, 17 July 1901. *JC*, 30 Aug., 6, 13 Sept., 15 Nov. 1901, 17 Oct., 12 Dec. 1902.

28 *JC*, 24 Feb. 1905. The Independent Tailors' Union, formed in September 1896, would be another example. The Sunday course of lectures provided political spokesmen with a responsive forum, but the union itself divided rather than concentrated worker support.

29 *JC*, 30 Aug. 1901.

30 *JC*, 6 Jan. 1911. Mark Moses took a hard line on labour matters. He had early recommended a practice, neither practicable nor ever actually attempted, comparable to the notorious French *livret*, the worker's passbook. Employers would only hire workers whose previous employer had signed them off as satisfactory. *JC*, 23 May 1884; Fishman, *Jewish Radicals*, 136–7. Stuart M. Samuel hoped to revive the Jewish National Tailors' Association in 1901 to act in concert with worker organizations to bring better order and predictability to the clothing industry. See the meeting of 15 Jan. 1901. *JC*, 18 Jan. 1901.

The workmen's association agreed to do the best it could to find replacements for any employee in violation of the rules. Both sides agreed to operate 'in all matters concerning labour and disputes' under the same conditions as English firms.[31] The Jewish Master Bakers' Association struggled on two fronts. It campaigned for strict sabbatarianism to protect observant members and, incidentally, to ascertain that community leaders were prepared to lend their influence and support. But it also found itself involved in guerrilla warfare with the London bakers, who took violent exception to Jews baking on Sunday and initiated harassing prosecutions under sabbatarian statutes.[32]

For those lying outside the precariously sheltering network of friendly societies or trade unions, collecting banks or self-help loan societies enjoyed some popularity, particularly in the mid-1890s. Unlike friendly societies or trade unions, however, these organizations enjoyed little if any success without substantial commitment from some middle- or upper-class advocate. The Charity Organisation Society warmly endorsed such plans. The Self Help Labour Loan Society, borrowed from the German idea of People's Banks, started in St Pancras and Ealing. The Reverend J. H. Cardwell, vicar of St Anne's, Soho, a pioneer of collecting savings banks, took the idea up for his parish. Workers and small business people created their own capital, putting in a weekly sixpence, a shilling, or whatever their means would permit. From this fund, loans would be made to members needing temporary assistance. Two other members were to act as sureties, and no borrower could draw more than the sureties had on deposit. Losses thus became theoretically impossible. Cardwell's society was, by 1896, handling £1,000. All depositors who did not borrow drew 7.5 per cent interest, a substantially more attractive rate than Post Office savings or competing thrift institutions. Borrowers paid 5 per cent for their money, but interest had to be paid first, so the effective interest rate was 8 per cent. With 0.5 per cent for management costs, the arrangement looked foolproof on paper. Small Jewish dealers and tailors used the Cardwell society. One woman, for instance, dealing in second-hand clothing needed £5 to purchase a parcel of goods. She had thirty shillings of her own in the bank, sought out two friends who had thirty shillings and £2 respectively. Would they stand surety for her? Once assured that she would do the same for them, the deal was settled.[33]

31 Settlement of 14 Dec. 1896. *JC*, 8 Jan. 1897.

32 See, among other occasions, the December 1896–January 1897 campaign in *JC*. The Board of Deputies turned the matter over to its law and parliamentary committee and authorized Sir Samuel Montagu to negotiate with the Home Secretary. See BDBJ B 2/18/4.

33 The Jewish Board of Guardians loan funds provided much the same opportunity without the problem of finding sureties. The trade-off, however, was the loan committee's prying oversight. Making such institutions work, however, required an active, committed volunteer at the head who could continue to recruit deposits in slack times and in the face of losses. That seems to have been the source of Dr Oliver's success in St Pancras and Ealing and Cardwell's in Soho. *JC*, 14 Aug., 6 Nov.1896. The scheme developed for the Provident Society for Jewish Workpeople in Birmingham, which operated on threepence to half-a-crown deposits, depended on 'collectors' to keep going, a seasonally effective form of operation at best. *JC*, 14 Aug. 1896.

SOCIALISTS AND ANARCHISTS

Just as many in the East End responded selectively to Anglo-Jewish initiatives and teachings, other voices within the community demanded a hearing. Fresh from his struggles with the Vilna rabbis and their subservience to oppressive Russian authorities, Aron Lieberman reached London in August 1875. With nine fellow Litvaks, Lieberman organized the Hebrew Socialist Union (Augdah Hasozialistim Chaverim) in May 1876. With its vision of the international brotherhood of all workers, the Socialist Union devoted itself to quibbling about criteria for membership and details of ideology. Lieberman's 'Call to Jewish youth' (18 July 1876) may or may not have made him an inspiration for the 'Bund' and an apostle of Socialist Zionism ('Poale Zion').[34] The 'call' drew a wrathful response from Chief Rabbi Nathan Adler and the Jewish establishment press. A public meeting on 26 August 1876 disintegrated into a verbal, then a physical brawl. The Tailors' Union wanted no part of Lieberman or the disorder he engendered. Lieberman vanished to Germany and a crusade for Russian liberation and social democracy, but Morris Winchevsky carried Lieberman's ideological torch in the *Arbeter Fraint* (The Worker's Friend), a Yiddish-language, Socialist paper which began publication on 15 July 1885. Establishing a market for itself by trading in Marxism and anti-clericalism, *Arbeter Fraint* became a sounding board for anti-establishment resentment and an object of radical ambitions. The International Workers' Educational Club, organized by a group of Jewish socialists in 1884, sought to radicalize all trade union movements. The Berner Street club resounded to heady rhetoric and regularly listened to William Morris summon workers and intellectuals for fellowship and economic emancipation. The club took control of *Arbeter Fraint*, converting it from a monthly to a weekly publication, and using it to stimulate unionization drives in London and the provinces. By 1887, *Arbeter Fraint* was waging its own civil war with Anglo-Jewry.

Sir Samuel Montagu and Chief Rabbi Adler won hands down. *Arbeter Fraint's* campaign of blasphemy and desecration worked against any possible radical success. A Yom Kippur ball finished the job. By 1888, the anarchists, organized as the Knights of Labour, who captured paper and club could not have cared less. Labour was becoming militant, the combined forces of the Social Democratic Federation and the anarchists saw themselves catapulting to communal command in a general strike of tailors and sweated workers in August 1889. They had the year right – 1889 saw the emergence of the new unionism in such historic disputes as the dock strike – but they had underestimated communal leadership, particularly Sir Samuel Montagu and Lord Rothschild. Taking the stance of mediators, Montagu and Rothschild settled the strike, then counterattacked. Anglo-Jewish East End club life was enriched to attract more participants. The Federation of Synagogues launched its aggressive campaign to hold believing Jews in familiar institutions but under the authority of the Chief Rabbi.

---

34 As W. J. Fishman argues in *Jewish Radicals*, 111. Fishman, chapter 4 onwards, remains the most useful summary of Jewish political radicalism from the 1870s to 1914, and I have drawn heavily on it for this section.

S. Yanovsky and the anarchists seized Berner Street and *Arbeter Fraint* in 1891, the older social democrats organizing a new journal, *Die Freie Welt*. Neither captured the hearts and minds of its would-be constituents. *Arbeter Fraint* claimed two hundred subscribers, but by no means all were paid up. *Die Freie Welt* claimed over five hundred, but many of those sales were in the United States. Threatened with condemnation by a London Council Council inspector, Berner Street shut down, residual club members enrolling in the London International Working Men's Association. The chattering and quarrelsome Yiddish radical press was no match for Montagu's not-very-secret weapon, the great Yiddish preacher Chaim Z. Maccoby. Maccoby's pulpit charisma attracted thousands, crushing atheistical radicalism in religious revivalism from 1894 to 1914. Anarchist outrages, the terrorism of an earlier generation, achieved nothing and served only to underscore how far such self-appointed voices of the people had strayed from the aspirations of those who lived and laboured in the East End.[35]

London anarchists became tabloid fair game after President McKinley's assassination in 1901. The *Standard*, which led the charge, contended that 4,000 heads of families in the Berner Street club were anarchists and communists advocating violence and assassination. The accusation, although it recurred from time to time in modified form during the testimony before the Royal Commission on Alien Immigration, ran so counter to the evidence that it was disregarded. The Russian Free Library in Church Lane was run by a Russian Christian, not a Jew. Since printing the simplest news-sheet or journal demanded £3 to £5 merely to set the type, the radical appetite for words had to be fed with imports from Russia or New York. Jewish workers preferred religion and reacted strongly against atheism and blasphemy.[36]

Immigrants and refugees also brought the Bund, the General Jewish Workmen's Union of Russia and Poland, to Britain. A proto-organization started in Vilna in 1885 and 1886 among Jewish students, it presented itself as the elite leaders of a worker vanguard promoting revolution through worker action. It combined an educational programme for the working classes with the accumulation of strike and benefit funds that were of some service in the 1888 strikes. Those strikes changed the tactics of Jewish socialists and spread the movement from Minsk to Warsaw. These intellectual enthusiasts celebrated May Day in 1896 by dispatching their representatives of the Jewish Proletariat of Russia to the International Socialist Congress in London. While this had little impact upon either Western socialism or East End Jewry, it did convince Russian authorities to take the organization seriously. Persecution magnified their sense of self-importance. The first Jewish Socialist Conference, convened in September 1897, saw the formal constitution of the Bund. While Bundists initially joined the Russian Working Men's Democratic

---

35 Fishman, pt iii, deals with the ascendancy of Rudolf Rocker and the revival of *Arbeter Fraint* from October 1898. German and Gentile, Rocker re-established Berner Street as the Worker's Friend Club, secular in philosophy and anarchist in politics, in 1906.

36 *Standard*, 14 Sept. 1901. For replies the *Standard* was willing to print, see *Standard*, 17, 19 Sept. 1901, and for the replies it would not print, see *JC*, 20 Sept. 1901. Even Arnold White conceded that Jewish leaders had no use for Jewish anarchists, a point made clear in the testimony of most Anglo-Jewish spokesmen before the Royal Commission on Alien Immigration. A. White, *English Democracy* (London, 1894), 156–7.

Party, they separated again to act in concert but retain their autonomy. As earlier, the effective Bundist contribution in ensuing years was principally to recruit and administer strike funds, the five Bundist congresses between 1897 and 1903 emphasizing industrial action. But industrial action threatened to make the much-touted workers the real powers within the faction, and frustrated intellectuals preferred to think of themselves as the elite of a revolutionary political party. The tsarist government was glad to oblige with persecution, and upwards of 2,200 of their 'intellectual proletariat' were arrested and deported in 1901, 1902 and 1903. Like Zionist workmen in Russia, who preferred Poale Zion, the Bundists stood apart from the Russian Socialist party, proud of their Jewishness and ideological purity. As these enthusiasts drifted in the refugee stream, they brought their ideology westward to London, to Paris, and those centres of reception overseas. In the earlier years of the twentieth century, however, Bundists in Britain were principally another voice of political discord, more intent on preserving doctrinal purity than finding effective grounds of agreement and cooperation with the British political left and labour movement.[37]

The communal response to the Kishinev massacres of 1903 laid down the lines of political division within the community for a generation. Anglo-Jewry, for a variety of reasons, divided but declined to organize a public protest, unlike its counterparts in other Western countries. Relief funds were organized, and behind-the-scenes pressure brought to bear, but the responses seemed, to many critics, weak, even craven. This appeared to offer radicals an opportunity to steal a march on the Jewish leadership. They had misfired badly in the summer of 1902 when they attempted to establish a branch of the International Labour Federation, patterned on the Parisian organization of the same name. Neither trade unionists nor the East End masses took the slightest interest. Kishinev offered the radicals another chance. An International Kishinev Massacre Protest Committee sprang into being. It managed one East End meeting and then sought to translate its transient popularity into some durable institutional form. The committee itself was short-lived, winding up its affairs at the end of July 1903, but it bequeathed a General Jewish Workers' Organisation Committee to the East End.

All of this suggested a unity of purpose that was nowhere to be found, even among the organizers of the original Kishinev demonstration. A small but articulate faction of dogmatic idealists wanted no part of trade unions, calling them nothing more than 'a silly palliative'. They thought they had translated the Kishinev outrage into a potential general strike, that the abolition of capitalism was at hand. Trade union leaders wanted no part of such premature notions. They responded by trying to vote non-unionists out. But unionists, who saw the organization committee as the long-sought umbrella organization for all Jewish trade unions, found that the committee actually spawned new splinter groups within their own bodies, the ultimate divisive legacy of radical political propaganda. A Plain-Hands Trade

37 They did, however, always make the ceremonial gesture. The London branch of the Bundists, Association Wecker, invited 'advanced' political organizations to a Trafalgar Square demonstration on 8 June 1902 to protest at the brutal repression of Bundists by the Vilna police. *JC*, 13 June 1902.

Union and an allied Anti-Sub-Contracting Union withdrew, denouncing stodgy union leaders and passive union policies.[38]

From time to time small groups of intellectuals among the immigrants did attempt to combine 'to spread education of a highly advanced nature'. In the autumn of 1902, for instance, a few political discussion groups managed to convince the Independent [Furniture] Carvers' Union to join them in establishing a Labour Institute, to be modelled on the Maison du Peuple of Brussels. One large hall for public meetings would be needed in a building that would also have smaller rooms for trade union or political society offices. Fantasies of 1,000 people contributing one penny per week wafted briefly through the East End and then, like others before and after, vanished with scarcely a trace. Rudolf Rocker, a German Gentile who learned Yiddish and preached his doctrine of worker solidarity in the East End from the late nineteenth century until his internment as an enemy alien in 1914, hoped among other things to build a people's protest on the even more unlikely basis of the Jewish women's trade union movement.[39]

Anglo-Jewish leaders were invariably attentive to those problems upon which political grievances could focus and fester. Housing, for instance, was one area in which the philanthropic impulse launched a multiple attack. Not only did such organizations as Rothschild's 4% Industrial Dwellings Company provide model housing, but Sir Samuel Montagu donated twenty-six acres of land to the London County Council to erect housing for the poor. Jewish leaders were active in spurring local authorities to act against sanitary violations and breaches in the housing codes. Since numbers outran ingenuity, popular impulse and Anglo-Jewish leadership allied, for instance, in the winter of 1898–9 to form the Tenants' Protection Association. Chaired by Canon Barnett of Toynbee Hall and organized by Progressive party members of the London County Council, association meetings gave the aggrieved an outlet for their grievances and the leaders an opportunity to display their virtue.

East End Jewish housing needs helped to create an opportunity for exploitation. Landlords bought up unsanitary dwellings, made inexpensive, cosmetic repairs, and rack-rented the tenements. Hanbury Street homes valued at £600 turned over for £1,400 with more than proportionate raises in rent. Thirteen two-room houses inhabited by Christians in a dark court off Quaker Street, Spitalfields, were sold, the tenants evicted and newcomers forced to pay premiums of thirty to forty shillings for the privilege of becoming weekly tenants. The rent on each was raised by half (from 5s to 7s 6d). New tenants could only meet such charges by sub-letting or substantially overcrowding the buildings. The ease with which new tenants could be found inspired the new landlord immediately to sell six of the buildings. The landlord recovered much of his original investment. Tenants saw their rents bumped up to eight shillings. Better housing commanded greater premiums. A relatively new row of houses on Old Montagu Street changed hands several times,

38 'Childish action of this description,' observed the *Jewish Chronicle*'s labour correspondent, 'will show on what flimsy ground some labour men are ready to bring into play the forces of disintegration that cause the stagnation of which they complain and which constitutes the only real menace to their interests.' *JC*, 19 Feb. 1904. See also, *JC*, 2 Sept. 1902, 31 July, 7 Aug. 1903, 22 Jan. 1904.

39 *JC*, 17 Oct. 1902; 17 July 1903. For Rudolf Rocker, see his autobiography, *In Shturem. Golus Yorem* (London and Buenos Aires, 1952).

the rents rising on each transfer. Two rooms and a kitchen on the ground floor which were originally let for 9s 6d had risen to 15s. Only repeated exertions by the Whitechapel sanitary aid committee sustained marginally acceptable conditions.[40]

Housing hysteria grew. The observant pointed at Hanbury Street housing brokers doing business in the synagogues on the Day of Atonement. Jew-baiters saw the opportunity to substantiate their indictments. Those forced to pay higher rents were roused to protest and to demand action. From such tinder could dangerous political fires be kindled. Anglo-Jewry could not allow the movement to run its course. Sir Samuel Montagu, in particular, had personal and well as institutional interests at stake. His strong political base might be endangered if he failed to take decisive action. Since Montagu planned, among other things, to bequeath his Whitechapel parliamentary seat to his nephew Stuart M. Samuel, he made certain that he chaired the mass public meeting on high rents on 19 December 1898. At that gathering, Montagu denied the 'vicious rumour' that he owned East End property, denounced 'house usurers', demanded more model housing, and discoursed on the merits of suburban dispersion. Then, as his legacy to his Whitechapel constituents, he announced that he would offer the London County Council twenty-six acres of land he owned at Edmonton as a site for 700 homes to house 3–4,000 people. Montagu had once again put his finger on the pulse of real public opinion. In so far as the agitation for the Royal Commission on Alien Immigration had a real grievance propelling it, that unrest pivoted on skyrocketing housing costs in the borough of Stepney. The leadership, having recaptured the initiative, proclaimed its virtue. displayed warm sympathy for 'the people', and initiated an institution to sustain its control. The Chief Rabbi denounced any Jewish landlords who exploited the poor as 'transgressing Jewish law'. H. W. L. Lawson, proprietor of the *Daily Telegraph*, member of the London County Council, and shortly to be Conservative MP for Mile End, called for urban authorities to take the lead in constructing more model housing. Pious hopes for the future, however inspirational, did not answer immediate needs. Montagu had the answer for that. He proposed that a solicitor be appointed to act on behalf of tenants facing illegal eviction. Thus came into being the East London Tenants' Protection Committee.[41]

Once again, as they had done so many times before and would again, inchoate needs bubbled in a cauldron of popular discontent. Whether that agitation could have boiled up into sustained political activity independent of, even hostile to, the leadership or not, it could have fed any number of well or casually mounted challenges. Anglo-Jewry stepped in, recaptured 'its people', and then established yet one more institution to bind community and leadership. Everyone recognized Montagu's handiwork. George Vandamm was his choice as solicitor, although Toynbee Hall and Canon Barnett provided facilities and kept the books. Anglo-Jewry understood the importance of describing the Jewish East End as no more than one part of a larger working-class housing problem. By 1904, the existence and exertions of the committee combined with reduced pressure for

40 Each issue of the *Jewish Chronicle* from early 1898 brought more examples to communal attention. Harry S. Lewis, who led his crusade for reform from Toynbee Hall, made certain that public agitation never flagged. The *Star*, among other tabloids, picked up and publicized the displacement of Gentiles by Jews.
41 Tenants' Protection Association meeting, 14 Jan. 1899. *JC*, 20 Jan. 1899.

housing to ease the burden of litigation. The East London Tenants' and General Legal Protection Committee, as it came to be called, sat every Tuesday night. Committee members, skilled in such things, gave advice, 'providing professional assistance for people who need legal redress for wrongs of all kinds, and who are too poor to pay for a solicitor's service'. Benjamin Schewzik's short-lived and ill-starred arbitration bureau was recreated under Anglo-Jewish auspices. The committee heard about forty cases each week. In most instances advice sufficed, so costly and embarrassing litigation could be prevented. The committee still placed more than a hundred cases each year in Vandamm's hands, principally questions of worker compensation, disputes between employers and employees, husbands and wives, and the increasingly common claims arising from street accidents. The Jewish Board of Guardians worked hand-in-glove with the committee, and the committee had the cooperation of the Bet Din, the rabbinical court, legally enforcing awards the Bet Din had made.[42] From angry popular protest yet another of the threads had been spun that wove working-class Jews into a web of Anglo-Jewish dependency.

ZIONISTS AND JEWISH NATIONALISTS

Yet a different challenge to Anglo-Jewry arose at least in part from within its own ranks. Sir Moses Montefiore, the very model of an Anglo-Jew, supported Jewish settlements and development in Ottoman Palestine. Colonel A. E. W. Goldsmid of Jewish Lads' Brigade fame was a principal in organizing the Chovevei Zion Association, committed to the active colonization of Palestine. It formally organized at Montagu's Jewish Working Men's Club on 31 May 1890. The luminaries were there: Rothschild and Montagu, Sir Benjamin Louis Cohen, Hermann Adler and Moses Gaster. Although a few, including the great preacher Rabbi Chaim Z. Maccoby who would regularly speak for Chovevei Zion, undoubtedly believed that the great work must ultimately restore the entire Jewish people to its scriptural home, the Anglo-Jewish leaders believed nothing of the sort. Whether alienated by Anglo-Jewish insistence that Chovevei Zion work in tandem with the Paris-based Jewish Colonisation Association (ICA) in a clearly limited conception of Jewish nationalism or whether the great majority of East Enders were actually unmoved by this early phase and diluted version of Zionism is unclear. It did not prove to be one of the more sturdy bridges the West End built to the East. Nor is the evidence clearer that Theodor Herzl's version of modern Jewish nationalism would have attracted a more substantial following in England had it not merged with other political tensions and strains within British Jewry.

As Zionism became not merely an idea but an organized movement aspiring to assume a major place in communal organization, it gathered about itself both the committed and the ambitious, the discontented and the dreamers. Zionism, more clearly than any political issue, challenged the assumptions on which Anglo-Jewish institutions had been constructed and the goals Anglo-Jewry defined and

---

42 East London Tenants' Protection Committee, *Sixth Annual Report, 1904* (London, 1905); West London Tenants' and General Legal Protection Committee, *Twelfth Annual Report, 1910* (London, 1911). The census of 1911 showed moderate or substantial population declines in Stepney (down 18,756) and the adjoining areas, dramatically easing the housing shortage.

pursued.[43] Zionism never captured a majority of British Jews either before, during or immediately after the First World War, but it did achieve impressive support. By the turn of the century, communal statisticians numbered twenty-six bodies belonging to the English Zionist Federation, twenty-four Zionist benefit or tontine societies, and two chapters of Chovevei Zion. Some served broad-gauge ideological and utilitarian purposes, among them the social and educational friendly society instituted by committed Labour Zionist young intellectuals. They hoped to combine education with benevolence, having as their first object:

> The mutual improvement of the intellectual, social and moral tone of the members by means of social gatherings, conversations and discussions on scientific and other questions of the day, whilst the second object is to collect a fund with a view of assisting members during sickness, death, misfortune, and emigration.[44]

In the great tradition of Labour Zionism, this society admitted members usually rejected by benefit societies: women, those over forty, and those who could not secure a doctor's health certificate. Since the society was not financially suicidal, the latter, however, were only permitted to subscribe to a special fund providing access only to the cultural benefits and, for an additional contribution, to the tontine.

The passions Zionism aroused and the debate it engendered made the movement appear far larger than lifesize. Neither organized Zionism nor the politically far less effective anti-Zionist League of British Jews, founded in 1917, captured the community. Zionism, however, did succeed in dividing Anglo-Jewry itself, appealing, for various reasons, to limited numbers among the elite. Zionism more quickly attracted restive spirits within the Jewish middle classes. No more effective club was available with which professionals could smite their pretentious betters.

MACHZIKÉ HADASS

The East End made not only economic, social, and political but also its religious declarations of independence, challenging Anglo-Jewish Orthodox concessions to modernity, convenience, or being British. Solomon Herz led one of the most visible of such insurrections. Born in Germany and attached to Rabbi Hirsch's ultra-Orthodox *schul* in Frankfurt, Herz migrated to New York City where he founded the Chevra Shomré Shobbos and then came to London, establishing himself in 1881 as leader of the ultra-Orthodox community. Nothing remarkable transpired for a decade, although grievances festered about mixed choirs, forms of worship and Jewish observances. Then a *shechita* issue precipitated a public breach between Herz and the Chief Rabbi. Adler gave notice in 1891 that the sale of kidney fat could not be permitted. The ultra-Orthodox approved, but the Jewish Butchers, organized and restive, protested. They informed Adler that the discontinuation of such sales was 'impracticable'. Adler retreated, withdrew the

---

43 For a discussion of these, see Cohen, *English Zionists*. On Zionism in general, see D. Vital, *The Origins of Zionism* (Oxford, 1975).

44 The society held its first public meeting in December 1902. *JC*, 2 Jan. 1903.

prohibition, and endorsed fresh regulations. Herz exploded and formed a society to promote ultra-Orthodox principles with its separate organization for *shechita* regulation.[45]

The community grew slowly in numbers, more rapidly in ambitions. Funds were laboriously procured to hire a rabbi, Abba Werner, whose hopes for the community ran far beyond rigorous *shechita* enforcement, although that proved an attractive starting point in the East End. While the society counted no more than 250 members by the end of 1896, ten butcher shops enjoyed Machziké Hadass endorsement. Society popularity reached far beyond the boundaries of its organization. Rigidly Orthodox schools proved attractive. A Talmud Torah educating 'truly observant' East End children was the first step in society plans leading to the organization of an Orthodox Yeshiva. Society leaders justified their programme by attacking the compromises that had been made in traditional Judaism. Machziké Hadass, moreover, argued that it was not a whit less dedicated to anglicization than the West End establishment. Being better Britons, society leaders argued. was not achieved by compromise, rather, 'by strictly observing our holy religion, one would become a much better loyal British subject than those who discard traditional law'. Many Anglo-Jews felt the the weight of this argument in their purse, if not their heart. The costly patronage system sustaining West End domination seemed to have no limits, particularly as philanthropies outgrew their facilities and required new ones, not to mention each expensive East End scheme as it was costed out. If Anglo-Jewry's object were to encourage self-sufficiency, then Machziké Hadass testified to zealous East End Jews religiously ministering to themselves.

In 1896, the Brick Lane Talmud Torah, needing space for Hebrew and religion classes, assumed the lease of a Wesleyan chapel that stood next door. Methodists being few and far between in that part of Spitalfields by the 1890s, the chapel was let 'for the worship of God'. The financial responsibilities involved in maintaining such a large building weighed heavily upon the Talmud Torah managers, and they eagerly passed the obligation over to Machziké Hadass for its synagogue. And so on Sunday, 11 September 1898, the Rav (congregational rabbi) led a parade through the narrow streets. Musicians playing violins and trumpets struck up, symbolically, the royal Windsor march. Bewildered Gentiles, out for a Sunday stroll, saw the Rabbi Werner bearing the sacred scrolls, followed by dancing men, women and children, march up Brick Lane to the synagogue doors. Society officials and musicians, crowd and policemen tumbled in helter-skelter as they were flung open. Rabbi Werner, with his traditional thin sing-song, was inaudible beyond the first row or two, but a *maggid*, powerful of voice and dramatic in pose and gesture, captured the crowd. An estimated two thousand were held spellbound. 'Altogether,' reflected one observer, 'it was a deeply interesting manifestation Oriental rather

---

45 See Herz's article, 'Kosher butchers', *JC*, 8 May 1891. The minute book of the Machziké Hadass Society and Community in English, Hebrew and Yiddish from February 1891 (5 Adar II 6551) to 1904 is AJ/121 in the Mocatta Library. Volume II continuing to 1915 is in AJ/126. Bernard Homa has written a tribute to these stalwarts in *A Fortress in Anglo-Jewry: the Story of the Machzike Hadath* (London, 1953). See also, A. M. Hyamson, *The London Board for Schechita, 1801–1954* (London, 1954), chapter 9.

than Western, picturesquely devout rather than sternly solemn, loud and unrestrained, yet with the saving grace of deep and intense sincerity.'[46]

Three months later, having led his society so far, Solomon Herz was dead. He had established his own Bet Din to adjudicate religious and civil matters and appointed two *dynanim* (rabbinical members of the Bet Din), and he bequeathed a legacy of East End religious independence. Here there would be no mixed choirs, no creeping Anglicanism, nor, for that matter, any of the preaching the Adlers had made so central to services. Rabbi Werner was 'a Rav of the old type', very learned, dealing at length in his services with Talmudic questions and answers (*shaaloth-u-teshuboth*). The great synagogue of Spitalfields was open all day every day. Sabbath services were packed. Support came almost exclusively from the working classes, their halfpennies and farthings sustaining Machziké Hadass charities. No poor person appeared on a Friday evening for whom a Sabbath meal would not be provided. Special collections were regularly undertaken for those in distress. Machziké Hadass may have lacked order and discipline. Certainly the synagogue was neither as clean nor well kept as the fashionable, if much less used, monuments of the West End, but the society's Talmud Torah taught 1,000 children in Hebrew and Talmud using Yiddish as the medium of instruction, a standing reproach for the anglicizing Jewish Religious Education Board.

Self-help was one thing, but a declaration of total independence, not to mention one of moral superiority, was intolerable. Machziké Hadass had to be brought within the Anglo-Jewish order of things. The growing controversy over alien immigration restriction revived Anglo-Jewry's sense of the need for communal political control. Sir Samuel Montagu, as head of the Federation of Synagogues and president of the Shechita Board, first used Machziké Hadass separatism to win representation for his Federation on the Shechita Board and bring *shechita* income to the Federation. Had Federation representation been there from the start, he reminded recalcitrant United Synagogue representatives, the split would not have arisen in the first place. Sephardic representatives agreed, and United Synagogue delegates divided. Then Montagu turned to the thirteen-year-old quarrel. Machziké Hadass and the Shechita Board finally came to terms in February 1905, with Montagu scolding both sides and announcing:

> The great and urgent necessity of to-day is that our foreign coreligionists should be brought more and more within the influence of English Jews rather than be estranged from them by needless dissensions, and we hope that this necessity is now well understood in those quarters in which the Machziké Hadass secession originated.[47]

46 *JC*, 16 Sept. 1898. The building, originally built by Huguenots in 1743, had passed to the Wesleyans in July 1849. Acquiring it, Machziké Hadass possessed the largest synagogue in the East End. The demand for stricter Orthodoxy struck home among many Jewish leaders, conscious of the many compromises made in observance and religious training. Not surprisingly, therefore, a correspondent reviewing the Day of Atonement services in the East End in 1904, took perverse delight in twitting the *Machziké Hadass* synagogue. He was amused that a congregation which found the Chief Rabbi insufficiently *fromm* (precise in observance) was one in which not one member of the choir wore a *talis* (the fringed stole worn by observant Jews at prayer). 'The decorum,' he wrote smugly, 'left very much to be desired.' *JC*, 23 Sept. 1904.

47 The touchiest point remained *kashrut*. Machziké Hadass continued to select its own special *shochetim* (ritual slaughtermen), but their appointments required the Chief Rabbi's sanction. *JC*, 17, 24 Feb. 1905.

Montagu re-established the authority of the Chief Rabbi over the society, which was gradually amalgamated within the Federation of Synagogues. Like politics and trade unionism, Anglo-Jewry might waver, even compromise, but there remained limits to the freedom it would permit.

COMMUNAL SELF-ASSERTION

East End Jews, as they developed their sense of self, took pride in their own world. At one end of the scale, this consisted in refusing to be bullied. Such acts of self-assertion were seen as 'manliness', and met with unspoken, if not open, community approval. Gentile hooligans often roughed up Jewish boys. In March 1898, a ten-year-old Christian boy was killed in a street fight. The flood of mutual condolences and testimony of goodwill that followed brought out evidence of more than a little feuding between Jew and Gentile over 'turf'. While formally decrying violence on anyone's part, some understood this as a desirable manifestation of Jewish pride when it could be domesticated in the militant, patriotic garb of the Jewish Lads' Brigade. The fact of the matter was that some parts of the East End were areas in which Gentiles needed to be circumspect. The rector of Christ Church, Spitalfields, who was both philo-Semitic and in a position to know, blamed the students attending the Brick Lane Talmud Torah classes for causing trouble.[48]

At the other end of the scale, the East End developed its own 'social' institutions. The Jewish Social Working Men's Club, for instance, may have modelled itself on the Montagu example, but it was East End-organized and led. The club invited Stuart M. Samuel to a July meeting in 1896 for the formal purpose of establishing its funding commitment for the Home and Hospital for Jewish Incurables, to which Samuel had such a personal commitment and for which he constantly sought working-class support. The president, when thanking Samuel for attending, 'mentioned the desire of himself and fellow members to prove to the community that Jewish working men's clubs were formed for higher purposes than drinking and gambling.'[49]

The principal beneficiaries of metropolitan London charity may have resided in the East End, but the East End participated in communal philanthropies, even mounting several of its own. East Enders raised an estimated £10,500 for charity each year by the beginning of the twentieth century, an estimate which, if correct, meant contributions of about £1 for each Jewish family in the East End. Some sixteen East End-organized societies alone raised almost £2,700, while documented East End support to communal charities exceeded £2,400 in 1901. More than those sums again came in contributions to local winter charities, payments to distress funds of friendly societies, not to mention the almost interminable number of special benefits for individuals in distress, charity for Palestine, even remittances to Russian Yeshivas. Children and women came first. The East London Orphan Aid

---

48 *JC*, 1 Apr. 1898. The leadership was clearly embarrassed, preferring to leave physical defence to constituted authorities. They made much, for instance, of Justice Courser's vigorous handling of two cases of Sunday Jew baiting in Worship Street police court in August 1896 announcing that 'sport will henceforth be less popular as a Sunday afternoon pastime on Mile End Road.' *JC*, 18 Aug 1896.
49 *JC*, 31 July 1896.

Society topped the contribution list of specifically East End philanthropies with £400 for Norwood. The Central Marriage Portion Society, the Jewish Lying-In Charity, the Foreign Jewish Ladies' Benevolent Society and the Israelite Widows' Society, among others, were witness to those rites of passage through life and death, the aid and care given between friends and neighbours.

East End philanthropy also made revealing social, even political, statements. Just behind the Orphan Aid Society came the Hebrew Society for Brotherly Help with its £300. Initiated in 1897, to assist 'respectable tradesmen in reduced circumstances' with non-interest loans 'to recover their former position', the Society for Brotherly Help testifies to the rich complexity of East End Jewish society and the strong sense of community east of Aldgate. The scale of loans might have been small, from £2 to £5, but their social impact was great. Such modest grants enabled lower middle class small businessmen, the ballast of any society, to tide themselves over adversity and regain their economic footing without loss of status. A firm, self-sustaining, proudly independent group, such a petty bourgeoisie provided stable social and political leadership in what might otherwise have been a volatile almost unmanageable community.[50]

The world of the East End was, in several respects, a proud one that grew more so with the passing of time. Yiddish became, as the nineteenth century gave way to the twentieth, less a badge of shame to be discarded as soon as English could be learned than a proud communal self-assertion. Union meetings would shout down English speakers and applaud those addressing them in Yiddish. Drawing on a Russo-Polish past and an active New York present, a Yiddish theatre started in Kenmure Road, Hackney. Without any particular fanfare, it opened its doors in April 1902, playing good or inferior works to sell-out audiences of about 700. Opening night saw 2,000 turned away. After a false start in Aldgate and occasional performances at Shoreditch, the Orient rose on Commercial Street with accommodation for 2,000.[51] The English press might sneer at the clumsy staging and overdrawn acting and the Jewish press might wring its hands, but Yiddish culture would remain one of the voices of the East End before the First World War.

And when Anglo-Jewish institutions appeared to fall short of the mark, such assertive East End bodies as the Society for the Protection of Jews organized themselves to do the job. The Stepney borough council, stung into action by alien radical politics in 1911, passed resolutions demanding further alien immigration restriction that reeked of ill-disguised anti-Semitism. The Board of Deputies, guided by its cautious law and parliamentary committee, preferred to do nothing and say nothing, hoping that matters would soon pass and tempers cool, although it watched Home Secretary Winston Churchill's policies very carefully. Local East End leaders contended that the board was apathetic. That was untrue. The Deputies were frightened. Understanding that would not have made the East Enders happier. They organized to protest against the borough council resolutions, sought a mass meeting to which Gentiles would be invited, and considered ways in which an anti-defamation campaign should be conducted.[52]

50 The communal statistician who compiled the estimate pointed out that his figures, if correct, worked out to 3s a head or about £1 per East End Jewish family. *JC*, 15 Apr. 1898, 20 Sept. 1901.

51 *JC*, 2 May 1902, 10 June 1904.

52 See the account of the 3 February 1911 meeting at Stepney Jewish Schools. *JC*, 10 Feb. 1911.

8

Independence and Communal Control: Women and Social Discipline

Revolutions often have a date of convenience marking an event, significant in itself, although actually but one episode in a revolutionary process long in the making. The Conference of Jewish Women on 13 May 1902 was such a moment, striking, unique, a point of no return, but simultaneously just another step in a long development. Mrs Nathaniel Cohen certainly had no sense of striking a blow for freedom when she opened the proceedings at Portman Rooms, Baker Street that morning. She spoke of a fruitful division of philanthropic work between women and men. Women, she suggested, should tend to 'detail work' while men could better grapple with such 'larger issues' as the housing problem. Women were best placed to advise mothers on matters of health, sanitation and hygiene or to teach girls the lessons of domestic economy.

The speakers that followed, whether that veteran Rothschild, Lady Battersea, with her campaign against sexual exploitation through preventative and rescue work, or Lily Montagu championing controlled adolescent self-development through prayer meetings and girls' clubs, touched areas in which Jewish women were already a presence. Mrs Lionel Lucas of the old guard and Alice Model of the new joined forces if not social philosophy to champion professional nursing and proper childcare. Hannah Hyam and Nettie Adler touched on the importance of professionalizing social work, developing sounder education and improving philanthropic organization. Some participants came from highly traditional backgrounds. Mrs Meyer A. Spielmann's important Jewish Ladies' Clothing Association grew out of a traditional synagogue *dorcas*, women's guilds that provided clothing for the poor. Others represented the latest developments. Hilda Joseph uncompromisingly championed academic professional training or supervised experience for every aspiring philanthropic visitor.[1]

---

1 The inspiration was American. Mrs Meyer A. Spielmann and Mrs Lawrence M. Simmons took to heart the promptings of a touring group of American Jewish activist women who had started their own such

British Judaism had long defined women's roles in traditional terms, but the facts of late nineteenth-century society were undermining that position. The feminist challenge to the traditional order developed from above within established and affluent Jewish society and from below as increasing numbers of working-class women discovered new economic opportunities and new roles in the world of the late nineteenth and early twentieth century. Jewish women's history in Britain followed a course charted earlier, to some degree, in mainstream society. By the mid-1890s, Anglo-Jewry had become increasingly conscious of the need to be involved in, contribute to, and learn from their organized peers in English society. The National Union of Women Workers issued its official report on the October 1895 conference at Nottingham in January 1896. Jewish organizations were conspicuous by their absence. The Jewish press asked why, reminding readers that National Union meetings had been held in conjunction with that of the Women's League for Mothers and Women in Positions of Responsibility. Jewish women played expanding roles and demanded greater scope within communal organizations, but, like Jewish trade unionists, they still had not coordinated their aspirations with those of an increasingly articulate and organized British women's movement. Miss Gertrude E. Mosley, a district visitor for the Jewish Board of Guardians, addressed the National Union meeting, but no other Jewish organization contributed to the meetings, although they touched on every aspect of social and industrial life and the roles women play in it.

The *Jewish Chronicle*'s editorial question, while by no means representative, was symptomatic. Some Jewish women as individuals had already begun to march to the franchise drummer, although save for Lady Battersea (Constance de Rothschild before she married Cyril Flower), few took up the feminist-inspired cause of temperance work. Jewish organizations already served education and settlement houses or provided care of and clubs for girls and working women. Beatrice Webb suggested that she and other social activists had more to learn from Jewish women's organizations. Organized feminism was poised to invade the world of Anglo-Jewry. When the Countess of Aberdeen established the National Council for Women in 1897 as a British chapter of the International Council over which she presided, Lady Battersea joined forces with her in an effort to create an umbrella organization under which Jewish activist women's organizations might join with others.[2]

The increasing intervention of women in social work and social policy, Jewish and otherwise, played to mixed official reviews. John Burns, a cabinet member with impeccable working-class credentials, complained that fluttering feminists aggravated rather than eased his task at the Local Government Board.

We are confronted with all the philanthropic mischief of the social butterflies and sentimental busybodies. Lady Bountiful competing with Lady Prodigal

---

organization two years before. The *Jewish Chronicle* was highly supportive, offering considerable publicity both before and after the 13 May meeting. For the meeting itself, see *JC*, 16 May 1902. Biographical sketches of the leading Jewish women appeared during the first half of the year while texts of the papers presented appeared week by week in the *Jewish Chronicle* through the summer and autumn.

2 *JC*, 7 Feb. 1896, 23 July 1897.

for the smiles of the poor and the bibulous cheers of the loafers in distributing other peoples money, at the cost of the character of all the poor.[3]

Burns, as was often the case, had it wrong. The mobilized ladies of the Union of Jewish Women meeting in 1902 accepted traditional male philanthropic philosophy. Sensitive as they were to issues of parenting and childcare, all accepted the stern philosophy of the Jewish Board of Guardians and the Charity Organisation Society. Relief must never pauperize. Aid must always be calculated to assist each recipient to become self-respecting and self-supporting. The union debated the relative benefits and consequences of relief in cash or in kind. Without exception speakers criticized the dilettante, warned against patronizing the less fortunate, and praised those who sought coherent, achievable goals.

The union leadership undoubtedly had no sense of the feminist implications of their meeting. Had anyone bothered to ask, most of them would have answered that their proposals were merely clarifying technical and administrative details of existing social policy. But both form and substance were changing. Just as Britain had finally permitted women to stand for local office, Anglo-Jewry had allowed, with equal resistance and quite as many misgivings, let it be said, women to be elected to the governing bodies of the Jewish Board of Guardians and such other leading communal charities as the Jews' Hospital and Orphan Asylum. Reform Jews already allowed women owning seats in their own right to vote in annual elections. By the early twentieth century, even the hallowed premises of the United Synagogue were not secure.

Feminism and feminist issues cut various ways. On the one hand, Anglo-Jewry organized to impose control upon women, particularly single women. A rhetoric of 'protection' could be invoked wherever family constraints were lacking or seemed insufficient. Thus could the Jewish image of high standards of sexual behaviour and strong family ties be sustained within the community and for the wider public. For those innocent of or impervious to the blandishments of genteel moral persuasion, a vigilance society, with the blessing of the Chief Rabbi and the Bishop of London, helped to enforce community intolerance for moral deviance.

Women themselves, on the other hand, independently advanced a broader agenda of a role for women, one step, as it were, leading inexorably to the next. The Union of Jewish Women was merely one starting point. The Women's Industrial Council held a conference of representatives of organizations interested in women's work in January 1904 at the offices of the London School Board. There, under the watchful eye of Margaret Macdonald, social activist and wife of the future Labour Prime Minister, and Nettie Adler, daughter of the Chief Rabbi, middle-class social activists considered proposals to improve life and prospects for 'girls of the industrial class'. Their first concerns were to reduce the high rate of infant mortality. Education was their chosen front line on which to do battle, and the Jewish Crêche in many ways the ideal model to follow. They hoped to establish a technical day school programme to that end at the Sir John Cass Institute in Aldgate to serve Jewish and Gentile poor alike. The Women's Industrial Council sought support from the various London Poor Law Boards of Guardians, and such private

3 Burns to Margot Asquith, 15 Aug. 1914, Burns Papers, Add MS 46,282, f. 164 in the British Library.

organizations as the Society for Waifs and Strays and the Dr Barnardo Foundation. Hackney Technical Institute seemed another possibility drawing once again on Jewish philanthropic groundwork, and the Battersea Polytechnic might apply Jewish models to underprivileged Gentile girls.[4]

Without exception, leaders of the Union of Jewish Women had individual histories of increasingly wide-ranging charitable and educational work. Lady Battersea organized the Jewish Association for the Protection of Girls and Women with Lady Rothschild, Claude Montefiore and A. R. Moro among others in 1885. Lady Battersea worked in the trenches from early years, not merely as a social obligation, but as a matter of deep conviction. She learned on the scene. From the early 1870s, she served her mother's Jewish Ladies' Benevolent Loan Society, visiting the poor, distributing loans of one to ten pounds, and personally making collections. Her commitments expanded through the years moving far beyond the confines of communal philanthropy. The Home Office appointed her and the Duchess of Bedford prison visitors in 1896. An executive of Lady Henry Somerset's National British Women's Temperance Association and active in the Society for the Prevention of Cruelty to Children, she bridged Jewish and mainstream British women's organizations as President of the National Union of Women Workers.

Most of the other Jewish leaders had honed their skills almost exclusively within Jewish organizations. Mrs Lionel Lucas, a Goldsmid and a strong-willed kinswoman of Frederic D. Mocatta, proclaimed herself an unreconstructed traditionalist, although hers was a pioneering career. Wealthy and determined, she was a major contributor to Sir Benjamin L. Cohen's new building for the Jewish Board of Guardians. President of the ladies' conjoint vistation committee since 1880, Mrs Lucas organized an adult workroom at the board through which she ran her own putting-out system. An average of 120 women, principally widows or wives with sick or disabled husbands, made up articles of clothing in their own homes. Every Tuesday morning, Mrs Lucas could be found perched on her high chair at the board, keeping her detailed logbook on each woman, paying for the finished goods and distributing cut-out garments. Neither payment nor material would be given to anyone who failed to meet Mrs Lucas's rigorous standards of personal neatness and cleanliness. The woman forgetting to wear a bonnet would be turned away. The board enthusiastically approved, appointing Mrs Lucas in 1896 president of the workrooms, adding her as an executive of the apprenticeship department, and selecting her to be the first female member of the executive committee of the board itself. She had earned it. Single-handedly and at her own expense, Helen Lucas added professional nursing to Jewish Board of Guardians activities, even building a residence, Victoria House, next door to the Board of Guardians for her nurses and other paid Board workers.

Mrs Lucas, who was, in fact, hewing out new roles for Jewish women, considered herself a guardian of the old ways. She fought the organization of girls' clubs tooth and nail and strongly opposed the institution of crèches. Girls, she insisted,

4 Women's Industrial Council report of 29 Jan. 1904 meeting to secretary, education committee, National Union of Women Workers, March 1904 and confidential supplementary report. Macdonald Papers, PRO 30/69/1366.

belonged at home helping their mothers after school or after work, and mothers should tend their children, not place them in day care. Modern mothers, she believed, were all too prone to shirk their responsibilities to their offspring. Moral responsibility meant everything to Mrs Lucas, and she was determined to extend it from herself to all she could reach. Religious worship was close to her heart, and she tolerated no change in services. A mainstay of the Reform congregation, she stood foursquare against all change, even the intrusion of any more English into services, and, observed an essentially flattering biographer, 'it is largely [due] to her influence that the Reform ritual has suffered so little change during sixty years.'[5]

Mrs Herman Tuck, whose husband figured prominently on the council of the United Synagogue and in the affairs of Jews' College, was a variation on Mrs Lucas's theme. Another stalwart of the Jewish Board of Guardians visiting committee, she was stirred into independent action when a friend suggested that the West End sustained Jewish philanthropy while North Londoners, like the Tucks, shirked their philanthropic responsibilities. Inspired by Booth's *In Darkest England*, Mrs Tuck hit upon the North London Grocery Fund as a way of ministering to immediate needs while preaching the text of self-improvement. For twenty weeks each year, every Thursday at the Jewish Working Men's Club, she and a cohort of volunteers distributed parcels of grocery 'valued at not less than 2s 6d' and scaled by size of family to assorted, investigated cases. Old men, overburdened women and poverty-pinched children shuffled through receiving their packages of tea, coffee, sugar, rice, haricot beans, barley and soap. Potatoes were dropped because they made the parcels too heavy for children to carry, and bread omitted because the Jewish Soup Kitchen provided it. A ritual of manners ensued. Men were reminded to take off their caps. Individuals arriving unwashed received Mrs Tuck's reminder that their next parcel would consist entirely of soap. Anyone pushing was ejected and sent to the rear of the line. Some 380 souls would be processed in each conventional weekly hour and a half session, over 6,000 through the winter season. Preliminary investigations, often through the Jewish Board of Guardians or the ladies' conjoint visiting committee, identified those deserving benevolence. Each received a ticket inscribed with the applicant's name, residence, the number in the family, and identifying the individual recommending the case. Mrs Tuck, meticulous in such details, used her own private coded marks to follow the course of each ticket. Not until 1903 did Mrs Tuck concede that the North London Grocery Fund had outgrown her capacity for personal management. Where £94 and volunteers' enthusiasm cared for thirty poor families in the winter of 1890–1, by 1902–3 almost £600 and a veritable army of enthusiasts provided aid for 7,660 families.

5 *JC*, 14 Mar. 1902. Charles S. Loch of the Charity Organisation Society convinced the Jewish Board of Guardians that the poor widow without skills should not be carried at home with an allowance. That policy was 'a weak course to adopt without a more definite aim. If continued it would render the recipient dependent, and deaden the natural impulse to self-support. In such a case . . . some of the children should be provided for otherwise than by the mother, until such time as the mother could be taught a trade which would enable her to resume their support. It might not seem desirable that the family should be thus broken up, but the touch between the mother and her family could be kept intact, and it was found in such cases that the family feeling continued strong.' C. S. Loch to the visiting committee, JBG, 19 Apr. 1901. Nathan Joseph strongly endorsed this position. 'The days had passed when people allowed their hearts to run away with their heads and were led mainly by sentiment in the administration of their charity.' *JC*, 8 May 1901.

Lady Magnus, wife of Sir Philip, a substantial woman of sturdy face and physique, committed herself to education. Daughter of the Mayor of Portsmouth, she not only taught sabbath classes from the age of sixteen but began writing improving literature that proved to have abiding popularity. 'H.M.' produced *Little Miriam's Bible Stories*, *Holiday Tales*, and *Maurice's Barmitzvah Story* before she married in 1870. She continued as a regular correspondent for the Jewish press, was much involved with the the Jews' Deaf and Dumb Home over which her husband long presided, but was best known as a pioneer in the girls' club movement. The East London Jewish Girls' Club, founded in 1886, was her pioneeering enterprise, the model for later imitators. Her later works – *About the Jews since Bible Times* and *Jewish Portraits* – enjoyed a continued popularity into the mid-twentieth century, and *Outlines of Jewish History* (1885) became the principal textbook of the Jewish Religious Education Board. Every Jewish prisoner, by order of Home Secretary Matthews at the turn of the century, was presented with a copy of her *Light on the Way* as a beacon for self-improvement and rehabilitation.

Bella Löwy, daughter of the kindly scholar-philanthropist who was for so long the administrative mainstay of the Anglo-Jewish Association, peered through her steel-rimmed glasses at a world needing moral improvement and uplift. She managed mothers' meetings for the Jewish Board of Guardians at home and founded a Société de Bienfaisance aux Jeunes Filles at Constantinople in 1893 to save young Jewish women from being caught up in 'the white slave trade'. She helped to translate the ideas of others into action. Mrs Alfred Nathan needed her help to begin the Domestic Training Home, where 'friendless girls' were to be turned into respectable Jewish domestic servants. The home aspired simultaneously to solve the problem of their moral well-being and address the growing servant shortage for affluent Jewish families. Alice Model could never have launched her Sick Room Helps' Society without Bella Löwy's aid. Miss Löwy alone could secure the first year's expenses from Frederic Mocatta. Like her father before her, she combined scholarship and a commitment to aiding East European refugees, She laboured for ten years to edit and partly translate five volumes of Graetz's *History of the Jews* and also translated Errera's *Russian Jews* from the original French. At the same time she, as president of the Ladies' Clothing Association, worked with the Russo-Jewish Committee to clothe the newcomers and with the dispersion committee to move East Enders to Brixton.

The Chief Rabbi's wife had been plunged into the philanthropic pond as a young girl by her mother. The future Mrs Adler started in the Ladies' Loan Society, organized well before the Jewish Board of Guardians created its loan department. The ladies sat each week in a room at the old Jews' Infant School personally interviewing cases, taking their shillings and half crowns. Even Baroness de Rothschild took her turn every two months. Mrs Adler's forte, one which her famous daughter Nettie would enlarge on, was education. To make life tolerable and education possible for the poorest children, she organized and presided over Jewish Children's Penny Dinners, ably seconded by Hannah Hyam, then extended supplementary aid by organizing the Boot Fund. The Holiday Fund, the Thrift Society, and the Jewish Children's Happy Evenings followed apace. A champion of the Domestic Training Home and the communal day care centre, the Jewish Crêche, she also sat on the council of the Anglo-Jewish Association, actively overseeing affairs at the Evelina de Rothschild School in Jerusalem.

Nettie Adler championed professionalization and aggressively expanded the scope of Jewish and state social concerns. She revolutionized the Committee of Wage Earning Children, leading a deputation to the Home Secretary, Sir John Gorst. Extracting a promise of government action, the committee went to work, investigating and documenting some 7,000 cases of children working for wages out of school hours. Testifying before the inter-departmental committee, Nettie Adler's evidence not only stirred Salisbury's government to action but set a direction of subsequent social legislation and policy. A school manager under the London School Board in the East End, Nettie Adler sought to enrich and extend the opportunities school offered East End girls. Not only was she a mainstay of the happy evenings and country holiday programmes for students, but she sought to bring more extensive vocational training to the last years of school. Capitalizing on the camaraderie of schooldays, she created old scholars' guilds for the schools with which she was involved. These guilds were a half-way house between school and girls' clubs. Offering entertainment, improving lectures and concerts or dances they provided a pleasant weekly reunion for fifty or sixty graduates who had gone into the workforce. The guilds, moreover, became a second stage in Nettie Adler's long campaign to lessen the dependence of Jewish women by moving their girls towards the more promising trades and better apprenticeships.

Parents had what Nettie Adler considered the unfortunate habit of setting their daughters to work for the best short-term return on the assumption that their girls would soon marry and that industrial independence was unnecessary. Nettie Adler, as a member of the visiting committee and industrial committee of the Jewish Board of Guardians, saw too many cases of distressed widows lacking skills, unable to make their way in the world. Their dependence on charity, so she argued, sapped their character. Independence, however, once set as a goal, could not easily be constrained. Its implications were more than obvious, so the guilds, whatever their intention, were preaching a doctrine of women's emancipation. Nettie Adler wanted young girls thrust out as breadwinners to have real options, to be self-sufficient. Much, she argued, depended upon training them and their 'view of life'. By such increments were adolescent Jewish women to move, in little steps, from tradition to modernity, from convention to choice.

The Union of Jewish Women, from its inception, not only coordinated and sought out opportunities for women in educational and social work; it sought to find places for growing numbers of Jewish women seeking positions beyond the working classes. The union recruited and placed Jewish governesses, teachers, and clerks. One Irish Jewish woman, for instance, unable to find a teaching post for herself had taken a factory job. The union found a position for her in a London school, brought her to town with the chaperonage of the Traveller's Aid Society, and found her accommodation near her work at the Sara Pyke House. Other girls were apprenticed in the same way and often by the same people who would have processed their cases at the Jewish Board of Guardians or the Jews' Hospital and Orphan Asylum, but from their numbers the union recruited a few promising candidates to be trained as nursing probationers.[6]

6 First annual committee general meeting, Union of Jewish Women (UJW), 27 May 1903. *JC*, 5 June 1903.

'Girls of the industrial class', although they received less publicity, also asserted themselves. Efforts, like Miss Barry's Society for the Protection of Women Workers in Birmingham, which proposed to embrace all trades and establish a separate trade union, were still-born, but even such failures spoke to a new feminist consciousness. Jewish women who began to discover independence in the workplace may have started a generation behind their Gentile counterparts but were beginning to catch up. By the turn of the century, male Jewish workers could have learned something about union solidarity, discipline and persistence from Jewish females. Jewish tailoresses in Leeds showed firmness even when their well-organized male counterparts began to lose solidarity, and London Jewish tailoresses were undaunted by decades of male Jewish failure when they began to unionize on their own behalf in 1903. The Cardboard Box Makers, not exclusively but principally made up of Jewish girls and women, held out for three months in 1905 and won a settlement in their favour. They had no funds and only modest public support, but they had already had a history of success that sustained them through their strike. A few years before, the same women and the same union had held the line.

Cigarette- as opposed to cigar-making created hand and machine work for which women were as or more qualified than men. Women were usually paid only three-quarters of men's wages for the same work. Women workers, although subjected to considerable male abuse in the workplace, joined the Amalgamated Cigarette Makers' and Tobacco Cutters' Union, but severe competition worked against effective collective action. Organized in 1893, the union fell on harder and harder times, its effectiveness almost inversely proportionate to the number of women employed in the trade. Staggering in 1900, the union suddenly dissolved in May 1903. Like the tailoresses of Leeds, the women cigarette-makers then struck out on their own. With the help of S. Ellstein, one of the better organizers of the day, they established their own trade union in March 1903, originally intending to allow only female members. Some combination of the spirit of worker solidarity that Ellstein always preached and a utilitarian sense that the trade could never be organized without the participation of men led the militant ladies to open their ranks. But it was all in vain. Male antagonism and the steady introduction of labour-saving machinery doomed their efforts.[7]

Girls and young women were not easily constrained. Mrs Lucas or Mrs Tuck might break the spirit of the charity garment-maker or the girl or woman waiting humbly in line for her package of groceries, but over and over again Anglo-Jewry could see, if it looked, that East End girls were unsubdued. Free School Concerts for the Poor, organized in 1893, was given up in 1898 since 'our efforts were not duly appreciated by the classes for whose benefit they were originally organised'. Shorn of rhetoric, the complaint revealed much.

> We do not seem to get the right class of audience. The hall is generally full, but it has been necessary during the last year or two to have a good many

---

7 *JC*, 24 Sept. 1897, 29 May, 17 July 1903, 1 Sept. 1905. The Jewish Tailoresses' Union developed as a branch of the Amalgamated Society of Tailors. The tailoresses' plan of benefits was intelligently designed to hold members and suggests that the women in the trade were by then better disciplined than the men. Each woman paid 3d per week in dues. After twelve months, she was eligible for strike pay, sick benefits, and an unemployment benefit. *JC*, 5 Aug. 1904.

more stewards at each concert, otherwise it was difficult to maintain order. Lately a number of grown-up girls from the cigar factories have come, and have given an enormous amount of trouble; in fact some of them had to be removed for disorderly conduct. These girls come to talk to their friends and not to hear the artistes.[8]

Some Anglo-Jewish leaders took this new self-assertion of young Jewish women and built on it. Lily Montagu defended the girls of her Soho club, refusing to rein in the enthusiasm which gave the West Central such vitality merely to satisfy some stuffy would-be donors, offended by such vulgarity. The existence of the clubs themselves testified to Anglo-Jewry's sense that adolescent females must 'be brought under wise influences' in those years between leaving school and becoming young adults.

The greater involvement of women in Jewish social work brought both increased freedom and control. Family issues and child care, as might have been expected, assumed ever-greater importance. An 1896 report on infant mortality in *The Hospital* suggested that Britons, as a people, had much to do. Almost a quarter of the deaths in England were of children under the age of ten. When Jewish philanthropies appointed a committee to investigate, however, they discovered that while only 20 per cent of deaths among the wealthiest Jews were children under ten, among Jewish paupers, the rate was almost 82 per cent. The numbers reflected badly on the community and were becoming worse. Deaths among Jewish children under ten, as a percentage of deaths among Jews, ran at more than double the national average and was rising (54.5 per cent in 1891, 60.25 per cent in 1893). To argue, as the committee did, that more than three-fifths of the population in Whitechapel had arrived in the previous ten years, that most immigrants were between twenty and forty, the hardiest and most prone to take risks, that they married early and were 'highly improvident', was merely to restate the problem, not to attack it. Badly-paid workers overcrowded under unsanitary conditions would almost certainly have higher child mortality rates.

Women social workers sought to 'improve' the habits and adjust the customs of newcomers. Ironically, thus, the expanding freedom, role and authority for middle-class Jewish women came, in effect, to be based on constraining the 'freedom' of the 'ignorant' poor. Some problems common in mainstream English society were rarely found in poorer Jewish families. Drink was an insignificant problem. Illegitimacy rates were very low. Abortion and infanticide were either well-concealed or rarely occurred. Poor Jewish parents, moreover, cared for their children. They just did not understand 'proper' household management, and corrective education would take time. Their rooms were often heated by coke stoves, and newcomers, in particular, seemed to believe that cold fresh air was a greater risk than a stifling, unventilated room. Perhaps it was back in Russia. These young people, moreover, had little sense of 'proper' infant nutrition. Starvation was almost unheard of, but diet was a serious problem. Once breast-feeding stopped, immigrant mothers would feed their children 'a bit of what's going', all too often something tough and indigestible. Diseases of the digestive system were blamed for at least 120 of 317 deaths the committee investigated. A large proportion of these, committee experts felt, could be attributed to overfeeding or improper feeding.

8 Amelia B. Davidson was outraged, but little better evidence can be offered for the growing self-assertion of girls and women. The days of passive deference had gone. *JC*, 21 Oct. 1898.

In this way yet another attack was levied against East End culture. The ubiquitous visitor, usually a woman, more rarely a rabbi, distributed papers giving rules of health for women and children printed in English and Yiddish. All visitors were instructed to invoke sanitary inspectors and factory inspectors to prevent facilities used as workrooms during the day being used as bedrooms for children at night. Anglo-Jewry's coercive machinery was brought into play. Those homes refusing to adapt to the new rules were, in theory at least, to be cut off from charitable relief.[9] At the same time, each intervention, however justifiable in itself, could work against that very spirit of independence and self-help communal leaders were at such pains to develop. Philanthropy threatened to become part of the way of life for a substantial subculture within the East End. Some thousand families were regular recipients of Jewish Soup Kitchen bounty throughout the winter. They made the transition to warmer weather by drawing on the Matzos Fund and Passover relief distributions. Their children attended Jews' Free School, clothed, shod and fed by ancillary charities. The Jewish Board of Guardians undertook their apprenticeship when they completed their education. Jewish wards in hospitals attended them when they were ill. If the husband died, the Board of Guardians widows' fund cared for them. But balancing risk and gain, there was no contest. The more fortunate must teach the underprivileged as effectively as possible how to be like themselves.

The underprivileged, of course, had their own ideas. Even by the early twentieth century when they were well organized and well financed, for instance, the Children's Country Holiday Fund outings only moved about 2,000 of the 30,000 Jewish children out of the East End ghetto. Most Chedarim and Talmud Torahs were open, and parents with children not in school but underfoot, often dispatched them thither. The girls not at a Cheder could often be found 'elping muvver', and boys often assisted their fathers at work. Many, however, showed an impressive streak of independence and struck out to earn money for themselves. Making and selling toffee apples was one choice. Boys, who could shout louder than the cacaphony of East End sounds sold halfpenny newspapers. At night they employed their small profit to go to the music-hall. 'The Foresters' in Cambridge Road was particularly popular and appears to have been the agency for bringing the latest songs to the East End. Girls, who functioned under more constraints, crowded around the barrel-organ on the street, did cotton skirt dances, and popularized that new craze, the cake walk.

Children, once freed from the tutelage of school and tasks of home, wanted to play. Victoria Park was so popular it was called 'the Polish Brighton', and the tram or bus heading there 'the Polish Express'. They walked, they larked, some swam in the bathing pond. Cricket was popular, Victoria Park providing more ample fields than Tower Moat closer to home. For those who had drained the East End cup, the fashionable West End beckoned. Little clusters of ghetto boys could often be found negotiating with a conductor in Cannon Street for a bargain fare to Westminster. They were not always well received. Mr Justice Denman incurred some communal ire when remarking, when fining a young Jew at Marlborough Street police court for disorderly conduct in 1903, 'Hyde Park would be a decent place on Sundays but

9 See the extensive discussion in *JC*, 10 Apr. 1896.

for your Jews of the East End, who go there for the purpose of making cads of yourselves.'[10]

Political and cultural populism surged generally through Western societies, including Britain, during the late nineteenth and early twentieth centuries. Among other aspects, populism assumed a strong social moralizing thrust. Its sources were many and varied, often contradictory and lie beyond the scope of this study. At one level, populism was 'class war', a neo-puritanism, pitting often-*arriviste* middle classes and lower middle classes against idle, amoral upper classes and feckless, undisciplined lower classes. At another level, the late nineteenth-century religious revival inspired Jews and Christians alike to dedicate themselves to moral and theological reclamation. Just as the eighteenth-century enlightenment, with its secular concerns, had its counterpoint in popular evangelical religious revivals – whether German Pietism, French Jansenism, English Wesleyanism, the American Great Awakening, or Jewish Hasidism, so the social and political secularization of the Victorian world inspired religious recommitment. British Jews, as we have seen, insisted on formal observances, although many questioned the gap between form and content. Most immigrant Jews brought belief and commitment that helped to give meaning to their daily lives. Among Christians, a denominational spectrum from the Salvation Army and competing Church Army to Christian Socialists, from the Free Church to Roman Catholics, sought to bring religious moral discipline to Britain, refining weapons of social persecution and, where they could not prevail, demanding that the state take action.

MORAL CONTROL

Some parts of the Christian revivalist agenda troubled Anglo-Jewry. Renewed agitation for legislated sabbath observance, for instance, raised troublesome public issues of Jewish exceptionalism. On other aspects of the moral crusade, however, some Anglo-Jews were determined not to be left behind. Jewish concerns were of two kinds, each pointing to the same solution. On the one hand, Anglo-Jewry confronted the increasingly visible and dramatically overpublicized involvement of Jews in prostitution and what contemporaries had come to call the white slave trade.[11] This raised issues of public image and shortcomings in communal policies. If Jews took the lead in attacking the criminal and rescuing the abused, one real or potential source of anti-Semitism would be removed. The rising number of immigrants and the unsocialized poor, moreover, could fall prey to the unscrupulous.

Anglo-Jewry took credit for the sharply lowered incidence of prostitution and reduced number of brothels in the East End. While the facts were correct, Jewish settlement was only one, although a very important, cause. The steadily declining

10 *Daily Telegraph*, 14 July 1903; BDBJ minute book, 16 July 1903; 'Children of the ghetto at holiday time', *JC*, 11 Aug. 1905. On the general issue, see Stephen Humphries, *Hooligans or Rebels? An Oral History of Working-Class Childhood and Youth 1889–1939* (London, 1981).

11 For a sprightly discussion, see E. J. Bristow, *Prostitution and Prejudice: the Jewish Fight against White Slavery, 1870–1939* (Oxford, 1982). V. D. Lipman discusses the institutional evolution in *A Century of Social Service*, Appendix I.

TABLE 8.1 Arrests for prostitution in the Whitechapel police division, 1892–1901

Year	Number charged	Gentile	Jewish
1892	344	331	13
1893	334	320	14
1894	225	214	11
1895	227	354	23
1896	251	229	22
1897	231	210	24
1898	322	290	32
1899	352	204	48
1900	228	200	28
1901	272	220	52

Source: Evidence Presented to the Royal Commission on Alien Immigration, 17 July 1902.

importance of the London docks through the 1880s and beyond removed many traditional patrons. Jews, with their stress on family life and virtues, moved in, and prostitutes, like publicans, undoubtedly suffered a severe loss of trade. S. Charrington, the wealthy brewer who won the Mile End parliamentary seat in 1885, joined forces with the East End Mission to 'clean up' the district. Like other purity campaigns, Charrington's had a brief salutary effect, but the police, who had to deal with the question every day, reported it to be short-lived. Church missions, the National Vigilance Association and Jewish groups nagged the authorities into somewhat sporadic but increased activity. Between 1892 and 1900, the number of those charged with prostitution fell from 344 to 228. The number of Jewish prostitutes rose both proportionately and in absolute numbers, although not nearly in proportion to Jewish population in the Whitechapel police division. The figures were understated to the extent that a Jewish woman adopted or used an 'English' name when arrested.[12]

Reimposing moral discipline demanded sexual stewardship, creating, among other things, institutions that would provide the protection and supervision that modern families could not or would not furnish. Adequately serving communal needs demanded some facility to retrieve those who had 'fallen'. Thus was founded Charcroft House, the first Jewish rescue home and hostel for unmarried mothers, established in Mile End and later moved to more substantial facilities in Shepherd's Bush.

William T. Stead, the sensationalist editor of the *Pall Mall Gazette*, gave focus to a rising revulsion with Victorian sexual exploitation and vastly exhanced the circulation of his newspaper. He actually purchased a young girl and published a lurid, if accurate discussion of how easy it was. Stead's brief stint in prison for

12 Lord James discussed the statistics with Inspector Stephen White of the CID. The numbers showed what both restrictionists and Anglo-Jewry wished to see. S. Charrington, the eminent brewer, held Mile End as his political fief from 1885 to his death in 1905. Charrington provided beer, work and moral uplift for the borough of Stepney. His brewery was one of Stepney's greatest industries, its substantial expansion contributing to the local housing shortage.

embarrassing the authorities brought a dramatic increase in his newspaper's sales and heroic status in a moral crusade taking institutional shape. The White Cross Crusade, the moral ascetics of the Anglican Church establishment, worked hand-in-glove with the leading Wesleyan layman, Sir Percy Bunting, editor of the *Contemporary Review*, a supporter of William T. Stead's sensational journalistic campaign against white slavery and fomenter of the National Vigilance Association. By the early twentieth century, most of these religious and secular agencies associated in the London Purity Alliance under the presidency of the Bishop of London. The Twentieth Century League, founded in 1901, addressed itself to the tasks of combating the growth of 'hooliganism' in the metropolis, a convenient catch-all term for adolescent misbehaviour, and 'to provide counter-attractions for girls and boys who frequent the streets and are prone to develop criminal or semi-criminal tendencies'. The Bishop of London and Chief Rabbi Adler marched arm in arm as president and vice-president.[13]

Anglo-Jewry was already there. Rothschild women (Lady Rothschild and Constance Rothschild, later Countess Battersea), Claude G. Montefiore and Arthur R. Moro took up the cudgels and organized the Jewish Ladies Society for Preventative and Rescue Work in March 1885 and Charcroft House, the first of several institutions ultimately to amalgamate in the Jewish Association for the Protection of Girls and Women. Gentlemen attended to the sordid details. Ladies created regimens of moral regeneration. 'Rescued' women entered the redemptive regimen of washtubs, needlework and substantial doses of prayer. A society representative cruised the docks as immigrant ships arrived, providing 'protection' for unaccompanied women and moving them off, as best he could, to society facilities or those of the Poor Jews' Temporary Shelter.

From its inception the Jewish Association for the Protection of Girls and Women pursued an aggressive policy in dealing with strays or those in presumptive danger. The association existed

> To shield and protect Jewish girls and women, to rescue them, when necessary, from evil, to check and combat the causes which bring them to danger and ruin, to cheer and befriend the helpless, the homeless, the struggling and the troubled, to hunt down and punish the malefactor, to uphold the honour of the Jewish name, to prove that Jews are no less zealous for purity, no less keenly anxious to 'prevent', to shelter and to redeem, than members of any other religious denomination – all this, & more than this is our aim. The task is gigantic.[14]

Anglo-Jewry had associated itself with one of the great campaigns of the age. The broader cause was scarcely one the leadership would endorse, although politics often produces strange alliances. In this instance, the Jewish elite stood shoulder to shoulder with the advanced feminists. Militant feminism evolved from Josephine

---

13 The great question of the day was how to manage adolescents. Twentieth Century League, *First Annual Report* [1902] (London, 1903). Much of the early work emphasized continuation and technical schools, the usefulness of boys' brigades and cadet corps, and particularly the creation and expansion of institutes and clubs 'for working lads and girls'. For the work of the London Purity Alliance and the National Vigilance Association, see the National Vigilance Association archives in the Fawcett Library.

14 AIU Angl II/H/12/6245.

Butler's long struggle to repeal the Contagious Diseases Acts, those public health measures that mandated inspection of prostitutes in certain military garrison towns. The mobilized feminists, having secured repeal, moved in 1886 into the vanguard of the campaign against white slavery. Those feminists who contended that the Acts were a declaration of sex war by men seeking to institutionalize the humiliation and debasement of women, saw vigilance campaigns, preventative and rescue work as the stuff to begin redressing the balance between the sexes. Christabel Pankhurst, the militant suffragette, proclaimed 'Votes for Women and Purity for Men'. This formidable battle cry may not have appealed to Anglo-Jewry, whose philosophy on the place of women ran in a very different direction, but the opportunity to use the fervour of vigilance crusaders to socialize its own community was both irresistible and, in its eyes, necessary.

Through the ensuing years, what would become the Jewish Association for the Protection of Girls and Women extended its network of operations. The Sara Pyke House in Highbury Quadrant provided a hostel for girls not earning enough to sustain themselves in 'suitable' surroundings and for those needing temporary assistance while searching for work. The Sara Pyke House also served as an auxiliary hostel for Stamford Hill, the certified industrial school for Jewish girls to which girls might be committed by magistrates if they appeared to be in 'undesirable surroundings or liable, lacking proper supervision, to enter a life of crime'. The Intermediate Home, at association headquarters in Aldgate, provided refuge for girls and women while their cases were in court or awaiting trial or where they could stay while visitors investigated their 'dangerous or evil surroundings' to determine what action to recommend. By the 1920s, a girls' club on the premises provided 'recreation and instruction' for girls association workers had 'befriended'. Highbury House, also a later addition, answered wartime and postwar needs by providing a home for 'orphans and friendless children'. In yet another effort to provide for the privileged, girls were trained for domestic service.[15]

Girls' clubs regularly proclaimed their 'preventative' purpose. The Reverend Simeon Singer laboured diligently for moral improvement and sexual restraint. When dedicating new facilities for the West Central Working Girls' Club, he praised Lily Montagu for 'drawing city girls from the temptations of music-halls and dancing-saloons'.[16] The Sarah Pyke House and Domestic Training Home were more explicitly 'preventative' organizations. Charcroft House, another branch of the Jewish Association, dealt with rehabilitation. Retrieving women from the streets, brothels, or their pimps was considered both indelicate and dangerous, so a gentlemen's vigilance committee was assigned the actual 'rescue work'. The staff of Charcroft House then attempted to rehabilitate the victims, restore them to their families, or find them suitable employment. Vigilance organizations pressed their services on the government. The National Vigilance Association, of which the Jewish Association was a constituent member, offered to escort girls and young women brought before the magistrates on charges of prostitution out of the country, although it did hope that the government would underwrite its costs. The

15 See the Jewish Association for the Protection of Girls and Women brief history in AIU Angl II/H/12/6245.
16 *JC*, 24 Jan. 1896.

arrangement was, so the Home Office felt, economical. The metropolitan police, who viewed vigilantes as troublesome busybodies, disapproved of any measure that might encourage them, but politicians recognized the electoral appeal of purity. While Claude G. Montefiore, the Reverend Simeon Singer, and Gabriel Lindo joined Rothschild ladies in advancing the organized cause of Jewish purity, David L. Alexander, president of the Board of Deputies, sat on the executive committee of the National Vigilance Association and served on its legal subcommittee in the decade before the war. Anglo-Jewry could give no clearer endorsement of the national campaign for moral uplift. Home Office administrators also saw potential value in organizations which could 'forcibly' accomplish things the government wished to have done but feared being criticized by civil libertarians should it undertake them.[17]

The Jewish Association for the Protection of Girls and Women, the clearest community response to working-class women's independence, involved issues of both self-assertion and control. The Jewish community made much of the fact that Jewish colonization of the East End had meant a striking improvement in moral behaviour. Anglo-Jewry proclaimed the virtues of self-help, but crime and moral deviance were not on the list of approved trades. To police the world of single women, the rhetoric of protection was brought into play. The association, indeed, was more than merely a vigilance society. It found itself itself drawn into a miscellany of community issues. In some instances, the association appears to have been an institution of last resort in Jewish concerns for which only persuasion rather than recourse to law could address the issue. The Tottenham congregation appealed to the Board of Deputies for assistance in the case of three girls: eighteen, sixteen and thirteen, whose father had died two years before and whose mother had died the previous year. Two of the girls had already been baptized in the Mormon faith, and the third was about to be baptized. Since the mother had been on good terms with the Mormon Elders, the law and parliamentary committee did not consider that the Board of Deputies had *locus standi* in the case. The committee, however, referred the matter to the Jewish Association for the Protection of Girls and Women for its consideration.[18]

OTHER ISSUES OF LIBERTY AND CONTROL

Far from lowering the quality of life in Stepney, Anglo-Jewry argued with some merit, Jewish colonization had greatly improved it. Formerly, police would only patrol many Whitechapel streets in pairs. Montagu reminded the Royal Commission on Alien Immigration that he knew those streets well. Leman Street, now the heartland of Jewish philanthropic institutions, had been a dangerous place in 1885 when he first ran for parliament. Criminal statistics documented the communal case. Robbery and larceny had fallen nearly 25 per cent in the 1890s alone. Production from illegal stills boomed just prior to Jewish holidays among

17 Coote to Chalmers, 3 Jan. 1905, HO to MEPO, Jan. 1905, and passim Nov. 1905–Jan. 1906, HO 45/10327/132181/5.
18 Law and parliamentary committee, 23 Apr. 1919. BDBJ C 13/1/2.

newcomers in the 1880s, but that trade had all but vanished from the Jewish East End by 1900. Jews introduced some skilled crimes, particularly forgery, and gambling was certainly the East End Jewish vice. A sign advertising a Jewish restaurant was, as often as not, merely a cover for a gaming house. Only Jewish shops, reported the medical officer of health and public analyst for Stepney, adulterated pepper and mustard, and proportionately more Jewish than Gentile shops offended gravely enough to be prosecuted or cautioned. Jewish coster-mongers, vigorously competitive, were frequently before the magistrates on charges of obstruction, but that scarcely represented a crime wave. The police of 'H' (Whitechapel) Division often complained about the difficulty of explaining the law to foreigners, who doubtless understood less and less English as the occasion demanded. In ethnic mix, police recruitment lagged, as it usually does, far behind that of the population. As late as 1902, not one police officer in H Division could speak Yiddish.[19]

The common generalization that a slum or ghetto is synonymous with impacted poverty and downward mobility is simply untrue. For some, certainly for more than anyone would wish, the East End might have been just that, but for the overwhelming majority it was not. However difficult life might have been in Stepney, it furnished opportunity, scope and freedom beyond anything known, even imagined, in the Pale of Settlement. Jews, perhaps more than any other minority, turned themselves to 'betterment'. Growth, mobility and increased independence – all of which Anglo-Jewry had so tirelessly preached – simultaneously underscored the problem of misfits and deviants within the community. For Jews, cultural convention served the needs of social discipline more effectively and longer than for most groups in Britain. But by the turn of the century, disciplinary problems demanded new institutions. If the Jewish subculture wished to maintain its identity and substance, as Anglo-Jewry understood those things, then the community must attempt to set limits on freedom and resocialize the deviant.

It all started, as might have been expected, with issues growing out of the increasing independence of women and children. Confronting the issue of girls in trouble forced Anglo-Jewry to consider the broader issue of punishment and rehabilitation. Victorian Britain provided the precedent to follow. Decades before, the British had accepted the principle of segregating juvenile offenders, but placing them in institutions that continued to be privately endowed and managed. This appealed, as we have seen in so many other areas, to the liberal tradition of minimalist government. Exchequer grants would assist and government inspectors would ascertain that minimum standards were sustained, but responsibility for social discipline was a partnership between public and private institutions.

Lord Shaftesbury and Mary Carpenter had been among the leaders in a campaign to segregate, rescue and rehabilitate those who might otherwise turn to a life of crime. Inspired at least in part by their philanthropic example, the British had, by the middle of the nineteenth century, developed and accepted two institutions to manage those children. Reformatories served juveniles guilty of serious offences and existed, at least in theory, 'to root out these bad habits'.

---

19 Testimony of Dr D. L. Thomas, 16 June, Inspectors Stephen White and Richard Hyder, 17 July, and Superintendent John Mulvany, 24 July 1902. RCAI.

Industrial schools, on the other hand, trained minor offenders and those destitute children 'whose circumstances would encourage them to commit crimes'. Industrial schools were a substitute for ineffectual parental guidance for, as Mary Carpenter had argued, neglect, not poverty was the source of most difficulty. Children should always be understood to be unable to guide themselves.[20]

Anglo-Jewry, with few cases needing such attention, entered into a sequence of arrangements with established private institutions, but these invariably came undone. Rabbinical and communal visiting posed no problem, but dietary laws and Jewish sabbath observance were not easily accommodated in rigorously regulated secular institutions. Jewish authorities were willing to 'pay' for one day's 'lost' labour, but institutional authorities disliked having their routines disrupted. Anglo-Jewry created the Hayes Industrial School in 1901 to deal with boy offenders. Few Jewish girls were institutionalized before 1905. The Jewish leadership found the use of Christian industrial schools unsatisfactory and a source of constant aggravation. To construct an institution for a handful of offenders, on the other hand, seemed an unwarranted expense. After much debate within the community, the Montefiores and the Rothschilds jointly sponsored the establishment of an industrial school for Jewish girls.

Such institutions were not urgent needs before the twentieth century. The numbers involved were simply too small, and the individuals who might have been institutionalized could usually be managed in other ways. Like the poor law workhouse, the reform school was rarely invoked. Jewish pride in the family and community social programmes for family assistance seemed to render such an institution irrelevant. The community managed such cases through foster homes, apprenticeship and emigration. Jews' Hospital and Orphan Asylum taught upwards of three hundred boys and girls a standard academic and vocational curriculum 'to turn out children with the same education, the same habits, and the same chances in life, as any other well-cared for, well taught, English girls and boys'.[21] As in everything else, expanding community size raised the problem of boys and girls lacking proper supervision and 'difficult' children more starkly for the first time in the late 1880s. Anglo-Jewry's initial concern with children who were disciplinary problems was to ascertain that they followed Jewish observances wherever they might be placed. The Board of Deputies, after extensive negotiations, reached an agreement in July 1889 with the managers of the East London Industrial School in Lewisham to take all Jewish boys committed to industrial schools. The Jewish authorities agreed to pay £50 for each boy's maintenance, £25 for the extra officer and increased superintendance required, and one shilling per boy each week for the loss of the boy's work on the sabbath. Thirteen lads were initially admitted. Within a year the number soared to twenty-eight, and the school insisted on better terms.[22]

---

20 See, in particular, Report of the Select Committee of the House of Commons on Criminal and Destitute Juveniles. *PP* (515), VII (1852).

21 *JC*, 16 Apr. 1897.

22 Felix A. Davis's well-conceived and active programme dealing with released prisoners certainly helped by keeping recidivism low. *JC*, 10 Feb. 1911. Home Secretary Matthew White Ridley constructed a synagogue within Wormwood Scrubs Prison in 1898, although only thirty-seven Jewish prisoners were incarcerated there. See also, BDBJ, London Committee of Deputies, *Annual Report* (April 1890), 17–20; *Annual Report* (1891), 27–8.

These arrangements were a temporary palliative. Complaints grew about the ways in which Lewisham handled its inmates. Anti-Semitism was a real problem, to a minor degree with the staff and a greater extent among other inmates. The omnipresent conversionists seemed always to be near, rumoured to have easy access to Jewish boys. Lewisham, not Jewish authorities, terminated the agreement in 1898, and Anglo-Jewry had no choice but to establish the Hayes Industrial School which opened in 1901.

The lack of any Jewish industrial school had, to communal leadership despair, become a matter of public comment and criticism. Jewish criminals were few and far between. Visiting statistics also showed a steady decline. While 717 Jews were imprisoned in 1904, the number dropped to half that (358) by 1910. A substantial number of those were, so Jewish authorities contended, there for non-payment of fines rather than indictable offences.[23] The number of juveniles was also low, but here statistics were misleading. Nathan Joseph, who agreed that something must be done to rescue community children on the verge of crime, reminded proponents that the average number of Jewish children committed to industrial schools in any one year since 1888 was eight, of which only about two per year had actually been convicted of a criminal offence. Thirty-three consigned to industrial school was the maximum ever detained at any one time. Of all offenders placed in industrial school that year, five were charged with 'being beyond the control of their parents', ten with the frightful crime of begging, nine for the still more terrible crime of 'wandering', twelve for 'being in bad company', twelve for stealing, and only one for felony. If the leadership were determined to have such a facility, a small house would surely suffice, not an institution to house eighty.[24]

Anglo-Jewry's great social policy engineer was brushed aside, for the community image was in danger. Friendly magistrates like Dickinson of the Thames Police Court moved from raised eyebrows to criticizing the community about its juvenile offenders.

> I have very little doubt this lad [a nine-year old runaway caught picking a pocket in Aldgate Station] is an expert thief, and am sorry to say these cases of theft by little Jewish boys are becoming sadly numerous. I have spoken time after time from this bench, but no notice has been taken. It is a crying shame there is no industrial school to receive these boys, and I have to discharge them. Their parents know that, and so do the boys themselves, for there are none sharper. They all know the Court is absolutely powerless in the matter. I cannot send the lad to a reformatory, for he is far too young.... I have protested time after time respecting this serious state of things, and still nothing is done. I shall remand the boy to the workhouse for a week, and suppose at the end of that time, I shall have to discharge him.[25]

---

23 Doing so triggered a parliamentary question about the number of Jews in prison and whether the numbers justified the cost. Benjamin L. Cohen supported Ridley, protesting about the question of numbers by denomination. Ridley made the not-very-subtle point to the House that constructing this small synagogue next to the very large Roman Catholic chapel satisfied a long-standing grievance. *JC*, 6 May 1898.

24 Visitation committee meeting, United Synagogue, 5 July 1898. *JC*, 8 July 1898.

25 *JC*, 23 Sept. 1898.

Was the community's good name worth the £15,000 that Hayes Industrial School would cost? Rothschild said yes and put up £5,000 for starters. With rumbling anti-Semitism, with Conservatives taking up alien immigration restriction as a party measure, and with the certainty that after constructing the school, the government would defray almost all of the costs, Joseph's counsels of moderation were overborne.[26]

From its start, Hayes was a model enterprise consistently winning high marks from government inspectors and reasonable financial support from Anglo-Jewry. Hayes boys displayed an extraordinary capacity to monopolize athletic awards, which, as other educational institutions have discovered, much accelerated the flow of financial support. But Hayes translated that pride into academic achievement. A tribute to sound management and policy, Hayes did precisely what industrial schools were, in theory, supposed to do. It removed boys from problem situations and settings, re-educated them, offered them a fresh start in life. The school managers remained in contact with their old boys, suggesting that the relationship at Hayes was both utilitarian and pleasant. Hayes could claim that 'our lads are become respectable and industrious citizens with a robust outlook on life.' Within two years of its founding the government's inspector of schools would observe, 'The progress made by the school is little short of wonderful.' So it was. Boys at Hayes spent half their time pursuing a conventional education curriculum and half their time on 'industrial' subjects: carpentry, gardening, sewing and laundry work. Hayes managers considered the sound body the foundation of a disciplined and orderly mind. Drill, gymnastics, and competitive sport were much in favour.[27]

An industrial school for girls grew out of the Jewish campaign against the 'white slave trade', and anxiety about the Jewish involvement in it. Some mixture of moral revivalism and class assertion lay, as elsewhere, behind the resolutely middle-class phenomenon that focused upon the 'protection of girls and women' and sought to destroy 'the ubiquitous traffic'. For Jews as for mainstream English society, this attack had strong class overtones, being directed against both the 'immoral' lower classes needing discipline, education, and order, and an idle, corrupting elite. In England, the crusade furnished a basis for political self-assertion by an aspiring, ambitious middle-class group and a launching pad for a new phase in feminist militancy. The impeccably high bourgeois Jewish elite had no such political needs;

26 Felix Davis and Louis Davidson led the struggle for Hayes. Davis reminded a United Synagogue meeting that 90 per cent of industrial school income in 1897 came from the state and a further six per cent from the sale of goods made in schools. While the average cost per head per inmate was £19 13s, he proclaimed, £18 10s came from public sources. Girls were not yet considered a sufficient problem, the existing arrangement with the King Edward Schools seeming satisfactory. Hayes was one of Walter (later second Lord) Rothschild's first major communal undertakings. He acted as treasurer in the fund-raising and for the school. *JC*, 17 Apr. 1896, 10, 17, 24, 31 Dec. 1897, 14 Jan., 8 July, 23, 30 Sept., 14 Oct., 4 Nov., 9, 30 Dec. 1898, 11 Jan. 1901.

27 Law and parliamentary committee, 12 May 1901, BDBJ C 13/1/6; *JC*, 29 Mar. 1903, 3 Mar., 21 Apr., 7 July 1905; 13 Jan. 1911. Hayes opened with fifteen inmates, six of whom were committed for 'being beyond the control of their parents'. *JC*, 22 Feb. 1901. Hayes also reinforced Anglo-Jewry's belief in schools and clubs as socializing institutions. Of the twenty-one boys admitted in 1902, twelve could neither read nor write, and nine could do so only 'very imperfectly'. Hayes was proud of what it did with these lads who teetered on the edge of a life of crime. Of the ten boys discharged that year, one enlisted in the army, one was sent to sea, four emigrated, and three entered trades, results the Hayes managers found very pleasing. Hayes Industrial School, *Second Annual Report*, 1902 (London, 1903).

PLATE 1   A market in the heartland of East End Jewry:
Petticoat Lane in December 1912.

PLATE 2   Community and sociability: Jewish women and their East End world in a
rare moment of relaxed conviviality around 1900.

PLATE 3 A hearing before the Bet Din, the Jewish religious court, Chief Rabbi Hermann Adler presiding (c.1900).

PLATE 4 Dr. Nathan Marcus Adler. First Chief Rabbi of Great Britain and the British Empire, he anglicanized Ashkenazic Orthodoxy.

PLATE 5   Leonard Lionel Cohen. He led the Jewish Board of Guardians into the twentieth century in partnership with the evolving welfare state.

PLATE 6   Sir Samuel Montagu, Bt, First Baron Swaythling.

PLATE 7   Frederic David Mocatta.

PLATE 8   Economic independence and the growing emancipation of Jewish women:
Frankenburgs' workroom in 1909.

PLATE 9 Hebrew language instruction and religious education were indispensable to the preservation of Jewish culture. The Brick Lane Talmud Torah at the turn of the century.

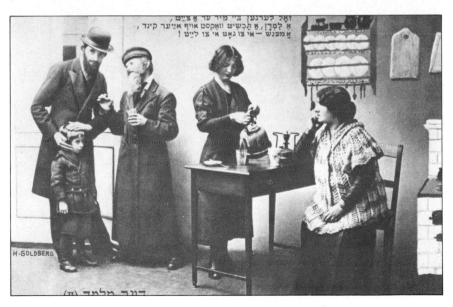

PLATE 10 East End culture blended the old and the new. A *melamed*, a Hebrew and religious teacher, enlarges on his qualifications to instruct the family's young son.

PLATE 11 The communal political crisis: Anglo-Jewry pleads for military
volunteers in 1916.

PLATE 12 'Peripatetic Philosophers of the Ghetto.' The Sabbath in the East End.

THE ILLUSTRATED LONDON NEWS,

REGISTERED AT THE GENERAL POST-OFFICE FOR TRANSMISSION ABROAD.

No. 2696.—VOL. XCVII. SATURDAY, DECEMBER 20, 1890. TWO SIXPENCE.
WHOLE SHEETS BY POST...

PLATE 13 Russian persecution proved to be Anglo-Jewry's best weapon to mobilize
the English community on its behalf.

its authority was already established. What the campaign offered Anglo-Jewry was an opportunity to display British Jews as staunchly moral, prepared to discharge unpleasant civic duties, standing as peers with the leaders of other religious denominations.

Such communal stalwarts as David L. Alexander, president of the Board of Deputies until 1917, and Claude G. Montefiore, president of the Anglo-Jewish Association were also active in the leadership. Sir Samuel Montagu personally investigated the Constantinople to Cairo traffic in women. The Reverend Simeon Singer led rabbinical activists at home and abroad. Each of these men acted from a strong sense of moral rectitude, augmented, to be sure, by concern for the public image of Jews. The purity campaign also helped to animate Jewish feminism, just as it worked to mobilize British feminism as a broad-based movement.

Claude Montefiore and his wife, both of whom were crusading activists, took it upon themselves to establish an industrial school for girls. They presented a house on Stamford Hill in 1905, and the Rothschilds wrote some cheques. Stamford Hill was intended 'to secure the welfare of children, now in danger of mental and moral ruin, often through no real fault of their own'. The very news that Stamford Hill existed was enough, so the Montefiores announced, to produce better behaviour in Jewish families, an impressive claim, if somewhat difficult to demonstrate. Stamford Hill was to be 'an industrial school', not a reformatory. Initially, at least, it accepted no criminals. Stamford Hill was 'a refuge for children living in debased and immoral surroundings or convicted by Magistrates of minor offences'.[28]

Beyond the operational problems of institutionally managing difficult or deviant children lay broader issues of children's rights, ones that the community leadership rarely addressed. But children, like women, had more options in life and were gaining greater independence. The majority of communal leaders perceived this to raise issues of discipline and refined new institutions to address that problem. The Jewish Association for the Protection of Girls and Women and the reformatory movement were two of the more obvious approaches taken to bring wayward women and youth back under communal control. A minority of Anglo-Jews opted to hasten the emancipation, even at some cost to tradition and habit. Nettie Adler was one of the moving spirits in the Committee on Wage-Earning Children, which sought to rouse public interest in and support for the Employment of Children Act. Child labour, however, was not the most popular of causes in the East End. Adler's committee, moreover, sought to extend children's rights, a sentiment which, however modish in advanced British society, ran against the grain of the close-knit Jewish family structure. Nettie Adler and her associates pressed on. Children should be understood, encouraged, and protected. In 1904, the committee enrolled

28 *JC*, 21 July 1905. Even after the war, in 1920, Anglo-Jewry confronted a series of undesirable alternatives. Neither Hayes nor Stamford Hill was intended for serious juvenile offenders, so various special arrangements had to be made with other institutions. Netherton took up to thirty Jewish boys from London but refused to promise to take alien children. The LCC considered taking over a house for Jewish boys to be administered by the Hayes management. For girls, ironically, only the Church Army ran institutions which would accommodate Jewish offenders and make satisfactory arrangements for them. See law and parliamentary committee, 31 Mar., 12 May, 16 June 1920, BDBJ C 13/1/8.

in the campaign to secure separate courts of justice for children.[29] An active Jewish minority joined an aggressive British minority in protecting the rights and expanding the opportunities for youth. Herbert Samuel's Children Act of 1908 would be a landmark along the way.

---

29 *Report of the Committee on Wage-Earning Children* (1904); *JC*, 24 Feb. 1905.

9

The Alien Question

British Jews had developed a smoothly running machinery to assimilate newcomers by the 1870s. Migrants had been principally West European in outlook, products of Jewish communities in Holland and Germany, so the task was culturally easy if economically demanding. Even this system, however, was quite new. Before 1859 and the founding of the Jewish Board of Guardians, no formal system had existed to assist the poor or socialize the immigrant. No sooner was the system in place, however, than demographics and economics accentuated by politics threatened its workings. The Russian Empire housed most of Europe's Jews, and the Russo-Jewish population multiplied at an even faster rate than the general European increase. From some million and a half in mid-century, over four million Jews remained in the Empire in 1900 in spite of substantial out-migration.

One major impulse to leave was economic. The West was perceived to be a world of unparalleled opportunity, an impression made even more attractive than it was by the contrast at home. But the West was also strange and far away, so most Jews who migrated moved to other places within the Russian Empire. Defeat in the Crimean War dislocated the Russian economy. Polish nationalism in the 1860s recruited considerable Jewish support; its repression added to the numbers of those for whom migration was a salutary choice. When the Russian government adopted overt anti-Semitism as national policy in 1881, a growing number of adventurous Jews pursuing economic opportunity in the West were joined by waves of refugee Jews fleeing from pogroms. Once established, kin communicated with kin, former townsman with those of his community who remained behind. Most Russian Jews, nevertheless, remained in Russia. When they migrated in search of opportunity, the majority moved to other parts of that Empire.[1] Jewish internal and external migration had already begun and would have accelerated whatever the Russian domestic political situation. Western Jewish leaders, however, argued and believed

---

1 Some of the most interesting and sophisticated work on this subject has been done by Michael Stanislawski of Columbia University.

that, were Russia to behave as a Western liberal state, Jews would stay, vastly enriching Russian life as they had that of Western nations.

West European Jewish leaders, moreover, feared what substantial immigration might mean to themselves and for Jewish life in the countries in which they lived. Most emigrating Jews hoped to go and actually went to the United States. Others by choice or an inability to go further settled in the countries of western Europe. Britain had the advantage or disadvantage of standing athwart the northern sea lanes. That meant not merely that tens of thousands of transmigrants passed through on their way to points beyond the seas but that the British Jewish population at least quadrupled. Most of that increase, moreover, was highly visible, being concentrated in the East End of London and smaller-scale ghettos in a handful of major industrial cities.[2]

Immigration restriction and control came to be a matter of concern for the governments of all Western nations. But when the immigrant became a refugee, the liberal conscience was touched, and places had to be found. Westerners resented Russia for 'dumping' its social problem on them. Russian persecution also indelibly branded the autocracy as hopelessly obscurantist. Such resentment and perception helped to fuel and fan fires of western Russophobia that bedeviled late nineteenth- and early twentieth-century diplomacy. Although Western Jewish leaders decried Bismarck's expulsion of foreign Jews from Prussia in 1886, no one sought to bring Great Power diplomacy to bear in protest.

The British Jewish elite may not have been as exclusionist as its French counterpart, but Anglo-Jewry did what it could to discourage immigrants, whether westernized poor Jews or strangers from the *stetls*, the ghettos of Eastern Europe. Anglo-Jewry was proud of its achievements, its successful evolution as an assimilated subculture within Britain, and was ill-disposed to those who might disrupt the smooth workings of the community. Some Anglo-Jews had weighed restriction as a communal option, and the Jewish Board of Guardians practised an ineffective version of it as policy. The board, in its early years, allocated £50 to placard the Pale with printed notices discouraging immigration to England. No sooner had

2 The provincial population rose proportionately more than the London Jewish population, moving from slightly less to slightly more than one-third of the total. See the statistics of the *Jewish Year Book*, the somewhat more elaborate data of the Royal Commission on Immigration (1903), and Lipman, *Social History*, 102–3. Argentinian footdragging on the Baron de Hirsch plan scotched that early effort to create an adequate escape route for mass migration. 'No country,' reported Sir A. Paget to Lord Salisbury, 'was willing to receive them, and to bring them into some foreign land without the prospect of their being able to establish themselves and earn a livelihood would probably expose them to as great an amount of misery as they will have to endure by remaining in the country of their birth.' 11 May 1892, HO 45/10062/B2840A/ 39. The Foreign Office felt certain that no plan could deal with 'deporting' 3,000,000 Jews in twenty-five years. Howard to Salisbury, 21 June, and memorandum, 27 June 1892. For an example of mid-century Dutch Jewish immigration, see Emanuel Shinwell's reflections on his family background in *Conflict without Malice* (London, 1955), chapter 1. The starting point for any consideration of this problem remains Gartner, *Jewish Immigrant*, which every student of this question should consult. B. Gainer, *The Alien Invasion: the Origins of the Aliens Act of 1905* (New York, 1972) deals at length with the anti-alien agitation and the passage of restrictive legislation. J. A. Garrard, *The English and Immigration 1880–1910* (London, 1971) studies the problem in the light of more recent Commonwealth immigration since 1948. For the numbers involved, S. Rosenbaum carefully reworked the Registrar General's Report for 1903 to find 232,000 Jews in England and Wales (148,000 in London), 262,000 in the United Kingdom (26,000 in Scotland, and no more than 4,000 in Ireland). *JC*, 10 Mar. 1905.

substantial Russo-Polish migration begun, however, than the Board of Guardians and Russo-Jewish Committee reinstated the old practice in 1882 as a matter of routine. The Foreign Office, the Board of Trade and the Home Office monitored the developing cooperative efforts of Jewish organizations to regulate the flow of human beings. By the 1890s, East European committees refused any financial assistance to those proceeding to the United Kingdom, and Anglo-Jewish contributions came on the express conditions that Central European Jewish agencies assist no Jew to settle in Britain.[3]

Western Jewry, in general, and Anglo-Jewry in particular, lacked accurate information about, not to mention understanding of, the largest Jewish settlement in the world. Only when Russian pogroms began in the 1880s did refuge for persecuted co-religionists begin to outweigh resistance to strangers. Anglo-Jewry repeatedly sought to understand precisely what was going on. Albert Löwy, secretary to the Anglo-Jewish Association, investigated the situation in Eastern Europe on behalf of the Anglo-Jewish Association and the Alliance Israélite Universelle. His graphic description and frightening analysis pried open the doors for refugees.[4] To preserve some degree of order, Löwy and the committees developed a screening network in Germany, centred on the port of Hamburg.

The Alliance Israélite, which had done much to develop a general West European policy of 'pay to move them on or accept them', attempted to keep immigrants far from France. As early as 1870, the Alliance toyed with the idea of coordinating a universal Jewish emigration society, one that would screen younger, more promising prospective migrants from the older and those 'unfit to be removed'. The Alliance, led by men who thought of themselves as political realists, thought its strategy would benefit all parties and might not prove too costly. Anti-Semites, the Alliance mused, might even assist in defraying expenses. The governments of Russia, Prussia and Roumania did not like Jews. Perhaps they would help to defray the costs of being rid of them. But neither the French nor English leadership wished to have these displaced people with their strange habits and unassimilable ways. Planned colonies overseas were the answer.[5] The Alliance, in particular, always pursued such grand designs whenever the opportunity seemed appropriate, but the immediate situation demanded short-term, practical answers. Working through the Liverpool branch of the Anglo-Jewish Association, the Alliance paid transportation and maintenance expenses to move 'its refugees' from Germany onwards to North America.[6]

Any such policies were palliatives and could never cope with the millions of Jews in the Russian Empire. Any realistic solutions, Western Jewish leaders believed, depended on changing the state of affairs in Russia. Virtue was born of necessity. Western Jewish leaders in every country came to say, even sometimes to believe, that Russian political misbehaviour was the principal cause for massive Jewish

3 See, e.g., Giffen to Lushington, 24 May 1892, HO 45/10063/B2840A/41. Magnus, *Jewish Board of Guardians*, 20; Testimony of Sir Samuel Montagu to the RCAI, 23 Mar 1903.

4 'nous ne voudrons pas créer une nouvelle Pologne outre mers.' Mocatta à Loeb, 27 nov, encl Lzwy to Meyer, 23 Nov. 1881, AIU Angl II/D/35/9986. See, generally, A. R. Rollin, 'Russo-Jewish immigrants in England before 1881', *Transactions of the Jewish Historical Society*, XXI, 202–13.

5 Beratheil à Crémieux, 10 mars 1870, AIU Angl II/D/30/1017a-c; *JC*, 4 Mar. 1870.

6 Silver to Loeb, 4 Oct. 1881, AIU Angl II D/35/9216.

immgration. Politics became a convenient explanation, and the myth that equality for Jews would keep them in the East was born. Convenience, however, did not render it less a myth. Habsburg Galicia, where Jews had been fully emancipated since the creation of the Dual Monarchy in 1867, produced, as Lloyd Gartner reminds us, the same proportion of Jewish emigrants from its population as left Imperial Russia.[7]

The problem of the indigent migrant had two dimensions in Britain, one of impression and one of reality. Generations of poor Dutch Jews created the stereotypical image of Jewish poverty, immortalized from generation to generation in Fagin of *Oliver Twist*. 'Dutch' Jews came to be a description of any poor Ashkenazi, Dutch or German in origin. Among them, downward mobility seemed a fact of life. Through the 1870s, although they conceded the impressionistic nature of their statistics, Anglo-Jewry saw immigration into England principally as a European Jewish response to economic conditions. By the 1850s and 1860s, Jews from the Pale constituted a larger and larger proportion of this 'floating' population. Traditional explanations, however, still appeared to work. Immigration declined markedly during any economic slump. Emigration – and a committee of the Jewish Board of Guardians worked hard to promote it – usually meant returning to the continent and those moved consisted overwhelmingly of Polish Jews. Slowly, very slowly, the stereotype of the poor alien changed. Polish and Russian Jews displayed an impressive capacity to adapt and get on in the world. This seemed to validate Anglo-Jewry's utilitarian social philosophy. But even after a generation of East European immigrants had displayed its capacity to grow and prosper, the British Jewish elite made no compromises in its commitment to anglicize all resident Jews.[8] At the same time, while the Jewish establishment came to have a clearer sense and appreciation of East European Jewish immigrant potential, Anglo-Jewry still saw itself primarily as a processing agency moving refugees onwards. As it had done in the middle of the nineteenth century, Anglo-Jewry continued to discourage migration from the continent and, failing that, sought to deflect it to other shores.[9]

7 Gartner, *Jewish Immigrant*, 41. For Nathan Joseph's early letter raising the issue of restriction, see *JC*, 26 Feb. 1880.

8 Emigration counted by the JBG was 490 in 1878, a drop of nine from the previous year. Of these 72 per cent returned to the continent, and ten per cent moved to other parts of the UK. Only 18 per cent went on the United States, Australia, the Cape and Canada. Transmigrants, those who arrived from European ports and trans-shipped to the United States, were not included in this count. JBG, *Annual Report* (1878); J. Jacobs, *Studies in Jewish Statistics* (London, 1891), 20; I. Zangwill, *Children of the Ghetto*, volume I (London, 1892), 37–8.

9 The Cape Colony and, subsequently, the Union of South Africa offered a realistic option, although the Board of Deputies and Jewish Board of Guardians had to conduct negotiations on language difficulties (migrants to the Cape Colony were supposed to know English) and regulations requiring immigrants to work through embassies of their countries of origin. Law and parliamentary committee, 4 Mar., 14 Apr. 1902; 18 Feb., 3 Mar. 1903, BDBJ C 13/1/5; Abraham to Emanuel, 18 July 1902. B 2/1/11; and the correspondence and notes from the Jews' Temporary Shelter to Emanuel, 19, 21, 16 Oct., 2 Nov., 28 Dec. 1911, 29 Jan., 21 Feb. 1912 and Gladstone to Secretary of State, Colonial Office, 15 Jan. 1912, B 2/1/17. Gartner, 45n, quoting Wagstaff to Foreign Office, 14 May 1892, FO 65/1426. The Foreign Office, Board of Trade and Home Office monitored the international efforts Jewish organizations made to regulate immigration. East European committees refused any financial assistance to those going to the United Kingdom. Anglo-Jewish money came on the express condition that no Jew be assisted to settle in Great Britain. Giffen to Lushington, 24 May 1892, HO 45/10063/B2840A/41. Beatrice Webb describes the chaotic scene at the initial landing stage in London in Booth (ed.), *Life and Labour*, volume I (London, 1889), 582–3. Cf. the description in *JC*, 12 Feb. 1904. See AIU Angl II/D/25 for various plans, 1882–99 for settling refugees.

While acculturation animated almost every Anglo-Jewish social institution, processing immigrants meant, in the first instance, moving as many of them as possible through England and on to the United States. Husbands without work often moved on to America, leaving wives and children behind until the husbands could find employment and housing. In many cases this brought the family to the local Jewish Board of Guardians, whether in London or the provinces. Frustrated boards repeatedly threatened to turn such 'abandoned' families over to the untender mercies of poor law workhouses but rarely did so. From time to time, however, the London board did dispatch wife and children to America whether they had been summoned or not. This philanthropic sleight of hand prompted bellicose reactions from the United Hebrew Charities of New York.[10]

Canada, South Africa, other parts of the Empire, and Latin America were secondary targets because they offered fewer economic opportunities, cost more to reach, and had less well articulated infrastructures to aid newcomers. Ultimately Canada and then, after the Boer War, South Africa became favoured alternatives to the United States. Emigration, moreover, did not prevent East End overcrowding, for perhaps one in ten Jews arriving in England stayed there. When not moving Jews on to points overseas, Anglo-Jewry sought to sift them to other parts of Britain. Sir Samuel Montagu's dispersion society, established in the face of restrictionist agitation in 1902, enjoyed considerable community support in scattering Jewish 'settlers' through provincial Britain. Reading, however, proved the one striking example of a Federation colony that prospered. Dispersion generally demanded a pre-existing, cooperative provincial Jewish infrastructure. Leeds, which numbered scarcely more than a dozen Jewish families in the mid-1840s, had more than 5,000 Jews by 1890, most of whom were recent migrants from Poland and Russia. Leeds, however, was particularly attractive. A local Jewish board of guardians assisted immigrants upon arrival and 'paid a machiner to teach them', sliding them smoothly into the local tailoring trades. The demand for Leeds clothing rose steadily through the 1880s, creating opportunities for all and minimizing many of the conflicts and problems that haunted the East End of London. When growth slowed at the turn of the century, Leeds became the scene of bitter industrial disputes and class tension.[11]

Even among refugees, Anglo-Jewry also demanded that those who were in a position to help themselves do so. All institutions processing refugees developed elaborate tests and screening techniques to ascertain that only genuine refugees received aid and that only those fit for and willing to endure the hardships of pioneering were supported. Anglo-Jewry could deal sharply with those who appeared to compromise its policies. Simon Cohen, a baker who was called 'Simha

---

10 Gartner, *Jewish Immigrant*, 170–1; RCAI (1903), qq 15318, 15583 ff. The JBG began taking stringent measures on wife desertion by refusing to offer any relief except in cases of illness or dire necessity. This practice, initiated in 1872, had short-term success, but by 1878 had no appreciable effect. JBG, *Annual Report* (1878), *JC*, 28 Feb. 1879. By the time anti-alien agitation had reached its crescendo, the JBG conceded that the category was meaningless. By then they were ready to concede that husbands and fathers would save their own fares, migrate across the Atlantic, establish themselves, and then send for their families. JBG, *Annual Report* (1904).

11 Report of the Select Committee of the House of Commons on the Sweating Trades. *PP* (1889), qq 30825–40, 30871, 30917–20, 30976.

TABLE 9.1   Relief by the Jewish Board of Guardians, 1885–1914

	1885	*1890*	*1895*	*1900*	*1905*	*1910*	*1914*
Applicants for aid:							
Native	424	419	524	508	720	626	508
Foreign (resident 7 yr+)	1,113	1,192	1,773	2,122	3,200	3,149	3,589
Foreign (resident 7 yr−)	1,871	1,740	2,497	2,809	2,826	584	411
Nationality (newly arrived):							
Russian/Polish	376	220	129	1,199	572	40	21
German/Austrian	79	34	15	71	68	9	7
Dutch	3	9	6	4	0	0	0
Roumanian	—	—	—	493	14	2	2
Other	9	7	10	18	9	0	0
Emigrants:	817	1,043	614	1,838	1,611	372	174

Source: Jewish Board of Guardians, *Annual Reports.*

Becker', established the original Poor Jews' Temporary Shelter in his shop, where survivors of the journey from Eastern Europe could find at least a degree of warmth and comfort as they began their new lives in that strange, sometimes hostile land called Whitechapel. The Jewish Board of Guardians, led by Mocatta and Montagu, had the establishment branded as unsanitary and closed. No inducements to pauperism would be tolerated. Judging from their own statistics, few were.

The Jewish Board of Guardians came, as we have seen, to act as Anglo-Jewry's social welfare board, broadly supplemented by and usually coordinating its efforts with a panoply of specialized philanthropies and charitable institutions. Two other major institutions, the Poor Jews' Temporary Shelter and the Russo-Jewish Committee, evolved to process immigrants and refugees.

THE POOR JEWS' TEMPORARY SHELTER

The Poor Jews' Temporary Shelter, an Anglo-Jewish 'improvement' upon Simon Cohen's 'unsanitary' refuge, was re-established in slightly more capacious and better-organized quarters. The heavily used facilities, to judge from the organization's own reports, continued to leave much to be desired in terms of cleanliness but answered Anglo-Jewish demands for the orderly processing of deserving individuals. Even the facilities were ultimately, by 1901, shifted into a capacious £10,000 facility. Samuel Montagu and some friends took matters in hand. Montagu and Hermann Landau, himself a Polish immigrant, a stockbroker-banker, and the first Pole to be accepted in the 'cousinhood', sought to recreate the Shelter as an institution, animated by 'sound' social philosophy and sincere humanitarian conviction, to fill an institutional void in the processing of newcomers.

The shelter proved indispensable, since the Jewish Board of Guardians had no intention of deviating from its six-month residence requirement before considering any candidate for relief. The new Jews' Temporary Shelter undertook the initial care of transmigrants and immigrants. A kindly man, Hermann Landau, who served as president from the foundation of the shelter in 1885, nevertheless applied the steely social philosophy of Victorian philanthropy.[12] Able-bodied males took a 'labour test'; they had to do work of some sort – usually a menial task like chopping wood – to receive free shelter. Since needs were great and resources scanty, even the most humane people and institutions were forced to cheese-paring economies. Contemporaries saw this as sound and generous benevolence. That great repository of social policy wisdom, the Charity Organisation Society, had taught all British philanthropists the debilitating and degrading effects of casual handouts or any form of assistance that did not inspire recipients to improve themselves.

No individual fought harder for the often-victimized migrant than Hermann Landau. He wanted all European Jewish agencies to create a network that would provide security for refugees. But he confronted a paradox. If word leaked back into the Pale that such an institution as the shelter existed, all authorities feared that Russian and Polish Jews would inundate the West. Landau attempted to balance these incompatible aspirations. He argued in terms of costs, quite apart from the toll of human suffering, that providing protection when refugees first arrived was far less expensive than the subsequent drain on the philanthropic purse were they allowed to shift for themselves. His case was easy to document. Unscrupulous agents fleeced even the most wary immigrants from the time they first considered leaving Eastern Europe until their arrival in London.[13]

Although the Jewish agencies attempted to provide protection for those who migrated through their network, such victimization was never fully checked. Many more Jews came or attempted to come on their own, with or without the assistance of family or friends who had migrated earlier. Unscrupulous agents, often colluding with one another, fished in these streams of human traffic. Five unfortunate men, to cite but one instance of a kind repeated countless times, paid eighty-five roubles each in Brest-Litovsk as their fare to Boston, Massachusetts. The Brest and London agents to whom they were sent denied that they had been paid and refused to help them further. In spite of the efforts of the shelter, the Russo-Jewish Committee and the Board of Guardians, nothing could be done. Reasoning that nothing effective could be done for those who moved outside of controlled channels and to dissuade others from taking any but 'approved' courses, Anglo-Jewry deported the five back to Russia and took pains to see that their story received the widest possible circulation 'to act as a warning to other intended emigrants'.[14]

For many who had kin or friends already established in London, the greatest problem on landing was to find them in the chaos of Tilbury Dock. Whether they moved through the Jewish organizational network or on their own, immigrants had often heard of the shelter in Poland or Russia. Others were told of it on the docks by

---

12 Typescript short biographical sketches of Landau and other leading figures in the Jews' Temporary Shelter by Abraham Mindy, secretary to the shelter, are in AJ/328 in the Mocatta Library.

13 Landau testified that immigrant and refugee Jews were as victimized in London as they had been in Russia. First Report of the Select Committee of the House of Commons on Alien Immigration. *PP*, 1888. (Cd. 1742), qq 2163–90. See also the discussion in *JC*, 21 Aug. 1891.

14 The shelter ran at a slight deficit for 1895, reporting income of £1,302 and expenditure of £1,334. Poor Jews' Temporary Shelter (JTS), *Tenth Annual Report* (1896).

a shelter official in an effort to save the unwary from the 'land sharks', as Landau called them, who parted new arrivals from their limited means.[15] However they learned of it, many found their way to the shelter. With a few years, shelter officials met all incoming ships, assisting, as it happened, both Jewish and Gentile arrivals. Once at the shelter, newcomers were registered. The superintendent took their names, asked if they had friends or relatives in London, what trade they practised or what skills they had, and relieved them of their money 'for their own protection'. Those who had London kith or kin were united with them as quickly as possible. Those staying at the shelter were fed two meals each day, three after 1897, sanitized in a Russian steam bath, and expected to attend daily prayers. The shelter safeguarded the refugee's cash or, when he was impecunious, an advance from its own funds and purchased drafts available to the migrant only when he arrived at his final destination. This hastened the individual along, removed any temptation to stay in England, and protected those who might otherwise be victimized – all at a total cost to the community of not more than £500 per year.[16]

The shelter preferred to handle 'worthy' people who had appropriate testimonials and had moved with the assistance of approved Jewish agencies. But how was worthiness of immigrants and their families to be determined? Sir Samuel Montagu thought that certificates of good character, attested by a would-be immigrant's rabbi, might be the best way to deal with the issue of undesirable Jewish aliens and even offered that formulation to the royal commission investigating the problem.[17] Religious testimonials, however, never became an explicit criterion for the shelter, although participation at services certainly was. Whether because of or in spite of such notions and rules, Herman Landau's yeoman work at the Jews' Temporary Shelter, the first contact of most immigrants with Anglo-Jewry, proved equal to severe strains, although not without generating much anxiety and demanding the cooperation of other communal organizations.

15 Numbers of immigrants began to decline in the mid-1890s. The JTS processed 3,540 (1895–6), 2,811 (1896–7), and 2,060 (1897–8). Of the 2,060 served in 1897–8, 1,683 'were provided with the means to make their way in the world', which translated into partial or full subsidy. A further 1,582 passengers were assisted en route (conventionally a description of those passengers handled for the steamship companies). The JTS provided 12,219 meals (with a substantial assist from the Sabbath Meals Society) and furnished a night's lodging in 7,595 cases. When, that year, 'land sharks' shifted to prey on the smaller group of arrivals in Grimsby, the JTS dispatched a superintendent to that port who put an end to the abuses. *Thirteenth Annual Report of the Poor Jews' Temporary Shelter, 1897–1898* (London, 1898), JTS annual meeting, *JC*, 13 Jan. 1899.

16 'Eine Schilderung des Misehandlungen, welche die jüdischen Auswandern aus Russland und aus Polen zu erleiden haben.' Landau believed five per cent of all refugees left Russia with 500 to 10,000 roubles, usually in banknotes. Most were robbed while sleeping if not swindled en route. Agents on the Russian border, in Berlin, Hamburg, and Bremen, could much improve the situation. Landau to Bigart, 14 Feb 1898, AIU Angl I/B/37/6429. Landau expounded on migrant trials and tribulations before the House of Commons Select Committee on Emigration and Immigration. First Report, 27 July 1888. *PP*, XI, qq 2163–90. Montagu organized a protest meeting against the JBG visiting committee action in closing Cohen's shelter. Mocatta defended the action, arguing that the existence of such a shelter would be an inducement to pauper immigration. Landau, Montagu, and Ellis Franklin then developed the new facilities, opening them in October 1885. *JC*, 15 May 1885; Gartner, *Jewish Immigrant*, 52–3.

17 HO 45/10303/117267/18, 49. *The Lancet* established a special sanitary commission on the 'Polish colony of Jewish tailors' which reported on 3 May 1884, leading the *Jewish Chronicle* to demand that the JBG take both housing and 'unscrupulous masters' in hand. *JC*, 16 May 1884.

During 1895, the Poor Jews' Temporary Shelter processed a record 2,236 immigrants in contrast to the 1,874 of the previous year. Most of those received were 'birds of passage', inspired by the spring and summer transatlantic rate wars. Substantially increased numbers began migrating to South Africa, so many that outward bound ships were fully booked weeks ahead of sailing. The opportunity to sail fully loaded also led some ships to delay their departure for one to two weeks, imposing considerable strain on shelter resources. The shelter provided over 1,000 meals each week throughout the year. Representatives of the Jews' Temporary Shelter met each ship and took charge of those who had landed who had no relatives or friends to care for them. In July 1895, for instance, the shelter handled three substantial groups, shipping most of them on, within a week, to South Africa and the others to the United States. In those instances where the South African immigrants lacked full passage money, the shelter provided the balance. After the Boer War, the shelter worked closely with the Board of Deputies, the Jewish Board of Guardians and the Russo-Jewish Committee to move as many immigrants as possible to the Cape Colony.[18] Whenever possible, however, the shelter investigated and shifted the responsibility and cost of caring for immigrants to family or friends in London.[19] The shelter never discriminated against Gentiles who knew no English, although few availed themselves of its services. Landau usually handled such cases on an individual basis with the aid of Gentile friends. Board of Trade regulations laid responsibility upon the captain of any vessel and the shipping company for the safety and comfort of passengers arriving from the continent. They also left the shipping company responsible for the safe return of any passenger not admitted to the United Kingdom. This created a mutual bond of interest between those lines bringing immigrants into London and the shelter. By the turn of the century, principal shippers had worked out agreements with the shelter to process their batches of transmigrants.[20]

An elaborate infrastructure developed to serve immigrant needs and answer Anglo-Jewish concerns. The Poor Jews' Temporary Shelter was, in effect, an accommodation station for the transatlantic or South African trade, moving its wayfarers out through Liverpool and Southampton. Costs of these operations constituted two-thirds of the shelter's annual expenses. Those whose business it was to know, however, contended that the Temporary Shelter only handled a trifle over 20 per cent of the Russian and Polish transmigrants between 1890 and 1902.

18 In early 1903, for instance, the Cape passed an Immigration Act demanding that would-be settlers know a European language. The immediate issue was, did Yiddish qualify? Alexander negotiated the matter with Fuller, the Agent General for the Cape Colony. Fuller secured a favourable ruling on the question of Yiddish but exacted a promise, in return, that Landau would deliver properly washed and dressed candidates to Fuller for immigration certificates. Fuller to Alexander, 10 July, BDBJ minute book, 22 March to 16 July 1903.

19 Of ninety-five who landed on 5 July, eighty-three were sent by Castle Line to South Africa. All of the 122 who landed on 16 July appear to have been sent to South Africa, and the seventy-five landed on 26 July were sent to New York. Another 429 arrived between 3 and 21 July from Hamburg in parties not exceeding twenty-five. The police had no information on their disposition. MEPO to HO, 25 Oct 1895, HO 45/10063/B2840A/79.

20 The shipping companies paid £1,562 for passengers bound for South Africa in 1897–8. Once shipping company income was arranged, the Russo-Jewish Committee cancelled its £125 subsidy. JTS, *Twelfth Annual Report, 1896–97* (London, 1897); JTS, annual meeting, 9 Jan. 1898. *JC*, 14 Jan. 1898.

The majority proceeded to Liverpool on their own. Well before the Aliens Act of 1905 the government had the capacity, if it chose to do so, to know the actual numbers involved, but the form in which the Board of Trade published its statistics confused rather than clarified the issue. Local authorities licensed transmigrant facilities in houses or hotels under the supervision of the shipping companies themselves.

The Beaver Line carried the majority of North American passengers. Passage brokers, also licensed, supplied contract tickets for the port of arrival and were required to furnish lists to local authorities with particulars. The broker was responsible for seeing that initial lists and disposition lists agreed and could lose his licence if they did not. By 1904, the Home Office had a clear idea of where most newcomers went. Jews clustered in the East End or Soho. Germans went to Finsbury, Belgians to St Pancras, and Italians to Saffron Hill. Jews, so the Home Office reported, often arrived without plan or purpose. Most had been invited by and had help from family or friends. Once landed they then considered the problem of where to live and what to do. But Jews also went through a double screening process. Beyond what the shipping companies did themselves, only Jews, however, had institutions both in Europe and in England sending back 'undesirables' and those who could not adjust to their new setting. The shelter played an ongoing role in this process. A sudden surge in the number of Roumanian refugees in 1900 fleeing through Britain seemed an opportunity for some local layabouts who were seeking to secure a subsidized passage to Canada. A group of 'foreign Jews' representing themselves as penniless Roumanian refugees assembled at the shelter. Closer investigation revealed that they were the 'riff-raff of Eastern Europe, Galicians, Russian, and Poles', so they were told to find work and sent away.[21]

In economically hard years in the United States, refugees and immigrants sometimes drifted back, retracing the steps they had taken on their original exodus. Revived American prosperity invariably reduced the number travelling from west to east. But returnees were many in difficult years. About 16 per cent of immigrants (298) in 1894 found 'that they cannot make progress in America' and came through the shelter on their way back to Russia. Only 53 (2.5 per cent) returned in 1895. Although the numbers going to the United States rose sharply, from 291 (1894) to 509 (1895), the shelter reported happily that most were in their productive years with few denizens of the shelter having 'passed middle age'.

The shelter was twenty years old when the Aliens Act of 1905, the first modern statute restricting immigration into Britain, was passed. It was never busier. Another transatlantic shipping rate war, individuals moving in anticipation of restrictive legislation and refugees fleeing military service in the Russo-Japanese war made 1904–5 the most active year in the institution's history. Political sensitivities made efficient shelter processing more important than ever. Anglo-Jewry, frightened by the potential scope of restrictive legislation in the bill that failed in 1904 and that which passed in 1905, was anxious to have as many arrivals as possible sent onwards out of the country. Landau reported that over £34,000 had

21 JTS, *Fifteenth Annual Report, 1899–1900* (London, 1900); JTS annual meeting, 30 Dec. 1900. *JC*, 4 Jan. 1901. Ellis reported in 1904 that only 29,511 Russian and Polish immigrants stayed at the Poor Jews' Temporary Shelter (20.6 per cent). F. E. Ellis, Report on Alien Immigration (May 1904), HO 45/10231/B37811/15.

been spent in the last quarter of 1905 to settle refugees in the United States, Canada and Argentina. All this was done with a minimum of publicity. No public appeal was made. Almost £10,000 came from the Russo-Jewish Committee and the Jewish Colonization Association. Most of the rest came from the Rothschilds and people to whom they appealed privately. The shelter handled almost 6,800 of the approximately 48,000 who landed at London docks. Nearly 50 per cent of them arrived in the last half of 1904. Inmates of the shelter were increasingly travelling on their own resources. In that most unusual year, over 45 per cent (3,046) were paying their way. The usual number in the recent past had been over 60 per cent (2,400 or more). Looking back on the year, Anglo-Jewish estimates were that some 5,000 immigrants moved on who, with their families, would otherwise have added 25,000 to British Jewry. Had they paused, as so many had done in the past, they would have been 'a burden to the community and little benefit to themselves'. Thanks to this great communal effort, they were moved onwards at once. The shelter believed that it had been instrumental in limiting the numbers who remained in England, even among those who had, in the past, paused for several months of menial work to save money to bring along their wives and children.[22]

For several years Landau had sought to render his institution self-sufficient, using shipping line income and the small endowment funds, but special needs invariably frustrated him. The Rothschilds came to his aid and celebrated the achievements and two decades of shelter communal service by raising the money for a new substantial facility. The Aliens Act of 1905 had its psychological preventative effect, and the new hundred-bed shelter served steadily declining numbers of increasingly self-supporting individuals. A significant number of shelter inmates, moreover, were self-sustaining transmigrants for whom the shipping lines paid room and board. This precipitated some communal carping about whether the shelter was a philanthropy or a business.

By 1910, of 2,300 male passengers passing through the shelter, only thirty-seven 'had no calling', the 'highest employment factor' in shelter history. Travellers deposited £26,390 that year as compared with £8,000 in 1908–9, an average for the years immediately after the Aliens Act. Shelter representatives turned increasingly to 'protective work' at railway stations and docks in coordination with the Jewish Association for the Protection of Girls and Women. Of the 219 immigrants rejected at the Port of London under the Aliens Act in 1909–10, shelter intervention helped obtain permission to land for 114. In one instance a Russian child travelling with its mother and seven siblings to join the father in North America was rejected for medical reasons, although the others were allowed to go on to their destination. The shelter, aided by Herbert Bentwich, managed to get the decision reversed, the shelter promising to see that the child received proper medical care. Shelter officers cooperated with public health officials during the 1909 East European cholera epidemic.[23] The Jews' Temporary Shelter, however much it enjoyed official confidence and leadership approbation, never developed a substantial contributor base. Some critics reasoned that it should pay its own way; others seemed disinclined

22 JTS, *Twentieth Annual Report 1904–1905* (London, 1905); *JC*, 2 June, 15 Dec. 1905; 24 Feb. 1911.
23 JTS, *Twenty-fifth Annual Report 1909–1910* (London, 1911); JTS annual meeting, 18 Jan. *JC*, 24 Feb. 1911.

to give, believing that the Aliens Act rendered it unnecessary. The institution, undaunted, soldiered on.

THE RUSSO-JEWISH COMMITTEE

Russian persecution so accelerated the wave of Jewish emigration that institutions had to be refined to manage it. All the practical issues surrounding immigration and transmigration remained, but pogroms gave Anglo-Jewry one important advantage. Russian brutality mobilized Jewish and Christian philanthropy for the cause of refugees. Baron Henry de Worms could assemble a spectrum of English culture at the Carlton Club to sign the January 1882 manifesto summoning a great public meeting. The Archbishop of Canterbury, Cardinal Manning, Lord Shaftesbury (everybody's favourite philanthropist), Matthew Arnold, the novelist Charles Reade, and Charles Darwin signed up on the spot. J. Whittaker Ellis, Lord Mayor of London, presided at the initiation of the Mansion House Fund for the victims of Russian outrages. Money poured in. Not only contributions but a ready-made network of European and English Jewish agencies to process the victims came into being.[24] The Lord Mayor of London and Cardinal Manning mobilized funds and supporters. Anglo-Jewry and the Alliance Israélite refined the technique of handling. The Mansion House Committee, established to administer these funds, dealt with the immediate crisis of 1881–2. The Mansion House Fund was then placed in the hands of a new body, the Russo-Jewish Committee, built on the administrative experience of the fund's first two years. The Russo-Jewish Committee managed refugees, keeping them off the books of the Jewish Board of Guardians and preventing them from becoming a public charge. A Conjoint Committee of the Board and Russo-Jewish Committee administered cases of concern to both bodies.

Since the Russo-Jewish Committee considered only refugees, the rhythm of cases reflected the intensity of persecution or, in the special case of 1905–6, individuals and their families fleeing from military obligations in the Russo-Japanese War. The Conjoint Committee's concerns were those refugees who remained in England but required assistance. Aid was sparingly given and very often came in the form of assisting the applicant and his family to leave England. Anglo-Jewry insisted, in so far as possible, that those who received assistance had reasonable prospects of adjusting satisfactorily to British life. Those who might prosper elsewhere were helped to go. Those who could not seem to adapt, for whatever reason, were sent back from whence they had come, human tokens to the Russo-Jewish Committee's rigorous policy of triage.

Russo-Jewish Committee activities – developing colonies of settlement, subsidizing refugees in transit and as they attempted to adjust to life in the United Kingdom – were costly. Continued Russian brutality worked to the committee's benefit. Abuse sanctioned anguished public appeals that regularly replenished funds.

---

24 *Daily Telegraph*, 23 Jan. 1882; de Worms to Loeb, 23 Jan., Ellis to AIU, 14 Feb., New York to Mansion House Fund, 1 Apr., Ellis to Loeb, 2 Apr.; Löwy to Loeb, 17 Mar, AIU Angl II/D/24/821, 1120, 1673; AIU Angl II/D/25/1497.

TABLE 9.2 Emigration and repatriation by the Russo-Jewish Committee–Jewish Board of Guardians Conjoint Committee, 1882–1906[25]

Year	New Applications	Persons	Emigrated	Repatriated	Cost (£)
1882	1,591	2,749	1,207	579	7,248
1883	48	114	55	105	523
1884	55	149	58	38	502
1885	67	174	49	35	339
1886	103	177	65	107	509
1887	90	215	110	65	753
1888	337	673	216	162	1,246
1889	468	863	221	215	1,237
1890	335	815	341	74	1,224
1890	537	1,636	410	111	2,185
1892	1,456	3,277	835	508	4,765
1893	1,155	2,649	740	440	5,781
1894	534	1,324	292	490	2,899
1895	336	901	286	223	2,414
1896	350	852	172	146	2,035
1897	417	1,181	183	191	2,559
1898	583	1,443	336	461	2,617
1899	432	1,128	379	226	2,775
1900	531	1,184	361	392	3,019
1901	342	729	111	285	1,732
1902	291	543	26	296	1,448
1903	395	720	57	288	1,428
1904	450	688	55	186	1,370
1905	2,706	3,847	174	927	3,241
1906	1,528	2,796	839	577	6,784
Total	15,137	30,827	7,578	7,127	60,651

Source: Stettauer Papers, AJ/22 in the Mocatta Library.

Committee resources underwrote the periodical *Darkest Russia*. Lucien Wolf's prose and management kept the adrenalin and cash contributions flowing. The intelligence network that Wolf developed for that periodical was to prove invaluable to him in later negotiations for Anglo-Jewry with the British Foreign Office. Wolf's pen, however. could only keep a simmering pot a-boiling. In the generally calmer 1890s, emigration was generally self-propelled and financed. Kinfolk brought kinfolk; friends encouraged former neighbours. In slacker years, processing agencies like the Russo-Jewish Committee devoted their attention to assimilating

25 As parliamentary discusion of legislation on the subject of aliens rose to a peak, the conjoint committee began to understate total numbers involved. In 1904, 800 others emigrated at conjoint expense directly from Antwerp to Canada but do not appear in the total for that year. In 1905, the Russo-Jewish Committee also funded all or part of the expenses of 2,830 individuals emigrated through the Jews' Temporary Shelter. In 1906, with the legislation in place, the Russo-Jewish Committee paid for 444 emigrated directly from continental ports, and 8,142 more were emigrated from Europe at the expense of continental Jewish agencies. Stettauer Papers, AJ/22.

refugees at home, to the development of settlements overseas, and to refining predictive techniques to sort out sound prospective colonists.

Initially, the Russo-Jewish Committee's screening network operated in Germany. Most Jewish refugees poured into Hamburg. A local selection committee was empowered to select those fit to pioneer in North American colonies. At the other end, committee managers on the scene overseas were directed to acquire the most promising sites, to husband committee financial resources, and to cultivate local political leaders.[26] Canada became increasingly popular when resistance to immigration stiffened in the United States. Sometimes, as in the case of Philadelphia Jewry, Americans even demanded financial support for their emigrant aid societies from those Europeans who had shipped immigrants over. As new colonies for Jewish settlement were organized in New Jersey, Texas, or California, constant, although often futile, efforts were made to turn tailors and pedlars into farmers.[27]

Independent promoters, whose enthusiasm outran their conception of the problem, often disrupted the delicate machinery managing emigration. One Konstantinowsk, 'unaware of his incompetency to cope with the emigration question', gathered a party of Roumanian Jews for resettlement in Palestine. Floundering 'in a state of utter helplessness and despair' in Constantinople, he appealed to the London committee for help. That body, standing firm against 'self-elected or others' promoting emigration from Roumania or Russia declined either to aid or advise him.[28] As more and more places of settlement had to be found, Latin America seemed to offer possibilities. While Argentinian enterprises flourished, although the authoritarian management aroused much resentment, Brazil was hopeless. An attempt to plant four hundred colonists in Nova Odessa near Sao Paulo failed. Few of the colonists were of 'the right stamp'. 'Most of them', reported the president of the Sao Paulo Jewish Benevolent Society, 'were Poles from Whitechapel, and the women came with big hats, silk blouses, and gloves.' Within a few weeks, most had abandoned any effort to till the soil and returned to Sao Paulo, utterly destitute and a drain on local resources. Farmers, 'not the sweepings of the streets', were needed. Brazilian authorities, moreover, were unlikely to be supportive.[29]

Almost all immigrants were or were encouraged to be transmigrants, moving through the elaborate screening network that the Alliance Israélite, the Austrian and German committees and the Russo-Jewish Committee erected from centres of East European Jewish settlement to the borders of the Russian Empire. As genuine a philanthropist as Frederic D. Mocatta argued that any meaningful emigration programme depended on 'triage'. The huge British and French investment for East

26 Subscriptions of £60,000 (1,500,000 francs) were already in hand. Cooperation also demanded that the French stop shipping unwanted emigrants from Paris to London. Mocatta à Loeb, 12 mars 1882, AIU Angl II/D/35/1491.

27 Lyon to AIU, 16 Oct; Loeb à Lyon, 9 nov. 1884, AIU Angl II/D/35/9960. For one effort to educate, see Mark Samuel, *How to Promote and Develope [sic] Agricultural Pursuits among the Jews* (Liverpool, 1883) which Löwy furnished to Loeb, 9 Jan. 1884, AIU Angl I/B/44/8588.

28 Löwy to Loeb, 5 Mar. 1883, AIU Angl II/D/35/5780.

29 'The Brazilian authorities,' commented another Jewish Sao Paulo leader, 'would treat the immigrants just as they would treat any other poor immigrants, which is not saying much.' Reports in Davidson to Stettauer, 7 May 1909, AIU Angl I/H/7/7063.

European refugees might otherwise be jeopardized. The elderly, the sick, and those lacking the skills to make a new life must be left behind or manage through their own means and at their own risk.[30]

West European Jewry knew that it could never cope with massive migration from the Russian Empire. Having convinced itself and telling anyone else who would listen that Russian misgovernment lay at heart of the immigration problem, considerable efforts were made to stimulate developments in Russia itself which would encourage the restless to stay. Jewish philanthropists and even organizations contributed to facilities to educate and resettle Jews within the empire. Individual Jewish notables made fruitless pilgrimages to senior Russian officials. Almost as ineffective were efforts to bring Western diplomatic pressure to bear on the Imperial Russian government to remove unfair restrictions on Jews, to act forcefully to prevent persecution and pogroms, and to create an environment comparable to that in Western Europe and America where Jew and Gentile alike could prosper.

The migrants of the 1890s were, in many ways, a pleasant contrast, in Anglo-Jewry's eyes, to the frightened refugees of the 1880s. The Jewish Board of Guardians had finally come to appreciate the remarkable adaptability of East European Jews. It reported that newcomers adjusted well to British conditions when they remained in England and called them 'capable and self-reliant'. Since these people had moved on their own initiative and at their own expense, they had already demonstrated their acceptance of the ethics of self-help Anglo-Jewry was so anxious to inculcate.[31] The Russian-Polish emigration remained so substantial that Central and West European Jewry was forced continually to refine its processing institutions. The fear of renewed persecution, moreover, always threatened to overwhelm the existing network. The Russo-Jewish Committee used the breathing space of the 1890s to consider the more general issue of colonization. But the relative calm between 1891 and 1899 also created some problems. Russian persecution was indispensable for fund-raising. Fortunately for the committee, official and popular East European anti-Semitism could be counted upon to generate publicity-worthy horrors. None was missed. Lucien Wolf's *Darkest Russia*, with William E. Gladstone's approving endorsement, saw to that.[32] Basic Anglo-Jewish policy remained unchanged. Self-propelled immigrants were still urged to move on. Colonization, the creation of sanctuaries where Jews could construct new lives for themselves, remained a stage in emancipation.

Planners, however, confronted one difficulty after another. Russia and Poland, the largest areas of Jewish settlement, demanded more resources than Western Jews could mobilize, but the 'evil empire' of an earlier generation had no monopoly on abuse and repression. Roumania systematically violated the principles it had

30 Mocatta à Loeb, 12, 20 mars 1882, AIU Angl II/D/35/1491, 1949.

31 JBG, *Annual Report*, 1897, 16. On the rhythm of immigration, see Gartner, *Jewish Immigrant*, 38–49, 283 and his article, 'Notes on the statistics of Jewish immigration to England, 1870–1914', *Jewish Social Studies*, XXI.

32 See, e.g., the arrangements for the City of London meeting of 10 December 1890 and the effort to maximize both British and French press coverage to develop the broadest possible base of philanthropic support. Joseph to Loeb, 23, 30 Nov., 7, 11, 18 Dec.; Loeb à Joseph, 29 nov., 16 déc.; Loeb à Löwy. 2 déc.; Joseph to Bigart 17 Dec. 1890, AIU Angl I/H/7/9829, 9852, 9876, 9904, 9920, 9939. See AIU II/D/25 for various plans, 1882–99, to settle refugees.

guaranteed in the Treaty of Berlin of 1878 and abused its Jewish population. Roumania, while a problem infinitely smaller in scale, generated its own waves of migrants for whom adequate arrangements did not exist. In 1899 and 1900, for instance, Roumanian Jews clogged the overstrained arteries of organized Jewish resettlement. Their sudden, unpredicted exodus could not have come at a worse moment for Western Jewry. Anti-alien agitation appeared to be gathering force everywhere. While France continued to reel with Dreyfus afterquakes, the British Conservative government caught up in the chauvinism and racism of the Boer War would shortly endorse immigration restriction as a government measure.[33] East End overcrowding and social problems, so embarrassing for acculturated West End Anglo-Jewry, were the stock-in-trade of every would-be social reformer. 'We simply dare not,' warned Claude Montefiore, 'help to establish batches of penniless emigrants in this country.' That meant the repatriation of those who could not be trans-shipped, crushing hopes, costing money, and engendering untold suffering. Somehow emigration had to be 'regulated and limited'. A conference in Paris on 26 and 27 June 1900 determined that some system be developed. Anglo-Jewry fully agreed. Nothing 'can be more dangerous than a haphazard, planless and aimless emigration on the part of the Roumanians.' Were matters not taken in hand immediately, the British government would be compelled to act 'preventing any alien immigration in the future'.[34] Given the saturation of New York and the problems with United States immigration regulation generally, Canada seemed to offer the best prospect. Anglo-Jewry would have preferred to direct emigrants and refugees directly from the continent to their final destination, in order to avoid problems of trans-shipment, the unpleasant publicity which fed anti-alien agitation of statistics of immigrant landings, and the ten per cent who for various reasons stayed in Britain.[35]

Roumanian, as opposed to Russo-Polish emigration, was too erratic in volume to be regulated by a coordinated West European Jewish network. This created occasional chaos, uncoordinated if well-meaning intervention that strained every agency. Seventy-five Roumanians, for example, arrived unannounced at the London docks on 30 June 1900. They were but the first of no one knew how many. Four hundred more were preparing to come from Rotterdam and Frankfurt. Anglo-Jewry had to improvise aid for these seventy-five who were literally on their doorstep. Theirs was a common story. All were men. About half of them were artisans. All came from Bucharest. They had met their civil obligations in Roumania only to confront few job opportunities and severe discrimination. Since they had fulfilled their Roumanian military service, the government would permit them to leave at their own expense. They funded their exodus through a benefit performance at the Bucharest Jewish Theatre. With that money they purchased their passports and tickets to Kronstadt. Passports were expensive – 20 francs each – so the men wished to save travel costs by walking to Hamburg. This the

33 See, e.g., Chief Rabbi Adler to his French counterpart, 'I have great anxiety, lest the war stir up Anti-Semitism here.' 9 Jan. 1900, AIU Angl I/B/54 bis/8927.

34 Adler to Bigart, 9 July 1900, AIU Angl I/B/54 bis/9994.

35 An article, datelined Bucharest, 30 June, discussed the problem Roumanian Jewish flight created for all the countries through which refugees passed. 'Die rumänische Judenswanderung', *Frankfurter Zeitung*, no. 185, 7 July 1900.

Roumanian government would not permit. The Budapest Jewish Relief Society found money to pay their train fares from Kronstadt to Vienna. In Vienna the local Alliance Israélite bought them tickets for Rotterdam but gave them nothing more.

All wished to go to Canada. When they arrived in Rotterdam, the police refused to allow them into the city. They were kept under strict surveillance in the police court while their case was considered. The magistrates informed them they would have to go back to Bucharest. The men asked for a forty-eight hour delay, sold some of their possessions to raise the money to eat, and sent a deputation to Frankfurt. Frankfurt relief organizations paid their fares to London and promised to inform London and Paris of their decision. With tickets in hand, they were placed by Rotterdam police on board their steamer, but no one bothered to tell London. When the group landed, it dispatched a deputation to the great champion of Roumanian Jews, Dr Moses Gaster, Haham of the Spanish and Portuguese congregation, and asked for the money Frankfurt authorities promised would be forthcoming from France to pay for the next leg of their journey. Gaster, who had nothing, sent them to Claude Montefiore, the president of the Anglo-Jewish Association.

Montefiore immediately took the group to Hermann Landau who arranged for their feeding and accommodation at the Poor Jews' Temporary Shelter. The two of them examined the new arrivals and felt that most of them seemed 'strong and capable'. The party was still determined to settle in Canada, and, unlike many groups, the men appeared to have a reasonable prospect of making new lives for themselves. Montefiore gambled. He decided to dispatch all seventy-five, arranged berths for them on a ship from Liverpool departing on the night of 2 July. He wrote to Narcisse Leven, president of the Jewish Colonisation Association in Paris, for reimbursement for the funds advanced, presuming that the Jewish Colonisation Association would pay. Montefiore explained proudly that he had used his influence to achieve a 'group rate'. He convinced the shipping company to reduce the usual £5 4s fare to £3 17s 6d. The seventy-five would reach Montreal in ten days. Montefiore telegraphed Canada and arranged to open a line of credit charged to the Jewish Colonisation Association to settle the new arrivals. No one from the group, warned Montefiore, must be permitted to drift into the United States. Impressed that the refugees, who clearly knew what questions they were going to be asked and what answers they should give, were 'anxious to work on the land', Montefiore suggested that Leven recommend to the Montreal committee that these immigrants could do harvest work when Leven sent the money Montefiore had authorized. Roumanians, he observed, had one advantage. Some could speak French, so their adaptation would be simpler than it was for many Jewish immigrants. They would, of course, need warmer clothing, but that should be provided in Quebec. Montefiore, properly schooled in Russo-Jewish Committee and Poor Jews' Temporary Shelter policies, proudly announced that the Roumanians were given no money for incidental expenses, for such people 'should not be encouraged'.[36]

Complicated and difficult as it was for them, the seventy-five Roumanians were a special case, rather easier than most. Their success depended on finding just the right help from just the right people at just the right time. Matters could rarely go so

36 Montefiore to Leven, 1 July 1900, AIU Angl I/D/17/9911.

smoothly. Canada, moreover, was not a fully satisfactory destination. The country could only absorb experienced, capable agriculturalists. Few migrants were, most being 'hawkers and dealers'. Those going to Canada, moreover, often found it or hoped to use it as a way of slipping into the United States. Canadian Jewish administration was 'very defective', although Montefiore and Rothschild hoped that matters might be improved by bringing experienced people from New York to manage affairs in Montreal. When numbers ran out of hand as, given Roumanian emotions and Austro-German anxieties, they were likely to do, Anglo-Jewry often threatened to pack any refugees who landed in Britain, even those who were ticketed transmigrants, back to the continent, insisting that they be processed direct to their final destinations.

The most charitable of Anglo-Jewish leaders issued an ultimatum to their continental counterparts. British Jewry would only be a party to fully coordinated migration. They would 'refuse absolutely to be the means or conduit pipe for sending any more out'. Leven and the Jewish Colonisation Association had helped these Roumanians get to England. Were they to fail in Canada, Anglo-Jewry would send them right back to the French. The British used this occasion to refuse to be a party to any further unsystematic migration. Their French counterparts acceded, agreed, and used the Alliance and Jewish Colonisation Association connections and European offices to bring matters back under control.[37]

Ultimately Montefiore and Anglo-Jewry hoped to find other options, perhaps in Australia and New Zealand for suitable, able-bodied refugees, but any effective response demanded a screening of potential refugees in Roumania, simplifying the migration route (preferably keeping it out of England or France), and a considerable amount of money. Since New York was now as anxious as London and Paris to shunt immigrants to other points, it, too, could raise money, particularly for Canadian settlements. When French and English Jews discussed 'ransom' in connection with refugees, they literally meant it. Cash contributions, funding the refugee and migration network, was the price they would pay to keep migrant poor out of their own countries. Pay for them or take them were the accepted alternatives. Other Jewish committees accepted the same principle.

> We, on our part, conscious of the difficulty of adding to the number of the refugees in this Country, when the market is already glutted with labour, have already agreed to pay 'ransom' money, £30,000, as our contribution towards the emigration and settlement in America, and are prepared to abide by our bargain.[38]

37 The English found themselves with three groups of nearly two hundred Roumanian Jews each deposited in London in a matter of a few days. The Temporary Shelter could not accommodate them. Liverpool could not export them. Some forty-six found work but displaced other Jews by working for lower wages. Over a hundred were 'floating about in London'. The matter was urgent. The sudden inrush triggered discussion in the House of Commons on 5 July. Rothschild to Leven, 6 July; Bigart à Montefiore, 8 juil. 1900, AIU Angl I/D/17/9898, 9911, 9964.

38 Joseph reminded the French that if they had not yet paid their ransom 'as the price of exemption from refugees', they must be prepared to take all refugees permitted to pass through Germany. Joseph to Bigart, 20 Jan. 1892, AIU Angl I/H/7/7730. The Stettauer Papers show the 1906 allocations. Britain and abroad (including Hirsch funds and money from the United States) would contribute £444,284 12s. The Hilfsverein paid 550,000 marks, the AIU 350,000 francs, the Hilfszentrum, 130,000 marks, the Vienna Allianz 19,201.91 roubles. A further 434,028.15 roubles would come from Russia, while 'other' groups would provide 10,737.56 roubles. Stettauer Papers, AJ/22.

To meet the immediate problems of Roumanian refugees, the Russo-Jewish Committee contributed £1,000, and British Jewish leaders prodded the Jewish Colonisation Association to continue its capitation contributions. They also demanded that the Alliance Israélite maintain discipline over its Central European branches to prevent any further uncoordinated dispatch of refugees.[39]

Polish and Russian refugees were more manageable in that the numbers were substantial and constant enough to justify creating and maintaining a system for processing would-be immigrants. Anglo-Jewry had sprung into action to organize and process those fleeing the pogroms of 1881 and 1882. During its the first year of operation, the Mansion House Committee (later called the Russo-Jewish Committee) dispatched 8,500 'carefully selected' refugees to the United States, but almost 15,000 Russian Jews 'many of whom were sent by various irresponsible persons and Committees' reached New York. The British took strong exception to American bills. Anglo-Jewry felt professional New York Jewish agency officials created unjustifiable administrative costs and managed matters inefficiently, but Anglo-Jewry's power to remonstrate or influence was no stronger than New York's need for English money. Jewish Aid Societies in Chicago and Cincinnati, the two most important centres outside New York, were no better, being too busy quarrelling with one another to process refugees efficiently. Ettinger's Jewish colony failed in Los Angeles. Philadelphia showed no capacity to manage its own. Newly-arrived refugee colonists tended to drift back to New York. Alternatives were badly needed.[40]

By mid-1882, the Mansion House Committee which managed the substantial funds contributed for refugee aid classified their charges in three groups. The first were those whom Anglo-Jewry, in cooperation with the Vienna Allianz, processed through their own local committees in Lemberg and Brody. Dr Asher Asher and Samuel Montagu had organized these for the Mansion House Committee during their special mission to Galicia. Paid committee agents selected refugees at the Russian frontier. The chosen travelled at committee expense to a camp at Brody. Here they underwent a further screening. Those approved were sent to Lemberg for yet another screening. Those finally accepted were then shipped from Lemberg to Hamburg, processed through the Jews' Temporary Shelter, on to Liverpool, and from thence overseas. The Mansion House Committee paid for clothing and housing as needed. Refugees were dispatched, fares paid, to their final destinations in the United States or Canada. On-site committees, particularly the Hebrew Emigration Aid Society of New York, received a small contribution to be given to each immigrant to start his new life. This arrangement, orderly and bureaucratic as it was, affected only a fraction of migrants. The committee also assisted fugitives dispatched to London by the Hamburg and Berlin committees and considered case-by-case those who arrived in England at their own expense. Some remained in

39 Montefiore to Leven, 6 July, 6 July; Montefiore to Bigart 16 June, 21 June, Bigart à Montefiore, 24 juin 1900, AIU Angl I/D/17/9686, 9778, 9959, 9964.
40 Goldsmid to Loeb, 31 July,1 Aug; Cohen to AIU, 2 Apr; Joseph to Loeb, 4 , 19, 23, 29 June, 4 July,19 Dec. 1882, AIU Angl I/B/15/3329,3340; I/B/54 bis/1707; I/H/7/2534, 2724, 2778, 2858, 2918, 4953.

England. Most, however, continued, with full or partial committee aid, to the United States.

Those arriving on their own initiative created the most difficulty. Were they refugees or just emigrants? The Conjoint Committee of the Mansion House Fund (which became the Russo-Jewish Committee) and Jewish Board of Guardians attempted to screen the deserving and undeserving, but they confronted the serious difficulty of those too old, too weak, or unfit for emigration. Since they reached England at their own expense, Jewish agencies might cajole but could not force them to return to the Russian Empire. Anglo-Jewry did its best to do so, but the inevitable numbers who remained grew, creating a growing burden for communal relief agencies.[41]

Triage, to which Anglo-Jewry had never been hostile in principle, was a policy of necessity. However necessary, triage posed a moral dilemma and administrative burden. Not surprisingly, some Jewish leaders began to see some form of legislative immigration restriction, so long as legitimate refugees were protected, as a positive good. Others, who participated regularly in their own exclusionist policies, felt strongly that Jews should never voluntarily relinquish such decisions to state authority.

Processing agencies occasionally found themselves with Jews who could neither be moved onwards nor repatriated. The Russo-Jewish Committee ultimately supported several hundred Bessarabian Jews. When the territory was awarded to Roumania, they had refused to register as Russians, were treated as Turks, expelled and sent to Salonika. Unwelcome there in a community dominated by privileged Sephardim, the survivors of malaria-ridden Salonika slums came to England. The Russo-Jewish Committee found them to be unassimilable and wished to repatriate them. But to where? They denied being Russian, were not acceptable to Roumania, and had no home in the Balkans. The only option available to the committee, as Nathan Joseph tartly observed, was to drown them. Even these seemingly intractable cases, however, ultimately adapted to life and work in England, although not without drawing heavily on committee funds. If they could grow strong and prosper in England, Joseph argued, perhaps any immigrant, properly supported, could do so.[42]

Refugees, no less than other migrants, sometimes had second thoughts. Those who fled from Poland and Russia in the pogroms of 1881 and 1882 did not all wish to stay where they were placed. By mid-1882, a small but significant number began to drift back to Europe and homes left behind. For some the familiar world of the Pale, however bad, was no worse than what they felt they confronted in new and strange places. A few were homesick. Others just could not cope. Some had been troublesome – such as the twenty-five adults and children returning to Antwerp from the United States in July 1882 who pestered the Hebrew Emigrant Aid Society for help in New York but refused to do any work.

Each returning individual and family meant money lost. Returnees, moreover, had prevented some other 'deserving case' from escaping under committee

---

41 Joseph to Loeb, 17 May 1882, AIU Angl I/H/7.
42 Joseph testimony before RCAI, 12, 20 Mar 1903.

auspices. Anglo-Jewish leaders, understandably frustrated, condemned the lay-abouts and homesick as 'in all probability the most helpless or the most idle of those who found their way over the sea'. Some advocated yet another screening test. Sir Julian Goldsmid, then president of the Anglo-Jewish Association, asked the Alliance Israélite to offer the Jews at shelters in Baltic ports or in the refugee camps passage back to their native country to catch those having second or third thoughts about the new world. Criteria for selection were made more rigorous, and the Brody processing centre became a byword for turning people back. To some extent, Anglo-Jewish readiness to assist was a function of its capacity to dispose of those who shared its bounty. New York had been quickly saturated, and no alternatives save the more costly options of Natal or the Cape Colony seemed readily available in 1882. Attenuated persecution, moreover, appeared to mean that matters were improving in Russia. Rather than risk failures and costly returns, Nathan Joseph considered that repatriation 'will soon be the safest and most desirable course'.[43] Joseph, who had done so much to design English policies, was whistling in the dark. Improvement was temporary and illusory. The Frankfurt committee, which met regularly to arrange the shipments and set quasi-quotas, needed more and more colonies.

If Los Angeles failed, Vineland, New Jersey, a Russo-Jewish Committee project developed in 1885, prospered. Sir Alexander Galt, the Canadian statesman, undertook to settle nearly fifty families in Manitoba. A new Emigrants Aid Society and Labor Bureau in Philadelphia offered better prospects than the thornier United Hebrew Charities Committee of New York. Samuel Montagu crossed the Atlantic 'and found even that body adverse to any action tending to moderate the harsh tendency of local port authorities'. Demands were greater than ever. Expelled Russian-Jewish students, yet another target of the Russian authorities, became a constant charge on Anglo-Jewry's books by 1885. Imperial German restiveness with large numbers of 'foreign' Jews meant that only Jews with through tickets would be allowed to enter the country. That laid on British, French, Dutch and American shoulders the problem of creating still more agricultural colonies, principally in Palestine and North America.[44]

Anglo-Jewry, to its annoyance, found itself put in the same position that it had placed the United States. When Bismarck, responding to Prussian pressure, expelled Polish nationals from Prussian territory, many Jews opted to migrate to England rather than return to Russian oppression and Polish anti-Semitism. Anglo-Jewry could not send them back through the normal channels, for they could not land in Hamburg without showing that they had tickets or the fare to return to

---

43 Joseph to Loeb, 19, 23, 29 June, 4 July 1882, AIU Angl I/H/7/2724, 2778, 2858, 2918; Goldsmid to Loeb, 28, 31 July, 1 Aug. 1882. AIU Angl I/B/15/3303, 3329, 3340. On the general theme of encouraging Eastern Jews to stay put and strive, with Western aid, for political emancipation, see Zosa Szajkowski, 'Emigration to America or reconstruction in Europe', *Publications of the American Jewish Historical Society*, 42/2 (1952), 157–88.

44 See, e.g., Joseph to Loeb, 27 March, 25 Apr., 23 May, 22 Oct 1884; 15 Jan. 1885, 25 Oct. 1886; 4 July,19 Sept., 23 Dec. 1888; Loeb circular letter, sept. 1885, AIU Angl I/H/7/8991, 9107, 9139, 9221, 10000, 8609, 8629, 7292, 6633, 6663, 6925.

Russia. An alternative landing site was finally arranged in Rotterdam, and an arrangement made whereby the burden of costs could be met in instalments and shared.[45]

Russo-Polish Jewish settlers, refugee or immigrant, still poured into and settled in the East End. By the 1890s, Anglo-Jewry's social institutions were working at or beyond their capacity to socialize those who, for whatever reason, chose to remain in England. After six months, newcomers technically became eligible for Jewish Board of Guardians assistance and support. Few who failed to meet the demanding standards of the board applied for aid. Over 90 per cent of cases the board investigated received some assistance. This might, to be sure, be no more than a steerage ticket outward to the United States or back to the Russian Empire, but the overwhelming majority of applicants, native or alien, were clearly 'deserving' in Anglo-Jewish eyes. By the mid-1890s, the burden, while heavy, was shifting. Russo-Jewish aliens imposed the greatest burden on the board, but the longer they had been in the country, the less likely they were to need assistance.[46]

Anglo-Jewry's patience and support never appeared to waver, but by 1900, a continual querulous tone runs through the private correspondence. Benjamin Louis Cohen, president of the Board of Guardians, and Conservative member of parliament, had already made a public statement in favour of immigration restriction, provided always 'that precautions were taken to preserve inviolate the right of asylum'.[47] Cohen's Board of Guardians, so burdened with debt, blamed Russo-Polish Jewish immigration. American Jews, staggering under far heavier welfare costs, suggested that the English were not doing enough. As early as 1890, New York was urging British, French and German Jewish relief organizations to support the families of poor emigrants in their own countries, while the wage earners went to the United States and established themselves.[48]

Western Jewry held simultaneously contradictory opinions about what East European Jews should know. Since they assumed that Jews who could escape to the West would prefer to do so, Western Jewish organizations provided as little information or encouragement as possible. Once again, they invoked the principle of 'less eligibility'. Only those whose survival depended on escape would make their way to the frontiers. Once there, processing agencies and camps turned 'the helpless hopeless cases' around and sent them back to Russia, considering their act a kindness. As a result, rumour, fantasy, and information from those who had already migrated West blended with equal weight. Efficiency demanded some cost-effective and humane institutions to process and protect the emigrants. But

45 Gartner, *Jewish Immigrant*, 44n; *JC*, 5, 15 Nov. 1886.

46 JBG, *Annual Report* for 1897 (London, 1898), 41ff.

47 *The Times*, 21 Mar. 1894. Cohen's position remained consistent over the next decade, and he voted for the Aliens Act of 1905. Gartner implies, I think unfairly, that his baronetcy, was a reward for his advocacy and this vote. The honour, well deserved, came for his leadership of the JBG through difficult years, for his personal and financial support of the Conservative party, and for his role in the life of the City. Joseph believed, as Gartner observes without the same criticism, that immigration restriction was 'humanitarian'. *JC*, 6 Apr. 1906. Cf. Gartner, *Jewish Immigrant*, 55.

48 Cohen to Loeb, 14 Dec.; Joseph to Loeb 16 Dec. 1890; Adler to Lévi, 1 June 1893, AIU Angl I/B/54 bis/5039, 9907; I/H/7/9939.

well-publicized processing agencies, so Western Jewry believed, would exacerbate the difficulties by creating a westward stampede of East European Jews. As a result, frontier handling posts fulfilled some of the worst anxieties of their sponsors.[49] News of vast philanthropic enterprises, moreover, were presumed to rouse excessive expectations, so would-be immigrants were often totally in the dark about what could and could not be done. Philanthropic assistance to refugees, moreover, also might imply that Russia had the right to expel her Jewish subjects, an intolerable notion to Western Jewry. Persecution should not, they felt, be seen as a 'chronic disorder', but only as 'an acute and temporary insanity of Russia and her Czar'.[50]

Colonization, whether the ambitious plans of Baron de Hirsch, the several enterprises initiated by Franco- and Anglo-Jewry, or the Palestinian colonies of Baron Edmond de Rothschild, could at best handle but a small percentage of the five million Jews of Imperial Russia. Functioning effectively, such enterprises could only process suitable colonists:

> for those who have been clerks, shopmen, dealers, pedlars, hawkers, glazers, old clothes' men, there is no future in any colony, least of all in a new colony – that for the aged, the decrepit, the diseased, the weak and incapable [Hirsch's] scheme has no chance of success . . .[51]

New York, for all the problems involved, remained the greatest hope. Colonel Weber, chief commissioner of immigration at the Castle Garden depot, had been among the champions of immigrant and refugee Jews. His latitudinarian standards minimized repatriation. When Weber came to Europe to investigate the problem of Russian persecution and Jewish refugees, he was carefully briefed and much fêted. While the best prospects for Jewish resettlement, the Russo-Jewish Committee believed, remained the United States, 'except overcrowded cities', British colonies in the temperate zone, South American republics, and possibly Egypt, Central America and the West Indies offered some prospects. Alexandria was conveniently close for settling Odessa refugees, but was not well regarded. Palestine, given the unpredictability and capriciousness of Ottoman officials and poor economic prospects even when settlements could be established, did not figure on the Russo-Jewish Committee list, although that body made no final judgement about Chovevei Zion plans laid before it. Argentina remained the best hope in Latin America. A German conjoint committee investigation repeated the depressing social and political news the British had already learned about Brazil.

Even the British Empire, save for Canada, seemed expensive and to offer limited possibilities. Travel to Cape Town cost too much, and that city still lacked Jewish-sponsored projects and seemed to hold little commercial opportunity. Port Elizabeth was still more expensive, Johannesburg prohibitively so, and the cost of

49 See, e.g., Joseph's observation that any agency, at the frontier or elsewhere, would be a constant invitation to emigration 'and would probably increase the evil it was intended to cure'. Joseph to Loeb, 16 Dec 1890, AIU Angl I/H/7/9939. For the best general discussion, see Gartner, *Jewish Immigrant*, chapter 2.

50 Joseph to Loeb, 30 May 1891, AIU Angl I/H/7/5659.

51 Ibid. See also Joseph to Bigart, 24 Mar. 1892, AIU Angl I/H/7/7972.

living in each was 'enormous'. Black Africans provided a strong, capable manual labour force with which Jewish immigrants could not possibly compete. India was not considered. Australia and New Zealand, with their high transportation costs, offered scanty prospects even when reached. Not only were known opportunities limited to able-bodied, young, single men, but the ascendant Labour party built its programme on protecting high wage rates, so politics militated against opportunities for new workers.[52] Given the problems of resettlement and colonization, small wonder that Anglo-Jewry and the Alliance Israélite toyed with Arnold White's proposal for Jewish agricultural settlements in southern Russia. Much de Hirsch money and effort, after all, was expended to make better lives for Jews within that Empire.[53]

The Russo–Japanese war abruptly increased the number of immigrants to be processed, principally across the Atlantic. Jewish reservists and conscripts understandably displayed even less enthusiasm for Mother Russia's wars than Russian and Polish Jewish aliens were to show for service in the British forces between 1914 and 1917. The cry of political persecution brought in fresh funds, but the reality almost overwhelmed the now well-seasoned agencies. Volunteers from the Jewish Board of Guardians, the Anglo-Jewish Association, and the Russian-Jewish Committee assisted in the demanding rota sittings to process the new arrivals, and the immediate crisis passed.[54]

So smoothly did the operations go that the increasing numbers being processed almost evaded the hawk eyes of anti-alien agitators. The winter of 1903–4, however, severely depleted resources. The Poor Jews' Temporary Shelter had to arrange the housing and feeding of 4,247 over the winter, before dispatching the majority to Canada and substantial numbers to Argentina and the United States. A considerable number of would-be Canadian emigrants, moreover, were deflected from Vienna to Antwerp and shipped directly from there without ever landing in England. Impostors coming to England were rigorously weeded out and repatriated as a warning to others about abusing the status of political refugee, and as a demonstration to British authorities that Jewish agencies ran an adequate programme of immigration control.[55] Repatriation, moreover, was not free. The Board of Guardians and Russo-Jewish Committee charged a minimum of 15s 'from such persons who could

52 'Such a staunch friend of our people should be well received wherever there are Jews', wrote Joseph to Loeb, suggesting that he make certain Weber be introduced to the Rothschilds when in Paris. Joseph to Loeb, 24 July, 30 May, 9, 22, 24, 30 Sept., 17 Nov. 1891; Joseph to Bigart, 26 Feb., 24 Mar. 1892, AIU Angl I/H/7/6663,5659, 7027, 7108, 7126, 7156, 7416, 7875, 7972; Russo-Jewish Committee, *First Report of the Intelligence Department* (December 1891).

53 Joseph to Bigart, 29 Oct. 1891, 11, 18, 24 Mar., 6 May 1892, AIU Angl I/H/7/7324, 7921, 7950, 7972, 8139.

54 See the discussion of the JTS appeal in *JC*, 27 Jan. 1905. 'The industrial conditions of this country prevent the settlement here of any large number of these refugees, so the majority of the fugitives from Russian military service are being emigrated to Canada and Argentina, where special arrangements are being made for their reception and employment.' Report of the Russo-Jewish and Board of Guardians Conjoint Committee, JBG, *Annual Report* for 1904 (1905).

55 Russo-Jewish Committee, *Annual Report* (1904). The *Daily Mail*, king of the tabloids, warned against the growing influx of aliens, aliens as a threat to public health, and forgery as particularly an immigrant crime. The paper's attention turned, however, within a day from Jews to Macedonian gypsies. *Daily Mail*, 1, 2 Dec. 1904.

show no valid reason for coming'. After 1900, the charge rose to a minimum of £1 and a maximum of 30s regardless. The Board of Guardians offered repatriation as its only form of relief to more and more applicants.[56]

By the early 1890s, the Board of Trade, the Home Office, the Metropolitan Police and such Jewish agencies as the Russo-Jewish Committee and the Poor Jews' Temporary Shelter had begun to attack the problems of immigration with a shared understanding, if not a common policy. By 1891 the Jewish Society for the Protection of Girls and Women stationed a man in uniform to interview and collect those travelling without adult males. A representative of the Temporary Shelter met all boats and attempted to move those lacking family connections through the shelter. From July 1897, the police protected lady social workers on the docks who were attempting to shepherd newly-arrived unaccompanied women. The Russo-Jewish Committee and Jewish Board of Guardians also made every effort to deflect Hamburg arrivals (and also made a point of informing public authorities about their efforts). The Jews' Temporary Shelter, for instance, conceded that while its more than 2,000 immigrants in 1890 represented a 45 per cent rise from 1889, the proportion of transmigrants had risen from 27 per cent to 55 per cent. These were new, more promising immigrants and transmigrants. Less than ten per cent of shelter's clients 'lacked a trade'. At the same time, almost three hundred newcomers were returned to their native land. The shelter believed that those now settled in England and the United States had by the 1890s passed the word back to Poland and Russia that any male 'without a calling' risked rejection at his port of entry.[57]

PROCESSING AND ADAPTATION

Once landed in England, immigrants confronted a panoply of socializing institutions. Those who brought them had their own ideas. Montagu, Landau and their colleagues were as determined as Cohen and Mocatta to socialize foreign Jews in appropriate ways. Such differences as existed between, for instance, the Jewish Board of Guardians and the Russo-Jewish Committee were merely tactical, ones of degree not of kind. Montagu, Landau and those who thought like them may have been slightly more sympathetic to the shock of first arrival. Certainly they preserved familiar rituals and exploited a spirit of *Landsmannschaft* as the most effective way to move aliens towards anglicized Jewish life. They coaxed more than they bullied. Montagu's Federation of small, linked synagogues drew newcomers gradually but surely into English life. They seemed less threatening, overpowering and strange than United Synagogue facilities. But Montagu and Landau were as determined to anglicize their 'foreigners' as any other Anglo-Jewish leaders. Newcomers confronted the world of

56 Cohen testimony to RCAI, 12 Mar. 1903.

57 Landau to Warren, 24 July 1887; Police Order, 'H' Division, 30 July 1887; Supt Roberts' Report, 11 Jan. 1891; Board of Trade (BT) to MEPO, 22 Dec. 1890, 19 Jan. 1892. A police report of 2 January 1891 described the Jews' Temporary Shelter as an institution with the 'principal objective to diminish, insofar as possible, the number settling in the East End.' MEPO 2/260; *Fifth Annual Report, Poor Jews' Temporary Shelter, 1889–1890* (London, 1890); *Sixth Annual Report, Poor Jews' Temporary Shelter ,1890–1891* (London, 1891); F. E. Ellis, 'Alien Immigration (May 1904)', HO 45/10241/B37811/15.

Samuel Smiles and self-help even in the Temporary Shelter, where the able-bodied were expected to perform labour service. From that tattered building on Leman Street, the newly-arrived began their socialization.

Old institutions and new were brought to bear. The 'foreign' Jews learned English. They were taught sanitary habits that were not only good for them but would render them less offensive to their English neighbours. They were offered opportunities to prosper in the English world by English rules and English criteria. And, within the clear limits of the situation and class opportunity, many of them did. East European Jewish immigration built the British cheap clothing trade, developing both significant British exports and furnishing a wide and inexpensive range of clothes for the least affluent members of British society. The 'democracy of modern dress' was, to a great degree, their creation.[58] They created a new world of entrepreneurship and opportunity, and they exploited kith and kin to make it grow. The putting-out system revived in the sweatshop of 'bespoke' tailoring. The modest capital required for very small workshops and the constant supply of 'greener' labour simultaneously provided human exploitation and opportunities for mobility comparable only to those of the early days of British industrial development. Within broad and significant limits, the ideal world of Samuel Smiles had been recreated in microcosm. Nothing, however, was predictable in that world. The father's success or failure, so ran the common assumption, determined the fate of the family.

Meir Bloomstein, of a relatively prosperous Hasidic family, landed in England in about 1888 with his second wife and four children. He failed in a small woollen business in England just as he had earlier failed as a timber merchant in Poland. Meir and his wife returned to Poland, but their sons were left in England. They lived with a widow from the same home town to avoid returning and being conscripted into the Russian army. Henry Bloomstein, who clung to Hasidism and Yiddish, ultimately prospered in London, a tribute to his own version of the self-help that Anglo-Jewry preached. His path was anything but easy, and success actually came only in the 1920s. Through the years of adversity, if Henry needed assistance, he found it among his kin, his Hasidic synagogue, or landsmen, and never, apparently, turned at any time to that plethora of institutions Anglo-Jewry had been at such pains to construct.[59]

Arnold White, the great apostle of national efficiency who devoted much effort to attacking the alien menace, also brought forcefully to the attention of authorities the fact that the worst abuses in sweating were not in the East End but at Chatham. The

---

58 A. A. Baumann, 'Possible remedies for the sweating system', *National Review*, XII/69 (November 1888), 292–3. Tailoring led all occupations. Jews as masters and workforce swarmed to it, and tailoring continued to lead London Jewish occupations through the First World War. Jacobs, *Jewish Statistics*, section 5, pp. 33–40; RCIA (1903), statistical appendix, table LXI. Booth's survey describes the tailoring trade in *Life and Labour*, I, 209–40.

59 See John Cooper, 'Two East End Jewish families: the Bloomsteins and the Isenbergs', in Newman (ed.), *Jewish East End*, 59–73.

master tailor of the marine barracks established a putting-out system exploiting soldiers' and pensioners' wives. A court of inquiry found witnesses intimidated and the practices difficult to untangle but concluded: 'The fact of the master-tailor receiving no official salary, and therefore being obliged to make his profit out of the workers appears to your Committee to be a premium on sweating.'[60] Strange people, crowded housing, industrious people anxious to work and willing to take low wages and harsh conditions – all these forced some measure of upward social mobility among the native English among whom they settled. But for the tradesmen whose more affluent customers moved onwards, for the marginal craftsman in under-capitalized industries, for those hostile to new people and different ways, those aliens represented a threat that must be brought under control.

Sir Samuel Montagu, who had as much experience in all aspects of the business as any Anglo-Jew, believed that Jewish immigrants adapted well. They were 'orderly and peaceable', 'grateful and loyal to countries in which they were fairly treated'. 'If I thought they would injure the state, I would keep them out, but since they ultimately benefit the state as well as themselves, I would like them to come in.'[61]

Official British policy concerning alien immigration developed only after the problem, in its acute form, had passed. East European Jewish immigration had peaked and was already beginning to subside by the end of the nineteenth century. Anxiety about what might happen rather than something that was happening served as an excuse for legislation. The United States adopted a law in 1903 more clearly defining the unsatisfactory immigrant, adding a slightly ambiguous literacy test. Even the more sensible British officials feared that such legislation might wash the least desirable immigrants back on to British shores. Officials on the scene in Eastern Europe, like Alexander Murray, British consul in Warsaw, fed these anxieties. Murray spoke warmly of the 'better' immigrants, but

> The unfortunate part of the Jewish element is that almost all who emigrate from here are petty hawkers and men without definite occupation, who cannot work at any trade and would not if they could; it is the disadvantage even of the Jewish workman, hardworking and clever craftsman as he is, that so soon as he has got a little money together he abandons work to open a shop.
>
> As to morals, the trading Jews, though personally free from sexual immorality and its consequences, and good family men, are an active poison wherever they are, as they are the receivers of stolen goods, procurers of girls, swindlers in business and at the back of every description of fraud.[62]

---

60 Report of the Select Committee of the House of Commons on the Sweating System. (1889), qq 1330–33, 1598, 15925, 15944–5, 16177, 16193, 16233, 16236, 16240–8, 16277, 16428, 16439, 16451–4, second report appendix D; fifth report, p. xxxviii.; qq 29322–634. The Manchester Society of Tailors joined the chorus decrying the influx of Jewish tailors who cut rates, although the president of the union also contended 'the greatest possible harmony' existed between Jews and Christians and that both worked together in shops, qq 29771–30939.

61 Montagu's testimony before the RCAI, 23 Mar. 1903, was candid, firm and reasonable. It is also extremely informative about communal assumptions and institutions.

62 Murray to Lansdowne, 10 Feb. 1905, HO 45/10303/117267.

Every myth, every fear had become inextricably linked with the development of public policy. That Anglo-Jewry shared such anxieties without being able publicly to say so was counterbalanced by Anglo-Jewish determination to continue to make the rules for its own community. From such a confusion of motives and purposes grew the agitation for what would become the Aliens Act of 1905.

10

The Struggle for the Aliens Act

The splendid benefactions of the Rothschilds and other leaders of the Jewish community to their co-religionists in the East-end are as a lamp set on a hill to those in Eastern Europe who are tormented by the agents of resolute government until they consent to emigrate. The absence of military conscription, the existence of an indiscriminating people, and the reputation enjoyed by England for sympathy with distress in every form, are forces which not only draw the pauper foreigner to these shores in ever increasing numbers, but spread the impression that England is a place where, at all events, the wicked cease troubling, and where a quiet and supportable existence for those whose standard of comfort and cleanliness are lower than our own are certain to be found.

So wrote Arnold White in yet another of his frenetic efforts to mobilize public opinion against 'the alien menace'.[1] Most such campaigners began by disavowing any hostility to Jews. But audience and author alike knew what they meant. Whether avowing protection for native labour, national efficiency, or wrapping itself in the Union Jack, immigration restriction meant, first and foremost, keeping East European Jews out of England. Anti-Semitism, while a commonplace of modern British culture, expressed itself more generally in attitudes rather than action. But the 1880s were unusual times. The 'Great Depression' (1873–96), the first sustained check to Victorian economic growth, shook British confidence more than it damaged the British economy. Economic competition, particularly the rapid growth of Germany and the United States, forced the British to confront a simple reality. The United Kingdom had become one of the leading economic powers, rather than the dominant one. Weaker sections of the British economy suffered

1 Arnold White letter to *The Times*, 30 May 1887. See the effective reply of Stephen N. Fox, 'The invasion of pauper foreigners', *Contemporary Review* (June 1888), 855–67 to Arnold White's article in *Nineteenth Century* (March 1888) where Fox points out, among other things, that Booth's estimate of the entire Jewish community from which White was demanding protection was 45,000 out of a metropolitan population in excess of five million.

most, as they were bound to. Economic growth always proceeds by displacement, where more effective activities supplant less competitive ones. But that development, 'forced efficiency', aggravated tensions always present in the more marginal quarters of society. The word 'unemployed' officially entered the *Oxford English Dictionary*. The considerably higher rates of economic growth in Imperial Germany and the United States precipitated a spate of British proposals for easy cures. Economically counterproductive, socially deceptive, politically illusory and often morally repugnant, these ranged from the ostensible, if fictitious, benefits of imperialism to panaceas of economic and social protectionism. The heady nationalism of nineteenth-century Europe encouraged an English cult of patriotism in all its less attractive forms. From Oxford common-rooms to children's literature, from Pall Mall clubs to the music-halls, the foreigner was belittled and 'being British' elevated to a way of life. The Irish had long felt this cutting edge of prejudice and responded by increasingly opting for their own national existence. English Jews, however, wanted to be British and had gone to considerable lengths to ensure that more recently arrived Jews did too.

Immigrant Russian and Polish Jews encountered this different culture and newly sharpened prejudices. They also augmented a Jewish community that was now highly visible. Being concentrated in the East End of London, rather than the docklands of Liverpool or the industrial sprawl of Glasgow or Manchester, they were more likely to be singled out by journalists and politicians as 'the Jew'. The disruption of local culture, a process in which newly arrived Jews were but one of many factors, generated discontent and fear. Anglo-Jewry understood all this and attempted through its network of educational and social institutions to respond as rationally as possible. Rationality, however, is not necessarily a highly effective response to deeply felt emotional problems.

East European immigrants on balance, quickly generated demonstrable gains for the British economy. They created a ready-made clothing trade that enabled British workers to emancipate themselves from used clothes dealers and shoddy goods. That same industry carved out substantial markets overseas for a British export economy increasingly hard pressed to compete. But immigrant Jews were different. They could be singled out as a source of social dislocation and poverty. The numbers of Jewish immigrants involved, even during the years of greatest movement, remained modest, but the newcomers clustered, for understandable reasons, not merely in London but in the East End. That area, moreover, was itself undergoing substantial change, Jews or no Jews. The old trades, particularly sugar refining and the London docks, were in sharp decline. As in all districts adjoining the City of London, housing could not compete with commercial and business needs. That meant the steady displacement of houses for factories, warehouses, railway sidings and public buildings.

Jewish settlement grew most rapidly in two parishes of the borough of Stepney: Whitechapel and St George's-in-the-East. Whitechapel housing stock shrank substantially. The East End, moreover, was a convenient laboratory for a boom generation of would-be social scientists anxious to study and learn but still carrying old prejudices and assumptions. Unsophisticated observers saw the departure of the Irish and English poor and their replacement by Jews, and presumed a causal relationship. Upwardly mobile Jews already had their well-defined migratory routes from the ghetto, principally to the north and west of London. Whitechapel conveyed a sense of class as well as ethnic concentration. Since its Jews were increasingly newcomers, aliens easily recognizable through appearance, habits and language, relatively small numbers could be made to appear even greater than they were and to pose an easily exaggerated threat to things British.

Arnold White, one of the leading journalistic spokesmen for 'national efficiency', conveyed a deputation of aggrieved workers to the Home Office in December 1887. As 'exhibits', the term he used, he also produced four Poles, two of whom had arrived in England during the past week. The Poles knew no trade and were presently paying a sweater to teach them one. The rudimentary skills they sought to learn, argued White, given the low wages they would accept, would enable them to displace the young women garment-makers in his deputation. The late Victorian world, while not disturbed by the fact that women earned far less than men for comparable tasks, was unprepared to cope with male immigrants who would actually undercut women's wages. White's point ran beyond the argument that these Jews displaced native labour, adding to the serious problem of unemployment. He played on a moral theme, well calculated to appeal to the tabloid mind of late Victorian England. Young women thus displaced had to survive, and some would be forced to turn to prostitution. White produced a report on the St George's Rescue Home to prove it. For a government committed, as this one was, to the moral well-being of society and the protection of girls and women, the answer should be immigration restriction. That titillating turn-of-the-century issue, white slavery, could be turned to effective political account. Citing Chief Rabbi Dr Adler:

> The extension of the social evil [of unchaste maidens] to my community may be directly traced to the overstocked labour market and to the Russian persecutions continuing to this day which cause thousands of Jewish girls to arrive at these shores without any means of subsistence.[2]

White then turned Adler's jeremiad round. 'Innocent' English girls lacked the supporting apparatus of the Jewish community. Thus immigration drove hundreds of poor English girls to prostitution. In addition to this increasingly modish 'morality' argument, White produced another law-and-order theme. He offered his

> intimate knowledge of the unemployed and of the Park speakers and drunken rioters, [about whom] I have no hesitation in saying that a very considerable portion of these revolutionary spouters and agitators are of foreign origin. . . .
> By the continuance of this system of unrestricted pauper immigration you are contributing very largely to the present restlessness and to the manner in which English workers and the unemployed are being led astray.[3]

The government, White charged, compounded this problem. The Home Secretary spent £180,000 to shift Scottish crofters to British Columbia to start a new life but failed to close the door through which pauper immigrants poured in to take their

---

2 Deputation to Mr Matthews and Mr Ritchie on pauper immigration, 15 December 1887, HO 45/10062/B2386/8.
3 Ibid.

places. The politics of Jewish alien politics, White continued, were of a piece with their sanitary habits. No snide inference was omitted. Quoting the Jewish Board of Guardians and the Whitechapel district board of works, White embellished his point about uncleanliness, turning it to the 'ironic' point that Jews spread disease to their English neighbours, but they, having adapted themselves to a life of filth, suffered a surprisingly low death rate.

Responding to the argument of the economic benefits Jews had brought to Britain, White contended that they had brought them by driving down the wage rate in the clothing industry by 40 per cent over the past ten years. The easy days were over, and hard times were settling in. Jewish poverty was on the rise. Each year the Jewish Board of Guardians pleaded its greater and greater burden and incapacity to manage in the future. That much-vaunted Jewish claim that they cared for their own, White continued, was untrue. The situation was untenable, and a frightening burden was about to fall on the shoulders of the British taxpayer. Steps could be taken at once. The Foreign Office should instruct all consuls

> in the neighbourhood of the parts whence these foreigners come, to articulate, in the most unmistakable and wide spread manner, the fact that so far from there being a living for these poor people here, directly the contrary is the fact. And it is the more necessary to do that because it is the custom of certain sweating tailors to advertise in Hebrew papers on the borders of Poland that there is plenty of work in England in order to bring people over here that they may make more money as middlemen by keeping wages down.[4]

Great Britain should follow the example of the United States, in so far as possible, to prevent further erosion of native stock. Russian governors were expelling Jews from their provinces. Germany and France had made regulations to protect themselves. England would find itself taking the worst and least fit. Unrestricted immigration weakened Britain's economy, unsettled social order and contributed to moral degeneracy. If the government failed to act, moreover, an aroused public might take matters into its own hands. Look at what was happening not just in Russia but elsewhere on the continent. The longer the alien problem was ignored, the greater the possibility of *Judenhetze*, mass anti-Semitic violence in England itself.[5]

White's rambling indictment appeared in various forms. Others, far less well informed than White, served even more strident fare. White and other restriction-ists usually went to great lengths to deny or conceal hostility to Jews as such. Others showed no interest in camouflage and played maliciously on British prejudice. Hilaire Belloc and G. K. Chesterton, for instance, would shortly bring

4 Ibid.
5 Ibid. White three times attempted to exploit his notoriety from the anti-sweating, anti-immigrant campaigns to win a seat in parliament. Unlike Vincent in Sheffield Central and Evans-Gordon in Stepney, he failed to translate xenophobia and social reform into electoral victory. White ran as a Gladstonian Liberal for Mile End in 1886. Charrington crushed him (2,110 to 1,281). Riding the national restrictionist campaign, White then tried Northumberland, Tyneside division, in 1895, as a Liberal Unionist, only to lose to Gladstonian Liberal J. A. Pease (5,486 to 5,018) in a constituency the Conservatives did not contest. White enjoyed no better fortune in the Liberal landslide of 1906. He lost Londonderry County, Northern division, to the Conservative, H. T. Barrie (4,806 to 2,699).

their literary skills to anti-Semitism. Anglo-Jewry publicly counterattacked in various forums. The Dreyfus case played to its advantage. Overt anti-Semitism became bad form or at least in poor taste. To some extent, representing restrictionism as veiled anti-Semitism was a sound tactic. Jewish patriotism during the Boer War could be cited to counter the suggestion that Jews shirked the obligations of citizenship. Even very poor Jews embodied Victorian bourgeois virtues with their sobriety, morality and strong family life. Few showed better than Britain's Jews how far the virtues of self-help could carry the dedicated practitioner. Community spokesmen lauded and publicized the positive communal achievements.

But Anglo-Jewish success and acculturation left it believing or fearing the potential accuracy of parts, at least, of the indictment. Most of the rambling anti-alien rhetoric had been overwhelmed by facts, although that demonstration merely rendered more strident the words of true believers. Board of Trade reports swept away the 'pauper' myth. Not only did immigrant Jewish aliens not burden the poor rates, but also they did not, as the chairman of the Whitechapel board of guardians reminded the royal commission, displace others and force them into poverty. The Royal Commission on Alien Immigration found no evidence that native workers had been displaced by the newcomers. The 'unwashed' arrivals soon set standards of cleanliness, industry and behaviour far higher than those of their British social counterparts.

The only substantive charge against immigrants, as restrictionists found to their annoyance, concerned housing. Aliens poured into Stepney, spilling over from Whitechapel into St George's-in-the-East and did so far more rapidly than communal institutions could disperse them. Although relatively few penetrated the docklands of Limehouse, Mile End (the other Stepney parish) and the adjoining borough of Bethnal Green saw substantial Jewish growth by the early 1900s. Both positive and negative causes were at work. Newcomers clustered to the reinforcement of kin and co-religionist. Their synagogues, their social institutions, schools for their children and their Yiddish culture centred on the streets radiating from Aldgate. Work, particularly jobs permitting sabbath observance, could be found there. Those seeking to disperse Jewish settlement found that the poor would not move unless these institutions, opportunities, and even sociability could be recreated. The native workers and poor, however, were not significantly displaced by this movement. They were already leaving. The old industries of Stepney were gone or in sharp decline. Sugar refining was no more, and the business of the Port of London continued to fall.[6] The dock strike of 1889, so famous in the annals of labour history, was like so many turn-of-the-century East End trade disputes, a protest against the realities of British economic development. Native workers were already moving away to better opportunities before aliens moved in. Land values everywhere on the perimeter of the City, moreover, made residential housing economically uncompetitive with industrial or commercial use. Unless housing properties delivered a higher and higher return, market pressure would mean conversion.

Many East End immigrant Jews lived in rack-rented rabbit warrens, turned all too often to the same few overcrowded trades, but they were set apart in their deficiencies

6 On the general problem, see *inter alia* D. L. Munby, *Industry and Planning in Stepney* (Oxford, 1951). Montagu reminded the Royal Commission on Alien Immigration that he and his colleagues had attempted to settle Jews in an agrarian colony near Aylesbury (where Rothschild influence should count for much) only to run afoul of Sunday observance laws. RCAI, 23 Mar 1903.

by their affinity for Yiddish and the remembered culture of Eastern Europe. Anglo-Jewry responded by building model tenements for Jewish workers and by bringing communal and local government authority to bear against those who failed to meet minimal sanitary standards. Montagu's dispersion committee laboured to move overcrowded East Enders out to the greater opportunities and more salubrious setting provincial cities might provide. Jewish Board of Guardians and Jewish Hospital and Orphan Asylum apprenticeship programmes sought to move Jewish youth away from the overcrowded and sweated clothing and shoemaking trades. Jewish relief agencies calculatedly repatriated those who could not adapt to British life. Every Anglo-Jewish institution attacked Yiddish. The Russo-Jewish Committee, not content to wait for the socialization of the next generation, subsidized evening English classes for adult foreign Jews. Jewish organizations worked with the London School Board in evening technical education courses to upgrade the skills of young people and adults already in the workforce. Youth clubs and the Jewish Lads' Brigade sought to continue the anglicization board and voluntary schools had so earnestly begun.

Social deviance was intolerable to the ever-watchful communal leaders. They were, in many respects, the puritans of the turn of the century. The Jewish Association for the Protection of Girls and Women fought prostitution and the sexual exploitation of women both as a matter of principle and to remove any taint from the Jewish public image. Jewish industrial schools were established and reform schools would later be founded both to control the wayward and publicly to demonstrate the community's commitment to law and order. Translators paid by the community worked in police and county courts to keep Jews from making fools of themselves and to minimize adverse magisterial comment. Political radicalism received short shrift, the elite moving to minimize any potential appeal anarchism or socialism might have. Labour and industrial organization were endorsed to the extent that they made for stabler trade conditions, emphasized self-help and upward social mobility, and contributed to a favourable communal image. Anglo-Jewry, while differing in party politics, remained impeccably mainstream. Some were Liberal, others Conservative or Unionist. Labour began to attract supporters, particularly among professionals and the more secure working classes, but only as it became a clearly respectable political party. Every communal institution, each Anglo-Jewish social principle worked to one purpose above all: creating Jewish Britons.

The pressure for some official action continued to build in spite of the facts of the case. That helps to explain why the issue of immigration restriction was never really susceptible to argument on the merits of the case. The first flurry of activity grew, as might be expected, in response to the immigration in the 1880s. Arguments about worker displacement and the growth of sweated trades played against a background of sustained underemployment during those trying years of the so-called Great Depression. Investigations of sweating revealed it to be far more widespread than tailoring in the Jewish East End. Alien immigration, while seen as a potential problem, was not deemed worthy of legislation. The investigative reports of 1888, however, merely postponed political confrontation. The Trades Union Congress continued to complain until the early 1890s. Immigrant numbers, which had dipped after the surge from 1881–3 to something of the order of 3,000 per year, rose again in 1890 and 1891 when the Russian government attempted to drive some 400,000

Jews back into the Pale of Settlement. Although the numbers slid fairly steadily downwards to about 2,500 per year for the rest of the decade, that brief surge reactivated the restrictionists.

Colonel Sir Howard Vincent and Major Evans Gordon, who led the parliamentary charge, harassed the government from the House of Commons. Arnold White and other publicists played on a popular mind now tempered in the daily heat of yellow journalism to demand oversimplified answers to complicated issues. As is so often the case, however, the sense of there being a problem heightened as the actual issue receded. Although Salisbury's government considered the issue of immigration and the sweated trades in June 1892, parliament dissolved and new elections were held before any pledge could be acted on. Jewish immigration to Britain was declining by the time legislation was seriously mooted. Alien restriction became a Conservative party issue playing simultaneously on a generalized, unfocused malaise growing out of a sense of relative decline and a determination to re-establish Britain's place in the world with a broad programme of protection and national efficiency. The xenophobia of imperialism, the Boer War, and the inability of the Salisbury–Balfour administration to develop an effective domestic programme helped to make immigration restriction an attractive policy that would convey a sense of purposeful government.[7]

Immigration restriction attracted protectionists. The campaign initially grew outside the House of Commons, although the temptation to play the alien card, particularly for members of parliament campaigning in constituencies with a visible but substantially powerless Jewish presence, would soon prove irresistible. Of East London members, only Sir Samuel Montagu and his nephew and successor, Stuart M. Samuel, in the Whitechapel seat, never endorsed some measure of restriction.

7 CAB 37/30 (1892)/30–1. Precedent and legislation already existed for some things about which much restrictionist heat and passion were to be spent. *The Times*, 2 Apr 1901; HO 45/10063/B2840/10–11. The right to expel aliens for a variety of offences had never been in question. See.e.g, Lovell to Harcourt, 1 Apr. 1882, MS Harcourt 96, ff. 73–5, in the Bodleian Library. Some of the more devoted advocates of civil rights saw restriction of immigrant freedom as a dangerous intrusion upon British liberty. See, 'The outlawry of unpopular persons', *Journal of the Vigilance Association*, 15 Sept .1883, 89–90.

One can easily underestimate the sense of an elite beleaguered and see the drive for immigration restriction as a mixture of tabloid virulence and the leadership of a handful of Anglo-Saxon racists. See, e.g., A. V. Dicey to Bryce, s.d. [1898], MS Bryce 3, f. 39, in the Bodleian Library, who wished to use the papers concerning the proposed aliens bill. On the other hand, English tabloid journalism has its unique qualities. The *Daily Mirror* of 6 December 1904 offered, among others these headlines: ALIEN SCOURGE//HUNDREDS OF UNDESIRABLES ARRIVING EVERY DAY//GYPSY SCOURGE IN ESSEX//DISEASE-STRICKEN IMMIGRANTS with story lines about the wreckage of Eastern Europe floating ashore in England. 'Few are not physically and morally degenerate. Their manner of life would disgrace any self-respecting community; the occupations which the majority of them drift into are opposed to law and order.' *Judenhetze* was not an impossibility in England. Colin Holmes reminds us how extremely sensitive the metropolitan police were to the potential violence of unconstrained anti-Semitism and did everything possible to prevent 'Ripper riots' in 1888. C. Holmes, 'East End crime and the Jewish community, 1888–1911', in Newman (ed.), *Jewish East End*, 114–15. By 1914, the government had a sense that at least the underlying economic problems that might feed it were being brought under control by state action. See, e.g., McKenna to Lloyd George, 6 Oct. 1914. Lloyd George Papers C/5/12/10 in the House of Lords Record Office. On the agitation for and passage of the Aliens Act, the standard work and one on which I have drawn heavily for this chapter is Bernard Gainer, *The Alien Invasion: the Origins of the Aliens Act of 1905* (New York, 1972). See also the points Wolfgang Mock and Gisela Lebzelter make in their contributions to P. Kennedy and A. Nicholls (eds), *Nationalist and Racialist Movements in Britain and Germany before 1914* (London, 1981).

Extraparliamentary agitation built up during the 1880s as a product of economic and social discontent, East End change, and the formulation and popularization of racist thought, and it was fed by a nagging loss of self-confidence. When the United States began to limit immigration in 1882, some Britons argued that this would turn unprotected England into the dumping ground for the least desirable settlers.[8]

The debate settled, whatever the rhetoric of the moment, along free trade/fair trade lines. So long as Britain held an unchallenged world position, it actively pursued a policy of free trade. Unionists, among others, felt that Britain was endangered in an increasingly threatening world and sought 'protection' in the broadest sense of that term. Liberal politicians generally clung to the principles of free movement for human beings quite as much as free trade in goods. Responding to a parliamentary question, Sir Michael Hicks-Beach as Liberal president of the Board of Trade tried to restore some perspective. He reminded the Commons that British emigrants to the United States were barred in far greater proportions by poverty restrictions than were Russian Jews. The British Treasury order of 1887 already barred immigrants 'who were likely to become a public charge' and, as interpreted by the Home Office, rendered contract labour illegal. As with any blanket decision, such administrative overkill produced an outcry for 'special cases'. Exceptions made for domestic servants, actors, singers, artists and 'persons in new industries' soon rendered the 1887 rule all but unenforceable.[9]

While the Russian policies of 1890 and ensuing persecution and pogroms triggered another successful Mansion House meeting and enabled the Russo-Jewish Committee to replenish its depleted coffers, the rising numbers of immigrants also stimulated restrictionist organization. A start had previously been made. The Earl of Dunraven, an apostle of 'fair trade', and Arnold White took an early flutter with a Society for the Suppression of the Immigration of Destitute Aliens in 1886, which vanished into well-merited oblivion without making any particular mark. Along the way, their anti-alien campaign had picked up the Earl of Meath, a generous man who championed planned emigration as the cure for British working-class ills. Alien immigration of any sort undercut his simplistic formulas. So, too, Lord Charles Beresford enrolled, being a self-appointed champion of the native English traditional craftsman. Colonel Howard Vincent, shortly to be knighted, was trying the cause on for size. The restrictionist movement suited his personality, his 'fair trade' ideology and could prove useful in his artisanal

---

8   The United States imposed sanitation conditions on immigrant ships as early as 1855 and banned the 'importation' of women for prostitution in 1875. The Act of 1882 imposed a duty of fifty cents per alien (which raised the transatlantic fare) and excluded convicts, lunatics and 'persons unable to care for themselves without becoming a public charge'. The Americans added moral turpitude, polygamists and persons suffering from 'loathsome or dangerous contagious disease' in 1891. In 1893, a further statute demanded that the immigrant shipmaster testify to literacy, means of support (at least $30), and whether the immigrant had a job, a family, and other personal information. The capitation tax was doubled to one dollar in 1894, and doubled again to two dollars in 1903. Of 60,764 'Hebrews' reaching the United States in 1900, 444 were barred as 'paupers,' 114 refused for 'loathsome disease'. Over the next two years, the numbers declined slightly. Material for the Royal Commission on Alien Immigration, 22 Mar. 1903, HO 45/10062/B2386/19.

9   HO 45/10062/B2386/4, 7; Lushington to Harcourt, 28 June 1882, HO 45/9623/A18445/1 encl 2–5.

Sheffield Central Division constituency.[10] Vincent convinced the Conservative party conference of October 1887 overwhelmingly to adopt a 'fair trade' motion addressed to the issue of foreign imports and 'the influx of destitute foreigners'. The issue of restricting alien immigration must thereafter be seen as what it, in fact, was – an important part of the struggle against the mid-Victorian gospel of free trade. Protection, in whatever form and to whatever degree, meant limiting in one way or another the free flow of people, capital and goods. Since this represented an apparent reversal of the policies Britain had pursued for half a century, the political campaign needed targets of opportunity. Jewish immigrants were visible and conveniently located. At times as part of a broader strategy, at times a way of keeping the protectionist pot boiling, Jewish newcomers were almost necessary victims. Anti-Semitism, covert or overt, certainly helped but was, all in all, a minor factor. The continued preposterous exaggerations of those who certainly knew better, not to mention the degree to which much of the Jewish leadership was prepared to cooperate, are best understood through seeing alien restriction as part of a broader attack on the very foundations of nineteenth-century liberalism.[11]

Whether the flurry of refugees in 1890 and 1891 or unsettled economic and housing conditions in East London sparked the revival or not, a full-blown – actually overblown, as it happened – restrictionist organization came into being. Lord Dunraven presided over the Association for Preventing the Immigration of Destitute Aliens, founded in May 1891. Its constituency expanded as numbers of migrants rose. The association, as might be expected, combined the usual decorative but dim peers, careerist xenophobes and a sprinkling of radical cranks and crackpots with some devoted fair traders. The Duke of Norfolk and the Duke of Sutherland endorsed the organization, as did a handful of members of parliament. The association denied that it singled out any specific group.

> There was no feeling of politics, religion, or nationality in this matter, [insisted Lord Dunraven] except that it was recognized to be the duty of all to protect our own nation and our own kith and kin. The conditions under which these people could live, with the commonest food and in the vilest air, crowded together like the lower animals, would lead to the survival of the unfittest. He added that if the immigrants only now attacked a few industries they would attack others and their low wages would set a low

10 The only foray the 'society' (if it ever was formally organized) made into the East End was a public meeting in April 1887 ostensibly on the issue of the sweated trades. Montagu, Mocatta and Alfred L. Cohen sat on the platform with these 'concerned philanthropists' but opposed the resolution calling for immigration restriction. *The Times*, 20 Apr. 1887. Arnold White claimed that he and the Earl of Dunraven financed such an organization. RCAI, Pt II (Cd. 1742), *PP*, IX (1903), q 330.

11 This also explains one of the reasons why so few Liberals, save for those running in East London constituencies, took a restrictionist position. Churchill appears to have understood this and made his first great parliamentary coup as a Liberal the defeat of the Aliens Bill of 1904. Sir Howard Vincent took charge of the Union of Conservative Associations in 1894 in his unrelenting campaign for protection. Gainer deals with this problem in Alien Invasion, chapter 6. See also J. Chamberlain, 'The labour question', *Nineteenth Century*, 32 (Nov 1892), 677–710; B. H. Brown, *The Tariff Reform Movement in Great Britain 1881–1895* (New York, 1943); S. H. Zebel, ' "Fair trade:" an English reaction to the breakdown of the Cobden treaty system', *Journal of Modern History*, 12 (1940), 161–86. Churchill proclaimed that the Aliens Bill of 1904 was 'protectionism'. See his letter to *The Times*, 31 May 1904.

standard throughout the country. He warned the public that they must guard their country from being swamped by those who in their habits and mode of living degraded the national life.[12]

But the association sounded no resonant trumpet. It failed to focus East London frustration or to excite national attention. It evaporated, having mobilized no broad campaign, in premature self-congratulation when Salisbury's government mindlessly pledged to bring in an aliens bill just three weeks before it dissolved parliament in 1892.

For the first although not the last time, Conservatives burned themselves on the issue of free trade. The McKinley tariff of 1890 in the United States led Salisbury's party to raise the question of retaliation. As it would do again in 1906, protection spelled disaster at the polls, and Gladstone's last Liberal government staggered haplessly into office. Retaliation was discreetly buried, but restriction remained alive. Salisbury offered a private bill in 1894, and the Unionist party formally adopted the idea of restriction for the election of 1895, but the pledge may have been little more than window dressing designed for working-class appeal. The Trades Union Congress, which regularly debated such issues, passed restrictionist resolutions from 1892 to 1895. To what extent labour leaders felt the pressure of anti-alien agitation and to what degree they were hitting out against the frustrations of continued high unemployment are unclear. Importing strike-breakers, of course, had been and remained a bitter issue. The London Trades Council endorsed anti-alien resolutions in 1891 and 1892, undoubtedly feeling the hot breath of the British Brothers League down its back. After 1895, however, organized labour reversed its position. The gradual return of prosperity certainly contributed. Socialist labour argued the brotherhood of workers. Liberal labour, by far the majority of unionized workers, correctly identified restriction with protectionism. Adopting it as a party issue may actually have proven politically counterproductive for Conservatives. Organized labour only returned to the restrictionist cause when it joined the rest of the country, including Anglo-Jewry, in that orgy of patriotism in the summer of 1914.

As an administrative matter, ministers fumbled the matter back and forth from department to department. Conservatives, who tottered out of office in 1893, and Liberals, who limped in, saw a potential issue but either wished to avoid it or did not know what to do with it. Those who dealt with the issue on a day-to-day basis seem not to have been particularly disturbed one way or the other. The Home Office and metropolitan police tended to take an *ad hoc* and prudential approach to the issue.[13]

---

12 *The Times*, 4 May 1891. Sir William Marriott, Sir John Colomb, William Lowther, Howard Vincent, Sydney Buxton and M'Arthur (all MPs) were among the founding members. Arnold White and his unpleasant associate, the Reverend G. S. Reaney, W. H. Wilkins, and the ubiquitous Montague Crackenthorpe played prominent roles in its founding and development. See also: *The Times*, 28 Nov. 1890; 21 Apr., 4, 22 June, 29 Aug. 1891; 30 Mar., 7 May 1892. see also HO 45/10063/B2840A/11a.

13 While the Home Office developed files, it was not of one mind on the subject. The department finally prepared a general Memorandum of the Laws relating to the Landing and Residence of Aliens in Great Britain for the cabinet in July 1894 [CAB 37/36/21], distributing it in January 1895. HO 45/10063/B2850/ 5 supplemented by a Memorandum on the Powers to Expel, in October 1899, HO 45/10063/B2850/8.

Civil servants appeared to be alternately bemused and annoyed by restrictionist noises. Sir Kenelm Digby of the Home Office, whose department would have ultimate responsibility for administering whatever legislation might be put in place, joined Lord Rothschild in a stinging minority report for the Royal Commission on Alien Immigration.[14] Some members of parliament returned in the Conservative victory of 1895 still saw restriction as the easiest way to win increasingly important working-class support. They touted restriction as an easy palliative for endemic unemployment and declining wages growing out of falling prices for consumer goods. They appealed for votes by, among other things, pledging to exclude pauper aliens and prison-made goods. Official statistics suggested that pauper aliens were a poor target. Board of Trade numbers, as confusing as they were in many ways, showed that the number of foreigners in the United Kingdom had slightly declined in 1895. Provincial police reported fewer 'tramping foreign Jews' in 1895 than 1894, and relief figures for both the Jewish Board of Guardians and the Conjoint Jewish Board of Guardians/Russo-Jewish Committee were down.[15]

Facts about immigration, however, proved increasingly irrelevant, for facts were only incidentally involved. Statistics were manufactured or manipulated to fit personal prejudices. The census of 1901 revealed that Britain, with 7.6 million foreigners by birth and nationality had fewer aliens within its borders than any other European country except Spain and Sweden.[16] That fact swayed no restrictionists. They needed prejudice to sustain their campaign and chose to find other 'facts'. The newly emerging field of social investigation brought amateur enthusiasts and would-be professionals into that most convenient laboratory, East London. Hard evidence about the sweated trades and social conditions, particularly in housing, poured into print from private investigations, philanthropic enterprises and government enquiries. Busybodies from such moral uplift institutions as the National Vigilance Association, who spent much of their time nagging the police and Home Office, argued that a general crackdown on aliens would prove a formidable strike against prostitution.[17] Statesmen and civil servants still hesitated. The Board of Trade realized, correctly, first that it lacked reliable numbers and, second, that immigration and even the world of sweatshops produced significant economic benefits as well as social and political difficulties. Native worker displacement was marginal, and the new Jews had, in fact, contributed to a dramatic

14 See, particularly, Digby's three letters, 'The Aliens Bill and the Home Office', *The Times*, 3, 31 May, 4 July 1904.

15 See the discussion in *JC*, 15 May 1896.

16 On the other hand, there were three million British aliens resident in foreign countries, 2,791,403 in the United States alone, making Britain the most notorious 'offender'. *JC*, 20 Jan. 1905.

17 See, e.g., their agitation in February 1895. HO 45/9745/A56729/1–4. Claude Hay regularly introduced measures for the National Vigilance Association. His Aliens Bill of July 1909, expanding on a variety of 'morals' offences, was dropped before its second reading. HO 45/10403/184435. When Goulding's Aliens Bill in 1911 sought to expand restrictions to ban certain criminal categories, NVA members sought to tack on elaborate 'morals' amendments. HO 45/10641/206332/1.

TABLE 10.1   Landed immigrants and transmigrants, 1885–1888

	1885	1886	1887	1888
Landed aliens	8,901	8,829	7,900	11,156
Transmigrants (Hull to Liverpool and USA)	29,657	44,715	59,754	63,819

Source: Giffen to Moran, 19 June 1889. Statistics prepared for the Select Committee on the Sweated Trades. HO 45/10063/B2840/1.

improvement in the standard of living of the poorer classes and created significant exports to some of Britain's most important trading partners.[18]

Extraparliamentary pressure continued unabated. The Foreign Office, responding to the hectoring of Arnold White and others, deployed its consular forces to slow the tide of immigrants and, in a somewhat random way, to develop some sense of the nature and scope of the problem.[19] The Local Government Board, awash in sanitation and housing violations and concerned about its crumbling poor law administration, suggested the immediate prohibition of the immigration of destitute Russian Jews as early as 1892. By the end of 1901, the Association of Poor Law Unions of England and Wales was demanding some restrictive action.[20] The House of Commons Committee on Foreign Immigration and the House of Lords Committee on the Sweated Trades in 1888 provided a reasonable basis from which to consider the issues involved, although their statistics, too, remained inadequate. The problem of immigration, the Board of Trade found, was not serious in terms of the entire population. Four-fifths of landed immigrants moved on to other points, most out of the country altogether.

But transmigrants still might be newcomers. Jewish immigrants from Rotterdam to New York, given the price-setting of shipping pools, saved 16 per cent on their fares by sailing from Rotterdam to London and then London to New York. The terms of trans-shipment, however, required a six-week stay in England before

18 HO 45/10063/B2840/10–11; Giffen to Lushington, 24 May 1892, HO 45/10063/B2840/41. See also Giffen to Moran, 19 June 1889, HO 45/10063/B2840/1. Llewellyn Smith, the Board of Trade's statistical expert, continued to produce numbers undercutting the restrictionist arguments. Reports to the Board of Trade on Alien Immigration into the United States, PP (1892–3), LXXI (C. 7113); Board of Trade (Alien Immigration), Reports on the Volume and Effects of Recent Immigration from Eastern Europe into the United Kingdom, PP (1894), LXVIII (C. 7406); and the Annual Reports on Emigration and Immigration for 1903 [PP (1904), CVI]; 1904 [PP (1905), XCVIII.]
19 Morier to FO 29 Mar., 2 Apr. 1892; Dundas to Malet, 30 July; FO to HO, 9 Aug. 1895, HO 45/10063/B2840/35, 41, 76–8. The Moscow Gazette helped to fuel British hysteria by announcing that Russia would dump 60,000 of its poorest Jews in the United Kingdom during the winter of 1891–2. Jennings and Smith reports to HO, HO 45/10063/B2840/1.
20 Ritchie to HO, 8 Apr 1892, HO 45/10062/B2386; CAB 37/59/146 (Dec 1901 for cabinet of 7 Jan. 1902).

embarking for the United States.[21] Adding a few thousands to the population, particularly when a substantial portion of the newly arrived were concentrated in Stepney, still gave rise to 'social and industrial anger among those with whom they came in contact'.[22]

Fundamental change in Stepney antedated any significant Jewish immigration. Stepney was a borough in transition. While the Jewish population rose to just under 40 per cent of the total by 1901, the actual available housing stock in the borough had been significantly reduced.[23] Displacement was, in the first instance, the product of a shift from residential housing to commercial and industrial property and the considerable dislocation of railway development. Stepney buildings themselves, save for those constructed by Jewish and other philanthropies, were old, dating back to the early nineteenth century. Most of Stepney knew neither drains nor sewers before 1855 and the creation of local boards of works. Water was a tribute to the misconduct of private enterprise. The East London Water Company, which enjoyed the local monopoly, often placed only one tap in each building. Water was poor in quality, delivery erratic at best. Space contracted as ground floors were pressed into shops to service the area. Gardens and front areas, where they existed, were converted. The transition, however, began in the 1840s. The native population was already moving or being moved out before immigrant Jews moved in, for their principal sources of employment were in decline or moving elsewhere. The developments reinforced one another. The reduction of housing stock continued apace as population grew. All this made the shift of street after street to become wholly or almost wholly Jewish appear an even more dramatic change than it was.

In December 1900, riding the sick jingoism of the Boer War, came Major William Eden Evans-Gordon, an old Indian Army officer, newly elected MP for Stepney and moving spirit of the British Brothers League. The league's actual founder, William Stanley Shaw, never emerged from the shadowy world of xenophobic agitation, and the shock troops were Evans-Gordon's highly organized East End residents. The league had no dues although it encouraged its partisans to make small donations; one joined simply by signing on. Evans-Gordon seems to have paid the bills, and well he and his fellow East End Unionist MPs might. The league, with its regular, enthusiastic East End public meetings, kept the

---

21 Simple economics explained the phenomenon. An 1895 pool agreement between British and German shippers on immigrant traffic set the Rotterdam–New York fare at £7 10s, but Rotterdam–London was 11s, and London–New York £5 15s (a total of six guineas). The Rotterdam agent managing the traffic, bound by the terms of the agreement, had to be 'ignorant' of the fact that the applicant was a transmigrant. May 1904. HO 45/10241/B37811/15. See also: House of Commons, Select Committee on Immigration and Emigration (Foreigners), First Report, *PP* (1888), XI; Second Report, *PP* (1889), X; House of Lords, Select Committee on the Sweating System, which issued five reports and minutes of evidence between 1888 and 1890: *PP* (1888), XX-XXI; *PP* (1889), XIII-XIV; *PP* (1890), XVII. For another valuable contemporary study, see Georg Halpern, 'Die jüdische Einwanderung-Bevölkerung Londons', in A. Nossig (ed.), *Jüdische Statistik* (Berlin, 1903), 322–35.

22 CAB 37/30/30 (2 June 1891). The metropolitan police made one of the more intelligent concise summaries of the issues. Memorandum for Response to Select Committee, 16 June 1888, MEPO 2/260.

23 The Whitechapel population rose from 75,552 in 1871 to 78,768, a modest increase. During those same years, however, the number of 'houses' (although that term is very misleading) dropped dramatically from 8,264 to 5,735. Census of England and Wales 1901 (Cd. 875), *PP*, 1902, table 9. See generally Munby, *Industry and Planning in Stepney*.

electioneering spirit going and reminded the enfranchised voters who their true friends were. Evans-Gordon proclaimed himself the new political messiah for beleaguered Gentiles, and Arnold White was his prophet. A veritable orgy of patriotism and alien-baiting shook the People's Palace, where, on the same evening, aliens would attend iron-working and wood-working classes. The organist whipped up the audience by playing *Soldiers of the Queen* and *Home, Sweet Home*. Eleven speakers outdid one another to bring joyous shouts of 'Wipe them out' from the overflow crowd of two thousand. London dockers and other burly 'native' working men acted as stewards, hustling out the occasional protestor. Within eighteen months the Brothers had signed up 45,000 members,. After all, it cost nothing to join, and signing on seemed a good way of defining 'virtuous us' and 'inferior them'. League partisans were by no means merely unsophisticated working people. Arthur Conan Doyle donated half a guinea, and open sympathizers and members included a surprising number of clergymen.[24]

Immigration restriction was a convenient way to avoid dealing with difficult, even intractable social problems. The government, for instance, had no intention of dealing with restriction in 1901, when it had its 'khaki election' majority and gave priority to those issues it considered important.[25] Prime Minister Arthur Balfour knew better but chose to misrepresent the matter in oversimplified terms. This debate provides an insight into what Balfour would do later in his partially principled but partially cynical exploitation of Zionism. A brilliant man and skilled debater, although one of the least effective first ministers, Balfour beat the drums of immigration restriction for Conservative party advantage.

> Let me translate this into the actual facts of Whitechapel. It means that the foreign immigrant first drives the British workman out of Whitechapel and then the small remnant has to pay the rates in order to carry out the sanitary arrangements and the Poor Law arrangements which are to remedy the state of things of which he is the victim. How can you justify it? The truth is that the evil is not only great and pressing in these districts where it prevails, but it is one which these districts are perfectly incapable of dealing with unassisted. I listened really with some shame to the loud professions of philanthropic

24 Gainer, *Alien Invasion*, 67–73. See also the testimony in Royal Commission on Alien Immigration, *PP*, (1903), IX, qq 8557ff. Rothschild supported Evans-Gordon's parliamentary candidacy, and Weizmann admired the Major. C. Weizmann, *Trial and Error* (London, 1950), 118–19. Evans-Gordon travelled to Russia and Eastern Europe, wrote compellingly about the conditions under which Jews lived there, and sympathized with their desire to better themselves. He just did not want them 'flooding' into England. He applauded Israel Zangwill's Jewish Territorial Organisation and, naturally, found Zionism an attractive solution. W. Evans-Gordon, *The Alien Immigrant* (London, 1902); letter to *The Times*, 1 Dec. 1905; 'The attack on the Aliens Act', *National Review*, 48 (Nov. 1906), 460–70; 'The stranger without our gates', *Nineteenth Century and After*, 49 (Feb. 1911), 210–16. By the beginning of the twentieth century, the alien question had come to divide Britain's elite. Edwin Montagu, Sir Samuel's brilliant son and a future cabinet minister, generally stood aloof from 'Jewish' concerns. While at Trinity and president of the Cambridge Union in 1902, however, he organized a debate on 18 February 1902 upon and spoke for the proposition 'That this House would disapprove of an attempt to restrict by legislation the immigration of "Pauper" Aliens.' He lost in a close division.

25 See the material assembled for an answer to T. R. Dewar's parliamentary question, 27 Mar. 1901; Bateman (Commercial Department, Board of Trade) to HO, 29 Mar. 1901, HO 45/10063/B2840; *The Times*, 2 Apr. 1901.

altruism on the part of gentlemen who pay neither from their own pockets nor from the pockets of their constituents, nor from any section or class with which they have to deal.[26]

'We have a right,' he concluded, 'to keep out everybody who does not add to the strength of the community.'

ANGLO-JEWISH RESPONSES: A STUDY IN AMBIGUITIES

The exclusionists and the Anglo-Jewish elite shared assumptions and conclusions, although the Jewish establishment could never openly admit it. Had not the Jewish Board of Guardians been willing to allocate £50 from its meagre resources early in its history to post notices throughout the Pale discouraging emigration to England? The Board of Guardians deported back to Europe or Russia any applicants for relief who could not, in their view, become self-sufficient 'Englishmen'. The Board of Deputies of British Jews would willingly support any measure 'so far as it should be effectually directed' to bar 'aliens of immoral or criminal character'. Board of Deputies president David Alexander sat on the executive committee of the National Vigilance Association. Nothing could delight him more, in both capacities, than to see the government act to bar prostitutes and those profiting from immorality. Sir Samuel Montagu thought restricting immigration to those who could secure a certificate of good character from their rabbi a good idea, an opinion which delighted Evans-Gordon. Leonard L. Cohen, president of the Jewish Board of Guardians, publicly endorsed the exclusion of criminals and the physically or mentally ill or disabled. Nathan Joseph preferred an alternative system whereby the government would repatriate those who failed to adapt to a useful life in Britain rather than the more difficult task of deciding on arrival which immigrants might or might not be 'liable' to be a burden on the community. Benjamin L. Cohen, past president of the Board of Deputies, and Harry S. Samuel both endorsed Sir Howard Vincent's Alien Immigration Bill of 1903. That private bill was a tactical move to force the royal commission to end its hearings and the government to act. It also sought to establish the principle of limiting immigration by finding the broadest area of agreement between Anglo-Jewry and the restrictionists.

While actual victims of persecution should never be denied asylum in Britain, Anglo-Jewry, with few exceptions, advocated and practised its own policy of exclusion and repatriation. Quite as much, if not more, than the host culture, Anglo-Jewry sought a community of the highest moral standards. But they stoutly and correctly denied misleading restrictionist arguments. On every occasion, Anglo-Jewry proclaimed that Russian and Polish Jews did not lower 'the native

26 *The Times*, 19 May 1905; HO 45/10303/117267/62. The senior civil servants at the Home Office had as much trouble as their former chief, Sir Kenelm Digby, in attempting to define the vaguer terms of the various aliens bills. Officials puzzled in particular about the question: under what circumstances might 'offences of a religious character' be considered 'political offences' and thereby allow persecuted Jews the status of political refugees. 2 May 1905, HO 45/10303/117167/49. Gartner, *Jewish Immigrant*, 274–80 has a highly compressed, although generally sound, brief summary of the politics of alien restriction.

standard of life'.[27] Even the most outspoken opponents of Jewish immigrants conceded that Jews were sober, thrifty, industrious, able, determined to rise and had 'perfect family life and a love of sound education'. They embodied, in fact, the ostensible virtues of Victorian Britain. While migrant and poor Jews lived in overcrowded housing under unsanitary conditions, the issue was one of class, not ethnicity. Sanitary officials of the London County Council reported precisely the same conditions among the poorer native classes throughout the metropolis in districts in which few if any aliens lived.[28] Provincial towns and villages, with few if any Jewish inhabitants suffered from comparable or worse conditions. The problem of overcrowding clearly demanded uniform enforcement of existing sanitary regulations and a proper housing code, not an attack on aliens.

Just such a mission Dr David Lewis Thomas, physician and barrister, set for himself. As medical officer of health, first, for the Limehouse district board of works and then, after the creation of the metropolitan borough, the medical officer of health for Stepney,

> He set himself . . . the task of improving the sanitation and health of the Jewish quarters. By degrees he got matters into a much better state, particularly as regards food supplies and the slaughter methods. His campaign for clean milk shops has resulted in vastly improved conditions, and Stepney is the only Borough where steps have been taken to get barbers' shops and hairdressing saloons in a respectable and safe condition. His system of voluntary certification, accepted by the local trade is unequalled.[29]

That campaign made Dr Thomas less than popular. He himself visited shops, checking shelves for dust, demanding regularly swept floors, and, less usefully, that milk and fish not be sold in the same room (presuming, as he did, that organisms from fish could contaminate milk). Fish, not milk, produced shop profits, for delivered milk cost but one farthing a pint more. Thomas's licensing authority was a

27 Both sides employed suspect numbers in the debate. The Jewish Board of Deputies used Llewellyn Smith's statistics on labour displacement, but for reasons not altogether clear, Llewellyn Smith partially disowned his own figures as the debate became heated. The alien immigration committee of the Jewish Board of Guardians used the estimate of 200,000 foreign workers in Britain. See, e.g., Evans-Gordon to Akers-Douglas, 17 May 1904, HO 45/10303/117267/18.

28 Spurred on by anti-alien agitation, the LCC surveyed sample areas to compare the East End with non-alien districts. Overcrowding per 100 houses (not using the census base of more than two inhabitants per room as overcrowded regardless of size of that room, but 'genuine overcrowding', based upon the number of cubic feet of air space per person) showed Lambeth (26 per cent) and St Pancras (31 per cent) as far worse than Mile End Old Town (two per cent) and Whitechapel (nine per cent). Even Kensington (14 per cent) ran higher than the East End. Cited in BDBJ, *The Aliens Bill*, 1905 (London, 1905), 4–5.   Walter Long, president of the Local Government Board, hoped, by turning to the East End boards of guardians in February 1905, to elicit some politically useful data. He demanded the swiftest possible return on the number of aliens on the rates during 1904, the character of the relief given, and the countries from which the aliens came. *JC*, 3 Mar. 1905. The choice was apt, for the Jewish Soup Kitchen, one of the best indicators of short-term desperation, had a 24 per cent rise in applicants in the winter of 1904–5 compared to the previous year (also a bad one), and 65 per cent above a 'normal' year. Slack trade and East End unemployment brought applications from persons 'who have resided in London many years, and have never before received relief from the Kitchen'. *JC*, 24 Feb. 1905.

29 Obituary in *East London Observer*, quoted from N. A. Cohen, 'Dr. Thomas and the Milkroom', in Newman (ed.), *Jewish East End*, 55–7. Cohen's essay is an admirable presentation of regulation from the point of view of the regulated.

powerful weapon, so in response the shopkeepers organized the Stepney Grocers and Provision Dealers Association. The result appears to have been a truce with some benefits accruing to both communal health and East End organization.

The Jewish leadership once again found secular authorities performing tasks that it would have been politically troublesome to do itself. Here as elsewhere the issue cut both ways. Improving local conditions worked to the benefit of all, but the publicity surrounding such problems fuelled the fire of immigration restriction. Anglo-Jewry hoped that the community and the wider political public would be able to distinguish between the important and the trivial. The leadership, from the beginning of the restriction campaign, fully endorsed barring some categories of immigrants. The Chief Rabbi spoke for most when he said:

> I would unhesitatingly declare, on behalf of the community, that we should hail with the extremest gratification any measure, however drastic, that would deal with those who have the slightest taint of criminality, either in regard to the exclusion or deportation of those who are not merely aliens in respect to this country, but who are aliens from Judaism.[30]

At the same time, Anglo-Jewry and many others who thought seriously about such problems realized that the actual numbers of immigrants were so small as to make the necessary bureaucracy of control far more expensive than any benefit that might flow from its creation. The British seemed bent on imitating the American system, but Britain did not have a million migrants flowing in each year; the numbers were closer to 7,000 and diminishing. The campaign, however, actually spoke then as it continued to do later to deep irrational, emotional needs, not significant national issues. Supposedly competent social investigators and theorists like the Webbs or J. A. Hobson were no less prejudiced in their assumptions and prone to conceal their biases than the Arnold Whites of the day. Endemic unemployment is a problem. Blame immigrant paupers. After centuries of the urban history of substandard housing and deficient sanitation, a nation finally begins to recognize the human and economic costs involved. Blame Polish Jews. A genteel elite of modest skills and political competence shows itself less and less capable of sorting out the complex issues of modern states, economies and societies. Blame alien political agitators.

The facts were not difficult to unearth. The total size of the Jewish community was, so the Jewish leadership believed, not more than 120,000 in the London County area. The total number of aliens dependent on the rates in 1904 was 1,600. Increasing demand for parish relief came, not from aliens or Jews as such, but from 'a larger class in this country who has great faith in the virtue of medicines and drugs, who take advantage of the fact that medical relief is given gratuitously by the parish officer, and that medical relief does not disfranchise anyone or render them likely to any other disability.'[31] If the issue was public cost, the Jewish community would meet that issue head-on as it had done for so long. Lord Rothschild, speaking for the Jewish Board of Deputies, informed the Home Office that the Deputies

---

30 Speech to the festival dinner of the Jewish Religious Education Board, 15 Feb. 1905. *JC*, 17 Feb. 1905.
31 Statement of Lord Rothschild as leader of the deputation from the Jewish Board of Deputies to the Home Secretary. 19 May 1904, HO 45/10303/117267/18. See also the Alexander–Emmanuel discussion of clauses and amendments the following year. 4, 11 May 1905, BDBJ C 13/1/5.

would guarantee that no Jewish immigrant would become a public charge during his first two years residence in Britain. Anglo-Jewry was prepared to pay that price in order to retain for itself the decision about which Jews should be allowed in Britain and which should be returned from whence they came.

Restrictionists generally sought to have it both ways: to target Jews while disavowing anti-Semitism. Parliamentary leaders of the anti-alien movement like Major Evans-Gordon, who enjoyed substantial Jewish support, insisted that 'the most undesirable elements of all in our foreign population are not Jews. There are quarters in London infested and infected by the riff raff and scum of all nations. I need not name their professions.' 'Why should we not exclude foreigners who are diseased or of bad character or hopelessly destitute?'[32] Such an effective appeal to nativism, to the prejudices of the displaced native marginals of Whitechapel, who were far from lacking in local political influence, and to the anxieties of those concerned with the new cult of national efficiency proved effective political building blocks. Cost–benefit arguments rarely appeal to the economically displaced, and parliament had, throughout the nineteenth century, paid consider- able attention to such complaints. Parliament had no interest in repealing economic growth, but on this issue nagging anxiety about unemployment and economic displacement tended to obscure the simple fact that Jewish migrants had significantly expanded the British economy. Evans-Gordon, moreover, had little difficulty in finding Jewish witnesses to testify for restriction before the Royal Commission on Alien Immigration in spite of real or implied pressure from co-religionists.

For most Anglo-Jewish institutions, restrictionist agitation had little direct impact. They continued to serve their particular constituents, ever vigilant against the potential corrupting influence of generosity. Some rippling influence of anti-alienism could be felt in the heightened efforts at the Jewish Board of Guardians and the Jewish Hospital and Orphan Asylum to apprentice youngsters away from the overcrowded trades. Such concerns certainly lay behind Nathan Joseph's severe strictures on the board's industrial committee conservatism in its apprenticeship policies.[33] New board schools eased the burden of educating Jewish children, although they also imposed new demands on the overstrained funds of the Jewish Religious Education Board. Houses were torn down to make way for the new schools, a form of urban renewal that eliminated slums but placed additional strain on remaining Stepney housing. Model estates of the 4% Industrial Housing Corporation continued to go up, serving as showcases of Anglo-Jewry's determination to help ease the housing crisis, but the Rothschild–Joseph flats in and around Stepney could not answer local needs completely. Those constructed further afield proved unattractive to poor Jewish tenants who preferred the unsanitary and overcrowded familiar to the clean and airy distant.

---

32 *East London Advertiser*, 30 Apr. 1904. D. L. Alexander speaking for the Board of Deputies accepted the Balfour and Akers-Douglas assurance 'that this Bill is not the off-spring of anti-Jewish feeling' and that they would regard the growth of any such sentiment 'as a great national calamity'. BDBJ Deputation to HO, 19 May 1904, HO 45/10303/117267/18. Moses Gaster, who never avoided calling a spade a damned shovel, for his part called it blatant anti-Semitism.

33 The JBG meeting debating industrial committee policies and Joseph's minority report was held on 11 Nov. 1901. *JC*, 15 Nov. 1901.

The burden on the Jewish Soup Kitchen reflected the immediate state of the economy and the severity of the weather, both of which had little to do with the ebb and flow of restrictionist agitation.

In other respects the community was spurred to action. The community felt itself besieged and began to draw its disparate governing elements together. The Board of Deputies finally conceded that constitutional modifications must be made. Like the Anglo-Jewish Association, the Board of Deputies moved to improve representation and participation of provincial Jews. Anti-alienism certainly helped to bring the United Synagogue to terms with Montagu's Federation of Synagogues. Resolution might well have come regardless, but restrictionism, by forcing Jews to band together in common cause, much accelerated the process. Unable to devise a viable East End programme of its own, the United Synagogue made peace with the Federation as the most appropriate religious anglicizing influence in the East End. The Federation was finally allowed representation on and a share in the profits of, first the Shechita Board, then the Flour Committee. By 1902, the Federation rabbi was invited to sittings of the Bet Din, the Chief Rabbi's ecclesiastical court. Anglo-Jewry endorsed the affiliation scheme, a proposal Montagu made to small, provincial congregations to join the Federation.[34] Montagu, for his part, also worked to further communal unity by bringing the most important London separatists, the Machziké Hadass into the Federation and under the Chief Rabbi's authority.

The Russo-Jewish Committee intensified its adult education programme in the East End and funded local Jewish Boards of Guardians from Birmingham and Manchester to Edinburgh and Glasgow to accelerate the policy of dispersion. Jewish women, who by the beginning of the twentieth century were finally being permitted to take a major role in communal social activity, met for the first time as the Union of Jewish Women in May 1902, seeking to bring provincial and London experience together as a guide for future activity. Every effort was made to encourage viable Jewish communities outside London. Montagu, in his personal imitation of the Garden City Association, hoped the dispersion committee could move factories to the suburbs and develop Jewish settlements entirely outside London. That in Reading proved the most viable success. Far too often property speculators gobbled up savings and hopes. East Enders trying to escape to Benfleet and Portsea in Essex were 'fleeced', and communal leaders drew scant consolation from the fact that they had warned would-be purchasers that there were potential hazards.[35]

Once aliens were suspect, new anxieties augmented old. Political phobias joined economic ignorance and a cultural fear of these strange Jewish people with their odd habits and capacity to work hard and get on in the world. Britain as a refuge for the politically persecuted had helped to create wide national sympathy for the Mansion House and Russo-Jewish Committees. But did political persecution license subversive ideas? Even Liberal sympathizers became increasingly concerned as the nineteenth century gave way to the twentieth. By the Russian revolution of

---

34 See *JC*, 1902 passim, for the affiliation scheme.
35 On the early work of the dispersion committee, see RCAI, 23 Mar. 1903; *JC*, 13, 20 June 1903. For Benfleet, see *JC*, 20 Aug., 3, 10, 17, 24 Sept., 15, 22, 29 Oct., 12, 16 Nov., 10 Dec. 1897, 21 Jan. 1898.

1905, an increasing number of Britons began to fear that Jewish migrants brought politically radical ideas as well as socially offensive habits.[36]

Extraparliamentary pressure groups reinforced what had started, in part, as Conservative party opportunism, finding an issue to unite a party hopelessly divided on tariff policy and tarnished by the aftermath of the inglorious Boer War. Even militant morality waded into the fray. The crusade against the 'white slave traffic' reinvigorated the older anti-alien social and economic arguments while conveniently providing 'virtue' for political cynics and opportunists. Nobody, especially the Jewish leadership, denied the unpleasantly conspicuous role of Jews in prostitution and the traffic in human beings, and nobody was more anxious than Anglo-Jewry to eradicate that problem. Constance Rothschild and Claude Montefiore had already sponsored the Jewish Ladies Society for Preventative and Rescue Work in March 1885, adding a Jewish organization to the mushrooming societies particularly concerned with juvenile prostitution. The Jewish Association for the Protection of Girls and Women, formally constituted as such in 1896, became a model which even the parent National Vigilance Association came to imitate both in its domestic work and international organization. Charcroft House, a Jewish institution founded in the best traditions of Victorian philanthropy, joined a miscellany of settlement houses and refuges redeeming the fallen with needlework, laundry and substantial doses of prayer. Anglo-Jewry took its concerns well beyond the British Isles. Sir Samuel Montagu, visiting Cairo in the winter of 1904–5, used the occasion to have a well-publicized interview with Lord Cromer on behalf of the movement for the suppression of the white slave trade.[37]

As with other contemporary vigilance organizations, the Jewish Association's domestic balance sheet is hard to reckon. Were the achievements in human terms commensurate with the costs? Perhaps they were, but rescue from risk also offered new opportunities for social management. The cause of purity also provided a convenient instrument for those anxious to reassert control over a wayward community. David L. Alexander and Claude Montefiore worked actively to draft and promote morality legislation.[38] Those fighting white slavery sought not only new criminal sanctions against individuals involved in prostitution or any form of moral laxity; they also attempted to restrict the free movement of prostitutes and their exploiting managers. Once again Anglo-Jewish leaders, for very different reasons, shared some of the restrictionist views of White, Vincent and Evans-Gordon. At one level, the racists and anti-immigrationists were performing a task Anglo-Jewry dared not overtly take upon itself. Quite beyond issues of sustaining communal social control, statutory restriction or persecution could be a useful weapon to purify English Jews. One can always do what is right with even more enthusiasm when one knows that it is also in one's own interest. The imposition of

36 Chalmers to Gladstone, 10 Jan., 6, 19 Mar. 1906, Herbert Gladstone Papers. Add MS 45,933,ff. 10–11, 17–20, in the British Library.

37 *JC*, 17 Feb. 1905.

38 Jewish vulnerability to anti-Semitic sniping could be attributed, in substantial part, to the increasingly visible Jewish presence in English vice and crime. Bristow, *Prostitution and Prejudice:*, part 3. Mossley of the Anglo-Jewish Association was also much involved with organizations to combat the white slave traffic. He contended that criminals would easily evade the regulations proposed while 'many excellent persons might be kept out'. BDBJ Deputation to HO, 19 May 1904, HO 45/10303/117267/18.

moral discipline and control – to which no leading Jews were likely to object – offered a popular and publicly endorsed additional way to reinforce elite communal control.[39]

While many Anglo-Jews at the turn of the century still privately shared Goldsmid's strident 1859 views about aliens, most ultimately succumbed to community pressure and laboured, however half-heartedly, against restrictive legislation. Some did not. Sir Harry S. Samuel, then MP for the Limehouse division of Tower Hamlets took an outspokenly active role in the British Brothers Association. Communal activists like L. J. Greenberg chided the Board of Deputies for its passivity. The board refused to be flustered or stampeded into ill-considered action. Its principal concern, and the one issue on which almost all British Jews were united, was that actual victims of political or religious persecution should never be deprived of refuge. Ambiguous restrictions on this point in the government's measure unsettled both Anglo-Jewry and many Liberal MPs and helped to confound the 1904 Aliens Bill. To be assured that asylum would be preserved was all that was needed to secure Anglo-Jewry's tacit acceptance of the 1905 measure. The issue, after all, was not whether certain immigrant Jews should not be in England. Jewish organizations had been repatriating 'undesirables' (usually on the grounds of unadaptability) for decades. Immigration management and control, even restriction, had long been part of Anglo-Jewry's own agenda. Those whose dedication had contributed to Jewish emancipation and social opportunity worked among the socially deprived and the newcomers to ascertain that the community's achievements would not be undone. Thus they had erected schools, social welfare institutions, clubs and even friendly societies to shape their world as British and Jewish.

After half a century of almost unbroken, if slow, success, Jewish leaders perceived their work endangered everywhere in the West. One indisputable source seemed to be the unrestricted and massive flow of East European Jews. Their bizarre appearance and bad habits seemed somehow to feed the Dreyfusian sickness of France, the growing *Judenhetze* of Germany and Austro-Hungary, and the drive for immigration restriction in Britain and the United States.[40] Formal and informal conferences of national Jewish organizations designed programmes for and processed immigrants through the 1880s and 1890s. All shared the same concerns and, within the constraints of their assumptions, they were both effective and humane.

But neither the effort to give order to Jewish migration from Eastern Europe nor the elaborate and costly attempts of West European philanthropists like Hirsch to improve Jewish conditions and opportunities within the Russian Empire seemed to stem the rising swell of anti-Semitism in its various national and regional forms. Anglo-Jewry hastily summoned an Emigration Conference to meet in Frankfurt in November 1904. Even the United States, although not formally represented, dispatched two observers. Hermann Landau represented the Anglo-Jewish

39 *The Third Annual Report of the Emily Harris Home for Jewish Working Girls* (1905). The home, an institution housing twenty girls and feeding a substantial number who worked in the area, spoke proudly of its role as a sanctuary for the respectable in Soho, observing as well that many of its girls 'come from undesirable homes, and are much benefited by the moral and physical advantages they receive'.

40 See, e.g., 'Unsere Lage', *Allgemeine Zeitung des Judenthums*, 6 Jan. 1905.

Association as well as his own Poor Jews' Temporary Shelter, while Stettauer spoke for the Jewish Board of Guardians and Russo-Jewish Committee. Both discussed the recently resisted Aliens Bill of 1904 and the certain prospect that some measure would pass in 1905.

On one point all delegates and observers tacitly agreed. They wished, through financial contributions, to move the refugees away from themselves. The meeting explicitly disclaimed any intention to pass emigrants from one country to another. The conference sought, formally at least, no more than to keep all member countries informed about the volume and direction of emigration 'so that no large movement would take place without that country's consent and cooperation.'

> It has been agreed, in the people's own interests, not to encourage emigration at present, but to try as much as possible to improve the conditions in the countries from which the emigrants mostly came, particularly in the way of founding industrial undertakings.[41]

The conference, like others before it, confronted a litany of migrant abuse. German and Austrian Jewish organizations found themselves with growing numbers of recently fleeced sheep. Agents and border guards shook down Jews fleeing the Russian empire to their last penny. Even those would-be immigrants who had started with some money now reached Central and Western Europe with nothing. Immediate relief and some system of immigrant protection were urgently needed. The Austro-German groups had already expended 150,000 kronen. The Alliance Israélite Universelle contributed 50,000 francs to maintain nearly 1,000 Russian immigrants in Galicia, a sum matched by the Hilfsverein der deutschen Juden, the Frankfurt Committee and the Vienna Alliance.

But where were they to go? Money was one thing, domestic politics were yet another, and the issue of sending them somewhere else remained paramount. Shipping companies were cooperative. Canada seemed a possibility. The companies offered cheap fares and facilities for kosher food. Not only that, but the companies arranged to go directly without touching England. Anglo-Jewry heaved a sigh of relief. Explorations continued. Texas seemed a possibility. Some Jews had managed to find homes in Scandinavia. It all cost money, but it did keep refugees away from British shores.[42]

DEALING WITH LEGISLATION

Having made yet another attempt to stem the flow of Jewish immigrants, Anglo-Jewry turned back to the problem in domestic politics. The Conservatives had placed immigration restriction in their political arsenal. Lord Salisbury, shortly to be back in office as Prime Minister, introduced an Aliens Bill in July 1894 to exclude destitute aliens and anarchists. Salisbury somewhat disingenuously avowed that he, as a private member, was responding in the great Tory tradition to Trades Union Congress wishes. Rosebery's Liberal government stood firm against the

---

41 Landau's report to the AJA, *JC*, 16 Dec. 1904.
42 Landau's report, *JC*, 16 Dec. 1904, 6 Jan. 1905.

measure and prevailed, but the Conservatives in 1895 added a restriction plank to their election platform. Joseph Chamberlain, without giving the matter great consideration, added an aliens bill to the Unionist programme at the same time. He had already taken the position that immigration restriction should be part of a fair trade programme, and he had no great love for Jews. Since Tories and Unionists had adopted the issue, Conservative Jewish MPs could run with it, particularly those for whom good politics coincided with their private views. Benjamin Louis Cohen, although past president of the Board of Guardians, was a devoted Conservative MP whose only concern was that the right of political and religious refuge be preserved. Otherwise an aliens bill would merely place on the statute book policies that Jewish agencies themselves pursued at their private expense. Harry S. Samuel (Limehouse) spoke for more council members of the West London Synagogue than himself when he vigorously campaigned for total prohibition of pauper immigration, and Harry Marks, who was the soul of commitment and generosity with the Jewish Hospital and Orphan Asylum (St George's-in-the-East), repeatedly attacked pauper aliens.

The Labour Party in its formal pronouncements remained more unshakably anti-racist than much of its membership. The Trades Union Congress and several individual trade unions urged parliamentary consideration of the issue in 1892 and 1893.[43] But individual working-class leaders, such as John Burns, declined to fall in line. Burns denounced the oppression of individual Jews, particularly poor immigrants, but he could not resist some upper-class Jew-baiting. Jewish capitalists were oppressive, but the Jewish poor should not be persecuted. George Lansbury, the socialist humanitarian, took a wider view when he told the Christian Social Union that Christian working men would do well to imitate the Jewish example of 'industry, sobriety, and thrift'. For such Fabian enthusiasts for national efficiency as the Webbs, however, investigative experience in the East End served to sharpen their class and racial prejudices.[44]

External events cut both ways. British revulsion over the Dreyfus case in France probably weakened the anti-immigrant cause. Blatant anti-Semitism again became somewhat unfashionable. That did not deter the Earl of Hardwick from introducing an aliens bill in 1898. Although a private measure, the government may well have been testing the political waters with it. The Earl of Derby, a member of the administration, seconded Hardwick's bill, but the proposal proved stillborn. From 1899 into 1905, however, immigration rose once more. Bessarabia and Kherson sustained famine and anti-Semitic riots. Then in 1900, Roumanian Jews, fleeing appalling abuses, appeared in substantial numbers, themselves reversing several years of generally declining East European immigration. 'Those dirty immigrants'

43 The TUC meeting in autumn 1892 in Glasgow instructed the parliamentary committee 'to use every legitimate means in its power to have brought and passed through the House of Commons a Bill to prevent the immigration of pauper aliens to our shores.' James Lowther, using the debate on the Address from the Crown as the occasion to raise the issue of destitute alien immigrants (11 Feb. 1893), also cited forty-three labour organizations, six town councils, fourteen metropolitan boards of guardians, and sixteen boards of vestries as petitioning for restriction. *The Times*, 13 Feb. 1893; HO 45/10063/B2840A/69.

44 See, for instance, Burns's remarks on 25 April 1904 concerning the Aliens Bill. 4 *Hansard* 133, 1149–50, 1158–60. Beatrice regularly gave voice to such views, and Sidney and Beatrice both published their opinions in *Industrial Democracy*, vol. 2 (London, 1897), 698n, 744n. For Lansbury's St Paul's address, see *JC*. 10 Mar. 1905.

were once more an issue. The 'khaki election' of 1900, a Conservative attempt to capitalize on the jingoism of the early Boer War, does little to improve the image of late-Victorian political leadership and responsibility. Restrictionist positions were but frosting on the chauvinistic cake. Thomas Dewar conducted an anti-alien crusade as he contended for the St George's seat. Sponsored by Lord Rothschild and Sir Francis Montefiore, he defeated his Liberal opponent, the Jewish candidate, Bertran S. Straus. No one won in an East London constituency who had not partially endorsed at least a restrictionist position, except Stuart M. Samuel, who barely managed to keep his uncle's long-time Whitechapel seat in 1900. Even some losers like Straus endorsed barring the ill and criminals. Rothschild vigorously supported Major Evans-Gordon's Stepney campaign, which reflected, among other things, Anglo-Jewry's mixed feelings about restriction.[45]

After the government's 1904 bill had been talked out in the Grand Committee but before the modified 1905 measure came forward, a by-election for Mile End in January 1905 afforded all parties the opportunity to test restriction as an issue in one of the centres of anti-alien agitation and in what had been a safe Conservative seat. Charrington, the eminent brewer and Conservative MP, who had sat for the constituency for a long time, had enjoyed substantial Jewish support. Charrington had held the seat in 1900 by a comfortable 1,160 majority, polling almost two-thirds of the votes cast. Harry Lawson, son of Lord Burnham, proprietor of the *Daily Telegraph*, sought to succeed Charrington, who was retiring, as Unionist member. Lawson's grandfather, Joseph Moses Levy, had been an active member of the London Jewish community, but Lawson's father married out of the faith. Lawson took pride in his background and made no attempt to conceal it, although he dwelt on it in detail for the *Jewish Chronicle* rather than in the *Daily Telegraph*. The divisive issue of tariff reform that would produce a Liberal landslide in the general election of 1906 mattered very little. Such protectionist posters as appeared in the constituency came from the Tariff Reform League. Lawson and Straus differed little on such issues.

The *Jewish Chronicle* hoped that ordinary party lines had been sufficiently obliterated so that 'Jewish and non-Jewish electors alike have been left free to cast their votes primarily on the merits of the alien question.' Bertran Straus, the Liberal, trying yet another East End constituency, hoped to draw the overwhelming majority of the Jewish vote while nibbling away at neutral electors on the conventional Liberal issues of the day – 'peace, retrenchment and reform, economy and efficiency.' Straus proudly announced his pride in being Jewish, reminding voters in a sharp dig at Lawson that his name was the same as his father's and grandfather's. Even Straus, however, was a 'restrictionist', as was every East London member of parliament except Sir Samuel Montagu and his nephew and

---

45 Evans-Gordon narrowly lost a by-election in 1898 on the death of the sitting Conservative member to W. C. Steadman (2,492 to 2,472), and Rothschild's endorsement probably contributed to the huge reversal of the poll in 1900 when Evans-Gordon defeated Steadman (2,783 to 1,718). Fishman, *Jewish Radicals*, 86–90, presumes that such Anglo-Jews were themselves politically ambitious and cynically endorsed restriction. Even his evidence, however, demonstrates that their restrictionist views were sincerely held. Fishman's book is less valuable for his critique of the establishment than for his treatment of East End anarchism, particularly the inspirational work of Aron Lieberman. Most leading Jews accepted Major Evans-Gordon's repeated assurances that he was hostile to aliens, not Jews. See Weizmann, *Trial and Error*, 90–1.

successor as MP for Whitechapel, Stuart M. Samuel. Straus chose to represent himself as a moderate who advocated 'excluding the diseased and criminal alien'. For the rest, he stood for free trade, an end to contract Chinese labour in South Africa, trade union wage rates for all government employees, for reform of the land laws (always a good and meaningless cry in an urban constituency), and equalization of rates (a matter of considerable local consequence in a poorer district of London).

The voters showed more concerned for bread-and-butter issues – the high price of provisions and unemployment relief. Although the politicians and parties devoted much attention to the alien issue, hoping to use the election result as a mandate one way or another, campaigners in the field quickly discovered that the rising price of sugar mattered more than allegations about alien competition and displacement. Neither Lawson nor Straus let restriction go, both feeling still that victory ultimately would hinge on that issue. Then Straus began to backpedal. By the end of his campaign he talked at length about which aliens he would keep out. The results could give satisfaction either way. Lawson held this safe Conservative seat by a scant seventy-eight votes, breaking a string of government losses. Restriction ultimately was not the issue on which the voting turned. Lawson, however, acted as if it were. Immediately after the election, he pledged, in Stepney, to use his considerable influence with Balfour to bring in a drastic aliens bill.[46]

Some measure to limit alien immigration was certain to pass. Once the Balfour government had brought in its bill in 1904, it found the measure ill-suited to the purpose it proclaimed. The veneer of debating rhetoric did not disguise the actual legislative intent – slowing the flow of East European Jews. From time to time the rhetorical veneer vanished. 'Stepney is not Palestine,' shouted Hayes-Fischer, 'and these aliens might find a Promised Land elsewhere.' The House of Commons rocked with approving laughter. Serious issues, preposterous speculations, thoughtful concern and blatant prejudice tumbled over one another during the discussion. The economic argument was too complicated and subtle to influence the debate. The Royal Commission on Alien Immigration investigating the alien question reported in 1903 that English skilled labour had suffered no serious displacement. As to unskilled labour, the evidence cut both ways. The Board of Trade stressed the new, substantial export trade that the aliens had built from nothing. In London, Manchester and Leeds immigrant Jews had created or revived industries employing not only Jews but native labour. Labour displacement was too tricky an issue for the conventional oversimplification of political debate, almost too complex for objective analysis. Alien Jews moved principally into trades already in decline, paying wages and offering conditions that British workers would not accept. Were the job to be done, only immigrant Jews would do it. Housing in Stepney was an undeniable problem, but the rigorous enforcement of existing sanitary legislation could resolve much of it. The voluminous testimony to the commission, often highly charged both ways, was of mixed value, the commission's summary an uneasy balance, and the recommendations for strong legislation on which Evans-Gordon

46 See Straus to the editor, *JC*, 10 Feb. 1905. Straus felt confident the forthcoming Aliens Bill would be quite moderate. The restrictionist issue had been milked for all it could give in Mile End with severely disappointing results. Were the Mile End election to be repeated in the next general election, few Tory seats would remain in London. The *Jewish Chronicle* reported all constituency and political club meetings concerned with the forthcoming Aliens Bill.

above all insisted, squared so little with either evidence or report that Lord Rothschild and Sir Kenelm Digby, senior permanent secretary at the Home Office, sharply dissented.[47]

Some critics, among them spokesmen of established British textile industries, contended that a reputation for 'cheap and shoddy goods' was, on balance, harming British trade. The short-term benefits of the new exports placed the British traders' reputation for quality, built up over generations, at risk. Opponents of restriction pointed out in response that London slop tailoring pre-dated substantial Jewish immigration, having formerly being been done by an Irish colony in Soho. Those workers had not been 'driven into destitution by the aliens; they had drifted into occupations more congenial to them.' Much of the garment trade, to be sure, was conducted in sweatshops, but that issue did not lend itself to any easy solutions. The sweaters themselves were as poor as their hands, working long hours under the most marginal conditions. Sweating could be addressed through more vigorous enforcement of existing factory and workshop legislation and the local sanitary codes. Other critics argued that the severe undercapitalization of sweatshop industries adversely affected British businessmen. Aliens, so they argued, were prone to go into bankruptcy 'with a large amount of unsecured liabilities'. John Burns turned the economic argument on its head. Why not, he asked, exclude the rich Jews of the West End rather than 'begin a system of petty persecution against men whose only crime was their poverty'. On other issues, the facts were only a trifle more clear. No one disputed the statistics of 'colonization' within the borough of Stepney. But those numbers gave rise to more petulance than purpose. Canon Barnett of Toynbee Hall social work fame had testified before the royal commission that Stepney was less crowded than it had been before the alien incursion. That did not interest one of the most dedicated populists, Thomas Fowell Buxton. Aliens disrupted his Fabianesque local government reforms.

> The County Council had gone to great expense in dealing with the housing question, and at the present moment in their model dwellings in Boundary-street no less than 24 per cent of the residents were aliens. I object as a ratepayer of London to being called on to provide model dwellings for the unhoused population of the East of Europe.

For the measure before the House in 1905, Buxton conceded that he just did not like poor Jews.

> The objection I have to them is that they are in a totally different state of civilization from what we desire in this country; that neither in race, religion, feeling, language, nor blood were they suitable or advantageous to us, and they were by far the most destitute of all aliens who come to these shores.[48]

---

47 For the Report, see *PP* (1903), IX (Cd. 1741–43). Gainer, *Alien Invasion*, chapters 7–8, is an excellent, thorough discussion of the Commission and the 1904 and 1905 parliamentary debates. Conservative constitutionalists understood some of the more troublesome questions in the Alien Bills. See, e.g., Dicey to Bryce, s.d.[1904], MS. Bryce 3/39 in the Bodleian Library.

48 Debate on the second reading of the Aliens Bill (Passed 211 to 59), House of Commons, 18 May 1905. Cutting in HO 45/10303/117267/62.

Alien criminality was much bandied about, but no statistics supported such charges. East European Jews were, by all accounts, law-abiding, industrious, sober, and anxious to improve themselves. The occasional Jewish alien in the workhouse – and one had to look far to find one – was, more often than not, there 'for the purpose of reminding their friends that they are bound to support them'. Everyone agreed that Britain could and should exclude 'undesirables'. But who were they? Few took exception to banning the immoral, although almost everyone conceded that hard-core criminals were unlikely to be caught in an immigration officer's net. Deportation of aliens who abused English hospitality was acceptable to all parties. The Aliens Bill, however, established an important precedent, instituting a summary procedure without judicial appeal, a matter that troubled even some partisans of alien restriction. Those committed to civil rights found the idea intolerable. James Bryce, the scholar-statesman, called the Aliens Bill 'a sort of scarecrow to frighten alien immigrants, which was neither a sapient nor a dignified course for this country to adopt'. The bill was a 'sham', and its authors knew it would not work.[49]

The bill was supposedly designed to bar the immoral and criminal. It would do neither. Both could enter with ease for the simple price of a first- or second-class ticket. Only the poor would be affected. Just as in the United States, only 'alien steerage passengers' were regulated. Evidence was available about the movement of foreign prostitutes. Newhaven, Folkestone and Dover, their most conventional ports of entry, would lie outside the new regulations. Restrictionists did not care. The definitions of those to be excluded left everything to be desired. As with so much 'anti-white slave' legislation, the words the proposal used were magnificently imprecise. What did 'decently' mean? Who was to define decency? Only the poor remained. But Home Secretary Akers-Douglas and the government argued at considerable length that they wanted self-sufficient immigrants. Why, then, bring in this measure, for Russian and Polish Jews rarely failed to become completely self-sufficient? Minimal communal aid had enabled the overwhelming majority of them to adjust successfully to their new community.

Many then and since have puzzled as to why Arthur Balfour, who knew how to use parliamentary procedure as well as any man, should have directed the 1904 bill into Grand Committee. Once there, Liberal sharpshooters, led by their most recent convert, Winston Churchill, sniped the measure to death. Gladstone had created the Grand Committee in 1882 to counteract Irish nationalist parliamentary obstruction. By moving non-contentious bills through this select body, minor clauses and details of law and phraseology could be smoothed out. Putting such a controversial measure in Grand Committee invited its decimation. Various explanations could be offered, the most cynical being that Balfour disliked the measure as passed and wanted it killed without taking the blame for it. Certainly Balfour was much distracted by the highly divisive controversies on free trade that

49 Debate on the second reading of the Aliens Bill (May) 1904 (Passed 241 to 117). Cutting in HO 45/10303/117267/8.

were shaking the Conservative and Unionist parties. But Balfour's only procedural alternative, the Committee of the Whole House, was not that much more inviting.[50]

The Jewish leadership found much to its taste in the Aliens Bill. Anglo-Jewry had no objection to barring the mentally unfit or those who, through infirmity, were likely to become chargeable to the public. Nor, save for criticizing the ease with which such a provision could be evaded, did community leaders object to excluding an alien sentenced in a foreign country 'for an extraditable offence'.[51] Anglo-Jewry rejoiced to see in the 1905 bill that England would not renounce its sanctuary for political refugees. But the leadership took the strongest possible exception to the omission of refugees from religious persecution. Moses Gaster, in a characteristic outburst, charged the government with drawing up an alien's bill combining 'the worst features of Rumanian hypocrisy with the draconic legislation of Russia'.[52]

The tradition of political refuge must, all Jewish leaders felt, hold for religious refugees. Otherwise, as the Board of Deputies reminded the government, preposterously inhumane results must follow from the legislation as drafted. The board offered a telling example. Two Jews barely escaped with their lives from the massacres at Kishinev and Gomel. One, a proscribed member of a revolutionary society, would be safely welcomed to England as 'desirable'. The other, who had joined no society, would, by definition, be excludable. Both sides realized that opening the door to religious refugees might, in effect, prevent the exclusion of any East European Jews, save perhaps those from the Ottoman Empire.[53] Russian, Polish, and Roumanian Jews, moreover, could obtain official certificates of character or passports only with great difficulty and some bribes. Russian police certificates of character were 'a farce'. They cost about ten roubles. With one, an individual could then be granted a passport, after paying 'moderate' bribes for about £3 10s. But

> no workman, however good his character, who has been involved in a trade strike, or who is suspected of Progressive views, can obtain his Certificate, while the keeper of a disorderly house and the fraudulent Bankrupt get theirs as a matter of course.

50 Balfour's papers and private correspondence cast no light on this point. Akers-Douglas, the Home Secretary, found himself in Grand Committee with a hopeless task. The following year, Balfour's government made no pretence about 'non-contentious', and introduced the bill under the 'guillotine', which imposed strict time constraints on debate and gave any administration whose whips could control its majority a sure win.

51 Leonard Cohen, president of the Jewish Board of Guardians referred to them as 'those who never ought to have come here'. 27 July 1904, HO 45/10303/117267/18.

52 Chalmers memorandum. 17 May 1904, HO 45/10303/117267/18. The case of Moische Smolenski tested the issue. Smolenski was a Russian Army private stationed in Krementschug when an anti-Jewish riot took place. Smolenski left his barracks to protect a friend, also a Jew, threatened by the rampaging mob. By leaving the barracks and not returning within a certain time, he was liable for two years hard labour and deserted to avoid it. The Immigration Board had to determine whether this was a religious or a political act and whether or not it fell within the stipulated exceptions to the 1905 statute. The Home Office ruled it political, since martial law had been declared. Smolenski's motive had to be considered as well as his offence. Since he did not leave the barracks for any personal reason but in consequence of the disturbances, he was allowed to remain in England. HO 45/10327/132181/11.

53 H. L. W. Lawson, editor of the *Daily Telegraph* and victor in the Mile End by-election, raised the matter as a parliamentary question on 3 May 1905. Home Office officials wrestled with the issue and ultimately decided the answer must depend on the facts in any individual case. HO 45/10303/117267/49.

Possession of these documents was but the first step. Were certificates of character and passports to be made mandatory, as the Aliens Bill required, any Jew's

> chance of escape merely depends on the mood of the series of functionaries through whom their application passes, and at best will simply depend on the extent of the rapacity of such officials. This process of extortion must have an adverse effect on the Alien's small savings, which should form their capital on arriving here and the English regulations will throw these hapless people still further into the hands of their oppressors.[54]

Behind the objections on principle lay problems in both law and administration. The legislation empowered the Home Secretary and various ill-defined authorities with a wide measure of authority without judicial review. Such an accretion of administrative authority and power brought liberal and radical critics to the barricades. Led by Winston Churchill in his newly tailored Liberal party costume, Charles Trevelyan, and Sir Charles Dilke, the 1904 bill was slaughtered in committee. The issue of constitutional safeguards, which much concerned the Jewish Board of Guardians, led ultimately both to the dropping of the 1904 measure and the amendment of the bill that passed in 1905. Given the wide range of administrative discretion still involved,[55] local immigration boards would lack the sophistication to understand 'the peculiar qualities of the immigrants, whose fate and future they are called on to decide'. The Board of Deputies believed, however, that 'if some member of the Jewish Community, possessing a thorough knowledge of these people, be appointed a member of each immigration board, . . . the chance of miscarriages of justice will, to some extent, be lessened.'

This heated debate on one small, if significant point of the religious refugee conveys an erroneous impression of Anglo-Jewish resistance to restrictionist legislation. The Jewish leadership found many of its objectives served by a statute of which it could never openly approve. Anglo-Jewry would have preferred to make its own decisions about who should be allowed to land and who refused, as to some extent it had done for so many years. Jewish institutions had finally managed to have it both ways. They had stood up for the cause of the community, while the government assumed one of their tiresome and expensive burdens, repatriating undesirables and those who could not adapt to British life. The Aliens Act of 1905 continued, to a considerable degree, policies that the Jewish elite had pursued for decades.

> Had the Bill only limited its operation to criminals, prostitutes, persons with infectious diseases, idiots, or even persons of notoriously bad character, [Board of Deputies president David L. Alexander told the Home Office] I

---

54 BDBJ, Objections to the Aliens Bill, July 1904, HO 45/10303/117267/16.

55 The bill provided, for instance, that any alien in receipt of poor relief brought before a court of summary jurisdiction within twelve months of landing, found wandering without 'ostensible means of subsistence', or 'living under insanitary conditions due to overcrowding' could be expelled. Once more the vagueness of the terms was painfully clear. What made matters worse, the shipping company was liable for the expenses of supporting and returning the alien and his dependants to his port of departure. To Liberals like Walter Runciman, who also happened to hold a major interest in shipping lines and acted as a spokesman for shipping interests, this made the measure doubly impossible. Runciman Papers, *passim*. and HO 45/10303/117267/3, 5, 6, 20, 26, 54, 58, 60.

may say that the Jewish community would not have offered a murmur of opposition, nor is there the slightest objection to that power which is proposed to be given by clause 3 of ordering an alien on conviction to leave these shores.[56]

Agitation to secure the bill that failed in 1904 and the one that passed in 1905 forced the Jewish leadership to take careful stock of its own attitudes and interests. Sharing restrictionists' hopes that limiting immigration would ease downward pressure in the labour force, Anglo-Jewry focused more intensely than ever on the possibilities of moving surplus Jewish workers onwards. The Jewish Board of Guardians, for instance, created a Jewish Emigrants Information Board to advise would-be emigrants where their best prospects lay. The information board drew on a network of correspondents that the Jewish Board of Guardians had built over the years through its emigration committee. Screening all applicants, the information board could guarantee advisers and 'certificates of respectability' for approved immigrants.

> We urge the many Jewish workmen who, owing to overcrowding and continued absence of regular employment, are earning but a precarious livelihood, or who desire to better their conditions, and to live in a land where the rent is not so high, and where the air is fresher, to consider carefully the possibilities of emigration.[57]

Canada afforded the most openings, had synagogues and facilities for Jewish life. But what started as an orderly effort to siphon marginal Jews from the East End became, with the Russo–Japanese War, almost a panic-stricken effort to process refugees out of England as quickly as possible. Fleeing Jewish Russian reservists were bustled onwards to Canada or Argentina lest yet more fuel be added to the anti-alien fire. The watchful popular press approved, applauding the attentive supervision of Jewish institutions, but always hinting that behind each army 'deserter' was a wife who had sold off whatever assets the family had and who would follow her husband to whatever his final destination might be. Magistrates courts also yielded their quota of data for the restrictionists. Abraham Galob, a Russian Army deserter, drew a three-month sentence for theft. In London for three weeks with no prospects, he turned in desperation to housebreaking.[58]

The debate did not stop with the Aliens Act of 1905. The issue now became administration. Restrictionists badgered Home Secretary Herbert Gladstone about his 'deficient' enforcement. The Tottenham murders of 1909 and the Sidney Street affair in 1911, which combined crime and radical politics, triggered renewed anti-alien agitation, but in general all parties settled down to living with the Act.

---

56 HO 45/10303/117267/18. Evans-Gordon reminded the Home Secretary, 'The Jewish Community is as much interested in the exclusion of undesirable persons as the rest of the people of this country. When sending emigrants to their own colonies they make the most careful inquiries into the character, health, and antecedents and general suitability of the people they send.' Evans-Gordon was willing to accept Sir Samuel Montagu's suggestion that certificates of character should be given by the local rabbi. Evans-Gordon to Akers-Douglas, 17 May 1904. HO 45/10303/117267/18.

57 C. Waley Cohen and Frank Goldsmith to the editor, *JC*, 10 Mar. 1905.

58 *Daily Chronicle*, 6, 7 Dec. 1904; HO 45/10404/117267/8; JBG, *Annual Report for 1904* (1905); *JC*, 10, 17, 28 Mar 1905.

Anglo-Jewry continued to worry about civil rights and administration. Restriction-ists portrayed a nightmare of loopholes. But the facts were irresistible. The number of immigrants steadily declined, continuing a trend reaching back into the 1890s. Anglo-Jewry drew more and more heavily on new state institutions, and continued to refine its own socializing institutions. State collectivism continued to merge well with Anglo-Jewish philanthropic social control. Newly arrived British Jewry prospered and grew restive at the old elite's continued demands for deference. When alien legislation next became a serious issue, the target would be German subversives, not East European Jews. A Home Secretary of impeccable Liberal credentials, Reginald McKenna, put through the Aliens Restriction Act of 1914, a measure that swept aside every restriction on the right of the Home Office to bar or deport without appeal. With provisions and controls much extended, it remains in force today.

11

Endorsing the Unthinkable

The attitude of Jews towards the aliens has been the subject of criticism, not always in the best taste. But an equally interesting point is the attitude of Judaism, the religion, to the stranger. One is proud to recall that the teaching of our faith in this regard is unfailingly humane.

'Judaism and the alien', *Jewish Chronicle*, 24 February 1905

POLITICIZING THE COMMUNITY

The Board of Deputies, to the annoyance of community activists, rarely took political initiatives. The executive preferred discreet negotiations, a strategy to which it made few exceptions. Judicious discussions, as far removed from the glare of publicity as possible – so ran leadership thinking – best served the community. Before the twentieth century, the board rarely appealed to Jewish members of parliament as a 'bloc', although individual Jewish members conducted behind-the-scenes lobbying on its behalf. This Anglo-Jewish preference for discreet diplomacy in both domestic and foreign affairs had much to commend it. British Jews, a trivial numerical minority of the British population, were themselves politically hypersensitive. England had furnished Jews great scope. Patience, diligence and unity delivered Jewish opportunities and rights over the first two-thirds of the nineteenth century, and those gains, Anglo-Jewry believed, must never be placed at risk. Anti-Semitism, even *Judenhetze*, seemed real risks in the world of the Dreyfus affair in enlightened France or Jew-baiting in the highest German Imperial circles. Had not anti-Jewish violence broken out in New York? Sinister power and influence was attributed to Jewry even in the English world of tabloid journalism and in the music-hall culture that traded on the manipulation of recognizable symbols. Under these circumstances, political discretion seemed the rational course. Allowing any issue to be defined too clearly as in the Jewish interest could, in Anglo-Jewish eyes, do more harm than good.

Jewish political needs were best served when communal wants could be represented not as Jewish but as in the best national interest. What happened when this was not the case? Anglo-Jewish efforts to bring British diplomatic pressure to bear on Russia and Roumania to ease the persecution of their co-religionists continually foundered on this quandary. Britain supported individual freedom and liberty of conscience as abstract principles, but in the post-Bismarckian world, gratuitously offending either Russia or Roumania, let alone both, was not perceived as serving British national interests. Conservative and Liberal governments alike made sympathetic noises about persecuted Jews, but *Realpolitik* imposed its unsentimental demands. By the same token, Anglo-Jewry preferred to have Gentile sympathizers take the lead in parliament on domestic issues of communal concern. Sir Charles Dilke, Sir Charles Trevelyan and Winston Churchill, for instance, took command in the Grand Committee's parliamentary massacre of the Aliens Bill of 1904.

The leadership's responsive, if not passive, strategy left it vulnerable to communal criticism. Leopold Greenberg, the publisher who was shortly to take over the *Jewish Chronicle*, communal activists Herbert Bentwich and Joseph Cowen, and Haham Gaster, among others, goaded institutional leaders at every opportunity for their failure to endorse activist positions on alien immigration, Russian and Roumanian persecution, and Zionism. Each was a sorely contentious issue. Anglo-Jewry had mixed views on immigration restriction and did all that could have been done, given the political realities of the times, about Russia and Roumania. Anglo-Jewry was overwhelmingly hostile to Zionism and Jewish nationalism, whatever sympathy such doctrines might have elicited among the East End rank and file. To the great majority of the Jewish establishment, accepting Zionism meant surrendering a century of real achievement within the diaspora for an unrealizable and to them undesirable fantasy.

On each of these issues, however, a constituency of indeterminate size took the contrary view. Championing unrestricted immigration, denouncing East European misgovernment and pogroms, whether sponsored or spontaneous, purged the individual soul and proved effective communal politics by the beginning of the twentieth century. Kishinev, for instance, offered East End radicals an opening they attempted to exploit. Anglo-Jewish tactical sensitivities could not assuage communal anger. A combination of trade union activists and veteran political agitators organized the International Kishinev Protest Committee in June 1903 and sponsored the public meeting the leadership declined to convene. Proclaiming that Jewish security depended upon revolution in Russia may have stirred the angry crowd, but those resolutions conveyed a highly misleading impression of East End political sentiment. Having given voice to precisely those views Anglo-Jewry had been at tactical pains to conceal, the organizers attempted to translate the transitory euphoria of one public meeting into effective institutional form. They reorganized themselves as the Jewish Labour Defence Committee.[1] Although that grandiose conception fared as poorly as other efforts to build effective Jewish trade unions, the committee was symptomatic of a newly emerging world of Jewish politics. While communal deference persisted, the personalities to whom it was paid and the institutions through which it worked were subject to increasing competition. The entrenched conservative Jewish establishment was no longer in undisputed command.

These divisive issues were symptoms of deeper change within the community. British Jewry was becoming restive. East European Jews were not merely a substantial

1 *JC*, 17 July 1903.

majority of Jews in Britain but were increasingly self-confident and self-assertive. The politics of deference on which the Anglo-Jewish elite had built its structured community were under attack. A growing number believed the old guard had guarded too long. Zionism, since it also enjoyed support of a few within the charmed circle, became a rallying point for both true believers and those who saw in Zionism a vehicle to seize power within a democratized Jewish community. Denouncing Russian and Roumanian abuses was like being against sin. Those who had no communal responsibilities also laboured under no political or tactical constraints. Unlike Yiddish-speaking political radicals and Jewish Hampdens, moreover, these bourgeois communal Jacobins flaunted untarnished religious credentials. Greenberg belittled Liberal Judaism and the Jewish Religious Union and denounced anything that smacked of compromises in Orthodoxy. Greenberg and Bentwich, arguing that Anglo-Jewry was selling Jews out, demanded to testify before the Royal Commission on Alien Immigration in 1903. There they denounced every compromise. Restrictionists were, they argued, anti-Semites.

The lines played well in the East End, but Anglo-Jewish influence carried the day. Deference was a long time a-dying. The ageing lions of Judah still had teeth and claws. The brutal Kishinev massacres of 1903 in which government officials were culpable if not actually sponsors of the pogrom roused Western opinion. Theodore Roosevelt, that American master at combining virtue and political opportunism, took a hard anti-Russian line. Christians and Jews jointly sponsored French and German public meetings denouncing the perpetrators. Anglo-Jewish leaders, however, counselled a measured response. David Alexander of the Board of Deputies and Claude Montefiore of the Anglo-Jewish Association believed that a Jewish-sponsored public protest would be counterproductive, but they were hard pressed to restrain their organizations. They would publicize the facts. They arranged subscription funds to relieve the victims. But Christian sponsorship was not forthcoming, and they did not want an Anglo-Jewish sponsored mass public meeting, particularly just when the whole issue of the Jewish East End and alien immigration were so much in the public eye.

The Conjoint Foreign Committee fended off a proposal for such a public gathering, but Greenberg, Bentwich, Cowen and Gaster were determined to try to override the committee at special meetings of the parent bodies. Sir Samuel Montagu brought his wisdom, experience and authority to the special meeting of the Board of Deputies in June. He not only slew but drew and quartered activist enthusiasts. Public meetings already held in the East End and Hyde Park, Montagu observed, disgraced the community and endangered Russian Jews. 'Apart from the fact that socialists and nihilists had presided and taken part in those meetings, the resolution that had been passed urged that the first step in the emancipation of the Jews was the abolition of Tsarism.' These little people glorified themselves and accomplished nothing. Important non-Jews organized the New York and Paris meetings, and they produced good results. Had English Christians been as forthcoming and wished to sponsor a meeting in London, Anglo-Jewry would have been overjoyed to cooperate.

Montagu would have nothing to do with a wholly Jewish meeting. The United States was, he continued, 'the only country which Russia fears.'

The United States holds, and perhaps will continue to hold, the balance between nations in the far East, and if anybody could do anything, America, with her million Jewish subjects, is the right country to take the lead. . . . The Mansion House meeting [of 1882] was necessary because Russia had promulgated laws avowedly affecting the Jews, and they had been bound to protest against what was admittedly a Government action.[2]

After Kishinev, Montagu reminded his listeners, the Russian government expressed its apologies and took action. To call the Russians liars and denounce them would be 'risking the lives of the five million Jews that remained in Russia'. Joseph Prag was gavelled and voted down when he appealed to Alexander at the Board of Deputies to cut through the red tape and be a true leader of British Jews. Greenberg attempted a flanking attack through the United Synagogue but was ruled out of order trying to bring the issue before its governing body.[3]

The Anglo-Jewish Association was another matter. Even old Frederic Mocatta felt that there could be no harm in a public protest meeting, and Claude Montefiore, strongly of Montagu's opinion, lay stricken with influenza. It fell to Lucien Wolf, now moving to the forefront of establishment Jewish foreign policy, to try to hold the meeting. He won the debate but lost the vote.

Those who clamoured for a public meeting did so in the pain and mortification caused by a close contact with the facts of the situation. But what they had to consider in this matter was not how much they felt but how much good they could do. They had had a public meeting in 1882, and in 1890, they had had another. What really happened? The outrages of course ceased, but they ceased before the meetings were held. During the eight years that had elapsed between the two the alien question had been born.[4]

Those eight years, Wolf explained, also gave rise to repressive legislation in Russia, the extension of the anti-Jewish May Laws. Tsar Alexander III thereafter considered Jews to be enemies of his dynasty and nation. A Jewish-sponsored indignation meeting could accomplish nothing. It would only do harm, exciting the patriotism of even those Russians who might be well disposed towards us. Enthusiasts should reconsider their own motives, he warned and not demand a public meeting 'for the purpose of relieving their chests of an indigestion of indignation'.

The Conjoint Foreign Committee again beat back the proposal, and Montefiore retrieved the Anglo-Jewish Association at a subsequent meeting. Montefiore was named as the British representative to go to an international conference of West European leaders sponsored by the Hilfsverein in Berlin to consider Kishinev, the international management of Jewish immigration, and the white slave trade. Still

2 BDBJ Minute Book, special meeting, 28 June 1903. Bentwich's proposal lost, 30 to 1, all partisans save the sponsor scattering before the broadsides of Montagu and Leopold de Rothschild. Montagu knew his East End far better than his intellectual critics. Even Israel Zangwill was grist for Sir Samuel's mill two days later at the board meeting of the Federation of Synagogues. *JC*, 3 July 1903.

3 BDBJ meeting, 17 June, BDBJ Minute Book, 17 June 1903; United Synagogue council meeting, 16 June, reported in *JC*, 19 June 1903.

4 Wolf would argue in very similar terms during the war in 1915 and 1916 (see chapter 12). AJA council meeting, 14 June, *JC*, 19 June 1903.

concerned about his health, he deputed Wolf to act in his place. With control once again vested safely in establishment hands, cooler councils prevailed at home and abroad.

This pragmatic, case-by-case approach to politics meant that Anglo-Jewry responded pragmatically to issues as they arose rather than refining and acting on any comprehensive programme. Anglo-Jewry had general objectives but was principally concerned that no measure should injure the community or thwart observant Jews. Should some general benefit be involved, so much the better. Each nineteenth- and twentieth-century education bill, for instance, was considered on its specific merits as it came forward. Neither the education nor the law and parliamentary committee of the Board of Deputies had defined positions or desiderata, although they carefully considered the impact each proposal might have on British Jews in both state and voluntary schools. Given the national clash of Christian denominational passions whenever an education bill came forward, Anglo-Jewry was well advised to stand aside, urging only minor amendments as the bills progressed, and let Nonconformists and Anglicans battle it out. Sunday closing proposals, annually brought forward by Lord Avebury and Christian sabbatarians, always involved Jewish interests, but Anglo-Jewry acted with great restraint, intervening only when it appeared that one of the annual private bills might pass. As issues involving broadened state social commitments came forward, Anglo-Jewry sought to secure provisions within each statute, and administrative decisions once they came into operation, to secure those benefits to all co-religionists, native, naturalized or alien.

Some measures – immigration restriction was one – permitted no evasion or temporizing. Anglo-Jewry had private mixed feelings: a determination to retain, as far as possible, the selection of 'appropriate' Jewish newcomers in its own hands, a commitment to the principle of the right of asylum, tempered by complete agreement with those who sought legislative exclusion of the criminal, the incapacitated and the unsuitable. Anglo-Jewry could not, however, afford to appear remiss in defending Jews. Gaster touched a sensitive nerve when he denounced the leadership's refusal to bend their administrative rules for Roumanian Jewish refugees in their hour of need. At the conference held to consider what to do,

> not a single trace of high principle, not a word of sympathy and encouragement fell from any of the so called leaders of the Jewish community. Not a word was uttered save such which were promoted by timid fear or by the idea that Jews could be expelled from England. . . . The belief that the Jews of England were erecting barriers against them and barring their doors could but intensify their misery and add to the weight of the chains that already oppressed them.[5]

Gaster alone would have had little impact on Anglo-Jewry's natural tendency to evade and delay, but his words were increasingly heard and felt in wider circles of

---

5 AJA meeting, 2 June. *JC*, 7 June 1901. No issue of the *Jewish Chronicle* from the 1880s onwards lacked its litany of Roumanian abuse. Publication of Edmond Sincerus, *The Jews of Roumania. The Laws and Their Consequences* (London, 1901), coincided with this communal debate. Originally published in French, the book cogently restated the systematic Roumanian evasion of Article 44 of the Treaty of Berlin and shredded apologist arguments.

British Jews. Aliens, now a majority of British Jews, were moving up in the world, possessed a stronger sense of self, and were less inclined to defer or automatically to toe the leadership's line.

Anglo-Jewry acted. Community testimony was organized for parliamentary committees and royal commissions. Communal notables responded to media criticism through letters to the editor and responsive articles. Once restriction had become a matter of party politics, the board could temporize no longer and established its own alien immigration committee. Of all of the tasks immediately at hand, the first was to develop the most accurate possible statistics. Friends and foes of immigration restriction were equally ignorant of facts. Whatever Llewellyn Smith and the Board of Trade statisticians might have done, accurate numbers proved difficult if not impossible to develop.[6]

Committee minutes reveal two major related activities. The first were efforts to amend bills as they appeared and moved through their several parliamentary stages. The second was more subtle, reflecting the fact that Anglo-Jewry had its own 'exclusionist' agenda. Foreign Jews, the committee found, actually were living in deplorable conditions and undercutting wages at Merthyr and Dowlais in Wales. Could something be done to secure the cooperation of the Jewish Colonisation Association to move these unfortunates onwards to Canada as quickly as possible. If they remained, they might become evidence for our enemies?[7]

The other Anglo-Jewish strategy was to cast foreign Jews in a favourable light. Hannah Hyam, a social worker and philanthropist with more insight and judgement than most, presented a strong, sensible case to the most receptive part of the government coalition, the Women's Liberal Unionist Association. Since Joseph Chamberlain was running up the restrictionist standard on his Unionist party protectionist flagpole, her statement was apt and timely. Foreign Jews, she reminded her listeners, had a far higher standard of living than the public realized. As evidence, she cited the large number of butcher shops in the East End, a point that Montagu had emphasized before the royal commission, which testified to the excellent diet of the newcomers. The Commission on Physical Deterioration, established in some public panic after the Boer War, revealed an intolerably high number of rejects for military service, but the commission found Jewish children an exception, well cared for and in sound physical condition. The high percentage of foreign Jewish children in school, the determined upward economic mobility of the newcomers, and the intense patriotism of the Jewish aliens made them a national asset to be encouraged, not a problem.[8]

6 C. H. L. Emanuel (BDBJ secretary and solicitor), Report on the State of Emigration and Immigration, 1897, 1898. BDBJ B 2/1/1; Report of the alien [immigration] committee, 26 Oct. 1903, BDBJ B 2/1/1; B 2/3/6.

7 Committee minutes, 10 Mar. 1904, BDBJ C 13/1/5. Wales was a sore point. Not only had it been the scene of one of the only outbreaks of anti-Jewish violence, but Cardiff authorities, in particular, systematically fanned restrictionist flames. *JC*, 7 June 1901.

8 Meeting of the Kensington branch, 10 Feb. 1905. *JC* 17 Feb 1905. Much agitation seems to have gone into keeping Jewish spirits up on the subject rather than convincing anyone else. Charles Rosenfelt, for instance, produced a little pamphlet, *Progress or Retrogress* (London, 1905), ostensibly addressing the issue from the perspective of 'religion, psychology, and morals'. His tract was much more likely to make the Jewish community feel good about itself than have any significant impact on the general public, although Earl Spencer, Sir Charles Dilke and Winston Churchill's endorsements appear on the flyleaf applauding its message.

The Aliens Act actually passed in 1905 appeared far less threatening than the measure defeated in 1904. Some Jewish leaders, and not merely the more activist among them, thought the Liberal government of Sir Henry Campbell-Bannerman would deliver them from the more troublesome clauses of the measure and rigorous, at times almost capricious administration. Was not Herbert Gladstone, now Home Secretary, the son of one of religious liberty's greatest public spokesmen? And was not young Herbert Samuel, that rising star among Jewish members of parliament, the Under-Secretary? But the Home Office, although receptive to administrative suggestions and anxious to secure the cooperation of Jewish organizations, at least in part to simplify its own administrative burden, had no intention of repealing or substantially amending any part of the Act of 1905.[9] When, moreover, activists pressed the Board of Deputies and its relevant committees to memorialize the government, Lord Rothschild, to whom the board appealed as the leading figure in Anglo-Jewry, absolutely refused to be a party to anything more than 'a moderate letter asking for improved administration'. Were the matter to be raised in parliament, he warned, the Jewish community was likely to find itself confronted with a more severe rather than a modified measure.[10]

Kishinev, set as it was in the midst of the controversies swirling around the Royal Commission on Alien Immigration, established the lines on which Jewish foreign and domestic policy would be fought out through the First World War. The overwhelming majority of Anglo-Jewry stood against Zionism and Jewish nationalism as a threat to every goal Western Jewry had won since emancipation. Russia and Roumania must be convinced that their own national best interests were served by granting Jews equal rights. While the leadership continued to move substantial numbers of East Europeans onwards to the Americas or the British Empire, Anglo-Jewry stood firm on the principle of immigration exclusions or communal repatriation. The differences of opinion between the Anglo-Jewish establishment and the more moderate restrictionists was one of degree and authority, not one of substance. Both wished to exclude criminals, the immoral, and the physically or mentally incapacitated. The Jewish leaders preferred to repatriate those who failed to build independent lives for themselves in England, while others preferred the authority to exclude those 'likely' to be unable to do so from landing in the first place. Anglo-Jewry, moreover, was not happy to see the state making decisions it would prefer to make for itself. Once the government began to determine matters

9 See, *inter alia*, Chalmers to Gladstone, 10 Jan., 6, 19 Mar. 1906, Gladstone Papers, Add MS 45,993, ff. 10–11, 17–18, 19–20; Churchill to Gladstone, 8, 28 Feb. 1907, Gladstone Papers, Add MS 45,986, ff. 127–30, and HO 45/10327/132181; HO 45/10335/138344; HO 45/10341/139774; HO 45/10515/135080, HO 45/10517/135339, and HO 45/10522/139441 passim. The 'little H.O. Jew', as one of Walter Runciman's annoyed correspondents called Herbert Samuel, did far more than the Board of Deputies activists would allow, to ease the problems of administration and attempt to find the broadest basis of cooperation between the government and the Jewish organizations. See, R.W.L. to Runciman, 26 May 1906, Runciman Papers, WR 14.

10 D. L. Alexander, the Caesar of the Board of Deputies and usually the soul of discretion and moderation on such points, initially sided with the activists, only to have Rothschild very sharply slap him down. Alien immigration committee minutes, 7, 11, 14 Nov., 12, 13 Dec. 1907, BDBJ C 13/1/5. The board went ahead with a much watered-down Memorial which drew an annoyed response from the Home Office. ibid, 15 Jan., 7 May 1908.

hitherto decided by Jewish organizations, where would it all stop? While making enthusiastic common cause with the state on domestic policies as central and local authorities standardized and underwrote the principal costs of social welfare, Anglo-Jewry still attempted to preserve social institutions which served its social, religious, and political philosophy.

ALIENS: THE QUESTION OF ADMINISTRATION

Implementing the Aliens Act proved almost as controversial as passing it. Both extremes, partisans and critics, remained carping and dissatisfied. Restrictionists portrayed loopholes as sluice gates through which the residue of Eastern Europe continued to pour. Critics contended that screening standards were capriciously and inconsistently applied. Confusion reigned from the beginning. Akers-Douglas, the Conservative Home Secretary, did not even have time to sign the administrative procedure orders before Balfour's government was out of office. Restrictionists feared that Liberals would gut the measure. Herbert Gladstone as Home Secretary and Herbert Samuel as Under-Secretary were suspect in their eyes. Few Liberal voices had mouthed restrictionist rhetoric. The new Liberal government was seen at best as disinterested in and at worst as disinclined to rigorous enforcement. Samuel as a Jew and Gladstone as a champion of civil liberties were closely watched. For almost nine years, until the First World War resolved the issue on terms no restrictionist would previously have dared to ask, Vincent, Evans-Gordon and Claude Hay in a steady barrage of parliamentary questions demanded sterner administration and fewer exceptions.

Opportunities for criticism were immediately forthcoming. The Sylvia Rosenbaum case created just the publicity Anglo-Jewry wished to avoid and exactly the kind of issue with which Evans-Gordon and other restrictionists hoped to embarrass the Government. Sylvia Rosenbaum, recently arrived in London, had slipped through or rejected the usual Anglo-Jewish institutional screening. A young and attractive orphan, she drifted into prostitution, into the hands of a notorious pimp, and was soon up on charges of robbery in a brothel. Magistrate Dickenson lacked the evidence for a felony conviction but hoped, with the cooperation of the Jewish Board of Guardians, to have her voluntarily deported to her native country. She declined. Her pimp paid her fine. The Home Office, not informed of these details, refused to consent to Dickenson's deportation order. Within three months, Sylvia had robbed a Norwegian sailor of thirty shillings and was once again on remand. This time she was deported, but not before the press and public had gained an exaggerated sense of Jewish involvement in vice and crime, the National Vigilance Association had been given an opportunity to offer its undesired services to save the government from 'future embarrassment' in such cases, and the Home Office developed long-overdue improved communications with magistrates.[11]

Leonard Cohen, who as president of the Jewish Board of Guardians and unchallenged spokesman for Jewish social welfare institutions, had ridden out the

---

11 HO 45/10334/137764/4–7; *Observer*, 3 June 1906; *The Times* , 4 June 1906; *Globe*, 4 June 1906; *Daily Telegraph*, 12 June 1906.

communal storm of criticism that had blown up when he testified in favour of statutory restriction in 1903, now argued for further legislation. Board of Guardians resources were overstrained (a fact that Rothschild, who invariably found his pockets being picked to cover any deficit, also mentioned). Provisions should be tightened, Cohen argued, to deal with 'diseased aliens' who took advantage of the provision exempting boats with fewer than twenty passengers from inspection to slip ashore. This was not an issue of the right of refuge. Such newcomers, Cohen argued, overtaxed limited Jewish resources and strengthened the case of anti-Semitic agitators.[12] Cohen had told the Home Office in 1904 that he looked forward to the government absorbing the costs of repatriating undesirables. The burden, at the time, fell upon the Jewish Board of Guardians, comparable societies in other countries, and the shipping companies. 'Undesirables', however, were those who arrived 'with a physical incapacity, obvious to the eye, and [men] of very poor physique, and, of course, persons who are engaged in immoral trade, such as souteneurs, procurers, and that class of person, and of course, prostitutes.' The new legislation proposed to fix responsibility for these costs on the shipmaster.[13]

The records of the Jewish Board of Guardians from 1905 to 1914 tell a story of close cooperation with the Home Office. A working relationship grew easily between a government with a history of respect for the rights of legitimate refugees and an Anglo-Jewry always sensitive to domestic political nuance. The Board of Deputies settled happily for administrative consultation and participation. Its president, David L. Alexander, sat on the Home Office Departmental Committee on Receiving Houses. In the best British tradition, the Jewish establishment understood that immigration control, like so many other things, would be a matter of men, not measures. The Board of Deputies immigration committee, in cooperation with the Jewish Board of Guardians, named the Jews to sit on immigration boards. Both government and Anglo-Jewry welcomed the partnership. The Home Office defused possible Jewish establishment resistance. Although Anglo-Jewry would have preferred to screen its own community, the government was performing a task Jewish organizations had laboured at for years, and doing so at the taxpayer's expense.

For the Jewish elite, important internal political issues were at stake. The establishment secured its flank against communal critics by ascertaining that the precious right of asylum was protected. Home Secretary Gladstone was delighted to give reassurance on the point. Under his administration, any new arrival could assert that he or she was a political refugee, placing the burden of proving otherwise upon the immigration officer. An appeal system, which never fully satisfied any group, restrictionist or otherwise, worked reasonably well for those who could find support ashore. The poor who were not English-speaking, who lacked British connections or sponsors and who could not prove that they had useful economic skills, on the other hand, had little chance. However awkward and unpredictable this system might be, most of Anglo-Jewry would find little fault with its general results.

12 Alien immigration committee minutes, 10 Mar. 1907., BDBJ C 13/1/5.
13 'They are now voluntarily undertaken because no public fund available for the purpose exists; but in these struggling days, even charitable societies are loath to assist the Treasury in self-imposed responsibilities.' May 1904, HO 45/10241/B37811/15.

Administrative details required constant fine tuning. Sanitary issues loomed increasingly large in the pre-war spate of local government social intervention. Various London County Council and borough council authorities wanted clarification of public health requirements in transmigrant housing facilities. Debate about what impact restriction might have on the British shipping trade concerned the royal commission and members of parliament considering the 1904 and 1905 bills. Already burdened with financial responsibility for removing would-be newcomers rejected by immigration authorities, the shipping trade, being as competitive as it then was, tried to cut other corners and costs, contending, among other things, that ordinary common lodging house requirements should not obtain in transmigrant facilities.[14] Piecemeal adjustments created overlapping and contradictory decisions and results. By March 1910, the immigration committee was undertaking a wholesale revision of Home Office procedures in processing aliens. Communal controversy was quickly suppressed. Herbert Bentwich of B'nai B'rith and David Alexander of the Board of Guardians agreed on the format and procedures for the aliens legal aid committee. While under the aegis of the Board of Guardians, the committee included involved experts, like Stettauer and Landau, and those apt to raise problems, like Haham Gaster. The Russo-Jewish Committee and B'nai B'rith shared the expenses. Alexander and Emanuel remained firmly in command. As in other instances, control of appropriate organizations meant tactful and effective management of a sensitive issue. Much of the difficulty revolved round the unsatisfactory nature of promises of employment for those seeking to land. Home Office figures suggested that four out of five immigrants did not take up or stay with the employment named in the undertaking they had made when landing. Committee investigation suggested that the market was working too well. Immigrants broke their original engagements to take other jobs at higher wages, although Home Office numbers were inaccurate. The board and Home Office ultimately shelved the question in 1913 when the Home Office accepted employment 'options' as well as specific employer engagements. What once had been protests now became tactful negotiations with Under-Secretary Pedder at the Home Office.[15]

Both sides continued to grumble, but little more was changed. Troublesome cases would be matters for special negotiations. A foreign-born couple long resident in England were sentenced to prison and subsequent deportation for neglect of

14 For the sensitive negotiations between the LCC, the Home Office and Kahan and Co. (acting for the Royal Mail Steam Packet Company) between 1906 and 1907, see HO 45/10336/138914/3–4. Landau's Poor Jews' Temporary Shelter, although its interests were much involved given its boarding-out facilities, opted to stand aside from the discussion in this instance.

15 Pedder did not always find them tactful or accurate and his irritation can be seen in file marginalia. See, e.g., the correspondence, 13–19 May 1910, HO 45/10522/139441. For the alien immigration committee, see BDBJ C 2/1/1; the aliens legal aid committee (1911–4) C 2/1/2. The committee heard sixty-eight appeals at nineteen sittings (1911–12) and eighty-two appeals at twenty-eight sittings (1912–13), the majority of which were allowed to land. Of fifty-eight cases heard between August 1911 and February 1912, for instance, forty-five appeals were allowed, thirteen denied. For the operation of a small provincial organization, see the files of the Grimsby Hebrew Immigration Society in BDBJ B 2/1/13. Would-be immigrants sometimes managed their own cases without assistance or counsel. See, e.g., the three young man who appealed on 9 June 1911 and won admission. *JC*, 16 June 1911. See also, BDBJ to Akers-Douglas, 9 May 1905, enclosing BDBJ, *The Aliens Bill*, 1905. HO 45/10303/117267/56.

their five children. Alexander approached Pedder on humanitarian grounds to stay the deportation, assuring him that a special fund had been raised in the East End 'to give the couple, who were in poor circumstances, a fresh start after serving their sentence'. At the same time, a newly-married wife asked that the board appeal to prevent a deportation order being made against her husband. Alexander determined that the offence was too serious for the board to interfere. Members of parliament, particularly advanced Liberals representing London constituencies, occasionally weighed into this comfortable alliance, attempting to cut through bureaucratic routine in individual cases for humane considerations and to score political points with their constituents.[16]

Not all Jewish leaders, needless to say, cheerfully accepted these compromises. The Haham, Moses Gaster, striking a characteristically didactic and bellicose pose, demanded that Winston Churchill and Herbert Samuel take the lead in securing a mild administration of the 1905 Act. He then insisted that the new Liberal government amend the measure to give refuge for victims of religious 'persecution', not merely of religious 'prosecution'. Jews, Gaster warned, would remember their friends and punish their foes at the next general election.[17] But Anglo-Jewry as a whole confined itself to token criticism or resistance. Sir Samuel Montagu (who had become Lord Swaythling) took a more matter-of-fact attitude. He asked Home Secretary Herbert Gladstone if there were any chance of repeal. If not, he observed laconically, he would attempt to prevent Jews 'from knocking their heads against a stone wall'. Since his nephew, Herbert Samuel, was Under-Secretary, Swaythling was satisfied that the Act would be administered in a benevolent spirit.[18]

While the Aliens Act of 1905 proved a measure with which the Jewish leadership could come to terms and with which they were in underlying agreement, it, like Kishinev, left residual bitterness in the Jewish community. The measure's intended selectivity helped to underscore the lines of conflict between part of the community and their leaders. All British Jews were 'immigrants', but official scrutiny was now reserved for those who resembled the more recent newcomers. British Jews of East European origin, often not yet naturalized, shared their culture, their background, and, increasingly, their ideology. Much of the future sympathy for Zionism, just as past and current episodic enthusiasm for varieties of socialism and anarchism, grew from the mobilized sentiments of

16 As did Wedgwood Benn, among others. Chalmers to Gladstone, 23 Aug. 1906, Gladstone Papers, Add MS 45,993, ff. 37–8; *Daily News*, 23 Aug. 1906. For the Rosenfeld and Silverman Cases, see law and parliamentary committee, 16 Mar. 1913, BDBJ C 13/1/7. For the implementation of the Home Office administrative procedures, see HO 45/10517/135339/1–42; HO 45/10327/132181/1–28; and HO 45/10515/1350801/36; MEPO 2/986, 2/1006, 2/1155, 2/1178, 2/1678..

17 Gaster to Churchill, 13 Dec., Gaster to Samuel 13 Dec. 1906 [*sic.*, 1905]. Gaster Letter Book, March 1905-June 1906. Religious 'persecution' potentially opened the door for uncontrolled immigration; much effort had gone into securing religious as well as political 'prosecution'. See, e.g., HO 45/10303/117267. Even Gaster was willing to concede that the Aliens Bill would undoubtedly be of relatively low priority 'from a party point of view' for the new Liberal administration. Churchill's role in killing the 1904 bill in committee was doubly significant. It marked his first major contribution as a Liberal and established him as a hero for the significant Jewish element in what would be his Manchester constituency. For his flamboyant play to the Jewish gallery, see R. Churchill, *Winston Churchill*, II, 81–3; Marsh to Gladstone, 15 Apr 1908. Gladstone Papers, Add MS 45,986, f. 131.

18 Swaythling to Gladstone, 13 Dec. 1907, Samuel Papers A/24/10 in the House of Lords Record Office.

poorer and foreign Jews. They did, as Gaster said they would, remember their friends and enemies. Zionism, simply by affronting so much of the Jewish elite, helped to mobilize and politicize the new against the old, the poor against the rich, the outsider against the establishment.

The Aliens Act of 1905, of course, applied to all aliens, not merely Jews. Anti-restrictionists derived ironic consolation from some unintended results of the legislation. The Foreign Office, for instance, often found itself tidying up after over-zealous officials. The Folkestone immigration officers seemed, in Foreign Office eyes, intent on disrupting Anglo-French relations. Such well-publicized difficulties merely hinted at the problems the measure created. 'This wretched Aliens Act,' remarked Foreign Secretary Grey, 'will end by leaving us without a friend in Europe.'[19]

Even deportation could be a two-edged sword. The metropolitan police reported the case of an individual who either could not or would not speak who was arrested for wandering round Margate without any apparent means of support. He was deported as a Russian Pole of unknown name. The Russians refused to have him since his identity and national origin were unclear. In January 1906 he was once again in police custody, and no one could determine who or what he was, or even whether he was merely pretending to be dumb.[20] The Home Office, with, to be sure, considerable prodding, allowed a Russian refugee, rejected by the United States, to land as a victim of 'religious persecution', although only on the understanding that he would collect his family from Russia and proceed to the United States as soon as he could save sufficient funds to qualify for entry.[21] 'Political' offences opened Pandora's Box. One Jewish petitioner claimed to have escaped from Odessa where he had refused to fire upon his brethren. Investigation revealed, however, that he had been living in London, robbed his father, spent the money in Hamburg, and was now attempting to slip back into England.[22] Was the Jewish reservist fleeing call-up in the Russian army a political refugee or an 'undesirable'? And what about the intransigent politics of violence, which the English always liked to believe was the peculiar monopoly of other people? Did Britain actually wish to open its doors to the terrorists of the day? The sensationalist press was always there, ready to pounce. The *Daily Express*, for instance, notified Scotland Yard with some enthusiasm about the anarchist Voitchevsky, who had settled into the Whitechapel Jewish Co-operative Stores, with his reputation for terrorism.[23] In 1909, two men, ostensibly anarchists, murdered a policeman in

19 Grey to Gladstone, 13 Feb. 1906, Gladstone Papers, Add MS 45,992, f. 125; Cambon à Grey, 31 jan. 1906 in FO to HO 9 Feb. 1906, HO 45/10327/132181/17 and L. Paulian à Bertie, 6 fev. 1906. Ibid., 18. For the tortuous negotiations with various countries and rules on repatriating foreign lunatics, see Foreign Office memorandum, 28 July 1903, HO 45/10289/110706. The French lost a lengthy struggle with the British with each anxious to dump a group of troublesome Serbian gypsies on one another. *The Times*, 8 Feb. 1905; HO 45/10303/117267/8.

20 Only Gilbert and Sullivan could have done justice to this case. MEPO 2/931.

21 Case of Meir Rodenovich. Apr. 1906, HO 45/10341/139774/1–3.

22 Chalmers to Gladstone, 31 Aug. 1906, Gladstone Papers. Add MS 45,993, ff. 41–2. From time to time, Jewish authorities burned their fingers very badly on ill-chosen cases. See, e.g., the Marks case. Emanuel to Gladstone, 22 June 1908 and Troup's sharp rebuke to Alexander, 3 July 1908, BDBJ B 2/1/15.

23 Their information actually preceded that from the Russian chargé d'affaires. Chalmers to Gladstone, 19 Mar 1906, Gladstone Papers, Add MS 45,993, ff. 19–20.

Tottenham. Whether the gang of aliens who killed one policeman and wounded two others in Houndsditch on 16 December 1910 were anarchists, as they claimed, or merely burglars, they raised the spectre of the politically dangerous and criminal alien who might slip into England. Home Secretary Winston Churchill literally called out the army to arrest them in the famous 'siege of Sidney Street' on 3 January 1911. Public hysteria had been roused, and even this one-time outspoken defender of free Jewish migration sought to tighten immigration controls.[24]

Churchill conceded that no practical legislation or system of administration could totally 'prevent the entry or return to this country of undesirable individuals', nor should the Liberal party concede the principles it had proclaimed on excluding aliens 'or upon the right of asylum'. All Liberals, including Prime Minister Asquith, however, had suggested that 'the principle of expulsion for abuse of hospitality' could be more effectively developed. On grounds like this, Churchill believed, no responsible citizens would disagree. Anglo-Jewry had no more use than the government for the criminal alien. Framing such a measure, however, required that the government simultaneously safeguard the mass of unnaturalized aliens from any sense of harassment and satisfy the public demand for more effectively 'ridding this country of common alien criminals of the most dangerous type'. Anglo-Jewry could enjoy the luxury, once again, of having the government assume a task that it could not politically do itself. Churchill understood the difficulties.

> Two naughty principles are involved in it. First, a differentiation between the alien, and especially the assimilated alien, and a British subject, and second, that an alien may, in certain circumstances, be deported before he has committed any offence. Both these principles can be effectively sustained. The Bill aims, however, at removing the great mass of non-naturalised alien population from the fear of being harshly used by the new provisions. If an alien has lived here for five years free from crime, he will, except in respect of bearing arms, suffer no disability or risk of expulsion, although he may not afford to become naturalised.[25]

24 Churchill to Asquith, 3 Jan.; Churchill to George V, 19, 29 Apr. 1911. M. Gilbert (ed.), *Winston Churchill: Companion Volume*, II/2, 1032, 1066, 1072. See also, CAB 37/105/2(1911) and the memoranda of Chalmers and Pedder, January 1906 in HO 45/10327/132181/11. Sir Robert Anderson, the highly respected police commissioner, weighed into the fray with 'The problem of the criminal alien', *Nineteenth Century and after*, 69 (February 1911), 217–25. Sidney Street led some magistrates and immigration committees to take a far more rigid line. See, e.g., Wolfe to Emanuel, 13 Feb. 1911, BDBJ B 2/1/11 and the collection of Grimsby cases in HO 45/10341/139774/1–6. Grimsby, however, had a history of being capricious. See, e.g., the Haffenberger case, where a man with £40 cash, a shopowner with other property, was refused the right to land for want of means and had his request to appeal denied. Law and parliamentary committee, 10 Mar. 1908, BDBJ C 13/1/6. The Southampton immigration board rejected a Russian journeyman cabinet-maker from Montevideo (no evidence was given as to whether he was Jewish or not) in spite of the appearance of a master cabinet-maker before the board to offer the applicant a job. *JC*, 27 Jan. 1911.

25 Churchill, Criminal Aliens, 19 Jan. 1911, Lloyd George Papers, C/18/2/1. The cabinet committee on Home Office bills included Lord Crewe, Lord Beauchamp, Herbert Samuel, Walter Runciman, and Birrell, each of whom had strongly civil libertarian views of aliens. In spite of the treaty establishing the legal aid committee, Bentwich continued to snipe at the board when it failed to take what he considered to be a strong enough line against impending aliens bills. See, e.g., his charged that, in failing to oppose Churchill's 1911 measure, the board 'had abdicated its right to protect Jews'. BDBJ Minute Book, 29 May 1911. The *Jewish Chronicle* editorially echoed Bentwich on 9 June 1911.

As Churchill's measure moved forth, however, the new concerns of the Committee of Imperial Defence also came into play. Questions of aliens and national security, which would come into greater and greater importance during and after the First World War, were tacked on to the bill. Broad clauses and the power of regulation through Order in Council cloaked the legal circumscription of civil rights with the all-important mantle of national security. Anglo-Jewry still approved, so long as the legal right of appeal to an expulsion order was maintained. Jews were, after all, patriotic Britons.[26]

Alien restriction, simply by being on the books, produced its intended effect, one to which the Anglo-Jewish leadership was by no means hostile. The flow of aliens slowed dramatically. The causal connection, while universally presumed then and since, was not necessarily correct. Immigration had already declined and would almost certainly have continued to do so, interrupted by spurts such as the Russo–Japanese War and the 1905 revolution produced. The difference with or without legislation was a matter of degree, not of kind. Britain was no longer the attractive opportunity it once had been. Many Jews who originally settled there understood this and chose to move on. America, in spite of economic booms and busts, remained a more attractive labour market. Given the ample cultural and institutional support in the new world, whether in the United States, Canada or Argentina, immigration streams would, of their own accord, have moved away from the British Isles. Emigration from Britain continued more or less apace, although immigration steadily declined. Jewish processing agencies meeting regularly at Frankfurt conferences worked effectively to route the flow around England and onwards to the western hemisphere. The 110,700 transmigrants of 1907 going through the British Isles sagged to 61,680 by 1908. East European Jews were, moreover, as their western co-religionists had hoped they would, working out viable lives within the Russian Empire, however precarious they might be.

Anglo-Jewry took no less pleasure in the impact of 'liability to expulsion' clauses on alien crime. Within three years, the number of aliens charged with offences before the Central Criminal Court had dropped to a third of those in the years immediately before the Act. Criminal alien expulsions (by no means all Jewish) were running at slightly over three hundred a year by 1907. From 1906 to 1909, the Aliens Act also enabled the government to deport '384 aliens of an extremely objectionable character' who had entered the country as transmigrants but declined to move on. Shipping companies, now bonded under the provisions of the Act, better policed the character of the passengers they landed.[27] Jews and crime remained a serious problem for the communal image. Anglo-Jewry decried the readiness with which the press would identify this or that malefactor as 'a Jew', but the popular media dealt in sensationalism. Little adrenaline ran when identifying a housebreaker as a Wesleyan.

26 See Churchill's explanation, 12 Apr. 1911, to the King; Alexander to Churchill, 15 May; Pedder memorandum, 16 May, Ruggles–Brise memorandum, 17 May 1911, and Churchill's firm directive about the Board of Deputies to the Home Office staff: 'Keep them friendly . . .' Gilbert, *Winston Churchill: CV*, (II/2)1251–3, 1256–7.

27 Akers-Douglas, Home Secretary during the Balfour administration, proudly paraded Haldane Porter's statistics while complimenting himself and Home Secretary Gladstone on their administration of the Act. 14 June 1909, 5 Hansard 6, 739–83. Gladstone also took prompt action against immigrants with criminal convictions. Ibid., 815.

On issues of procedure, Anglo-Jewry never secured all it asked for, but the evidence is murky that those matters topped its crowded agenda. Between the Act of 1905 and the outbreak of war in 1914, Jewish leaders were anxious to define legal protection for aliens. While Anglo-Jewry accepted and even quietly endorsed measures of discrimination, it demanded fair process before immigration boards, particularly the provision of interpreters in court on appeals from board decisions. The Board of Deputies, in spite of its bold stance on this matter, needed full board endorsement to commit substantial funds for its own alien immigration committee, and that membership hated to spend money. While prepared to deal with cases on an *ad hoc* basis, the board had no intention of expending more than £30 to £50, scarcely a massive commitment to civil rights. Critics of such niggardly behaviour commented tartly that poor aliens were badly served by British Jewry's allegedly 'most representative' body. This was a class, not a mass, society. East European Jews would never forget that the 'old guard' of the Board of Deputies refused to extend itself for Jewish newcomers. But meanness of spirit or 'class prejudice', to whatever degree they might have been involved, were only part of the explanation. The Board of Deputies had little money. Other institutions, religious and social, managed the communal purse. They, as we have seen, had evolved in a haphazard manner, resisting almost all attempts to rationalize or coordinate their activity. The protection of would-be immigrants was nobody's central concern. The Poor Jews' Temporary Shelter, increasingly funded by and working with the shipping companies, specialized in transmigrants. The Russo-Jewish Committee had been established to deal with Jewish victims and refugees. The Board of Deputies believed that the committee was the logical body to bear those expenses. Self-propelled immigrants were, all Anglo-Jewish institutions agreed, on their own and at their own risk. Relief institutions served 'refugees', a term used, however, with some measure of discretion and flexibility.

The Russo-Jewish Committee, however, was running low on funds and high on commitments: English language training for immigrant adults, subsidies for provincial communities accepting Jewish newcomers, loans and social services for worthy beneficiaries not yet eligible for Board of Guardians support, contributions to the international Jewish immigration processing network, and even relief for Jews in Russia. The Board of Deputies, thrashing about for some funded body to underwrite immigrant appeal legal expenses that the board would not or could not pay, pointed to the Russo-Jewish Committee. When the committee pleaded overcommitment and poverty, the Deputies replied that the committee should appeal to the whole Jewish community, not send the bill to the Board of Deputies. This bickering underlined an important Anglo-Jewish assumption. The market was an acceptable test of communal priorities. Success in annual or special fund-raising was, in Jewish establishment eyes, the best measure of community endorsement for institutions, programmes, and policies.[28]

28 Alien immigration committee minutes, 5, 23 Oct., 3, 15 Nov. 1910, BDBJ C 2/1/1/1. The Board of Deputies took great care but paid surprisingly little for such important and demanding appointments. Court interpreters had to know German, Russian Yiddish, and English. Rehfisch, translator at Whitechapel County Court and clearly the most able, eventually had to go during the war because he was of German origin. BDBJ B 2/10/12. The salary of £150, if not princely, brought out thirty-four candidates in January 1899. See BDBJ B 2/1/6; BDBJ Minute Book, 23 Nov., 21 Dec. 1899; Emanuel memorandum, 15 Oct. 1896, BDBJ C 13/1/4.

NATURALIZATION

Naturalization further complicated the tangled problem of aliens and immigration. The Board of Deputies had for years urged the government to secure reciprocal rights for naturalized subjects. Naturalization brought the alien Jew in England the full rights of any Briton, but should the naturalized Jew return, for instance, to his native Russia, he was still treated as a Russian Jewish subject. Just as problematical were third-country problems where Britain had no treaty covering issues of citizenship and naturalization. The Golden case, where a Russian-born, English-naturalized Jew residing in Prussia was expelled without cause as a Russian Jew, frustrated the board. The Conjoint Foreign Committee, to which the issue was sent, thereafter urged the Foreign Office to secure full rights for naturalized as well as native British subjects.[29] Naturalization policy affected the immigrant who had long since landed. Traditionally, any child born in Britain was, by right, a British subject, but a surprising judgement clouded that principle. It arose in a 1904 voting registration decision. A Pontypridd registering barrister decided in 1904 that a child of immigrant parents, although born in Britain, did not have the franchise since his father was still not naturalized. Thus naturalization, not merely the security of being accepted as a landed alien, came to assume still greater importance. Naturalization, moreover, was an issue about which the Board of Deputies had strong feelings. Applying for British citizenship was one of the ways in which newcomers to the community demonstrated their ultimate adjustment to and full participation in British life. They felt the prize of citizenship should be made as accessible as possible.

Problems, in so far as any existed, were of degree, not kind. Neither the board nor Liberal party leaders found the existing rules inappropriate. The Naturalization Act of 1870 demanded a £5 fee (although other costs involved meant that a candidate would normally expect to spend nearly £10), five years, residence, and testimonials from four householders as to the applicant's character. Two major issues, cost and literacy, nagged the Jewish leadership. The £5 naturalization fee excluded the poor. That was potentially politically dangerous, underscoring economic and social divisions within the community and further taxed communal charitable resources. Every government felt that the fee had the salutary effect of checking capricious applications from marginal social groups.[30] The Jewish leadership had mixed

29 BDBJ Minute Book, 18 July 1897.

30 The fee had been £1 after the implementation of the Act of 1870. Home Secretary Harcourt, who had a tidy, cost-accounting mind, raised it to £5 in 1880, not to deal with any inrush of applicants, but to cover costs and the time involved. Childers, in a moment of political passion, reduced it to £1 again as a response to the Franchise Act of 1884 and the urgings of Sir Samuel Montagu. Matthews raised it again in the Conservative government of 1886 on the grounds that during the six months the £1 fee had been in force, applications for naturalization doubled. The metropolitan police could not cope without adding extra staff. Herbert Gladstone, as Home Secretary, believed that naturalization agents were behind the renewed agitation. The only pressure for change came from the Manchester Liberal Association and Sir Stuart Samuel, the Jewish activist MP for Whitechapel. 'I have received,' he observed in a confidential memorandum for the cabinet, 'no representations from the leaders of the Jewish community.' 29 July 1907. Churchill urged Gladstone to set a £3 fee which was estimated to meet costs in 1908, although he did not move in that direction after he became Home Secretary. Churchill to Gladstone, 24 Feb. 1908, in Gilbert (ed.), *Winston Churchill: CV* (II/2), 762–3. See also, CAB 37/89/75; HO 45/10063/B2840A; HO 45/9952/B31998; HO 45/45/9682/B13456.

feelings about the literacy requirement. Communal institutions, after all, strove to create Jewish Englishmen. Knowing English was part of being British. But Anglo-Jewry, like the host culture, prized demonstrated moral qualities above all. What about those long resident in England of unimpeachable character who lacked the time or opportunity to master the language? 'An elderly man usually got naturalized,' reported the secretary of the Metropolitan Naturalisation Society, 'not for himself, but so that his children under age might get naturalized with him for one fee.' The Board of Deputies felt that such cases should remain exceptional and that the matter was best managed through case-by-case negotiations with the Home Office.[31]

Neither cost nor language was a problem for the more prosperous aliens, so those issues smacked of class discrimination within Jewry and heightened that invidious distinction between rulers and inferiors. On this issue, provincials, being more politically sensitive to newcomers and resentful of London domination, tended to take a stronger line for amendment than most of Anglo-Jewry. Manchester, with a well-organized naturalization society, was often in the lead. The Manchester organization protested at the mechanics of naturalization administration and argued that the literacy requirements had merely become a device for excluding acceptable applicants solely because they were Jewish or 'different'. The police determined literacy, and in Manchester they reputedly had anti-Semitic attitudes. The Board of Deputies, after much discussion, particularly in the London and provincial committees most directly concerned, compromised. The committees ultimately acknowledged the undesirability of eliminating all tests, but felt that the capacity to write one's name and 'reasonably understand and speak the English language' should suffice. Were the requirement to be more severe, authority should not lie in the hands of the police.[32] Manchester continued to agitate to promote its own case, but it needed more friends than Winston Churchill. The Home Office dug in its heels. Herbert Gladstone and Herbert Samuel had formulated Liberal policy in 1906. The candidate for naturalization should have sufficient English language skills to understand and to discharge the duties of citizenship.

> Mere conversational facility when he meets a gentile does not suffice to show that a Jew is identifying himself with English life. On the contrary, if the only newspapers he can read are the Jewish ones, the likelihood is that his ideas are kept widely apart from those of the ordinary English citizen.[33]

Both London and provincial clubs aided aliens to secure naturalization. Partly benefit societies, such clubs enabled individuals slowly to save the substantial sum

31 De Hass testimony to the law and parliamentary committee, 5 Apr. 1905, BDBJ C 13/1/6; Law and parliamentary comittee, Sept. 1912, BDBJ C 13/1/7. B. A. Fersht, who was to play so active a role in communal friendly societies, was also president of the Spitalfields Naturalisation Society, continually urged the Board of Deputies to negotiate removal of the language restriction from the requirements. The board somewhat uneasily refused, although it consistently thumped for a substantial reduction in fees. See, e.g., law and parliamentary committee, 6, 22 Mar. 1906, BDBJ C 13/1/6.

32 Law and parliamentary committee minutes, 4, 14 Dec. 1911, BDBJ C 2/1/1. The Manchester Jewish Naturalisation Society, organized in 1894, claimed that it had helped to secure 340 certificates in its first ten years. *JC*, 31 Mar. 1905.

33 Pedder memorandum, 27 Dec. 1912, HO 45/10687/226279/6. See also ibid., 1, 4–5; *JC*, 9 Aug. 1912.

TABLE 11.1   Jewish naturalization, 1902–1910[34]

Year	Total naturalized	Russian total	Russians from London
1902	766	458	220
1903	868	544	273
1904	961	464	217
1905	652	240	101
1906	811	321	126
1907	654	232	90
1908	545	174	42
1909	849	242	81
1910	1,091	390	205

Source: Board of Deputies of British Jews Papers C 2/1/1.

required to secure naturalization. Not only did candidates have to accumulate £5 for the fee, an agent who expedited matters needed to be paid, sponsors had to be found and certificates attested to. As if this were not enough, the alien must purchase the 2s 6d Inland Revenue stamp, even pay another 2s 6d fee to take the oath of allegiance. When the Home Office regulations on language tests came into force, they seemed most unfair, a cruel stumbling block for the hundreds who had been putting their pennies and shillings into their naturalization society. The Board of Deputies protested at the behest of the Metropolitan Naturalisation Society:

> This pressed hardly on men who had been subscribing for some time to Naturalisation Societies and to certain Jewish tradesmen whose occupations did not permit their acquiring a good knowledge of English.[35]

to which the Home Office responded only with a promise to consider each case on its individual merits. Having made an effort but certainly no fuss, the board returned to consider weightier matters.

Manchester's naturalization society was open to all, Jews or Christians. Although initiated in 1893, the practical work of the organization only began in February 1895, when forty-eight members were enrolled. By the end of the year 123 subscribers were on the books, and during the year, twenty-six members had

34 No official statistics were kept on religion or ethnicity, merely prior nationality. Both Jewish and governmental agencies believed numbers of 'Russian' and 'Jewish' to be approximately the same. There could be no doubt that the Home Office 'literacy' policy of 1905 sharply reduced the percentage of Russians among those naturalized. The figures suggest that provincial naturalization societies were the more active from 1905 until 1910 and that in spite of their efforts, Jewish naturalization never approximated to the 60 per cent or more of the total as it had done before 1905.

35 BDBJ Minute Book, 28 Mar., 19 Nov. 1905. See also HO 45/10687/226279/5; Law and parliamentary committee, 21 Apr. 1904, BDBJ C 13/1/5. In March 1905, for the first time since 1895 (when Russians and Poles coming in the great migration would have begun to be eligible for naturalization), Germans moved ahead of Russians as the most substantial nationality becoming British. Jews were a substantially lower proportion of Germans than Russians. *JC*, 7 Apr. 1905.

received their certificates of naturalization while fourteen more were pending. Members subscribed one shilling or more each week towards their ultimate naturalization fees and expenses. The society held classes to bring applicant English literacy up to the mark and also arranged for the appropriate testimonials as to character. Whenever enough funds were in hand, a ballot was taken among those eligible, and the winners received their certificates.[36] The Leeds Jewish leadership created a naturalization club to assist landed Jews to become British subjects and acted as a screening agency to ascertain that certificates were granted only 'to people of exceptional character'. The club claimed to have helped more than a hundred Jews obtain naturalization in 1903 and 1904 as the agitation for immigration restriction reached its parliamentary peak. Suddenly, as the Balfour government determined to have its bill in 1905, that society found its work at a standstill when Home Secretary Akers-Douglas refused to grant naturalization to anyone who could not write and read English 'besides trying to put other obstacles in the way'.[37] Manchester Jews seconded Leeds frustration, taking particular exception to being fobbed off with the Home Secretary's suggestion that applicants prepare their own applications and avoid any but official charges.[38]

After a few angry editorials in the Jewish press coupled with protests and the occasional provincial deputation, Anglo-Jewry fell back into its former habits. Those alien Jews who were willing to sacrifice time and money to undertake those things necessary for citizenship would, in the elite's view, become responsible British subjects meeting their obligations and enriching the life and substance of Anglo-Jewry. Those who would not did not, in the final analysis, deserve to share fully in British culture. They were and would remain, to some degree, strangers. But the war clouds settling over Europe would soon raise again the question of

---

36 First annual meeting of the Manchester Naturalisation Society, Jews' School, 26 Jan. 1896, J. Salomon presiding. Some half a dozen benefited from the drawing at this meeting. *JC*, 31 Jan. 1896. Manchester Jews continued to press for eased requirements. See, particularly, the letter of the president of the Manchester Liberal Federation to Home Secretary McKenna, 18 July 1912. HO 45/10687/226279/1, 4–6. Naturalization requirements confused even the most expert. See, e.g., A. V. Dicey to Lushington, 20 Nov. 1893; Lushington to Dicey, 22 Nov. 1893 (HO 45/9877/B15365) and the bundle of law officer's opinions in HO 45/9862/B13456. For a sense of the range of cabinet concerns about naturalization, see CAB 37/88/48 (1907); 37/89/75(1907); and 37/91/31 (1908); Churchill to Gladstone, 24 Feb. 1908; Dulberg to Churchill, 25 Apr. 1908. Gilbert, *Churchill CV*, II/2, 762–3, 785.

37 Hurwitz to the editor, *JC*, 24 Feb. 1905. Whatever else may have been the case, this did Gerald Balfour, MP for Leeds Central, no good among Jewish voters in the forthcoming general election. See also, *JC*, 25 Oct. 1901, 26 Sept. 1902. Russian and Polish Jews, while they had become the largest single group naturalized, were still only about 40 per cent of the total. The Home Office reported forty-five naturalizations for February 1905, for instance (with names, addresses, and occupations given in the *Jewish Chronicle* for 10 March), showing eighteen Russians, twelve Germans, three Austro-Hungarians, three Italians, two Swedes, two from the United States, and one each from Venezuela, the Netherlands, France, Denmark and the Ottoman Empire.

38 HO 45/10687/226179/4–5; *JC*, 9 Aug. 1912.

who and what were British Jews. Wartime brought restrictions even on naturalized British subjects and their children.[39]

Anglo-Jewry also found itself once again fair game in domestic political wars. The parliamentary elections of January and December 1910 produced an almost exact balance of Liberal and Conservative party strength. The Liberal government, to survive, depended on its Labour party and Irish Nationalist allies in what came to be, in effect, a radicalized progressive coalition government. Some leading Anglo-Jews, the Cohen family of Board of Guardians fame, for instance, had always been Conservative members of parliament. Rothschild supported Evans-Gordon, the Conservative immigration restrictionist, for his Stepney seat. North Hackney, Mile End and both Bethnal Green seats passed, in 1910, into Conservative hands. Although Herbert Samuel was the first practising Jew to sit in a British cabinet in 1909, shortly to be followed by Rufus Isaacs and Edwin Montagu, Liberals as politicians could be as offensive to Jewish sensitivities as the most backwoods Tory. David Lloyd George singled out Lord Rothschild, who had joined the campaign to reject his 1909 budget in the House of Lords, for a savage attack. Hilaire Belloc made anti-Semitism a cornerstone of his 1910 Liberal election campaign in Salford South.[40]

THE COMING OF WAR

From the turn of the century onwards, delicate matters of legal procedure coloured debate, legislation and administration on matters of immigration restriction. Liberals, in general, spoke sensitively on such issues, although Churchill had sought to tighten the law in 1911 as it touched on criminals and, by implication, political radicals. Both E. A. Goulding's private bill and Churchill's government measure died in committee, and the weighty agenda of constitutional reform, rearmament, Irish Home Rule and welfare state legislation monopolized parliamentary attention. When war came in 1914, the long debate abruptly ended. Reginald McKenna, reaching into Committee on Imperial Defence files, introduced what became the Aliens Regulation Act on 5 August. With scarcely a murmur or second thought, all safeguards, reviews and appeals vanished. Parliament granted the Home Secretary absolute summary power to regulate immigration and landed

39 The British steadily tightened their rules against the appointment of naturalized subjects and even native-born children of aliens to government positions, continuing, even extending, wartime restrictions after the end of hostilities in 1918. See, e.g., Leith Ross to [Drummond], 2 Nov., Dormer to Leith Ross, 4 Nov., Leith Ross to Dormer, 5 Dec. 1916, Grey Papers, FO 800/101/239–41; Report of the Committee . . . to Consider the Cases of Persons in Government Offices Not of British or Allied Parentage. (Cmd. 195) (London, 1919); CAB 24/5/251; GT-5073–4, CAB 24/57/176–8; Government Employees Whose Parents Are Not Natural-Born British or Allied Subjects, 28 Sept.–26 Oct. 1918, GT-6100, CAB 24/67/278–9; Aliens or Non-Wholly British in Government Departments, 26 Nov 1918, GT-6378, CAB 24/70/244; Aliens in Command of British Ships, 21 Feb 1919, GT-6869, CAB 24/75/306–307; Employment of Enemy Aliens in British Industry, 6 Mar. 1919, GT 6944, CAB 24/76/265–6. The usual chauvinist press kept the issue hot. See, e.g., *Pall Mall Gazette*, 20 June 1918. The War Cabinet understood these excesses perfectly well but preferred to use, not counter them. See: War Cab 24 June, 10, 11, 29 July 1918, CAB 23/6/435/9, 23/7/443/11, 444/7–10, 453/10.

40 *The Times*, 18 Dec. 1909; 10 Jan. 1910; *JC*, 17, 31 Dec. 1909, 7, 14, 21 Jan. 1910; Lipman, *Social History*, 169; G. Alderman, *The Jewish Community in British Politics* (Oxford, 1983), 81–5.

aliens. This 'temporary' wartime measure was extended in 1919 to make aliens 'attempting to cause mutiny, sedition, or disaffection' liable to deportation and created a new offence, 'the promotion by aliens of industrial unrest (as distinct from particular trade disputes in which the alien may himself be concerned)'. Gone was the statutory protection of 1905 for political asylum, Home Secretary Shortt observing tartly 'that the changed and changing circumstances of the world and particularly of Russia (whose subjects were the main object under the right of asylum . . .) render it unnecessary and undesirable to maintain this statutory provision.' The unrestricted movement of people, axiomatic in a free trade economy, checked in 1905, was closed in 1919. Anti-Bolshevism completed what anti-Semitism had begun. The 1919 Aliens Act, renewed biennially thereafter, remained undebated policy until the Alien Order of 1953 and the Alien Act of 1956.[41]

War raised the issue of patriotism in its starkest form. But it also created a double paradox. Germanophobia placed established Jews at jeopardy. East European newcomers, after all, were identified as 'friendly' aliens. Most assimilated Jews, to be sure, if not English born, were naturalized. War with Germany led many Jews like others to change their names, yet another step in anglicization.[42] War made the issue of 'enemy' aliens and what was to be done about them a matter of immediate concern. Imperial Russia was a fighting ally, so most Jewish aliens represented no immediate problem. Polish Jews, however, sometimes came from Prussian Posen or Austrian Galicia. Those not yet naturalized were enemy aliens, and the Home Office proved generally unsympathetic to their claims for exemption or special status in spite of considerable pressure from Anglo-Jewry on their behalf in specific cases. The Board of Deputies refused to take up the cause of any German, Austrian or Hungarian person merely because he was Jewish, acting only when loyalty to Britain could not be questioned. The board appealed to government officials only when specifically Jewish questions were involved. An Austrian Jew received a life sentence in Belgium for espionage. The matter received close scrutiny, and the board declined to interfere. Detention sometimes even served communal interests. A man representing himself to the Board of Deputies as a Roumanian Jew interned as an enemy alien appealed for help. After enquiries to the Home Office revealed that the man in question had been convicted on at least five occasions, the board lost interest in whether he was a Roumanian or not.[43]

41　A subcommittee of the Reconstruction Committee appointed in 1916 ultimately reported in January 1918 along the main lines the 1919 bill was to take. The 1905 Act was deemed inadequate, both for keeping 'undesirables' out and for the latitude it gave the courts. E. Shortt, Aliens Bill, 12 Mar. 1919. GT-6971, CAB 24/76/356–9. 5 Hansard 65, 1986–90; 5 Hansard 114, 2745–818; 5 Hansard 120, 57–166, 183–241, 325–43. When the Board of Deputies and Lord Rothschild asked that a Jew be allowed to sit on, and the board be permitted to give evidence before the aliens committee of the Home Office considering the problem in 1918, both requests were denied, although the board was invited to make any suggestions it might choose to submit in writing. Emanuel to HO, 18 Feb., HO to Emanuel, 27 Feb.; Law and parliamentary committee, 9 Apr. 1918, BDBJ C 13/1/8.

42　Sir Edward Troup, reviewing matters in 1918, observed that two Home Office civil servants had German names. They changed them at the outbreak of the war. One had a German grandfather who had come to England before 1800 and whose other grandfather and father were both British army officers. 'The other is a Jew whose family settled in England some 70 or 80 years ago, who long before the war was markedly anti-German, and who was one of the founders of the Civil Service Cadet Corps and an officer in the A.S.C. (T.F.).' Troup also observed that Polish Jews 'as a class ought, I believe, to be distrusted'. E. Troup, Enemy Aliens, 26 June 1918, GT-4961, CAB 24/55/212–4.

43　Law and parliamentary committee, 14, 21 Nov 1917, 19 Jan 1918, BDBJ C 13/1/8.

Board president David Alexander sat proudly as Anglo-Jewry's representative on the Central Committee for National Patriotic Organisations.[44] Sir Stuart Samuel, his successor in 1917, was no less active. Their own German extraction lay in a distant and irrelevant past. They were English. Anglo-Jews were patriots. They would not compromise with Britain's foes, Jewish or Christian. Even on matters of censorship, when letters in Yiddish were stopped unless written in Roman characters, the board sought accommodation – would printed characters be permitted? – not confrontation.[45] German nationals were the most numerous 'enemy' Jewish aliens, predominating by more than five to one over any other. Of the 66,000 individuals of enemy nationality over eighteen, some two-thirds were men. Of the 23,000 women, more than 12,000 were British born and acquired foreign nationality only by marriage. Women were not interned, although they were restricted as to residence and movement.

Lord Kitchener insisted on a large-scale internment programme in October. Within two or three weeks, about 20,000 enemy aliens had been rounded up and placed in camps under military control. Kitchener then reversed himself once more and began releasing substantial numbers on parole, about 2,700 in February 1915 alone. The Home Office, itself subject to much popular pressure on the issue, remonstrated to the Prime Minister. Internment fell most severely on Germans. Austrian and Hungarian subjects, many of whom came to be considered 'friendly' nationals by the end of the war, suffered far less than Germans. 'Ottoman subject' encompassed many ethnicities, a number of which Britain was cultivating, so only about ten per cent were actually detained. The civil service was repeatedly cleansed in screenings that reached to the humblest levels. Rehfisch, who had served so long and effectively as translator at the Whitechapel county court, lost his post because he had been born in Germany. Foreign-born special constables in London were discharged.[46] Genuine concerns about security and chauvinistic emotion both contributed to such purges.

Although empowered to take whatever action it chose, months passed before the government made up its own mind. On 13 May 1915, after the sinking of the *Lusitania*, Prime Minister Asquith announced the official policy. The government opted to intern enemy alien men of military age while repatriating enemy alien women, children, and men over military age. An advisory committee 'of judicial character' was empowered to make exceptions for men

who, by reason of close ties with this country, arising from long residence, or dating from boyhood, might be considered to have become practically British,

44 Law and parliamentary committee, 28 Oct 1914, BDBJ C 13/1/7; HO 45/10740/162173.

45 Law and parliamentary committee, 9 Apr 1918, BDBJ C 13/1/8.

46 See the law and parliamentary committee report, 14 Jan 1915, BDBJ B 2/10/12. The law and parliamentary committee attempted, from 4 March 1915 to secure the same rights for Jewish Turks as had been granted Christian inhabitants of the Ottoman Empire, but found themselves stumbling over accusations that Jews figured significantly among the Young Turks. BDBJ C 13/1/7. Gaster asked Herbert Samuel to intervene and release a harmless Belgian refugee interned as a Turkish subject of Sephardi origin. 22 Aug. 1916, Gaster Papers 68/328/1. Gaster often presumed upon his personal friendship with Herbert Samuel. See, e.g., his unsuccessful intervention on behalf of Mort Kegrinberg, alias Max Grinberg, in 1916. Samuel to Gaster, 23 May 1916, Gaster Papers 108/325/1. See also, McKenna to Kitchener, 16 Oct. 1914; Bryce to Asquith, 23 Nov 1914; and undated [late 1914] War Office memorandum, signed H.E.B., on the release and repatriation of enemy aliens. Kitchener Papers, PRO 30/57/75/WT 1–3.

and men belonging to what may be broadly described as friendly nationalities or races subject to hostile rule, while the enemy alien women and men over military age who have been exempted from repatriation are persons whose ties with this country by reason of marriage, children, or otherwise were such that no danger to the national interest was to be apprehended from their remaining here, and the enforcement of their return to their country of origin would have involved unnecessary suffering in many cases to British subjects.[47]

Males not interned were 'called on to volunteer for national service', a test which allowed constant review of their cases. Those declining to serve faced internment or compulsory repatriation. Each Home Secretary – Simon, Samuel, and Cave – applied these rules with increasing severity. The policy was repeatedly defended in the House of Commons. Exceptions were made principally to augment the agricultural workforce and, in some 1,650 cases, for their 'work of national importance'.[48]

War relief for all brought the communal rank and file out in force. Anglo-Jewish grand enterprises were remarkable in scope and substance, but Jewish workers taxed themselves without hesitation for the benefit of interned co-religionists and those impoverished by circumstances of war. The Jewish Workers' War Emergency Relief Fund challenged Anglo-Jewish and Zionists alike to set aside partisanship in the great common cause. The Mantle Makers' Union, however chequered its history as a trade organization, led the way. It refused to bend to the criticism of the Jewish press and dismissed criticism from Poale Zion. The Workers' Relief Fund was not embarrassed when the Federation of Yiddish Speaking Anarchists enrolled, reminding East Enders that Jews must help Jews in every land. Paole Zion, anxious to preserve its ostensible popularity among the people, immediately crept aboard. With Haham Gaster approving, the Workers' Relief Fund sponsored a million penny bazaar. While it fell far short of that goal, the fund had much to take pride in. Between March 1915 and April 1917, it had raised more than £7,500 and paid relief benefits in excess of £6,200. At least 20 per cent of its income went to interned Jews and their families, the Fund proudly proclaiming that it never discriminated between Jew and Jew.[49] Anglo-Jewry, for its part, did nothing to protect Yiddish newspapers, the *Jewish Times* and the *Jewish Voice*, when they were prosecuted under provisions of the Defence of the Realm Act for aiding and

47 Report of the aliens committee, 25 January 1918, CAB 1/26. The law and parliamentary committee sought to secure Jewish membership on the Home Office Aliens Committee or, failing that, to give evidence before the standing body only to be fended off by the Home Office. Emanuel to HO, 18 Feb. ; HO to Emanuel 27 Feb. 1918. Law and parliamentary committee, 9 Apr. 1918, BDBJ C 13/1/8. The cabinet was still of mixed minds in May 1915. 'We had some talk about aliens, some being for interning *all*, but W[alter] R[unciman] and W[inston] S. C[hurchill] were for observing the scrap of paper which naturalised aliens have acquired. K[itchener] remarked that no injurious action had been traced to any alien at large, while P.M. [Asquith] declared that nothing would induce him to repudiate any grant of the full privileges of citizenship to all naturalised persons'. 10 May [1915]. Hobhouse, *Inside Asquith's Cabinet*, 240–1.

48 Treatment of Enemy Aliens, June 1918, GT-1931, CAB 24/55/129–32. Kitchener's parole of Germans and Austrians, for instance, outraged the Scots. CAB 37/122/185 (9 Dec. 1914). See also, McKenna's CAB 37/122/182 (7 Dec. 1914) and CAB 37/123/10) (5 Jan. 1914 [*sic*, 1915]).

49 *Jewish Workers' War Emergency Relief Fund Bulletin, March, 1915 to April, 1917* (London, 1917), 2–13.

abetting the Amalgamated Society of Tailors in their efforts to 'impede work' on government contracts, although it was more than willing to unravel misunderstandings that led the Jewish section of the St John Ambulance Corps at Toynbee Hall to refuse to enrol naturalized Jews.[50]

Jewish prisoners of war also had to be attended to. By October 1914, the Board of Deputies was working with internment camp officers to ascertain that kosher food and facilities for worship were made available. Both proved problems so long as Jewish prisoners of war were scattered among the several internment camps. A destitute aliens committee, assisted by the Home Office, helped to provide kosher food for civilian internees and military prisoners of war. By mid-1915, the board's officers began to urge segregation of Jewish prisoners to ease the problem of providing for their diet and religious observance. In just the same way, when conscription came to Britain, the board suggested that the Home Office transfer Jewish conscientious objectors to one centre to deal with the lack of religious facilities for them.[51]

As the war progressed, British foreign policy redefined questions of nationality. Individuals, formerly 'enemies', were reclassified as 'friends'. Lucien Wolf, acting for the Conjoint Foreign Committee in 1917, intervened with the government to secure an Order in Council granting Baghdad Jews 'the special advantages asked for.'[52] The Board of Deputies sought concessions from some provisions of the Aliens Restriction Act for Polish Jews resident in Britain who were technically German or Austro-Hungarian subjects, a problem that became more acute as the Foreign Office began serious negotiations with the Polish National Committee. That committee, with its anti-Semitic leaders and attitudes, wished to limit all exemptions 'to the Polish race'. Delicate but firm negotiations on this point secured the broader definition and gave Lucien Wolf and the Joint Foreign Committee the opportunity to demand and secure Jewish representation on the Polish National Committee. That tokenism did not remove the Home Office order making a distinction between Polish Jews and other Poles. Only in 1919, when the Polish National Committee actively sought Anglo-Jewish support in its diplomatic campaign at the Paris peace conference, did it ask the Foreign Office to end the distinction. Anglo-Jewish negotiations then proceeded with the Polish National Committee on how to certify Polish-Jewish nationals. The National Committee, in spite of its anti-Semitism, felt that it needed Anglo-Jewish support for Polish national pretensions at the peace conference. Anglo-Jewry and the National Committee, moreover, shared a hostility to the more extreme claims of Jewish nationalists. Perceived common interests ultimately outweighed prejudice, as Lucien Wolf always argued that it could. A Polish Jewish Committee was established under the aegis of the National Committee to make recommendations on individual cases. By April 1919, negotiations – clearly linked to those Wolf was

50 *JC*, 5, 12, 19 Jan. 1917.
51 Law and parliamentary committee, 28 Oct., 11 Nov. 1914, 10 June 1915, 21 Nov. 1917, BDBJ C 13/1/7, B 2/1/11, C 13/1/8. Sebag Montefiore to Gaster, 21 Sept., Wallach to Gaster, 26 Sept. 1915. Gaster Papers.
52 Nathan Laski and representatives of Baghdad Jews in Manchester were particularly grateful to Wolf for his long efforts to secure this exception. Law and parliamentary committee, 1 Aug. 1917, BDBJ C 13/1/8; AJA/FAC, 3 Oct. 1917, AJ/204/4/56.

conducting at the Paris peace conference – produced a settlement. Jewish evaluation of Jewish interests was accepted coupled with Polish Jewish subordination to the Polish state. The compact finally concluded, the Home Office ended its distinction between Polish Jews and other Polish nationals.[53]

Such hard-won gains were offset by heightened nationalist paranoia. The war began with a blizzard of stories about spies that lost nothing in the telling. Demands that Germans be arrested whether any evidence existed against them or not might have been expected at the outbreak of the war. The House of Lords engaged in an extended, unprofitable debate on the spy peril on 25 November 1914. No one was exempt. An anonymous letter from a waiter at the Constitutional Club that Scotland Yard took seriously accused Asquith and others in July 1916 of acting in German interests. J. A. R. Marriott, the distinguished historian and member of parliament, repeatedly spoke out for an uncompromising policy of internment and segregation of aliens on behalf of himself and the British Empire League. The substantial dowager dreadnoughts who sponsored the league had little trouble in rousing tradesmen to sign their petition by appealing overtly to their patriotism and covertly to their desire to eliminate business competition. Closer at hand, Cuthbert Wilkinson, secretary of the League of Londoners, bombarded everybody who would listen and more who would not with abuse of aliens, enemy and otherwise.[54]

Wartime chauvinism aggravated other residual communal problems. B. A. Fersht, Anglo-Jewry's leading expert on friendly societies, struggled until late 1917 to amend the Health Insurance Act of 1911 and remove the anomalous provisions excluding aliens from benefits. By the end of the war, contributing aliens finally obtained the same terms as British subjects. What the right hand gave, the left hand threatened to take away. The civil service came sharply to discriminate against even British-born children of foreign parents, naturalized or not. The British Nationality and Status of Aliens Bill of 1918 proposed to strip children, even those born in Britain, of their citizenship should their parent's citizenship be revoked. London County Council schools sought to deny Jewish children of foreign parents the right to sit for county council scholarships.[55]

Anglo-Jewry was itself caught up in wartime euphoria and hysteria. Many communal luminaries, including Chief Rabbi Hertz and Lucien Wolf, organized the Jewish Peace Society to give effect to the meaning of Judaism by working for arbitration of international disputes, but the basic Anglo-Jewish agenda was the

53 Law and parliamentary committee, 23 Apr. 1919. See also, Samuel to HO, 6 Mar.; Memorial of the Polish National Committee to the Home Secretary, 18 Mar.; Lucien Wolf, Memorandum of Zaleski interview, 6, 22 Mar.; Law and parliamentary committee, 4 Nov. 1918, 9 Apr., 15 May 1918; Cave to Samuel, 6 Mar. 1918; Polish National Committee to Cave, 18 March 1918, BDBJ C 13/1/8.

54 Director of Public Prosecutions, Spies in England, Aliens File, 4 Oct. 1914; Troup–W. Graham Greene conference, 27 Oct 1914; CID file, 20 July 1916, Pedder memorandum, 5 Jan. 1917; Marriott to Cave, 29 Sept. 1917, 16 Oct. 1917 (in both of which Marriott softens his position); British Empire League petition, 28 Sept. 1917, HO 45/10756/267450/1, 90. 117. 514, 533, 622, 721; Wilkinson to Hankey, 23 July 1917, GT-1514, CAB 24/21/50.

55 Reconstruction Committee, Report of the Aliens Committee, 25 Jan 1918, CAB 1/26/46–71; H[ome] A[ffairs] C[ommittee] 27/2, 8 May 1919; HAC 35/3, 18 July 1919; Persons of Alien Extraction in the Civil Service, CP-812, CAB 24/98/48–52. There is also some related discussion of questions arising from the marriage of Jews in the United Kingdom in 1921. See MEPO 2/1804; PRO 79/45/3445.

patriotic prosecution of the Great War, pure and simple.[56] While generally seeking the widest possible definition of friendly aliens, Anglo-Jewry turned its back on alien Jews attempting to avoid military service. The Board of Deputies 'were of opinion that friendly aliens were liable to Military Service and unfriendly aliens to internment'. Aliens who had failed to apply for identity books during the war were subject, not only to fine or imprisonment, but to deportation. Anglo-Jewish authorities, lest they assist foreigners who had been avoiding military service, declined even to intervene in those cases of individuals who were over military age. Many had originally failed to apply through ignorance, and then feared to do so later for fear of the heavy penalties involved.[57]

While the community would have undertaken its extensive fund-raising to relieve Jewish war victims in Poland and Russia regardless, the confidential papers of the principals involved echo traditional concerns. The Petrograd committee reported 350,000 needing relief in the Pale of Settlement by the end of 1915. Were they not effectively settled and relieved, the number of Jewish paupers would rise by hundreds of thousands 'and will cause a tremendous emigration abroad'.[58] The chilling phrase served to inspire where humanitarism might have flagged. Concerns initially focused on Russian Poland, and communal support was easily found to organize the London Central Committee for the Relief of Polish Jews. That organization, however, had sympathies that were too strongly Zionistic for many community leaders, and it was also too narrowly defined. Jewish expulsions from the military districts in October and November 1915 scattered the needy well beyond Polish borders. Leopold de Rothschild and young Lord Swaythling, drawing heavily on American support, organized the Fund for the Relief of Jewish Victims of the War in Russia in mid-1916. Elkan Adler, working with Lucien Wolf, prepared a confidential report in August that became the basis of communal policy. Baron Gunzberg and the Petrograd committee oversaw the work of some 350 agencies in the Russian Empire and acted as a conduit for all Anglo-American funds. Wolf helped to arrange a treaty between the Polish and Russian relief organizations that coordinated fund-raising, ratified the Gunzberg management, but reserved 15 per cent of the Polish Relief Committee collections for Palestinian Jews, as a concession to Zionist interests.[59] Wolf's memorandum concerning collections through 30 November 1916 is doubly revealing. Not only does the preference for Russian or Polish contributions indicate more precisely where Jews of Eastern European actually came from, but the proportions and sources of contributions suggest important underlying changes within the British Jewish community itself.

56 Jewish Peace Society, *First Annual Report*, 1914–1915 (London, 1915).

57 Law and parliamentary committee, 14 Nov. 1917, 17 June, 8 July, 4 Nov., 9 Dec. 1918, BDBJ C 13/1/8.

58 L. Wolf, Memorandum of Jewish Relief Work in Russia, 28 Dec. 1915, Wolf Papers, Unclassified Russo-Jewish, in the Mocatta Library.

59 Wolf and the British used 16 million as the estimated Jewish population of Russia and Russian Poland in 1911. E. Adler, Jewish War Victims [Aug 1916]; Fund for the Relief of the Jewish Victims of the War in Russia, executive committee 4 July, general committee 11 July, Report of 27 Aug. 1916; Moshowitz to Wolf, 9 Dec. 1916, Wolf Papers, Unclassified Russo-Jewish. See also, 'Save our starving brothers!' *JC*, 26 Jan. 1917.

TABLE 11.2   Polish and Russian wartime relief, 1916

Source	For Poland (£)	For Russia (£)
Colonies	9,590	25,048
Provincial communities and synagogues	7,202	1,983
London synagogues	1,256	3,281
Donations	16,648	29,130
Totals	34,696	59,442

Source: Wolf Papers, Unclassified Russo-Jewish, in the Mocatta Library.

PEACE AND RECONSTRUCTION

By the end of the war, the Bolshevist bogey further clouded the issue of alien restriction. Aliens had been, so far as possible, eliminated from the civil service during the war. The war cabinet determined, in July 1918, that 'no one should be employed in Government offices or departments during the war unless he was the son of natural-born British or Allied subjects, but exceptions might be made for definite reasons of national importance.' By the time that the Treasury came to formulate a general policy in January 1919, the anti-alien position had become much harder. For general civil service positions, the Treasury preferred that any candidate be born a British subject, the child of a father also born a British subject, although with certain qualifications for the Foreign Office. A modification allowing foreign-born mothers was acceptable only on the urgent plea that so many army and navy officers had, for example, American-born wives. Sir Edward Troup, the retired senior civil servant from the Home Office, regularly sought to bring rationality to official outbursts of chauvinism with regrettably little success. He reminded the cabinet's Home Affairs Committee, 'There was no single case where a person of alien parentage engaged in any of our Government departments had done anything detrimental in the war, or was suspected of doing so.' And he reminded the department heads that Britain would have been far the poorer in scientific and technical matters had such a rule been enforced. H. A. L. Fisher, a sophisticated man who certainly knew better and chairman of the committee, personally disliked all rules, 'but it was pretty clear that in deference to public opinion some change would have to be made.' With careening public chauvinism available to take the blame, Britain retreated one step further.

Anglo-Jewry found itself attempting to undo what it had encouraged during the war in the spirit of patriotism. The Home Office used its discretionary powers during the war to deport individuals without trial or even without letting them know the charges against them. Some may have deserved their fate, but the government employed its authority simply to be rid of 'suspicious persons'. Once Britain turned to conscription, it also concluded a Military Convention allowing aliens either to serve in the British forces or to return to serve in their own allied country's army.

Those who opted to return to Russia found it almost impossible to return to England. The British government took the position that, unless they were recently arrived in England, they should have opted for military service in Britain. Some had done military service in Russia before coming to the United Kingdom and thought they would be better off there. Others had parents or relations who needed to be looked after. Few actually did military service since the Bolshevik revolution took Russia out of the war so quickly. Those who did serve for short periods often could furnish no proof of service, even if they had been captured by the Germans. One, lacking any papers, arrived back with a shrapnel wound, was refused permission to land, and had his appeal denied in spite of Board of Deputies support. British consuls were supposed to grant visas to Military Convention returnees who had their documents in order, but British immigration authorities, in spite of Board of Deputies protests, rejected many. Anti-Bolshevism, anti-Semitism and anti-foreign sentiments and prejudices mixed easily with an avowed policy of admitting only those with well-validated claims to return. Anglo-Jewry found itself with wives and children to support in England while husbands were sent back to Poland.[60]

The flotsam and jetsam of war drifted into Anglo-Jewish hands. Mrs Rachel Swerling, the wife of a Galician Jew living in London, had gone abroad for her health in July 1914 taking her two English-born children with her. The war stranded them. One child had died. She had escaped the Galician war zone to Vienna and, in April 1919, pleaded to be permitted to return to England. The Board of Deputies was sympathetic. Russian Jews who had returned to fight in the Russian army during the war under the Allied Military Convention found themselves barred from re-admission to Britain 'unless they can shew that since leaving the United Kingdom, they have been fighting for the Allied Cause'. The board undertook only to press the cases of selected individuals who had left wives and children in the United Kingdom. The wife of a Jewish soldier in the French Foreign Legion needed a permit to go to Paris when he was on leave. The board declined to strain the purse of Jewish philanthropy further but recommended that 'she should make the necessary declaration which would enable her husband to come over here on leave.'

The Home Secretary, unsettled about the infiltration of Bolsheviks, had denied two women, the wives of Russians, who had returned to Britain through Shanghai, permission to land. Both had children born in England. After the board was able to reassure him that they were politically harmless, they were allowed to re-enter the country. Russian veterans, who had left England for service during the war, were often unable to secure visas to return. Since they had families in England, they re-entered the country illegally and were arrested and ordered to be deported. Sir Basil Thomson, head of British counter-intelligence, remained unmoved by their pleas. They were, in his view, likely to be Bolshevik sympathizers. Sir Stuart

---

60 About deportations, on the other hand, the Board of Deputies had very few complaints. The French government acted in much the same way. The Minister of the Interior, acting on police reports, deported those Jews from Poland who had been civilian prisoners in Germany but were released after the Armistice and drifted into France without papers. Bigart à Wolf, 8 avr.; Emanuel to Bigart, 16 Apr.; Bigart à Emanuel, 21 avr. 1920, AIU Angl I/H/1/7684.

Samuel pointed out to him that many families thus became burdens on the state, given the 'enforced absence of the breadwinner'.[61]

SHARING THE BENEFITS OF BRITISH SOCIETY: NATIONAL INSURANCE

The National Insurance Act of 1911 offered British workmen generally enhanced benefits. Lloyd George, however, patterned his state sick and disability insurance on the model of the Old Age Pensions Act. Only British subjects benefited. Approved Societies managed benefits for employed contributors, one-third of the funds coming from the employer, one-third from the employee, and one-third from the state. Under the terms of the legislation, aliens could not become 'employed contributors' in an Approved Society. While the Board of Deputies proposed that the Chancellor of the Exchequer rethink his formula, it had little hope of success.[62]

The political climate, in spite of Stuart Samuel's somewhat frenetic efforts to mobilize the friendly societies, was unfavourable. The community had already expended its political energies on the Shops Bill and Aliens Bill of that year. In each instance, Jewish interests collided, or appeared to collide, with public opinion. Winston Churchill's Shops Bill, an effort to bring badly needed reforms to retail trades, raised the sensitive issue of Sunday trading. Anglo-Jewry preferred to minimize any public discussion that identified Jews as 'other' or 'different' people. The Aliens Bill of 1911 was, in many ways, worse. Questions about Jews as criminals and Jews as political subversives spurred the Home Secretary's efforts to tighten existing immigration legislation. Anglo-Jewry, as we shall see, preferred to cooperate in efforts to segregate undesirables and to deal with alien exclusion from old age pension and national insurance benefits by easing the process of naturalization. And so the exclusions remained. Political conflicts broadened and intensified between 1911 and 1914. The politics of consensus threatened to evaporate in something approximating civil war. When war did come, it refocused uninhibited political passion. Patriotism may or may not have been the last refuge of scoundrels, but it severely tested Anglo-Jewry. Enemy aliens were interned. Even many Jews who considered themselves impeccably English found themselves tarred with the alien brush. If Russian Jews were seen as malingerers, refusing military service and seizing the servicemen's business, Jews of German background could be represented as subversives.

Anglo-Jewry's social tasks and commitments remained. The war accelerated the process of feminizing social services. Patriotic Anglo-Jews marched off to national service and war. The old leadership who had forged the network were dead or standing down. Helen Lucas finally passed away in 1918 bequeathing £2,000 for her precious Adult Workroom and £1,000 for the Ladies Conjoint Visiting Committee. The following year, a frugal, retrenching Jewish Board of Guardians closed the workrooms for good. In spite of substantial government subventions, the

---

61 Law and parliamentary committee, 23 Apr., 5, 20 Nov., 2 Dec. 1919, 12 May 1920, BDBJ C 13/1/8. Sir Basil Thomson's agency turned in monthly intelligence bulletins to the cabinet on 'foreign revolutionary movements'. Each issue praised the efforts of Western countries waging war against 'Extremists, who are mainly aliens'. Bulletin no. 14, Dec. 1919, CP-308, CAB 24/95/36.
62 BDBJ Minute Book, 29 May 1911.

TABLE 11.3   Pre-war and post-war caseloads and costs for the Jewish Board of
Guardians

Year	Cases	Individuals	Emigration		Loan		Industrial		Health		Total (£)
			No.	£	No.	£	No.	£	No.	£	
1913	3,348	13,931	830	3,162	3,079	21,617	284	3,389	134	3,511	26,415
1918	2,024	7,418	—	—	628	5,305	66	935	884	3,656	27,308
1923	2,418	9,133	68	1,244	2,575	23,918	228	2,223	774	4,272	34,390
1928	2,503	9,242	19	353	2,156	25,975	273	2,075	834	10,864	36,745

Source: Jewish Board of Guardians, *Annual Reports.*

board could barely stay afloat. Leonard L. Cohen finally stepped down as president in 1920 after thirty years of service, exhausted by one financial crisis after another. The Jewish Board of Guardians had become increasingly dependent on government support. Treasury grants paid for the care of Jewish refugees. After the war, prolonged negotiations produced a compromise. The Board of Guardians agreed to supervise those refugees from Belgium, France, Poland, and other allied nations who could not return to their country of origin. The Treasury provided £1,000, a board-sponsored special fund a further £800. The government also provided temporary allowances for the dependents of repatriated Russian soldiers left behind in England. Pioneering in sanitation and public health had long been a source of Board of Guardians pride. The cost proved far too much, the work duplicatory with that of the expanding welfare state. The board discontinued the services of its five health visitors in 1921 on the grounds that their work was now being undertaken by borough councils. But nothing could remove wartime inflation. Fixed benefits devoured income. In 1913, the last year before the war, the Board of Guardians expended £10,888 on 619 allowance cases. In 1919, the board spent over £19,500 on 620. While old costs almost doubled, staggering new ones had to be met at once. Wartime demobilization demanded special funding and a new committee. Apprenticeship, however, was not helpful, and loans, the other tried and true board policy, threatened financial stability. In less than a year the loan account was overdrawn, and the board books balanced only by the use of bequests as current income. Stringent economies and a special appeal stemmed the tide in 1921. The allowance and relief committee cut the scale of relief by 15 per cent, and communal purses provided almost £42,000.[63]

Small, independent charities, themselves facing collapse, sheltered under the board's wing. The Jewish Ladies' West End Charity transferred its declining funds to the board in 1920, and the Joel Emmanuel Almshouses were accepted in 1922 after Viscount Bearsted underwrote a £5,000 endowment.

Other bellwether communal institutions confronted the same difficulties. Gerald G. Samuel, former honorary secretary of the Board of Guardians, was killed in action in 1917. He bequeathed a Home for Orphan Working Boys funded by a

---

63 The windfall was soon lost, and only £62,000 from the residual estate of Anthony Muller in 1925 tided the board throught the 1920s.

£10,000 endowment that complemented the work of Norwood. Although that eased some pressure on the Jewish Hospital and Orphan Asylum, Norwood also was forced to contract its commitments. Norwood could no longer provide the social cushion it once had. By 1925, it resolved, 'where the home is respectable, poverty – if it can be and is being relieved elsewhere – shall not determine in favour of the admission of a child to the Institution.'[64]

The council of the United Jewish Friendly Societies, on the other hand, buoyed up by a plan and some support from B'nai B'rith in the United States, suggested to the Board of Deputies that the community undertake yet another task. It proposed a specifically Jewish body 'in an advising intermediary or even executive capacity' to cooperate with the Ministry of Pensions in the board tasks of demobilization. The board's committee, however, divided. While accepting the several assumptions – that Jews showed special aptitudes for certain trades, that some trades gave better opportunities to observe the sabbath than others, that Jews had their particular needs if choosing emigration – the board realized that Ministry of Pensions money would be needed to make any plan work. Most members of the law and parliamentary committee preferred to have Jews appointed to the three sets of London committees rather than sponsor a new communal institution. But Jews sitting on local war pensions committees, local advisory committees, and a central disablement committee, would always be a minority, even in London, and every community with a substantial number of Jews would have to go through the same process in its own locale. B. A. Fersht, Anglo-Jewry's current expert on such matters, undertook to sit on the Stepney committees himself and report on any problems that might arise. Economy and efficiency carried the day, and Anglo-Jewry elected to participate but to allow the state, through the Ministry of Pensions, to pay the bills.[65]

64 See the files in AJ/19.
65 Law and parliamentary committee, 27 June, 3 Oct., 4 Nov. 1918, BDBJ C 13/1/8.

12

Foreign Policy: Jewish and National

The First World War, Winston Churchill once suggested, saved Britain from internal conflicts that were threatening to sunder the nation. Party violence, class war, the militancy which had come to dominate the women's movement created an impression to outside observers of a country close to total disintegration. The coming of war, Churchill observed, created 'a higher principle of hatred'. Labour became an estate of the realm, duly absorbed within the government. Ireland, whether green or orange, was shelved. Peers patriotically marched off to slaughter Germans instead of Liberals.[1] Quite the reverse was to be the case for British Jewry. The war, far from unifying the community or papering over those small rifts in its world, turned even minor fissures into yawning divisions.

The problem had been long in the making, and generational change accelerated it. Death and retirement claimed many nineteenth-century Anglo-Jewish stalwarts. Adler died, replaced by Hertz. Old Lord Rothschild survived only until 1915. Mocatta passed away in 1905. Sir Samuel Montagu, who spent his last years as Lord Swaythling, died in 1911, failing health having already forced him to curtail his activities. The community they had done so much to shape had quadrupled in size and become far less deferential and submissive. Restive intellectuals who had, for lack of anything better, seized on Zionism as the most effective ideological weapon with which to mobilize the 'masses' and strike at the 'establishment', were shortly to discover that the war did for them what they could not do for themselves. The fertile ground was there. The Rothschilds, the Mocattas, the Montefiores, the Montagus, the Samuels, the Cohens, the Adlers and the other great families had created a network of social and religious institutions which sustained and animated British Jews. Working against this impressive, effective voluntaristic network were the weight of numbers, the increasing proportion of newly-arrived East European Jews with their own ideology, values and needs, and the elementary facts of social

---

1 Such is the concluding argument of George Dangerfield's *The Strange Death of Liberal England* (London, 1936), a pioneering enterprise in the study of *mentalités*. Dangerfield's compelling prose continues to give his thesis more weight than modern scholarship would support.

and cultural change. Anglo-Jewry was entering the British establishment. Rufus Isaacs become the Attorney General and then Lord Chief Justice. Sir Samuel Montagu's nephew, Herbert Samuel, had launched that long and impressive political career which would take him through cabinet office to the first high commiss-ionership for Palestine. Montagu's son, Edwin, would counsel two Prime Ministers and help to shape the path to Indian self-government. Rothschilds and Sassoons moved through high politics and high society. The generation of philanthropists, embodied at its best in Frederic D. Mocatta, had passed or was dying; its progeny and successors, while never forgetting the world of Jewish charity and obligation, had visions and ambitions that increasingly drew them away from the tight network of kinship and obligation that controlled Anglo-Jewry. Success and economic prosperity also created a larger and wealthier Jewish middle class with its own ambitions and needs, far less committed to the traditional institutions for which they had usually been allocated little more than roles in the supporting cast. Some among them, often professionals or intellectuals, aspired to reshape the community in their own image or to suit their own vision and ideology. More appreciated how far they had made it in the world and sought to go further. Beyond that lay the simple fact that provincial Jewry had come, by 1914, to have a life of its own and a social and cultural existence apart from the London focused world of Anglo-Jewry. Like the restive businessmen and professionals who had formed the Birmingham Political Union, so important in the struggle for the Reform Bills of 1830 to 1832, or their counterparts in Manchester, who led the Anti-Corn Law League in the 1840s, provincial Jewry was increasingly asserting its class and regional claims.

The substantial masses of poorer Jews, working people, struggled with the daily problems of life and living, coping with the nagging inroads of inflation, with competition and technological change, and with the problems of marginal economies. Little interested in the debates and politics which rocked the middle class and elite, they were slowly but surely being emancipated from communal tutelage and care. State institutions increasingly served the secular needs of poorer Jews. While the world of voluntarism continued, as it continues today, to contribute significantly to Jewish life and leisure, the welfare state was coming, for Jews as for all citizens, to manage the necessities of life. Where formerly each social institution wove the Jew into a communal network of order and deference, secular institutions were anonymous, faceless, and instrumental. While the West End may have physically withdrawn from the East End, the long arm of its influence had been felt everywhere – where the poor Jew went to school, turned for medical help, sought relief in times of distress or looked for spiritual and cultural support. Now, increasingly, Whitehall and local authorities told the poor what to do and how to do it, regulated their lives and ministered to their needs.

For the foreign poor, yet another negative remained – the memory of a land left behind, the opportunities it had denied, and the pain it had inflicted. Many of the more recent migrants had fled from Russian military service. Few Jews from Poland or Russia were prepared to fight and die for their former homeland, although that was exactly what Anglo-Jewry would call on them to do in the Great War. Nothing could have mobilized the substantial majority of England's Jewry more dramatically than first the summons, then the demand, that they do battle in the allied patriotic cause. Zionism, as an English mass movement, owed little, if anything, to popular ideology and culture and less to the fulminations of journalists. Zionism, as a mass movement, owed almost everything to the war. The demands of patriotism, how they were perceived and acted upon at the highest levels of Anglo-Jewry and the British government, explain much of the soi-disant revolt in British Jewry.

Anglo-Jewry and their colleagues in the Alliance worked with Jewish organizations in Germany and Austro-Hungary to refine elaborate Jewish communal networks to process refugees and migrants onwards and out of Europe. Governmental authorities permitted, even abetted this process. Governments generally, however, resisted any appeals of organized Jewry to remonstrate with other governments, particularly when national interests demanded cultivation of the criticized power. When they did meddle – King Edward VII of England actually chided his cousin, Tsar Nicholas II for his anti-Semitic policies – the results often appeared to be counterproductive. The British Foreign Ministry knew that Russia officially encouraged, even participated in pogroms. The Russian bluntly responded to criticism, and British officials, even when they did not sympathize, understood.

> The fact that half the Jews in the world live in Russian territory is one for which they are not responsible. There were originally few, or even no, Russian Jews and Russia acquired her Jewish subjects when she took over, gradually, the possessions of Poland. What the Russian Govt. are now doing is merely to insist that the Jews must remain where they were when the territory which they inhabit became part of the Russian Empire. The Government have a perfect right to deny to the Jews access to the rest of Russia.
>
> Secondly, Russians contend that the policy which the Government have adopted towards the Jews is forced on them by circumstances. Self-preservation is the first law of nature and if the Jews were allowed a free hand they would, by dint of their energy, honesty, sobriety, intelligence, and thrift, squeeze the Russians out of existence. There is probably much truth in this contention. It is difficult to conceive a being more deficient in the qualities above enumerated than the average Russian, who is inferior in every respect to all other races who have the misfortune to live under his rule and who fails to compete with any of them on equal terms.[2]

The Jewish elites of Britain and France knew that substantial Jewish immigration would not be tolerated in their countries. Those elites had come to understand, even to share, the sensitivities of their host cultures. Neither the British nor French Jewish establishment wished to be embarrassed by unmanageable masses of 'the great unwashed', so some alternative had to be found. Thus the exhausting efforts to make the Hirsch colonies work. Zionists, of course, pursued the single-minded reconstruction of a homeland in the Holy Land. Israel Zangwill's Jewish Territorial Organization, a body quite hospitable to a sense of Jewish nationalism, saw the issue as one of immediate sanctuary for the persecuted amd sought settlements for Jewish refugees anywhere they could establish communities and prosper. Assimilationists, principally for lack of alternatives, also developed colonies in Palestine and

---

2 [H. Norman] to Tyrrell (file notes, 'most confidential'), 10 Feb. 1911, given by Sir Edward Grey to Lord Morley who passed them on to Claude Montefiore. See the response, Montefiore to Morley, 13 Feb. 1911, Grey Papers, FO 800/100/435–40.

attempted to create an infrastructure that would ease the life of Jews. Ottoman policies against immigrant Jews in the Holy Land, however, offered little encouragement for building substantially upon those small settlements in Palestine.

Narcisse Leven, president of the Alliance Israélite, also chaired the international board of the French-sponsored Jewish Colonisation Association to which the Edmond de Rothschild colonies had been given in 1899 with an endowment of 15 million francs. British, like other West Europeans, shared both costs and benefits. Palestine, however, was not merely one of several interests. Zionism had made Palestinian development a centrepiece of communal politics. Given North American resistance to immigration and the saturation of Latin American settlements, new viable refuges had to be found somewhere. The Colonisation Association, however, was so caught up in the Zionist issue that, when examining possibilities within Ottoman domains, it sought to avoid Palestinian questions even by resettling refugee Jews in Kurdistan and Iraq. The British weighed up Madagascar, Kenya, and even new Latin American alternatives. No solutions, Zionist or otherwise, adequately addressed the immediate issue. All plans were wanting either in practical or psychological terms.

The diplomacy of immigration remained a central issue for Western Jewish leaders. All parties continued to pay their 'ransom', and regular conferences designed strategies to move East European Jews to countries safely removed from their own. Almost as a microcosm of world events, the Alliance Israélite and Hilfsverein engaged in endemic sniping that demanded regular English pacification, but generally the processing system worked well until suddenly disrupted by the outbreak of war in 1914.[3] Between 1904 and 1914, the Jewish Colonisation Association established over five hundred emigration committees in Russia. A government-endorsed committee office in St Petersburg coordinated their operations. Working with the Hirsch Fund Jewish Agricultural and Industrial Aid Society, the association established Jewish Removal Committees which moved more than 70,000 immigrants through predominantly family-linked channels by 1912. While making emigration as orderly as possible, the association strove to develop institutions that would make life better for Jews in Russia.[4] With some significant setbacks, the strategy of making Russia more attractive succeeded. The association founded or supported schools, funded agrarian programmes, and even organized producer and marketing cooperatives. The Russian Imperial government, happy to have someone else pay the bills, permitted the association after 1905 to develop a network of cooperative savings banks which served some 450,000 members through 680 banks and held a capital of 40 million roubles.[5]

3 See, particularly, Joseph to Wolf, 14, 18 Dec. 1907; AIU resolutions, 17 déc. 1913, Bigart à comité centrale, 29 avr.; AIU comité centrale résolutions, 13 mai 1914. AIU Cdc S236/326, S237/266, 299.

4 The Jewish Colonisation Association (ICA) sponsored an investigation in 1898 about what could be done within Russia. *Recueil des matériaux sur la situation économique des israélites en Russie* (Paris, 1904) sketches out the master plan. See the useful article on the ICA in *Encyclopedia Judaica*, X, 44–51.

5 Baron de Hirsch, so Jacques Bigart of the AIU reported, offered in 1887–8 to contribute 50 million francs to educate Russian Jews, but the Russian ministers, uncertain as to what course to take, attached so many conditions that he withdrew it. He also attempted to go directly through Pobedonestzev offering a bribe of a million francs for Russian Orthodox education. Pobedonestzev kept the money, checked attacks on Jews, but did nothing more for their welfare. Bigart, 'Note, 14 nov. 1919 re. Baron de Hirsch', AIU Cdc S243/346–7.

DEVELOPING A JEWISH AGENDA

The Conjoint Foreign Committee committed itself, at the beginning of the war, to act as a watchdog for Jewish interests and to lobby the British government. The committee provided information for various departments, trading this for some measure of influence and privileged standing. Information being a useful commodity, the Conjoint Committee, the Alliance Israélite and other Jewish organizations in allied and neutral countries developed and traded elaborate archives. This raised the issue of more formal institutional cooperation. But belligerents and neutrals had unique problems and, often, very different obligations. Neutrals could raise questions belligerents felt obliged to avoid. Each time proposals for general meetings to concert a Jewish agenda were raised, the Conjoint Committee and the Alliance Israélite found them inopportune, fraught with political problems, and just dangerous. Not until the Paris peace conference of 1919 would the various Jewish organizations, meeting together, attempt to hammer out a joint Jewish agenda.[6] The Alliance and Conjoint Committee, however, could not have worked more closely had they been meeting together as a matter of routine. In a sense they did, for Lucien Wolf and Jacques Bigart, the secretaries and principal designers of policy of each, corresponded almost daily, harmonizing the interests and activities of the two bodies.

Cooperation between the two organizations reached well back into the nineteenth century. They had pursued an essentially joint strategy concerning emerging Balkan states. They had struggled through their foreign ministries to soften Russian anti-Semitic policies. Since they shared attitudes concerning new immigrants, they had designed joint strategies to fund, to screen and to process the human tide that flooded out from Eastern Europe. They organized relief and philanthropy through North Africa and the Ottoman Empire. The intimate linkage that prevailed through the First World War, however, was not forged until the war had been on for some months. Both the Alliance and Conjoint Committee had more than enough problems in adapting their institutions to the demands of war. Each confronted wartime dislocation: stranded refugees, disrupted international operational networks, Jewish internees and Jewish prisoners of war.[7] As with the governments themselves, Anglo-Jewry moved ahead of Franco-Jewry in considering the general problem of 'war aims', but the Alliance Israélite invited the institutional coordination.

Then it all happened very suddenly. The French sought to nip in the bud what they regarded as a Zionist crisis before it started. Anglo-French Jewry drew together to resist the Zionists, and what they perceived as the Zionist threat to

---

6 See, e.g., the efforts to fend off a Swiss-sponsored conference. Wolf to Bigart, 16, 21, 23, 28 June; Bigart à Wolf, 30 juin; Bigart et Sée à Paris Consistoire des Juives, Bigart à Sereni, Bigart à Brandeis, 30 juin 1916. Then, when the Italians asked for a 'belligerents only' conference, the inability of a Russian delegation to attend was used as an excuse to fend off the suggestion. Bigart à Sereni, 21 juil; Bigart à Wolf, 6, 11 août; Wolf to Bigart, 30 Aug. 1915, AIU Cdc S 239/371–3, 375, 393, 434, 440–3, 482.

7 The French found themselves even more overwhelmed than their English colleagues. When war broke out, some 50,000 dislocated Russian Jews in Paris threatened to bankrupt Jewish charities. Leven et Lévy à Marshall, 27 août 1914, AIU Cdc S 238/36–7.

Western Jewish values. Zionists had their clearly defined post-war agenda and exploited every opportunity to advance it. Most Anglo-French Jewish leaders feared the havoc Zionist principles, if they ever became ascendent, would wreak in Western Europe. They saw Zionism as the dream of every anti-Semite. When Yehiel Tschlenow and Nahum Sokolow, bearing news of Russian outrages against Jews in wartime Poland and flying their Zionist standards, visited Paris in February 1915, Jacques Bigart sprang into action. He brought the Alliance scurrying to Anglo-Jewry, pleading for a completely coordinated policy. From February 1915 to the Paris peace conference and beyond, the Alliance Israélite and the Conjoint Committee (reconstituted in 1918 as the Joint Foreign Committee) worked hand-in-hand.[8] Bigart, Wolf's opposite number at the Alliance Israélite, was a 'career official', who enjoyed an ever stronger personal position within his organization. Bigart's scope derived from his dedication and ability combined with the disinterest or incapacity of Alliance leaders, particularly after the death of the president Narcisse Leven in January 1915. Wolf, for his part, enjoyed great scope while always presenting himself merely as the humble servant of Anglo-Jewry. He knew his masters well, shared their assumptions and values, and possessed their confidence.

After developing an easy working relationship by correspondence on a variety of difficult and sensitive issues, Wolf visited Paris in September 1915. Agreement had already been reached on general policies. Wolf had been asked to tidy up the details of a common policy with the Alliance and leading members of the French Jewish community.[9] Controlling the agenda meant controlling the result. Wolf and Bigart defined and ordered the agenda. The standing Jews had among Western leaders would determine the influence they could wield during the war and the extent to which their voice would be heard in the peace settlement to follow. It all began, Wolf and Bigart understood, with cultivating access to those who made policy. That meant developing personal rapport and displaying political sensitivity, reasonableness, and restraint. The Jewish agenda, whatever it was to be, must be realistic and practical. Patriotism was indispensable and should be as visible as possible. Jews must mobilize to serve the national interest. Being liberals and champions of the culture of diaspora Jewry in Western civilization, Wolf and Bigart, like those they served, identified the best interests of all with what they, their culture, and their class perceived to be their own best interest.

The Jewish image mattered. Were Jews wronged or slighted, they must immediately set matters right. Wolf used his well-placed political contacts, for example, to counteract any official British statements which reflected badly on Jewry. John Buchan, author and future Governor General of Canada, then much

8 See, particularly, Bigart à Simonsen, 29 déc.; Bigart à Montefiore, 30 déc. 1914, 9 fév.; Bigart à Wolf, 4 mars 1915, AIU Cdc S 238/136–7, 139, 186, 214. See also Leven et Levy à Marshall 27 août, Bigart à Duparc, 11 nov.; Bigart à Leclerc, 13 nov. 1914, AIU Cdc S 238/36–7, 86, 90–2. Bigart had already shown how easily he could be roused on the subject of Zionism. See, e.g., Bigart auf Winz (Berlin), 8 Okt. 1913, AIU Cdc S 236/10. 'Tshlanoff and Zakoloff' from Moscow had previously joined Dr Blank from St Petersburg before the Conjoint Committee, but they apparently seemed far less dangerous in London. Conjoint Foreign Committee confidential file (CC Conf), 11 Jan. 1915, AJ/204/4 in the Mocatta Library.

9 Wolf, Report on His Paris Mission. CC Conf, 23 Feb. 1916, AJ/204/4; Confidential statement to the council of the Anglo-Jewish Association and the Board of Deputies by the presidents on 10 and 17 October1915. BDBJ minute book, interleaf pp. 11–12.

involved with the dissemination of war news, reported that the poverty of Polish Jews had led some to spy for the Germans. The statement, whether causally correct or not, happened to be true, but it would not do. Such thoughts lay behind Foreign Office resistance to Jewish memorials and growing coolness to Jewish diplomatic desiderata. Wolf called Buchan to account, developed substantial counter-documentation, and then called upon his Foreign Office contacts to help refute the charges.[10] Such tasks were unpleasantly familiar. As they had done before the war and would continue to do afterwards, the Conjoint Committee worked hand-in-hand with the Alliance to counter anti-Semitism, pooling information and sharing research for refutation.[11]

With the essentially complete cooperation of the Alliance, Wolf and his associates wielded impressive influence. They went on the attack for Jews anywhere and everywhere when the occasion offered. When M. Bark, the Russian Minister of Finance, came humbly hat in hand to London in 1915 to plead for war loans, the Conjoint Committee directly confronted him on the triviality of the concessions made to Russian and Polish Jews. Were Jewish opinion in Western Europe and America to be conciliated, real reforms must be enacted. Anglo-Jewry inferred that purse-strings might then be untied to support the Russian war effort. Bark promised to do the best that he could, which proved not to be much. That troubled those who, like Wolf, agreed that the most intelligent Jewish policy must be predicated on winning the good will of key Russian officials.[12] Since the division over Kishinev in 1903, the 'conciliators' had stood by this approach. Wolf continued to adapt and pursue it through the war.

Both French and English Jews exerted considerable pressure on visiting members of the Duma, the Russian parliamentary asembly, when they came to the West in 1916

10 CC Conf, 27 July, 6 Sept., 10, 17 Oct., 15 Dec. 1915, AJ 204/4; Buchan to Wolf, 12 Oct.; Wolf to Buchan,14, 18 Oct.; FO to Wolf, 19 Oct. 1915, BDBJ C 11/2/6. The Alliance fought the same libels using Wolf's information. Wolf to Bigart, 25 Mar.; Bigart à Wolf, 1 avr. 1915, AIU Angl I/J/8/5133; Paléologue à MAE, 4 fév; AIU à MAE, 23 juillet 1915, M[inistère des] A[ffairs] E[trangères.] [Archives diplomatiques]. [Séries] A [Guerre, 1914–1918]/1197/44, 47–52. This and related problems of official 'libels' concerning Russian Jews continued throughout the war. The elaborate counter-documentation demanded can be sampled in CC Conf, AJ/204/1–3. When the source could be identified, as in the case of Professor Bernard Pares attached to the Russian army, Wolf and the Conjoint Committee responded to that individual as well as the Foreign Office. CFC Conf, 8 Jan. 1917, AJ/204/4.

11 See, e.g., Wolf to Bigart, 26 Aug. 1918; Bigart à Wolf, 29 août 1918; Wolf to Bigart, 6–7 Sept. 1920; Bigart à Wolf, 8, 10 sept. 1920; Emanuel to Bigart 20 Oct. 1921, AIU Angl III/D/52. For Wolf's impressive cutting and translating files, see, *inter alia*, Wolf Papers ER-4 and Wolf Papers, Unclassified, Russo-Jewish in the Mocatta Library.

12 Although the formulae varied slightly from one proposal to another, unrestricted settlement, ending restrictions on education, the abolition of religious discrimination in visas and passports were always demanded. The reforms were, moreover, to be enacted by the Duma and ratified by the Tsar. BDBJ Minute Book, 1916, interleaf, pp 4–6. Baron Edmond de Rothschild took a very strong line with Bark in support of the Anglo-French position, and Wolf went to considerable lengths to keep Cyrus Adler and the American Jewish Committee supporting the same programme. Wolf, 'Circular Letter', 30 July, Wolf to Adler, 16 Sept., Bigart à Wolf, 22 août, 1,17, 22, 28 sept., 5, 6, 10 oct.; Wolf to Bigart 20 Sept., 12 Oct. 1915, AIU Angl I/J/8; AIU Cdc S 238/404–405, 420bis-3bis, 429–32; CC Conf, 10, 17 Oct. 1915, AJ/204/4. The second time round, Anglo-French Jewry was unwilling to commit much effort to Bark, although Wolf saw Berthellot, the chef du cabinet, on that matter among others. See CC Conf, 23 Feb. 1916, AJ 204/4; Bigart à Wolf, 30 juin; Wolf to Bigart 3 July; Bigart à Wolf, 5 juil. 1916, AIU Cdc S 239/384, 392. Jewish bankers, both English and German, had boycotted Russian government loans at various times in futile attempts to win concessions for Russian Jews. See, e.g., Grey to Revelstoke, 6 Apr.; Asquith to Campbell-Bannerman, 7 Apr. 1906, Grey Papers, FO 800/100/26–30.

with some effect, particularly among the centre-left members. That heartened Wolf and Bigart. But the strains of war were also telling by 1916. A crucial economic conference of the allies was scheduled for Paris. Wolf spurred the Alliance to demand that the economic conference hear a Jewish deputation. The French government, however, considered the proposal presumptuous and potentially disruptive and declined to give such a group access.[13]

Anglo-French Jewish activities attracted attention and respect, even envy. Wolf and the Conjoint Committee found odd fish in their widely cast net. The papacy, for instance, sought allies to make its views felt at any post-war peace conference. François Deloncle was the not very secret weapon of Cardinal Gasperri, the Vatican Foreign Secretary, in this campaign. Deloncle, a French journalist, former diplomat, and former deputy, set off in quest of Vatican allies, hoping to have Conjoint, Alliance and American Jewish Committee cooperation. The French and the American Jews took these overtures seriously, but Wolf, appointing himself to speak for the Anglo-French organizations, suggested that the Pope could best demonstrate his good intentions and most usefully employ his influence by improving Roman Catholic relations with Jews in Poland. The Alliance immediately fell into line.[14] The Deloncle problem breezed discreetly through in 1915 but arose in a more complicated form with Zionist implications in 1916. Wolf understood the dangers of involving Jews 'in our corporate capacity as a religious community with the questions of the representation of the Holy See at the Peace Conference and of the appointment of Papal Legates at the Courts of London and Petrograd'. He understood British and Italian sensitivities on the point of papal territoriality. He also recognized, as the French were slower to do, that any support for papal territoriality, by extension, implied a quasi-endorsement of Zionist claims for Palestine. Polish independence, which Deloncle also championed to all parties, was a point of emotional sensitivity among the French, and of religious importance to the Vatican. But it was an issue on which Poles were themselves divided and about which Russian liberals, upon whose ultimate success Western Jewry pinned such high hopes, felt very strongly. Polish nationalism was no place for Western Jewry to meddle. Wolf called the Vatican offer a cynical bargain: a statement against anti-Semitism that it should have made on principle was made on condition that

---

13 Wolf recruited Lord Bryce and Lord Rosebery to help. Wolf to Bigart, 18 May 1916, AIU Angl I/J/8/5559; Bigart à Wolf, 15 fév. 1915, 15, 21 mai, 5 juin 1916; Bigart à Sereni, 15 mai, 15 juin; Bigart à Simonsen, 21 juin 1916; Sée à Ministre de Commerce, 13 juin, Sée à MAE, 14 juin, Bigart à Wolf, 19, 30 juin; Bigart à Sereni, 30 juin; Bigart à Behar, 4 juil., 2 août 1916, AIU Cdc, S 239/140, 273, 275, 282, 302–3, 321–6, 336, 350, 356–7, 376–83, 390, 430–2; 'Un Tournée parlementaire', *Archives Israélites*, 24 août 1916; Board of Trade to CC, 29 Jan. 1916, CC Conf, 23 Feb., 17 May, AJ/204/4.

14 Wolf to Deloncle, 17 July; Bigart à Wolf, 18 juil.; Wolf to Montefiore, 16 July 1915, in which he observes that the Vatican must be 'pretty hard up' to be seeking Jewish support for its projects. BDBJ C 1/2/6. Bigart à Wolf, 18, 22 juil., 22 août, 1 sept.; Wolf to Bigart 20, 25 Aug. 1915, AIU Angl I/J/8/5271; AIU Cdc S 238/375–6, 404–5. Successive lead stories in *Archives Israélites* on 27 avril and 4 mai 1916 took the Wolf line. For an extensive file including both Alliance and American Jewish Committee material, see MAE A/1197/121 ff. On the Deloncle mission and Benedict XV's statement for American Jews, see MAE A/1197/39, 44, and *passim* and then, retrospectively, 'Le Sionisme et le Saint Siège', 19 juil. 1917. MAE A/1199/98–101. Wolf reported on Deloncle in detail to the Conjoint Committee. CC Conf, 16 July 1916, AJ 204/4.

Jewish organizations intervene in international politics in ways 'which would involve the Jewish community in considerable danger'.[15]

Wolf played a rough game of politics. He brooked no rivals and sought to discredit competitors, particularly those who threatened his carefully limited but 'realistic' goals. 'You will see,' he wrote to the Foreign Office when sending a list of names of the Zionist Action Committee and the Inner Action Committee in 1915, 'the majority of the members are enemy aliens.'[16] That observation, meanly intended, was in the most profound sense correct. The real struggle within British Jewry at the time lay between the cultural and political assumptions of traditional Anglo-Jewry, with its strong sense of deference, control and acculturation, and those who sought to change this world. The would-be 'revolutionaries', who were supported only by a minority of the Jewish establishment, had two cards to play. They could appeal to the growing sense of self among provincial Jewish communities against the London-focused traditionalists, and they could seek allies among the more recently arrived foreign Jews and attempt to recruit them with East European Jewish ideology, particularly Zionism.[17]

Wolf pursued policies in the old Anglo-Jewish tradition: developing and sustaining Jewish rights at home while attempting to secure civil and political liberty for all Jews in Eastern and south-eastern Europe. Wolf was no laggard campaigner. He had spent his lifetime fighting for Jewish rights in Russia and Roumania and was infuriated by anything that appeared to distract from that campaign. Wolf simply presumed that the inevitable expansion of liberalism would bring to Jews everywhere what had been won in the West over the past century. His objectives were time-honoured if slightly out-of-date. While willing to make tactical concessions to the Zionists, he believed that they threatened hard-won Jewish liberties, offered no practical solutions to deeper problems, and played a politically destructive role in western Europe and America. Jewish nationalism – the demand for special Jewish rights and the identification of Jews as a separate nationality – was anathema. It challenged the basis of western assimilation and would be intolerable to the passionate nationalities of Eastern Europe.

Wolf haunted the Foreign Office on issues of immediate concern while simultaneously seeking to secure British commitments to strong policies in defence of minorities in transferred territories. He and Georges Leygues, president of the Paris Comité d'Action and chairman of the Foreign Affairs Committee of the Chambre des Deputés, cooperated in defining and agitating for identical programmes with the Foreign Office and Quai d'Orsay.[18] A year and a half of constant labour bore fruit. Foreign Minister Grey finally asked the Conjoint Committee to provide desiderata for the peace settlement on the Jewish question.

---

15 Alexander and Montefiore to Marshall, 28 Apr. 1916. AIU Angl I/D/13/5559; Bigart à Wolf, 15 mai; Wolf to Bigart, 14 July 1915; 18 May, 18 Oct. 1916. I/J/8/5559, 5738; I/G/4/5271; Bigart à Duparc, 12 juin, Bigart à Wolf, 5 juin, 5 juil. 1916. AIU Cdc S 239/298–9, 304, 320, 392; *JC*, 9 June 1916; CC Conf, 27 June,16, 27 July 1916, AJ/204/4.

16 Wolf to Archer, 11 Feb. 1915, CC Conf, AJ/204/4. Wolf also had an engaging way of attempting to draft the Foreign Office's replies to his queries. See, e.g., Langley to Wolf, 15 Sept. 1915, BDBJ C 11/2/7.

17 See Cohen's rigorous *English Zionists*.

18 Wolf, Report on his Paris mission. CC Conf, 23 Feb. 1916, AJ/204/4; Wolf to Alexander, 20 Mar. 1916, BDBJ C 11/2/8. Wolf to Bigart, 28 July; Bigart à Wolf, 30 juil. 1915, AIU Angl I/G/4/5286.

Wolf had his committees in order. He secured official endorsements from the Alliance Israélite, the St Petersburg Committee and the Italian Committee. So armed, the Conjoint Committee presented the Foreign Office with a non-Zionist agenda. Grey himself favoured Wolf's modest proposal on Palestine. The Foreign Office consulted the French ambassador, Cambon, who also endorsed the general principles involved, then packed the proposals off together with supporting documentation to the Quai d'Orsay. The British had finally decided that Jewish issues were important and asked for French views on the most desirable policy to adopt.[19]

The French government, far ahead of the British on this point, already had a Jewish consultative body in place. The Quai d'Orsay asked, in April 1915, for a Franco-Jewish committee to conduct propaganda for the entente, particularly in the United States. Simultaneously, the Alliance created a comité d'études 'comme une sort d'émenation du Comité de Propagande, mais indépendamment de lui'.[20] Much the same was happening in England. Lord Robert Cecil, acting for the Foreign Office, subsequently had private discussions with Wolf about the same question. Propaganda for America meant saying something about Palestine. Wolf understood, even stressed, that something must be offered to gain American Zionist sympathy. What Wolf did not realize was that the Foreign Office would dig in its heels at what it saw to be the counterproductive task of yet again hectoring Russia on the issue of equal rights for Jews. Nothing had come of that over the years, and Britain was desperate to keep Russia in the war. Gratuitous offence did not seem an intelligent strategy.

Wolf began with the premise that equal rights for Jews would have to be a proclaimed Allied peace aim. Considering that point made – it had been but was not yet accepted – Wolf turned his fertile mind to some limited concessions for Zionists. He suggested a declaration on Palestine promising unrestricted Jewish settlement, equal rights, and a degree of communal autonomy for Jewish towns and colonies. Wolf knew that he had competition. Sir Mark Sykes, a strategically placed, over-enthusiastic amateur whose grand ideas betrayed his ignorance of Middle East realities, had been wooed and won by Gaster and Russian Zionists. A devout Roman Catholic, Sykes was bumbling towards a design for the Middle East that would assemble a vast, harmonious Arab kingdom, a Zionist state, and an Armenian agglomeration which, under the ever-benevolent oversight of British and French mandatories, would bring peace and prosperity to humanity's homeland. The Zionists were delighted to have well-placed contacts with the British and French governments and were preparing the next stage in their campaign. Wolf hoped to forstall them with his Palestine formula. His tactical information, however, was limited. Conjoint Committee discussions with the Zionists had broken down. Wolf

19 1 oct.–27 oct.1916, MAE. A/1198/54–103; Briand told Lord Bertie that he thought the Arabs would object. Bertie to Grey, encl Bertie à Briand, 13, 21 Mar. 1916. Bertie Papers, FO 800/176/3–5; Wolf to Bigart, 9, 18 Oct., 22 Nov 1916, AIU Angl I/J/8. CC Conf, 18, 24 Sept.1916, AJ/204/4.

20 S. Lévi, Question Juive en Russie, 21 oct. 1916, MAE A/1198/100. The French quickly developed some useful lines of propaganda. See, *Appeal of the Consistory of the Jews of France to Jews of Neutral Countries* (Paris, 1915); Bigart à Wolf, 7, 10 déc. 1915, 30 juil., 28 sept., 6 oct.; Wolf to Bigart, 28 July, 5, 12 Oct., 30 Nov., 7 Dec. 1915; Bigart à Blank, 25 jan., Bigart à Sereni, 24 oct.; Bigart à Durkeim, 14 avr. 1916, AIU Angl I/J/8/5311, AIU Angl I/G/4/ 5286; AIU Cdc S 239/35, 39–40, 107, 223; S 240/15–16.

had nothing to give, the Zionists nothing to gain. On the one hand, this made Wolf's task of a common formulation much easier. Zionists thus were not involved in the programme he developed with the Alliance, the Italian Committee and the Petrograd Committee. Wolf presented these recommendations to the British government on 3 March 1916, suggesting to dubious officials as he would later to American Zionists that the difference between Zionists and moderates like himself was merely one of timing.[21]

The British government, however, saw Jews divided and was nestling into its own negotiations with the Zionists. The Palestinian option was extremely attractive. It would not offend their Russian ally, might serve some vague British interests, and would give the appearance, particularly to American Jews, of making a major concession to world Jewry. The Quai d'Orsay, doing precisely the same sums and arriving at exactly the same answer, voiced no interest in the Lucien Wolf formula. Capitalizing on French coolness, the British told the Conjoint Committee,

> The formula [on Palestine] has been the subject of correspondence with the French Government, and the latter have taken the view that it would be useless to make such an announcement at the present moment, as they have ascertained that it would not satisfy a very large body of Jewish opinion.[22]

That response reflected two facts. The Zionists did not approve, and the Ministère des Affaires Etrangères had its own Zionist and American agenda.

---

21 'On the subject of Palestine, let me say that in essense there is no difference of opinion among the Jews of this country. What difference exists is really only a difference of method. Those who think with me, desire that the Zionists should proceed prudently and slowly, so that their ultimate success may be all the more certain and solid. Above all, we are anxious that, in whatever they do, they shall not shipwreck the cause of Emancipation in other countries.' Wolf, Typescript of 1916 address to the American Jewish Congress, BDBJ C 11/2/8; Wolf, confidential memorandum, 6 June 1917. BDBJ C 11/2/11. Wolf to Bigart, 6, 20 Mar.; Bigart à Wolf, 29 mars 1916, AIU I/J/8/5479, 5636. The Foreign Office gave Wolf access to its files for his documentation. He used this material for his *Notes on the Diplomatic History of the Jewish Question* (London, 1919) which was to be so influential during the Paris peace conference. Wolf's general principles are set forth in Wolf to Bigart, 2 Mar. 1915, AIU Angl I/J/8/5628; AIU Cdc S239/416–47. See, also, Wolf, Notes for a Pro-Allies Propaganda among the Jews of the United States, 16 Dec 1915, BDBJ C 11/3/1/3; Wolf to Bigart, 24, 30 Nov., 14 Dec. 1915, 13 Jan. 1916; Bigart à Wolf, 7, 10 déc. 1917, 9 jan. 1916, AIU Angl I/J/8. Anglo-Jewry struggled with a 'legal' definition of Jewish citizenship. The BDBJ law and parliamentary committee ultimately settled for a statement that Jewish allegiance must be 'to the country in which they have their settled home or are temporarily resident'. Meeting of 3 Oct. 1918, BDBJ C 11/2/13. Lord Robert Cecil contended, with some annoyance, that the Jews were building their political position on the 'Russian difficulty'. Cecil to Spring-Rice, 29 Mar 1916, Cecil Papers, FO 800/196/141–4.

22 De Bunsen to Wolf, 4 July 1916. Wolf immediately asked Bigart to find out what assurances 'he was empowered to communicate confidentially to the American Jewish communities by the French Government'. Wolf to Bigart 18 July 1916, AIU Angl I/J/8/5698. Bigart à Wolf, 26 nov. 1916, AIU Cdc S 240/68. Montefiore and Alexander protested to Grey, 1 Oct. 1916. Wolf, while in Paris, had discussed matters with leading Zionists who 'disavowed any hostility to the proposed declaration'. The French government, Wolf felt, 'had some other reason, unconnected with Jewish opinion, for the attitude they had taken up.' CC Conf, 18 Sept., 1 Oct. 1916, 8 Jan., 6 Feb. 1917, AJ/204/4. See also, FO to Bertie, 11 Mar. 1916, Bertie Papers, FO 800/176/1–2.

WHAT IS TO BE DONE?

War or no war, Anglo-Jewry had its international tasks. Nothing became easier, much became more difficult, and some things became or appeared to become impossible. Relief for the distressed failed to reach those in friendly zones for lack of transport and because of the priorities of war. What, for instance, could be done for Austrian and German Polish Jews who wished to secure special status, not merely to be recorded as enemy aliens? Not very much, as things turned out, until the British government itself opted for a policy of national self-determination for Poland.[23] War blocked Jewish emigration, leaving those in transit stranded wherever they happened to be. Jewish organizations in each belligerent country attempted, as best they could, to care for Jewish needs in the lands their nation controlled, and Jewish committees in neutral lands handled resources and information for all. The pain of war also multiplied the expectations of the peace which must follow. Such massive suffering must somehow be turned to good account. Anglo-French Jewry resolved, during the fighting if possible, in the peace to follow for certain, to resolve their traditional concerns. In a partial division of labour, the Alliance Israélite conducted most business with the Italian Committee, and Wolf worked with his non-Zionist Russian contacts, principally Dr Ruben Blank and the Petrograd Committee. The Conjoint Committee and Alliance dealt independently, although coordinating their approaches, with organizations in the United States. The principal desiderata remained what it had always been: full civil and religious equality for all East European Jews.

One area of Anglo-French Jewish concern lay within the sphere of entente military operations. Salonika Jews had already figured on the Alliance and conjoint agendas before the war of 1914. The only Jewish city in the world outside the Pale of Settlement was a delicate issue in both Jewish and international politics. The Alliance Israélite, with considerable interests there, made Salonika its special study. The Conjoint Committee wished to safeguard Jewish rights in some enforceable way. The Greeks were indecently anxious to acquire Salonika after the Balkan Wars in 1912 and even to pay a substantial price to Jewish opinion, should that seem a way to gain French and British support. Anglo-Jewry felt cooperation with the Alliance on the issue 'very desirable'.[24] The Alliance trusted the Greeks. The Conjoint Committee questioned Greek intentions and reliability and held back. Wolf understood that Russia had emerged as the dominant power in the Balkans. Treaty concessions to Jews, if wrested from unwilling Balkan states, would be so much window-dressing. The great powers would not fight Russia on the issue of anti-Semitism or minority rights. Wolf, unfortunately, proved to be correct. Just as Roumania had dug in her heels about minorities in spite of treaty commitments, Greece, with Salonika in hand, proved far from willing to come to terms with the Jews.[25]

23 See the files on these appeals in HO 45/10740/262173.
24 Montefiore to Nathan 29 Nov.; Wolf to Montefiore, 9 Dec. 1912, BDBJ C 11/2/3. CC petition to FO, 4 Mar. 1911; CC to Grey 17 Nov. 1913, AIU Angl I/D/7/9044, 9522.
25 Wolf to Montefiore, 22 July 1913, BDBJ C 11/2/4. Emanuel to AIU, 12 Nov. 1912, and 1913, AIU Angl I/D/10/7579, 8291. Anglo-Jewry's tortuous negotiations with the Greeks on issues relating to Salonika after everything was ostensibly settled can be found, in part, for 1921–4 in AIU Angl I/G/6, AIU Angl III/D/47/6526.

Salonika Jews were understandably anxious. Greeks were unlikely to forget how favoured Jews had been during the Ottoman supremacy. Some of the wealthier Salonika Jews, working through Alliance contacts, attempted to place themselves under the protection of the Spanish government. The ostensible influence and role Salonika Jews played in the Committee of Union and Progress and Young Turk movement gave rise to yet more misgivings. Friends of the Young Turks allegedly maintained ties with Germany. Such identification with major and minor Central Powers worked against equal rights, let alone privileges, for Salonika Jewry.[26]

In spite of Conjoint appeals to the Foreign Office, little had been resolved by 1913. Failing there, Wolf turned to private negotiations with senior Greek officials to secure pledges for rescue and security.[27] After the Turks entered the First World War, however, the issue of Salonika Jewish citizenship proved to be a problem in domestic as well as foreign policy. The Alliance secured from the French government the same 'capitulation-protected' status for Ottoman Jews that Christian minorities enjoyed. The Conjoint Committee, however, failed to convince either the Foreign Office or the Home Office to consider Salonika Jews who had failed to take Greek citizenship after the Balkan Wars as anything other than hostile aliens.[28] Negotiations dragged on until 1918. Salonika Jews also came under attack from Greeks who represented them, possibly correctly, as Turkish sympathizers. Familiar forms of harassment became all too common. Then, in 1917, much of the Jewish quarter went up in flames. Contemporary rumour suggested arson, a deliberate attempt to burn the Salonika Jews out. Even after pressure from British and French military occupation authorities, Salonika Jews received scanty

26 A. J. Toynbee, Memorandum of the Panturanian Movement, GT-1981, 7 Sept. 1917, CAB 24/25/361–70; Arab Bureau, Cairo, report, May 1916, FO 438/9/36/73–4. Bigart à Montefiore, 15 juin 1914, AIU Cdc S 237/397/5229. 'L'Italie, l'Espagne et les juifs', 21 juin 1917, MAE A 1199/59–78.

27 Wolf to Montefiore and Alexander, 5 Feb., 4 July 1913. Wolf also attempted to persuade Adler to convince the Greek Patriarch at Constantinople to issue a strong pronouncement against the 'blood accusation', which, he felt 'will do wonders for the Jews of Salonika'. Wolf to Adler, 8 July 1913, BDBJ C 11/2/4. F. D. Mocatta had, long before, attempted to bring AIU influence to bear with the Greek king to damp down manifestations of anti-Semitism. Mocatta à Loeb, 2 août 1891, AIU Angl II/D/34/6744.

28 The Treaty of Athens which brought Salonika to Greece gave those inhabitants resident abroad six months in which to register and become Greek subjects. Those who failed to do so remained whatever they had been before. On 7 January 1915, however, a revised British Royal Proclamation relieved 'Armenians, Greeks and Syrians of the Christian religion who were technically Turkish subjects from all the restrictions of alien enemies'. Stavrick to Wolf, 24 Feb. 1915. The Home Office balked at extending this to Ottoman Jews, so Wolf attempted to negotiate through the Greek legation and the Foreign Office. Wolf to Oliphant, 19 July 1915, BDBJ C 11/2/6. Wolf to Oliphant, 24 Nov 1915, BDBJ C 11/2/7; CC Conf, 15 Dec. 1915, AJ/204/4. see also Sykes to the Director of Military Operations, 7 July 1915, FO 438/7/198/96–9.

compensation for their lost property.[29] Anglo-French Jewry organized relief, while Wolf and his French colleagues attempted to secure guarantees for community safety and some reasonable compensation.

Prime Minister Venizelos considered Jewish matters a minor problem. He supported the Greek plan to expropriate the burned-out area, design a modern city and develop it through the sale of the confiscated land sites. The wealthy, whether Jewish or Greek, could benefit from both speculation and development. Small proprietors, most of whom were Jewish, would be squeezed out. Unremitting Anglo-Jewish diplomatic pressure finally led Venizelos to promise that small Jewish owners would not be entirely cut out of the redevelopment. Even this modest concession proved politically controversial in Greece, so Venizelos then appropriated half of the profits as a 'betterment tax'. That effectively eliminated most small owners. After balking for several more months, Venizelos finally accepted Wolf's minority rights clauses, a curious proclamation of principle on the ashes of Jewish shops, homes and hopes.[30]

Salonikan Jewry, conscious of how rapidly their position had deteriorated, also proved responsive, much to Conjoint and Alliance annoyance, to the attractions of Zionism. A French-language local newspaper, *Israél-Sion*, took up the cause in 1916. The old life of privilege under Ottoman rule would not return. Dramatic loss of power and status was bad enough. Now active persecution seemed to be increasingly their fate. As the Salonika Jewish community finally began to bestir itself, the assertive and aggressive politics of Zionism seemed attractive. Through Zionism, Salonika Jews could give vent to their feelings and frustrations.[31]

---

29 Wolf to Simon, 16, 18 Oct.; Assaël à Herz, 22 sept. 1915, BDBJ C 11/2/7. Wolf to Stavridi, 13 Mar. 1916, BDBJ C 11/2/8. Such constant negotiations in individual cases were a nuisance. See, e.g., the October 1917 correspondence, BDBJ C 11/2/11. See, also, 'Situation de la population israélite sous la domination grecque', [Dec 1918]; Lubin to Schiff, 29 Mar. 1918, BDBJ C 11/2/13; 'Prerogatives dues à la Commaunauté Israélite de Salonique: Raison d'être de ces prerogatives'. [1921], BDBJ C 11/2/16. For the very tangled legal issues involved, see the report of the BDBJ law and parliamentary committee., 3 Oct. 1918, BDBJ C 11/2/13. The Home Office finally ruled that Sephardi Jews who were Ottoman subjects would be eligible for certificates 'entitling them to treatment as alien friends, without regard to the portion of the Ottoman Dominions in which they were born'. They might, however, then have to demonstrate their loyalty by accepting any 'work of national importance' assigned them by the Ministry of National Service. Williams to Laski, 4 Oct. 1918, BDBJ C 11/2/13. Wolf developed a substantial dossier on the 'systematic ill treatment of the Jews of Salonika by the Greeks' for use at the peace conference. Wolf to Bigart, 5 Feb. 1919, AIU Angl III/D/52/6738. At the same time, Wolf was careful to avoid mindless service to AIU interests in Salonika. See, e.g., Wolf, Peace Conference Diary (PCD) in the Library of University College, London, 14 Feb. 1919.

30 Venizelos also reminded the Joint Committee and the Alliance that Greek elections were held on Sundays and that the substantial Salonika Jewish community was exempt from the Sunday Rest Law. Wolf to Venizelos, 23 Aug., 28 Aug., 8 Sept.; Venizelos to Wolf 27 Aug. 1919, CC Conf, 3, 23, 31 Oct., 11 Dec. 1917, AJ/204/4; JFC, *The Peace Conference*, 108–10; Wolf to Bigart, 21 May 1918, AIU Angl III/D/52/6403. Abuse of the Sunday Closing Law led to Greek crackdowns and restrictions in the years after the war. See, e.g., Wolf to Bigart 15 Jan., 16 Mar., 26 May, 26 July 1925, AIU Angl IV/D/54/6701, 6800, 6910, 7031. On Salonika relief, see, e.g., Wolf to Bigart 27 Sept.; 2, 6, 13, 15 Nov. 1917, AIU Angl I/J/8/4228, 6200, 6209, 6221.

31 Commanding General, Salonika to Hankey, 'Zionism', 17 Dec. 1917, GT-3032, CAB 24/26/120. Graillet à Pichon, 9 jan. 1918 [misdated 1917 and misfiled by MAE], MAE A/1198/111–12; de Billy à Ribot, 12 juin; Graillet à Ribot, 3 juil., 20 sept. 1917. See also Graillet à Pichon, 18, 20 déc. 1917, 12 fév. 1918, MAE A/1199/57, 87–8, 144–6; MAE A/1199/ii/116–7, 120, 157–9.

Conjoint Alliance pressure could effectively be brought to bear in Salonika because the region was under Anglo-French military control. While General Serrail was in command, of course, they actually might have lost it.[32] However incompetent the military commander and however sensitive some of the issues of Greek diplomacy, reasonable settlements in Salonika once negotiated could be enforced. Allies, or potential allies, however, could be worse than enemies. Roumania was a lynchpin in entente Balkan strategy, and little Roumania had proven totally intractable on issues of Jewish civil rights since the Congress of Berlin in 1878. Nothing, with the exception of Russian pogroms and oppression, infuriated Western Jewry so much as Roumania. Almost every issue of the *Jewish Chronicle* for thirty-six years pilloried Roumanian misbehaviour.

The Roumanians pledged to grant their Jews full civil rights in Clause 44 of the Treaty of Berlin. Having ratified it, every Roumanian government classified Jews as aliens, granting them civil and political rights only when they became naturalized. This the government rarely allowed. The total number of Roumanian Jews naturalized between 1878 and 1914 was in the low hundreds. Roumanian citizenship, moreover, did not come automatically to children born in the country, so once an alien meant always an alien. The situation actually became worse, for the child was more totally stateless than its parents. Western Jewry, having exerted itself to secure a minority rights clause, was forced to watch it being judicially perverted. Roumanian Jews suffered, if anything, more oppression after than before they were protected by international treaty. Over the next decades, dissensions among the great powers prevented any effective reconsideration or redress. Once major powers began to bargain for Roumanian support, the diplomatic stakes became too high for Jewish rights to matter.[33] But what was to be done? Raising the Roumanian question 'in an aggressive way', irritated British government officials. It also appeared to validate Roumanian anti-Semite claims that 'an international Jewish conspiracy' was intervening in Roumanian domestic affairs. Lofty promises, such as those the Conjoint Committee received from the Foreign Office in July 1914,

---

32 Serrail combined military incompetence with an unparalleled capacity to infuriate the Greeks. Grey to Kitchener, 2 Feb.; Kitchener to Grey 3 Feb. 1916, Kitchener Papers PRO 30/57/77/WU 40; Briand à Cambon, 23, 29 mai 1916, MAE A/Grande-Bretagne/539/84, 103.

33 L. Wolf, Correspondence with *H.M. Government Relative to the Treaty Rights of the Jews of Roumania* (London, 1919), 45–57; Wolf, *Diplomatic History of the Jewish Question*, esp. Appendix III, 48–59, 83–7; JFC, *The Peace Conference. Paris, 1919* (London, 1920), 10 ff. The Balkan Wars aggravated this already bad situation. Close observers feared correctly, like Wolf, a significant rise of religious persecution in the region, 'more indeed than when the Turks were the dominant power.' Wolf to Alexander, 26 Nov. 1913. The Conjoint Committee protested Roumanian behaviour, particularly in territories taken from Bulgaria. The Foreign Office responded, as it did most of the time, that the 'timing' was 'inappropriate' for any action. Conjoint Committee to FO, 11 Jan; Mallet to Wolf, 17 Jan., 6 Feb., 9 June, 24 July, 29 Oct. 1913, BDBJ C 11/2/4. See, also, Montefiore to Bigart, 9 Dec. 1919, AIU Angl I/B/54 bis/7730. During the Balkan War of 1913, Roumania promised immediate naturalization for the 14,000 Jews serving in their army and then reneged when the war ended. Ehrenpreis à Clemenceau, 19 nov. 1917; Clemenceau à Pichon, 27 jan. 1918, MAE A/1200/100–6.

proved as unredeemable as the original pledges given to Crémieux two generations before.[34]

Roumanian Jews staggered under wartime oppression. Wolf and the Conjoint Committee urged discretion, but the outraged French took a stronger line. The new Franco-Jewish Commission de Propagande opened an extensive campaign dwelling, particularly, on the economic basis of Roumanian anti-Semitism. This approach, Wolf argued, if followed logically, would teach 'the Roumanian anti-Semites, who are very powerful, that the Germans are their best friends'.[35] Persecution worked. Cowed Roumanian Jews, meeting in January 1916, even declined to push for Jewish emancipation for the duration of the war. Roumanian Jewry had a vociferous lobby in England as well as France. But Roumanian Jews understood, as many of the British and French partisans did not, that any wartime agitation would be represented as treason and made the excuse for even harsher measures against the community. Wolf believed that any action taken by exiles or by British or French organizations on behalf of Roumanian Jews would rebound to their detriment, if not actual danger. Entente diplomats, moreover, would scarcely appreciate British and French Jews agitating on this issue while those governments were attempting to curry favour with Roumanian politicians and public opinion.[36] Once again, Roumanian Jews were to be sacrificed to the higher needs of statecraft. Roumanian military hysteria generated anti-Semitic paranoia. A Roumanian Army order of 27 August 1917 said: 'All the Jews must be placed in the front line at the beginning of an attack.' Another:

All the boy scouts, as well as all the women and men belonging to the lower sanitary personnel, and who are not of Rumanian nationality, are to be excluded. Jews cannot be tolerated in the hospitals for wounded and sick. There must be no humanitarian feelings and sentimentality displayed toward them. It has been proved that, approaching our wounded with a mask of pity and innocence of boy scouts, they are in fact spies.[37]

Just as Russian domination of the region after the Balkan Wars cast a pall over any hopes for improvement, the February Russian Revolution suddenly appeared to offer hope for Roumanian Jews. Obscurantist tsardom, the bulwark for anti-Semitism everywhere, had been overthrown and replaced by an avowedly liberal order committed to a programme of ethnic civil and political rights. The Roumanian Foreign Minister, Take Ionescu, sought to placate this new Russian government

---

34 Montefiore to Leven, 29 Sept., 12 Oct. 1913, AIU Angl I/B/54 bis/8883, 8912; Montefiore and Alexander to Grey, 14 July; Eyre Crowe to Montefiore and Alexander, 28 July 1914, AIU Angl I/J/8/9917. Early files show the same complaints and problems. See, e.g., the Goldsmid–Crémieux correspondence in 1866 and 1867, AIU Angl II/D/29/11–13, 112–13 or Mocatta à Leven, 18 août 1879, AIU Angl II/D/34/923; Löwy to Loeb, 1, 6 May, 11 Nov 1884, AIU Angl I/D/16/9134, 9136, 9148; Gaster's voluminous correspondence à Loeb, 7 oct. 1883 to 3 mai 1891, AIU Angl I/D/16; Montefiore to Bigart, 17 Oct 1909.

35 Wolf to Lord R. Cecil, 13 Jan. 1915, BDBJ C 11/2/8. St. Aulaire à Ribot, 12 mai 1917, MAE A/1199/10–12.

36 Mitrany to Wolf, 6 June; Wolf to Mitrany, 8 June; Wolf to Montefiore, 8 June 1916, BDBJ C 11/2/9. For a general file of Foreign Office correspondence on Roumania in 1916, see BDBJ C 11/3/2/1.

37 Wolf to Misu 4 Feb. 1918 quoting Army Orders 14,798 and 40,164 of 27 Aug. 1917, BDBJ C 11/2/13; AJA foreign affairs committee, confidential file (FAC Conf), Sept.–Nov. 1917, AJ/204/4.

and find favour with the Western entente by taking an enthusiastically liberal position on the Jewish question. Following confidential soundings of the Conjoint Committee and Alliance, Ionescu accepted their demands that legislative concessions on Jewish rights must precede the grant of any new territories to Roumania. Ionescu liberalism, however, was predicated on entente success. Military events proved catastrophic. The Bolshevik revolution and collapse of Russia also brought Roumania down. Iorga, the leading political anti-Semite, recovered his nerve and the king's ear as any hopes for a greater Roumania waned and Roumania was forced to sue for a separate peace with Germany in May 1918. The Russian revolution, moreover, dramatically politicized social conflict in Roumania. A newly-formed Labour party, adopting the full emancipation of Roumanian Jews in its programme, identified Jews with the 'radical' cause. That raised Anglo-French Jewry's hackles. Wolf, the Conjoint Committee, and the Alliance could not allow Jewish emancipation to be in any way identified with social radicalism, particularly Bolshevism. They had fought socialism and anarchism within their own immigrant communities. They not only understood, they shared western repulsion at the political contagion of Bolshevism.

The Treaty of Bucharest (7 May 1918) which took Roumania out of the war, also granted enough concessions to Jews to recharge Roumanian anti-Semitism but by no means enough to satisfy the Jews themselves. Now, however, Roumanian Jews were not only 'social radicals', they were also 'pro-German'.[38] Roumanian Jewry was spared the worst possible consequences of these turns of events by Roumanian cupidity. Roumania wanted substantial territorial gains, particularly in Transylvania and Bessarabia. Ionescu, anxious to secure a broad consensus of Western support, sought once again, among other things, the support of Roumanian Jews and Jewish opinion abroad. Roumania might, after all, have trouble almost doubling its size at the Peace Conference if she were under constant attack as a morally unfit state. But when Ionescu publicly attempted to commit Roumania to the guarantees his country gave in Article XLIV of the Treaty of Berlin, he could not redeem his pledge. The Joint Committee and Alliance reminded the peace conference 'that the vindication of the sanctity of Treaties has been one of the chief moral aims of the Allies,' so 'no enlargement of the present frontiers of Roumania shall be sanctioned until all the laws necessary to give effect to the stipulations of the Powers relative to Jewish emancipation have been duly enacted'.[39] To do less would be to diminish the political and civil rights of more than 400,000 Jewish Roumanians.

38 FO, political intelligence report, 19 Sept. 1918, CAB 24/67/105; Bigart et Sée à MAE, 1917, MAE A/1199/169–70; Lord Robert Cecil publicly committed Britain to Roumanian Jewish enfranchisement on 30 May 1918, GT-4830, June 1918, CAB 24/54/99–118.

39 JFC, *The Peace Conference. Paris, 1919* (London, 1920), 74–5. For the 1918 negotiations with Ionescu see, Wolf to Bigart 5, 9 Apr., 21 May; Ionescu to Wolf, 11 Oct.; Bigart à Wolf et entretien Bigart–Ionescu, 30 oct. 1918; Wolf to Bigart 6 Nov.; Bigart à Wolf 13 nov.; Wolf to Bigart, 16 Nov. 1918, AIU Angl III/D/52/6169, 6181, 6361, 6365, 6404, 6540; Bigart à Wolf, 25 Feb.; Wolf to Bigart, 21 May 1918; Confidential appendix [26 mai 1918]; Interview Wolf–Ionescu, 9 Aug. 1918; Wolf to Bigart, 23, 30 Sept. 1918; Interview Wolf–Ionescu, 7 Oct. 1918; Wolf to Ionescu, 7 Oct. 1918, AIU Angl III/D/49/6404, 6485, 6518, 6524, 6540; Mitrany to Wolf,14 June 1917, BDBJ C 11/2/14. AIU Angl III/D/49–54 has a vast collection of Anglo–French negotiations concerning Roumania. For the delicate negotiations between January and October 1919, see also Wolf, PCD, *passim.*

Roumania was the battle that Lucien Wolf and Jacques Bigart were determined to win. The American Jewish Committee was quickly mobilized to cooperate, and the Italian Jewish Committee agreed to join any campaign. Nowhere would they allow the peacemakers to permit future evasions 'in the Rumanian manner'. Minorities must be guaranteed their full rights, and they must have the right of appeal beyond national courts to the League of Nations and the International Court of Justice. But another contest remained to be fought in Roumania between moderates and Jewish nationalists. Roumanian Jews, Wolf contended, might have equal rights, but they had no claim to special privileges. Wolf prevailed. Jews became 'full Nationals of Roumania without any formality or conditions; ... they obtain equal civil and political rights with the Roumanian Nationals of other creeds, together with complete religious toleration.' The Zionist-supported demands for special rights were rejected. Of the five million Roumanians who were racial, religious, or linguistic minorities, only 800,000 were Jews. To claim special rights not available to other minorities would be to invite the spread of anti-Semitism. 'The interest of the Jews is to act with these Minorities in their common interest against the roumanising Roumanians, and not to give cause for the extension of Roumanian anti-Semitism to the non-Jewish Minorities.'[40] For those Jews identifiable as Roumanian residents before, even during the early years of the war, citizenship did finally become attainable. For others, little changed. The litany of abuse continued, and international protest tended to aggravate it.[41]

Western Jewish organizations had never digested Russian Jewish policy. Most Jewish organizations convinced themselves that Russian persecution produced the massive westward migration of Jews. The fact that the vast majority would probably have migrated anyway was uncomfortable and not one that Jews or non-Jews

---

40 Wolf to Carr, 1 Dec.; Wolf to Bigart, 9 Dec. 1919, BDBJ C 11/3/2/2; Wolf to Marshall, 28 Nov. 1918; see also Samuel and Montefiore to Balfour, 18 June; Graham to Wolf, 28 June; Minutes, JFC Conf, 14 Nov. 1918, AJ/204/4; Graham to Wolf, 19 Nov. 1918, AIU Angl III/D/49/6443; BDBJ C 11/2/1340. Wolf worked very carefully with the Alliance on the limits of concessions that should be permitted to the Roumanians. He suggested amendments for the Roumanian constitution to Lord Robert Cecil, who was in charge of treaty arrangements in this region for the British Foreign Office. He discussed details at length with the British treaty draftsman, Headlam-Morley, who proved understanding and supportive. Wolf then returned to London to prepare and orchestrate a press campaign, while making clear to his more agitated French colleagues why certain concessions exacted in Poland were undesirable and counterproductive in the case of Romania, particularly clauses granting special educational rights to Jews alone. Bracing the British, coaxing the French, Wolf secured a workable and just Roumanian treaty. Wolf, PCD; Cecil to Wolf, 5 June 1918, BDBJ C 11/3/1/1; Wolf to Montefiore, 17 Sept.; draft lead article, 'The high hand of Rumania'; Wolf to Meyer, 27 Oct. 1919, BDBJ C 11/2/14; Carr to Wolf, 10 Nov.; Wolf to Carr, 1 Dec.; Wolf to Bigart, 9 Dec. 1919, BDBJ C 11/3/2/2; Bigart à délégués, mars; Bigart à MAE, 26 mars; Bigart à Labin, 30 mars, Sée et Bigart à Conférence, 21 avr.; Bigart à Stern, [c. 1 mai 1919], AIU Cdc S 242/389–91, 395–6, 401–2, 440–2, 450; Sée et Bigart à Carr, 2 juil.; Bigart à Filderman, 3 juil.; Bigart à Wolf, 5, 7, 10 déc. 1919, AIU Cdc S 243/75–7, 416, 425, 446–7. Herz to Wolf, 23 Jan.; BDBJ to Lloyd George, 24 Feb. 1920, BDBJ C 11/3/2/3; 'L'Entente capitulerait-elle?' *Archives Israélites*, 11 déc. 1919. See also *Archives Israélites*, 9, 30 jan., 10, 17 avr. 1919. Zionism and Jewish nationalism had made Wolf's task no easier. See the problem, e.g., of a Palestine-born Roumanian Jew forced to seek British protection to avoid 'being sequestered as being an enemy subject'. Barclay to FO, 23 Jan. 1919, FO 608/98/44634/251.

41 Even Wolf, who had laboured for moderation and concessions to secure the broadest possible minority guarantees, ultimately agreed with Bigart when the AIU veteran howled about 'un nouveau témoignage de la perfidie roumaine' and observed sadly that the actual policy of the Roumanian government had remained unchanged from 1878. Bigart à Wolf, 18 Jan. 1923, AIU Angl III/D/49/5353.

preferred to believe. To accept that truth would have required confronting directly the question of why Western European Jewry resisted playing host to those coming in search of the same opportunities that their own forebears had found. Western Jews needed to believe that Russians were, by and large, dreadful people and to ignore the westward migration of all other East European peoples to the greater economic and social opportunity the West provided. To face reality required confronting their own shortcomings. Normal Russian abuse, they preferred to argue, worsened as Russia creaked towards modernization.

The observation, although true, concealed rather than explained the problem. Segregated and stigmatized, Jews were convenient targets. Anglo-French Jewish leaders understood and acted upon the broad spectrum of problems Russian anti-Semitism presented to them. Nineteenth-century pogroms, by frightening refugees westward, heightened anti-Semitic tensions in the countries to which they fled and triggered a wave of immigration restriction legislation. The new migrants also underlined the social distinction within the Jewish community between the more stable, affluent and integrated elements in Britain, France and America and the poorer, less assimilable strangers in a new land.

Anglo-Jewry's long memories of Russian mission, as we have seen, reached back to the first appeals from Russian Jews to their Western co-religionists. Sir Moses Montefiore, then president of the Board of Deputies, made their cause his. In 1846 and again in 1872, he travelled to Russia, and his efforts contributed to substantial, if temporary, relief for the persecuted. He also established a precedent; every succeeding president of the board adopted the cause of Russian Jewry. Adolphe Crémieux mobilized Alliance resources in the same campaign, although his immediate objectives concerned the emerging Balkan national entities. The evolving Franco-Russian alliance effectively ended Alliance hopes to bring effective diplomatic pressure to bear through the Quai d'Orsay. Anglo-Jewry, particularly Lucien Wolf, never flagged in the campaign to 'reform' Russia through pressure from Western public opinion.

Such agitation, while frustratingly ineffective, had many benefits. Russian persecution animated Western Jews. Pogroms, for instance, made Anglo-French Jewry consciously act upon their moral obligations. They met, contributed, petitioned, prayed. Such victimization, moreover, 'secured for the persecuted Jews the interest and sympathy of the whole world'. Russian behaviour elicited Gentile sympathy and support for various Jewish causes. On the other hand, the unpleasant reality of refugees and immigrants remained. Efforts to fend them off, to deflect them to other shores, even to develop new, substantial colonies of settlement proved expensive and still left the problem unresolved. Panic about uncontrolled immigration animated many leading Zionists. Balfour, Brandeis, Frankfurter and Lord Eustace Percy, exchanging views in Paris in 1919, each agreed that Zionism would provide the sanctuary their own countries should not. Not one of them wanted 'that' kind of Jew in his country.[42]

The struggle for Jewish rights constantly energized Anglo-Jewry itself. Fighting persecution renewed the communal sense of purpose. That, in turn, reinforced

---

42 Their 24 June 1919 meeting was 'strictly confidential'. FO 800/217/187–8. For a more favourable view, see Ben Halpern, *Weizmann and Brandeis* (New York, 1987).

Anglo-Jewry's sense of superiority. In foreign affairs, as when ordering its domestic world, Anglo-Jewry reaffirmed its sense of emancipation and acculturation as the best route to a fulfilling and a Jewish life. Zionism and Jewish nationalism challenged these assumptions. The conflict between Zionists and assimilationists that reached its first climax during the war was profound and complete. Jewish nationalism, in any form, endangered a century and a half of achievement and mission and denied the basis upon which Western Jewry stood.

Anglo-French Jewry, therefore, never wavered in its campaign to make Russia another liberal Western community. Russia proved uncooperative. She showed no sign of mending her ways with the coming of the war. Incompetent Russian generals, including the Grand Duke Nicholas, sought to make scapegoats of Jews to excuse their own military incompetence. Germans 'liberated' Polish Jews just as they were to do in Roumania. Germans later sought to satisfy Polish nationalism, with its strident anti-Semitism, in preference to Jewish civil rights, when the two were in conflict. Polish Jews had ample reason to prefer Germans to Russians. Russian generals acted as if all Jews were German agents, actual or potential, who should be forcibly removed from the war zone as a matter of internal security.[43] Rumours of poverty-stricken Polish Jews spying for the Germans appeared in the British press, threatening to intensify already smouldering English anti-Semitism. Wolf read this as a warning. Such stories hampered his negotiations with the Foreign Office. The chauvinism that fuelled the British war effort targeted the stranger. Jews, even alien Jews, must be patriots. To counter-attack, Wolf went to great pains to 'correct' Ministry of Information releases. Wolf also encouraged East End friendly societies to play an active role in socializing and integrating foreign Jews into English life. Friendly societies, Wolf believed, were the institutions that best overlapped Anglo-Jewish elite and artisan Jewish values. Through them, both the merchant banker and the immigrant tailor shared a common ideological and material interest. Philanthropy and self-help, the traditional principles of Anglo-Jewry, remained an effective cry. British Jewry usually responded well to such appeals. The war, however, particularly a war in alliance with Russia, proved another matter. The demand for patriotism as well as philanthropy would be the issue on which Anglo-Jewish communal control would founder.

The Russian government understood the damage their anti-Semitic policies could do. The United States, under President Woodrow Wilson, acceded to Jewish pressure and refused to renew its commercial treaty. British and French Jewish bankers pointedly boycotted Russian loans. With more than enough difficulties, the mindlessly obscurantist Russian government added gratuitously to them by hammering out still more anti-Jewish regulations. No French or British Jewish contractors or businessmen were permitted to conduct wartime commerce in Russia. Lord Grey attempted to put off the outraged cries of the mobilized Jewish community and refused to raise the matter at the 1916 entente economic conference. Britain could not, Grey argued, intrude into Russian domestic affairs. The Alliance reminded the Quai d'Orsay that the French foreign minister had

---

43 After much pushing and shoving, Sazanov made an explanatory report in which, he contended, 'Les faits exposés prouvent à l'évidence, combien les accusations d'antisémitisme militant lancés contre le Gouvernement russe sont injustes et mensongères.' 15 sept. 1915, encl in Paléologue à Delcassé, 15 sept. 1915, MAE Arch dipl A/1197/99–101.

promised action on these matters as far back as 1909.[44] Although beaten on the specific issue, the point was made. Threatened with serious disruption of supplies, the Russians retreated. Their Western allies then attempted to put the best face on matters by 'applying pressure'.

For those like Wolf deeply committed to the worldwide cause of Jewish civil rights, the war complicated a difficult situation. First Grey, then Balfour, resisted pressure to remonstrate with one Russian abuse after another on the grounds that they could not interfere in the domestic affairs of an ally. Uninhibited Zionist attacks on the Russians delighted West European Jewish crowds while making matters worse for Wolf and the moderates. Such assaults stiffened official resistance. Anti-Semites pointed to them when making vague accusations, as Zionists predicted they would, about an international Jewish conspiracy. The moderates had the unenviable if not impossible task of demonstrating that diplomacy would work. Zionists could indulge in uninhibited crowd-pleasing at no political cost, while every delay, each failure, eroded moderate support. Even significant moderate successes – the pogroms averted through diplomatic pressure at Easter 1916, for instance – had a negative aura to them.[45] To the costs of patience, tact and restraint were soon added the price of patriotism. Asquith's government, desperately short of manpower, compounded the problems of the moderates when it sought to recruit or conscript Russo-Jewish 'refugees'. The bed-rock of English patriotism, about which Anglo-Jewry felt so strongly, proved to be the reef on which the anti-Zionist ship would founder.

Some matters, on the other hand, went remarkably smoothly. As Russia collapsed and splintered, the Alliance and Conjoint Committee moved swiftly in an effort to secure full civil rights for Jews in the fragments that splintered off. At times, for example with Finland, the partners had some difficulty in sorting out just who spoke with what authority. The Finnish delegates, during their London stay, sought Wolf out and pledged that their government would satisfy 'all doubts in regard to the equal rights of Jews in Finland'.[46] Czechoslovakia assured Jewish equal rights and then asked Wolf in what form he would prefer the guarantees. Even the Ukraine, by 1919, was seeking Jewish organizational endorsement. With the Ukraine, however, the patent incapacity of any government to govern except, ultimately, the Bolsheviks, was to make the extensive negotiations intellectual exercises.[47]

The Jewish problem was, if anything, more acute in Poland than in Russia. The initial euphoria over Polish enfranchisement in 1914 quickly evaporated.[48] Almost all of what had been the Pale of Jewish Settlement – about 80 per cent of Russian Jewry according to contemporary estimates – was now a separate Poland. As Wolf and others privately feared, liberalization could make matters even worse than they

44 Sée(AIU) à MAE, 13 juin 1916, MAE A/1198/13–17; Wolf to Grey, 6 June 1916, AIU Angl II/D/26/5598.
45 Alexander to Bigart, 28 Apr. 1916, AIU Angl I/G/4/5529; Wolf to de Rothschild, 29 July; Wolf to Montefiore, 30 July 1915, BDBJ C 11/2/6.
46 AJA, FAC Conf, 11 Dec. 1917, 31 Jan. 1918, AJ/204/4; Bigart à Wolf, no 6734. 10 fév. 1918; Report of the JFC [6 Mar 1918], BDBJ C 11/2/13. Wolf to Bigart, 25 Jan; Bigart à Wolf, 30 jan. 1918, AIU Angl III/D/52/6283; Cdc S 241/293.
47 See Wolf, PCD and AIU Angl III/D/52.
48 Leven à Feinberg, 16 sept. 1914, AIU Cdc S 238/44–6.

had been before. A widespread anti-Jewish boycott, begun before the war, actually expanded under independence. Dmovski's National Democratic party, anti-Semitic to the core, presented itself to Britain and France as the proper 'government in exile and true spokespeople of the Polish nation'. National Democrats also systematically refused to recognize as Polish any but those of 'Polish race'. To qualify one had to prove that he had not been Jewish for three generations. Much agitation with the Foreign Office produced token Jewish representation.[49] The Joint Committee and Alliance directly confronted the ongoing savagery of Polish politics as the peace conference assembled. Zionists and the Jewish People's Group in Poland composed their considerable differences by 1916 to help to create a united front on the particularly troublesome issue of the sizeable but threatened Jewish minority. Since the National Democratic party had committed itself to a policy of 'the forcible elimination or reduction of the Jewish population', not only were Polish Jews subject to growing harassment, but those thousands of Jewish fugitives, victims of the 'barbarous deportations' and refugees from the war were obstructed in their efforts to return. The German occupation increasingly appeared to be the good years in Polish-Jewish history, although German policy, too, had taken its twists and turns. Then, with the collapse of Russia, Germany began to play to the Ukrainians at the expense of Poles and with renewed or expanded benefits for Jews.[50] Under Russian administration, economic boycotting of Polish Jews, applied with increasing severity since 1912, was pushed 'to nationalise Polish trade and industry in a narrow racial sense'. Such a policy not only threatened 'a law-abiding and hard-working community' resident in Poland for more than seven centuries but held out the prospect to other countries, particularly Britain and the United States, of 'vast streams of indigent emigration'.[51]

Once again the spectre of the last years of the nineteenth century was reinvoked with its unmanageable hordes of East European Jews draining Western resources and arousing nascent anti-Semitism. Anglo-Jewry, characteristically, thought tactful but discreet diplomacy the best counter-measure.

> My Committee are of opinion that any public manifestations of Jewish international activity are to be deprecated in view of the misinterpretations to which they give rise in certain organs of the public press. They realise, however, all the importance of studying the emigration question and of taking

49 Bigart à Wolf, 7 juin.; 7, 13 nov.; Wolf to Bigart, 15 Mar., 21 May, 13 June, 16 Nov. 1918, AIU Angl III/D/52/6181, 1403, 6344, 6424, 6830; Wolf to Bigart, 5 Nov. encl sub-committee on negotiations, 28 Oct.; Wolf to FO, 31 Oct. 1917; Bigart à Wolf, 8 nov. 1917, AIU Angl I/J/8/6183, 6193. Wolf, confidential memorandum, 14 June 1916, AIU Angl II/D/41/5731. For the various approaches to the issue, see CFC Conf 27 July 1915, 17 May 1916, 3, 23 Oct., 11 Dec. 1917; 31 Jan. 191, AJ/204/4.

50 L. B. N[amier], FO intelligence report on Poland, GT-2192, 4 Oct 1917, CAB 24/27/379 seq; GT-3912, 12 Mar 1918, CAB 24/45/34–41. See also, Sée à MAE, 18 juin, 1916, MAE A/1198/18–19.

51 JFC, Peace Conference, 74. Wolf and his associates also attempted to have the international community guarantee Jewish Sunday trading in Poland, a point far from settled anywhere in the West. Anti-Semitic passions rose in Poland with the armistice on the Western Front. Supporting and attempting to strengthen a Polish government that would act against pogroms, however, was a sensible policy, aggressively pursued. Archives Israélites, 29 mai, 3, 17 juil. 1919; Blank to Wolf, 29 Nov. 1918, BDBJ C 11/2/13. See also confidential report: Wolf–Blank–Oliphant interview at FO, 2 July 1915, AIU Angl II/D/26/5271. For the continuing problem, see Wolf's report on the second meeting of the Assembly of the League of Nations [16 Nov 1921], AIU Angl III/D/52/9143.

measures to deal with it, and they suggest that this may be effected by means of correspondence.[52]

Such a threat was one to which the French were even more sensitive than the British. They wanted results, not publicity.

We must agree among ourselves on those measures we must eventually take to canalize and regulate emigration when it comes, to see to what extent and in what areas of economic activity it will be possible to find them employment. I have no doubt that a substantial exodus will come from all the countries of Eastern Europe as soon as the frontiers are opened. We are already having large groups of poor people arrive.[53]

On this point such Zionist enthusiasts as Balfour and Brandeis agreed with Wolf, Bigart, and the vast majority of establishment Jews – they did not want 'those people' in their countries. The moderates hoped to 'liberalize' Eastern Europe and thus render emigration unnecessary. Establishment Zionists saw Palestine as the way to deflect immigration whether Eastern Europe was 'liberalized' or not.

Poland became, thus, increasingly a focal point in which all Wolf's diplomatic skill and resources would be tested. First he had to convince the Polish government to accept the special nature of the Jewish problem.

To refuse to recognise their separateness would be to martyrise this very separateness and thus to prolong the Jewish question indefinitely. It would be better to make reasonable concession to them on the facts. This, at any rate, would make for friendly relations between the two races, and time and economic constraint might be trusted to do the rest in the way of bringing them still closer together.[54]

If Polish leaders would make formal pledges, if Poland would publicly accept properly framed minority treaties, and if – perhaps most important – economic viability and social stability could be brought to the new nation, then moderation would be vindicated.[55] But before Wolf could realize his ambitions, his struggle with Zionism and Jewish nationalists remained to be fought out.

---

52 Wolf to Bigart, 9 Feb. 1920, AIU Angl III/D/52/7518.

53 Bigart à Wolf, 9[sic] fév. 1920, AIU Angl III/D/52/7518. Both communities consistently attempted to prevent 'any oppressive country from dumping down here the refuse of that country, people afflicted with disease and with vice, and who would never have been sent her[e] had there been the least scintilla of capacity in the people who sent them'. Cohen to Wolf, 11 June 1901, BDBJ C 11/2/2. These sentiments of the turn-of-the-century crisis came to be repeated even more sharply in the years following the war. On the original issue, see chapters 9–11. Nancy Green of the Institut des Hautes Etudes in Paris is currently completing research on a general study of Jewish emigration.

54 Wolf, PCD, 5 Mar. 1919.

55 'The magnitude of the Jewish population renders it necessary that patience should be strained to its utmost in order to secure a stable social peace in that country. Moreover the alleged infractions while undoubtedly causing a widespread insecurity do not afford material for a reliable case before the League. Finally, the political situation was one which rendered great circumspection imperative.' Wolf was able to show that the Polish government had, in fact, acted decisively to stop 'real trouble'. The price being paid – the continuation of an organized anti-Jewish boycott and non-recognition of civil rights – would ultimately be redeemed once the Polish government was strong enough. Wolf, Report to the Joint Foreign Committee, 15 Dec. 1920, AIU Angl III/D/52/8253. Wolf's careful orchestration of the Jewish position can best be seen in Wolf, PCD and FAC Conf, 3, 23 Oct., 11 Dec. 1917, 31 Jan. 1918, AJ/204/4/54, 66, 71–2,unn.

13

Zionism Ascendant?

ZIONISM AS HIGH POLITICS

Herbert Samuel, at the time president of the Local Government Board in Asquith's Liberal government, saw war with Turkey as a way to find an appropriate solution for the Zionist issue. With appropriate asides for Moslems and Christians, Britain could find 'in yet another sphere her historic part of civiliser of the backward countries'. Prime Minister H. H. Asquith, who wished to commit himself to the fewest possible new imperial commitments, found the idea preposterous, but Samuel returned three months later with a slightly modified proposal. Edwin Montagu, Samuel's cousin and long a person on whom Asquith had depended for political advice on delicate issues, responded sharply in a private memorandum to Asquith and a confidential paper to Lloyd George.[1] The substance of the debate on what would eventually become the Balfour Declaration would not shift from these positions, although the emotional impact certainly did. Lloyd George's somewhat frivolous and Arthur Balfour's more serious interest in Zionist goals left friends of

1 H. Samuel, 'The Future of Palestine', January 1915, CAB 37/123/43; 'Palestine', March 1915, CAB 37/126/1. Montagu answered in two memoranda. Montagu to Asquith, 16 Mar. 1915, original in MS Asquith 27, ff. 38–41; copy in Reading Papers, MSS Eur F 118/95 in the India Office Library (with Reading's marginalia and Montagu's notes for cabinet discussion); Montagu to Lloyd George, 16 Mar. 1915. Lloyd George Papers C/25/14/1. Samuel also lobbied unsuccessfully with Reading. Samuel to Reading, 3 Feb. 1915. Reading Papers. MSS Eur F 118/99. See also, Montagu to Asquith, Mar. 1915. MS Asquith, 27, f. 38. Asquith, although close to Montagu, had mixed views about Jews characteristic of the more liberal members of the upper classes. See, e.g., Asquith to Crewe, 23 Nov. 1913. Crewe Papers C/40. For Asquith's acid comments on the Samuel proposal, see M. and E. Brock (eds.) *H. H. Asquith Letters to Venetia Stanley* (Oxford, 1982), 402–7 and his bemused observations on Montagu's counter, 17 Mar. 1915, ibid, letter no. 354. Samuel continued to lobby Lloyd George, coordinating his efforts with Weizmann. Samuel to Lloyd George, 13 Jan. 1915. Lloyd George Papers C/7/8/6. Kitchener toyed with the idea of encouraging Zionists in Palestine as early as December 1914, but he rejected the idea because he believe the Zionists too closely connected with Constantinople and Berlin. Kitchener to Storrs, 22 Dec., Storrs to Fitzgerald, 28 Dec. 1914. Kitchener Papers. PRO 30/57/45/00/71, 73. Lloyd George, at this stage, wanted action and success. Lloyd George to Kitchener, 3–29 Jan. 1915, ibid., 80/WV/11–13. For the general question, see I. Friedman, *The Question of Palestine* (London, 1973) and L. Stein, *The Balfour Declaration* (London, 1961).

Zionism in governing circles even after Samuel had lost his cabinet post and moved into the opposition.

The cabinet discussions in March 1915 centred, not on the issue of Jews in Palestine, but on the question of what 'Moslem political entity' should be constructed on the ruins of the Asian Ottoman Empire. Anglo-Indian opinion had now begun to be mobilized, and, in later stages through Edwin Montagu, would have much to say on the issue throughout the protracted negotiations for a Middle East treaty settlement. At the cabinet meeting of 9 March, however, Montagu chose for whatever reason not to speak on the Palestine issue.[2]

The question of doing something for the Jews assumed greater importance in both France and Britain as the stalemated war dragged on and exhaustion made them increasingly dependent on American support. American Jewry, although estimated to be only two to three million, was considered to be strategically placed, particularly in Democratic party politics. President Woodrow Wilson was reported to be much influenced by German Jews and anti-entente Jews. A disproportionately large portion of the American Jewish community came from Eastern Europe with bitter recollections of Russian oppression. The facts were bad enough, but stories of Russian wickedness lost nothing in the telling. Jewish spokesmen, Zionist and anti-Zionist, hoped to exploit English and French fears. They had fertile ground. Something approximating panic developed in Paris and London as the 1916 presidential election moved towards its climax. Sir Cecil Spring-Rice, the British ambassador, wrote hysterical dispatches on the subject, while Jusserand, the far more intelligent French ambassador, discussed the same acute problems with much greater sensitivity.[3] Spokesmen for the English and French Jewish establishments – Lucien Wolf for the British and Victor Basch for the French – were dispatched to the United States to convey generous sentiments about East European Jewish civil liberties and some soothing Palestinian balm for American Jewry.[4] Spring-Rice,

2 So Hobhouse pointedly observed in *Inside Asquith's Cabinet*, 227–8. See also CAB 37/126/8. Martin Gilbert prints the war council discussions of 19 March 1915 in his *Winston Churchill: Companion Volume, 1914–1916* (London, 1979), 713–16. Prior committee discussions focused on the issue of the Balkans and the Ottoman Empire in Europe. The De Bunsen Committee of the Committee on Imperial Defence, sometimes called the 'Spoils Committee', took up the issue of Asiatic Turkey on 8 April 1915 and reported on 30 June. Committee on Imperial Defence (CID), Asiatic Turkey. Paper 220-B. CAB 4/6/74; Crewe MS M 17(15); 'The War', 14 Mar. 1915. G-16 CAB 24/1. All options were intelligently explored and deemed unsatisfactory in one way or another. Montagu to Asquith [c. 15 Apr 1915]. MS Asquith 27/93–9. The Conjoint Committee was not asked for what it considered to be the appropriate Jewish desiderata until more than a year later. Alexander, Montefiore and de Rothschild to Grey, 1 Oct. 1916, AIU Angl II/D/26/5722.

3 See, e.g., Spring-Rice to FO, 7, 18 July; Spring-Rice to Grey, 21 July, 16 Aug., 16 Dec. 1916. CAB 37/151/43; 37/152/14; 37/154/22; 37/161/4, 37. Spring-Rice to Balfour, 29 Dec. 1916, Balfour Papers, Add MS 49,740, ff. 32–38. Spring-Rice, however, always reported that American Jewry was anti-Russian rather than pro-German. See his regular reports in FO 800/241–42. Jusserand's correspondence on this subject is in MAE A/1197–201. French assumptions about American Zionists and their connection to French pacifism, however, must have coloured their attitude. E. de Billy memorandum, 10 fév. 1918. MAE A/1200/148–50.

4 The French government developed approaches to American Jewry far more rapidly than the British. See, e.g., [L. Wolf], Confidential Suggestions for a Pro-Allies Propaganda among the Jews of the United States, 16 Dec. 1915, BDBJ C11/3/1/3. Poincaré's confidential assurances, sent via Basch, were a vague formulation of what would be the Balfour Declaration position. Wolf attempted to pry the terms of the assurances from Moutet, deputy for Lyons and a principal Briand supporter. Wolf à Moutet, 19 juil. 1916. BDBJ C 11/2/9.

however, had dealt with Russians in various diplomatic positions and served in St Petersburg. He pointed directly at the entente quandary. As matters stood in 1916, the Zionist option was preferable to conceding 'moderate' Jewish demands.

> The difficulty is that the Jews will not be satisfied with anything short of a promise from Russia of equal treatment. As competition between Jews and Christians in Russia is out of the question in the country districts, the Jews could not be admitted to those districts without very serious consequences both for the Christians and the Jews themselves. This I believe the Jews resident in Russia themselves understand. If we make this demand from Russia we shall meet with a positive refusal and we shall not do the Jews any good. Some other means therefore must be taken of pleading their case and winning their sympathies.[5]

The Conjoint Committee and the Alliance attempted to resist the more problematical implications of Zionist nationalism. At the same time they understood that they must produce a programme that would answer some of those needs to which Zionism spoke. They settled for British and French government pledges of unrestricted immigration to and unimpeded Jewish colonization of Palestine. In simplest terms this meant: 'Equal political rights with religious liberty in all countries and with facilities for colonisation in Palestine with special rights in those parts where the Jews are in the majority would seem to me the right policy.'[6] The British and French Jewish establishments, overwhelmingly anti-Zionist, would go so far but no further. Once they had defined their desiderata, they worked unstintingly to gain a commitment to some such general principles from their respective foreign ministries. Wolf saw Premier Briand in July 1916 in Paris to impress on him the uniformity of Jewish opinion while simultaneously seeking to turn the Zionist flank by having extended negotiations with Baron Edmond de Rothschild.[7]

The moderate position, constantly subject to attack in England, would also soon be challenged in France. Max Nordau opened his French campaign in 1916 for a tripartite Zionist programme: enforced equal rights for Jews everywhere in the world, recognition of Jewish nationality 'if the Jews themselves so desire, in all cosmopolitan states where the Jews form a considerable, organized element of the population', and Palestine for the Jews.[8] Nordau followed in the footsteps of Nahum Slousch, lecturer

5 Spring-Rice to Cecil, 17 Mar 1916, Spring-Rice Papers, FO 800/242/77–8.

6 Reading to Montagu, 19 Mar. 1916, Reading Papers, MSS Eur F 118/95. The anti-Zionists consistently took the position that anti-Semites loved Zionism. Some of them did. C. Holmes, *Anti-Semitism*, 119–20.

7 Wolf to Samuel, 18 July; Wolf to Oliphant, 18 July 1916 BDBJ C 11/2/9. Bigart à Wolf, 5, 30 juin, 7 juil.; Wolf to Bigart, 2, 6 July, Wolf à Bigart, 7 juil. 1916. AIU Angl I/J/8/5590, 5604, 5610, 5635, 5649; Wolf to Bigart 14 July 1916. I/G/4/5271. Moutet, among others, told the French government to take Wolf seriously. See his confidential memorandum, 14 juin 1916, MAE A/1198/20–5. Wolf understood that some position on Palestine was essential, were any impact to be made in the United States. See, e.g., FO 800/210/136 ff. Knowing perfectly well that the Prime Minister made made of his own foreign policy decisions, he went to Reading, who enjoyed Lloyd George's confidence, to ascertain that the anti-Zionist position reached the Prime Minister. Wolf to Reading, 23 Feb 1916. BDBJ C 11/2/8.

8 'Ils seront soumis à l'autorité du gouvernement exerçant la souveraineté sur le pays.' *Le Peuple Juif*, no. 16, 15 jan. 1917. Ormsby-Gore summarized the 'Jewish Palestinian Question' in a confidential report to Balfour, 3 Feb. 1917, suggesting the political desirability and practicality of endorsing a Zionist position. Balfour Papers, FO 800/210/101–22.

in Hebrew literature at the Sorbonne. The Quai d'Orsay, understanding entente vulnerability to German propaganda among American Jews, had cleverly underwritten Slousch's lecture tour to the United States and Canada in 1915. Slousch advocated 'une sorte de Judé indépendante, au sud de Jerusalem et des Lieux Saints, de façon à ne pas froisser les chrétiens'.[9] The French Foreign Ministry endorsed nothing and denied nothing. It simply let Slousch talk.

The Jewish Board of Deputies and the Anglo-Jewish Association, the institutions for which the Conjoint Committee spoke, endorsed Wolf's minimalist, non-Zionist position as a programme acceptable for all entente Jews. Wolf then took this into the lion's den and attempted to convince Balfour that the committee represented the overwhelming majority of 'Jews of British birth, education and sentiment'. Acknowledging Balfour's interest in Zionism, Wolf also reminded him that Zionism was only part of the Jewish nationalist movement, a drive fuelled principally 'by the general struggle for Nationalist autonomy and independence in Eastern Europe'. He explained that the Conjoint Committee, a representative group and 'the only body authorized to speak for the Jewish communities, not only of the United Kingdom but of the British Empire' saw Zionism as 'no part of our practical political programme' since it offered no practical solution for the anomalous political and social conditions of the substantial Jewish communities of Eastern Europe. He underscored the assimilation of Western Jewry while allowing for

a deep sentimental attachment for Palestine for historical reasons, and we were, besides, interested in the welfare of that country through the many Jewish institutions which we either owned or controlled there. We should rejoice if the Zionists made Palestine the seat of a flourishing and reputable Jewish community. We should have no objections if that Jewish community developed into a local Jewish nation and a Jewish state. But, we stipulated that, in its political work, it should not claim the allegiance of the Jews of Western Europe ... [nor] adopt methods which might be calculated to compromise the position and aims of Jews in other countries.[10]

Balfour, for his part, conceded that he did not know much about the broader Jewish nationalist movement. Balfour acknowledged that the Zionists with whom he had been dealing also admitted that Zionism would not solve the overall problem of the Jews in Eastern Europe. Wolf, believing he had found his opening, turned the conversation to those issues that most concerned the Anglo-French Jewish leadership: the ill-treatment of Russian Jews and Russia's barbarities in Poland under its wartime emergency powers. Wolf observed that earlier representations from the Conjoint Committee to Grey and from the Alliance to Briand had ultimately produced representations to the Russian government and brought to an end the worst persecutions. Much damage, meanwhile, had been done in sections of neutral opinion, particularly in the United States. Much could be retrieved if the current government would proclaim peace aims that included a strong position on

9 Jusserand à Briand, 17 déc. 1915. MAE A/1197/115, encl. 116–18.
10 Wolf, Memorandum on the Jewish Question, 31 Jan. 1917, a summary of an extended interview between himself and Balfour, enclosed in Wolf to Drummond, 7 Feb. 1917. Balfour, Lord Robert Cecil, Lord Hardinge, Drummond, and Oliphant all reviewed Wolf's summary of the discussion and agreed that it was accurate. Balfour Papers, FO 800/210/138–55.

minority rights. As matters stood, it appeared that 'the Government did not quite realize what the Jewish question was. Both in magnitude and cruelty, it was the greatest scandal in the political life of Europe.'

Balfour fell back on the explanation the foreign ministry had offered for years. 'Injudicious interference' would only make matters worse. Wolf should understand, Balfour archly continued,

> the persecutors had a case of their own. They were afraid of the Jews, who were an exceedingly clever people, and who, in spite of their oppression, achieved a certain success, which excited the jealousy and envy of the peoples among whom they lived. No one persecuted the gypsies because no one was afraid of them, but wherever one went in Eastern Europe, one found that, by some way or other, the Jew got on.[11]

The Jews were, moreover, 'a distinct race' practising a religion that was 'an object of inherited hatred'. Since Jews were 'numbered by millions', in Eastern Europe, one could understand, though never justify, such persecution. Such factors must be considered when requesting that Western governments urge the Russians to emancipate their Jews.

Wolf tactfully reminded Balfour that the ostensible cleverness of the Jew was only true 'in comparison with the illiterate populations of Eastern Europe', that 'his wits had been preternaturally sharpened by persecution and by his confinement to town life.' Wherever they had been emancipated, Jews were comparatively no more clever than the populations of which they were a part. 'The greatest fortunes of the world were not Jewish, while the greatest poverty in the world *was* Jewish.' Since anti-Semitism came from the very top of Russian society, rather than springing from the masses, Wolf continued, diplomatic pressure could have an significant impact.[12]

While the first negotiations between the Conjoint Committee and the Zionists during the war broke down in 1915, Wolf concentrated on refining desiderata which would satisfy the French, the Italian, and the various British commonwealth and imperial Jewish committees. Full political and civil liberties for the Jews of eastern Europe had to be the first demand. Since the Zionist issue would not go away, some statement, however innocuous, must be made on Palestine. The various groups finally settled on 'such municipal privileges in the Towns and Colonies inhabited by [Palestinian Jews] as may be shewn to be necessary', another half-step towards Zionist demands. Events overran such evasions.[13] The Russian February revolution brought the long-awaited abolition of all restrictions on the Jews. For

11 Ibid.

12 Ibid. The Alliance also took the position that the Russian government and elite fomented anti-Semitism. See, e.g, AIU à MAE, 23 juil. 1915, MAE A/1197/47–53. A leading Dutch Zionist warned Balfour that the better-off Jews would not go to Palestine, that it was a pauper country which Zionism would make more so. Townly to Balfour, 22 June 1917, Balfour Papers, FO 438/10/43/81.

13 Wolf, Confidential Statement from the Conjoint Committee, 22 Oct 1916, Interleaf, BDBJ Minute Book, 1916, pp. 39–40. Wolf's suggested Palestine formula as presented to the Alliance is in AIU Angl, I/J/8/5731. See the discussion of Sylvain Lévi's translation for the MAE and the need to keep Conjoint–Alliance proposals to their governments confidential and out of the hands of the Zionists in Wolf to Bigart, 29 Sept. 1916, AIU Angl I/J/8/5722. CFC, *Statement on the Palestine Question*, 17 May 1917 appended to the minutes of the meeting overturning the long-time board, 52 to 50 with several abstentions. A second vote was ordered which produced the 56 to 51 margin. BDBJ Minute Book, 17 June 1917.

almost half a century, Western Jewry had ascribed Jewish difficulties principally to Russian persecution. Remove that, and Jews throughout Europe would become well-adjusted subcultures within each nation. Zionism, it was hoped, would then be irrelevant.

But the Russian revolution, paradoxically, improved the Zionist position. The framework of debate suddenly changed. Anti-Zionists had previously argued that Zionism would increase, even be used to justify, persecution. Nor, as Wolf had told Balfour, could Zionism solve the East European Jewish problem. But now with revolution and emancipation that problem appeared to have vanished. Jews now held, in theory, at least, those rights Western Jewish assimilationists argued were the essential condition for their becoming contented and effective parts of their host culture. That 'liberated' peoples and their spokesmen could persecute as vigorously as the tsarist regime, or more vigorously, remained a lesson to be learned. For the moment, the issue appeared to be simple. Zionism was no longer needed to secure American support, for the United States had entered the war in April 1917. Prospects for East European Jews appeared to be dramatically improved. But Zionism had acquired a momentum of its own once undertaken at cabinet level. Rather than a utilitarian sop to America or even a public concession to Jews, Zionism was translated, in cabinet debate into a question of British self-interest and a matter of competition with the Central Powers.[14]

In one of those casual, unofficial meetings at which the British seemed to make so many important decisions, Lloyd George, Lord Curzon and cabinet secretary Hankey cautioned Sir Mark Sykes in April 1917 against taking Arab matters further in his forthcoming mission to the Middle East. Lloyd George and Curzon insisted that absolutely nothing be done that might be 'prejudicial' to British interests. British relations with France in that region had become increasingly problematical. Sykes was, moreover, to make absolutely no agreements or concessions contrary to British interests or that might in any way inhibit the development of the Zionist movement under British auspices. The Jews, observed Lloyd George, might do us far more good than the Arabs. Sykes enthusiastically agreed, since he was already imagining himself as the planner of a vast composite Arab–Jewish–Armenian entity in the Middle East. But Curzon, always full of his own wisdom on matters oriental, was more concerned about French gains than troublesome and relatively trivial Jewish issues.[15]

The war, after all, created a Zionist paradox. Chaim Weizmann chose to gamble on entente victory. But the entente appeared to link the liberal, highly acculturated Jewish communities of Britain and France in common cause with the oppressive Russian regime, a tyranny that became dramatically worse for Jews with the coming

14 This explains the delicate but coordinated discussions between Sokolow and Balfour, who met with Cambon, Sykes and Picot. Their 'bienveillance', achieved by avoiding the issue of suzerain power for Palestine, was cabled to Brandeis. Sykes to Balfour, 9 Apr. 1917. Sykes Papers (Sledmere) 41A at St. Antony's College Library, Oxford. The Russians realized that the French were concluding Zionist bargains in the spring of 1917 and wanted to know the French position on Zionism and the creation of an independent state in Palestine. 29 mai 1917, MAE A/1199/39. At the same time Sokolow told Picot that the ICA and Petrograd Jewish Congress had endorsed Zionism and demanded a commitment from the French. The French, confused, scrambled to find out where the Foreign Office stood on the issue. J. Cambon à P. Cambon, 22 mai 1917, MAE A/1199/35/90.

15 Secret instructions, 3 Apr. 1917. Sykes Papers 38.

of the war. Germans, on the other hand, 'liberated' Jews as they occupied eastern territories. German and Austrian Zionists and anti-Zionists, moreover, working with American representatives in Constantinople, undoubtedly saved Ottoman, particularly Palestinian, Jews from the fate of Armenians and many Syrian Arab nationalists. The Germans, no less than the French and British, appealed to East European, neutral, and, particularly, American Jewish opinion. Chancellor Bethmann Hollweg proved far more sensitive to Jewish interests during the war than he had ever done before it. Bethmann Hollweg and Wangerheim, German ambassador to the Porte, repeatedly urged Talaat, the Turkish Minister of the Interior, to deal very carefully with any matters that might antagonize world Jewish opinion.[16]

Such intervention proved very important. Djemal Pasha, the Turkish commandant in Palestine, viewed alien Jews, most of whom were Russian, as actually or potentially subversive. He began to deport all Jews of Russian nationality in December 1914 and only reluctantly bowed to orders from Constantinople to stop.[17] But the Turkish alliance also constrained Germany. The British and French could make platitudinous statements about Jews in Palestine. Germany actually could do little more than issue a general, confidential instruction to its consular officials in the Ottoman Empire suggesting that the German imperial government was not ill-disposed to Jewish aspirations. Even this approach demanded a delicate balance between offending their Turkish allies, capitalizing on the popularity of German occupation rule among Jews in tsarist lands, and playing to what the Germans and the British both incorrectly assumed was pro-German sympathy among American Jews. The fact that the American ambassador to Constantinople was, as a matter of unspoken convention, Jewish also constrained potential persecution. The Turks did not forget that the Americans had remained neutral in their war.[18]

When the Balfour Declaration finally came before the cabinet, Edwin Montagu, son of the late Sir Samuel Montagu and Secretary of State for India, sustained the Montagu family position on Zionism, although he shared none of his father's religious views. Edwin Montagu fought a hard rearguard action, the principal effect of which was to lead to minor modifications at the behest of Curzon and significant ones in Lord Milner's alternative formulation. The British government, like British Jews, understood how important a coordinated stance with their American counterparts must be. Woodrow Wilson's initially cool response proved to be only a temporary, if unnerving, setback. Montagu had not, in fact, won cabinet support as

16 E. Zechlin, *Die deutsche Politik und die Juden im Ersten Weltkrieg* (Göttingen, 1969), 318; FO Intelligence Dept, Memorandum on the Attitude of Enemy Governments towards Zionism, GT-3635, February 1918, CAB 24/42/112–21. For the Kühlmann correspondence about the Jaffa deportations, see Allizé à MAE, 18 oct. 1917, MAE A/1199/189. Picot contended that the Bapst and Dernburg efforts in Berlin in March 1917 were nothing more than an effort to create difficult and disunion between the allies. Jules Cambon memorandum, 11 mars 1917, MAE A/1198/117–18. The Russian government displayed some anxiety about Russian Jews being 'expelled', and it offered to pay the British for keeping them in Egypt until after the war. Buchanan to Grey, 12 Jan. 1915, Grey Papers, FO 438/5/72/33.

17 More than 600 had been removed before deportations stopped in March 1915. Herbert Samuel was much concerned and maintained close contact with the Conjoint Committee to secure current Palestinian intelligence. BDBJ C 11/2/8–9.

18 Zechlin, *Die deutsche Politik*, 366ff.; W. Laqueur, *History of Zionism* (New York, 1972), 172ff.

Weizmann and Rothschild feared.[19] Curzon agreed with Montagu that the Declaration was ill-advised, but only because he felt that Palestine could never absorb significant numbers of settlers or develop a viable economy to sustain the hopes that such an announcement would encourage. Lord Milner, anxious to find some accommodation, formulated a compromise which, slightly more modified at the final cabinet meeting, became the text of the Declaration. Balfour contended that expert opinion divided on the economic potential of Palestine, that so far from committing Britain to a Zionist state, he was thinking only of 'some form of British, American, or other protectorate, under which full facilities would be given to the Jews to work out their own salvation and to build up, by means of education, agriculture and industry, a real centre of national culture and focus of national life.' Zionism would not, so Balfour argued, compromise or retard assimilation in the West, the appropriate analogy being that of an Englishman who migrated to the United States, his children 'becoming full nationals' of that country.

Balfour then played the theme of the German peril ever so gently to Lloyd George suggesting more serious Central Powers competition for Zionist favour than was actually the case.

> The French have already given an assurance of sympathy to the Zionists [the Cambon statement to Sokolow] on the same lines as is now proposed for His Majesty's Government, though in rather more definite terms. The Italian Government and the Vatican have expressed their sympathy, and we know that President Wilson is sympathetic and is prepared to make a declaration at the proper moment.[20]

19 Rothschild to Balfour, 3 Oct.; Weizmann and Rothschild to Balfour, 3 Oct. 1917, FO 371/3083/89–94. Balfour, milking Admiralty and Elkus reports, also suggested, 'It is not, indeed, impossible that there may be some connection between the Jewish wire pullers in Constantinople and the Jewish element in Petrograd.' Balfour to the cabinet, 17 July 1917, CAB 1/25/45–6. See also, House to Drummond, 10 Sept. 1917, GT-2015, CAB 24/26/39. Balfour attempted to convince House of the German threat to secure Jewish support through Zionism. FO to Wiseman, 6 Oct 1917, Curzon Papers, MS Eur F 112/267 in the India Office Library. Milner warned Lloyd George that Germans were appealing to Russian Jews. He thought Jews would have more power and influence in Russia than organized labour. Milner to Lloyd George, 31 May 1917, Lloyd George Papers F/38/2/6. The concern remained into 1918. See R. Lévy, 'Le Problème de la Palestine: un manoeuvre politique allemande', *l'Humanité*, 3 avr. 1918; P. de Margeris à Chiffré, 10 fév. 1918, MAE A/1200/146–7; A/1201/82.

20 CAB 23/4/261/12; CAB 23/4/227/2; CAB 23/4/245/18. Balfour to Lloyd George, 25 Oct. 1917, Lloyd George Papers F/3/2/36. Rothschild's original formula 'that Palestine should be reconstitued as the National Home of the Jewish people' (Rothschild to Balfour, 18 July 1917, GT-1803) gave way to Milner's alternative, 'a home for the Jewish people in Palestine'. (GT-1803A) CAB 24/24/12–14. On these details, see Ormsby-Gore to Oliphant, 21 Sept. 1917, FO 371/3083/96–7. Save for Curzon's laborious 'The Future of Palestine', 16 Oct. 1917, GT-2406, CAB 24/30/22–3 and Montagu's trenchant critical papers (q.v.), Hankey assembled a summary of pro and con views in 'The Zionist Movement, 17 Oct 1917', G-164, CAB 24/4. The position of the Central Powers is summarized in Memorandum on the Attitude of Enemy Governments towards Zionism, February 1919, GT-3635, CAB 24/42/112–21. Balfour was not correct and undoubtedly knew it. German Jewish policies moderated after, not before, the Balfour Declaration. See, e.g., FO intelligence, weekly report, GT-3912, 12 Mar. 1918, CAB 24/45/40. Rothschild (perhaps prodded by Weizmann) had originally suggested this argument to Balfour. Rothschild to Balfour, 22 Sept. 1917, FO 371/3083/98–99. Cambon's statement to Sokolow was far vaguer than the Balfour Declaration, and the Vatican position restated its post-1870 insistence on territorial rights for religious organizations. See Cambon à Sokolof[!], 4 juin 1917, FO 371/3083/143082/49; M. de Margerie note, Sionisme en Palestine, 22 mai 1917, MAE A/1199/33–4.

Curzon donned Islamic dress for the occasion and discoursed on the improving theme of Britain as the greatest Moslem power in the world. The cabinet, when finally satisfied that all circles could be squared, endorsed the Declaration on 31 October 1917.

Once again events soared ahead of understanding. The Bolshevik revolution took Russia out of the war more expeditiously than concessions to newly-emancipated Russian Jews might have served to keep her in. American Jewry's expectations appeared to heighten from the Declaration to Allenby's capture of Jerusalem, but those hopes took ironic twists and turns.

THE STRUGGLE WITH ZIONISTS

Wolf's standing with the Foreign Office, so clear in the discussions between London and the Quai d'Orsay in the summer of 1916, continued to be almost unassailable until the apparent overthrow of the anti-Zionist leadership of the Jewish Board of Deputies in the summer of 1917. From the destruction of the Conjoint Committee to the reconstruction of the Joint Foreign Committee at the close of the war, Wolf officially spoke for no more than himself and the Anglo-Jewish Association. His efforts to regroup anti-Zionist forces in the Union of British Jews enjoyed no success.[21] Increasingly, Wolf found himself forced to work through the resolutely anti-Zionist Alliance and to trade strictly on his experience and contacts when dealing with the Foreign Office.

Information rather than advice on policy had been and remained Wolf's best *entrée* to the Foreign Office, and Wolf understood how to play on it. Once the French connection was established, he also exploited the quasi-official Anglo-French Jewish involvement in the propaganda addressed to the United States to be heard at the British Foreign Office upon a variety of issues. Wolf contended that Anglo-French Jewish cooperation helped to secure the American Federation of Labor resolution of 1916 formally committing the United States labour movement to equal rights for Jews throughout the world. By the end of June 1916, the American Jewish Committee had been agreed to the Conjoint Committee–Alliance programme, and Wolf, at least, felt that this should allay Foreign Office anxieties about anti-entente Jewish inclinations.[22]

Lucien Wolf and the Anglo-Jewish leaders who served on the Conjoint Committee repeatedly asked those to whom they must answer for freedom to negotiate, a minimum of oversight and respect for the confidentiality of their dealings. This gave Wolf in particular the capacity to act with an extraordinary measure of freedom, the capacity to soar well beyond conventional institutional constraints. He never abused it and was always forthcoming with the results of his activities. In statements of October 1915 and February 1916, for instance, he discussed very candidly the ways in which he sought to coordinate the policies of the

21 See, e.g., Wolf to Bigart, 16, 21 Aug., 23, 30 Sept.; Bigart à Wolf, 12 août, 27 sept. 1918, AIU Angl III/D/52/6483, 6485, 6518, 6524.

22 Drummond to Wolf, 30 June, 15 July 1916; de Bunsen to Wolf 4, 5 July; Wolf to Montefiore, 7 July 1916; Wolf to de Rothschild, 1 Oct. and Wolf to Cecil, 1 Oct. 1915, BDBJ C 11/2/9; Reading to Wolf 23 Mar. 1916, BDBJ C 11/2/8; Bigart à Montefiore, 22 avr. 1917, AIU Angl I/J/8/5931.

South African Board of Deputies and the American Jewish Committee with regard to the future policies. His technique was almost invariably the same. Find all the possible areas of agreement, attempt to eliminate hopelessly controversial issues, and never dwell on disagreements. Efforts to raise troublesome issues were abruptly shunted aside. Much had been left open for negotiation. From August to October 1916 Wolf had brought the several bodies to agree on fairly simple formulations. All political and civil disabilities must end for the Jews of Russia and Roumania. Yet another half-step was taken to meet Zionist demands for Jews in Palestine by insisting on 'such municipal privileges in the Towns and Colonies inhabited by them as may be shewn to be necessary'.[23]

The Conjoint Committee also worked with the conference of American Jewish organizations to develop a cooperative programme to resolve the problem of 'the future of many millions of Jews in Eastern Europe'. Foremost on this agenda were the issues of Jewish rights and the peace conference. Palestine took third place behind the prospective status of Jews when transferred from one sovereignty to another and Jewish rights in the new and future Poland. The Conjoint Committee still hoped to work out some compromise with the Zionists and announced that it would consider 'any scheme of Jewish immigration and colonization, and for the free development of Jewish institutions and cultural life which will promote the Zionist aims without compromising the struggle for equal rights in other countries'.[24] Wolf, moreover, believed that the assimilationists now had communal support. The Anglo-Jewish broad-gauged programme had carried the day in foreign policy and was substantially supported, not merely by the leadership, but within the Jewish community at home. Presumptuous as it sounded, Wolf might have been correct, but his patriotic blinkers misled him. Mid-1916 might have proved the occasion to reaffirm Anglo-Jewish assimilationist command of British Jewry had not the issue of military service, as we shall see, suddenly polarized the community. The assimilationists misread the depth of anti-Russian feeling in the East End. Wolf forged ahead, seeing victory in hand on the foreign and domestic fronts. He planned a new British national union, uniting Anglo-Jewish organizations behind his 'non-partisan' programme.

23 Wolf, Confidential Statement from the Conjoint Committee, 22 Oct 1916, interleaf, pp. 39–40, BDBJ Minute Book. Wolf was, with Alexander's aid, attempting to unite the anti-Zionist establishment and the growing Zionist minority. Wolf believed that the unity of the various Jewish national committees could alone render Jewish diplomacy effective. See, e.g., Wolf to Bigart, 22 Feb., 2 Mar., 14 July 1915, 3, 6, 7 July, 20 Aug.,12 Sept. 1916; Bigart à Wolf, 9 fév. 1915; 5, 30 juin,15 sept. 1916, AIU Angl I/J/8/5590, 5604, 5610, 5620, 5628, 5635, 5649 9691, 9707; AIU Angl I/G/4/5271. *Pro Causa Judaica*, a Swiss organization in which Dreyfus-Brodsky of the AIU played an important role, agitated for a much stronger Zionist position from Western Jewry. Wolf and the Conjoint Committee responded very coldly. Bigart, embarrased by the conflict of interests, came down solidly on Wolf's side. The only policy for the AIU was 'une collaboration intime et permanente entre nos amis en Londres et nous'. Wolf to Bigart, 21 July; Bigart à Wolf, 24 juil.; Bigart à Lioni, 13 août 1916, AIU Cdc S 239/451, 418–19; PCJ à Ditasta, 27 mars, 22 avr. 1918, MAE A/1201/59–60, 112–3, 120–1.

24 Wolf to Adler, 16 Sept. 1915, included in BDBJ C 11/2/7–10. Edwin Montagu would take the same line with the cabinet in his two classic papers protesting at what would become the Balfour Declaration. 'The anti-Semitism of the present British government', 23 August 1917, GT-1868, CAB 24/24/256–7 and 'Zionism', GT-2263, 9 Oct. 1917, CAB 24/28. Montagu to Asquith, 16 Mar. 1915, MS Asquith 27, ff. 38–41. Hankey summarized the various positions, pro and con, for the cabinet in 'The Zionist movement', 17 Oct. 1917, G-164, CAB 24/4.

We are not going to be Nationalists, or Zionists, or Territorials, but simply Jews, claiming equal rights for Jews everywhere. I hope the result will be the restoration of a real unity in the Anglo-Jewish community. A big meeting is to be organised in the East End to launch the movement, and I want to get on the platform all our representative men.[25]

Wolf had two objectives:

In the first place I want to get a closer union and a freer and more continuous intercourse between our east-end and our west-end, and in the next place, I want to establish an organisation for the defence of Jewish rights, with a programmeme of essentials on which all parties can join.[26]

Wolf had been talking too long to people not fully in touch with East End opinion. He believed, probably correctly, that the Jewish friendly societies represented the stable, responsible lower middle and upper working classes in so far as any institution did. He presumed that they, with fathers, husbands, and sons fighting in the war, would rally behind their familiar leaders and institutions. They did not. The campaign against Zionism was not won, but lost – at least for the moment. The deferential Jewish community was rumbling, the intellectual Jacobins, seeing their opportunity to destroy the old authoritarian communal order, were ready to strike.[27]

Each apparent success seemed to produce more difficulties. Months of negotiation to develop a common Jewish agenda had divided not united the community. The war that should have unified the community seemed to split it. The Russian revolution should have proved to be that dawn at which it was bliss to be alive. The Conjoint Committee rejoiced, reserved public comment until the Russians abolished all restrictions on the Jews and then dispatched a congratulatory telegram to Prince Lvov, the Russian Prime Minister.[28] For the better part of half a century, Western Jews had told themselves and anyone who happened to be

---

25 Wolf felt over 35,000 members were already in hand. 'I believe all the friendly societies will come in, and already some of the Zionist societies have joined us.' Wolf to Zangwill, 17 Jan., 3 Mar.; Wolf to Lord Swaythling, 9 Mar.1916, BDBJ C 11/2/8. See also, Wolf to Green, 10 Feb.; Wolf to Dywien, 30 Mar.; Wolf to Montefiore, 7 Apr. 1916, BDBJ C 11/2/8.

26 Wolf to Zangwill, 3 Mar.1916, BDBJ C 11/2/8.

27 For the details of this struggle, see Cohen, *English Zionists*, and the forthcoming second volume of Jehuda Reinharz's biography of Weizmann (volume I, New York, 1986). The French government believed that the English Zionist movement was led by intellectuals grouped around the University of London consisting principally of professors, writers and artists. This frightened the older Anglo-Jewish leaders and the Jewish millionaires, the French concluded, who coupled the newer Zionist agitation with the older anarchist and socialist strains. The poor Jewish masses, however, were little attracted to Zionist propaganda, being patriotic (until British military service was demanded) and generally highly observant. A de Fleurian à MAE, 27 déc. 1917, MAE A/1199/ii/122–4. The Labour party resolved on 10 August 1917 (and reaffirmed as a joint Labour party–TUC statement on 28 December) that Jews should everywhere have equal rights of toleration, residence and trade, equal citizenship, and that there should be an internationally guaranteed Palestine so Jews could move 'free from interference' (the Conjoint–Alliance agenda). GT-1733, GT-3167, CAB 24/23/138; CAB 24/37/196. See also, Wolf, Memorandum, 'Confidential', 6 June 1917 responding to Gaster's accusations at the council of the Anglo-Jewish Association. BDBJ C 11/2/13.

28 BDBJ Minute Book, 22 Apr 1917. The AIU was less restrained until Wolf damped their enthusiasm. Bigart à Wolf, 22 avr., 3 mai; Bigart à Marshall, 22 avr.; Bigart à Montefiore, 22 avr.; Wolf to Bigart 26 Apr. 1917, AIU Cdc, S 240/309–10, 324; AIU Angl I/J/8/5931, 5938.

listening that massive Jewish immigration and the host of social and political problems it appeared to bring would dwindle once Russia joined the ranks of liberal, civilized nations. The pressure on Jews to seek refuge in flight and solace in Zionism would end.

Quite the reverse happened. Victory for the Conjoint–Alliance diplomatic position actually weakened their domestic strength. Jewish civil rights in Russia intensified rather than slowed the British Zionist campaign. Rampaging Zionists, confident of their friends in high places, unrelentingly pressed Wolf and the Conjoint Foreign Committee. Anglo-Jewish champions of Western liberalism and pluralism faced their own two-front war. David L. Alexander held the gate at the Jewish Board of Deputies, seemingly as invincible as ever, repelling growing numbers of Zionist invaders. Claude Montefiore continued to control the Anglo-Jewish Association. Their French associates were unshaken as Sylvain Lévi prepared to crusade against Zionism in the United States. The British and French governments, however, for reasons of their own – not the least of which was the ease of making Zionist concessions and the impossibility of forcing their Russian ally do anything – were moving in the opposite direction.

Wolf fought two campaigns. On the one hand, he went directly to Balfour with the argument that the Conjoint Committee spoke for British and Empire Jewry, and that Zionism was neither wanted nor desirable. Simultaneously he argued to Montefiore, Alexander, and their French allies, among others, that delay and silence were a greater danger than an open public quarrel with the Zionists. He knew, through Bigart and his French friends, that the Zionists were moving closer to official endorsement. Assimilationists must strike now, reasserting their communal leadership and capitalizing on the movement of events. The American elections had passed, and Wilson was closer to entering the war on the entente side than he had ever been. Matters in Russia were clearly moving to some crisis from which Jewish interests could not do otherwise than improve. The French government had agreed to remonstrate with the Russians on Jewish rights on the terms the Conjoint and Alliance had recommended.[29]

Wolf also went directly to the Zionists. Baron Edmond de Rothschild had insisted that every effort should be made to avoid public division. Wolf charged the Zionists with the failure to renew negotiations after they had proposed them themselves as far back as November 1916.[30] Nothing happened, but Weizmann did let slip information about tentative British government commitments. Wolf knew the old guard was in trouble. After the invitation to prepare a general statement of the Jewish desiderata in the peace settlement for the de Bunsen committee, the Foreign Office had set the statement aside as 'not opportune'. He knew the Zionists had been encouraged in France. While concerns about America waned by the spring of 1917, Russia remained crucial. American manpower could not be brought to bear until 1918 or 1919, and France, teetering on that brink of exhaustion which

29 Briand, Ministre des Affaires Etrangères, pledged the Alliance a strong remonstrance to the Russian government. Bigart à Sereni (président des Communautés Israélites d'Italie), 5 jan. 1917, BDBJ C 11/2/11; Wolf, Memorandum on the Jewish Question, 31 Jan. 1917, Balfour Papers, FO 800/210/138–55; Wolf to de Rothschild, 3 Jan., 5 Feb.; Wolf to Bigart, 3 Jan. 1917; Wolf to Oliphant, 4 Feb., 1 Mar.; Deputation of the Jewish community to Prime Minister Hughes (Australia), 7 Feb. 1917, BDBJ C 11/2/11.
30 Wolf to Sokolov, 4 Jan. 1917. BDBJ C 11/2/11.

produced mutinies in its army, desperately needed to keep the second front going. A flagging of the Russian war effort might release yet more German troops to be hurled against the western front in a decisive battle. The Zionists, always effective at self-advertisement, contended that their friends could help to keep Russia in the war. Sokolow promised the French government full Zionist support in a Jewish campaign against Russian pacifists. He also pledged to use Jewish influence in Italy to hold that tottering country in the war. What was said in France, moreover, was almost certainly urged in England. Wolf suspected that Lloyd George had made unauthorized promises, as Lloyd George was likely to do. Lloyd George, of course, could forget promises as easily as he made them, but the point was troubling.[31]

These last negotiations between the Conjoint Committee and Weizmann's Zionists broke down before they ever really began. The Conjoint Committee would only discuss the 'cultural programmes' accepted at the last two Zionist Congresses in 1911 and 1913, and the Zionists were far beyond that.

> This policy aimed primarily at making Palestine a Jewish spiritual centre by securing for the local Jews, and the colonists who might join them, such conditions of life as would best enable them to develop the Jewish genius on lines of its own. Larger political questions not directly affecting this main purpose were left to be solved as need and opportunity might render possible.[32]

Zionist expectations rose with Sokolow's success in Paris and the fruitful Weizmann–Rothschild negotiations with Balfour. Zionist representation, although nowhere near a majority, had increased on the Board of Deputies. The Wolf–Alexander–Montefiore 'hard-line' position, while apparently institutionally supported, rested upon a faltering majority in which 'trimmers' held the balance of power.

Ignoring any warning signals and seeking to launch a preemptive strike against favourable War Cabinet consideration, Alexander and Montefiore signed Wolf's statement 'Palestine and Zionism – Views of Anglo-Jewry' and sent it to *The Times*

---

31 Sykes to Balfour, 9 Apr. 1917. Sykes was also concerned that information might leak on the negotiations between Sokolow and himself. Sykes to Podrone, 29 Apr 1917, Sykes Papers 41A. The French government had a confused account of an alleged February 1916 meeting between Gaster, Lord Rothschild, James de Rothschild, Herbert Samuel, Asquith[!], Weizmann, Sokolov and delegates from Russian and the United States. Although not unanimous, the majority, Picot reported (quite possibly in a garbled way from Sykes), voted that the mainstream institutions had lost the right to speak on Jewish peace desiderata and authorized Sokolow to negotiate with the Allied states. This Zionist meeting had led ultimately to the Cambon meeting and commitment of 4 June 1917. Picot à Ribot, 5 mai; MAE à Sokolow, 4 juin 1917, MAE A/1199/2–7, 48–52. See also, Wolf to Bigart, 20 Aug., 12 Sept.; Bigart à Wolf 15 sept. 1916, AIU Angl I/J/8/5695, 5707, 6236; AIU Cdc S 239/482.

32 CFC, *Statement on the Palestine Question*, 17 May 1917, appended to the minutes of the meeting overturning the board, 52 to 50. There were several abstentions. A second vote then produced the more commonly cited 56 to 51 result. BDBJ Minute Book, 17 June 1917. The minutes suggest none of the heat and passion of this dramatic event. D. L. Alexander, long-time president, H. S. Q. Henriques, and J. M. Levy resigned on the spot. The turnover on the Board led Sir Philip Magnus, Bt, MP, B. A. Fersht, S. E. de Haas and I. Solomons (all staunch Wolf supporters) to resign their positions on the Conjoint Committee. Sir Stuart Samuel, Bt, MP became president of the board on Lord Rothschild's nomination, Rothschild and Magnus (representing the pro- and anti-Zionist positions respectively) vice presidents. The most intelligent analysis of what happened came from Edwin Montagu. Montagu to Cecil, 14 Sept. 1917, FO 371/3083/82–8.

where it was published on 24 May. Much is said in criticism of this precipitous act,[33] but Wolf believed it the only way to drive the Zionists back to negotiations or to discredit them before the British public. 'This Statement,' he told Bigart, 'is not necessarily a declaration of war. It is indeed, intended to be conciliatory, and we are perfectly prepared to make it a basis of fresh negotiations with the Zionists.'[34] Wolf knew that the Zionists were 'not disposed to take any action by way of assisting us in the emancipation of the Jews of Eastern Europe'.[35] They contended that the matter was one for Russian, not Western, Jews to settle. Bigart understood and agreed.

You have long known the opinion of the [Central] Committee of the Alliance concerning the Zionist movement. It has not varied and we would openly approve your manifesto, which agrees entirely with our conception, but our special situation in Turkey imposes considerable discretion upon us, and we prefer to make no public declaration on Palestinian questions.[36]

When the boiling dispute within English Jewry burst into the columns of *The Times* in May 1917, a coalition of Zionists and other malcontents challenged both the public statement and the old leadership. The Anglo-Jewish Association held firm, but the Board of Deputies, after a passionate debate, carried a vote of censure by a slim majority. The *Jewish Chronicle* proclaimed a revolution which had not, in fact, come, not, at least, within the organized ranks of British Jewry. The system had

33 Cohen suggests that Wolf did not know how far Sykes and Balfour had moved the British government. He cites Bigart à Wolf, 16 avr. 1917 from the Wolf Papers 5948, Mowshowitch Collection, at YIVO, New York City in his discussion in *English Zionists*, chapters 6–7. But Wolf had ample information, and the Sykes and Balfour point Cohen makes was only marginally relevant to Wolf's considerations. The diplomatic situation was askew. The Zionists already had their Paris coup, and they were working hard with their British government friends. Wolf also realized that the situation had reached crisis point within the Board of Deputies. The demand that the Conjoint Committee go back to the table with the Zionists under what were considered to be intolerable conditions was narrowly rejected, 26 to 33. BDBJ Minute Book, 20 May 1917. Alexander and Wolf were particularly incensed that those who pressed Zionist resolutions were also so naive as to demand that the Conjoint Committee do something about 'the expulsion and ill-treatment of Jews in Palestine.'

34 Wolf to Bigart, 23 May 1917, AIU Angl I/J/8/5979. The Quai d'Orsay followed the controversy with great interest. MAE A/1199/14–19. Tardieu, in New York, felt that the Germans were still in a position to outbid the entente on Zionism and urged his government to take a stronger stand than the Balfour Declaration on the issue. Tardieu à MAE, 17 jan.; Tardieu à MAE et Clemenceau, 9 fév. 1918, MAE A/1200/141–2.

35 Wolf to Bigart 26 Feb. 1917, AIU Angl I/J/8/5880. See also, Wolf to Bigart, 3, 9 Jan.,1, 23 Mar., 19, 26 Apr.; Bigart à Wolf, 5, 9, 12 jan., 22 mars, 9, 16, 17 avr. 1917. AIU Angl I/J/8/5821, 5834, 5880, 5885, 5904, 5938, 5931; Bigart à Wolf, 31 mai, Wolf to Bigart, 5 June 1917, AIU Angl I/G/5/5979, 5989.

36 My translation of the French. Bigart à Wolf, 21 juin 1917, AIU Cdc S 240/378. Bigart brusquely rejected an Italian Committee request for a conference 'concernant la question palestinienne'. 'J'ai lieu de penser que dans les circonstances actuelles, et avec l'évolution qu'a subie la question palestinienne à la suite de la lettre de M. Balfour, l'Alliance refusera de prendre aucune initiative dans cette question, et je ne sais même si il acceptera éventuellement de participer à une conférence quelconque sur ce sujet provoqué par d'autres organisations.' Bigart à Wolf, 18 nov. 1917, AIU Angl I/J/8/unn. Much later Wolf observed, 'Our present feeling is that we could not take any steps on the basis of the declaration of the British Government so long as that declaration assumes that the Jews all over the world constitute a separate nationality. I think I may say that we should have no insuperable objection to a "Jewish national Home in Palestine", but we cannot agree to a "National Home for the Jewish People in Palestine", seeing that that formula assumes that Palestine is the national home of the whole Jewish people, and that consequently they are only temporary sojourners and aliens in the countries of which they are now legally recognised nationals and citizens.' Wolf to Bigart, 30 Nov. 1917, AIU Angl I/J/8/6223.

not ended and would shortly be firmly reconstructed. 'A handful of self-elected persons' did continue 'to speak for Anglo-Jewry.' Foreign Jews did not displace English Jews. Provincials did not nudge Londoners aside. Professionals and intellectuals had not ousted plutocrats. The issue of Zionism had proved a convenient point on which to rally disparate forces, but Sir Stuart Samuel, who succeeded D. L. Alexander as president of the Board of Deputies remained faithful to elite traditions, values and style of management.[37]

The immediate impact was felt outside Jewry in the British Foreign Office. Wolf had gambled on being able to hold both parent bodies. Leopold de Rothschild's death and Wolf's miscalculation about how effective an opponent Chief Rabbi Hertz might prove led to this temporary setback within Anglo-Jewry. Wolf did not fully retrieve what he had lost at the Foreign Office until the Paris peace conference. 'This vote means the dissolution of the Conjoint Committee,' minuted Ronald Graham, 'and it will no longer be necessary to consult that body.'[38] After the great upheaval at the Board of Deputies, Wolf was written down, in official books, as but one among several who might appropriately be consulted. His value as an informant remained high, for his contacts in many worlds were unique. He never, however, fully regained his almost unchallenged position of 1916.

Some opponents appreciated his skills and did not underestimate his recuperative powers. Beware of Lucien Wolf and those who think with him or are inspired by him, warned Sir Mark Sykes. He is an anti-Zionist who wants to focus Jewish power at some point outside Palestine. He has masqueraded as a quasi-Zionist to forestall the Zionists. Weizmann also had a keen sense of the man and continued to regard Wolf as a powerful and dangerous adversary.[39] Wolf and the Conjoint Committee never abandoned the field. The rearguard action of creating a League of British Jews sponsored by Lionel de Rothschild, Sir Philip Magnus and Lord Swaythling (the older brother of Edwin Montagu) was a moral gesture, not politically viable. Sir Charles Henry, Swaythling and Sir Philip Magnus, however, saw Lloyd George in August 1918. Lloyd George, as usual, made pacifying noises. Henry then asked Beaverbrook to stop pro-Zionist propaganda. This brought Balfour scurrying to the Zionists' rescue. Wolf also displayed uncharacteristically

---

37 *The Times*, 18 June 1917; *Zionist Review* (July 1917), 37; *Jewish Chronicle*, June 1917. Balfour kept himself informed. See FO 800/210/83 ff. Edwin Montagu attempted to minimize the significance of the change although acknowledging the importance of the Board of Deputies in his letter to Lord Robert Cecil, 14 Sept. 1917, CAB 24/27/372.

38 Wolf fought gamely to recover lost ground with Oliphant on 18 June, but his explanation was lame. Wolf, however, bided his time and returned with the reconstructed Joint Foreign Committee. FO 371/3053/121745.

39 Sykes to Prodrome, 27 Apr. 1917, Sykes Papers 41A; Weizmann to Brandeis, 14, 16 Jan. 1918, FO 371/3394/21931/418–31.

bad judgement with his spiteful and ill-conceived efforts to launch Sylvain Lévi on an anti-Zionist rally in the United States in the late summer of 1918.[40]

When negotiations with the Zionists broke down, and once the Zionists and provincials secured a narrow but limited and transient ascendancy in the Board of Deputies of British Jews, the treaty with the Anglo-Jewish Association was terminated, and the Conjoint Foreign Committee was dissolved. The moderates retreated to the secure ground of the Anglo-Jewish Association with its own Foreign Affairs Committee and then reconstructed a conjoint committee in a new treaty with the Board of Deputies of British Jews called the Joint Foreign Committee. That agreement rested on both parties accepting the Balfour Declaration and making no efforts to undo it.[41] What that meant proved open to various interpretations. Wolf minimized Palestinian problems as far as possible in the hopes of securing a united Jewish front on what he regarded as the most significant issues. Privately he did everything in his power to undercut the Declaration or to minimize its implications. The Alliance Israélite shared Wolf's views, and the French government, having made its appeal to Zionism only to see the Zionists opt for the British, had no burning desire to forward the cause in a Palestine which was increasingly unlikely to be part of a French-managed greater Syria.[42] The Zionists were furious, and, as Wolf reported,

> The situation is, however, still very delicate, and the Zionists, although defeated, have not laid down their arms. I shall continue my work as long as I can, but I will not hide from you that the atmosphere of strife in which the work has to be carried on is not very congenial to me.[43]

Wolf was to lead the moderates to triumph at the Paris peace conference. With his French and American colleagues, with his carefully cultivated contacts in the

40 Balfour to Lloyd George, 22 Aug., Lloyd George to Balfour, 27 Aug. 1918, Lloyd George Papers F/3/3/29–30; Wolf to Bigart, 16, 21 Aug., 23, 30 Sept.; Bigart à Wolf 12 août, 27 sept. 1918., AIU Angl III/D/52/6483, 6485, 6518, 6524. Morganthau failed to develop an effective backfire against Zionism with his article, 'The future of Palestine', *New York Times*, 12 Dec. 1917, but his activity gave Weizmann and Brandeis considerable anxiety. See, e.g., FO 371/3394 *passim*. Morganthau's influence with Wilson, however, temporarily swung the President back to the position that an international, inter-religious body should govern Palestine. Jusserand à Pichon, 14 déc. 1917, MAE A/1199/ii/98–100. Lord Reading, who shared Montagu's views about Zionists, made pro-forma comments of political and personal sympathy for Zionism during his American mission but evaded substantial discussion of the issue. Reading Papers, FO 800/224/198–239.

41 Wolf to Bigart, 24 Sept. 1917. Bigart accepted the new arrangement and praised Wolf's struggle against the Zionists. The AIU never accepted the Balfour Declaration and had, as a result, more freedom of manoeuvre during the peace negotiations. Bigart à Wolf, 27 sept. 1917, AIU Angl I/J/8/6129. Wolf used AIU independence when he felt contrained about the draft treaty with Turkey in 1923. 'I do not think that my Committee will or can depart from the position they then took up [the previous year]. This however need not bind you as you have not formally accepted the Balfour Declaration as we have. We shall of course raise no objection to any action you may decide to adopt.' Wolf to Bigart, 27 Mar. 1923, AIU Angl III/D/49/5526.

42 For the emphasis of the next two years see, [L. Wolf], *The Peace Conference. Paris, 1919. Report of the Delegation of the Jews of the British Empire on the Treaties* (London, 1920). Sénateur Etienne Flandrin early defined and defended the French claim in 'Nos Droits en Syrie et Palestine', *Revue Hebdomadaise* (5 juin 1915).

43 Wolf to Bigart, 25 Jan. 1918, AIU Angl III/D/52/6283. For British Government discussions of the precipitous Turkish armistice, see War Cabinet 492A, 29 Oct. 1918, CAB 23/274–86.

British peace conference taskforce, and with the unwavering support of Claude Montefiore and Sir Stuart Samuel, he would win important concessions on Jewish rights.

By mid-June 1918, as the last desperate German offensive in the west had been broken, as Turkey lay crumbling, as the breakout from Salonika actually began (some four years too late), but before the great victories on the Western Front, the British government finally took that formal stand for which Anglo-Jewry had fought so long. To the long list of suppressed nationalities such as Serbs and Czechs, the British now added a set of formal declarations in favour of Jewish civil rights in Eastern Europe.[44]

COMMUNAL SERVICES AND THE DOMESTIC FRONT

International policy spoke to domestic issues as well as foreign affairs. Although the flow of immigrants dropped steadily after 1906, Anglo-Jewry continued to process newcomers, those long landed and the native-born through its educational and social institutions. The balance of numbers within the community swung significantly towards those either born in or long resident in England. The East Enders were people more experienced in living and working together both under and independent of communal tutelage. Whether labouring under the inequities of alien status or merely the relative inequalities of class, British Jews were both more self-sufficient and self-assertive. Anglo-Jewry told them to become self-reliant, and most of them did. As they became so, they also came to share pre-war restiveness. They nipped at the heels of the Board of Deputies, for instance, to act more forcefully on their behalf.

The National Insurance Bill of 1911, the cornerstone of the emerging welfare state, discriminated sharply against non-Britons. Aliens could not be members of 'approved societies' which meant that they could draw benefits based only on their own and their employer's contributions. The government contribution was reserved to British subjects. Aliens, moreover, had to pay their premiums at the Post Office in the same way as a native rejected by friendly societies. The statutory exclusion struck at the benefits of the most responsible part of the Jewish working classes. When the Board of Deputies waffled on the matters, the Jewish friendly societies took their case, unsuccessfully, to the government.[45] David Lloyd George, then Chancellor of the Exchequer, had a budget already overstrained by an arms race and new social commitments, and he had no intention of inviting further opposition criticism by legislating for the benefit of a small, not over-popular minority. Perceived wartime needs together with patient negotiations ultimately secured an amendment in 1917 allowing contributing aliens the same rights under national insurance as British subjects. Sustaining worker efficiency and morale for wartime production by then outweighed other considerations, and the additional expense seemed trifling given the unparalleled costs of war.

44 Wolf, The Jews of Eastern Europe. Statement by His Majesty's Government. [29 June 1918], BDBJ C 11/3/1/3.

45 See, e.g., Law and parliamentary committee, 3 July 1911, BDBJ B 2/10/10.

Anti-defamation work continued unabated, made all the more difficult by the chauvinism of war. The issue of Russian aliens assumed new proportions. As patriotic Britons marched off to serve king and country, Jewish aliens were accused of shirking service and stealthily appropriating servicemen's trade. What began as little more than a mumbling and whispering campaign grew into more overt anti-Semitism. A pamphlet, 'The Conquering Jew – A Vision of 1950', circulated widely in the East End during June 1918. Board of Deputies representatives consulted the Director of Public Prosecutions only to be told that a magistrate could not, in spite of the broad provisions of the Defence of the Realm Act, take summary action, and the case would eventually have to go before a jury. The government prosecutor feared 'that there was a likelihood under present circumstances of a Jury being unsympathetic,' and he declined to take action unless he could be certain of a conviction being obtained. The board, opting for discretion, retreated. The war's end and Western phobia about revolution magnified the problem. Conspiracy theory gained new popularity, and even the Protocols of the Elders of Zion were back.[46] The London Hospital staff was accused of anti-Semitism, of mistreating Jewish patients, and of barring Jews from its shelters during zeppelin air raids. On investigation it turned out that the standard of Jewish applicants for medical training had, like that of other males, declined, and the London Hospital had begun admitting better qualified Gentile women than Jewish men. Testy patients, it also turned out on investigation, had discovered that accusing the staff of anti-Semitism brought them attention they could not otherwise secure. The air-raid shelter problems were simply ones of overcrowding. Patients and staff came before local residents.[47] Such matters, which formerly would either never have occurred or would have been easily and quickly cleared up, dragged on, guaranteeing that still more would follow.

Anglo-Jewry attempted to counter revived anti-alienism by organizing the National Union for Jewish Rights. Lucien Wolf, the champion of and expert at counter-documentation, initiated a project that continued through the war of collecting data about foreign-born Jews and Jewish children of foreign parents serving in the armed forces or engaged in work of national importance. As alien Russian Jewish resistance grew against various proposals for their military recruitment in 1916, Wolf resigned the presidency, which passed to Haham Gaster. The National Union, for which Wolf had held such high hopes as an institution to counter communal Zionist appeal, shifted the work in concert with the Foreign Jews Protection Committee against Deportation and Compulsion. The protection committee became a bastion of East End resistance to Anglo-Jewish leadership during the communal struggles of 1917.[48]

---

46 The board did, however, consider asking for an amendment of DORA that would stop libels on Jews. Law and parliamentary committee, 17, 27 June 1918, BDBJ C 13/1/8. Lucien Wolf wrote *The Jewish Bogey and the Forged Protocols of the Learned Elders of Zion* (London, 1920) for the press committee the Board of Deputies organized to deal with such things. The specific inspiration was a series of articles in the *Morning Post*, 12–30 July 1920.

47 Law and parliamentary committee, 15 May, 27 June 1918. See also 14, 21 Nov. 1917, 19 Jan., 9 Apr. 1918 for some of the others ways in which issues of anti-Semitism were confronted or avoided. BDBJ C 13/1/8.

48 See Abraham Bezalel's form letter from the protection committee, 10 May 1917, Dywien to Gaster, 15 Aug., 21 Sept. 1916, 22 May 1917, Gaster Papers 45/37/2, 36/328/1, 86/329/1, 94/327/2; *JC*, 5 Jan. 1917.

Jewish agencies, in spite of government support, found themselves overstrained. As in British society itself, women assumed more substantial roles as military service devoured ever larger numbers of men. The feminization of Anglo-Jewish institutions, however, proceeded only within well-defined limits. Religious institutions remained run and managed by men. While the Anglo-Jewish Association had admitted women, the Board of Deputies did not, neither did women enter the well-guarded premises of the Conjoint Foreign Committee. Schools, clubs and social service agencies increasingly depended for day-to-day operation on women, returned demobilized veterans, and older men. Recruitment proved as taxing a burden for Anglo-Jewish agencies as it did for the military. Who, asked 'Mentor' in the *Jewish Chronicle* from his communal armchair, will carry on the fight for Judaism? Jewish institutions found themselves paying a heavy price for their history and structure. They were awkward and inflexible, dependent upon the time and resources of the committed few to whom the many deferred. Organized in heirarchical, authoritarian layers, newcomers were expected to serve long apprenticeships. Independence in thought or action was unwelcome. 'The Pooh-Bah cult,' mused the communal sage, 'is not conducive either to general good work or the bringing forward of new men to do what the community needs should be done.'[49]

LOSING CONTROL: THE ISSUE OF MILITARY SERVICE

Tender concern for the legitimate refugee, fury with continued Russian insensitivity, and an awareness that language and culture represented a barrier to the effective use of Russian Jews ran counter to the clear obligations that Anglo-Jewry felt towards the British war effort. The manpower concerns and demands of the Western entente powers lurked behind the issue of military service for foreign Jews Anglo-Jewry confronted rumbling anti-Semitism in the East End arising from avoidance of military service by 'foreign Jews'. Non-Jewish males fought and died, so the argument ran, to give these aliens jobs and business opportunities. For their part, the alien Jews, almost exclusively Russian, regarded recruitment as a thinly disguised scheme to take away their hard-won East End homes, jobs and sanctuary. Supported by Weizmann and the Zionists, the Benenson Committee on Recruiting, sometimes called the Russian Committee, took a strongly civil libertarian stand and thereby defined yet another point of dispute between British and foreign Jews, one in which the moderates could not fail to lose, whatever the outcome in the specific instance.

Herbert Samuel, in his official capacity as Home Secretary and as the leading Jew in the government, hoped to find some viable formula for recruitment.[50] Wolf hoped the question would not be treated as a Jewish question but as one affecting all

49 'Compulsory enlistment. Jewish "slackers" and "shirkers"', *JC*, 7 Jan. 1916.

50 Wolf to Samuel, 1 June; 9 June; Wolf to de Rothschild, 2 June; 9 June 1916. Zangwill thought it particularly brutal to threaten repatriation of Russian Jews to Russia and feared that Jews would be subject to harrassment in the British army. His solution, like Jabotinsky's, was the formation of exclusively Jewish units. Wolf felt that such a proposal appealed to neither Zionists nor anti-Zionists. Zangwill to Wolf, 16 June; Wolf to Zangwill, 19 June; Wolf to B. Zusman, 24 July 1916, BDBJ C 11/2/9.

friendly aliens who, by virtue of their residence in Britain, 'are escaping their military obligations'. But how could service be demanded of Jews, aliens at that, when Britain was still avoiding conscription for her own subjects? The Conjoint Committee recommended that all aliens from allied powers of military age residing in Britain be offered the choice of service in the British or their own country's army. Should they opt for British service, they ought to be eligible to be naturalized as British subjects. That would ease the hostility to compulsion.[51]

The French, as outspoken champions of the right of political asylum, reacted dramatically, seeing this as an issue of civil liberties for refugee Jews. Emile Durkheim led a revolt against any such proposal when Wolf sought to secure Alliance support for a common policy. Durkheim had, moreover, a strong contingent of non-Jews behind him including Georges Leygues, president of the foreign affairs committee of the Chambre and M. Moutet, deputy for Lyons and a leader of the Briand group. Such an approach, they believed, would merely accelerate and deepen the threatening anti-Semitic and nationalist propaganda in France. Not only did they prevent the Alliance supporting the British, but Moutet travelled to England to put the case to Samuel.[52] British officials retreated. They reassured Moutet, then sought some compromise formula. Wolf and the British Jewish elite saw the issue as neither more nor less than 'slacking and malingering' in a way that would generate a wave of British anti-Semitism. Disapproval of Russian persecution was no reason to refuse to serve in the British army.

Negotiations moved backwards and forwards through the summer of 1916. Separate Jewish units appeared as bait, then disappeared. In September, Herbert Samuel and the government finally accepted one month of voluntary recruitment to see if enlistments would answer the need. Wolf and the Benenson committee hammered out the details. Naturalization, including the privilege for any casualty's dependents, would be the incentive.[53] Matters appeared calmer, for the unilateral threat of conscription was not reinvoked. While order and propriety might appear to

51 Wolf to de Rothschild, 2 June 1916, BDBJ C 11/2/9.

52 Wolf to de Rothschild, 18 July; Wolf to Samuel, 18 July; Montgomery to Wolf, 19 July; Wolf to Moutet, 19 juil.; Wolf à E. Durkheim, 19 juil.; Wolf to J. Schapiro, 19 juil. 1916; Moutet saw Samuel and Lord Newton (Under-Secretary of State for Foreign Affairs) and was much reassured. Wolf responded tartly to Durkheim, 'La question est, néanmoins, d'une certaine gravité, car on a découvert par des recherches officielles, qu'il y a 25,000 Russes d'âge militaire en Angleterre qui ne font rien pour le défense du pays.' Wolf to Durkheim, 31 juil. 1916, BDBJ C 11/2/9. Bigart tried to pacify Wolf, explaining that Durkheim's principal concern was to prevent an emotional outcry among Jews in neutral countries. Wolf to Bigart 6, 18 July 1916, AIU Angl I/J/8/5658; Bigart à Wolf, 7 juil. 1916, AIU Angl I/G/4. The French government resisted any recruiting for Jewish units identified as such, even for the Zion Mule Transport Corps that served in Gallipoli. Foreign Jews could only serve in the Foreign Legion. Wolf to Zangwill, 8 Aug. 1915, BDBJ C 11/2/7.

53 Wolf was delighted to be quit of his role as middleman between Benenson's Russian Committee and the Home Office. The 'aliens' wanted 'unconditional exemption', and the War Office would have preferred 'to draft them all into labour battalions'. Wolf to de Rothschild, 15 Aug., 23 Aug.; Samuel to Wolf, 17 Aug.; Wolf to Sebag-Montefiore, 5 Sept., 8 Sept.; Wolf to Alexander, 6 Sept. 1916. 'So far our friends in the East End have not made any proposals whatever to serve this country in the present emergency, but seem to have had no other idea than to avoid, by hook or by crook, any sort of military service whatever. This has made a deplorable impression upon everybody.' Wolf to Dywien, 12 Sept. 1916, BDBJ C 11/2/9. For two official views on a Jewish Corps, see GT-353, 24 Jan. 1917, CAB 24/9 and GT-447, 14 Apr. 1917, CAB 24/10. Gaster strongly opposed segregating Jews in the British army. Gaster to Daiches, 10 Sept. 1917. Gaster Papers 61.

have been restored in Jewish ranks, Wolf realized that the Jewish nationalist movement had gained much momentum from the controversy.[54]

Anglo-French Jewry shared the priorities of their national leaders. On the new Russian government's decree of emancipation in 1917, the Conjoint Foreign Committee, the Alliance Israélite and the Italian Committee appealed to the Russo-Jewish community to cooperate in a campaign 'to secure the liberation of other Jewish communities which are still languishing under political and religious diabilities'. Beyond this point, on which there was no disagreement, the Western Jewish leadership demanded that Russian Jews demonstrate their gratitude

> by rallying in their full strength to the appeal for men which has been addressed to them by our Government. It is only by victory in the field that the Russian Revolution can be finally consolidated, the liberties of the Western World founded on a sure and permanent basis. No Russian Jew, wherever he may be, can hold aloof from the fight for this victory without proclaiming himself unworthy of the rights which have now been so gallantly won for him.[55]

Opinion divided sharply on this point. Assimilationist leadership contended that Jewish grievances were now settled within the entente, that past persecution was only something in the past, that the consolidation of victory demanded sacrifice and commitment. Refugee Jews saw matters differently and failed to appreciate the price of liberation. Why should they fight for their recent tormenters? Official grand pronouncements, in fact, belied substantial and profound differences of opinion, divisions that aggravated the Zionist and anti-Zionist rift and more clearly defined that struggle as one between the old Anglo-Jewish leadership and an increasingly substantial part of its constituency. To some extent, the problem was one of class and a significant measure of elite insensitivity. A hearty handshake from Colonel de Rothschild no longer sufficed to recruit cannon-fodder. But the struggle for control in the Jewish community and the implications of Zionism as an ideology rendered the debate heated and shrill. Weizmann was charged with encouraging East End Jews not to serve in the British forces when Weizmann had actually said 'that he had no influence or power to force them to do so, and that the English government must conscript them'.[56]

The dramatic turn of events with the Emancipation Decree and the February revolution offered promise and problems. The need for Russian Jewish refugee status appeared to have evaporated. Russian Jews would now cooperate in the war effort either by serving Mother Russia or enthusiastically enrolling in British or French forces. The Bolshevik revolution and peace offensive, however, destroyed whatever illusions might remain. Bolshevik representatives worked actively to block the recruitment of Russian Jews into the British or French forces, and Jews repatriated from the West to Russia proved vociferous and effective critics of the

---

54 Wolf to Montefiore, 4 Aug. 1916, BDBJ C 11/2/9.

55 Statement by BDBJ president, D. L. Alexander. BDBJ meeting, 22 Apr. 1917. Interleaf in BDBJ Minute Book, 57–8. The 27 to 18 vote on a subsequent motion implicitly dividing the issues of Jewish emancipation and Russian Jewish military service better reflects sensitivities on this issue.

56 Rothschild, who reported this incident in detail, believed it to be a thinly disguised effort to block the Declaration. Rothschild to Balfour, 20 June 1917. FO 800/210/87–9.

West.[57] Rightly or wrongly, Jews came to be increasingly identified in Western official eyes as much involved, not in the liberal revolution, but in the Bolshevik and anti-Western cause. Anglo-Jewry twisted and turned as reports flowed in from their own sources documenting a highly visible Jewish presence among the extreme socialists. While the great majority of Jews were Mensheviks and moderate Social Democrats, English and French Jewish leaders feared (and their own information often confirmed) what was for them an unpleasant set of facts.[58] Fears about East European Jewish radicalism reinforced ingrained elite prejudices about immigrants, nourishing their own sense of self-righteousness and superiority. The Anglo-French leadership devoted much effort and considerable anxiety to public statements that East European Jews were not radical. Contrary information flowed from Wolf to the Foreign Office. Wolf developed 'cordial relations' with Lloyd George's information bureau. English newspapers gave stories of Jewish moderation in the Russian revolution 'a wide and salutary publicity'. At the same time, the Anglo-French Jewish elite shared all class prejudices about what was happening in Russia and privately worried endlessly about property rights and expropriation.[59]

PEACEMAKING: PALESTINE, JEWS, AND VERSAILLES

Peacemaking, as should have been expected, proved almost as difficult as levying war. Edwin Montagu, shaken by an Imperial War Cabinet meeting at which his colleagues staked out preposterous aspirations, appealed to Arthur Balfour.

57 The issue came under extensive discussion in the war cabinet meeting of 21 January 1918 at which Sir George Buchanan, who ran the British Russian mission, and Balfour spoke candidly. Balfour, for instance, referred to Radek as 'an International Jew of the same type as Trotzki', sliding, with unpleasant ease, into the vocabulary of anti-Semitism. CAB 23/5/327.

58 Ruben Blank reported that six of the twelve deputies to the Petrograd constituent assembly were Jews, four of whom were Bolsheviks. The more moderate Jewish elements attempted to take every precaution, even to founding a daily paper (shortly to be suppressed in the Bolshevik revolution). Blank to the Foreign Affairs Committee of the AJA (FAC), 4 Dec. 1917; AJA Stockholm agent to FAC, 2 Jan. 1918; FAC Conf, 31 Jan 1918, AJ/204/4.

59 Reports abound on this point throughout the summer of 1917. See, e.g., CAB 1/25/127. Field intelligence, on the other hand, generally ran the other way. See, e.g., report of Major J. F. Neilson, 31 Mar. 1917, GT-525, CAB 24/11/109–12. The Foreign Office intelligence bureau consistently reported that the majority of Jews supported the more moderate parties. See, e.g., GT-1426, 16 July 1917, CAB 24/20/168–71; GT-2174, 1 Oct. 1917, CAB 24/27/311–13; GT-2442, 29 Oct.1917, CAB 24/30/270–4; GT-2841, 1 Nov. 1917; CAB 24/34/206–9. Virulent attacks also circulated. James Colquhoun, chairman of the Caucasus Copper Company, complained that Germans and Jews had totally corrupted southern Russian life in as letter that found its way to the British cabinet via the Chief of Naval Operations. 21 Aug. 1918, GT-5466, CAB 24/61/210–18. Such anxieties persisted in informed circles. See, e.g., D'Abernon to Curzon, 16 Aug 1920, D'Abernon Papers, Add MS 48,923, ff. 132–4 or the interdepartmental meeting of 18 Nov. 1919 with its reference to 'ruthless Jews, who are making use of the Bolshevik movement'. Curzon Papers, MSS Eur F 112/175/101 or the Kerr–Kerensky interview, 24 June 1918, GT-4948, CAB 24/59/163–74. Among other private expressions of Anglo-French Jewish anxiety about Bolshevism, see Bigart à Wolf, 23 sept. 1917. The issue grew more acute in 1919. See, *Le Temps*, 21 déc. 1919 and the refutation in *Archives Israélites*, 25 déc. 1919. Wolf furnished the documentation needed to calm Lord Robert Cecil and Clemenceau on the question of Jewish politics and Russian Bolshevism. 6, 12 Nov 1917. AIU Angl I/J/8/6200, 6221. See also, FAC Conf, 12 Sept., 3 Oct., 11 Dec. 1917, 31 Jan. 1918, AJ/204/4/52 ff.

So we go on. It is fatal to let the French here. It is appalling to think even of ourselves as mandatories there. The idea of an American Fleet in the Mediterranean is unspeakably horrible. And we are going into these negotiations with our mouths full of fine phrases and our brains seething with dark thoughts.[60]

A whimsical critic once asked a mid-Victorian painter who had just completed an elaborate mural about the Arthurian legend, 'And pray, sir, what were they going to do with the Holy Grail once they found it?' Such a question occurred to the British cabinet a number of times as the war ended. Ironically, once the British confronted actual options and costs, they considered leaving Palestine, Armenia and Constantinople in American hands. That would limit French and Italian claims in the Middle East or or at least remove a considerable source of tension between the old allies. Americans would be a friendly buffer should British relations with France or Russia become troublesome. American mandates could thus achieve British strategic goals while enabling the British to limit their costs and commitments. The United States, moreover, was perceived to have precisely that delicate balance of Christian missionary and Jewish interests and pressure groups to operate the Palestine mandate evenhandedly in spite of its inexperience in international politics.

But the question always remained about American inexperience and ineptitude. Woodrow Wilson was much given to lurching unilaterally in almost any direction in pursuit of some momentary enthusiasm, and Wilson had enormous European standing and prestige at the end of the war. He revelled in the role he could now play of the great crusader. Narrow national interests had produced generations of war. Now all that could change. Wilson, in this instance, chose to be disingenuous. Although Balfour had personally told him about and shown him the various secret Middle-Eastern agreements early in 1917, Wilson chose to forget that fact once the Bolsheviks published those documents. In one of his more manic moments in October 1918, Wilson decided that narrow nationalism must end. Specifically translated, this meant that Britain should gain nothing from the war. Then, when he met Weizmann in January 1919, the French, not the British, became the great threat. When presented with the opportunity to assume mandatory responsibility themselves, however, the Americans quickly retreated from any major Middle-Eastern commitments.[61]

---

60 Montagu to Balfour, 20 Dec. 1918, Balfour Papers, Add MS 49,748, ff. 304–5. See also, Cecil to Loyd George, Dec. 1918, Lloyd George Papers F/6/5/54; Curzon, German Colonies and Turkish Possessions, GT-6015, 16 Oct. 1918, CAB 24/67/48–51.

61 Henderson to Northcliffe, 14 Nov. 1918, Lloyd George Papers F/41/8/22; FO 608/98/44634/142–4; Weizmann to Brandeis, 14 Jan. 1918, FO 371/3394/21931/418–27; *The Times*, 18 Jan. 1919. Montagu doubted that the Americans had sufficient experience to manage a Moslem country like Palestine. 18 Oct. 1918, CAB 1/27/80–1. Amery was terrified lest the British actually put the Americans in Palestine. Amery to Curzon, 19 Oct. 1918, Curzon Papers, Eur F 112/267. The American State Department wanted to know the terms of the St Jean de Maurienne agreement between France, Italy and Britain. Since neither Britain nor France proposed to honour that agreement, neither had any desire to be further embarrassed by revealing its contents. Wiseman to Reading and Northcliffe, 10 Nov. 1918, Balfour Papers, Add MS 49,741, ff. 230–1; Wilson, although he feigned ignorance, had been informed about the Sykes–Picot agreements when Balfour went to the United States in 1917. Add MS 49,687, ff. 244–8; Henderson to Northcliffe, 14 Oct. 1918, Lloyd George Papers F/41/8/22; Balfour to Lloyd George, 26 June 1919, FO 800/217/96–9; Drummond to Wiseman, 8 Feb. 1918, Reading Papers, FO 800/222/574; CAB 1/28 ii/81; FO

On the diplomatic front, the peacemakers seemed to confront an almost perfect inverse relationship between effective wartime contributions and post-war expectations. The Italians, who had proved unable to defend their own frontiers against significantly inferior forces, displayed an insatiable appetite for reward, a demand for symbolic and political equality with the Big Three, and a determination to assume responsibilities they were totally unable to meet.[62] The British and French complicated matters further, quarrelling when they needed maximum accord. Clemenceau and Lloyd George engaged in a six-month artillery duel over the Middle East. Lloyd George fired the first round. Against all advice, he accused the French to their face of sending 'a few niggers to prevent us from stealing the Holy Sepulchre'.[63] Since the British were trying, in every possible way, to rewrite their diplomatic incompetence in the Sykes–Picot agreement at the expense of the French, Clemenceau, not surprisingly, turned the matter into a diplomatic Verdun. The firing eventually ceased, at least on the more obvious aspects of this issue, by

---

800/216/224–5, 232–45 (on Italy); Balfour to Curzon, 16 Dec. 1918; Curzon Papers, MSS Eur F 112/274/64 (on the reality of costs); cabinet meeting, 3 Oct. 1918, CAB 23/14/482A (on the balance of interests in America); Wise to Balfour, 30 Dec 1918, FO 800/210/421–8. The British Labour party and Trades Union Congress enthusiastically endorsed the idea of American rather than British mandates. Labour was still in its innocent, anti-imperialist phase. G. N. Barnes, Notes on the War, 30 Dec. 1917, CAB 1/25/226–30; A. Henderson's dissent from Curzon, 1 May 1917, CAB 21/78/6–9; and the Labour party and Trades Union Congress war aims, GT-3167, 28 Dec. 1917, CAB 24/37/194–6. In a moment of even less lucidity than usual, the British weighed using the Italians as a counterweight to squeeze the French out of Palestine. Hardinge to Curzon, 23 Apr. [1917], Curzon Papers, Eur MS F 112/118A/120–1. See also, Montagu to Balfour, 20, 26 Feb.; Balfour to Montagu, 25 Feb., Balfour Papers, Add MS 49,471, ff.184–8; Curzon to Cecil, 1, 5, 15 Aug. 1918, Cecil Papers, Add MS 51,007, ff. 10–23. See also Montagu to Balfour, 21 June 1919, FO 800/217/69–71; Montagu to Curzon, 28 Aug. 1919, Curzon Papers, MSS Eur F 112/213B/160–6; Amery to Balfour, 21 Dec. 1918, FO 800.209/625–6; and Montagu Papers AS-IV-3(689–93); AS-1V-6(802, 811–12, 822, 855, 869, 873–5, 888).

Just as Britons began to rethink their conflicting Palestine engagements, they also realized that they had not properly considered the issue of which Arabs should be supported where, let alone what the British really should be attempting to accomplish in the Middle East. This issue lies outside the scope of the present study, but the files of the Eastern Committee of the War Cabinet are the best place to see it evolve. Curzon's own copies and notes are in Curzon Papers. MSS Eur F 112/274. Having been unable to decide about Middle Eastern settlements while the Turks recovered strength and confidence and having to some degree alienated both Zionist and Arab constituencies, the British also confronted the real issue of peace costs. The fantasy of an independent Armenia had vanished. The sons of Hussein grumbled or were in revolt. Zionists realized that the British had no intention of exerting their power to create a Jewish state. Lloyd George, ultimately to his own political destruction, preferred incompetent Greeks to increasingly strong and confident Turks. The United States had withdrawn into isolation and a sense of moral superiority. Winston Churchill, with his unfailing genius to have the wrong answer for the right question, suggested that the Americans be offered either or both the Palestine and Mesopotamia mandates. Cabinet 342, 24 Dec. 1919, CAB 24/95/190; Lloyd George to Churchill, 11 June 1921. Lloyd George Papers F/9/3/54.

62 Curzon to Bonar Law, 30 Nov. 1918, Bonar Law Papers 84/3/25 in the House of Lords Record Office; Wiseman to Drummond, 23 Jan. 1918., Balfour Papers, Add MS 49,471, ff. 2–6.

63 Hankey to Curzon, 5 Nov. 1918. Such rhetoric did, apparently, help to bring Mosul into the British zone. The French representative in Egypt raised the issue of problems in squaring the Balfour Declaration and Sykes–Picot agreement much more intelligently than either Government. MAE A/1199/171–5, 196–7. Pichon had also, in December 1917, stated that France was interested in assuming control of Palestine. War Cabinet, 31 Dec. 1917, CAB 23/4/308/8. For French thoughts on the urgency of clarifying the 1916 agreements, see, e.g., Picot à Pichon, 6 déc. 1917; Cambon à Gout, 15 jan.; de Margerie à Cambon, 17 jan. 1918, MAE A/1199/ii/79; A/1200/80, 84.

mid-September 1919 with the most distressing problems papered over or resolved.[64]

The Joint Foreign Committee, as part of its constitution, was drawn further into the Palestine question than its more recalcitrant anti-Zionists would have wished. The committee accepted the Declaration, specifically reserving the point 'that nothing in that letter shall be held to imply that Jews constitute a separate political nationality all over the world or that Jewish citizens of countries outside Palestine owe political allegiance to the Government of that country.' Beyond this, the Joint Committee recommended that the mandate be vested in Britain, that the boundaries of Palestine be capacious enough 'to afford room and favourable conditions for a large settlement of Jews, care being taken to safeguard the vested interests and rights of the existing non-Jewish population'. While demanding 'complete religious equality' and 'the fullest equality of political and economic rights for the members of all races and religious communities', the committee cautiously accepted Zionist arguments for extended boundaries and: 'That the political, economic and moral organisation of the country be such as to facilitate the increase and self-government of the Jewish population with a view to its eventual predominance in the government of the State, in accordance with the principles of democracy.'[65] Wolf hoped to see Balfour in Paris, particularly now that he could argue that the Zionists and Joint Foreign Committee were acting in unison. But Balfour acted as he had done with the Zionists, declining to be identified with the Anglo-French Jewish coalition, asking only to be informed of their proposals. Only the peace conference itself could act on their requests.[66]

Zionist and Alliance delegations were in place in Paris from the beginning of the peace conference. The Joint Foreign Committee, while selecting its representatives, dispatched Lucien Wolf to coordinate the work of the various Jewish delegations in advance. He arranged for a central bureau, the offices of which would be in the Alliance Israélite headquarters.[67] The design of the bureau, carefully coordinated by Wolf and Bigart, met the approval of all of the leading members of the Franco-Jewish community including Baron Edmond de Rothschild. United action about preliminary arrangements brought some important benefits. The Foreign Ministry and Quai d'Orsay responded, for instance, to central bureau pressure to

64 M. P. A. Hankey, Summary of the Proceedings in Paris, September 1919, CAB 1/29/21–3, 33–4; Lloyd George to Clemenceau, 18 Oct.; Clemenceau to Lloyd George, 9 Nov. 1919, FO 406/41/169; Curzon to Derby, 22 Oct. 1919, FO 406/41/129. Pichon compiled a list of twenty-five basic grievances for Lord Milner, 'Relevé de Quelques-unes des Menées dirigées contre l'Influence française et contre les Accords Franco-Britanniques sur l'Asie-Mineure,' 12 mar. 1919, FO 406/41/22 and Curzon's response to Cambon, 19 Mar. 1919, FO 406/41/25.

65 JFC, Statement of Policy of the Palestine Question, 4 Feb. 1919 in *The Peace Conference. Paris, 1919* (London, 1920), 112–13.

66 Wolf to Drummond, 10 Feb., Drummond to Wolf, 12 Feb. 1919, FO 800/215/179, 190.

67 Wolf encountered much delay in securing his visa for no particularly clear reason. Wolf to Bigart, 11, 15, 28 Nov., 23 Dec. 1918, 6, 29 Jan. 1919, AIU Angl III/D/52/6182, 6193, 6576, 6643, 6648, 6666, 6716. He then found himself waiting five hours at the Préfecture de Police to get his identity card. Wolf, PCD, 3 Apr. 1919.

oversee the production of a Polish Jewish delegation, badly needed where the national delegation had shown itself unswervingly anti-Semitic.[68]

Eugène Sée, Sylvain Lévi, and Dr Netter joined Salomon and Joseph Reinach in a distinguished, veteran Alliance delegation to the Paris peace conference. Anglo-Jewry also selected its leading active luminaries. Sir Stuart Samuel and Claude G. Montefiore, as presidents of the Board of Deputies and Anglo-Jewish Association respectively, led the Anglo-Jewish group. They were to be joined by Lord Rothschild and Lord Swaythling, the leading titled representatives of Zionist and anti-Zionist opinion. Rothschild and Swaythling had obligations in London, so Henriques and Prag, seasoned veterans of the old elite and both cool towards Zionism, served in their places. Anglo-Jewish delegate selection had been tortuous and bitter, for the wounds of 1917 had never fully healed. Rothschild and Montefiore, for instance, had no sooner come to a tentative agreement than Montefiore publicly denounced Zionism once more. Rothschild, furious about what he regarded as a betrayal, then captiously demanded that Balfour refuse to hear Montefiore on any Jewish issues at the Paris peace conference.[69] Calmer heads prevailed. Lucien Wolf was selected to act as secretary, the Zionists deriving slight consolation from the proviso that, to serve, Wolf must give up his places in the Board of Deputies and the executive committee of the Anglo-Jewish Association.

Wolf preceded the Anglo-Jewish delegation. Zionists and their sympathizers contined to regard Wolf as a danger and viewed his appointment as an affront. He exerted his considerable charm and great tact to minimize such difficulties without ever surrendering what he considered to be the most crucial principles.[70] Since Wolf could work with singlemindedness of purpose and the Zionists suffered internal division and personal conflict, he manoeuvred very successfully through the political labyrinth. A man of moderation, he turned underlying Alliance anglophobia, which bubbled to the service on the issue of Palestine and Zionist-Jewish nationalist extremism, to his own advantage. Once in Paris, Wolf established close ties with the key figures among the British peace conference taskforce. Through those contacts and friendships he was to render yeoman service in the Minority Clauses of treaties establishing the Succession States of Eastern Europe. Simultaneously, he worked hand in hand with the Alliance to influence the Quai d'Orsay, using Sylvain Lévi as his principal contact at the Foreign Ministry.

While the great names of Anglo-Jewry mattered for public relations, most of the work would be done at the central secretariat. One of the least well-kept secrets of diplomatic history is that preliminaries and quiet, behind-the-scenes negotiations between those involved in doing the work are crucial to the outcome. Wolf's sense

---

68 Report of the Joint Foreign Committee, Meetings of 28 January and 4 February 1919. interleaf in BDBJ Minute Book, pp. 128–9. The Zionists feared the central bureau would give Wolf too strong a position and wavered between obstructing it and taking advantage of its services. Wolf, PCD, 10 Feb. 1919. Sokolow and Weizmann produced a Polish Jewish delegation elected in a series of Zionist-Jewish nationalist coups. When a conservative, religiously Orthodox delegation elected by over 600 communities finally appeared in Paris, the Zionists first tried to intimidate, then to denounce it.

69 Rothschild to Balfour, 15 Dec., 19 Dec.; Balfour to Rothschild, 16 Dec. 1918, Balfour Papers, FO 800/210/93–100.

70 See, e.g, Wolf's meeting with the Zionists and Jewish nationalists on 16 February. Wolf, Peace Conference Diary (PCD), 16 Feb. 1919.

of timing and priorities, his understanding of what mattered and what did not, allowed him to have most matters in train or in hand even before the lords of Anglo-Jewry arrived in Paris. The Joint Foreign Committee, the Alliance Israélite and the Zionist organization reached agreement on the arrangements for a Central Bureau in January 1919. The Zionists, confident that their aspirations were about to be realized, looked on the bureau as more of a convenience than a threat. Franco-Jewish and Alliance resistance was subtle and muted, the Alliance, in particular, always seeking to avoid controversy and sensitive to the pressure of and upon its own schools and institutions in the Middle East. More ambitious plans to have all Jewry speak with one voice foundered on the issue of Jewish national rights. Eastern European delegations, carefully hand-selected by Weizmann and Sokolow, refused to accept the traditional Anglo-French programme of equal rights for the Jews of Eastern Europe; they demanded recognition as a separate nationality in their respective countries.

The Joint Foreign Committee and Alliance, knowing the strongly Zionist commitments of the American delegation, attempted to find some formula to rein in while still accommodating runaway Jewish nationalism. The Zionists, confident that victory was at hand, demanded still more Palestinian concessions, even floating the idea of a Jewish Commonwealth. With that singlemindedness that had carried them so far, they shunted aside issues of East European civil rights as secondary or irrelevant. Zionists also displayed an unusual lack of political sense, bullying any critics and tactlessly frittering away their considerable advantages. Sokolow told the Alliance that 'the Jewish masses were now in the saddle, that the old "charitable" traditions of the Alliance and similar bodies were no longer applicable', sentiments ill-calculated to promote cooperation and develop some sense of common purpose. Abraham Ussishkin, the 'King' of Odessa and Zionist-denominated spokesman for the Jews of the Ukraine, told anyone who cared to listen that the Zionists were masters of the situation. They had no need to consult other organizations. If the Alliance or Joint Committee wished to transact any Jewish business, they must do so through the Zionist Central Committee. Wolf and Bigart agreed that Anglo-French Jewry would not 'be paralyzed by a conspiracy of Zionist Organisations masquerading as Foreign Jewish Delegations'. The greatest immediate danger, Wolf understood, was that inexperienced, naive and enthusiastic Americans might be drawn into the Zionist and Jewish nationalist camp. Wolf sincerely attempted to narrow the grounds for disagreement, to move beyond questions of personality and behaviour to reach an accommodation. After toying with the idea of using Baron Edmond de Rothschild, Wolf cleverly settled on placing the matter of agreement squarely in the hands of Marshall and the American delegation.

Sylvain Lévi inflicted the first serious blow to the Zionists when he, as French 'Zionist' representative, undercut their presentation before the peace conference on 27 February 1919. Weizmann denounced Lévi, 'Je ne vous connais plus. Vous êtes un traître.'[71] Sokolow and Weizmann realized that they must somehow retrieve political momentum. All that remained for them were European Jewish affairs

---

71 '[Sylvain Lévi] strongly supported the essential idea of a National Home, but he doubted the wisdom and practicality of much of the Zionists' Proposals. He insisted that the scope of the Zionist scheme was out of proportion to the limited resources of Palestine, and he suggested narrower limitations and the slower and

which had passed, through their overconfidence and default, to Wolf. They ran up the extreme Jewish nationalist banner and sought to rally their forces. Wolf, on the other hand, ran Anglo-Jewish foreign policy himself. He struck out in no new directions but pressed forward on a programme Anglo-Jewry had repeatedly endorsed. He carefully secured conjoint endorsement from London on any specific issue as soon as he had settled it. When confronted with an unpalatable alternative, he often avoided direct confrontation, invariably pleading the need to consult his masters. Wolf also dominated Franco-Jewish diplomacy. Anglo-French Jewry had filed their Memorials (almost invariably Wolf's texts with occasional Bigart emendations) and made themselves consultants, however unofficial, in the various treaty negotiations. As the moderates moved forward, Palestine, to Zionist fury, had been shelved until a peace conference committee could investigate and report. Frustration contributed to a flurry of Zionist attacks. They demanded that the Alliance and the Joint Foreign Committee withdraw their Memorials. They attempted to make themselves the only authorized channel for transacting Jewish business. Sokolow and his colleagues thoughtlessly attacked and belittled Wolf and the Alliance to their own subsequent embarrassment. Wolf had coped with detractors all his life. He always carefully documented his case and maintained written records. Sokolow behaved in ways that tended to lose him the respect of friend and foe, repeatedly shifted position, misrepresented, and even lied about matters easily checked. American Jews and peace conference officials, before whom this drama was staged, were quickly disabused. Zionist excesses became one of Wolf's strongest weapons and best arguments.

Zionists had carelessly given Wolf his opening when they refused to be drawn into elaborate negotiations for East European Jewish rights. Such matters were irrelevant, distracting, and could prove destructive of Zionism in the unlikely event that they worked. By the time Zionists realized what had happened, the issue had moved beyond their control. The Alliance and Joint Foreign Committee had not fought so long and hard to compromise their *raison d'être*. Their Memorials to the peace conference demanded 'autonomous rights in regard to [Jewish] communal institutions and social life for all Religious and Cultural Minorities'.[72] The Zionists initially attempted to prevent anything from happening. They then split from their Western colleagues to join their own East European national Jewish deputations in a separate committee. Weizmann, with that sublime confidence that had carried

---

more prudent action. He denounced the scheme of dual nationality and the underlying ideas of Zionist Pan-Jewish nationality generally. He opposed privileges and preferences for Jews and even asked that in the matter of immigration they should enjoy no favours which were not equally extended to others.' Since Lévi also insisted that France should play its 'historic role' in Palestine, he elicited Pichon's warm congratulations. Balfour fell asleep when the session began. Secretary of State Lansing twittered. Only Baron Sonnino of Italy showed himself enthusiastic. Wolf, PCD, 28 Feb.–1 Mar. 1919.

72 Delegation of the Jews of the British Empire to the President and Members of the Peace Conference, 21 Feb 1919, BDBJ C 11/3/2/2. Wolf orchestrated arrangements, as best he could. See his memorandum, 'The Peace Conference', 2 Jan. 1919, BDBJ C 11/3/2/4. Sereni, president of the Comitato delle Communite Israelitiche Italiane, approved. 23 Dec. 1918, BDBJ C 11/3/2/4. When matters became tense but Wolf wanted to keep Anglo-Jewry's hands clean, he would invoke the AIU to take a hard line. See, e.g., Wolf, PCD, 18 Jan., 13 Apr. 1919.

him so far, simultaneously launched a frontal assault on the entente governments. He sought to wring Zionist backing from a victorious but nervous coalition by playing the Bolshevik card, a thinly veiled threat that Jews might, without Zionism, become potential world-revolutionary shock troops. Zionism was, he argued, the West's best antidote to Bolshevism. Sykes believed all this.

> There is no doubt that the storm centres in this and other countries of the subversive and anti-institutional forces exist in the Ghettos and Jewish pauper or submerged colonies. The one thing which makes these centres quiescent and which devitalises the subversive and anti-institutional motor force is Zionism, as the Jewish intellect becomes centred in an ideal which has connection with existing institutions.[73]

Such an argument could be counterproductive. Weizmann's 'Bolshevist bogey' helped to convince Baron Edmond de Rothschild that putting Zionists in charge in Palestine would be 'handing over control of the National Home to European Bolsheviks'. Weizmann also coupled Bolshevism and Western paranoia about immigration. He told Oscar Straus that 'a failure of Zionism would mean a great immigration of Russian-Jewish Bolshevists in America,' to which Straus tartly replied, 'Well she shall hang them.'[74]

Louis Marshall of the American Jewish Committee, whose intrusive vanity ultimately alienated allies and enemies alike, sought to find some compromise. The Eastern and Western delegations assembled for two long night sessions on 5 and 6 April. Sokolow, as head of the Zionist Organization, Rabbi Osios Thom of Cracow (who had just been elected a member of the Polish Diet), and Abraham Ussishkin argued for the extended Jewish national programme, contending that only the privileges of separate nationality would prove 'an effective protection against Anti-Semitism'. Institutional separatism, they added, was but the first step in a vast Jewish nationalist programme, the ultimate object of which would be to federate all Jewish communities in one Jewish nation, with a 'claim to be admitted to the League of Nations on an equal footing with all other nations'.

The issue was immediately joined. Eugène Sée for the Alliance Israélite, Sir Stuart Samuel, Claude Montefiore and Joseph Prag for the British spoke at length on 'the unwisdom of a separatist policy and pointed to the experience of Western Europe and America as convincing justification of the policy of Equal Rights'. Not only was the nationalist position unwise; the East European states would never accept nor would the great powers force them to swallow such an indigestible lump.

---

73 Sykes to Balfour, 27 Feb. 1918, FO 800/210/129. Balfour also believed Jews were 'to a large degree, leaders in such [revolutionary] movements.' He passed on the preposterous rumour, very popular in upper-class British circles, that Lenin 'on his mother's side was a Jew'. Brandeis, to whom he was talking, told him that was nonsense, that Lenin 'on both sides is an upper class Russian.' Paris, 24 June 1919, FO 800/217/187. '[Weizmann] tried to frighten Wilson with Bolshevism,' explained Hogarth to Clayton, 'but I gather without much success; and he will try it on A. J. B[alfour] tomorrow. I am personally backing him wholeheartedly so long as he is moderate, but I fear things have gone too far in Palestine for us to take over, with that Jew Council in Evidence, without trouble. Still – there stands H.M.G.'s Declaration about the National Home! It must mean something, and this is about the least it could mean!' 30 Mar. 1919, Hogarth Papers 14(iv).

74 Wolf, PCD, 20 Jan., 25 Mar. 1919.

The religious and cultural minority clause of the Alliance and Joint Foreign Committee would best serve Jews everywhere.

The Americans assumed a Wilsonian posture. With Judge Mack in the lead, they supported the nationalists 'on the ground that they were the best judges of their own interests'. If they could not agree with the nationalists. Mack continued, 'our duty was to leave them alone, even though we knew that they were mad and headed for self-destruction.' Sokolow, who had opened the two sessions by making vaguely accommodating noises, closed them by shifting from English to Yiddish and restating the uncompromising Jewish nationalist position. Louis Marshall begged for a small committee to frame a compromise which would allow the Jews of the various East European countries 'the right of being treated as a National Minority should they so desire it'. The British, not anxious to refight their own wars of 1917, wriggled but accepted the formula provided no Jews 'should be compelled to become members of National Minorities'. Such an opting-out proviso would never pass Jewish nationalist muster but was designed to appear accommodating in American eyes. Wolf and his friends then carefully and disingenuously demanded only that the ultimate compromise should be acceptable to all parties. Wolf, Montefiore and the anti-Zionists knew the Alliance Israélite would have none of it. A special Alliance meeting considered the issue on 16 April 1919. Arguing powerfully that such a formulation would destroy everything for which French Jewry had worked since the French revolution, they rejected any compromise.

The British, or at least Lucien Wolf, heaved a sigh of relief. Attempting to integrate Zionists and assimilationists would not work. The Joint Foreign Committee and Alliance could now press their demand for religious and cultural minority rights without nationalist opposition and avoid public criticism of the Eastern delegations and Zionists in their application for national rights.[75] Wolf had executed a masterful coup. While working privately and assiduously for the treaty terms and arrangements he preferred, he stood publicly beyond Zionist criticism. He and his friends kept to the letter of his bargain. The peace conference would do their work for them and reject Jewish nationalist demands, which it did.

The Anglo-French moderates could now address the problem with which they had wrestled for half a century. The Congress of Berlin formula, in spite of Roumanian abuse, had worked reasonably well in the emerging Danubian and Balkan principalities. But that formula

> treated the question as exclusively one of difference of religious creed between the nationals of a given state but omitted to give any definition of nationality. The result was that it afforded the Anti-Semites an opportunity of differentiating between Jews and Christians by arbitrarily excluding Jews from the local nationality and relegating them to an abnormal class of stateless

---

75 Wolf, Comité des Délégations, Report on the Visit of the Delegation to Paris, [April 1919], BDBJ C 11/3/1/4; Wolf, PCD, 24 Mar.–16 Apr. 1919. The Joint Foreign Committee, including Lord Rothschild, approved and further instructed Wolf and the Paris delegation 'that they are not to agree to, or support the demands for Jewish national Rights.' 1 May 1919, BDBJ C 11/3/1/4. The Joint Foreign Committee also supported the BDBJ position that 'Great Britain's intention to accept the mandate for Palestine will not be abandoned', since, as Montefiore added, 'any other arrangement would greatly hinder the Immigration into that Country of those Jews who desire a new National Home.' BDBJ C 11/3/1/5. For the AIU debate, see Wolf, PCD, 16 Apr. 1919.

aliens. Thus their situation was rendered even worse than it was before for they became veritable outcasts without protection either in national or international law.[76]

Moderation and cautious diplomacy were the Joint Foreign Committee–Alliance Israélite way. It worked well enough that Jewish nationalists would later attempt to take credit for the results.[77] The Anglo-French decision to secure the best possible terms that could be realized and enforced was both honourable and reasonable. Confident of their social and cultural assumptions, satisfied that Western civilization was liberal civilization, that its pluralism allowed the Jew simultaneously to be citizen and self, taking comfort in the morality of the possible, they persevered. The peace treaties had many deficiencies, but the minority rights clauses as drawn were not among them. Those provisions had not come easily, but only after tortuous negotiations between Wolf and each one of the several national delegations of the Succession States. Zionists and Jewish nationalists were shunted aside. Word by word and clause by clause, Wolf hammered out the details with the British treaty draftsman.[78] The Alliance considered them Wolf's personal triumph. He was more modest. The success of 1919, he responded, was not the work of any one of them. They owed it to 'the complete loyalty and sympathy with which we all worked together'.[79]

Jewish nationalists, operating through the Comité des Délégations Juives, proved less and less effective. Dr Leo Motzkin, its secretary, claimed to the League of Nations in December 1920, that the Comité des Délégations represented twelve million Jews throughout the world and planned to petition for the admission of the 'Jewish People' to the League as a separate nationality. Such presumption led Lord Rothschild to move that Motzkin's proposals: 'are improper and dangerous

76 JFC to FO, [May 1919], BDBJ C 11/3/2/1. Wolf was pleased to see that the AIU remained entirely within the terms of his memorials, even on Salonika, and that Baron Edmond de Rothschild opted for Wolf's formula for Roumania. See, e.g., Wolf, PCD, 14 Mar. 1919.

77 Wolf, 'Report on the Minority Treaties', 15 Dec. 1920; Wolf to Bigart, 17 Dec. 1920. Sokolow privately admitted to Wolf that he had done nothing, leading to Wolf's observation, '*L'anguille!*' AIU Angl III/D/52/8253. When it came time to appoint an agent to act at the League of Nations, Wolf, Montefiore, Bigart and Sylvain Lévi rejected efforts of Zionists and Jewish nationalists to establish an International Jewish Committee. Such a body, Wolf observed, 'was undesirable and unnecessary' for 'we could not associate ourselves with the strong Nationalist policy of the Commitee of Delegations. Personally,' he continued, 'I regard the project with great anxiety, as I am sure we shall defeat the realisation of the Minority Treaties if we entrust their guardianship to a body pursuing the Nationalist aims which the Peace Conference rejected, and which the States concerned have been led to believe will not be pressed by the Jewish Communities.' Wolf to Bigart, 20 Jan., Bigart à Wolf, 31 jan. 1920; Wolf to Bigart 4 Feb.; Bigart à Wolf, 8 fév. 1921. The JFC and AIU, instead, worked out the procedure creating minority access to the Permanent Court of International Justice. See, e.g., Wolf to Bigart, 5 Oct. 1920, AIU Angl III/D/7471, 8006, 8253, 8444, 8458. Weizmann, after losing the presidency of the Zionist Congress and Agency, sought to revive Motzkin's proposal on a reduced scale by creating a small International Committee in London which he would chair that would 'deal with all political matters and direct the various European Committees'. The year was 1933, but even so, the idea remained intolerable. Laski to Adler, 6 Dec.; enclosed in Laski to Bigart, 6 Dec. 1933. See also Sylvain Lévi's response to Neville Laski, 11 déc. 1933, AIU Angl V/D/59/7680.

78 Wolf, PCD, esp May to October 1919.

79 Wolf to Bigart, 7 July 1920, AIU Angl III/D/52/7896. Wolf also owed his success to the great dexterity with which he had cultivated senior British staff at the Conference, particularly Sir William Tyrrell, Headlam-Morley, and E. H. Carr. See, e.g., Wolf, PCD, 18 Jan. 1919.

inasmuch as they are inconsistent with the loyalty and civil allegiance of Jews towards the countries of which they are nationals'.[80] The next year, 1922, the British would issue their two White Papers on Zionism, which, as Wolf triumphantly observed,

> very considerably diminish the concessions to the Zionists that were supposed to be implied by the Balfour Declaration. There will be no Jewish State and, although there will be a Jewish national Home, there will be no Jewish nationality. The functions of the Jewish Agency are restricted and Jewish immigration will be controlled by a body on which the Zionists are not likely to have a majority.

Only Jewish economic preference was left, 'but this really is all that remains of the extravagant hopes of the Zionists. As you may imagine they are profoundly disappointed'.[81] Wolf took advantage of the turn in attitude to negotiate for precise parity rather than privilege for non-Ottoman Jews residing in Palestine.

> In fact, while removing the disability of which we complained it creates for us a privilege which will not be shared by foreign Christians and Mohammadens who may also wish to reside permanently in Palestine. I dislike privileges as much as I dislike disabilities as I am certain they can only be dangerous for us. If you claim privileges in Palestine how can we refuse them to Christians in Poland or Roumania.[82]

The Anglo-French Jewish elite, operating through the Alliance and Joint Foreign Committee, stood as defenders of an order and culture refined with much effort before and since emancipation. They had struggled to make the dispersed Jew a full citizen of his state, endowed with the culture and beliefs of his forefathers, defining that which was owed to God and one's people in ways compatible with the civic freedom and responsibilities of liberal civilization. The elite feared that 'foreign Jews' would rend the delicate fabric of their culture. Education prepared immigrants to be British or French as well as Jewish, and it appeared to work. Since it did, Western Jews believed that liberal civilization and Jewish emancipation, once achieved, would ultimately bring the Jew of Eastern Europe, of the Ottoman Empire, or of North Africa to understand that the Western way was right. Some measure of self-interest coloured Anglo-French Jewish elite considerations. The Alliance and Consistory in France, the Board of Deputies, the Jewish Board of Guardians and the Anglo-Jewish Association in Britain had constructed ordered societies, Jewish in culture, liberal in outlook, but socially and politically deferential.

---

80 Minutes, JFC, 23 Feb. enclosed in Wolf to Bigart, 24 Feb. 1921, AIU Angl III/D/53/8526.

81 Wolf to Bigart, 6 July 1922, AIU Angl III/D/53/9897. PREM 1/24 shows how different the British perspective on Palestine had become at the highest levels by 1922. See also: Palestine: Correspondence with the Palestinian Arab Delegation and the Zionist Organization, June 1922 [Cmd. 1700]. Edwin Montagu's papers include a fascinating overview of these issues in 1920. Montagu Papers, AS-1–5/105/16–17.

82 Wolf to Bigart, 9 Jan. 1922. The Alliance agreed 'nous ne devons pas plus admettre un privilége qu'une infériorité'. Bigart à Wolf, 19 jan. 1922, AIU Angl III/D/53/9313, 9318. The problem arose through overcorrecting the 'disability' of Jews in the original article 123 of the Treaty of Sèvres. Wolf to Bigart, 2 May; Wolf to Curzon, 13 May 1921 and was still being tidied up in 1923. Bigart à Wolf, 13 mars 1923, AIU Angl III/D/52/8714, 8752; AIU Angl III/D/49/5467.

All this appeared endangered. Unassimilated or unacculturated Jews provoked anti-Semitism in the host culture, and Zionism, as an ideology, threatened to feed that poison.

And so they fought. They struggled within their own organizations, the French more successfully than the English. They sought to achieve their goals through the power of the states of which they were a part. Self-interest and principle were equally at stake. Their diplomatic accomplishments were considerable, if partial, and their view of the world survived, to a greater degree than they realized, until the cataclysm of Nazi madness. But even the Holocaust only drew more sharply the underlying paradoxes and problems of the Jew in the modern world.

14

Retrospect and Prospect

Anglo-Jewry, having negotiated and struggled for its place in the British world, determined that its achievements should not be lost. This interlocking cousinhood of wealth and privilege acknowledged its Jewish heritage without asking too many profound questions about it. The elite recognized its communal obligations and created institutions touching on the broadest range of social needs in Victorian Britain. Sometimes they dabbled, sometimes they sought to cure, but always they moved with a sense of purpose. A Spartan social philosophy animated Anglo-Jewry, but British Jewish philanthropy remained in advance of its times. Anglo-Jewry attempted to provide every co-religionist with the opportunity to practise his faith and live his life as fully and as constructively as possible. So Anglo-Jewry created schools, provided health care, constructed housing, cared for the aged, the infirm, the insane and the orphaned. The leadership attempted to weave British Jews into a rich tapestry of benefit societies and social clubs, recreational organizations and cultural associations. Social discipline operating through a complex network of voluntary organizations regulated life for late Victorian and Edwardian British Jews.

British Jews had dealt with newcomers and strangers in their midst since the Cromwellian readmission to the island. The great age of nineteenth-century free trade in goods, money and ideas was also an age of free trade in people. Emancipated human beings moved in unprecedented numbers both within and out from the European world. The partition of Poland, Jewry's historic refuge, created new opportunities and fresh dangers for Jews. Spurred by hope and driven by persecution, East European Jews drifted, then poured, westwards, most coming ashore in the United States. Many went through Britain, creating problems in the humane trans-shipment of people that Anglo-Jewry sought to address. Some stayed, concentrating an enormous underclass in but by no means limited to the East End of London. Had East European immigrant Jews not displayed an extraordinary talent for survival and adaptation, Anglo-Jewry's philanthropic labours could have accomplished little. As it was, a fruitful combination of immigrant inventiveness and establishment aid made that ghetto called Whitechapel an astounding laboratory in social mobility.

They did so many things. Facilities for religious observance – synagogues, kosher food, ritual baths, ecclesiastical courts and arbitration – grew in response to needs. The Jewish Board of Guardians, not to mention a host of smaller communal philanthropies, ministered to the poor and needy. Jewish schools served Jewish and secular needs, and the community provided religious education for those attending state institutions. Clubs brought males and females through the shoals of adolescence. Jewish philanthropies tended the aged, the disabled, the handicapped and the orphaned. And the East End community also provided for itself through friendly societies and trade unions, through a myriad of organizations that led one statistician to estimate that one Jewish person in every ten served on some communal organization.

Anglo-Jewry preached self help, Jewish observance, and British patriotism. The institutions created to socialize and maintain order and discipline, however, also helped to contribute to the ultimate emancipation of those who were supposed to be deferential and controlled. Women emerged to play active and powerful roles in communal affairs. Children were taught discipline but also learned self-confidence. No subculture within British society was more orderly, more industrious, or more upwardly mobile. Nor was any subculture more conscious of its public image and prepared to act against social deviants within its ranks.

Anglo-Jewry was not overwhelmed by a population that doubled and doubled again within a generation. But the newcomers did seem to threaten the world British Jews had constructed for themselves. The newcomers resisted pressure-cooker anglicization, appealed to their own forms of ethnic pride, and remained, for a time at least, a people apart. Since Western anti-Semitism seemed a concomitant of the new age of nationalism and democracy, Anglo-Jewry found itself on the defensive. Forced to choose between immigration restriction as public policy and heightened English ethnic tensions, Anglo-Jewry opted, somewhat covertly, for the former. Britain would remain, after all, hospitable to 'the right sorts of people', including Jews. They must not be too poor, too sick, too criminally-inclined or politically too subversive.

If they limited refuge, they also sought to create viable lives and opportunities for their East European co-religionists. Anglo-Jewry lobbied the British Foreign Office and other Western governments to use their diplomatic influence to secure full civil rights for Jews in Russia and Roumania. This transparent effort to ease a domestic Jewish problem ran aground on the reefs of international power politics. Neither Britain nor France, as war clouds gathered, could afford to antagonize their prospective East European allies. Anglo-Jewry's great friend, Edward VII, undertook to reason with his cousin Tsar Nicholas II on the issue of Jewish disabilities only to be told to mind his own business. Decades of diplomatic pressure produced ironic results. Britain and France, feeling the weight of Jewish criticism, sought some viable response. As a result, Zionists, not assimilationists, were the immediate beneficiaries of two decades of assimilationist diplomatic negotiations. Only during the Paris peace negotiations did Lucien Wolf manage to retrieve much, although never all, of the old Anglo-Jewish foreign policy.

Anglo-Jewry was a remarkable elite. A small, predominantly Ashkenazi group, it prospered in banking, investment, and, to a lesser degree, commerce. These ambitious leaders created the institutions to make an effective network of social control, stamped British Jews in their image and moulded them to their prudential philosophy. They were confident of their skills, in their achievements, of their status, and in their intentions. For almost half a century they held sway over their community, enjoying a fortunate combination of personal longevity, unchallenged economic success, and political supremacy.

In the decade and a half preceding the First World War, the old guard changed. A few retired. Illness or incapacity drove others to the sidelines. Death finally claimed its share. While the first Lord Rothschild survived until 1915, Samuel Montagu, Chief Rabbi Adler, Frederic Mocatta, not to mention Nathan Joseph, that prime mover of domestic philanthropy, passed away in the decade before. Sir Leonard Lionel Cohen still struggled to refurbish the Board of Guardians until 1920, and the seemingly immortal Morris Stephany, the board secretary, survived to 1918. But the great generation was going, if not gone. Some survived. Lucien Wolf survived, active to the end, until 1930. Claude G. Montefiore continued to preach his several gospels to the eve of the Second World War.

The next generation were very different people. Rothschild's title passed to no less committed but far less politically capable hands. Montagu's son, the second Lord Swaythling, had little of his father's commanding arrogance. Lord Swaythling's younger brother, Edwin Montagu, marched to a different drummer. One of the brightest young men of the revived Liberal party, Edwin's fortunes soared with Prime Minister H. H. Asquith, consolidated, then collapsed with Prime Minister David Lloyd George. Indian self-government, not Anglo-Jewry, commanded his attention. Edwin's cousin, Herbert Samuel, placed less distance between himself and the British Jewish community but could never be content merely to act on Anglo-Jewry's stage. Jews had arrived. The great generation had done its work. Tact, diplomacy, and firmness when needed carried the day. Rothschilds could become engaging, eccentric elite decorations and serious scientists. Montagu, Samuel, Sassoon, Isaacs, Nathan, and the ambitious of their privileged generation found the world of elite politics open to them.

The Anglo-Jewish world was too small for its new elite; the new professionals and businessmen were, whatever their ambitions and self-perception, too small to inherit that estate. Besides, the world that emerged from the carnage of war had no place for an elite of the old sort. Democracy had come into its own, and democracy had its own agenda. Time passed before democracy corroded the old vessels of deference and privilege, but they were already leaking well before the war. The old Anglo-Jewish establishment, however, was never successfully stormed from without. Anarchists, socialists, even trade unionists merged into their British environment or moved on. The vast majority of British Jews accepted, with token qualifications, the philosophy and values Anglo-Jewry had sought to impart – pride in being Jewish, anglicization, self-help and upward mobility. They became, in fact, what Anglo-Jewry wished them to be: English people of the Jewish persuasion.

Therein lay an unresolved tension, one that was played out in the tragic decades that followed. What was to be the relationship of this community with Zionism and Jewish nationalism? Claude G. Montefiore and Lucien Wolf championed Jewish civil liberties everywhere but resisted Jewish demands to be a people privileged or apart. Diaspora assimilation was Judaism's future. Jews must make their lives among, not apart from, the people with whom they lived. This liberal idea, the offspring of the enlightenment and economic modernization in the West, seemed somehow to have triumphed over all obstacles in 1919. The crash of the world economy, the triumph of totalitarianism, the madness of holocaust, and a world truly at war were all still far away. What remained to be done, believed surviving Anglo-Jewry, was simply to consolidate the great achievements of the past half century.

List of Sources

PRIMARY SOURCES

British Library, Additional Manuscripts

d'Abernon Papers. Balfour Papers. Burns Papers. Campbell-Bannerman Papers. Cecil Papers. Dilke Papers. Herbert Gladstone Papers. Northcliffe Papers.

Public Record Office (PRO), Kew

Board of Trade Papers (BT). Cabinet Papers (CAB): CAB 1; CAB 4; CAB 21; CAB 23; CAB 24; CAB 37. Home Office Papers (HO): HO 45; HO 145. Foreign Office Papers (FO): FO 371; FO 406; FO 608; FO 800 (Balfour Papers, Bertie Papers, Cecil Papers, Grey Papers, Nicolson Papers, Reading Papers, Sykes Papers). Metropolitan Police Papers (MEPO): MEPO 2. Ministry of Health Papers (MH): MH 10; MH 15; MH 51; MH 102. Public Record Office Papers (PRO): Kitchener Papers; Macdonald Papers. Prime Ministers's Papers (PREM): PREM 1.

House of Lords Record Office, London

Beaverbrook Papers. Bonar Law Papers. Lloyd George Papers. Herbert Samuel Papers. Stansgate Papers.

Fawcett Library, City of London Polytechnic

Louisa Twining Papers. National Vigilance Association Papers: Case Files and Reports; Confidential Executive Committee Minutes.

Board of Deputies of British Jews (BDBJ), Upper Woburn Place, London

Board of Deputies Minute Books. B Series. C Series, including: Alien Immigration Committee Papers; Conjoint Foreign Committee Papers; Education Committee Papers; General Correspondence; Joint Foreign Committee Papers; Law & Parliamentary Committee Papers.

Mocatta Library, University College, London

Anglo-Jewish Archives (AJ): Anglo-Jewish Association Papers; Conjoint Foreign Committee and Joint Foreign Committee Confidential Minutes; Education Aid Society Papers; 4% Industrial Buildings Society Papers; Federation of Synagogues Papers (Papers at 64 Leman St., London); Henriques Papers; Jews' Hospital and Orphan Asylum (JHOA) Papers (Norwood Archives); Jewish Lads' Brigade Papers; Jewish Religious Education Board Papers; Machziké Hadass Papers; Stettauer Papers; Swaythling Papers. Adler Papers. Gaster Papers. Mocatta Papers. Wolf Papers (Lucien Wolf's Peace Conference Diary, however, is in the University). College Manuscripts Library.

India Office Library (IOL), London

Curzon Papers. Montagu Papers. Reading Papers.

The London School of Economics and Political Science Library (LSE), London

Booth Papers. Webb (Passfield) Papers.

Bodleian Library, Oxford

MS Asquith. MS Bryce. MS Fisher. MS Harcourt. MS Simon. MS European (Milner Papers). MS dep. Church Mission to the Jews.

St. Antony's College Library, Oxford

Hogarth Papers. Sykes Papers (Sledmere).

Trinity College Library, Cambridge

Montagu Papers.

Cambridge University Library, Cambridge

Crewe Papers.

University of Newcastle-upon-Tyne Library (NUTL), Newcastle-upon-Tyne

Runciman Papers. C. P. Trevelyan Papers.

Samuel Montagu and Co. Limited, 114 Old Broad Street, London

Samuel Montagu & Co. Papers.

Alliance Israélite Universelle (AIU), Paris

Angleterre (Angl). Copies des correspondences (Cdc).

Ministère des Affaires Étrangères (MAE), Quai d'Orsay, Paris

Archives diplomatiques. Séries A. Guerre, 1914–1918. Séries A. Grande Bretagne.

Central Zionist Archive (CZA), Jerusalem

Sokolow Papers. Wolf Papers.

PRINTED SOURCES, OFFICIAL AND SEMI-OFFICIAL

Hansard's Parliament Debates
Parliamentary Papers
   Second Report of the Select Committee of the House of Lords . . . into the Execution of
      the Criminal Law, especially Regarding Juvenile Offenders , *PP* 1847, VII (534).
   Report of the Select Committee of the House of Commons on Criminal and Destitute
      Juveniles, *PP*, 1852, VII (515).
   First Report, Royal Commission for Enquiry into the Housing of the Working Clases, *PP*,
      1884–5, XXX. C. 4402.
   Royal Commission apointed to inquire into the Depression of Trade and Industry. First
      and Second Reports, *PP*, 1886, XXI, C. 4715. Second and Final Reports, *PP*, 1886,
      XXIII, C. 4893.
   Report to the Board of Trade on the Sweating System at the East End of London, by the
      Labour correspondent of the Board [John Burnett], *PP*, 1887, LXXXIX.
   Board of Trade, Memorandum on the Immigration of Foreigners into the United
      Kingdom, *PP*, 1887, LXXIX.
   Report . . . Proceedings . . . Minutes of Evidence and Appendix I: 27 July 1888; II, 8
      August 1889. House of Commons Select Committee on Immigration and Emigration
      (Foreigners). First Report, *PP*, 1888, XI. Second Report, *PP*, 1889, X.
   House of Lords, Select Committee on the Sweating System. First Report, *PP*, 1888, XX.
      Second Report, *PP*, 1888, XXI. Third Report, *PP*, 1889, XIII. Fourth Report, *PP*, 1889,
      XIV. Fifth Report, *PP*, 1890, XVII.
   Reports to the Board of Trade on Alien Immigration into the United States, *PP*, 1892–3,
      LXXI, C. 7113.
   Board of Trade (Alien Immigration), Reports on the Volume and Effects of the Recent
      Immigration from Eastern Europe into the United Kingdom, *PP*, 1894, LXVIII, C.
      7406.
   Royal Commission on Alien Immigration, *PP* (1903), IX. I, Report, Cd. 1741. II, Minutes
      of Evidence, Cd. 1742.. III, Appendix, Cd. 1741-I.. Royal Commission on Alien
      Immigration, 1904. IV, Index and Analysis to Minutes of Evidence, Cd. 1743
   Board of Trade, Annual Report on Emigration and Immigration. 1903, *PP*, 1904, CVI.
      1904, *PP*, 1905, XCVIII.
   Interdepartmental Committee on Physical Deterioration, *PP*, 1904, XXII (Report and
      Appendix, Cd. 2175; Minutes of Evidence, Cd. 2210; Appendix, Cd. 2186.
   Regulations . . . Made by the Secretary of State for the Home Department with Regard to
      the Administration of the Aliens Act, *PP*, 1906, XCVI, Cd. 2879.
   Expulsion of Aliens. Correspondence between the Secretary of State for the Home
      Department and His Honour Judge Rentoul, K.C., 11 March 1909., *PP*, LXX.
   Board of Trade, Accounts of Expenditures of Wage-Earning Women and Girls., *PP*, 1911,
      LXXXIX (Cd. 6953).
   Report of an Inquiry by the Board of Trade into Working-Class Rents and Retail Prices
      Together with the Rates of Wage in Certain Occupations . . . in 1912, 1913. *PP* (1913),
      LXVI (Cd. 6955).
   Local Government Board, Report on Infant and Child Mortality., *PP* (1913), XXXII (Cd.
      6909)
   Report of the Committee . . . to Consider the Cases of Persons in Government Offices Not
      of British or Allied Parentage. Cmd. 195. London, 1919.

Home Office. Comparative Statistics on Crime 1885–1919. London, 1921.

PRINTED SOURCES, PERIODICALS

Archives Israélites; Blackwood's; Charity Organisation Review; Contemporary Review; Daily Chronicle; Daily Mail; Daily News; East London Advertiser; Edinburgh Review; Le Figaro; Fortnightly Review; Globe; Independent Review; Jewish Chronicle; Jewish Quarterly Review; Jewish World; Jewish Year Book (which becomes the *Jewish Chronicle Year Book*); *Lancet; Morning Post; National Review; New York Times; Nineteenth Century* (which becomes *Nineteenth Century and after*); *Observer; Pall Mall Gazette; Quarterly Review; Standard; Sun; Le Temps; The Times; Transactions of the Jewish Historical Society of England; The Vigilance Record; Westminster Review; Yorkshire Evening News; Zionist Review.*

PRINTED SOURCES, ORGANISATIONS

Anglo-Jewish Association
Apprenticeship and Skilled Employment Association
Association for the Improvement of London Workhouse Infirmaries
Board of Deputies of British Jews
Boys' Life Brigade
Brady Street Club for Working Boys
Charity Organisation Society
Committee for the Prevention of Criminal Assaults on Children
Committee on Wage-earning Children
East London Jewish Communal League
East London Tenants' Protection Committee
Education Aid Society
Emily Harris Home for Jewish Working Girls
Federation of Synagogues
4% Industrial Dwellings Co. Ltd
Hayes Industrial School
Home and Hospital for Jewish Incurables
Home for Aged Jews
Hutchison House Lads' Club
Jewish Association for the Protection of Girls and Women
Jewish Athletic Association
Jewish Board of Guardians
Jewish Children's Penny Dinners Association
Jewish Colonisation Association
Jewish Convalescent Home
Jewish Day Nursury
Jewish Girls' Club
Jewish Ladies Society for Preventative and Rescue Work
Jewish Lads' Brigade
Jewish Peace Society
Jewish Religious Education Board
Jewish Schools' Boot Fund
Jews' Deaf and Dumb Home
Jews' Free School Happy Evenings
Jews' Hospital and Orphan Asylum
Ladies' Sanitary Association

Liberty and Property Defense League
London Purity Alliance
Mansion House Council on the Dwellings of the Poor
National Council of Women
National Social Purity Alliance (originally the Social Purity Alliance)
National Union of Women Workers
National Women's Labour League
National Vigilance Association
Poor Jews' Temporary Shelter
Russo-Jewish Committee
Sick Room Helps' Society
Society for the Evangelisation of Foreigners in London
Society for Promoting the Employment of Women
Society for Relieving the Poor on the Initiation of Their Children into the Holy Covenant
    of Abraham (Initiation Society)
Society for the Suppression of Mendicity
Soup Kitchen for the Relief of the Jewish Poor
Stepney Jewish Lads' Club
Travellers' Aid Society
Twentieth Century League
Union of British Jews
Union of Jewish Women
United Synagogue
Vigilance Association for Personal Rights
West Central Jewish Girls' Club
West Central Jewish Lads' Club
West Central Jewish Men's Club
West London Tenants' and General Legal Protection Committee
White Cross League
Women's Co-operative Guild
Women's Industrial Council
Women's Labour League
Women's Protective and Provident League
Women's Trade Union League

PRINTED SOURCES, CONTEMPORARY WRITINGS

Addison, Christopher, *The Health of the People and How It May Be Improved*. London, 1914.
Adler, Hermann, *Anglo-Jewish Memories*. London, 1909.
_____ *The North London Pulpit: A Special Series of Sermons*. London, 1892.
_____ *Religious Versus Political Zionism*. London, 1898.
Adler, M. N., *The Adler Family*. London, 1909.
Adler, Nettie, 'Children as wage earners', *Fortnightly Review*, new series, volume 71 (1903), 918–27.
'The alien immigrant', *Blackwood's Magazine*, volume 173 (1903), 132–41.
Anderson, Robert, 'The crusade against professional criminals', *Nineteenth Century and after*, volume 53 (1903), 496–518.
_____ 'How to put down "hooliganism"', *Nineteenth Century and after*, volume 52 (1902), 13–18.
_____ 'The problem of the criminal alien', *Nineteenth Century and after*, volume 69 (1911), 217–25.

———— 'The Punishment of Crime', *Nineteenth Century and after*, volume 50 (1901), 77–92.

[Asquith] Brock, Michael and E. (eds), *H. H. Asquith Letters to Venetia Stanley*. Oxford, 1982.

[Barnett, H. O.], *Canon Barnett, His Life, Work, and Friends*. 2 vols. London, 1918.

Bathurst, Kate, 'The need for national nurseries', *Nineteenth Century and after*, volume 57 (1905), 818–27.

Baumann, Arthur A., 'The Lords Committee on the Sweating System', *National Review*, volume 12 (1888), 145–59.

———— 'Possible remedies for the sweating system', *National Review*, volume 69 (1888), 269–307.

Battersea, Constance, *Reminiscences*. London, 1922.

Benjamin, Lewis S., 'The passing of the English Jews', *Nineteenth Century and after*, volume 72 (1912), 491–504.

Besant, Walter, *East London*. London, 1901.

Beveridge, William and Maynard, H. R., 'The unemployed: lessons of the Mansion House Fund', *Contemporary Review*, volume 86 (1904), 629–38.

Black, Clementina, *Sweated Industry and the Minimum Wage*. London, 1907.

———— (ed.), *Married Women's Work*. London, 1915.

Black, Clementina and Meyer, Adele, *Makers of Our Clothes*. London, 1909.

Booth, Charles, *The Aged Poor*. London, 1894.

———— *The Condition and Occupation of the People of the Tower Hamlets, 1886–87*. London, 1887.

———— (ed.), *Life and Labour of the People of London*, 2 vols. London, 1889.

———— (ed.), *Life and Labour of the People of London*, 9 vols. London, 1892–7.

Booth, William, *In Darkest London and the Way Out*. London, 1890.

Bosanquet, Helen, *Social Work in London, 1869–1912*. London, 1914.

Boulton, Harold E., 'The housing of the poor', *Fortnightly Review*, new series, volume 43 (1888), 279–86.

Bowley, Arthur L. and Burnett-Hurst, A. R., *Livelihood and Poverty*. London, 1915.

Bowmaker, Dr Edward, *The Housing of the Working Classes*. London, 1895.

[Braithwaite] Lloyd George's *Ambulance Wagon: Being the Memoirs of W. J. Braithwaite, 1911-1912*, ed. by Henry Bunbury. London, 1957.

Bray, Reginald, *Boy Labour and Apprenticeship*. London, 1911.

Breakell, Mary L., 'Women in the medical profession. By an outsider', *Nineteenth Century and after*, volume 54 (1903), 819–25.

Burns, John, 'The unemployed', *Nineteenth Century*, volume 32 (1892), 850–64.

Butler, C. V., *Domestic Service*. London, 1916.

Cadbury, Edward and Shann, George, *Sweating*. London, 1907.

———— et al., *Women's Work and Wages*. London, 1906.

Chamberlain, Joseph, 'The labour question', *Nineteenth Century*, volume 32 (1892), 677–710.

Chiozza Money, L. G., *Riches and Poverty*. London, 1904.

———— *Things That Matter*. London, 1912.

Churchill, Winston Spencer, *Liberalism and the Social Problem*. London, 1909.

Cohen, Lionel L., *Scheme for the Better Management of All the Jewish Poor*. London, 1860.

Committee on Old Age Pensions, *Old Age Pensions: The Case against Old Age Pensions Schemes*. London, 1903.

Crackenthorpe, Montague, 'New ways with old offenders', *Nineteenth Century*, volume 34 (1893), 614–32.

Cunningham, William, *Alien Immigrants to England*. London, 1897.

Daiches, Sameel, *Judaism in England*. Sunderland, 1907.

Drage, Geoffrey, 'Alien immigration', *Fortnightly Review*, new series, volume 57 (1895), 37–46.

———— *The Labour Problem*. London, 1896.

Dunraven, Earl of, 'The invasion of desitute aliens', *Nineteenth Century*, volume 31 (1892), 985–1000.

Dyche, John A., 'The Jewish immigrant', *Contemporary Review*, volume 75 (1899), 379–99.

———— 'The Jewish workman', *Contemporary Review*, volume 73 (1898), 35–50.

Elliot, Hugh S. R., 'Punishment and crime', *Nineteenth Century and after*, volume 70 (1912), 306–20.

Escott, Thomas Hay Sweet, 'The past, present, and future of the middle classes', *Fortnightly Review*, new series, volume 82 (1907), 109–21.

Evans-Gordon, William, *The Alien Immigrant*. London, 1903.

———— 'The attack on the Aliens Act', *National Review*, volume 48 (1906), 460–70.

———— 'The stranger within our gates', *Nineteenth Century and after*, volume 49 (1911), 210–16.

Faudel, Henry, *Suggestions to the Jews for Improvement in Reference to Their Charities, Education, and Central Government. By a Jew*. London, 1844.

'Foreign undesirables', *Blackwood's Magazine*, volume 159 (1901), 279–89.

Fox, Stephen N., 'The invasion of pauper foreigners', *Contemporary Review*, volume 53 (1888), 855–67.

Freeman, Arnold J., *Boy Life and Labour*. London, 1914.

Fyffe, H. H., 'The aliens and the Empire', *Nineteenth Century and after*, volume 54 (1903), 415–19.

Gidney, William Thomas, *The History of the London Society for Promoting Christianity amongst the Jews, from 1809 to 1908*. London, 1908.

Gollancz, Hermann, *Sermons and Addresses*. London, 1909.

Gorst, John, 'The Conservative programme of social reform', *Nineteenth Century*, volume 38 (1895), 3–16.

———— 'School children as wage earners', *Nineteenth Century*, volume 46 (1899), 8–17.

———— 'Social reform: an obligation of the Tory Party', *Nineteenth Century and after*, volume 53 (1903), 519–32.

Gould, E. R. L., 'The social condition of labour', *Contemporary Review*, volume 63 (1893), 125–52.

Gray, B. Kirkman, *A History of English Philanthropy*. London, 1905.

Great Synagogue, *Report of the Committee in Reference to the Duties and Emoluments Annexed to the Office of Secretary . . . to be Considered by the Vestry 5th February 5626 (1866)*. London, 1866.

Gregory, Alice S., 'Midwifery as a profession for educated women', *Nineteenth Century and after*, volume 63 (1908), 90–7.

Halpern, Georg, *Der Jüdischen Arbeiter in London*. Berlin, 1903.

———— 'Die Jüdische Einwanderung – Bevölkerung Londons' in A. Nossig (ed.), *Jüdische Statistik*. Berlin 1903.

Hamilton, Maud C., 'Mission women', *Nineteenth Century*, volume 46 (1884), 984–90.

Harrison, Frederic, *Autobiographic Memoirs*. 2 vols. London, 1911.

Hart, Ernest, 'Metropolitan infirmaries for the pauper sick', *Fortnightly Review*, new series, volume 4 (1866), 459–63.

Henriques, H. S. Q., *The Jews and English Law*. London, [c. 1909].

Herzl, Theodor, *The Complete Diaries of Theodor Herzl*, ed. by Raphael Patai, trans. by Harry Zohn. 5 vols. New York, 1960.

Higgs, Mary, *How To Deal with the Unemployed*. London, 1904.

Hobart-Hampden, Albinia, 'The working girl of today', *Nineteenth Century*, volume 43 (1898), 724–30.

Hobson, James A., *The Crisis of Liberalism. New Issues of Democracy*. Harvester Reprinted Edition. Croom Helm, 1974.

———— *The Social Problem*. London, 1902.

Holmes, Thomas, 'The making of the hooligan', *Contemporary Review*, volume 80, 562-75.

――― 'Youthful offenders and parental responsibility', *Contemporary Review*, volume 77 (1900), 845–54.

Hunter, Robert, 'The Future of City Charities', *Nineteenth Century*, volume 27 (1890), 72-88.

Hutchinson, James G., 'A workman's view of the remedy for unemployment', *Nineteenth Century and after*, volume 44 (1904), 331–42.

――― 'Can the working classes save? A workman's view', *Nineteenth Century and after*, volume 43 (1908), 285–96.

Inglis, M. K. 'The state versus the house: should there be a central government department for children?', *Fortnightly Review*. new series. volume 84 (1908), 643–58.

Jacobs, Joseph, *Statistics of the Jewish Population in London, 1873–1893*. London, 1894.

――― *Studies in Jewish Statistics*. London, 1891.

Jephson, Henry, *The Sanitary Evolution of London*. London, 1907.

'The Jewish Board of Guardians and the Lancet Report', *The Lancet*, no. 3169 (24 May 1884), 948.

Johnson, S. C., *A History of Emigration from the United Kingdom to North America, 1783–1912*. London, 1913.

Joseph, Morris, *Judaism as Creed and Life*. London, 1903.

Lambert, Brooke, 'Esau's cry', *Contemporary Review*, volume 44 (1883), 916–23.

Landa, M. J., *The Alien Problem and Its Remedy*. London, 1911.

Lilly, W. S., 'The cost of cheapness', *Fortnightly Review*, new series, volume 77 (1905), 711–25.

Lodge, Oliver, 'Some social reforms', *Contemporary Review*, volume 88 (1905), 1–20.

Ludlow, James Malcolm, 'Gilds and Friendly Societies', *Contemporary Review*, volume 21 (1873), 552–72, 737–62.

Macdonald, James Ramsay, 'Sweating – its cause and cure', *Independent Review*, volume 2 (1904), 72–85.

Macrosty, H. W., *Sweating, its cause and remedy*. Fabian Tract No. 50. London, 1894.

Magnus, Laurie, *Aspects of the Jewish Question*. London, 1902.

――― *The Jewish Board of Guardians and the Men Who Made It*. London, 1908.

――― *Old Lamps for New: An Apologia for the League of British Jews*. London, 1918.

Martin, Anna, *The Married Working Woman*. London, 1911.

――― *The Mother and Social Reform*. London, 1913.

Mason, Marianne H., 'Poor Law children and the efficient inspection of the "Divine System"', *Nineteenth Century and after*, volume 73 (1913), 1008–22.

Masterman, Charles F. G., *The Condition of England*. London, 1909.

Methuen, General Lord, 'Training the youth of England', *Nineteenth Century and after*, volume 57 (1905), 238–43.

Mocatta, Ada (ed.), *A Memoir of F. D. Mocatta (1828–1905)*. London, 1911.

Molesworth, Guilford L., 'Blundering social reform', *Nineteenth Century and after*, volume 74 (1913), 656–72.

Montagu, Lily H., *My Club and I: the Story of the West Central Girls' Club*, 2nd ed. London, 1954.

――― *The Jewish Religious Union and Its Beginnings*. London, 1927.

――― *Naomi's Exodus*. London, 1901.

――― *Thoughts on Judaism*. London, 1904.

――― *Samuel Montagu, First Baron Swaythling*. London, [1913].

Montefiore, Claude G., *Liberal Judiasm*. London, 1911.

――― *Liberal Judaism: An Essay*. London, 1903.

――― 'Nation or religious community?', *Transactions of the Jewish Historical Society of England*, volume 4 (1903), 1–15.

――― *Outlines of Liberal Judaism*. London, 1905.

_____ *Truth in Religion and Other Sermons*. London, 1909.

Mulhall, M. G. 'The rise of the middle class', *Contemporary Review*, volume 41 (1882), 325–34.

National Social Purity Alliance, *The Cleansing of the City*. London, 1908.

_____ *The Nation's Morals*. London, 1910.

Oliver, Thomas, 'Our workmen's diet and wages', *Fortnightly Review*, new series, volume 56 (1894), 513–26.

Pépin, E., *La Question des étrangers en Angleterre*. Paris, 1913.

Peppin, T. S., *Club-Land of the Toiler*. London, 1895.

Phelps, Sydney K., 'My friends among the home-workers of London', *Nineteenth Century and after*, volume 74 (1914), 834–44.

Potter, Beatrice [see also, Webb], 'East London Labour', *Nineteenth Century*, volume 24 (1888), 161–93.

_____ 'The Lords and the sweating system', *Nineteenth Century*, volume 27 (1890), 885-905.

_____ 'The sweating system', *Charity Organisation Review*, volume 4 (1888), 12–16.

Recueil des matériaux sur la situation économique des israélites en Russie. Paris, 1904.

Reeves, Maud Pember, *Round about a Pound a Week*. London, 1913.

Rentoul, Robert Reid, *Race Culture; or Race Suicide*. London, 1906.

'Report of the Lancet Special Sanitary Commission on the Polish Colony of Jew Tailors', *The Lancet* (3 March 1884), 817–18.

Rigby, L. M., *Working Lads' Clubs*. London, 1908.

Rocker, Rudolph, *In Shturem. Golos Yoren*. London and Buenos Aires, 1952.

Rosenbaum, Simon, 'A contribution to the study of the vital and other statistics of the Jews of the U.K.', *Journal of the Royal Statistical Society*, volume 68 (1905), 526–66.

Rosenfelt, Charles, *Progress or Retrogress*. London, 1905.

Russell, C. and Lewis, Harry S., *The Jew in London, a Study of Racial Character and Present-day Conditions*. London, 1900.

Russell, C. E. B. and Rigby, Lilian M., *Working Lads' Clubs*. London, 1908.

Salt, Henry S., *The Ethics of Corporal Punishment*. London, 1907.

Samuel, Herbert, *Liberalism*. London, 1902.

_____ *Memoirs*. London, 1945.

Schloss, D. F., 'Healthy homes for the working classes', *Fortnightly Review*, new series, volume 43 (1888), 526–37.

_____ 'The Jew as workman', *Nineteenth Century*, volume 29 (1891), 96–109.

_____ 'The sweating system', *Fortnightly Review*, new series, volume 42 (1887), 835–56.

_____ 'The sweating system', *Charity Organisation Review*, volume 4 (1888), 1–11.

_____ 'The sweating system', *Fortnightly Review*, new series, volume 47 (1890), 532–51.

Schreiner, Olive. *Women and Labour*. London, 1911.

Scott, Clement, 'The modern music-hall', *Contemporary Review*, volume 56 (1889), 683–90.

Seebohm Rowntree, B. (ed.), *Betting and Gambling*. London, 1905.

Simon, Oswald, 'The return of the Jews to Palestine', *Nineteenth Century*, volume 44 (1898), 437–47.

Singer, Simeon, *The Literary Remains of Simeon Singer*. Edited by Israel Abrahams. 3 vols. London, 1908.

Smith, H. Llewellen, *History of East London*. London, 1939.

'Social reforms for the London poor' by 'A London artisan', *Fortnightly Review*, new series, volume 35 (1884), 21–36.

Sokolow, Nahum, *History of Zionism, 1600–1918*, 2 vols. London, 1919.

Solly, Henry, *Working Men's Social Clubs and Educational Institutes*. 2nd Ed. London, 1904.

Stanley, Maude, *Clubs for Working Girls*. London, 1890.

Stefan, Gustav F., 'Six hundred years of English poverty: a study in the fluctuation of the purchasing power of wages', *Nineteenth Century*, volume 33 (1893), 932–51.

Stollard, J. H., *London Pauperism amongst Jews and Christians*. London, 1867.

Stuart-Wortley, James, 'The East End as represented by Mr. Besant', *Nineteenth Century*, volume 22 (1887), 361–77.

Surr, Elizabeth, 'The child criminal', *Nineteenth Century*, volume 10 (1881), 649–63.

Tawney, R. H., *The Establishment of Minimum Rates in the Tailoring Industry under the Trade Boards Act of 1909*. Studies in the Minimum Wage, no. 11. London, 1915.

Treloar, W. P., 'The cure of tuberculous children', *Nineteenth Century and after*, volume 84 (1918), 288–95.

Tuckwell, Gertrude, 'A seventeen hours' working day', *Fortnightly Review*, new series, volume 65 (1899), 783–8.

—— (ed.), *Women in Industry*. London, 1908.

Urwick, E. J. (ed.), *Studies in Boy Life in Our Cities*. London, 1904.

Warwick, Frances Evelyn, Countess of, *Afterthoughts*. London, 1931.

—— 'The cause of children', *Nineteenth Century and after*, volume 50 (1901), 67–76.

Waugh, Benjamin, 'Street children', *Contemporary Review*, volume 53 (1888), 825–35.

Webb, Beatrice, *My Apprenticeship*. London, 1926.

Webb, Sidney and Beatrice, *Problems of Modern Industry*. new edition. London, 1902.

Weizmann, Chaim, *The Letters and Papers of Chaim Weizmann*. Series A Letters. Ed. Meyer Weisgal et. al., volumes 3–9. Oxford, London, and Jerusalem, 1972–7.

—— *Trial and Error*. London, 1949.

Whelpley, James D., *The Problem of the Immigrant*. London, 1905.

White, Arnold, 'Alien immigration – a rejoinder', *Fortnightly Review*, new series, volume 57 (1895), 501–7.

—— (ed.), *The Destitute Alien in Great Britain*. London, 1892.

—— *Efficiency and Empire*. London, 1901.

—— *English Democracy*. London, 1894.

—— 'Europe and the Jews', *Contemporary Review*, volume 72 (1897), 733–42.

—— 'The invasion of pauper foreigners', *Nineteenth Century*, 22 (1888), 414–22.

—— *The Modern Jew*. London, 1899.

—— *Problems of a Great City*. London 1886.

—— *Tries at Truth*. London, 1891.

—— 'The truth about the Russian Jew', *Contemporary Review*, volume 61 (1892), 695–708.

—— 'A typical alien immigrant', *Contemporary Review*, volume 73 (1898), 241–50.

Wilkins, W. H., *The Alien Invasion*. London, 1892.

Wills, Alfred, 'Criminals and crime', *Nineteenth Century and after*, volume 57 (1907), 879–94.

Wilson, Andrew, 'Music halls', *Contemporary Review*, volume 78 (1900), 134–41.

Wolf, Lucien, 'Anti-Semitism', *Essays in Jewish History*. Ed. by Cecil Roth. London, 1934.

—— *Correspondence with H.M. Government Relative to the Treaty Rights of the Jews of Roumania*. London, 1919.

—— *The Jewish Boget and the Forged Protocols of the Learned Elders of Zion*. London, 1920.

—— 'The Jewish national movement', *Edinburgh Review*, volume 225 (1917), 1–17.

—— *Notes on the Diplomatic History of the Jewish Question with Texts of Treaty Stipulations and Other Official Documents*. London, 1919.

—— 'The Zionist peril', *Jewish Quarterly Review*, volume 17 (1904), 1–25.

Zangwill, Israel, *Children of the Ghetto*. London, 1909.

SELECT BIBLIOGRAPHY

Some but by no means all of the useful literature on this problem and its broader context is listed below. I have, for instance, cited little of the extensive journal literature. I offer these as some suggestions of informative and useful points of departure that I have found useful and helpful.

Adelson, Roger, *Mark Sykes: Portrait of an Amateur*. London, 1975.

Adler, Michael, *History of the Hammersmith Synagogue*. London, 1950.

Alderman, Geoffrey, *The Jewish Community in British Politics*. Oxford, 1983.

Aldcroft, Derek and Richardson, Harry W., *The British Economy, 1870–1939*. London, 1969.

Anderson, Olive, 'The growth of Christian militarism in mid-Victorian Britain', *English Historical Review*, volume 76 (1971), 46–72.

Ashworth, William, *An Economic History of England, 1870 to 1929*. London, 1960.

———— *The Genesis of Modern British Town Planning*. London, 1954.

Barnett, Arthur, *The Western Synagogue through Two Centuries (1761–1961)*. London, 1961.

Bayme, Steven, 'Jewish Leadership and Anti-Semitism in Britain, 1898–1918'. Doctoral Dissertation, Columbia University, 1977.

Bealey, Frank and Pelling, Henry M., *Labour and Politics*. London, 1958.

Benas, Betram B., 'A survey of the Jewish institutional history of Liverpool and district', *Transactions of the Jewish Historical Society of England*, volume 17 (1951–2), 23–38.

Bentwich, Norman, *Early English Zionists*. Tel Aviv, 1940.

———— *My First Seventy Years; An Account of My Life and Times, 1883–1960*. London, 1962.

———— *The Social Transformation of Anglo-Jewry, 1883–1960*. London, 1960.

Bermant, Chaim, *The Cousinhood: The Anglo-Jewish Gentry*. London, 1971.

Best, Geoffrey, *Mid-Victorian Britain, 1851–1875*. New York, 1972.

Bowle, John, *Viscount Samuel*. London, 1957.

Bowley, A. L., *Wages and Income in the United Kingdom since 1860*. London, 1937.

Briggs, Asa, *Seebohm Rowntree*. London, 1961.

Bristow, Edward J., *Prostitution and Prejudice: The Jewish Fight against White Slavery, 1870–1939*. Oxford, 1982.

———— *Vice and Vigilance*. Dublin and Totowa, NJ, 1977.

Brodetsky, Selig, *Memoirs: From Ghetto to Israel*. London, 1960.

Brown, Benjamin H. *The Tariff Reform Movement in Great Britain, 1881–1895*. New York, 1943.

Brown, Kenneth D. (ed.), *Essays in Anti-Labour History*. London, 1974.

Bruce, M., *The Coming of the Welfare State*. London, 1961.

Cardozo, D. A. Jessurun and Goodman, Paul, *Think and Thank: The Montefiore Synagogue and College, Ramsgate 1833–1933*. Oxford and London, 1933.

Clarke, Peter F., *Liberals and Social Democrats*. Cambridge, 1978.

Clegg, H. A., Fox, Alan, and Thompson, A. F., *A History of British Trade Unions since 1889*. volume I, 1889–1910. Oxford, 1964.

Cohen, Lucy, *Some Recollections of Claude Goldsmid Montefiore, 1858–1938*. London, 1940.

Cohen, Stuart A., *English Zionists and British Jews: The Communal Politics of Anglo-Jewry, 1895–1920*. Princeton, 1982.

Cowles, Virginia, *The Rothschilds*. New York, 1973.

Cronin, James and Schneer, Jonathan (eds), *Social Conflict and the Political Order in Modern Britain*. Croom Helm, 1982.

Daiches, David, *Two Worlds: An Edinburgh Jewish Childhood*. 2nd ed. Sussex, 1971.

Dangerfield, George, *The Strange Death of Liberal England*. London, 1936.

Davis, Richard, *The English Rothschilds*. Chapel Hill, 1983.

Deane Phyllis and Cole, W. A., *British Economic Growth, 1688–1959*. Cambridge, 1962.

Dent, H. C., *1870–1970: A Century of Growth in English Education*. London, 1970.

Dugdale, Blanche E. C., *Arthur James Balfour*. 2 vols. New York, 1937.

Dyhouse, Carol, *Girls Growing Up in Late Victorian and Edwardian England*. London, 1981.

Dyos, H. J. and Wolff, Michael (eds.), *The Victorian City*. 2 vols. London, 1973.

Elman, Peter, 'The beginnings of the Jewish trades unions movement', *Transactions of the Jewish Historical Scoiety of England*, volume 17 (1951–1952), 53–62.

Emy, H. V., *Liberals, Radicals and Social Politics*. Cambridge, 1973.

Endelmann, Todd, 'Communal solidarity and family loyalty among the Jewish elite of Victorian London', *Victorian Studies*, volume 28 (1985), 491–526.

—— *The Jews of Georgian England 1714–1830: Tradition and Change in a Liberal Society*. Philadelphia, 1979.

Epstein, I. and Levine, E. (eds), *Essays Presented to J. H. Hertz, Chief Rabbi*. London, 1942.

Finestein, Israel, 'The Lay Leadership of the United Synagogue since 1870', in *A Century of Anglo-Jewish Life*, ed. by Salmond S. Levin. London, 1971.

Fishman, William J., *Jewish Radicals: From Czarist Stetl to London Ghetto*. New York, 1974.

Fox, Lionel W., *The English Prisons and Borstal System*. London, 1952.

Fraser, Derek, *Urban Politics in Victorian England*. Leicester, 1976.

Friedman, Isaiah, *The Question of Palestine, 1914–1918: British-Jewish-Arab Relations*. London, 1973.

—— *Germany, Turkey and Zionism, 1897–1918*. Oxford, 1977.

Gainer, Bernard, *The Alien Invasion: The Origins of the Alien Act of 1905*. London, 1972.

Garrard, John A., *The English and Immigration, 1880–1910*. London, 1971.

Gartner, Lloyd P., *The Jewish Immigrant in England, 1870–1914*. London, 1960.

Gilbert, Bentley B, *The Evolution of National Insurance in Great Britain: Origins of the Welfare State*. London, 1966.

Gilbert, Martin and Churchill, Randolph, *Winston Churchill*. London, 1966–1988.

Gosden, M., *Self Help: Voluntary Associations in Nineteenth Century Britain*. New York, 1974.

Grigg, John, *Lloyd George: the People's Champion*. London, 1978.

Halévy, Eli, *Imperialism and the Rise of Labour*, trans. by E. I. Watkin. London, 1961.

—— *The Rule of Democracy, 1905–1914*, trans. by E. I. Watkin. London, 1961.

Halpern, Ben, *Brandeis and Weizmann*. New York, 1987.

—— *The Idea of the Jewish State*. 2nd ed. Cambridge, Mass., 1969.

Harrison, Brian, *Peaceable Kingdom: Stability and Change in Modern Britain*. Oxford, 1982.

—— 'Philanthropy and the Victorians', *Victorian Studies*, volume IX (1966), 353–74.

—— 'State Intervention and Moral Reform in Nineteenth Century England', *Pressure from Without in Early Victorian England*, ed. by Patricia Hollis. New York, 1974, 289–322.

Hobsbawm, Eric J., *Industry and Empire*. London, 1968.

Holcombe, Lee, *Victorian Ladies at Work*. Newton Abbot, 1973.

Holmes, Colin (ed.), *Immigrants and Minorities in British Society*. London, 1978.

Homa, Bernard, *A Fortress in Anglo-Jewry: The Story of the Machzike Hadath*. London, 1953.

Houghton, Walter E., *The Victorian Frame of Mind*. New Haven, 1957.

Humphries, Stephen, *Hooligans or Rebels? An Oral History of Working-Class Childhood and Youth 1889–1939*. London, 1981.

Hyamson, Albert M. H., *Israel Abrahams: A Memoir*. London, 1940.

—— *The Sephardim of England*. London, 1951.

—— *The London Board for Sechita, 1804–1954*. London, 1954.

Jabotinsky, Vladimir, *The Story of the Jewish Legion*. New York, 1945.

Jenkins, Roy, *Asquith*. London, 1964.

Jones, Catherine, *Immigration and Social Policy in Britain*. London, 1977.

Jones, Gareth Stedman, *Outcast London: A Study in the Relationship between Classes in Victorian Society*. Oxford, 1971.

Katz, Jacob (ed.), *Toward Modernity: The European Jewish Model*, New Brunswick, 1987.

Kedourie, Elie, 'Cairo and Khartoum on the Arab Question, 1915–18', *The Chatham House Version and other Middle Eastern Studies*. London, 1970, 12–32.

Kellett, J. R., *The Impact of Railways on Victorian Cities*. London, 1969.

Kennedy, P and Nicholls, A. (eds), *Nationalist and Racialist Movements in Britain and Germany before 1914*. London, 1981.

Koss, Stephen, *Asquith*. London, 1976.

Krausz, Ernest, *Leeds Jewry: Its History and Structure*. Cambridge, 1964.

Langan, Mary and Schwarz, Bill (eds), *Crises in the British State 1880–1930*. London, 1985.

Laqueur, Walter, *A History of Zionism*. London, 1972.

Laski, Neville, *The Laws and Charities of the Spanish and Portuguese Jews Congregations of London*. London, 1952.

Leftwich, Joseph, *Israel Zangwill*. London, 1957.

Levine, Ephraim, *The History of the New West End Synagogue*. London, 1929.

Lipman, Vivian David, *A Century of Social Service, 1859–1959: The History of the Jewish Board of Guardians*. London, 1959.

—— 'The rise of Jewish suburbia', *Transactions of the Jewish Historical Society of England*, volume 21 (1968), 78–103.

—— *A Social History of the Jews in England, 1850–1950*. London, 1954.

—— (ed.) *Three Centuries of Anglo-Jewish History*. London, 1961.

Loewe, Lionel, *Basil Henriques: A Portrait*. London, 1976.

Magnuson, Norris, *Salvation in the Slums: Evangelical Social Work, 1865–1920*. Metuchen, NJ, 1977.

Mandel, Neville J., *The Arabs and Zionism before World War I*. Berkeley and Los Angeles, 1976.

Marmur, Dov (ed.), *Reform Judaism: Essays on Reform Judaism in Britain*. London, 1973.

Marwick, Andrew, *The Deluge: British Society and the First World War*. London, 1965.

Mathew, W. R., *Claude Montefiore: The Man and His Thought*. London, 1956.

Meachum, Standish, *A Life Apart: the English Working Class 1890–1914*. London, 1977.

—— *Toynbee Hall*. London, 1987.

Mitchell, B. R. and Deane, Phyllis (eds), *Abstract of British Historical Statistics*. Cambridge, 1971.

Montagu, Lily H., *The First Fifty Years: A Record of Liberal Judaism in England*. London, 1950.

Morgan, Kenneth O. and Morgan, J., *Portrait of a Progressive: the Political Career of Christopher, Viscount Addison*. Oxford, 1980.

Morris, A. J. A. (ed.), *Edwardian Radicalism*. London, 1974.

Mowat, Charles Loch, *The Charity Organisation Society, 1869–1913*. London, 1961.

Munby, D. L., *Industry and Planning in Stepney*. Oxford, 1951.

Murphy, R. *The Religious Problem in National Education*. Liverpool, 1959.

Newman, Aubrey (ed.), *The Jewish East End 1840–1939*. London, 1981.

—— *The United Synagogue. 1870–1970*. London, 1976.

O'Day, A. (ed.), *The Edwardian Age: Conflict and Stability, 1900–1914*. London, 1979.

Olsen, Donald J. *The Growth of Victorian London*. London, 1976.

Owen, David E., *English Philanthropy, 1660–1960*. Cambridge, Mass., 1964.

Peacock, A. T. and Wiseman, J., *The Growth of Public Expenditure in the United Kingdom*. Princeton, 1967.

Pelling, Henry, *The Origins of the Labour Party, 1880–1900*. 2nd ed. London, 1965.

—— *Popular Politics and Society in Late Victorian Britain*. London, 1968.

Phelps Brown, E. H., *The Growth of British Industrial Relations*. London, 1959.

Pimlott, J. A. R., *Toynbee Hall*. London, 1935.

Pinchbeck, Ivy and Hewitt, Margaret, *Children in English Society*, 2 vols. London, 1973.

Prochaska, Frank, K, *Women and Philanthropy in 19th Century England*. Oxford, 1980.

Read, Donald, *England, 1868–1914: The Age of Urban Democracy*. London, 1979.

Reinharz, Jehuda. *Chaim Weizmann*, volume I. New York, 1986.

Robb, James H., *The Working Class Anti-Semite*. London, 1954.

Roberts, David, *The Victorian Origins of the British Welfare State*. New Haven, 1960.

Robson, William A., *The Government and Misgovernment of London*. London, 1939.

Rose, M. E., *The Relief of Poverty 1834–1914*. London, 1972.

Rose, Millicent, *The East End of London*. London, 1951.

Rosenberg, Edgar, *From Shylock to Svengali*. London, 1961.

Roth, Cecil, *The Federation of Synagogues*. London, 1937.

—— *The Great Synagogue, 1690–1940*. London, 1950.

—— *History of the Jews in England*. 3rd ed. Oxford, 1964.

—— *The Rise of Provincial Jewry*. London, 1950.

Rowland, Peter, *David Lloyd George*. London, 1975.

—— *The Last Liberal Governments: The Promised Land, 1905–1910*. London, 1968.

Sacher, Harry, *Zionist Portraits*. London, 1959.

Saul, S. B., *The Myth of the Great Depression, 1873–1896*. London, 1969.

Schama, Simon, *Two Rothschilds and the Land of Israel*. London, 1978.

Schwab, Walter, *B'nai Brith, the First Lodge of England: A Record of Fifty Years*. London, 1960.

Searle, G. R., *The Quest for National Efficiency*. Oxford, 1971.

Semmel, Bernard, *Imperialism and Social Reform*. London, 1960.

Shaftesley, John M. (ed.), *Remember the Days: Essays in Honour of Cecil Roth*. London, 1966.

Springhall, J., *Youth, Empire and Society: British Youth Movements, 1883–1940*. London,1977.

Stansky, Peter, *Ambitions and Strategies*. Oxford, 1964.

Stein, Leonard, *The Balfour Declaration*. London, 1961.

Sutherland, G. (ed.), *Studies in the Growth of Nineteenth Century Government*. London, 1972.

Sykes, Alan, *Tariff Reform in British Politics, 1903–1913*. Oxford, 1979.

Taylor, John, *From Self-Help to Glamour: The Workingman's Club, 1860–1972*. Oxford, 1971.

Thane, Pat, *The Foundations of the Welfare State*. London, 1982.

—— (ed.), *The Origins of British Social Policy*. London, 1978.

Thompson, Paul, *The Edwardians*. London, 1975.

—— *Socialists, Liberals and Labour; The Struggle for London, 1885–1914*. London, 1967.

Umansky, Ellen M., *Lily Montagu and the Advancement of Liberal Judaism: From Vision to Vocation*. New York and Toronto, 1983.

Vincinus, Martha (ed.),*A Widening Sphere: Changing Roles of Victorian Women*. Bloomington, 1977.

—— *Suffer and Be Still: Women in the Victorian Age*. Bloomington, 1972.

Vital, David, *The History of Zionism*. 3 vols. Oxford, 1975–87.

Waley, S. D., *Edwin Montagu: A Memoir and an Account of His Visits to India*. London, 1964.

Walkowitz, Judith, *Prostitution and Victorian Society*. Cambridge, 1980.

Weeks, Jeffrey, *Sex, Politics and Society: The Regulation of Sexuality since 1800*. London, 1981.

Whitaker, W. B., *Victorian and Edwardian Shopworkers*. London, 1973.

White, J. *Rothschild Buildings: Life in an East End Tenement Block, 1887–1920*. London, 1980.

Williams, Bill, *The Making of Manchester Jewry, 1740–1875*. Manchester, 1976.

Woodroofe, Kathleen, *From Charity to Social Work*. London, 1962.

Wrigley, C. (ed.) *A History of British Industrial Relations 1875–1914*. London, 1982.

Young, A. F. and Ashton E. T., *British Social Work in the Nineteenth Century*. London, 1956.

Young, Kenneth, *Arthur James Balfour*. London, 1963.

—— *Local Politics and the Rise of Party: The London Municipial Society and the Conservative Intervention in Local Elections, 1894–1963*. Leicester, 1975.

Young, Michael, and Wilmott, Peter, *Family and Kinship in East London*. London, 1957.

Zebel, Sydney H., 'Fair trade: an English reaction to the breakdown of the Cobden treaty system', *Journal of Modern History*, volume 12 (1940), 161–86.

Zechlin, E., *Die deutsche Politik und die Juden im Ersten Weltkrieg*. Göttingen, 1969.

Zubrycki, Jerzy, *Polish Immigrants in Britain*. The Hague, 1956.

Glossary of Terms

Ashkenazim Jews, chiefly of Central and Eastern European origin, following a rite slightly different from that of the Sephardim.

Bet Din chief rabbinical court. Adjudicates matters concerning Jewish observances, marriage, and divorce. Establishes rules and standards of *kashrut* to be administered through the Board of Shechita. Can act as court of arbitration on issues between Jews when both parties agree to abide by its judgement.

Beth Hamedrash (Bet Midrash) – the rabbinical place of study.

Cheder(im) literally 'a room': in this instance a one-room religious school teaching Hebrew language and Bible.

dorcas the women's service auxiliary to a synagogue, the term borrowed by Christian usage.

dayan (dayanim) a judge; a rabbi appointed to the Bet Din (q.v.)

Haham a scholar; the rabbi of the Spanish and Portuguese congregation in London.

halachah a system of law governing Jewish observance.

hasidism a pietistic sect deriving from Eastern Europe.

hebra (hebrot) an association for specific Jewish or ritual purposes.

kashrut (kosher) the Jewish rules of dietary propriety and observance.

landsmannschaft the bonds of common origin, usually describing the ties of those from the same village or region.

Machziké Hadass the self-denominated 'true upholders of the religion'. An Ultra-Orthodox congregation in London that rejected the authority of the Chief Rabbi in 1891.

maggid a popular preacher, usually using Yiddish.

matzo the unleavened bread that Jews must use at Passover.

melamed a teacher of the Hebrew language and Jewish religion in a Cheder.

mikva ritual bath for purification of the observant.

minyan the minimum of ten men who must be present to hold a Jewish service.

mitzva (mitzvot) a commandment; the obligations, religious and secular, for every observant Jew.

Purim the feast of lots, derived from the Book of Esther.

rabbi a Jewish 'clergyman', licensed by an appropriate body; a teacher, able to render advice and judgements on matters of observance.

rav a rabbi

reverend   a minister. In Great Britain, the title was used for Jewish 'clergy'.

schnorrer   a beggar.

seder   the ceremonial order, by extension, the meal on the first and second evenings of Passover.

Sephardim   Jews, principally descended from and practising the rites of those expelled from Spain and Portugal at the end of the fifteenth century.

Shechita Board   the administrative body overseeing the licensing of *shochet* and facilities for the provision of kosher meat.

shiva   literally 'seven'. The obligatory week of mourning for a deceased member of the family.

shochet   a ritual slaughterman.

stetl   an East European village.

stiebel (*stiblech*)   a small conventicle for worship or other purposes.

talis   the fringed stole worn by observant Jews at prayer.

Talmud   the authoritative body of rabbinic law.

Talmud Torah   Torah study; schools in which Talmud and Bible are studied.

Torah   the five Books of Moses; by extension the whole body of Judaic literature.

Index